THE PLAYBILL® BROADWAY YEARBOOK

INAUGURAL EDITION
2004-2005

ROBERT VIAGAS

Editor

AMY ASCH
Assistant Editor

KESLER THIBERT
Book Designer

AUBREY REUBEN
BEN STROTHMANN
Photographers

Cover design by IRA PEKELNAYA

MELISSA MERLO
Editorial Assistant

DAVID GEWIRTZMAN
Production Assistant

**PLAYBILL®
BOOKS**

The Playbill Broadway Yearbook: June 1, 2004–May 31, 2005
Robert Viagas, Editor

Library of Congress Cataloguing-in-Publication Data:
Library of Congress Card Number: 2005906049

ISBN 1-55783-682-5

Published by PLAYBILL® Books
525 Seventh Avenue, Suite 1801
New York, NY 10018
Email: yearbook@playbill.com
Internet: www.playbill.com

Printed by WALSWORTH PUBLISHING COMPANY
Commercial Book Group
389 Piedmont Street
Waterbury, CT 06706

Exclusively distributed by APPLAUSE THEATRE & CINEMA
BOOKS/Hal Leonard Corporation

Applause Theatre & Cinema Books
19 West 21st Street, Suite 201
New York, NY 10010
Phone: (212) 575-9265
Fax: (212) 575-9270

SALES AND DISTRIBUTION

North America:

Hal Leonard Corp.
7777 West Bluemound Road
P. O. Box 13819
Milwaukee, WI 53213
Phone: (414) 774-3630
Fax: (414) 774-3259
Email: halinfo@halleonard.com
Internet: www.halleonard.com

Europe:

Roundhouse Publishing Ltd.
Millstone, Limers Lane
Northam, North Devon EX 39 2RG
Phone: (0) 1237-474-474
Fax: (0) 1237-474-774
Email: roundhouse.group@ukgateway.net

SPECIAL THANKS TO:

James Babbin, Ira Pekelnaya, Melissa Merlo, David Gewirtzman, Pam Karr, Morgan Allen, Kesler Thibert, Gary Pearce, Aubrey Reuben, Ben Strothmann, Andy Buck, Andrew Ku, Pat Cusanelli, Maria Somma, Jim Steinblatt, Lynne Bond, Alan Eisenberg, Alex Barreto, John LoCascio, Phil DiChiara, Jenny Shoemaker, Kim Zahner, Pamela Engelhard, Jessica Thompson, Michael Griffin, Elizabeth Urcinoli, Catherine Ryan, the staff at Sardi's, Scott Newsome and Lillian Viagas, whose help, advice and guidance made this project possible.

And the Inaugural Edition Yearbook Correspondents:

Karmine Alers, William Barnes, Brig Berney, Brad Bradley, Jesse Shane Bronstein, Jeff Brooks, David Burnham, Mario Cantone, Chris Clay, Jill Cordle, Heather Cousens, Nick Danielson, Ray DeMattis, Teri DiGianfelice, Erin Dilly, David Elder, Melissa Errico, Susan Fallon, Jesse Tyler Ferguson, James FitzSimmons (twice), Dan Fogler, Beth Fowler, Artie Gaffin, Sriram Ganesan, Heather Goldenhersh, Milena Govich, Robert Guy, Roy Harris, Gregory Jbara, Jessica Hecht, Kevin Isola, Charlissa Jackson, Nikki M. James, Capathia Jenkins, Sara Kramer, James Lawson, Michael James Leslie, David Lowenstein, David Manis, Jackie Mason, Sean McCourt, Kenny McGee, Maureen McGovern, Alexander Mitchell (twice), Tony Montenieri, Michael Mulheren, Nancy Mulliner, Kris Koop Ouellette, Denis O'Hare (twice), Brad Oscar, Sarah Paulson, Jennifer Regan, Michelle Robinson, William Sadler, Ruben Santiago-Hudson, Justin Scribner, Tim Shew, Todd Michel Smith, Jeff Talbott, Josh Tower, Kim Vernace, Lee Wilkof and the cast of *Avenue Q*.

Also the many Broadway press agents who helped set up interviews and photo sessions: especially Chris Boneau, Adrian Bryan-Brown, John Barlow, Michael Hartman, Pete Sanders, Richard Kornberg, Bob Fennell, Philip Rinaldi, Sam Rudy and their staffs.

Plus the hundreds of backstage workers who took time out of their busy days to line up, smile, and say, "Hey-yyy."

PREFACE

Why a Yearbook?

When I hear PLAYBILL Publisher Philip Birsh's booming laugh coming down the hall, I can usually tell that something's up. When he sticks his head in my office with a Cheshire Cat grin on his face, I know that he has…

"An Idea."

I first heard and saw these portents in 1994 when he came to me with the idea that evolved into PLAYBILL.COM, our online theatre news service. I heard and saw them at regular intervals in the intervening years, leading to book, radio and recording projects that expanded the PLAYBILL brand name in innovative ways.

And then, in spring 2004, ten years almost to the day after our first PLAYBILL.COM meeting, I was working on the special Tony Awards edition of PLAYBILL when I heard the laugh, and moments later saw the grin. So I turned from my computer terminal in anticipation.

"What do you think of this idea?" Birsh said. "We'll do a yearbook, like a high school yearbook. Everybody loves their high school yearbook. But this one will be for the people who work on Broadway. We have half the material in-house already for the PLAYBILLS. But we'll include photos of *every person working on Broadway!*"

The result, which you hold in your hands, varies very little from that initial prime directive. We didn't get every last person, but we came as close as the cooperation of the subjects themselves would allow.

It was one of those natural ideas. Why hadn't anyone done one before? Yes, there had been other theatrical yearbooks through the years, some beloved and widely collected, but all were oriented toward researchers and archivists. None was a true yearbook in the school yearbook sense. And none was oriented toward the people who work, not only in front and in back of the Broadway footlights, but above and below them as well: not just the actors and writers, but the stagehands, the wardrobe people, the stage managers and the ushers. They're all part of the experience, too. No other yearbook was audacious enough to try including everyone.

But, considering that "everyone" eventually included more than three thousand faces, the project was far easier said than done. The creation of *The Playbill Broadway Yearbook* may someday be worth a book in itself. Certainly the cast of characters is compelling. That's a whole lot of star power. And ego. Considering how universal was the sense that this was a great idea, the obstacles turned out to be numerous. The first time you do any big project, you learn as you go along. Which is a gentle way of putting it.

The project began with brainstorming sessions. The cornerstone of the project was simple: Make a keepsake for everyone who works on Broadway

that would be infused with the same spirit of fun as a high school yearbook.

What should be in the book? Who should we include, and who, if anyone, should we exclude? How much material did we already have in the PLAYBILL files and generated by the PLAYBILL staff, and how much would we have to create? What information and images would make this project different and superior to other annual theatre books?

The matrix of the *Yearbook* would be faces: Not just the faces of actors who appear on Broadway's stages, but the faces of everyone behind the scenes as well. Did that mean stagehands? Did that mean musicians in the pit? Did that mean

The first Yearbook Committee (L-R): Ira Pekelnaya, Amy Asch, Ben Strothmann and Robert Viagas.

Photos by Ben Strothmann

ushers and box office people? We decided yes, yes, yes and yes, as many as we could get.

The artists and craftspeople would be like the student body. The producers and union leaders would be like the faculty. The organizations that support Broadway would be like the clubs. For the sports section we even had the Broadway Softball League. (We never figured out who corresponded to the lunch ladies, though.) Should we include just the forty new shows, or all sixty-five that were running at some point between June 1, 2004 and May 31, 2005? We decided on the latter. All decisions were based on including as many people as we possibly could. If any group has been left out of the inaugural edition, it's only because we failed to think of them in our brainstorming sessions.

One last touch: I'd always been impressed by actor scrapbooks, the ones that actors themselves compile, full of photos, memories, clippings and catchphrases to remind them of shows they'd been in. The initial concept here was to find one person on each show—perhaps an actor, but just as well a stage manager, doorman or makeup artist—to write down memories of each show, and supply us with backstage photos. We decided to call the person "*Yearbook* Chairman" and create a page that would be called "Callboard"

after the bulletin board each show has backstage. This concept was later refined, but the outline had been set.

Next, we assembled PLAYBILL's "*Yearbook* Committee," the staff that would put the book together. The actor photos are compiled for every Broadway PLAYBILL and updated weekly by staffer Pam Karr, who also updates the "Billboard Page"—the page that lists the show's title, stars and creative staff. It became her job to gather this material each week for the *Yearbook* as well. Playbill's tech guru Andrew Ku built electronic receptacles for the files. Designer Kesler Thibert came up with three basic page designs, of which one, a classic, low-frills high school yearbook look with color banners to set off each show, was chosen. Designer Ira Pekelnaya further refined those designs and helped choose fonts that would convey the simplicity and clarity of a classic yearbook. She also created an Art Deco gold cover that suggests an imaginary Broadway high school of the 1930s.

Because we knew that most of the project would consist of tracking huge quantities of names and photos, we needed someone with great database skills. Amy Asch, who has worked as an archivist for the estates of Irving Berlin, Oscar Hammerstein II and Jonathan Larson, had been working part-time for PLAYBILL.COM, and agreed to come aboard. Brainstorming sessions with Amy produced the list of questions we'd be asking each show to answer.

Aubrey Reuben, a photographer for the *New York Post* (and a tireless party animal), goes to every Broadway opening night, every party, every special events and every press conference and photographs them all. The PLAYBILL archives contain thousands of his photographs, priceless historical records, many of which would never see publication. Throughout the year, they capture moments in the life of Broadway that would otherwise vanish forever. When it became apparent that Chairpersons on each show could not always deliver usable photos, we decided to mine this trove for the *Yearbook*. PLAYBILL.COM's Morgan Allen fielded our barrage of requests for particular images.

The next task was to get Broadway people to understand the project and to accept that we were serious about doing it. It's hard to do something new in such a traditional business. Everything happens under the watchful eye of more than a dozen labor unions. Actors' Equity Association president Alan Eisenberg was the first to understand the project and endorse it. His letter of benediction opened many doors.

Back in 1995 when we were starting PLAYBILL.COM, it took months to convince some people that our reporters weren't computer salesmen, and to explain in those dawning days of the Internet how the information would get into people's computers. Similarly, many meetings about the *Yearbook* were conducted with Broadway's information gatekeepers, the press agents.

The initial positive reaction was almost universal: What a great idea! Why didn't anyone think of this before? But then came the questions about implementation. The press agents were dubious about the idea of taking photos backstage, dubious about setting up interviews that wouldn't see print for a year, and dubious about the idea of asking people to pay for something (even at a discount) in which they had participated. We explained that it was really no different from any other interview or photo session, and that students had to pay for yearbooks they appear in. We'd even bear the cost of photo sessions ourselves.

Chris Boneau of Boneau/Bryan-Brown was the first of the press agents to "get" the project and to instruct his staff to participate. He also suggested that the "Callboard" was very specifically a union institution, and that we'd be better off calling our page a "Scrapbook." We took his advice. He also suggested that the "Chairman" appellation for the Scrapbook page person was confusing. We changed that job title to "Correspondent."

Collaborating with the correspondents proved to be one of the *Yearbook*'s chief delights. The original idea was to post a questionnaire backstage and let the entire cast fill in thoughts and impressions. This sounded good in planning sessions, but in the end only one show did this: *Avenue Q*. More frequently, correspondents used e-mail to fill in the blanks. In about half the cases, the questionnaires were completed in a face-to-face or telephone interview, with yours truly asking the questions and the correspondent dictating the answers. This yielded an intimate, conversational feeling.

Many were witty, like actor Denis O'Hare, who wound up recording impressions of both *Assassins* and *Sweet Charity*, and taking some marvelous candid pictures of both shows. Jackie Mason of *Jackie Mason: Freshly Squeezed* did his Scrapbook interview entirely in the voice of his comic persona. The producer of Mario Cantone's *Laugh Whore* initially signed on as correspondent. But when he found he couldn't answer some of the deep backstage questions, Cantone himself stepped up to the plate.

Many were touching, such as Ruben Santiago-Hudson, who gave an account of *Gem of the Ocean*'s struggles out of town. William Sadler, who played the title role in *Julius Caesar* gave a memorable account of a stage-door fan encounter. David Lowenstein of *The Frogs*, Jessica Hecht of *After the Fall*, Tim Shew of *Wonderful Town* and Jennifer Regan of *Who's Afraid of Virginia Woolf?* spoke for actors everywhere when they told what it was like to work one-on-one with legends Stephen Sondheim, Arthur Miller, Betty Comden and Edward Albee, respectively. "The dream of my career was to be in that room," Lowenstein said.

We were delighted that several of our correspondents were nominated for Tony Awards, including Dan Fogler of *The 25th Annual Putnam County Spelling Bee* (who won Best Performance by a Featured Actor in a Musical), Heather Goldenhersh of *Doubt*, Cantone of *Laugh Whore* and Erin Dilly of *Chitty Chitty Bang Bang*. Congratulations to them all.

Not all the Correspondents were leading players. We heard from stage managers, dressers, stage doormen, understudies, company managers and personal assistants. They did a marvelous job, but that brings us to the struggles of the inaugural *Yearbook*. Getting photos of the backstage crews, orchestras and house staffs was mostly joyful, but sometimes also a daunting task.

When it became clear that the Correspondents could not be expected to take photos of these groups, we added another member of the *Yearbook* Committee, a talented young photographer named Ben Strothmann, whom we discovered posting photos of Broadway people and events on a Web site. His passion for the theatre is reflected in his clear, sharp portraits that always manage to capture the excitement of the theatre and the personalities of his subjects. Soon he was being scheduled almost around the clock ducking into the byways and offices of Times Square to capture the behind-the-scenes people who make Broadway happen. He climbed onto all manner of stages, desks, chairs, walls and even one forklift (at the PLAYBILL printing plant) to find new ways to make group photos interesting. His cry of "Say heyyy-yyy," to get people to smile was heard all over Broadway this season.

Scheduling these photo sessions around the busy lives of Broadway's movers and shakers sometimes seemed like trying to thread a rope up a twisting pipe. Some shows simply said no, and we respected that. In the end most shows participated. We hope that when the rest see how this project turned out, participation will increase for year two.

Brought on to help during this period was our "Quark Ninja," free-lance production man James Babbin, who wound up laying out the billboard and headshot pages using the difficult upgrade version of this widely used software. He was ably assisted by David Gewirtzman. Columbia University intern Melissa Merlo helped Amy Asch round up the nearly one thousand head shots of assistant directors, assistant stage managers and other elusive creative team members who rarely appear in print. They also worked out how to deal with the fact that the faces at long-running shows changed frequently over the season. They came up with the idea of dating the billboard pages used in each chapter, and calling the actors who left the show before that date "Alumni" and actors who arrived after that date, "Transfer Students."

Strothmann's photo sessions, possibly more than anything else, began to raise the Yearbook's profile. As the year progressed, industry attitude toward the project began to change. Organizations that had been neutral at first began to call and ask for photo sessions. People who had initially declined to take part began to call back to see if they could still get in.

Theatrical unions, in particular, began to get behind the project. Lynne Bond of the musician's union, Local 802, began contacting each show's orchestra to make sure they were participating.

The Theatrical Teamsters generously sent a car to pick Strothmann up from a train station so he could photograph them at their headquarters in suburban Nassau County.

Some of the organizations were very creative. The advertising company SpotCo asked to produce their own page, and came up with a wonderful design that posed all their employees in "school colors" in a layout that suggested classic high school yearbook. Not to be outdone, competing ad firm Serino Coyne submitted a page that used their employees' actual high school or college photographs.

People were starting to have fun with it.

As the Scrapbook questionnaires began to circulate, Correspondents began to know some of the questions before we asked them. Responses came in via e-mail, post, fax, courier, and some even scribbled on hotel stationery. The standard layout allowed for about 400 words, but some of the submissions were two or three times that. Melissa Errico of *Dracula* was one of the most enthusiastic contributors, handing in a pile of backstage photographs and more than 2,000 words of text, all of it entertaining. Kris Koop Ouellette of *The Phantom of the Opera* had more memories than we had space to list, so we adjusted the format to include as much as possible.

Birsh was urging us all to greater efforts. PLAYBILL Production Director Pat Cusanelli and Production Manager Gary Pearce offered valuable support during this time. But the *Yearbook* Committee was starting to feel the pressure. The last few weeks before the deadline coincided with the rush before the annual Tony Awards—the busiest time of the year at PLAYBILL and for the press reps. And that's when we sent them our lists of hundreds of missing photos of production personnel, some from shows long closed. No wonder they were cranky. What kept us going was the knowledge that we were creating something that would take the idea of *A Chorus Line* one step further: Not only would we recognize the dancers behind the star, we would salute *all* the people who create the theatre's magic.

On June 22, we hosted a four-hour "last chance" photo session on the fourth floor of Sardi's famous theatrical restaurant, complete with coffee and doughnuts, and gathered up the last few available photos. Among them was the board of the American Theatre Wing, which paid tribute to longtime leader Isabelle Stevenson by taking down her caricature from the walls and posing with it. We are proud to have her.

As we wrap up our effort, we're proud that we have created something unique and new in an old and tradition-bound industry. We hope that it will bring delight to the participants for many years to come. When they open the covers to show grandchildren or young theatre people of the future, they'll be able to say, "There, see? I was there. I worked at the top of my profession. I was, in my time, a part of the ongoing magic of Broadway."

Robert Viagas
June 2005

TABLE OF CONTENTS

HEAD OF THE CLASS

Most Tony Awards: *The Light in the Piazza* (6).

Most Cell Phone Rings at a Single Performance: 23 in *700 Sundays*.

Most Roles Played by a Single Performer in a Single Show: 38, Jefferson Mays, *I Am My Own Wife*.

Off-Site Hangout Most Frequently Named by Yearbook Correspondents: Angus McIndoe.

Trend #1— "Jukebox Musicals:" *Mamma Mia* (ABBA), *All Shook Up* (Elvis Presley), *Movin' Out* (Billy Joel), *Good Vibrations* (The Beach Boys).

Shows With Entirely Male Casts: 7 (*Democracy, Glengarry Glen Ross, Jackie Mason: Freshly Squeezed, I Am My Own Wife, Laugh Whore, 700 Sundays, Twelve Angry Men*).

Shows With Entirely Female Casts: 5 (*Golda's Balcony, The Good Body, 'night, Mother, Steel Magnolias, Whoopi*).

Shows With Men Playing Women: 7 (*Dame Edna, La Cage aux Folles, Spamalot, Pacific Overtures, Rent, Hairspray, I Am My Own Wife*).

Shows With Women Playing Men: 2 (*Avenue Q, All Shook Up*).

Trend #2—Shows About Child Abuse: *Frozen, The Pillowman, Doubt*.

Shows That Closed on Opening Night or Ran Less Than a Week: Oddly, none.

Shortest Regular Run: *The Good Body*, 40 performances.

Shows That Ran the Entire Season: *Avenue Q, Beauty and the Beast, Fiddler on the Roof, Hairspray, The Lion King, Mamma Mia!, Movin' Out, Phantom of the Opera, The Producers, Rent, Wicked*.

Longest-Running Show on Broadway This Season: *The Phantom of the Opera*, second-longest run on the all-time long-run list (see inset).

Long Runs That Ended This Season: *Aida, 42nd Street*.

Selected Actors Who Played Major Roles in Two Shows: Brían F. O'Byrne (*Frozen* and *Doubt*), Kelli O'Hara (*Dracula* and *Light in the Piazza*), Philip Bosco (*Chitty Chitty Bang Bang* and *Twelve Angry Men*), Marc Kudisch (*Assassins* and *Chitty Chitty Bang Bang*), Mario Cantone (*Assassins* and *Laugh Whore*), Denis O'Hare (*Assassins* and *Sweet Charity*), Roger Bart (*The Producers* and *The Frogs*), Phylicia Rashad (*A Raisin in the Sun* and *Gem of the Ocean*), Norbert Leo Butz (*Wicked* and *Dirty Rotten Scoundrels*), Hunter Foster (*The Producers* and *Little Shop of Horrors*).

Selected Authors Who Had Two or More Shows on Broadway: Donald Margulies (*Sight Unseen* and *Brooklyn Boy*), Tennessee Williams (*The Glass Menagerie* and *A Streetcar Named Desire*), Stephen Sondheim (*The Frogs, Pacific*

Broadway Long-Run List
Asterisk (*) indicates show still running as of May 31, 2005.

Cats 7485
* *The Phantom of the Opera* 7265
Les Misérables 6680
A Chorus Line 6137
Oh! Calcutta! (Revival) 5959
* *Beauty and the Beast* 4596
Miss Saigon 4097
* *Rent* 3821
* *Chicago* (Revival) 3590
42nd Street 3486
Grease 3388

Overtures and *Assassins*, the latter two with John Weidman).

Selected Directors Who Had Two or More Shows on Broadway: Joe Mantello (*Glengarry Glen Ross, Laugh Whore* and *Assassins*) and Daniel Sullivan (*Brooklyn Boy, Sight Unseen* and *Julius Caesar*).

Finalists for Best Noel Coward Parody: "Ruprecht" from *Dirty Rotten Scoundrels* and "You Won't Succeed on Broadway" from *Monty Python's Spamalot*.

If They Gave an Award for Best New Song, The Nominees Might Be: "The Song That Goes Like This," "And the Beauty Is," "Great Big Stuff" and

"Ariadne."

Trend #3—Flinging Things at the Audience: *Spamalot* (confetti cannon), *Chitty Chitty Bang Bang* (confetti cannon), *Dame Edna* (gladiolas), *Good Vibrations* (beach balls), *The 25th Annual Putnam County Spelling Bee* (candy and juice boxes), *Little Shop of Horrors* (giant man-eating plants).

Shortest Running Time: 75 minutes (*The Good Body*).

Longest Running Time: 175 minutes (*Who's Afraid of Virginia Woolf?*).

(Nearly) All Singing!: *Aida; Caroline, Or Change; The Phantom of the Opera; The Light in the Piazza* and *Rent*.

All Dancing!: *Movin' Out* and *Forever Tango*.

Puppets!: *Avenue Q, The Frogs, The Lion King* and *Little Shop of Horrors*.

Broadway Theatres Renamed: Schoenfeld (formerly the Plymouth), Jacobs (formerly the Royale) and Hilton (formerly the Ford Center).

Broadway Theatres Demolished or Gutted: Times Square and Henry Miller's.

Trend #4—Solo Shows: *I Am My Own Wife; The Good Body; 700 Sundays; Laugh Whore; Dame Edna: Back With a Vengeance!; Jackie Mason: Freshly Squeezed; Golda's Balcony; Whoopi*.

Nude Scenes: *Dracula* and *Julius Caesar*.

Shows with the Band on Stage: *Chicago, Boy From Oz, Spelling Bee, Wonderful Town, Brooklyn* and *Movin' Out*.

Trend #5—Wacky Pre-Show Announcements: *I Am My Own Wife* (in German), *The Light in the Piazza* (in Italian), *Dame Edna* (in which she urged people to leave their cell phones on and to have conversations—the better for her minions to find the talkers and throw them out) and *The Rivals* (reminding you cell phones didn't exist in the 18th century).

THE SHOWS

PLAYBILL®

AFTER THE FALL

CAST
(in order of appearance)

Quentin	PETER KRAUSE*
Holga	VIVIENNE BENESCH*
Mother	CANDY BUCKLEY*
Father	DAN ZISKIE*
Elsie	KATHLEEN McNENNY*
Louise	JESSICA HECHT*
Lou	MARK NELSON*
Mickey	JONATHAN WALKER*
Maggie	CARLA GUGINO*
Man in the Park	BAYLEN THOMAS*
Dan	KEN MARKS*
Secretary	ROXANNA HOPE*
Student	JAMES O'TOOLE
Nurse	LISA LOUTTIT
Lucas	CHRIS BOWERS

UNDERSTUDIES/STANDBYS
For Quentin – BAYLEN THOMAS*; for Maggie –
ROXANNA HOPE*; for Louise, Holga, Mother –
KATHLEEN MCNENNY*; for Father, Lou,
Mickey – KEN MARKS*; for Elsie, Secretary –
LISA LOUTTIT; for Man in the Park, Dan –
CHRIS BOWERS

Production Stage Manager: JAMES HARKER*
Stage Manager: ANDREA O. SARAFFIAN*

SETTING
Idlewild Airport, New York City, 1962.

* Members of Actors' Equity Association, the union of
professional actors and stage managers in the United States.

AMERICAN AIRLINES THEATRE

ROUNDABOUT THEATRE COMPANY

TODD HAIMES, Artistic Director
ELLEN RICHARD, Managing Director
JULIA C. LEVY, Executive Director, External Affairs

Presents

Peter Krause

in

Arthur Miller's

AFTER THE FALL

Carla Gugino   Jessica Hecht

Vivienne Benesch   Candy Buckley   Roxanna Hope   Kathleen McNenny

Ken Marks   Mark Nelson   Baylen Thomas   Jonathan Walker   Dan Ziskie

Chris Bowers   Lisa Louttit   James O'Toole

Set Design	*Costume Design*	*Lighting Design*	*Sound Design*
Richard Hoover	Michael Krass	Donald Holder	Dan Moses Schreier

Projection Design	*Hair/Wig Design*	*Production Stage Manager*
Elaine J. McCarthy	Paul Huntley	James Harker

Casting by	*Technical Supervisor*	*General Manager*
Jim Carnahan, C.S.A. and Mele Nagler	Steve Beers	Sydney Beers

Founding Director	*Associate Artistic Director*	*Press Representative*	*Director of Marketing*
Gene Feist	Scott Ellis	Boneau/Bryan-Brown	David B. Steffen

Directed by

Michael Mayer

Roundabout Theatre Company is a member of the League of Resident Theatres.
www.roundabouttheatre.org

9/5/04

Peter Krause (center) as Quentin with the women in his life (L-R): Vivienne Benesch, Jessica Hecht, Carla Gugino and Candy Buckley.

Photo by Joan Marcus

Peter Krause
Quentin

Carla Gugino
Maggie

Jessica Hecht
Louise

Vivienne Benesch
Holga

Candy Buckley
Mother

Roxanna Hope
Secretary

Kathleen McNenny
Elsie

Ken Marks
Dan

Mark Nelson
Lou

Baylen Thomas
Man in the Park

Jonathan Walker
Mickey

Dan Ziskie
Father

Chris Bowers
Lucas

Lisa Louttit
Nurse

James O'Toole
Student

Arthur Miller
Playwright

Michael Mayer
Director

Richard Hoover
Scenic Design

Donald Holder
Lighting Design

Dan Moses Schreier
Sound Design

Paul Huntley
Wig/Hair Design

J. Steven White
Fight Direction

James Harker
Production Stage Manager

Jim Carnahan
Casting

Gene Feist
Founding Director, Roundabout Theatre Company

Todd Haimes
Artistic Director, Roundabout Theatre Company

ROUNDABOUT THEATRE COMPANY STAFF
Artisitic Director ....TODD HAIMES
Managing Director ....ELLEN RICHARD
Executive Director, External Affairs ......JULIA C. LEVY
Associate Artistic Director ....SCOTT ELLIS

ARTISTIC STAFF
Director of Artistic Development/
Director of Casting ....Jim Carnahan
Artistic Consultant.......................Robyn Goodman
Resident Director.............................Michael Mayer
Associate Artists............................Scott Elliott,
  Bill Irwin,
  Joe Mantello,
  Mark Brokaw,
  Matthew Warchus
Consulting Dramaturg...........................Jerry Patch
Artistic Associate ....Samantha Barrie
Casting Director ....Mele Nagler
Senior Casting Associate ....Jeremy Rich
Casting Associate ....Carrie Gardner
Casting Assistant ....Jennifer Begg
Casting Intern ....Kate Schwabe
Artistic Intern ....Rachel Holmes

EDUCATION STAFF
Education Director ....Arlene Jordan
Senior Curriculum Advisor ....Renee Flemings
Director of Educational Programming ....Megan Waltz
Education Program Associate ....Lindsay Erb
Education Dramaturg.............................Ted Sod
Education Interns ....Gabrielle Eisenman,
  Anne Walbridge
Teaching Artists.............William Addis, Tony Angelini,
  Philip Alexander, Cynthia Babak,
  Victor Barbella, Brigitte Barnett-Loftis,
  Caitlin Barton, Joe Basile, Bonnie Brady,
  LaTonya Borsay, Mike Carnahan,
  Joe Clancy, Melissa Denton,
  Stephen DiMenna, Joe Doran,
  Alvin Eng, Tony Freeman,
  Jonathan Goldstein, Susan Hamburger,
  Karla Hendrick, Sarah Iams,
  Jim Jack, Alvin Keith, Jeannine Lally-Jones,
  Mark Lonergan, Padraic Lillis, Erin McCready,
  Andrew Ondrecjak, Marilyn Pasekoff,
  Laura Poe, Drew Sachs, Anna Saggese,
  David Sinkus, Olivia Tsang,
  Jennifer Varbalow, Leese Walker,
  Eric Wallach, Corey Warren,,
  Ryan Weible, Diana Whitten,
  Gail Winar, Kirche Zeile

ADMINISTRATIVE STAFF
General Manager ....Sydney Beers
General Counsel ....Laura O'Neill
Associate Managing Director ....Greg Backstrom
Associate General Managers ....Don-Scott Cooper,
  Jean Haring
Office Operations Manager ....Bonnie Berens
Human Resources Manager ....Stephen Deutsch
Network Systems Manager ....Jeff Goodman
Facilities Manager ....Timothy Santillo
Manager of Corporate & Party Rentals ....Jetaun Dobbs
MIS Associate ....Lloyd Alvarez
MIS Assistant ....Anthony Foti
Receptionists ....Jennifer Decoteau,
  Vanessa Bombardieri,
  Andre Fortson,
  Elisa Papa
Messenger ....Robert Weisser
Management Intern ....Andrew Jones
Information Systems Intern ....Jeremy Thomas

FINANCE STAFF
Controller ....Susan Neiman
Assistant Controller ....John LaBarbera
Accounts Payable Administrator ....Frank Surdi
Customer Service Coordinator ....Trina Cox
Business Office Associate ....David Solomon
Business Assistant ....Yonit Kafka
Business Intern...............................Danielle Tandet

DEVELOPMENT STAFF
Director of Development ....**Jeffory Lawson**
Director, Institutional Giving ....Julie K. D'Andrea
Director, Individual Giving ....Julia Lazarus
Director, Special Events ....Steve Schaeffer
Manager, Donor Information Systems ....Tina Mae Bishko
Associate, External Affairs ....Stacey L. Morris
Individual Giving Associate ....Glenn Alan Stiskal
Special Events Associate ....Elaina Grillo
Institutional Giving Assistant ....Kristen Bolibruch
Patrons Desk Liaison ....Cassandra Oliveras
Development Assistants ....Adam Gwon,
  Stephenie L. Overton
Development Interns ....Alison Johnson,
  Matt Freeman,
  Rachel Holmes

MARKETING STAFF
Director of Marketing ....David B. Steffen
Marketing/Publications Manager ....Tim McCanna
Marketing Associate ....Sunil Ayyagari
Marketing Assistant ....Rebecca Ballon
Marketing Intern ....Megan Fortunato
Website Consultant ....Keith Powell Beyland
Director of Telesales Special Promotions ....Tony Baksa
Telesales Manager ....Michel Morgan Noverre
Telesales Office Coordinator ....Anton Borissov
Telesales Intern ....J. W. Griffin

TICKET SERVICES STAFF
Director of Sales Operations ....**Jim Seggelink**
Ticket Services Manager ....Ellen Holt
Subscription Manager ....Charlie Garbowski
Box Office Managers ....Edward P. Osborne,
  Jaime Perlman,
  Jessica Bowser
Group Sales Manager ....Jeff Monteith
Assistant Box Office Managers ....Paul Caspary,
  Steve Howe, Megan Young
Assistant Ticket Services Managers ....Robert Kane,
  Kris Todd, David Meglino
Assistant to the Director of
Sales Operations ....Nancy Mulliner
Ticket Services ....Paola Arinci, Solangel Bido,
  Andrew Clements, Johanna Comanzo,
  Sean Crews, Barbara Dente, Nisha Dhruna,
  Kathryn Downey, Lindsay Ericson,
  Scott Falkowski, Catherine Fitzpatrick,
  Julie Hilimire, Talia Krispel,
  Krystin MacRitchie, Mead Margulies,
  Robert Morgan, Carlos Morris,
  Nicole Nicholson, Shannon Paige,
  Hillary Parker, Sarah Pesek, Benjamin Scott,
  Heather Siebert, Monté Smock,
  Melissa Snyder, Catherine Sorensen,
  Lillian Soto, Justin Sweeney,
  Greg Thorson, Nydia Zamorano-Torres
Ticket Services Intern ....Cheryl Kandel

SERVICES
Counsel ....Jeremy Nussbaum,
  Cowan, Liebowitz & Latman, P.C.
Counsel ....Rosenberg & Estis
Counsel ....Spitzer and Feldman, P.C.
Counsel ....Cleary, Gottlieb, Steen & Hamilton
Counsel ....Harry H. Weintraub,
  Glick and Weintraub, P.C.
Immigration Counsel ....Mark D. Koestler and
  Theodore Ruthizer
House Physicians ....Dr. Theodore Tyberg,
  Dr. Lawrence Katz
House Dentist ....Neil Kanner, D.M.D.
Insurance ....Marsh USA Inc.
Accountant ....Brody, Weiss, Zucarelli &
  Urbanek CPAs, P.C.
Advertising ....Eliran Murphy Group/
  Denise Ganjou
Events Photography ....Anita and Steve Shevett
Production Photographer ....Joan Marcus
Press Assistant ....Erika Creagh
Theatre Displays ....King Displays/Wayne Sapper

GENERAL PRESS REPRESENTATIVES
BONEAU / BRYAN-BROWN
Adrian Bryan-Brown Matt Polk
Jessica Johnson

ROUNDABOUT THEATRE COMPANY
231 West 39th Street, New York, NY 10018
(212) 719-9393

CREDITS FOR AFTER THE FALL
General Manager ....**Sydney Beers**
Company Manager ....Denys Baker
Associate General Manager ....Jean Haring
Production Stage Manager ....James Harker
Stage Manager ....Andrea O. Saraffian
Fight Direction ....J. Steven White
Dialect Coach ....Deborah Hecht
Associate Director ....Todd Lundquist
Assistant Set Designers ....Brian Harms,
  Jessica Kaplan
Associate Costume Designer ....Tracy Christensen
Costume Assistant ....Jessica Barrios
Costume Research ....Michael Silverstone
Associate Lighting Designer ....Karen Spahn
Assistant Sound Designer ....Catherine Mardis
Assistant Projection Designer ....Jake Pinholster
Master Technicians ....Trevor Brown,
  Susan Goulet
Assistant Master Technicans ....Amber Adams,
  Andrew Forste,
  Brian Maiuri
Assistant to the Technical Supervisor ....Elisa Kuhar
Wardrobe Supervisor ....Susan J. Fallon
Dressers ....Thom Carlson, Melissa Crawford,
  Kevin Mark Harris, Tamara Kopko,
  Kimberly Mark-Sirota, Vanessa Valeriano
Hair/Wig Supervisor ....Manuela LaPorte
Properties Supervisor ....Denise Grillo
Props Coordinator ....Kevin Crawford
Production Assistant ....Neil Korf
Vocal Coaching for Carla Gugino ....Deborah Lapidus
Sets built by ....The Shop, Inc.
Costumes built by ....Eric Winterling, Inc.
Costume Rentals ....ODDS Costumes
Fur Coat generously provided by ....Maximilian Furs
Lighting equipment by ....Fourth Phase
Sound equipment by ....Sound Associates
Driver ....John Pavich

AMERICAN AIRLINES THEATRE STAFF
General Manager ....Sydney Beers
Master Technician ....Glenn Merwede
Master Technician ....Susan Goulet
Wardrobe Supervisor ....Susan J. Fallon
Box Office Manager ....Edward P. Osborne
House Manager ....Stephen Ryan
Associate House Manager ....Zipporah Aguasvivas
Head Usher ....Edwin Camacho
House Staff ....Courtney Boddie, Peter Breaden,
  James Bruce, Oscar Castillo,
  Ilia Diaz, Elsie Jamin-Maguire,
  Sherra Johnston, Richard McNanna,
  Jacklyn Rivera, Chad Walters
Security ....Julious Russell
Additional Security Provided by ....Gotham Security
Maintenance ....Kenrick Johnson, Jesus Muñoz,
  Raphael Torres, Ronnie Hancock
Lobby Refreshments ....Sweet Concessions

Opening Night Gifts: Carla Gugino gave us ten pounds of fancy chocolate from an elegant shop in Soho. Director Michael Mayer gave us each a little piece of a note Arthur Miller had given him.

Backstage Rituals: We had a really silly one. Each night Kathleen McNenny would figure out what kind of Lifesavers and other candy to eat onstage during the scene in the airport waiting room.

In-Theatre Gathering Place: We'd gather each day in one of the dressing rooms and vent about our day.

Off-Site Hangouts: Vivienne Benesch would take everybody to Cafe Un Deux Trois or to Angus McIndoe's.

Favorite Snacks: Carla Gugino and Peter Krause would eat apples. Head dresser Susan Fallon was a genius pastry chef and would make a peanut butter chocolate cake. Every Sunday we'd go over to the theatre early to have these great brunches, provided by the crew, as a gift. Sometimes they'd have a special Southern-style brunch. There were some Sunday matinees where we literally could not get into our costumes afterward.

Record Number Of Cell Phone Rings: One night we had three, but it wasn't as annoying as the time someone's hearing aid was so loud, it deafened half of the audience.

Memorable Directorial Note: When we were working on the sex scene with the family sitting on the bed, Michael Mayer said, "Doesn't everyone have visions of their parents when they're having sex?" Occasionally the scene would get a round of applause, which made us think maybe Michael was right.

Each girl had a moment when Peter kissed her, which was very charming.

Therapies: Ken Marx was an amazing masseuse. If you had a problem, he could fix it. Personally, I found screaming at the death of Lou was very therapeutic.

Celebrity Visitors: Nicole Kidman was there but didn't come backstage. Mark Ruffalo, Jimmy Smits and Alec Baldwin came the same night and couldn't have been more flattering.

Favorite Moment: Being on stage with Arthur Miller for the opening night curtain call. That kind of thing takes you by surprise. Here was this icon, someone I grew up with, and someone whose world I always dreamed of being inside. When he came out on stage with us that night, it was genuinely moving.

Also: We were running at the same time as the Republican convention at Madison Square Garden, and all the protests surrounding that. There was a lot of strange anxiety in the air. I found that the audience was incredibly generous those nights. I think we all felt part of something connected to the political climate at that moment.

Correspondent: Jessica Hecht, "Louise."

Above left: Peter Krause and Carla Gugino arrive on opening night. Above right: Playwright Arthur Miller accepts applause from the first-night audience and the company on the stage of the American Airlines Theatre.

Above left: Cast members Roxanna Hope and Vivienne Benesch bracket Ethan McSweeney at the opening night party at the B.B. King Blues Club. Above right: Cast member Jessica Hecht arrives at the party.

Arthur Miller with companion Agnes Barley at the cast party.

Director Michael Mayer on opening night.

Photos by Aubrey Reuben

PLAYBILL®

✦N✦ PALACE THEATRE
UNDER THE DIRECTION OF
STEWART F. LANE, JAMES M. NEDERLANDER AND JAMES L. NEDERLANDER

DISNEY THEATRICAL PRODUCTIONS
PRESENTS

DEBORAH A. COX
IN

AIDA

MUSIC BY
ELTON JOHN

LYRICS BY
TIM RICE

BOOK BY
LINDA WOOLVERTON
AND
ROBERT FALLS & DAVID HENRY HWANG

SUGGESTED BY THE OPERA

STARRING
ADAM PASCAL   LISA BRESCIA
ERIC LaJUAN SUMMERS   ROBERT JASON JACKSON   TOM NELIS
AND
MICKY DOLENZ

ROBERT M. ARMITAGE   TERRA LYNN ARRINGTON   JEB BROWN   AFI BRYANT   TA REA CAMPBELL
TIM CRASKEY   JESSICA HENDY   CHEYENNE JACKSON   JOHN JACQUET, JR.   REGINALD HOLDEN JENNINGS
MAHI KEKUMU   YOUN KIM   NINA LaFARGA   ALLISON THOMAS LEE   KOH MOCHIZUKI   NOA NEVÉ
JODY RIPPLINGER   RAYMOND RODRIGUEZ   CHUCK SACULLA   SOLANGE SANDY   MICHAEL SERAPIGLIA
SLAM   LORI ANN STRUNK   SAMUEL N. THIAM   BROOKE WENDLE   SCHELE WILLIAMS   NATALIA ZISA

SCENIC AND COSTUME DESIGN
BOB CROWLEY

LIGHTING DESIGN
NATASHA KATZ

SOUND DESIGN
STEVE CANYON KENNEDY

HAIR DESIGN
DAVID BRIAN BROWN

MAKEUP DESIGN
NAOMI DONNE

FIGHT DIRECTOR
RICK SORDELET

MUSIC ARRANGEMENTS
GUY BABYLON
PAUL BOGAEV

ORCHESTRATIONS
STEVE MARGOSHES
GUY BABYLON
PAUL BOGAEV

DANCE ARRANGEMENTS
BOB GUSTAFSON
JIM ABBOTT
GARY SELIGSON

MUSIC COORDINATOR
MICHAEL KELLER

MUSICAL DIRECTION
ROBERT MIKULSKI

CASTING
BERNARD TELSEY CASTING

PRESS REPRESENTATIVE
BONEAU/BRYAN-BROWN

PRODUCTION STAGE MANAGER
LOIS GRIFFING

PRODUCTION SUPERVISOR
CLIFFORD SCHWARTZ

TECHNICAL SUPERVISION
THEATERSMITH, INC.

ASSOCIATE PRODUCER
MARSHALL B. PURDY

ASSOCIATE DIRECTOR
KEITH BATTEN

ASSOCIATE CHOREOGRAPHER
TRACEY LANGRAN COREA

PRODUCED BY
PETER SCHNEIDER & THOMAS SCHUMACHER

MUSIC PRODUCED AND MUSIC SUPERVISION BY
PAUL BOGAEV

CHOREOGRAPHY BY
WAYNE CILENTO

DIRECTED BY
ROBERT FALLS

ORIGINALLY DEVELOPED AT THE ALLIANCE THEATRE COMPANY IN ATLANTA, GEORGIA

9/5/2004

CAST
(in order of appearance)

Amneris	LISA BRESCIA
Radames	ADAM PASCAL
Aida	DEBORAH A. COX
Mereb	ERIC LJUAN SUMMERS
Zoser	MICKY DOLENZ
Pharaoh	TOM NELIS
Nehebka	SCHELE WILLIAMS
Amonasro	ROBERT JASON JACKSON
Ensemble	ROBERT M. ARMITAGE,

TERRA LYNN ARRINGTON,
AFI BRYANT, TIM CRASKEY,
JOHN JACQUET, JR.,
MAHI KEKUMU, YOUN KIM,
NINA LAFARGA,
ALLISON THOMAS LEE,
NOA NEVÉ,
RAYMOND RODRIGUEZ,
CHUCK SACULLA,
MICHAEL SERAPIGLIA,
SLAM, LORI ANN STRUNK,
SAMUEL N. THIAM,
BROOKE WENDLE,
SCHELE WILLIAMS, NATALIA ZISA

STANDBYS

Standby for Aida – TA'REA CAMPBELL; Standby for Radames – CHEYENNE JACKSON; Standby for Amneris – JESSICA HENDY: Standby for Zoser, Pharaoh – JEB BROWN

SWINGS:
REGINALD HOLDEN JENNINGS,
KOH MOCHIZUKI,
JODY RIPPLINGER, SOLANGE SANDY

UNDERSTUDIES:
Aida – SCHELE WILLIAMS; Radames – CHUCK SACULLA; Amneris – LORI ANN STRUNK; Mereb – MAHI KEKUMU, KOH MOCHIZUKI; Zoser – RAYMOND RODRIGUEZ; Pharaoh – CHUCK SACULLA; Nehebka – AFI BRYANT, SOLANGE SANDY; Amonasro – REGINALD HOLDEN JENNINGS, RAYMOND RODRIGUEZ

ORCHESTRA

Conductor: Robert Mikulski
Associate Conductor: Stan Tucker
Keyboards: Jon Werking, Bob Gustafson, Stan Tucker; Drums/Percussion: Keith Crupi; Bass: Gary Bristol; Acoustic/Electric Guitar: Bruce Uchitel, Jon Herington; Percussion: Dean Thomas; Concertmaster: Ron Oakland; Cello: Amy Ralske; Viola: Joseph Gottesman; Violin: Robin Zeh; French Horn: R.J. Kelly; Oboe/English Horn: Jim Roe; Flute/Alto Flute/Piccolo: Melanie Bradford
Music Coordinator: Michael Keller

Aida

MUSICAL NUMBERS

ACT ONE

Every Story Is a Love Story .... Amneris
Fortune Favors the Brave .... Radames and the Soldiers
The Past Is Another Land .... Aida
Another Pyramid .... Zoser and the Ministers
How I Know You .... Mereb and Aida
My Strongest Suit .... Amneris and Women of the Palace
Enchantment Passing Through .... Radames and Aida
My Strongest Suit (Reprise) .... Amneris and Aida
Dance of the Robe .... Aida, Nehebka and the Nubians
Not Me .... Radames, Mereb, Aida and Amneris
Elaborate Lives .... Radames and Aida
The Gods Love Nubia .... Aida, Nehebka and the Nubians

ACT TWO

A Step Too Far .... Amneris, Radames and Aida
Easy As Life .... Aida
Like Father Like Son .... Zoser, Radames and the Ministers
Radames' Letter .... Radames
How I Know You (Reprise) .... Mereb
Written in the Stars .... Aida and Radames
I Know the Truth .... Amneris
Elaborate Lives (Reprise) .... Aida and Radames
Every Story Is a Love Story (Reprise) .... Amneris

Deborah A. Cox as Aida.

Deborah A. Cox
Aida

Adam Pascal
Radames

Lisa Brescia
Amneris

Micky Dolenz
Zoser

Eric LaJuan Summers
Mereb

Robert Jason Jackson
Amonasro

Tom Nelis
Pharaoh

Robert M. Armitage
Ensemble

Terra Lynn Arrington
Ensemble

Jeb Brown
Pharaoh and Zoser Standby

Afi Bryant
Ensemble

Ta'Rea Campbell
Aida Standby

Tim Craskey
Ensemble

Jessica Hendy
Amneris Standby

Photo by Joan Marcus

Aida

Cheyenne Jackson
Radames Standby

John Jacquet, Jr.
Ensemble

Reginald Holden Jennings
Swing/Asst. Dance Captain

Mahi Kekumu
Ensemble

Youn Kim
Ensemble

Nina LaFarga
Ensemble

Allison Thomas Lee
Ensemble

Koh Mochizuki
Swing/ Dance Captain

Noa Nevé
Ensemble

Jody Ripplinger
Swing/Assistant Dance Captain

Raymond Rodriguez
Ensemble/ Fight Captain

Chuck Saculla
Ensemble

Solange Sandy
Swing

Michael Serapiglia
Ensemble

Slam
Ensemble

Lori Ann Strunk
Ensemble

Samuel N. Thiam
Ensemble

Brooke Wendle
Ensemble

Schele Williams
Ensemble

Natalia Zisa
Ensemble

Elton John
Music

Tim Rice
Lyrics

Linda Woolverton
Book

David Henry Hwang
Book

Robert Falls
Director/Book

Wayne Cilento
Choreographer

Bob Crowley
Scenic & Costume Design

Natasha Katz
Lighting Design

Paul Bogaev
Music Producer/ Conductor/Arrangements/Orchestrations

Gary Seligson
Dance Arrangements

Keith Batten
Associate Director

Tracey Langran Corea
Associate Choreographer

Christopher Smith
Technical Supervision

Bernard Telsey
Casting

Rick Sordelet
Fight Director

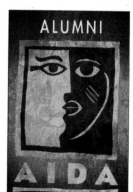

Tyrees Allen
Amonasro

Will Chase
Radames

Anika Ellis
Ensemble

Ashley Amber Haase
Swing

Grasan Kingsberry
Ensemble

Timothy Edward Smith
Ensemble

Allison Leo
Ensemble

Krisha Marcano
Swing

Darrell Grand Moultrie
Ensemble

Karine Newborn
Ensemble

Saycon Sengbloh
Aida Standby

Aida

STAFF FOR AIDA

PROJECT MANAGER ....LIZBETH CONE
Assistant to the Associate Producer ....Emily Powell

ASSOCIATE DIRECTOR ....KEITH BATTEN
Associate Choreographer ...TRACEY LANGRAN COREA

GENERAL PRESS REPRESENTATIVE
BONEAU/BRYAN-BROWN
Chris Boneau, Jackie Green, Adriana Douzos, Aaron Meier

COMPANY MANAGER ....LISA KOCH RAO
Assistant Company Manager ....Charlissa Jackson

PRODUCTION
STAGE MANAGER ....LOIS GRIFFING
Stage Manager ....Valerie Lau-Kee Lai
Assistant Stage Managers ....Elaine Bayless,
Beverly Jenkins
Dance Captain ....Koh Mochizuki
Assistant Dance Captain ....Reginald Holden Jennings
Fight Captain ....Raymond Rodriguez

Associate Scenic Designer ....Ted LeFevre
Scenic Design Assistants ....Mike Britton, Dan Kuchar
Prop Coordinator ....Denise J. Grillo
Prop Assistants ....Rebecca Haskins, Rashida Poole
Associate Costume Designer ....Scott Traugott
Costume Design Assistants ....Cory Ching,
Rick Conway,
Angela Kahler, Brian Russman
Associate Lighting Designer ....Edward Pierce
Lighting Design Assistant ....Karen Spahn
Assistant to Lighting Designer ....Richard Swan
Automated Lighting Tracker ....A. Cameron Zetty
Associate Sound Designer ....John Shivers
Hair Design Assistant ....Leslie Evers
Makeup Design Assistant ....Richard Dean

Production Carpenter ....Jeff Goodman
Assistant Carpenter ....Mike Kearns
Fly Automation ....Dave Brown
Flyman ....Joe "No" Abitante
Deck Automation ....Ann Cavanaugh
Production Electrician ....Salvatore Restuccia
Assistant Electrician ....Ronald Jacobson
Automated Lighting Technician ....Brian Dawson
Lead Follow Spot Operator ....Mike Lyons
Prop Supervisor ....Mike Smanko
Production Props ....Joe Redmond
Assistant Props ....Cavan Jones
Production Sound Engineer ....John Shivers
Sound Engineer ....Phil Lojo
Assistant Sound Engineer ....Alain Van Achte
Smoke and Atmospheric Effects ....Chic Silber
Associate to Mr. Silber ....Bill McComb
Wardrobe Supervisor ....Nanette Golia
Assistant Wardrobe Supervisor ....Peggy Kurz
Dressers ....Michael Berglund, Tom Bertsch,
Kristin Farley, Melanie Hansen, Michael Harrell,
Margo Lawless, Melanie McClintock, Marcia McIntosh,
Lisa Preston, Leah Redmond, Jessica Scoblick,
Shana Skop, Pam Sorenson, Dolly Williams,
Linda Zimmerman
Hair Supervisor ....Sonia Rivera
Assistant Hair Supervisor ....Gary Martori
Hairdressers ....Charlene Belmond
Andrew C. Lavenziano
Makeup Supervisor ....Jorge Vargas

BERNARD TELSEY CASTING, C.S.A.
Bernie Telsey, Will Cantler, David Vaccari, Bethany Berg,
Craig Burns, Tiffany Little Canfield, Christine Dall

Music Preparation Supervisor ....Peter Miller
Miller Music Service
Assistant to Mr. Margoshes ....Lawrence Rosen
Electronic Music Design .....Music Arts Technologies, Inc.
Electronic Drum Programming ....Gary Seligson

Show Accountant ....Jamie Cousins
Advertising..............................Serino Coyne, Inc.
Production Photography ....Joan Marcus
Orthopedic Consultant ....Dr. Phillip Bauman
Production Travel ....Jill L. Citron
Product Placement ....George Fenmore/
More Merchandising International
Personal Assistant to Elton John ....Bob Halley
Assistant to Tim Rice ....Eileen Heinink
Management for Ms. Cox ....Lascelles Stephens/
Overbrook Entertainment
Special Thanks............Lynn Beckemeyer, Harry Grossman
Original Project Manager ....Ken Silverman

CREDITS
Scenery and Automation by Show Motion, Inc. Lighting equipment by Four Star Lighting, Inc. Sound equipment by Masque Sound; Automated Lighting provided by Vari-Lite Production Services, Inc. Millinery by Rodney Gordon. 'Strongest Suit' Millinery by Bryan Crockett & Rodney Gordon. Armor by Julian Gilbert. Fabric Painters: Janet Bloor, Michele Hill, Mary Macy & Raylene Marasco. Digital Fabric Painting by Real Image. Custom Jewelry by Martin Adams. Custom Footwear by Frederick Longtin Handmade Shoes, J.C. Theatrical, K&D, Ltd., Montana Leatherworks, Rilleau Sandals, Sandalman. Feathers by American Plume & FancyFeather. Make up wipes courtesy of M.A.C. Hair by Ray Marston Wig Studio, Ltd. Trucking by Anthony Augliera, Inc. Henrietta Rinkell. Swimming Effect by Foy. Laser Effect by Norman Ballard. Steam Effect by Jauchem & Meeh NYC. Deck Smoke Systems by Sunshine Scenic Studio. Washing Silk Release by Feller Precision. Map based on Egypt and its trade network by Horner & Brooks Design Studio. Soft Goods and Fiber Optics by I. Weiss & Sons, Inc. Props by John Creech Design & Production, Tom Talmon, Westsun Scenic Edge. Prop soft goods by Cinaf Designs. Wilton Armetale Oasis Pitchers used. Chalices by Chiarelli's Religious Goods, Inc. Weapons by Lewis Shaw. Guitar Strings by DR. Guitar pickups by Seymour Duncan. Electric Guitar courtesy of Dean. Guitar pre-Amp courtesy of Crate Amplification. Acoustic Drums by Pearl Drums. Speaker Cabinet by Bag End. Drumsticks courtesy of Pro-Mark. Cymbals courtesy of Sabian Cymbals.

COSTUMES EXECUTED BY BARBARA MATERA, LTD.

NEDERLANDER
Chairman/President ....James M. Nederlander
President ....James L. Nederlander

Executive Vice President
Nick Scandalios

Vice President | Senior Vice President
Corporate Development | Labor Relations
Charlene S. Nederlander | **Herschel Waxman**

Vice President | Chief Financial Officer
Jim Boese | **Freida Sawyer Belviso**

Yamaha is the official piano of the Nederlander Organization.

Theatre insurance provided by Emar Group.

STAFF FOR THE PALACE THEATRE
Theatre Manager ....Dixon Rosario
Treasurer ....Cissy Caspare
Assistant Treasurer ....Anne T. Wilson
Carpenter ....Thomas K. Phillips
Flyman.....................................Robert W. Kelly
Electrician ....Eddie Webber
Propertymaster ....Steve Camus
Chief Usher ....Gloria Hill

DISNEY THEATRICAL PRODUCTIONS
President ....Thomas Schumacher
Senior Vice President & General Manager ......Alan Levey
Senior Vice President,
Managing Director & CFO ....David Schrader

GENERAL MANAGEMENT
Vice President, International ....Ron Kollen
Vice President, Operations ....Dana Amendola
Vice President, Labor Relations ....Allan Frost
Director, Human Resources ....June Heindel
Director, Domestic Touring ....Michele Gold
Manager, Labor Relations ....Stephanie Cheek
Manager, Information Systems ....Scott Benedict
Consultant,
Information Systems ....Christopher Diamond

PRODUCTION
Executive Music Producer ....Chris Montan
Vice President, Creative Affairs ....Michele Steckler
Vice President, Creative Affairs ....Greg Gunter
Vice President,
Physical Production ....John Tiggeloven
Purchasing Manager ....Joseph Doughney
Staff Associate Director ....Jeff Lee
Staff Associate Producer ....Florie Seery
Staff Associate Designer ....Dennis W. Moyes
Staff Associate Dramaturg ....Ken Cerniglia

MARKETING
Vice President ....Heather Epple
Vice President, Domestic Touring ....Jack Eldon
Director, New York ....Patricia Kellert
Manager, New York ....Michele Holland
Manager, New York ....Leslie Barrett
Manager ....Joel Hile

SALES
Vice President, Ticketing ....Jerome Kane
Manager, Group Sales ....Jacob Lloyd Kimbro
Group Sales Representative ....Juil Kim

BUSINESS AND LEGAL AFFAIRS
Vice President ....Jonathan Olson
Vice President ....Robbin Kelley
Director ....Harry S. Gold
Attorney ....Seth Stuhl
Paralegal/Contract Administration ....Colleen Lober

FINANCE
Director ....Joe McClafferty
Manager, Production Accounting ....Bill Hussey
Senior Business Planners ....Jason Fletcher, Justin Gee
Senior Analyst ....Sam Tello
Production Accountants ....Jamie Cousins
Alma LaMarr, Barbara Toben
Analyst ....Ronnie Cooper

CONTROLLERSHIP
Director, Accounting ....Leena Mathews
Manager, Accounting ....Erica McShane
Analysts ....Celia Brown, Adrineh Ghoukassian

ADMINISTRATIVE STAFF
Elliot Altman, Ann Marie Amarga, Amy Andrews, Alice Baeza, Jennifer Baker, Antonia Barba, Tiffany Casanova, Karl Chmielewski, Celena Cipriaso, Giovanna Cusicanqui, Dale Edwards, Carl Flanigan, Margie Freeswick, Jonathan Hanson, Jay Hollenback, Connie Jasper, Khadija Mohamed, Jeff Parvin, Roberta Risafi, Sarah Roach, Susan Rubio, Kisha Santiago, Christian Trimmer

Disney Theatrical Productions
1450 Broadway • New York, NY 10018
mail@disneytheatrical.com

BUENA VISTA THEATRICAL MERCHANDISE, L.L.C.
Director ....Steven Downing
Manager ....John F. Agati
Operations Manager ....Shawn Baker
Assistant Manager, Inventory ....Suzanne Jakel
Buyer ....Suzanne Araneo
Merchandise Assistant ....Renee Williams
On-site Retail Manager ....Kris Wright
On-site Assistant Retail Manager ....Katrina Bernard

Anniversary Gifts: The producers gave us a beautiful pen set.

Celebrity Visitor: My favorite was Will Smith. He came backstage during intermission and hung out for a little while. But then the audience members got a little crazy, and he had to leave.

"Easter Bonnet" Sketch: "It's Easy" (2004).

"Carols For A Cure" Carol: "The Holly and the Ivy."

Most Roles: Krisha Marcano. She was a swing and covered every track.

Backstage Rituals: To stay fit, the actors gather at every show by the stage manager's office for sit-ups.

Favorite Moment: When Aida gives Radames her hand. It's a combination of seeing her power and hearing the audience reaction. They've been rooting for her, and when it happens it's kind of unexpected, but people are glad it happens. It always gets a hand.

In-Theatre Gathering Place: The crew have a card room and the actors hang out in the swing room. They talk and play games. One game in particular everyone is addicted to: You go through the alphabet naming celebrities by the first letters of their names. You start with the initials AA, then AB, then AC, and so on. The person with the most names wins.

Off-Site Hangout: We're always going to clubs, because there's always someone who has been a part of the company performing somewhere.

Snack Food: Anything with chocolate in it.

Favorite Therapy: The actors work out with foam rollers. They worked them to death and we've had to order new ones.

Memorable Ad Lib: Heather Headley's mom in the audience at her first performance, yelled out, "Sing it, girl."

Stage Door Fan Encounter: For a while, Maya Days had a really dedicated fan. He was always there and always bought a ticket in the front row.

Busiest Day At The Box Office: When Toni Braxton missed a show.

Heaviest/Hottest Costume: Amneris. Also, there is the dancer who has the light-up dress in the runway scene.

Who Wore The Least: The East Indian trio in the belly dancing scene.

Orchestra Member Who Played Most Consecutive Performances Without A Sub: Dean Thomas, our percussionist, was always there.

Sweethearts: Raymond Rodriguez and Kenya Massey.

Also: The actors have several Walls of Fame backstage. One displays everyone's baby pictures. In the swing room we have cut-out pictures from magazines and newspapers that resemble people in the company. We also have a Bad Hair Wall right outside men's dressing room. It has pictures of people with bad hair, like a high school photo wall.

Correspondent: Charlissa Jackson, Assistant Company Manager

Photos by Aubrey Reuben

(L-R) Former Monkee Micky Dolenz, Deborah Cox, Adam Pascal, Lisa Brescia, producer Thomas Schumacher at the closing party at Cipriani 42nd St.

Deborah Cox and Will Chase at a reception welcoming Cox to the cast, at W Times Square Hotel.

Librettist David Henry Hwang and director Robert Falls at the final performance at the Palace Theatre.

Curtain calls on closing night.

Deborah Cox joins the cast.

PLAYBILL®

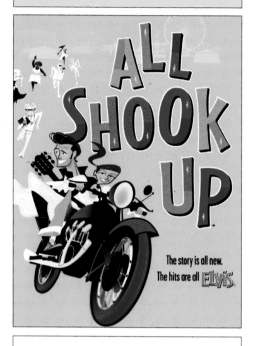

**The story is all new.
The hits are all ELVIS**

CAST
(in order of appearance)

Natalie Haller/Ed	JENN GAMBATESE
Jim Haller	JONATHAN HADARY
Dennis	MARK PRICE
Sylvia	SHARON WILKINS
Lorraine	NIKKI M. JAMES
Chad	CHEYENNE JACKSON
Mayor Matilda Hyde	ALIX KOREY
Dean Hyde	CURTIS HOLBROOK
Sheriff Earl	JOHN JELLISON
Miss Sandra	LEAH HOCKING

ENSEMBLE

BRAD ANDERSON, JUSTIN BOHON,
JUSTIN BRILL, PAUL CASTREE,
CARA COOPER, MICHAEL CUSUMANO,
FRANCESCA HARPER, TRISHA JEFFREY,
MICHELLE KITTRELL, ANIKA LARSEN,
MICHAEL X. MARTIN, KAREN MURPHY,
JOHN ERIC PARKER, JUSTIN PATTERSON,
MICHAEL JAMES SCOTT, JENNY-LYNN
SUCKLING, VIRGINIA WOODRUFF

Dance Captains:
RANDY A. DAVIS, JENNIE FORD
Assistant Dance Captain:
JENNY-LYNN SUCKLING

SWINGS

RANDY A. DAVIS, JENNIE FORD,
JENELLE LYNN RANDALL

continued on the next page

✺N✺ PALACE THEATRE
UNDER THE DIRECTION OF
STEWART F. LANE, JAMES M. NEDERLANDER AND JAMES L. NEDERLANDER

Jonathan Pollard   Bernie Kukoff
Clear Channel Entertainment   Harbor Entertainment   Miramax Films   Bob & Harvey Weinstein
Stanley Buchthal   Eric Falkenstein   Nina Essman/Nancy Nagel Gibbs   Jean Cheever   Margaret Cotter
in association with
Barney Rosenzweig   Meri Krassner   FGRW Investments   Karen Jason   Phil Ciasullo Conard

present

ALL SHOOK UP™
Inspired by and featuring the songs of ELVIS PRESLEY®

Book by
Joe DiPietro

Starring

Jenn Gambatese   Jonathan Hadary   Leah Hocking   Curtis Holbrook   Cheyenne Jackson
Nikki M. James   John Jellison   Alix Korey   Mark Price   Sharon Wilkins

Featuring

Brad Anderson Justin Bohon Justin Brill Paul Castree Cara Cooper Michael Cusumano Randy A. Davis
Jennie Ford Francesca Harper Trisha Jeffrey Michelle Kittrell Anika Larsen Michael X. Martin Karen Murphy
John Eric Parker Justin Patterson Jenelle Lynn Randall Michael James Scott Jenny-Lynn Suckling Virginia Woodruff

Set Design	Costume Design	Lighting Design	Sound Design	Wig & Hair Design
David Rockwell	**David C. Woolard**	**Donald Holder**	**Brian Ronan**	**David H. Lawrence**

Orchestrations	Dance Music Arrangements	Music Coordinator	Associate Director
Michael Gibson Stephen Oremus	**Zane Mark**	**Michael Keller**	**Daniel Goldstein**

Casting	Press Representative	Marketing	Associate Choreographers
Bernard Telsey Casting	**Barlow•Hartman**	**TMG** The Marketing Group	**Lorna Ventura JoAnn M. Hunter**

General Management	Production Stage Manager	Technical Supervisor	Associate Producers
Alan Wasser Associates Allan Williams	**Lois L. Griffing**	**Juniper Street Productions**	**Marcia Goldberg Greg Schaffert**

Music Supervision and Arrangements by
Stephen Oremus
Additional Choreography by
Sergio Trujillo
Choreographed by
Ken Roberson
Directed by
Christopher Ashley

Originally Produced for Goodspeed Musicals • Michael P. Price, Executive Producer • Sue Frost, Associate Producer
Original Cast Recording album from Sony BMG

All Shook Up and Elvis Presley are registered trademarks of Elvis Presley Enterprises, Inc.

5/20/05

All Shook Up

MUSICAL NUMBERS

TIME: A 24-hour period, during the summer of 1955
PLACE: A small you-never-heard-of-it town somewhere in the Midwest

ACT I

"Love Me Tender"	Natalie, Dennis
"Heartbreak Hotel"	Barflies
"Roustabout"	Chad
"One Night With You"	Natalie
"C'mon Everybody"	Chad, Company
"Follow That Dream"	Chad, Natalie
"Teddy Bear/Hound Dog"	Chad, Sandra, Dennis, Natalie
"That's All Right"	Sylvia, Lorraine, Chad, Dennis, Barflies
"(You're the) Devil in Disguise"	Matilda, Ladies Church Council
"It's Now or Never"	Dean, Lorraine, Company
"Blue Suede Shoes"	Ed, Chad
"Don't Be Cruel"	Chad, Jim
"Let Yourself Go"	Sandra, Statues
"Can't Help Falling in Love"	Company

ACT II

"All Shook Up"	Company
"It Hurts Me"	Dennis, Company
"A Little Less Conversation"	Ed, Company
"The Power of My Love"	Chad, Jim, Sandra
"I Don't Want To"	Chad
"Jailhouse Rock"	Chad, Prisoners
"There's Always Me"	Sylvia
"If I Can Dream"	Chad, Lorraine, Dean, Company
"Can't Help Falling in Love" (Reprise)	Earl, Jim, Sylvia, Matilda
"Fools Fall in Love"	Natalie, Company
"Burning Love"	Chad, Natalie, Company

Cast Continued

UNDERSTUDIES

For Natalie Haller: CARA COOPER, ANIKA LARSEN; for Jim Haller: BRAD ANDERSON, MICHAEL X. MARTIN; for Dennis: JUSTIN BRILL, PAUL CASTREE; for Sylvia: FRANCESCA HARPER, VIRGINIA WOODRUFF; for Lorraine: TRISHA JEFFREY, JENELLE LYNN RANDALL; for Chad: BRAD ANDERSON, JUSTIN PATTERSON; for Mayor Matilda Hyde: KAREN MURPHY, JENNY-LYNN SUCKLING; for Dean Hyde: JUSTIN BOHON, JUSTIN BRILL; for Sheriff Earl: MICHAEL X. MARTIN, JUSTIN PATTERSON; for Miss Sandra: MICHELLE KITTRELL, ANIKA LARSEN, JENNY-LYNN SUCKLING

ALL SHOOK UP BAND

Conductor/Keyboard: Stephen Oremus
Associate Conductor: August Eriksmoen
Reeds: Charles Pillow, Tim Ries, Andy Snitzer, Don McGeen; Lead Trumpet: Joe Giorgianni
Trumpets: Tino Gagliardi, Brian Pareschi; Trombone: Mike Davis; Organ/Keyboard 2: August Eriksmoen; Guitars: Ken Brescia, Chris Delis; Bass: Cary Potts; Drums: Steve Bartosik
Percussion: Joe Mowatt

Music Coordinator: Michael Keller
Music Copying: Kaye-Houston Music/ Anne Kaye & Doug Houston
Synthesizer Programmer: Andrew Barrett for Lionella Productions, Ltd.
Guitars provided by Gibson Guitars, Inc.

Elvis Lives: Cheyenne Jackson (center) and the cast.

All Shook Up

Jenn Gambatese
Natalie Haller/Ed

Jonathan Hadary
Jim Haller

Leah Hocking
Miss Sandra

Curtis Holbrook
Dean Hyde

Cheyenne Jackson
Chad

Nikki M. James
Lorraine

John Jellison
Sheriff Earl

Alix Korey
Mayor Matilda Hyde

Mark Price
Dennis

Sharon Wilkins
Sylvia

Brad Anderson
Ensemble

Justin Bohon
Ensemble

Justin Brill
Ensemble

Paul Castree
Ensemble

Cara Cooper
Ensemble

Michael Cusumano
Ensemble

Randy A. Davis
Ensemble/Dance Captain

Jennie Ford
Ensemble/Dance Captain

Francesca Harper
Ensemble

Trisha Jeffrey
Ensemble

Michelle Kittrell
Ensemble

Anika Larsen
Ensemble

Michael X. Martin
Ensemble

Karen Murphy
Ensemble

John Eric Parker
Ensemble

Justin Patterson
Ensemble

Jenelle Lynn Randall
Ensemble

Michael James Scott
Ensemble

Jenny-Lynn Suckling
Ensemble

Virginia Ann Woodruff
Ensemble

Joe DiPietro
Book

Christopher Ashley
Director

Ken Roberson
Choreographer

Sergio Trujillo
Additional Choreography

Stephen Oremus
Music Supervision/ Arrangements/ Orchestrations

David Rockwell
Set Design

David C. Woolard
Costume Designer

Donald Holder
Lighting Design

Michael Gibson
Orchestrations

Michael Keller
Music Coordinator

Bernard Telsey Casting
Casting

Alan Wasser
General Manager

All Shook Up

Jonathan Pollard
Producer

David Broser and Aaron Harnick
Producers

Marcia Goldberg, Nancy Nagel Gibbs
and Nina Essman
Producers

Harvey Weinstein
Producer

Margery Singer
Marketing

Photos by Ben Strothmann

Stage Management (L-R): Chris Zaccardi, Megan Schneid, Lois L. Griffing and Paul J. Smith.

Crew
Back Row (L-R): Aaron Straus, Mark Rampmeyer.
Center Row: (L-R): David Grevengoed, Mike Bernstein, Carlos Marqinex, Ian Michaud, Marvin Crosland, Bobby Kelly, Dave Brown.
Kneeling: (L-R): Jack Anderson, Geoff Vaughn.

Orchestra
(L-R): Tim Ries, Tino Gagliardi, Joe Giorgianni, Andy Snitzer, August Eriksmoen, Mike Davis, Don McGeen, Joe Mowatt, Chris Delis, Cary Potts and Steve Bartosik.

Front of House
In Front: Rose Zangale. Second Row (L-R): Alyson Handleman, Helen Geanolaes, Patricia Marsh, Sandra Darbasie, Dixon Rosario, Jr., Desteny Bivona. Third Row (L-R): Gloria Hill, Paul Vanderlinen, Edie Sanabria, Jennifer Butt and Bill Mullen.

STAFF FOR ALL SHOOK UP

GENERAL MANAGEMENT
ALAN WASSER ASSOCIATES
Alan Wasser Allan Williams
Lane Marsh Aaron Lustbader

GENERAL PRESS REPRESENTATION
BARLOW•HARTMAN
Michael Hartman John Barlow
Wayne Wolfe Andrew Snyder

CASTING BY
Bernard Telsey Casting
Bernard Telsey Will Cantler David Vaccari
Bethany Knox Craig Burns Tiffany Little Canfield
Christine Dall Stephanie Yankwitt

COMPANY MANAGER
Mark Shacket

PRODUCTION MANAGEMENT
JUNIPER STREET PRODUCTIONS
Hillary Blanken John Paull III
Kevin Broomell Guy Kwan

PRODUCTION STAGE MANAGER ....LOIS L. GRIFFING
Stage Manager ....Paul J. Smith
Assistant Stage Managers ...Megan Schneid, Chris Zaccardi
Associate Company Manager ....Maria T. Mazza
General Mgmt. Associates ...Thom Mitchell, Connie Yung
Associate Director ....Daniel Goldstein
Associate Choreographer ....Lorna Ventura
Music Coordinator ....Michael Keller
Rehearsal Pianist ....Jason DeBord
Dance Captains ....Randy A. Davis, Jennie Ford
Assistant Dance Captain ....Jenny-Lynn Suckling
Make-Up Designer ....Angelina Avallone
Associate Scenic Designer ....Robert Bissinger
Associate to Mr. Rockwell ....Barry Richards
Assistant Scenic Designers ....Ted LeFevre, Dan Kuchar, Todd Ivins, Michael Auszura, Ed Pisoni, Rob Andrusko, Richard Jaris
Assistants to Mr. Rockwell ....Nikita Polyanski, Corinne Merrill, Daniela Galli
Assistant to Mr. Harnick and Mr. Broser ....Lisa Lapan
Model Makers ....Rachel Janocko, Joanie Schlafer, Morgan Moore, Mike Dereskewicz
Associate Lighting Designer ....Jeanne Koenig
Associate Lighting Designer/ Automated Lighting ....Aland Henderson
Assistant Lighting Designer ....Michael P. Jones
Assistant to the Lighting Designer ....Jesse Belsky
Associate to Donald Holder ....Hilary Manners
Automated Lighting Programmer ....Richard Tyndall
Associate Sound Designer ....Mike Farfalla
Associate Costume Designer ....Kevin Brainerd
Assistant Costume Designers ....Daryl A. Stone, E. Shura Pollatsek
Costume Buyer ....Rebecca Bentjen
Costume Assistant ....Matthew Pachtman
Costume Interns ....Angie Harner (Chicago), Bretta Heilbut (NY)
Production Electrician ....Jimmy Maloney
Production Properties Supervisor ....Timothy Abel
Head Carpenter ....Jack Anderson
Assistant Carpenters ....Dave Brown, Matt Lynch, Geoffrey Vaughn
Head Electrician ....Carlos Martinez
Assistant Electricians ....Kevin Barry, Michael Taylor
Head Properties Supervisor ....Michael Bernstein
Assistant Properties Supervisor ....Marvin Crosland
Head Sound Engineer ....Aaron Straus
Assistant Sound Engineer ....TJ McEvoy
Production Wardrobe Supervisor ....Debbie Cheretun
Assistant Wardrobe Supervisor ....James Hall
Hair Supervisor ....Wanda Gregory
Assistant Hair Supervisor ....Mark Adam Rampmeyer
Hairstylist ....Charlene Belmond
Production Management Associates ......Ana-Rose Greene, Emily Lawson
Production Assistants ....Robert M. Armitage, Nellie Beavers, Dan Creviston, Sara Gammage, Annie Leonhart, Matthew Melchiorre, Blake Merriman, Chris Zaccardi
Production Associate to Mr. Pollard ....Susan Vargo
Synthesizer Programmer ....Andrew Barrett/ Lionella Productions LTD
Music Dept. Production Assistants ....Justin A. Malakhow, Alan Schmuckler (Chi), Joshua Salzman
Copyists ....Kaye-Houston Music, Inc.

Legal Counsel ....Franklin, Weinrib, Rudell & Vasallo/ Elliott Brown, Daniel Wasser, Jonathan Lonner
Insurance ....DeWitt Stern Group
Banking ....JP Morgan Chase & Co./ Richard Callian, Michele Gibbons
Accounting ....Rosenberg Neuwirth & Kuchner/ Chris Cacace, Patricia Pedersen
Audit ....Robert Fried, C.P.A.
Travel ....Road Rebel Entertainment Touring
Payroll Service ....Castellana Services Inc./Lance Castellana
Advertising ....SpotCo/Drew Hodges, Jim Edwards, Tom Greenwald, Jim Aquino, Lauren Hunter
Marketing ....The Marketing Group/ Laura Matalon, Tanya Grubich, Marti Wigder Grimminck, Jenny Richardson, Trish Santini, Jennifer Shultz
Merchandising ..SFX Theatrical Merchandising/ Larry Turk
Web Designer ....Simma Park
Theatre Displays ....King Displays, Inc.
Production Photographer ....Joan Marcus

Cover illustration by Jonas Bergstrand.
© Gladys Music 2004.
Elvis Presley is a trademark of Elvis Presley Enterprises, Inc.

For more information visit: www.allshookup.com.

CREDITS AND ACKNOWLEDGMENTS

Scenery and scenic effects built and electrified by ShowMotion, Inc., Norwalk, Connecticut and PRG Scenic Technologies, New Windsor, NY. Scenery painted by Scenic Art Studios, Cornwall, NY. Show control and scenic motion control featuring stage command systems® by PRG Scenic Technologies. Show control, fly automation and special effects using AC2 computerized motion control system by ShowMotion Inc. Soft goods built by I. Weiss and Sons, Inc., Long Island City, NY. Lighting equipment from PRG Lighting, North Bergen, NJ. Sound equipment from PRG Audio, Mt. Vernon, NY. Specialty props executed by The Spoon Group, Rahway, NJ; and Jauchem and Meeh, Brooklyn, NY. Additional hand props courtesy of George Fenmore, Inc. Acrylic drinkware by U.S. Acrylic, Inc. Costumes made by Barbara Matera Ltd, Parsons-Meares Ltd., Studio Rouge, Timberlake Studios Inc., Tricorne; uniforms by Park Coats; custom shirts by CEGO; custom leatherwear by Francis Hendy; custom gloves by Dorothy Gaspar; millinery by Arnold S. Levine, Inc., and Rodney Gordon, Inc.; uniform hats by Tanen Co.; custom sweaters by Maria Ficalora Knitwear Ltd.; shoes made by Capezio Dance-Theatre Professional Shop, JC Theatrical Shoes and LaDuca Shoes NYC; fabric dyeing/printing by Dye-Namix and Gene Mignola Inc. Leatherwear in part courtesy of SCHOTT NYC; men's undershirts courtesy of 2(x)ist. Study guide by Peter Royston/GUIDEWRITE. Special thanks to Goodspeed Musicals Costume Rentals. Custom wigs executed by D.H. Lawrence Enterprises, Inc. Interstate hauling by Clark Transfer, Inc. Natural herb cough drops courtesy of Ricola USA, Inc. Rehearsed at The New 42nd Street Studios. Special thanks to Fred Gallo.

SPECIAL THANKS

Susan Aberbach, Belinda Aberbach, David Beckwith, Jennifer Burgess, Carol Butler, Carolyn Christensen, Jennifer DeLange, Gibson Musical Instruments and Epiphone Guitars, Joanna Hagan, Alexander Hartnett, Gary Hovey, Debbie Johnson, Roberta Korus, Tom Levy, Richard Mincheff, Todd Morgan, Steven Rodner, Patrick Roy, Adina Schecter, Tim Schmidt, Abbie Schroeder, Jack Soden, Michael Sukin, Beth Williams, Scott Williams, Scott Yoselow

SONG CREDITS

"Love Me Tender" by Elvis Presley and Vera Matson; published by Elvis Presley Music (administered by Cherry River Music Co. and by Chrysalis Songs) (BMI). "Roustabout" by Bill Giant, Bernie Baum and Florence Kaye; published by Elvis Presley Music (administered by Cherry River Music Co. and by Chrysalis Songs) (BMI). "Heartbreak Hotel" written by Elvis Presley, Mae Boren Axton and Tommy Durden; published by Sony/ATV Songs LLC, dba Tree Publishing Co. (BMI). "One Night" written by Dave Bartholomew and Pearl King; published by Elvis Presley Music (administered by Cherry River Music Co. and by Chrysalis Songs) and by Sony/ATV Songs LLC (BMI). "C'mon Everybody" written by Joy Byers; published by Gladys Music (administered by Cherry Lane Music Publishing Company, Inc. and by Chrysalis Music) (ASCAP). "Follow That Dream" words by Fred Wise, music by Ben Weisman; published by Warner Chappell Music Inc. on behalf of Chappell & Co. Inc. (ASCAP) and by Spirit Two Music Inc. on behalf of Erika Publishing (ASCAP). "Hound Dog" written by Jerry Leiber and Mike Stoller; published by Gladys Music (administered by Cherry Lane Music Publishing Company, Inc. and by Chrysalis Music) and by Universal-MCA Music Publishing (ASCAP). "Teddy Bear" written by Kal Mann and Bernie Lowe; published by Gladys Music (administered by Cherry Lane Music Publishing Company, Inc. and Chrysalis Music) (ASCAP). "That's All Right" written by Arthur Crudup; published by Crudup Music and Unichapel Music, Inc. (BMI). "Devil in Disguise" written by Bill Giant, Bernie Baum and Florence Kaye; published by Elvis Presley Music (administered by Cherry River Music Co. and by Chrysalis Songs) (BMI). "It's Now or Never" written by Aaron Schroeder and Wally Gold Published by Rachel's Own Music [administered by A. Schroeder International Ltd,] and by Gladys Music [administered by Cherry Lane Music Publishing Company, Inc. and by Chrysalis Music] (ASCAP). "Blue Suede Shoes" written by Carl Perkins; published by Wren Music Co. Inc, on behalf of Carl Perkins Music, c/o MPL Communications, Inc. (BMI) "Don't Be Cruel" written by Otis Blackwell and Elvis Presley; published by Elvis Presley Music (administered by Cherry River Music Co. and by Chrysalis Songs) and by EMI Music Publishing (BMI). "Let Yourself Go" written by Joy Byers; published by Gladys Music (administered by Cherry Lane Music Publishing Company, Inc. and by Chrysalis Music) (ASCAP). "Can't Help Falling in Love" written by George David Weiss, Hugo Peretti and Luigi Creatore; published by Gladys Music (administered by Cherry Lane Music Publishing Company, Inc. and by Chrysalis Music) (ASCAP). "All Shook Up" written by Otis Blackwell and Elvis Presley; published by Elvis Presley Music (administered by Cherry River Music Co. and by Chrysalis Songs) and by EMI Music Publishing (BMI). "It Hurts Me" written by Joy Byers and Charles E. Daniels; published by Gladys Music (administered by Cherry Lane Music Publishing Company, Inc. and by Chrysalis Music) and by Warner/Chappell Music Inc. (ASCAP). "A Little Less Conversation" written by Mac Davis and Billy Strange; published by Elvis Presley Music (administered by Cherry River Music Co. and by Chrysalis Songs) (BMI). "The Power of My Love" written by Bill Giant, Bernie Baum and Florence Kaye; published by Elvis Presley Music (administered by Cherry River Music Co. and by Chrysalis Songs) (BMI). "I Don't Want To" words by Janice Torre, music by Fred Spielman; published by Gladys Music (administered by Cherry Lane Music Publishing Company, Inc. and by Chrysalis Music) (ASCAP). "Jailhouse Rock" written by Jerry Leiber and Mike Stoller; published by Jerry Leiber Music and Mike Stoller Music (ASCAP). "There's Always Me" written by Don Robertson; published by Don Robertson Music Corp. (ASCAP). "If I Can Dream" written by W. Earl Brown; published by Gladys Music (administered by Cherry Lane Music Publishing Company, Inc. and by Chrysalis Music) (ASCAP). "Fools Fall in Love" written by Jerry Leiber and Mike Stoller; published by Jerry Leiber Music and Mike Stoller Music (ASCAP). "Burning Love" written by Dennis Linde; published by Sony/ATV Songs LLC (BMI).

NEDERLANDER

Chairman/President ....James M. Nederlander
President ....James L. Nederlander

Executive Vice President
Nick Scandalios

Vice President
Corporate Development
Charlene S. Nederlander

Senior Vice President
Labor Relations
Herschel Waxman

Vice President
Jim Boese

Chief Financial Officer
Freida Sawyer Belviso

STAFF FOR THE PALACE THEATRE

Theatre Manager ....Dixon Rosario, Jr.
Treasurer ....Cissy Caspare
Assistant Treasurer ....Anne T. Wilson
Carpenter ....Thomas K. Phillips
Flyman ....Robert W. Kelly
Electrician ....Eddie Webber
Propertymaster ....Steve Camus
Chief Usher ....Gloria Hill

Memorable Celebrity Visitor: Priscilla Presley came the night before opening and asked to meet the whole cast after the show. She was so gracious and loved the show. She told Cheyenne that Elvis would be very proud!

Backstage Rituals: A few cast members gather in Jenn's dressing room for a prayer at the five-minute call. Our unofficial ritual is getting together to chitchat and stretch onstage before the overture begins!

Favorite Moment: Finale of Act I. "Can't Help Falling in Love." It's one of the only times during the show when the entire company is onstage together. The arrangement, by Stephen Oremus is beautiful and I get chills every night. I also LOVE "Now or Never." The bicycle makes me laugh every time I think about it.

Favorite In-Theatre Gathering Place: The stage management office. We don't know if we are welcome guests or not, but at any given moment, you will inevitably find more actors than stage managers in there. Thank goodness there are lots of chairs.

Favorite Snack Foods: Kirkland Trail Mix (you can find it at Costco), Twizzlers, and anything that Sharon Wilkins bakes for us.

Mascot: Rocco the pug, Joe DiPietro's little puppy, and Emma Curtis's little angel. She's a brussels griffon.

Favorite Therapies: I think our cast would overdose on Zicam and Wellness Formula, if it were possible.

Memorable Ad Lib: Alix Korey: "Have fun in the showers, boys," instead of "Have fun in the slammer."
Lorraine: "Have you ever kissed a girl?" Dean: "No, have you?"

Cell Phone Rings: Not a lot of cell phones, but many crying babies.

Strangest Stage Door Fan Encounter: A woman told Cheyenne that she had been waiting two hours to get her hands on his beefy thighs, and than grabbed ahold of him.

Who Wore The Heaviest/Hottest Costume: Sharon's wedding dress in Chicago weighed almost 20 pounds!

Catchphrases: "Pupeka!, "Curtie, help Grandma Chin," and "This is a song about tech."

Memorable Directorial Note: "Feel the body joy!"

Correspondent: Nikki M. James, "Lorraine."

Photos by Aubrey Reuben

Making the cast album at the Right Track Recording Studio.

Above left: Priscilla Presley and Cheyenne Jackson at the final preview. Above right: The cast rehearsing at the New 42nd Street Studios prior to going out of town.

Curtain call on opening night at the Palace Theatre.

Nikki M. James at the opening night party at Copacabana.

PLAYBILL

CAST

Proprietor	JOHN SCHIAPPA
Leon Czolgosz	JAMES BARBOUR
John Hinckley	ALEXANDER GEMIGNANI
Charles Guiteau	DENIS O'HARE
Giuseppe Zangara	JEFFREY KUHN
Samuel Byck	MARIO CANTONE
Lynette "Squeaky" Fromme	MARY CATHERINE GARRISON
Sara Jane Moore	BECKY ANN BAKER
John Wilkes Booth	MICHAEL CERVERIS
Balladeer	NEIL PATRICK HARRIS
David Herold	BRANDON WARDELL
Emma Goldman	ANNE L. NATHAN
James Blaine	JAMES CLOW
President James Garfield	MERWIN FOARD
Billy	EAMON FOLEY
President Gerald Ford	JAMES CLOW
Lee Harvey Oswald	NEIL PATRICK HARRIS
Ensemble	JAMES CLOW, MERWIN FOARD, EAMON FOLEY, KENDRA KASSEBAUM, ANNE L. NATHAN, BRANDON WARDELL

Production Stage Manager:
William Joseph Barnes
Stage Manager: Jon Krause
Assistant Stage Manager: Timothy R. Semon

STUDIO 54

ROUNDABOUT THEATRE COMPANY

TODD HAIMES, Artistic Director
ELLEN RICHARD, Managing Director
JULIA C. LEVY, Executive Director, External Affairs
Presents

Becky Ann Baker   James Barbour   Mario Cantone
Michael Cerveris   Mary Catherine Garrison
Alexander Gemignani   Neil Patrick Harris
Jeffrey Kuhn   Denis O'Hare   John Schiappa

in

ASSASSINS

Book by John Weidman

Music and Lyrics by Stephen Sondheim

James Clow   Merwin Foard   Eamon Foley   Kendra Kassebaum   Ken Krugman
Anne L. Nathan   Chris Peluso   Brandon Wardell   Sally Wilfert

Set Design by	*Costume Design by*	*Lighting Design by*	*Sound Design by*
Robert Brill	Susan Hilferty	Jules Fisher and Peggy Eisenhauer	Dan Moses Schreier

Orchestrations by	*Production Stage Manager*	*Hair and Wig Design by*	*Casting by*
Michael Starobin	William Joseph Barnes	Tom Watson	Jim Carnahan, C.S.A.

Technical Supervisor	*General Manager*	*Founding Director*
Steve Beers	Sydney Davolos	Gene Feist

Associate Artistic Director	*Press Representative*	*Director of Marketing*
Scott Ellis	Boneau/Bryan-Brown	David B. Steffen

Musical Direction by Paul Gemignani

Musical Staging by Jonathan Butterell

Directed by Joe Mantello

Generous support for *Assassins* provided by
The Diller-Von Furstenberg Family Foundation, Martin and Perry Granoff,
The Shen Family Foundation, Douglas S. Cramer Foundation, Diane and Tom Tuft.

**Major support for Roundabout Theatre Company's Musical Theatre Fund
provided by The Kaplen Foundation.**

From an idea by Charles Gilbert, Jr.
Playwrights Horizons, Inc., New York City, produced *Assassins* Off-Broadway in 1990.
Roundabout Theatre Company is a member of the League of Resident Theatres. www.roundabouttheatre.org

6/1/04

The cast: (L-R): Alexander Gemignani, Becky Ann Baker, Jeffrey Kuhn, Michael Cerveris, Neil Patrick Harris, Mario Cantone, Mary Catherine Garrison, Denis O'Hare and James Barbour.

Photo by Joan Marcus

Assassins

MUSICAL NUMBERS

"Everybody's Got the Right" .... Proprietor, Czolgosz, Guiteau, Fromme, Byck, Booth, Zangara, Hinckley, Moore

"The Ballad of Booth" .... Balladeer and Booth

"How I Saved Roosevelt" .... Zangara and Ensemble

"Gun Song" .... Czolgosz, Booth, Guiteau, Moore

"The Ballad of Czolgosz" .... Balladeer and Ensemble

"Unworthy of Your Love" .... Hinckley and Fromme

"The Ballad of Guiteau" .... Guiteau and Balladeer

"Another National Anthem" .... Proprietor, Czolgosz, Booth, Hinckley, Fromme, Zangara, Moore, Guiteau, Byck, Balladeer

"Something Just Broke" .... Ensemble

"Everybody's Got the Right" .... Moore, Byck, Czolgosz, Zangara, Fromme, Hinckley, Oswald, Guiteau, Booth

ORCHESTRA

Conductor: Nicholas Archer; Associate Conductor/Keyboard – Mark Mitchell
Keyboard – Paul Ford
Flute, Piccolo, Clarinet, Soprano Sax, Harmonica – Dennis Anderson
Oboe, English Horn, Piccolo, Clarinet, Alto Sax – Andrew Shreeves
Clarinet, Flute, Piccolo, Bass Clarinet, E-flat Clarinet, Tenor Sax – Ed Joffe
Bassoon, Clarinet, Baritone Sax – Mark Thrasher
Trumpet, Cornet – Carl Albach
Trumpet, Flugelhorn – Lorraine Cohen
French Horn – Ronald Sell
Trombone, Euphonium – Bruce Eidem
Guitars, Banjo, Mandolin – Scott Kuney
Bass, Electric Bass – David Phillips
Drums and Percussion – Larry Lelli

Cast Continued

UNDERSTUDIES

For Squeaky Fromme:
KENDRA KASSEBAUM

For Booth & Guiteau:
JAMES CLOW

For Czolgosz, Byck & Proprietor:
MERWIN FOARD

For Hinckley, Balladeer & Zangara:
BRANDON WARDELL

For Balladeer – CHRIS PELUSO

Swings – KEN KRUGMAN, SALLY WILFERT, CHRIS PELUSO

Neil Patrick Harris with (L-R): Alexander Gemignani, Jeffrey Kuhn, Mary Catherine Garrison, Denis O'Hare, Michael Cerveris, James Barbour, Becky Ann Baker, Mario Cantone

Photo by Joan Marcus

Assassins

Becky Ann Baker
Sara Jane Moore

James Barbour
Leon Czolgosz

Mario Cantone
Samuel Byck

Michael Cerveris
John Wilkes Booth

Mary Catherine Garrison
Lynette "Squeaky" Fromme

Alexander Gemignani
John Hinckley

Neil Patrick Harris
The Balladeer/ Lee Harvey Oswald

Jeffrey Kuhn
Giuseppe Zangara

Denis O'Hare
Charles Guiteau

John Schiappa
Proprietor

James Clow
James Blaine/ President Gerald Ford/Ensemble

Merwin Foard
President James Garfield/Ensemble

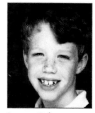
Eamon Foley
Billy/Ensemble

Kendra Kassebaum
Ensemble

Ken Krugman
Swing

Anne L. Nathan
Emma Goldman/ Ensemble

Chris Peluso
Swing

Brandon Wardell
David Herold/ Ensemble/Dance Captain

Sally Wilfert
Swing

Stephen Sondheim
Music/Lyrics

John Weidman
Book

Joe Mantello
Director

Paul Gemignani
Musical Director

Robert Brill
Set Design

Susan Hilferty
Costume Designer

Jules Fisher and Peggy Eisenhauer
Lighting Design

Dan Moses Schreier
Sound Design

Tom Watson
Wig and Hair Designer

Michael Starobin
Orchestrations

Jon Krause
Stage Manager

Jim Carnahan
Casting

Gene Feist
Founding Director, Roundabout Theatre Company

Todd Haimes,
Artistic Director Roundabout Theatre Company

Marc Kudisch
Proprietor

Assassins

Jeffrey Kuhn (Zangara) with Mario Cantone and Alex Gemignani in the background. "This was taken during tech while were hanging out in our *Assassins* booths. The booths became very odd little homes for us."

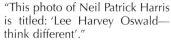

"During a moment of tech: Marc Kudisch, James Barbour with Mario Cantone in the background."

"Three moods of Becky Baker."

"This photo of Neil Patrick Harris is titled: 'Lee Harvey Oswald—think different'."

Michael Cerveris, Mary Catherine Garrison and Denis O'Hare during tech. "We were impersonating the bad publicity photos you see in *The Times* for small small theatre openings. It seems in really bad publicity photos, all the actors are talking and gesticulating at the same time. We decided that our bad play was probably a Molière."

Opening Night Gifts: The Sondheim Puzzle. Apparently, this is a tradition of Sondheim's: to create a puzzle that is linked to the show. In our case, each of us received a box with all the pieces of the puzzle in it. When finished, the puzzle was the *Assassins* poster with our initials carved out. Very cool and very hard to do. The pieces of the puzzles had strange shapes including a shoe, a clown a hammer, etc. One other gift that was absolutely brilliant was a t-shirt custommade for the opening by ensemble member Brandon Wardell. The T-shirt was the famous lineup of figures from *A Chorus Line* but their heads were replaced with the heads of the *Assassins*. Beneath it, in the proper font were the words: "*Assassins*...Studio 54."

Celebrity Visitors: It was really great to have the members of the original *Assassins* production—Deb Monk, Victor Garber, Patrick Cassidy, Lee Wilkof, Annie Golden among others—come back and visit us. Very nerve-wracking too.

Who Got the Gypsy Robe: Merwin Foard

Favorite Moment: I loved performing "The Gun Song," the quartet performed by Guiteau, Booth (Michael Cerveris), Czolgosz, (James Barbour) and Sarah Jane Moore (Becky Baker) and it was the most beautiful music I have ever sung. It was also the hardest and we didn't always get it right. There was a fairly long a capella section which was followed by the orchestra re-entering. On the nights we were off, the orchestra came back in and all four of us would fix our pitch—sliding up and down. But on the nights we got it right, it was one of the most exhilarating things I've ever been part of.

In-Theatre Gathering Place: Becky Baker and Mary Catherine Garrison's dressing room. It became the cafeteria for the entire cast. We would all show up early and sit on the floor and talk and eat until it was time to get ready. Between shows as well.

Mascot: There was a blow-up CPR doll named Trevor who used to hang from the ceiling of Studio 54. He was part of Robert Brill's original set idea. Well, he got cut and was adopted by certain members of the cast and lived in their room. Then, certain other members of the cast kidnapped Trevor and started sending notes to his adoptive parents. The kidnappers were called "Red Sky." It was all very mysterious and upsetting.

Trevor was returned to his family on Easter Sunday although some bitterness remained. The case was never solved. Trevor did fall on Kim Cattrall one night backstage and scared the bejesus out of her.

Cell Phone Rings: Remarkably, none that I can recall.

Strangest Stage Door Fan Encounter: The young Republican girl with the Bush button who told me that in five minutes she would convince me to vote for him. I smiled and told her that she was too young to be a Republican and in five minutes I would show her the error of her ways. She settled for an autograph and I went home.

Heaviest/Hottest Costume: Mario Cantone was in a Santa Claus suit and I think suffered the most although we all wore either wool or nylon, so no one was spared.

Also: Our best field trip as a cast was our gun field trip. We all had to go to a gun firing class in Brooklyn. That was a riot. We wore goggles and got lectured by a humorless man about how even blanks could take someone's eye out. We each got to fire into a hole.

Correspondent: Denis O'Hare, "Charles Guiteau"

PLAYBILL

GOLDEN THEATRE
A Shubert Organization Theatre

Gerald Schoenfeld, *Chairman*   Philip J. Smith, *President*

Robert E. Wankel, *Executive Vice President*

Kevin McCollum   Robyn Goodman   Jeffrey Seller
Vineyard Theatre   and   The New Group
present

Music and Lyrics by
Robert Lopez and Jeff Marx

Book by
Jeff Whitty

Based on an Original Concept by
Robert Lopez and Jeff Marx

with

Jennifer Barnhart, Natalie Venetia Belcon, Stephanie D'Abruzzo,
Jordan Gelber, Ann Harada, Rick Lyon, John Tartaglia

Puppets Conceived and Designed by
Rick Lyon

Set Design
Anna Louizos

Costume Design
Mirena Rada

Lighting Design
Howell Binkley

Sound Design
**Acme
Sound Partners**

Animation Design
Robert Lopez

Music Director & Incidental Music
Gary Adler

Music Coordinator
Michael Keller

Casting
Cindy Tolan

Technical Supervisor
Brian Lynch

Press Representative
**Sam Rudy
Media Relations**

Marketing
**TMG-The
Marketing Group**

General Manager
John Corker

Production Stage Manager
Evan Ensign

Associate Producers
**Sonny Everett
Walter Grossman
Mort Swinsky**

Music Supervision, Orchestrations and Arrangements by
Stephen Oremus

Choreographer
Ken Roberson

Directed by
Jason Moore

Avenue Q was supported by a residency and public staged reading at the
2002 O'Neill Music Theatre Conference of the Eugene O'Neill Theater Center, Waterford, CT

5/2/05

CAST

(in order of appearance)

Princeton, Rod .... BARRETT FOA
Brian .... JORDAN GELBER
Kate Monster,
Lucy & others .... STEPHANIE D'ABRUZZO
Nicky, Trekkie Monster,
Bear & others .... RICK LYON
Christmas Eve .... ANN HARADA
Gary Coleman ..NATALIE VENETIA BELCON
Mrs. T., Bear
& others .... JENNIFER BARNHART
Ensemble .... PETER LINZ,
HOWIE MICHAEL SMITH

Place:
an outerborough of New York City

Time:
the present

UNDERSTUDIES

For Princeton/Rod – PETER LINZ, HOWIE
MICHAEL SMITH; for Brian – PETER LINZ; for
Kate Monster/Lucy – JENNIFER BARNHART,
AYMEE GARCIA; for Nicky/Trekkie/Bear –
PETER LINZ, HOWIE MICHAEL SMITH; for
Mrs. T./Bear – AYMEE GARCIA, CARMEN
RUBY FLOYD, ANN SANDERS; for Christmas
Eve – AYMEE GARCIA, ANN SANDERS; for
Gary Coleman – CARMEN RUBY FLOYD.

AVENUE Q BAND

Keyboard/Conductor: Gary Adler

Keyboard/Associate Conductor:
Mark Hartman

Reeds: Patience Higgins

Drums:
Michael Croiter

Bass:
Maryann McSweeney

Guitars:
Brian Koonin

John Tartaglia (right) and Princeton react to their
latest setback.

Avenue Q

MUSICAL NUMBERS

ACT ONE

"Avenue Q Theme"	Company
"Opening"	Company
"If You Were Gay"	Nicky, Rod
"Purpose"	Princeton
"Everyone's A Little Bit Racist"	Princeton, Kate, Gary, Brian, Christmas Eve
"The Internet Is For Porn"	Kate, Trekkie Monster, Men
"A Mix Tape"	Kate, Princeton
"I'm Not Weaing Underwear Today"	Brian
"Special"	Lucy
"You Can Be As Loud As The Hell You Want (When You're Making Love)"	Gary, Bad Idea Bears
"Fantasies Come True"	Rod, Kate
"My Girlfriend, Who Lives in Canada"	Rod
"There's A Fine, Fine Line"	Kate

ACT TWO

"There Is Life Outside Your Apartment"	Brian, Company
"The More You Ruv Someone"	Christmas Eve, Kate
"Schadenfreude"	Gary, Nicky
"I Wish I Could Go Back To College"	Kate, Nicky, Princeton
"The Money Song"	Nicky, Princeton, Gary, Christmas Eve, Brian, Trekkie Monster
"For Now"	Company

Jennifer Barnhart
Mrs. T., Bear & Others,

Natalie Venetia Belcon
Gary Coleman

Stephanie D'Abruzzo
Kate Monster, Lucy & Others

Barrett Foa
Princeton/Rod

Jordan Gelber
Brian

Ann Harada
Christmas Eve

Rick Lyon
Nicky, Trekkie Monster, Bad Idea Bear #1 & Others/Puppet Conceiver & Design

Carmen Ruby Floyd
Understudy Gary Coleman/Mrs. T./Bear

Aymee Garcia
Understudy Kate Monster/Lucy/Mrs. T., etc.

Peter Linz
Ensemble

Ann Sanders
Ensemble

Howie Michael Smith
Ensemble

Kate Monster (Stephanie D'Abruzzo, left) accepts a mix tape of special songs from Princeton (John Tartaglia).

Jeff Marx and Robert Lopez
Music and Lyrics,
Original Concept

Jeff Whitty
Book

Jason Moore
Director

Ken Roberson
Choreography

Stephen Oremus
Musical Supervision/
Orchestrations/
Arrangements

Anna Louizos
Set Design

Howell Binkley
Lighting Design

Tom Clark, Mark Menard and
Nevin Steinberg
Sound Design

Michael Keller
Music Coordinator

Kevin McCollum
Producer

Robyn Goodman
Producer

Mort Swinsky
Associate Producer

Jeffrey Seller
Producer

Avenue
Q
Alumni

Christian
Anderson
Nicky/Trekkie
Monster

Angela Ai
Understudy
Christmas Eve

Leo Daignault
Understudy Brian

Alexander
Gemignani
Brian

John Tartaglia
Princeton/Rod

Darryl D. Winslow
Understudy Brian

The Orchestra
(L-R): Patience Higgins (Reeds), Brian Koonin (Guitar/Banjo), Jim Donica (Bass, sub), Zina Goldrich (Keyboards, sub), Dorothy Martin (Keyboard/Conductor, sub), and Michael Croiter (Percussion/Drums).

Photo by Ben Strothmann

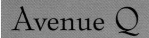

STAFF FOR AVENUE Q

GENERAL MANAGER
John Corker

GENERAL PRESS REPRESENTATIVE
Sam Rudy Media Relations
Sam Rudy
Dale Heller and Robert Lasko

CASTING
Cindy Tolan Casting
Laura Cass, Casting Assistant
Matt Schreiber, Casting Associate

COMPANY MANAGER
Mary K. Witte

Associate Company Manager ....Nick Lugo

PRODUCTION STAGE MANAGER ....**ROBERT WITHEROW**
Technical Supervision ....Brian Lynch/Theatretech, Inc.
Stage Manager ....Christine M. Daly
Assistant Stage Manager..Aymee Garcia
Resident Director ....Evan Ensign
Assistant Director ....Jen Bender
Associate Conductor ....Mark Hartman
Dance Captain ....Natalie Venetia Belcon
Production Assistant ....Alexis Prussack
Management Assistant ....Dawn Marie Bernhard
Assistant to Mr. Corker ....Kim Vasquez
Management Intern ....Andrew Jones
Producing Intern ....Robert Jones
Associate Set Designer ....Todd Potter
Assistant Costume Designer ....Elizabeth Bourgeois
Associate Lighting Designer/Programmer ....Timothy F. Rogers
Assistant Lighting Designers ....Douglas Cox, Ryan O'Gara
Production Carpenter ....Justin Garvey
House Carpenter ....Charles Zarobinski
Flyman ....Tom Anderson
Production Electrician ....Craig Caccamise
House Electrician ....Sylvia Yoshioka
Head Electrician ....Brady Jarvis
Video Programmer ....Paul Vershbow
Sound Board Operator ....Elspeth Appleby
Follow Spot Operators ....Joe Pfifferling, A.J. Gigerich
Deck Electrician ....Gretchen Metzloff
Production Properties Master ....Ron Groomes
House Properties ....Stephen McDonald
Wardrobe Supervisor ....John A. Robelen III
Dresser ....Jill Heller
Puppet Wrangler ....Phoebe Kreutz
Puppet Builders ....The Lyon Puppets/Rick Lyon,
Andrea Detwiler, Vanessa Gifford, Deborah Glassberg
Michelle Hickey, Michael Latini, Adam Pagdon, Laura Parè,
David Regan, Sara Schmidt Boldon, James Vogel,
James W. Wojtal, Jr., Entirely Different Design,
Tim Hawkins, Susan Pitocchi
Music Copying ....Emily Grishman/Alex Lacamoire
Keyboard Programmer ....Mark Hartman
Synthesizer Program Consultant ....Andrew Barrett
Costume Draper ....Karl Ruckdeschel
Assistants to Set Designer ....Heather Dunbar, Donyale Werle
Puppet Wig Consultant ....John James
Makeup Consultant ....Danielle Arminio
Sound and Video Design Effects............................Brett Jarvis
Animation/Video Production ....Noodle Soup Productions/ Jeremy Rosenberg
Marketing ....TMG-The Marketing Group/Tanya Grubich, Laura Matalon,
Greg Ramos, Ronni Seif
Advertising ....SpotCo/Drew Hodges, Jim Edwards,
Ilene Rosen, Jim McNicholas
Web Design ....Situation Marketing/Damian Bazadona
Concessions ....Max Merchandising, LLC/Randi Grossman
Legal Counsel ....Levine, Plotkin, Menin LLP/Loren Plotkin, Susan Mindell
Accounting ....FK Partners/Robert Fried
Bookkeeper ....Joseph S. Kubala

Insurance ..........................D.R. Reiff & Associates/Sonny Everett, Dennis Reiff
Banking ....JP Morgan Chase
Payroll ....CSI Payroll Services, Inc/Lance Castellana
Production Photographers ....Nicholas Reuchel, Carol Rosegg
Theatre Displays ....King Displays Inc.

THE PRODUCING OFFICE
Kevin McCollum Jeffrey Selle,
John Corker Debra Nir
Ryan Hill

AGED IN WOOD
Robyn Goodman
Associate Producer: Stephen Kocis

VINEYARD THEATRE
Douglas Aibel, Artistic Director
Jennifer Garvey-Blackwell,
Executive Director External Affairs

THE NEW GROUP
Artistic Director: Scott Elliott
Executive Director: Geoffrey Rich
Assoc. Artistic Director: Ian Morgan
Assoc. Executive Director: Amanda Brandes

CREDITS
Puppets built by The Lyon Puppets. Scenery by Centerline Studios Inc. 59th Street Bridge Photograph from Panoramic New York used with special permission by Richard Berenholtz. Stage portals by Atlas Scenic Studios. Lighting equipment by Fourth Phase. Sound equipment by ProMix Inc. Chain motors provided by Hudson Scenic. Christmas Eve wedding dress electrified by International Robotics/Mannetron. Ricola natural herb cough drops courtesy of Ricola USA, Inc. Props built by Prism Productions Services, Inc., Tom Carroll Scenery and Ken Larson. Animation operating system provided by ScharffWeissberg.

Avenue Q has not been authorized or approved in any manner by The Jim Henson Company or Sesame Workshop, which have no responsibility for its content.

Quote from "Something's Coming" (Bernstein/Sondheim) by permission of Leonard Bernstein Music Publishing Company LLC. (ASCAP).

SPECIAL THANKS
Amanda Green, Amy Kohn, Arthur Novell, Bobbi Brown Cosmetics, BMI Lehman Engel Musical Theatre Workshop, Brett Jarvis, Brian Yorkey, Chelsea Studios, Cheryl Henson, Craig Shemin, Doug Aibel, Ed Christie, Jana Zielonka, Jane Henson, Jean Banks, Jennifer Silver, Esq., Jodi Peikoff, Esq., John Buzzetti, Julia Sullivan, Kai Production Strategies, Kristen Anderson, Lara McLean, Manhattan Theatre Club, Maury Yeston, Nicole Rivera, Paulette Haupt, Peter Franklin, Pro-Mark Drumsticks and Mallets, Scott Elliott, Seth Goldstein, Splashlight Studios, Steven Greenberg, Teresa Focarile, The York Theatre, Lee Johnson.

ANY DONATIONS RECEIVED DURING THIS PERFORMANCE WILL BE GIVEN TO BROADWAY CARES/EQUITY FIGHTS AIDS.

 THE SHUBERT ORGANIZATION

Gerald Schoenfeld	**Philip J. Smith**
Chairman	President
John W. Kluge	**Lee J. Seidler**
Michael I. Sovern	**Stuart Subotnick**

Irving M. Wall

Robert E. Wankel
Executive Vice President

Peter Entin	**Elliot Greene**
Vice President, Theatre Operations	Vice President, Finance
David Andrews	**John Darby**
Vice President, Shubert Ticketing Services	Vice President, Facilities

House Manager ....Carolyne Jones

Photos by Aubrey Reuben

Above: The cast welcomes former President Bill Clinton (rear center) and Senator Hillary Rodham Clinton (right) backstage at the Golden Theatre.

Above: Harvey Fierstein congratulates author Jeff Whitty for his Best Book Tony Award at the 2004 Tonys.
Above right: Natalie Venetia Belcon recording the original cast album at Right Track.
Right: Ann Harada at the recording session.

Above left: John Tartaglia at "Broadway Bares 14." Above right: Curtain calls on opening night: Stephanie D'Abruzzo, John Tartaglia and Rick Lyon.

Opening Night Telegram Or Note: All the fake opening night faxes.

Opening Night Gifts: Steph's coloring books. Gary's name posters. Ann's pubic hair soaps. Mouse pads. Jen's "Bad Idea" wine charms. Jordan's puppet T-shirts. Rod and Carol singing the hits.

Celebrity Visitors: Former President Bill Clinton's "I'm friends with the director's father." The randomness that was Glenn Close and Jimmy Fallon. Luke Perry's "Will you marry me, Phoebe Kreutz?" Dame Judi Dench: and then she and her daughter sent a gift basket. Tom Hanks' "I hate musicals but I loved this." Helen Mirren's "Shit."

Who Got The Gypsy Robe: Carmen Ruby Floyd. Rick Lyon designed a beautiful sleeve with an *Avenue Q* panel and actual Trekkie Monster puppet head sewn onto the sleeve.

"Gypsy Of The Year" Sketch: Written by Rick Lyon.

"Carols For A Cure" Carol: "O Come, O Come Emmanuel."

"Easter Bonnet" Sketch: The 2004 Easter Bonnet sketch was written by Jordan, Rick, Stephanie and Gary in cooperation with the *Fiddler on the Roof* people. The sketch combined the two shows' casts with a brilliant parody of both shows, called *Avenue Jew*. The sketch won the 2004 Best Performance award.

Which Actor Performed The Most Roles: Tie between Peter Linz and Aymee Garcia. As well as performing his ensemble track, Linz covers Nicky/Trekkie, Princeton/Rod, Brian and is also puppet captain. As well as being assistant stage manager, Garcia covers Mrs. T, Bear and others, Kate/Lucy, Christmas Eve and the ensemble tracks.

Who Has Done The Most Shows: Hands down, Stephanie D'Abruzzo.

Backstage Rituals: At five minutes, Stephanie goes down into the orchestra and kisses everyone hello. After Natalie comes offstage from her scene near the top of Act I with Princeton, she is welcomed offstage with a daily charade. Before the show, John Tartaglia warms up to "Nobody's Side" from *Chess*. Johnny slaps Phoebe's ass as he passes during the Empire State Building scene. Johnny finds some way to make Natalie and Barrett crack up every night. Anne and Carmen sing all of Kate's songs as Jennifer Holliday. While Jen is doing Kate in in the Empire State Building scene, Rick puts stuffed bunny on a platform doing something different every night.

Favorite Moment : The orchestra simultaneously performs Christmas Eve's pubic hair speech, down in the orchestra pit.

In-Theatre Gathering Places: Girls' dressing room, green room, water cooler, stage manager's office.

Off-site Hangouts: Barrymore's, Tony DiNapoli, Virgil's, the bowling alley at Port Authority.

Favorite Snack Food: Krispy Kreme; candy; nuts; popcorn from Popcorn, Indiana; Aymee's cakes, cake, cake, more cake.

Mascot: Millie the Beagle, Bunny the Bunny, Hello Kitty.

Favorite Therapies: Ricola, grape juice (Rick's secret to Trekkie's voice), Singer's Saving Grace, water, bourbon, licorice tea, Entertainer's Secret, prayer to the Lord.

Memorable Ad-Libs: "Quite a lot of busy stuff to do for Gary Coleman.": Chandra Wilson as Gary Coleman exiting wedding.
"Like a slow tiresome walk downstream.": Natalie Venetia Belcon as Gary Coleman in the window after "Purpose."
"And fix the sign!": Jordan Gelber as Brian after the "Money" song when the Montessori School sign didn't deploy.
"It's all I have.": Ann Harada as Christmas Eve at the top of the "Money" song when Jordan forgot to bring the wallet out.
"That kid left me so sore!": Stephanie D'Abruzzo as Lucy T. Slut in the "One Night Stand" scene.
"I should had never had had hired a monster," Aymee Garcia as Mrs. Thistletwat in the morning-after scene.
"My purpose in life is to...[five second pause]...look for people.": Ann Harada.

Strangest Press Encounter: Aymee and Jen on Spanish television, with Mrs. Thistletwat speaking in Spanish.

Strangest Stage Door Fan Encounter: Every time Joe quizzes us about Nazis.

Who Wore The Least?: Kate and Princeton.

Orchestra Members Who Played The Most Instruments: Michael Croiter and Gary Adler.

Orchestra Members Who Played The Most Consecutive Performances Without a Sub: Mike Croiter and Brian Koonin.

In-House Parody Lyrics: "We could call you a car! You're a car, you're a car. Har! Har! Har!"
"Only four cows, four cows. Not just two cows: four cows!"

Memorable Directorial Note: "Da-da-da-da-da-da-off. End of 'Money Song.'": Note to Gary Adler.

Nicknames: "Big Fat Whore" (John Tartaglia). "Bad Idea Bear #1" (Estaban). "Bad Idea Bear #2" (Clover).

Jennifer Barnhart, John Tartaglia and Rick Lyon with puppets for John Kerry, Rod and George W. Bush at their election-season "debate" in Times Square.

Above: The cast is all smiles at the opening night party.

Right: *The Avenue Q* songwriting team of Robert Lopez and Jeff Marx in Times Square.

Catchphrase: Sha'mon.

Sweethearts: Mary and Millie. Gary Adler and Michael Croiter.

Superstition That Turned Out To Be True: "Break a leg." While *Avenue Q* was at the Vineyard Theatre, both Natalie and Rick actually did!

Correspondents: The cast.

Photo by Ernio Hernandez

Photos by Aubrey Reuben

PLAYBILL®

DISNEY's
BEAUTY AND THE BEAST

CAST

(in order of appearance)

Young Prince	BRIAN COLLIER
Enchantress	SARAH SOLIE
Beast	STEVE BLANCHARD
Belle	BROOKE TANSLEY
Bookseller	GLENN RAINEY
Lefou	ALDRIN GONZALEZ
Gaston	GRANT NORMAN
Three Silly Girls	TRACY GENERALOVICH, JENNIFER MARCUM, TIA MARIE ZORNE
Maurice	JAMIE ROSS
Wolves	ANA MARIA ANDRICAIN, CHRISTOPHER DeANGELIS, SARAH SOLIE
Cogsworth	JEFF BROOKS
Lumiere	PETER FLYNN
Babette	PAM KLINGER
Mrs. Potts	ALMA CUERVO
Chip at certain performances	MATTHEW GUMLEY PATRICK O'NEIL HENNEY
Madame de la Grande Bouche	MARY STOUT
Salt & Pepper	CHRISTOPHER DeANGELIS, BREK WILLIAMS
Doormat	BRIAN COLLIER
Cheesegrater	DENNY PASCHALL
Monsieur D'Arque	GLENN RAINEY

continued on the next page

✽N✽ LUNT–FONTANNE THEATRE

UNDER THE DIRECTION OF
JAMES M. NEDERLANDER AND JAMES L. NEDERLANDER

Disney Theatrical Productions
presents

STEVE BLANCHARD   BROOKE TANSLEY

in

DISNEY's
BEAUTY AND THE BEAST

Music by
ALAN MENKEN

Lyrics by
HOWARD ASHMAN & TIM RICE

Book by
LINDA WOOLVERTON

with

GRANT NORMAN   JEFF BROOKS   ALMA CUERVO   PETER FLYNN   JAMIE ROSS

ALDRIN GONZALEZ   MATTHEW GUMLEY   PATRICK O'NEIL HENNEY
PAM KLINGER   MARY STOUT

ANA MARIA ANDRICAIN   ANN ARVIA   GINA CARLETTE   BRIAN COLLIER   CHRISTOPHER DeANGELIS
BARBARA FOLTS   KEITH FORTNER   TRACY GENERALOVICH   DAVID E. LIDDELL
JENNIFER MARCUM   CHRISTOPHER MONTELEONE   BILL NABEL   BRIAN O'BRIEN
BRYNN O'MALLEY   DENNY PASCHALL   GLENN RAINEY   JOHN SALVATORE
SARAH SOLIE   MARGUERITE WILLBANKS   BREK WILLIAMS   TIA MARIE ZORNE

Scenic Design STANLEY A. MEYER	Costume Design ANN HOULD-WARD	Lighting Design NATASHA KATZ

Sound Design JONATHAN DEANS	Hair Design DAVID H. LAWRENCE	Illusion Design JIM STEINMEYER JOHN GAUGHAN	Prosthetics JOHN DODS

Associate Producer KEN SILVERMAN	Production Supervisor HARRIS PRODUCTION SERVICES	Production Stage Manager JOHN BRIGLEB

Casting BINDER CASTING/ MARK BRANDON	Associate Director KEITH BATTEN	Associate Choreographer KATE SWAN	Press Representative BONEAU/ BRYAN-BROWN

Fight Direction RICK SORDELET	Dance Arrangements GLEN KELLY	Music Coordinator JOHN MILLER

Orchestrations DANNY TROOB	Musical Supervision & Vocal Arrangements DAVID FRIEDMAN	Music Direction & Incidental Music Arrangements MICHAEL KOSARIN

Choreography by
MATT WEST

Directed by
ROBERT JESS ROTH

DISNEY ON BROADWAY

3/14/05

©Disney

Very Different From the Rest of Us: The cast performs the opening number, "Belle."

Photo by Joan Marcus

Beauty and the Beast

MUSICAL NUMBERS

ACT ONE

Overture
Prologue
"Belle" ....Belle, Gaston, Lefou, Silly Girls, Townspeople
"No Matter What"* ....Maurice, Belle
"No Matter What"* (Reprise) ....Maurice
"Me"* ....Gaston, Belle
"Belle" Reprise ....Belle
"Home"* ....Belle
"Home"* (Reprise) ....Mrs. Potts
"Gaston" ....Lefou, Gaston, Silly Girls, Tavern Patrons
"Gaston" (Reprise) ....Gaston, Lefou
"How Long Must This Go On?"* ....Beast
"Be Our Guest" ....Lumiere, Mrs. Potts, Cogsworth, Madame de la Grande Bouche,
                                                                                      Chip, Babette, Enchanted Objects
"If I Can't Love Her"* ....Beast

ACT TWO

Entr'acte/Wolf Chase
"Something There" ....Belle, Beast, Lumiere, Mrs. Potts, Cogsworth
"Human Again" ....Lumiere, Madame de la Grande Bouche, Cogsworth, Mrs. Potts,
                                                                                      Babette, Chip, Enchanted Objects
"Maison des Lunes"* ....Gaston, Lefou, Monsieur D'Arque
"Beauty and the Beast" ....Mrs. Potts
"If I Can't Love Her"* (Reprise) ....Beast
"A Change in Me"* ....Belle
"The Mob Song" ....Gaston, Lefou, Monsieur D'Arque, Townspeople
"The Battle" ....The Company
"Transformation"* ....Beast, Belle
"Beauty and the Beast" (Reprise) ....The Company

*Music by Alan Menken and lyrics by Tim Rice.
All other lyrics by Howard Ashman and music by Alan Menken.

THE BEAUTY & THE BEAST ORCHESTRA

Conductor:
MICHAEL KOSARIN

Associate Conductor:
KATHY SOMMER

Assistant Conductor:
JOSEPH PASSARO

Assistant Conductor:
AMY DURAN

Concertmaster:
Suzanne Ornstein

Music Coordinator:
JOHN MILLER

Violins:
Lorra Aldridge, Evan Johnson,
Roy Lewis, Kristina Musser

Cellos:
Caryl Paisner,
Joseph Kimura

Bass:
Jeffrey Carney

Flute:
Kathy Fink

Oboe:
Vicki Bodner
Clarinet/Flute:
KeriAnn Kathryn DiBari

Flute/Clarinet:
Tony Brackett

Bassoon/Contrabassoon:
Charles McCracken

Trumpets:
Neil Balm, James de la Garza

French Horns:
Jeffrey Lang, Anthony Cecere,
Robert Carlisle

Bass Trombone/Tuba:
Paul Faulise

Drums:
John Redsecker

Percussion:
Joseph Passaro

Harp:
Stacey Shames

Keyboards:
Kathy Sommer, Madelyn Rubinstein

Cast Continued

Townspeople, Enchanted Objects ....
ANA MARIA ANDRICAIN,
ANN ARVIA,
GINA CARLETTE,
BRIAN COLLIER
CHRISTOPHER DeANGELIS,
BARBARA FOLTS,
KEITH FORTNER,
TRACY GENERALOVICH,
DAVID E. LIDDELL,
JENNIFER MARCUM,
CHRISTOPHER MONTELEONE,
BILL NABEL, BRIAN O'BRIEN,
BRYNN O'MALLEY, DENNY PASCHALL,
GLENN RAINEY,
JOHN SALVATORE,
DARIA LYNN SCATTON, SARAH SOLIE,
MARGUERITE WILLBANKS,
BREK WILLIAMS, TIA MARIE ZORNE
Voice of Prologue Narrator ....
DAVID OGDEN STIERS

UNDERSTUDIES

Enchantress— GINA CARLETTE, BARBARA FOLTS;
Young Prince— KEITH FORTNER, DAVID E. LIDDELL;
Beast— CHRISTOPHER MONTELEONE, BRIAN
O'BRIEN, BREK WILLIAMS; Belle— ANA MARIA
ANDRICAIN, BARBARA FOLTS, BRYNN O'MALLEY;
Bookseller— KEITH FORTNER, DAVID E. LIDDELL;
Lefou— BRIAN COLLIER, KEITH FORTNER; Gaston—
CHRISTOPHER MONTELEONE, BRIAN O'BRIEN,
BREK WILLIAMS; Silly Girls— GINA CARLETTE,
BARBARA FOLTS; Wolves— GINA CARLETTE,
BARBARA FOLTS, KEITH FORTNER, DAVID E.
LIDDELL; Maurice— BILL NABEL, GLENN
RAINEY; Cogsworth— BILL NABEL, GLENN
RAINEY; Lumiere—CHRISTOPHER DeANGELIS,
BILL NABEL; Babette— JENNIFER MARCUM,
SARAH SOLIE; Mrs. Potts— ANN ARVIA, MAR-
GUERITE WILLBANKS; Madame de la Grande
Bouche— ANN ARVIA, MARGUERITE WILL-
BANKS; Salt and Pepper— KEITH FORTNER, DAVID
E. LIDDELL; Doormat— KEITH FORTNER, DAVID
E. LIDDELL; Cheesegrater— KEITH FORTNER,
DAVID E. LIDDELL; Monsieur D'Arque— BILL
NABEL, BRIAN O'BRIEN

SWINGS

GINA CARLETTE, BARBARA FOLTS,
KEITH FORTNER, DAVID E. LIDDELL,
JOHN SALVATORE,

Dance Captain:
DARIA LYNN SCATTON

Beauty and the Beast

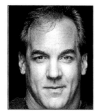

Steve Blanchard
Beast

Brooke Tansley
Belle

Grant Norman
Gaston

Jeff Brooks
Cogsworth

Alma Cuervo
Mrs. Potts

Peter Flynn
Lumiere

Jamie Ross
Maurice

Aldrin Gonzalez
Lefou

Matthew Gumley
*Chip at certain
performances*

Patrick O'Neil Henney
*Chip at certain
performances*

Pam Klinger
Babette

Mary Stout
*Madame de la
Grande Bouche*

Ana Maria
Andricain
Ensemble

Ann Arvia
Ensemble

Gina Carlette
Ensemble/Swing

Brian Collier
*Young Prince/
Doormat/Ensemble*

Christopher
DeAngelis
Ensemble/Salt

Barbara Folts
Ensemble/Swing

Keith Fortner
Ensemble/Swing

Tracy Generalovich
Ensemble/Silly Girl

David E. Liddell
*Fight Captain/
Ensemble/Swing*

Jennifer Marcum
Silly Girl

Christopher
Monteleone
Ensemble

Bill Nabel
Ensemble

Brian O'Brien
Ensemble/Pepper

Brynn O'Malley
Ensemble

Denny Paschall
*Ensemble/
Cheesegrater*

Glenn Rainey
*Ensemble/
Bookseller/Monsieur
D'Arque*

John Salvatore
Ensemble/Swing

Sarah Solie
*Enchantress/
Ensemble*

Marguerite Wilbanks
Ensemble

Brek Williams
Ensemble/Pepper

Tia Marie Zorne
Ensemble/Silly Girl

Alan Menken
Composer

Tim Rice
Lyrics

Beauty and the Beast

Linda Woolverton
Book

Matt West
Choreographer

Stanley A. Meyer
Scenic Designer

Natasha Katz
Lighting Designer

Jonathan Deans
Sound Designer

John Dods
*Prosthetics
Designer*

Keith Batten
Associate Director

Kate Swan
*Associate
Choreographer*

Rick Sordelet
Fight Director

John Miller
Music Coordinator

David Friedman
*Music Supervisor/
Vocal Arrangements*

Michael Kosarin
*Music Supervisor/
Incidental Music
Arranger*

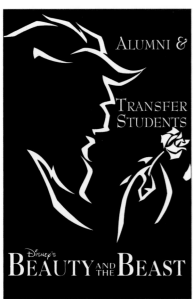

Disney's BEAUTY AND THE BEAST — Alumni & Transfer Students

Kevin Berdini
Ensemble

David deVries
Lumiere

Stacia Fernandez
Ensemble

Henry Hodges
Chip

Michelle Mallardi
Ensemble

Christy Carlson
Romano
Belle

Alex Rutherford
Chip

Billy Sprague, Jr.
Ensemble/Salt

Jennifer Hope Wills
Ensemble

Daria Lynn Scatton
*Dance Captain/
Ensemble/Swing*

Michelle Lookadoo
Silly Girl

Elizabeth Polito
*Enchantress/
Ensemble*

Jill Hayman
Ensemble

Beauty and the Beast

Wardrobe
(L-R): Dan Foss, Theresia Larsen, Ginny Hounsell, Suzanne Sponsler, Eric Rudy, Shannon O'Hara, Michael Piatkowski, Barbara Hladsky

Box Office
Kevin Lynch

Photos by Ben Strohmann

Front-of-House Staff
(Kneeling L-R): Melody Rodriquez, Evelyn Hynes, Joey Cintron, Madeline Flores, Carmela Cambio, Angalic Cortes
Second Row (L-R): Tracey Malinowski (House Manager), Jessica Gonzalez (Chief Usher), Marion Danton, Omar Aguilar, Lauren Banyai, Sharon Grant, Sheron James-Richardson, Honey Owen
Third Row (L-R): Christine Corrigan, Paul Perez, Maria Ortiz, Misael Reyes, Roberto Calderon, Carlo Mosarra
Back Row (L-R): Barry Jenkins, Paul Campbell, Robert McCloskey, William Pacheco

Beauty and the Beast

Photos by Ben Strohmann

Electrics
Seated (L-R):
Sebastian Schulherr,
David Brickman,
Gerald Schultz,
Peter Byrne
Standing (L-R):
Dennis Boyle,
James Travers Jr.
and Ed Crimmins

Hair Department
Seated (L-R):
Taurance Williams,
Thom Gonzalez
Standing (L-R):
Jackie Weiss,
Paula Schaffer and
Christina Grant (Makeup
Dept.)

(L-R): Joseph Riccio (Engineer), Bob Garner (Dooman)

Company Management
(L-R): Keith Cooper, Mark Rozzano

(L-R): David Bornstein (Props), Merv Haines (Pyro)

Photos by Ben Strothmann

STAFF FOR DISNEY'S BEAUTY AND THE BEAST

COMPANY MANAGER	MARK ROZZANO
Assistant Company Manager	Keith D. Cooper

Production Supervision	Harris Production Services

General Press Representative	Boneau/Bryan-Brown Chris Boneau/Jim Byk/ Juliana Hannett/Amy Jacobs

Production Stage Manager	**John Brigleb**
Stage Manager	**M.A. Howard**
Stage Manager	**John Salvatore**
Stage Manager	**Michael Biondi**
Dance Captain	Daria Lynn Scatton
Fight Captain	David E. Liddell

Puppet Design Consultant	Michael Curry

Special Effects Consultant	Jauchem & Meeh, NYC

Associate Production Supervisor	Tom Bussey
Production Manager	Elisa Cardone
Associate Scenic Designer	Dennis W. Moyes
Principal Set Design Assistant	Edmund A. LeFevre, Jr.
Set Design Assistants	Stephen Carter, Judy Gailen, Dana Kenn, Sarah Lambert
Associate Lighting Designers	Gregory Cohen, Dan Walker
Assistant Lighting Designers	Rob Cangemi, Maura Sheridan
Automated Lighting Programmers	Aland Henderson, Richard W. Knight
Associate Sound Designer	John Petrafesa, Jr.
Assistant to Lighting Designer	Richard Swan
Original Pyrotechnic Designer	Tylor Wymer
Automated Lighting Tracker	John Viesta
Projection Effects	Wendall K. Harrington
Associate Costume Designer	Tracy Christensen
Assistants to Ms. Hould-Ward	David C. Paulin, Markas Henry, Mark Musters, Fabio Toblini
Assistant to Mr. Lawrence	Linda Rice
Synthesizer Programming	Dan Tramon, Bruce Samuels

Production Carpenter	B.B. Baker
Production Flyman	Peter H. Jackson III
Production Electrician	Todd Davis
Production Property Master	Joseph P. Harris. Jr.
Production Sound Engineer	Scott Anderson
Production Wardrobe Supervisors	Sue Hamilton, Gerald Crawford
Production Hair Supervisors	Wanda Gregory, Valerie Gladstone
Production Prosthetics Supervisor	Angela Johnson

Head Carpenter	B.B. Baker
Flyman	Frank Frederico
Assistant Carpenter	Mark Hallisey
Automation Carpenters	Andrew D. Elman, Hugh M. Hardyman
Head Electrician	Tom Brouard
Assistant Electrician/Front Light	Peter Byrne
Assistant Electrician/ Special Effects Technician	William C. Horton, Sr.
Assistant Electrician/Vari*Lite Operator	Gregg Brooks
Sound Effects Engineer	Ned Hatton
Head Propertyman	David L. Bornstein
Assistant Propertyman	John Lofgren
Wardrobe Supervisor	Julie Ratcliffe
Assistant Wardrobe Supervisor	Eric Rudy
Ms. Tansley's Dresser	Ginny Hounsell
Mr. Blanchard's Dresser	Hope A. Flanigan
Wardrobe Crew	Suzanne Sponsler, Joseph Davis, Dan Foss, Billy Hipkins,

Barbara Hladsky, Rose Keough,
Kristin Socci, Richard J. Nash, Jr.,
Michael Piatkowski, Joan Weiss
Makeup/Prosthetics Supervisor ....Vincent T. Schicchi
Hair Supervisor ....Valerie Gladstone
Assistant Hair Supervisor ....Thom Gonzalez
Wig Crew...Tonya Bodison,
Anita Ragnovic,
Taurance Williams

Additional Orchestrations ....Michael Starobin,
Ned Ginsberg
Music Preparation Supervisor ....Peter R. Miller/
Miller Music Service
Assistant to Mr. Menken ....Rick Kunis
Assistant to Mr. Rice ....Eileen Heinink
Assistant to John Miller...............Matthew P. Ettinger
Rehearsal PianistsGlen Kelly,
Madelyn Rubinstein,
Amy Duran

Advertising.............................Serino Coyne, Inc.
Press Representative Staff ....Adrian Bryan-Brown,
Karalee Dawn, Adriana Douzos,
Jackie Green, Brian Harasek,
Hector Hernandez,
Jessica Johnson, Holly Kinney,
Aaron Meier, Genevieve Miller,
Jamie Morris, Joe Perrotta,
Linnae Petruzzelli, Matt Polk,
Susanne Tighe
Casting Associates ....Jack Bowdan, C.S.A.,
Laura Stanczyk,
Sarah Prosser
Payroll Manager ....Cathy Guerra
Production Assistants ....Bari Kkartowski,
Mika Hadani,
Alison Miller
Production Photography ....Joan Marcus,
Marc Bryan-Brown
Production Travel ....Jill Citron
Children's Tutoring................On Location Education
Chaperone ....Sarah Nadeau
Theatre Displays ....King Displays
Safety & Health Consultants..................CHSH, Inc.,
New York City
Originally Produced by
Robert W. McTyre ....Producer
Don Frantz ....Associate Producer

Based on the Disney Film Disney's
BEAUTY AND THE BEAST,
directed by Kirk Wise and Gary Trousedale.
Produced by Don Hahn.
Special thanks to all the artists and staff at
Walt Disney Feature Animation.
Tom Child, Initial Conceptual Development.
Anthony Stimac/Musical Theatre Works, Inc.

CREDITS
Scenic & Transformation Effect by
Motion Control Featuring
Stage Command Systems™
by Scenic Technologies.
Scenic construction, sculpting and
scenic painting by Scenic Technologies.
Additional scenery by Variety Scenic Studios;
Hudson Scenic Studios, Inc.;
Draperies by Showbiz Enterprises
and I. Weiss & Sons, Inc.
Lighting equipment by Four Star Lighting.
Automated lighting by Vari-Lite.
Pani Projection by Production Arts Lighting Inc.
Sound furnished by Sound Associates Inc.
Custom built props by Seitzer and Associates.
Table cloths by Decor Couture Designs.
Window treatments, hand and table linens by O'Neil.
Costumes executed by Barbara Matera Ltd.
Foliage by Modern Artificial.
Costumes executed by Grace Costumes, Inc.
Dying, screening and painting by
Fabric Effects Incorporated.

Surface designs and costume crafts
by Martin Izquierdo Studios.
Prosthetics by John Dods Studio.
Millinery by Douglas James, Arnold S. Levine,
Janet Linville and Woody Shelp.
Footwear by Capezio and J.C. Theatrical.
Vacuform costume sculptor by Costume Armour, Inc. Wigs
created by Bob Kelly Wig Creations, Inc.
Opticals by Fabulous Fanny's Myoptics.
Gloves by LaCrasia Glamour Gloves.
Beast muscle system by Andrew Benepe Studio.
Costume harness and supports by J. Gerard.
Additional supports by Danforth Orthopedic.
Special Adhesives by Adhesive Technologies, Inc.
Illusions by John Gaughan and Associates.
Invention and Magic Mirror by Tom Talmon Studio.
Pyrotechnical special effects materials
supplied by MP Associates, Inc.
Pyrotechnical Equipment supplied by LunaTech.
All sound recording by
Sound Designers Studio, New York City.
Emer'gen-C super energy booster provided by Alacer Corp.
Throat lozenges supplied by Ricola, Inc.

Cover Art Design © Disney

BEAUTY AND THE BEAST
originally premiered at
Theatre Under The Stars
Houston, Texas
December 2, 1993

Inquiries regarding the
licensing of stock and amateur productions of
BEAUTY AND THE BEAST
should be directed to
Music Theatre International,
421 W. 54th St., New York, NY 10019.
Tel: 212-541-4684
www.MTIshows.com

NEDERLANDER

Chairman/President ....James M. Nederlander
President ....James L. Nederlander
Executive Vice President
Nick Scandalios
Vice President•   Senior Vice President •
Corporate Development   Labor Relations
Charlene S. Nederlander   **Herschel Waxman**
Vice President   Chief Financial Officer
Jim Boese   **Freida Sawyer Belviso**

STAFF FOR THE LUNT-FONTANNE
House Manager..........................Tracey Malinowski
Treasurer ....Joe Olcese
Assistant Treasurer ....Gregg Collichio
House Carpenter ....Terry Taylor
House Electrician ....Dennis Boyle
House Propertyman ....Dennis Sabella
House Flyman ....Mike Walters
House Engineers ....Robert MacMahon,
Joseph Riccio III

DISNEY THEATRICAL PRODUCTIONS
President ....Thomas Schumacher
Senior Vice President & General Manager ......Alan Levey
Senior Vice President,
Managing Director & CFO ....David Schrader
General Management
Vice President, International ....Ron Kollen
Vice President, Operations ....Dana Amendola
Vice President, Labor Relations ....Allan Frost
Director, Human Resources ....June Heindel
Director, Domestic Touring ....Michele Gold
Manager, Labor Relations ....Stephanie Cheek
Manager, Information Systems ....Scott Benedict
Consultant, Information Systems ....Christopher Diamond

Production
Executive Music Producer ....Chris Montan
Vice President, Creative Affairs ....Michele Steckler
Vice President, Creative Affairs ....Greg Gunter
Vice President, Physical Production ....John Tiggeloven
Purchasing Manager ....Joseph Doughney
Staff Associate Director ....Jeff Lee
Staff Associate Producer ....Florie Seery
Staff Associate Designer ....Dennis W. Moyes
Staff Associate Dramaturg ....Ken Cerniglia
Marketing
Vice President ....Heather Epple
Vice President, Domestic Touring ....Jack Eldon
Manager, New York ....Michele Holland
Manager, New York ....Leslie Barrett
Manager ....Joel Hile
Sales
Vice President, Ticketing ....Jerome Kane
Manager, Group Sales ....Jacob Lloyd Kimbro
Group Sales Representative ....Juil Kim
Business and Legal Affairs
Vice President ....Jonathan Olson
Vice President ....Robbin Kelley
Director ....Harry S. Gold
Attorney.....................................Seth Stuhl
Paralegal/Contract Administration ....Colleen Lober
Finance
Director ....Joe McClafferty
Manager, Production Accounting ....Bill Hussey
Senior Business Planner ....Jason Fletcher, Justin Gee
Senior Analysts ....Sam Tello, Amir Feder
Production Accountants ..... Jamie Cousins, Alma LaMarr,
Barbara Toben
Analyst ....Ronnie Cooper
Controllership
Director, Accounting ....Leena Mathews
Manager, Accounting......................Erica McShane
Analysts ....Celia Brown, Adrineh Ghoukassian
Administrative Staff
Elliot Altman, Ann Marie Amarga,
Amy Andrews, Alice Baeza,
Jennifer Baker, Antonia Barba,
Tiffany Casanova, Karl Chmielewski,
Celena Cipriaso, Carl Flanigan,
Dayle Gruet, Jonathan Hanson,
Jay Hollenback, Connie Jasper,
Khadija Mohamed, Jeff Parvin,
Giovanna Primak, Roberta Risafi,
Sarah Roach, Susan Rubio,
Kisha Santiago, Christian Trimmer

Disney Theatrical Productions
1450 Broadway • New York, NY 10018
mail@disneytheatrical.com

BUENA VISTA THEATRICAL MERCHANDISE, L.L.C.
Director ....Steven Downing
Manager.................................John F. Agati
Operations Manager ....Shawn Baker
Assistant Manager, Inventory ....Suzanne Jakel
Buyer ....Suzanne Araneo
Merchandising Assistant ....Ed Pisapia
On-Site Retail Manager ....Keith Guralchuk
On-Site Assistant Retail Manager...............Anjie Maraj

Most Exciting Celebrity Visitor: Joe Torre, Manager of Yankees, came with his family. Steve Blanchard (who played the Beast) and I are big baseball fans, and we gave him a little tour of backstage. We chatted with him and he gave us a little inside stuff on the Yanks' next season. Afterward he sent us autographed baseballs. I have two boys, 12 and 6, and when he returned recently, he gave me a second ball so both boys could have one each.

"Gypsy Of The Year" Sketch: "I'm in a Cup" by Michael Piatkowski.

"Easter Bonnet" Sketch: "Neat Parody" by Billy Hipkins.

"Carols For A Cure" Carol: "Away in a Manger"

Backstage Ritual: We've celebrated many things: passing *Guys and Dolls* and *Fiddler on the Roof* on the all-time long-run list; passing 4,000 performances; our tenth anniversary. At all of these observances, our director Rob Roth, offers a prayer to lyricist Howard Ashman, who died during the writing of the movie. We always remember him.

Favorite Moment During Each Performance: Although Cogsworth is generally a humorous character, my favorite moment is not a humorous one. It comes just after Belle leaves and Mrs. Potts, Lumiere and I think the curse will follow through and we'll remain household objects forever. It's a tragic moment for all of us. It's the darkness before the dawn.

In-Theatre Gathering Place: There is a cross-under beneath the stage. In a corner on the stage left side is a workman's table once used by Mr. Lofgren, who was a much-beloved figure. He's moved on, but the table is still called Lofgren's Corner, and whenever we have a quick intermission birthday party or bon-voyage party, we have it there. You can tell when we're having one: The stage manager announces, "There's a phone call" for the person "at Lofgren's Corner."

Off-Site Hangout: The Café Edison, right around the corner. A lot also go to Hakata on 48th Street.

Favorite Snack Food: Cakes, constantly. We have a big cast and a big crew and they have a lot of birthdays, so we end up having a lot of cakes.

Mascot: Aldrin Gonzalez plays Lefou, sidekick to Gaston, the villain. One day a kid came backstage for a visit and met him, and said, "I know who you are, you're Gaston's dog!" So I suppose he's our mascot.

Favorite Therapy: Mucinex for the vocal cords. We have Ricolas in tubs everywhere.

Memorable Ad-Lib: One night I was on stage with Steve Blanchard, as the Beast, and he's singing "Something There" just as the table that has Chip's head, makes its exit. On this night, the Beast's tail got caught on the table and got yanked off as Steve was singing. We both looked down and saw it laying there on the stage, but Steve just kept going. The audience was in conniptions. At the end of the song, he has a line, "I want to

The cast performs their parody of "Big Spender" ("Big Blender") at the 19th Annual Easter Bonnet Competition at the New Amsterdam Theatre.

Left: Christy Carlson Romano at "Broadway on Broadway."

Right: Mickey Mouse gets ready to mix it up at "Easter Bonnet."

give her something—but what?" My line is supposed to be, "Well, there are the usual things: flowers, chocolate, promises you don't intend to keep." Instead I picked up the tail and said, "Well, there are the usual things: flowers, chocolate, your tail." And I handed him the tail.

Strange Stage Door Fan Encounters: There is a family, we call them The Dog Family, who have been coming to see the show again and again since it opened. They travel around the country in a Winnebago with their dogs—some of which are dead and have been stuffed. They used to follow the national tour from town to town, and now they come frequently to see the show in New York. The husband is a traveling minister and he doesn't fully approve of the theatre, but the wife and grown daughter have come, it must be approaching one hundred times. Some members of the cast actually visited the Winnebago when we were on tour, and saw the dogs. One more detail: They're very sweet, but they smell, and not faintly, of formaldehyde. One night, in the middle of a performance, we could smell it from the stage, and we all told each other, "They're here." And they were.

We also have a Japanese woman named Naomi who flies in from Japan and brings us origami and candy. She must have seen the show forty times. We know her so well that we say "Hello, Naomi!" when we see her at the stage door.

Heaviest/Hottest Costume: The heaviest costume is probably mine. It's close to 40 pounds and I have to run up and down stairs. Hottest would have to be the Beast. He's got all that hair—and a hump.

Who Wore The Least: The dancing napkins. They don't wear that much, which is a treat for the men in the audience.

Most Embarrassing Moment: During the scene where Lumiere and I are giving Belle a tour of the castle and trying to keep her from going to the library, I once completely went up on what came next in my line. So I started to just make things up. Patrick Paige was playing Lumiere, and I could seen him smiling next to me. At a certain point, the line was just not coming back to me, so I ad-libbed to Patrick, "Lumiere, what am I trying to say?" And he replied, in a perfect French accent, "You're on your own, my friend."

Correspondent: Jeff Brooks, "Cogsworth"

Photos by Aubrey Reuben

Bombay Dreams

| First Preview: March 29, 2004 | Opened: April 29, 2004 |
| Closed: January 1, 2005 | 30 previews and 285 Performances |

PLAYBILL®

CAST

(in order of appearance)

Akaash . . . . .MANU NARAYAN
Eunuchs (Hijira) . . . . .RON NAHASS,
BOBBY PESTKA, DARRYL SEMIRA,
KIRK TORIGOE
Ram . . . . .MUEEN JAHAN AHMAD
Salim . . . . .WILSON MENDIETA
Shanti . . . . .YOLANDE BAVAN
Sweetie . . . . .SRIRAM GANESAN
Munna (at certain performances) . . . .
NEIL JAY SHASTRI
or TANVIR GOPAL
Hard Hats .SURESH JOHN,
SEAN MacLAUGHLIN
Vikram . . . . .DEEP KATDARE
Mumtaaz . . . . .LISA STEVENS
Priya . . . . .TAMYRA GRAY
Madan . . . . .MARVIN L. ISHMAEL
Pageant Announcer . . . . .ZAHF PAROO
Rani . . . . .ANJALI BHIMANI
Policemen . SEAN MacLAUGHLIN, ZAHF PAROO
Shaheen . . . . .JOLLY ABRAHAM
Kitty DaSouza . . . . .SARAH RIPARD
Chaiyya Chaiyya Soloist . . .NATASHA TABANDERA
Movie Sweetie . . . . .DARRYL SEMIRA
Movie Shanti . . . . .GINA PHILISTINE
Movie Akaash . . . . .ZAHF PAROO
Lament Singer . . . . .IAN JUTSUN
Wedding Qawali Singers . . . . . .IAN JUTSUN,
SEAN MacLAUGHLIN, ZAHF PAROO

continued on the next page

⑤ BROADWAY THEATRE

1681 Broadway
A Shubert Organization Theatre

Gerald Schoenfeld, *Chairman* **Philip J. Smith,** *President*

Robert E. Wankel, *Executive Vice President*

WAXMAN WILLIAMS ENTERTAINMENT and TGA ENTERTAINMENT
in association with
DENISE RICH and RALPH WILLIAMS SCOTT PRISAND and DANNY SERAPHINE
H. THAU/M. COOPER/AD PRODS. INDEPENDENT PRESENTERS NETWORK
Present

TAMYRA GRAY   MANU NARAYAN
in

ANDREW LLOYD WEBBER'S Production of
A R RAHMAN'S

BOMBAY DREAMS

Starring

YOLANDE BAVAN   ANJALI BHIMANI   SRIRAM GANESAN
TANVIR GOPAL   MARVIN L. ISHMAEL   DEEP KATDARE   NEIL JAY SHASTRI

JOLLY ABRAHAM   MUEEN JAHAN AHMAD   AARON J. ALBANO   CELINE ALWYN   SHANE BLAND
WENDY CALIO   TIFFANY MICHELLE COOPER   SHEETAL GANDHI   KRYSTAL KIRAN GARIB   TANIA MARIE HAKKIM
DELL HOWLETT   SURESH JOHN   IAN JUTSUN   SEAN MacLAUGHLIN   WILSON MENDIETA   RON NAHASS
ZAHF PAROO   DANNY PATHAN   BOBBY PESTKA   GINA PHILISTINE   KAFI PIERRE   SARAH RIPARD   ROMMY SANDHU
DARRYL SEMIRA   LISA STEVENS   NATASHA TABANDERA   KIRK TORIGOE   J. R. WHITTINGTON   NICOLE WINHOFFER

Music by	Lyrics by	Book by
A R RAHMAN	DON BLACK	MEERA SYAL
		THOMAS MEEHAN

Based on an Idea by
SHEKHAR KAPUR and ANDREW LLOYD WEBBER

| Music Director/Dance Music Arranger | Original Additional Music Arrangements | Music Coordinator |
| JAMES ABBOTT | CHRISTOPHER NIGHTINGALE | MICHAEL KELLER |

Music Supervision, Arrangements and Orchestrations by
PAUL BOGAEV

| Production Manager | Casting by | Production Stage Manager |
| PETER FULBRIGHT | TARA RUBIN CASTING | BONNIE L. BECKER |

| Executive Producer | General Management |
| WAXWILL THEATRICAL DIVISION | THE CHARLOTTE WILCOX COMPANY |

| Press Representative | Marketing | Sponsorship |
| BARLOW•HARTMAN | MARGERY SINGER COMPANY | RHINO ENTERPRISES |

Associate Producer	Associate Producer	Associate Producers
SUDHIR VAISHNAV	THE ENTERTAINMENT PARTNERSHIP	ALEXANDER FRASER
		KEN DENISON

Lighting Design by
HUGH VANSTONE

Sound Design by
MICK POTTER

Scenery and Costume Design by
MARK THOMPSON

Choreography by
ANTHONY VAN LAAST & FARAH KHAN

Directed by
STEVEN PIMLOTT

The Original London Production was produced by The Really Useful Theatre Company and opened at the Apollo Victoria Theatre on June 19, 2002.

MUSICAL NUMBERS

ACT ONE

Scene One: Paradise Slum
Overture: "Salaa'm Bombay" ....Akaash, Sweetie and Ensemble
"Bollywood" ....Akaash and Ensemble

Scene Two: Shanti and Akaash's Home
"Love's Never Easy" ....Sweetie, Priya and Ensemble

Scene Three: The Miss India Pageant, Backstage

Scene Four: The Miss India Pageant, Frontstage
"Lovely, Lovely, Ladies" ....Rani and Ensemble
"Bhangra" ....Akaash, Rani and Ensemble

Scene Five: The Miss India Pageant, Backstage

Scene Six: Film Set of Diamond in the Rough
"Shakalaka Baby" ....Rani, Akaash and Ensemble
"I Could Live Here" ....Akaash
"Is This Love?" ....Priya

Scene Seven: Akaash's New Apartment
"Famous" ....Madan, Rani, Akaash and Guests

Scene Eight: Diamond in the Rough Premiere
Reprise: "Love's Never Easy" ....Priya and Sweetie

ACT TWO

Scene One: The Annual Indian Film Awards
"Chaiyya Chaiyya" ....Akaash, Rani and Ensemble

Scene Two: Akaash's Hilltop Mansion
"How Many Stars?" ....Akaash and Priya

Scene Three: Film Set of Bombay Dreams
Reprise: "Salaa'm Bombay" ....Rani and Ensemble
"Hero" ....Sweetie and Priya

Scene Four: Paradise Slum

Scene Five: Outside the Taj Royale Beach Hotel
"Ganesh Procession" ....The Company

Scene Six: Juhu Beach
"The Journey Home" ....Akaash

Scene Seven: Paradise Slum

Scene Eight: The Taj Royale Beach Hotel
"Wedding Qawali" ....The Company

Manu Narayan, Ayesha Dharker and company.

Photo by Joan Marcus

Cast Continued

ENSEMBLE
*(Slum Dwellers, Beauty Pageant Contestants, TV and Film Crew,
Feminist Demonstrators, Shakalaka, Chaiyya Chaiyya,
Film Salaàm Bombay Dancers and Fishermen)*
JOLLY ABRAHAM, MUEEN JAHAN AHMAD,
AARON J. ALBANO, CELINE ALWYN,
SHANE BLAND, WENDY CALIO,
TIFFANY MICHELLE COOPER,
SHEETAL GANDHI, KRYSTAL KIRAN GARIB,
TANIA MARIE HAKKIM, DELL HOWLETT,
SURESH JOHN, IAN JUTSUN,
SEAN MacLAUGHLIN, WILSON
MENDIETA, RON NAHASS, ZAHF PAROO,
DANNY PATHAN, BOBBY PESTKA,
GINA PHILISTINE, KAFI PIERRE, SARAH RIPARD,
DARRYL SEMIRA, LISA STEVENS,
NATASHA TABANDERA, KIRK TORIGOE

SWINGS
ROMMY SANDHU, JAMES R. WHITTINGTON,
NICOLE WINHOFFER

UNDERSTUDIES
For Akaash – AARON J. ALBANO, ZAHF PAROO,
DANNY PATHAN; for Priya – KRYSTAL KIRAN
GARIB, SHEETAL GANDHI, NATASHA TABAN-
DERA; for Rani – JOLLY ABRAHAM, SARAH
RIPARD; for Sweetie – SHANE BLAND, DARRYL
SEMIRA; for Shanti – ANJALI BHIMANI, SARAH
RIPARD; for Vikram – SEAN MacLAUGHLING,
ZAHF PAROO; for Madan – MUEEN JAHAN
AHMAD, SURESH JOHN, IAN JUTSUN; for Munna
– TANVIR GOPAL, NEIL JAY SHASTRI

BOMBAY DREAMS ORCHESTRA
CONDUCTOR: JAMES L. ABBOTT
Associate Conductor: Dan Riddle
Concertmaster: Sylvia D'Avanzo
Violins: Sean Carney, Nina Evtuhov, Pauline Kim,
Ming Yeh; Violas: Liuh-Wen Ting, Arthur Dibble;
Cellos: Ted Mook, Roger Shell; Flutes: Anders
Bostrom ; Oboe/English Horn: Charles Pillow;
Drums: Ray Grappone; Bass: Randy Landau;
Keyboards: Adam Ben-David, Dan Riddle,
Ann Gerschefski;
Onstage Percussion: Deep Singh, David Sharma
Music Coordinator: Michael Keller

Special thanks to Bombay Sapphire.

TRANSLATIONS OF HINDI EXPRESSIONS
Aaja Savariyan – "Come to me, my beloved"
Ulloo Ka Pattha – "Son of an owl "(dingbat)
Chhotu – "Teenie-weenie" *Shakh ti* – "Power"
Jodi Jug Jug Jiye –
"May the couple live for many years"

Bombay Dreams

Tamyra Gray
Priya

Manu Narayan
Akaash

Yolande Bavan
Shanti

Anjali Bhimani
Rani

Sriram Ganesan
Sweetie

Tanvir Gopal
Munna

Marvin L. Ishmael
Madan

Deep Katdare
Vikram

Neil Jay Shastri
Munna

Jolly Abraham
Ensemble

Mueen Jahan Ahmad
Ensemble

Aaron J. Albano
Ensemble

Celine Alwyn
Ensemble

Shane Bland
Ensemble

Wendy Calio
Ensemble

Tiffany Michelle Cooper
Ensemble

Sheetal Gandhi
Ensemble

Krystal Kiran Garib
Ensemble

Tania Marie Hakkim
Ensemble

Dell Howlett
Ensemble

Suresh John
Ensemble

Ian Jutsun
Ensemble

Sean MacLaughlin
Ensemble

Wilson Mendieta
Ensemble

Ron Nahass
Ensemble

Zahf Paroo
Ensemble

Danny Pathan
Ensemble

Bobby Pestka
Ensemble

Gina Philistine
Ensemble

Kafi Pierre
Ensemble

Sarah Ripard
Ensemble

Rommy Sandhu
Fight Captain, Swing

Darryl Semira
Ensemble

Lisa Stevens
Asst. Choreographer, Dance Captain

Natasha Tabandera
Ensemble

Kirk Torigoe
Ensemble

J.R. Whittington
Swing

Nicole Winhoffer
Swing

A.R. Rahman
Composer

Don Black
Lyrics

Meera Syal
Book

Thomas Meehan
Book

Bombay Dreams

Steven Pimlott
Director

Anthony Van Laast
Choreographer

Farah Khan
Co-Choreographer

Mark Thompson
Scenery & Costume Designer

Hugh Vanstone
Lighting Designer

Paul Bogaev
Musical Super. Orches. Vocal & Incidental Music Arrgmts.

James Abbott
Music Director/ Dance Music Arranger

Michael Keller
Music Coordinator

Margery Singer
Marketing

Andrew Lloyd Webber
London Producer

Charlotte Wilcox
General Manager

Anita Waxman
Producer

Elizabeth Williams
Producer

Scott Prisand
Producer

Ken Denison
Assoc. Producer

Alexander Fraser
Assoc. Producer

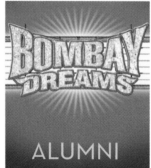

ALUMNI

Gabriel Burrafato
Ensemble

Ayesha Dharker
Rani

Madhur Jaffrey
Shanti

Miriam Laube
Mumtaaz, Chaiyya soloist

Aalok Mehta
Salim

Anisha Nagarajan
Priya

Michelle Nigalan
Ensemble

Front-of-House Staff

First Row (L-R): Laurie Bokun (Chief Usher), Ulysses Santiago (Ticket-Taker), Rosalies Aquino (Custodian).

Second Row (L-R): Svetlana Pinkhas (Usherette), Monssor Saidi (Usher), Not identified (Concessions).

Third Row (L-R): Not identified (Concessions), Mattie Robinson (Usherette), Barbara Arias (Usherette), Not identified (Concessions).

Fourth Row (L-R): Veronica Phelan (Usherette), Lisa Houghton (Usherette), Jason Coonan (Usher), May Park (Usherette), Joseph Pitman (Usher).

Fifth Row (L-R): Not identified (Concessions), Jorge Colon (Ticket-Taker), Not identified (Concessions), Not identified (Concessions), Elvis Caban (Usher), Darien Jones (Usher).

Photo by Ben Strohmann

Stage Managers and Swings
Front Row (L-R): Bonnie L. Becker, Charles Underhill, J. Philip Bassett
Back Row (L-R): Rommy Sandhu (Fight Captain), Lisa Stevens (Dance Captain), Nicole Winhoffer (Swing), James R. Whittington (Swing)

Electricians and Sound
Kneeling (L-R): Bob Beamers, George Milne, Peter Beeker, John Atkinson, Dominic Intagliato
Standing (L-R): Sandra Paradise, Lonnie MacDougal, Mike Milne, Jimmy Fedigan, Paul Verightny

Wardrobe Department
Standing (L-R): Kathleen Gallagher, Kelly Kinsella, Kathy Guida, Dawn Reynolds, Nancy Ronin, Jessica Chaney
Seated (L-R): Chip White, Ricky Yates, Rodd Sovar, Amber Isaac, Catherine Osborne, Alessandro Ferdico

Photos by Ben Strohmann

Bombay Dreams

Carpentry Crew
Back Row (L-R):
Robert Diaz,
Charlie Rasmussen,
Lia Nelson,
Mike Kelly.
Front Row (L-R):
Greg Burton,
Bob Gordon,
Paul Wimmer,
Erik Hansen.

Hair Department
(L-R): Joe Whitmeyer,
Leone Gagliardi,
John James,
Mary Malligan,
Hazel Higgins,
Kelly Reed

Props Department
(L-R): LauraMcGarty,
Rick Dal Cortivo,
Richard Anderson

Photos by Ben Strohmann

Bombay Dreams

Photos by Aubrey Reuben

Opening Night Telegram: One of my best friends sent a collage with the note, "If you mess up I'm going to have to kick you off the stage and take your role!"

Opening Night Gifts: Tom Meehan and his wife made us all beautiful collector's plates with an elephant and the *Bombay Dreams* logo, inscribed, "Thank you for all your hard work. Love and cheers, Thomas Meehan." Andrew Lloyd Webber gave us cards showing the Statue of Liberty wearing a colorful sari, and the opening date. The producers gave hard-carved pencil holders with the opening date. One of my friends who works at Barlow-Hartman had a picture of me superimposed on a *Playbill* cover with the title, "Sriram Ganesan starring in *Bombay Dreams.*"

Celebrity Visitor: I had a funny encounter with Mel Brooks and Anne Bancroft. I was in my bathrobe on the way to the shower. Mel Brooks said how much he enjoyed the show and how much he enjoyed my performance. But I was so nervous, all I could think of was that I was completely naked under this bathrobe. I wish I had a camera, but I'm also really glad I didn't.

Gypsy Robe: Rommy Sandhu.

"Gypsy Of The Year" Sketch: "Minorities Encouraged" by Vanessa Brown and Rommy Sandhu.

"Carols For A Cure" Carol: "Joy to the World"

Backstage Rituals: Since this was my first Broadway show, I had a religious ritual that I would do, starting two hours before the show. I also have a lucky coin I keep in my dressing room, a sentimental thing that was placed on my grandmother when she was cremated. I carried that coin with me during the audition and on the day I got the role, so I wore it during the critics' performances for good luck.

Favorite Moment: The fountain moment in "Shakalaka Baby." We get to have a nice shower after sweating for the first hour of the show. We also like the very opening of the show. When the violin starts to play, everyone gets excited.

Snacks: Candy and cookies, and occasionally Indian sweets (but they're really rich).

This page, clockwise from top: Ayesha Dharker, composer A.R. Rahman, Madhur Jaffrey and Tom Meehan at the cast party at Spirit. Co-producer Andrew Lloyd Webber on opening night. The cast performs at "Gypsy of the Year." Bollywood film star Padma Laxmi. Donald Trump and then fiancee Melania Knauss arrive for opening night. Sriram Ganesan and A.R. Rahman.

In-Theatre Gathering Place: The wig room. They always have goodies in there: cookies lozenges and hard candy. At Halloween they had candy corn.

Off-Site Hangout: Bombay Palace on 52nd Street. We have a lot of events there, and birthday parties. People also went to the Russian Vodka Room and The Divine Bar on 54th.

Mascot: The statues of Ganesh used in the parade scene. We prayed to one of the Ganeshas to remove all obstacles.

Therapy: I keep lozenges behind the set to keep my voice from drying out. And Throat-Coat Tea. I live off that stuff. A lot of people do Pilates, or go to the gym every day. There's also yoga, of course.

Memorable Ad-Lib: One night, in the scene when they ask for volunteers, there was a little kid in the audience who yelled, "I volunteer!!!" The show stopped for a second and the audience burst out laughing. It was a great, great moment.

Record Number Of Cell Phone Rings: Six! One night, during my death scene, no less than two cell phones rang, and one person took the call!

Strangest Fan Encounter: One night at curtain call a group of drag queens ran down the aisle to applaud me, and later they came to the stage door. It was amusing but also strange. I've had people at the stage door ask for my phone number!

Heaviest/Hottest Costume: The role of Rani wears the most costumes. Her heaviest piece is worn at the beginning of "Shakalaka Baby." The jewels alone weigh something like fifty pounds, and it's made of heavy, thick material.

Who Wore The Least: The female dancers in "Chaiyya Chaiyya" wear tube tops and hot pants. One member of the cast, Zahf Paroo, plays Rani's hairdresser, wearing short shorts and a tank top.

Also: The Hello Deli delicatessen across the street makes specialty sandwiches and we were always trying to get them to create a "Salami Bombay."

Correspondent: Sriram Ganesan, "Sweetie"

Photos by Aubrey Reuben

This page, clockwise from top: Curtain call on opening night. Anisha Nagarajan meets the press at the cast party. Filmmakers Ismail Merchant and James Ivory flank actress Susan Malick on the red carpet. Miss USA Shandi Finnessey arrives for opening night.

The Boy From Oz

| First Preview: September 16, 2003 | Opened: October 16, 2003 |
| Closed: September 12, 2004 | 32 Previews and 364 Performances |

PLAYBILL®

🅢 IMPERIAL THEATRE
249 West 45th Street
A Shubert Organization Theatre

Gerald Schoenfeld, *Chairman*   **Philip J. Smith,** *President*

Robert E. Wankel, *Executive Vice President*

BEN GANNON and ROBERT FOX
present
HUGH JACKMAN

Book by
MARTIN SHERMAN
Original Book by **NICK ENRIGHT**

Music and Lyrics by
PETER ALLEN & OTHERS

also starring
STEPHANIE J. BLOCK   **BETH FOWLER**   **ISABEL KEATING**   **JARROD EMICK**

with
MITCHEL DAVID FEDERAN   **MICHAEL MULHEREN**

Leslie Alexander   Brad Anderson   Todd Anderson   Roxane Barlow   Victoria Lecta Cave   Kelly Crandall   Timothy A. Fitz-Gerald
Christopher Freeman   Michael Halling   Jessica Hartman   Colleen Hawks   Curtis Holbrook   Tari Kelly   Heather Laws
Brian J. Marcum   Jessica Lea Patty   Nathan Peck   Josh Rhodes   Jennifer Savelli   Matthew Stocke   P. J. Verhoest

Scenic Design
ROBIN WAGNER

Costume Design
WILLIAM IVEY LONG

Lighting Design
DONALD HOLDER

Sound Design
ACME SOUND PARTNERS

Wig and Hair Design
PAUL HUNTLEY

Casting
**DAVE CLEMMONS CASTING
JOSEPH McCONNELL, C.S.A.**

Dance Music Arrangements by
MARK HUMMEL

Music Coordinator
MICHAEL KELLER

Consultant
STEPHEN MACLEAN

Technical Supervision
**NEIL A. MAZZELLA
DAVID BENKEN**

Press Agent
BONEAU/BRYAN-BROWN

Marketing
**HUGH HYSELL
COMMUNICATIONS, INC.**

General Manager
ALBERT POLAND

Production Stage Manager
EILEEN F. HAGGERTY

Orchestrations
MICHAEL GIBSON

Music Director/Incidental Music and Vocal Arranger
PATRICK VACCARIELLO

Choreography by
JOEY McKNEELY

Directed by
PHILIP WM. McKINLEY

8/30/04

CAST
(in order of appearance)

Peter Allen	HUGH JACKMAN
Boy (Young Peter)	MITCHEL DAVID FEDERAN
George Woolnough	MATTHEW STOCKE
Marion Woolnough	BETH FOWLER
Dick Woolnough	MICHAEL MULHEREN
Chris Bell	TIMOTHY A. FITZ-GERALD
Announcer	SHANE RHOADES
Judy Garland	ISABEL KEATING
Mark Herron	BRAD ANDERSON
Liza Minnelli	STEPHANIE J. BLOCK
Trick	SHANE RHOADES
Girl	EMILY HSU
Trio	COLLEEN HAWKS, HEATHER LAWS, TRISHA RAPIER
Greg Connell	JARROD EMICK
Dee Anthony	MICHAEL MULHEREN
Alice the Rockette	JENNIFER SAVELLI
The Ensemble	LESLIE ALEXANDER, BRAD ANDERSON, TODD ANDERSON, VICTORIA LECTA CAVE, TIMOTHY A. FITZ-GERALD, RAMÓN FLOWERS, ASHLEY AMBER HAASE, COLLEEN HAWKS, CURTIS HOLBROOK, EMILY HSU, HEATHER LAWS,

continued on next page

Hugh Jackman as Peter Allen.

MUSICAL NUMBERS

ACT ONE

Overture

Prologue   Peter in concert
"The Lives of Me" .... Peter

The 1950s

Scene 1   Various locations in Tenterfield, Australia: Peter's Grandfather's store
Peter's childhood home, Josie Mann's New England Hotel interior/exterior
"When I Get My Name in Lights" .... Boy & Ensemble
"When I Get My Name in Lights: Reprise" .... Peter

The 1960s

Scene 2   Australian Bandstand television performance
"Love Crazy" .... Chris, Peter & Ensemble

Scene 3   Hong Kong Hilton Hotel
"Waltzing Matilda" .... Peter & Chris
"All I Wanted Was the Dream" .... Judy

Scene 4   A small Chinese bar/Street in Hong Kong/New York City
"Only an Older Woman" .... Judy, Peter, Chris & Mark
"Best That You Can Do" .... Peter & Liza

Scene 5   Peter and Liza's apartment
"Don't Wish Too Hard" .... Judy
"Come Save Me" .... Liza & Peter

Scene 6   Peter and Liza's apartment, months later
"Continental American" .... Peter, Trick, Girl & Ensemble

Scene 7   Liza's act
"She Loves to Hear the Music" .... Liza & Ensemble

Scene 8   Peter in concert
"Quiet Please, There's a Lady On Stage" .... Peter & Judy

The 1970s

Scene 9   Peter and Liza's apartment
"I'd Rather Leave While I'm in Love" .... Liza & Peter

Scene 10   Marion's home
"Not the Boy Next Door" .... Peter

ACT TWO

The 1970s continued

Scene 1   Reno Sweeney
"Bi-Coastal" .... Peter & Trio

Scene 2   Peter's apartment
"If You Were Wondering" .... Peter & Greg

Scene 3   Dee's office/The Copacabana Club
"Sure Thing Baby" .... Dee, Greg, Peter, Trio & Male Ensemble

The 1980s

Scene 4   Radio City Music Hall, January 15, 1981
"Everything Old Is New Again" .... Peter & The Rockettes

Scene 5   Peter's dressing room – Radio City
"Everything Old Is New Again: Reprise" .... Marion, Dee & Greg

Scene 6   Peter's apartment
"Love Don't Need a Reason" .... Peter & Greg

The 1990s

Scene 7   Peter's apartment
"I Honestly Love You" .... Greg
"You and Me" .... Liza & Peter

Scene 8   Marion's home/The Australian concert/Peter in concert
"I Still Call Australia Home" .... Peter & Ensemble
"Don't Cry Out Loud" .... Marion
"Once Before I Go" .... Peter
"I Go to Rio" .... Peter & Company

Hugh Jackman is appearing with the
permission of Actors' Equity Association.

UNDERSTUDIES

Standby for Hugh Jackman – MICHAEL HALLING
Understudy for Peter Allen – BRAD ANDERSON; for
Boy (Young Peter) – P.J. VERHOEST;
for Marion Woolnough – LESLIE ALEXANDER,
HEATHER LAWS; for Dick Woolnough/Dee Anthony
– BRAD ANDERSON, MATTHEW STOCKE; for
Chris Bell – TODD ANDERSON, MICHAEL
HALLING; for Announcer – TODD ANDERSON; for
Judy Garland – VICTORIA LECTA CAVE, HEATHER
LAWS; for Mark Herron – TODD ANDERSON,
MICHAEL HALLING; for Liza Minnelli – HEATHER
LAWS, TRISHA RAPIER; for Trick – TODD ANDER-
SON; for Girl – JESSICA HARTMAN, HEATHER
LAWS; for Trio – VICTORIA LECTA CAVE,
HEATHER LAWS, JESSICA LEA PATTY; for Greg
Connell – BRAD ANDERSON, MICHAEL
HALLING; for Alice the Rockette – ASHLEY AMBER
HAASE, JESSICA LEA PATTY

ORCHESTRA

CONDUCTOR: Patrick Vaccariello
Associate Conductor: Jim Laev
Concertmaster: Fritz Krakowski
Violins: Victor Heifets, Katherine Livolsi-Stern,
Wende Namkung, Cecelia Hobbs Gardner
Cellos: Mairi Dorman, Vivian Israel
Lead Trumpet: Jeff Kievit
Trumpets: Tino Gagliardi, Earl Gardner
Trombones: Clint Sharman, Randy Andos
Reeds: Ted Nash, Ben Kono,
Ken Dybisz, Don McGeen
Drums: Brian Brake
Bass: Cary Potts
Keyboard 1: Mark Berman
Keyboard 2: Jim Laev
Guitars and Banjo: J McGeehan
Percussion: Dan McMillan

Music Coordinator: Michael Keller
Music Copying: Kaye-Houston Music/Anne Kaye

Hugh Jackman
Peter Allen

Stephanie J. Block
Liza Minnelli

Beth Fowler
Marion Woolnough

Isabel Keating
Judy Garland

Jarrod Emick
Greg Connell

Mitchel David
Federan
Boy (Young Peter)

Michael Mulheren
*Dick Woolnough/
Dee Anthony*

Michael Halling
*Standby for
Hugh Jackman*

Leslie Alexander
Ensemble

Brad Anderson
*Mark Herron/
Ensemble*

Todd Anderson
*Ensemble/Assistant
Dance Captain*

Victoria Lecta Cave
Ensemble

Timothy A. Fitz-Gerald
*Chris Bell/
Ensemble*

Ramón Flowers
Ensemble

Ashley Amber Haase
Ensemble

Jessica Hartman
*Asst. Choreographer/
Dance Captain/
Swing*

Colleen Hawks
Trio/Ensemble

Curtis Holbrook
Ensemble

Emily Hsu
Girl/Ensemble

Heather Laws
Trio/Ensemble

Jessica Lea Patty
Ensemble

Nathan Peck
Ensemble

Trisha Rapier
Trio/Ensemble

Shane Rhoades
*Announcer/Trick/
Ensemble*

Jennifer Savelli
*Alice the Rockette/
Ensemble*

Matthew Stocke
*George Woolnough/
Ensemble*

P.J. Verhoest
*Understudy Boy
(Young Peter)*

Martin Sherman
Book

Nick Enright
Original Book

Peter Allen
Music/Lyrics

Carole Bayer Sager
Musical Consultant

Philip Wm. McKinley
Director

Robin Wagner
Scenic Design

William Ivey Long
Costume Design

Donald Holder
Lighting Design

The Boy From Oz

Tom Clark, Mark Menard and Nevin Steinberg
Sound Design

Paul Huntley
Wig and Hair Design

Patrick Vaccariello
Music Dir./Incidental Music/Vocal Arranger

Michael Gibson
Orchestrations

Mark Hummel
Dance Music Arrangements

Michael Keller
Music Coordinator

Dave Clemmons
Casting

Joseph McConnell
Casting

Eileen F. Haggerty
Production Stage Manager

Neil A. Mazzella
Technical Supervisor

David Benken
Technical Director

Albert Poland
General Manager

Ben Gannon
Producer

ALUMNI
THE BOY FROM OZ

Roxane Barlow
Girl/Ensemble

Kelly Crandall
Ensemble

Christopher Freeman
Ensemble

Tari Kelly
Trio/Ensemble

Brian J. Marcum
Ensemble

Josh Rhodes
Announcer/Trick/ Ensemble

Isabel Keating as Judy Garland with Hugh Jackman as Peter Allen.

Photo by Joan Marcus

STAFF FOR THE BOY FROM OZ

GENERAL MANAGER
Albert Poland

PRESS REPRESENTATIVE
BONEAU/BRYAN-BROWN
Adrian Bryan-Brown, Jackie Green, Joe Perrotta

COMPANY MANAGER .... MARK D. SHACKET
Associate Company Manager .... Maria Mazza

Production
Stage Manager .... Eileen F. Haggerty
Stage Manager .... Richard C. Rauscher
Assistant Stage Manager .... Tina M. Newhauser

Asst. Choreographer/Dance Captain .... Jessica Hartman
Assistant Dance Captain .... Todd Anderson
Associate Scenic Designer .... David Peterson
Assistant Scenic Designers ..... Evan Alexander, Atkin Pace,
Thomas Peter Sarr
Associate Costume Designer .... Scott Traugott
Assistant Costume Designers .... Rachel Attridge,
Kevin Draves, Philip Heckman,
Brian Russman, Donald Sanders
Associate Lighting Designer .... Michelle Habeck
Assistant Lighting Designers .... Mike Jones,
Traci Klainer, Hilary Manners
Automated Light Programmer .... Seth Rapaport
Production Carpenter .... Hank Hale
Production Electrician .... Jimmy Maloney
Production Properties .... Heidi L. Brown
Head Electrician .... Carlos Martinez
Production Sound Engineer .... Robert D. Biasetti
Sound System Coordinator .... Paul Delcioppo
Automation Carpenters .... Scott Dixon, John Merritt
Carpenters .... Walter Bullard (House Head),
Terry McGarty (House Flyman),
Arthur J. Clark, Kevin Clifford,
Richard Fullum, Leon Stieb, Ken Wolff
Assistant Electricians .... Brian Aman, Kevin Barry
Electricians .... Paul F. Dean, Jr. (House Head),
David Brickman, Joan Griffenkranz,
Carie Kramer, Dennis Pfeifer
Sound Department .... Andrew J. Funk, John C. Cooper
Assistant Properties .... Justin J. Sanok
Prop Department .... James Satterwhite (House Head),
Freddy Bockwoldt, Joseph Hansen,
Ian McClarence, Kevin Nesbitt
Production Wardrobe Supervisor .... Nancy Schaefer
Assistant Wardrobe Supervisor .... Edmund Harrison
Dresser for Mr. Jackman .... Mark Caine
Dressers .... Dana Goodfriend,
Greg Holtz, Bob Kwiatkowski, Jeff McGovney,
Jane Rottenbach, Marisa Tchornobai, Janet Turner
Hair Supervisor .... Amy Solomon
Assistant Hair Supervisor .... Heather Richmond Wright
Hair Dressers .... Bobby Grayson, Eve Morrow
Makeup Consultant .... Melissa Silver
Associate Conductor .... Jim Laev
Assistant to Mr. McKinley .... Ryan Mackey
Assistant to Mr. Poland .... Michael Gesele
Assistant to Mr. Jackman .... John Palermo
Assistant to the Technical Director ...... Whitney Chapman
Chaperone .... Robert Wilson
Production Assistants ...... Nellie Beavers, Mary Birnbaum,
Sascha Connor, Amelia Frates
Children's Tutoring .... On Location Education
Physical Therapy .... Performing Arts PT
Advertising .... Serino Coyne Inc./
Greg Corradetti, Denise Geiger, Rebecca Russell
Marketing .... Hugh Hysell Communications, Inc./
Hugh Hysell, Michael Redman, Adam Jay,
Chris Alonzo, Lauren Appel, Kat Keller
Casting .... Dave Clemmons Casting/
Dave Clemmons, Rachel Hoffman,
Rye Mullis, Sara Schatz
Casting .... Joseph McConnell, CSA
Piano Vocal Score Prep .... Timothy Brown
Synthesizer Programmer .... James Lynn Abbott
Brazilian Percussion for "I Go to Rio" .... Roger Squitero
Merchandising ..SFX Theatrical Merchandising/Larry Turk
Legal Counsel .Paul, Weiss, Rifkind, Wharton & Garrison/
John Breglio, Esq., Olivier Sultan, Esq.
Accountant .... Rosenberg, Neuwirth & Kuchner, CPA/
Christopher Cacace, Jana Jevnikar
Banking .... JP Morgan Chase/Richard Callian
Insurance .... Marsh USA Inc./Robert Boyar

Payroll Service .... Castellana Services Inc.
Immigration Counsel .... Lawrence S. Yudess, Esq.
Dialect Coach .... Stephen Gabis
Web Design .... Pygmalion Designs/David Risley
Production Photographer .... Joan Marcus
Set Photographer .... Richard Lee
Rehearsal Studio .... New 42nd Street Studios
Travel Agent .... Tzell Travel/Ann McManus
Opening Night Coordination .... Jeffry Gray,
Suzanne Tobak/Tobak-Dantchik Events & Promotions, Inc.
Music Clearances .... Christine Woodruff
Promotional Merchandising .... George Fenmore/
More Merchandising Intern'l.

BEN GANNON
Assistant to Mr. Gannon .... Brian Abel
Administrator .... Cynthia Kelly

ROBERT FOX LIMITED
Assistant to Mr. Fox .... Hannah Bower
Accountant .... Karen Liverpool

CREDITS
Scenery constructed by Hudson Scenic Studio, Inc. Lighting equipment by Fourth Phase New Jersey. Sound equipment by Sound Associates, Inc. Props by Bratton Scenery & Display and The Rabbit's Choice. Dinnerware courtesy of Pfaltzgraff. Acrylic drinkware by U.S. Acrylic, Inc. Anchor Hocking Foodservice glassware used. Smoking supplies and accessories courtesy of Nat Sherman International. Hartmann luggage used. Additional set and hand props courtesy of George Fenmore, Inc. Soft goods and fiberoptics by I. Weiss New York. Costumes by Barbara Matera Ltd., Carelli Costumes, Inc., Euroco, Ltd., John David Ridge, Inc., Tricorne New York City, Brad Musgrove, Jen King. Men's custom shirts by Marc Happel, The Shirt Store. Custom knitwear by C.C. Wei. Finale costume frameworks by Jerard Studios. Feathers by American Plume & Fancy Feather. Additional millinery by Rodney Gordon. Shoes by La Duca Shoes, T.O. Dey Footwear, J. C. Theatrical. Custom fabric beading by Bessie Nelson, Artistic Beading, Sylvie's Costume. Custom fabric dyeing and printing by Gene Mignola, Dye-Namix Inc. Additional costume work by John Kristiansen NY, Arel Studio. Vintage clothing by Steppin' Out, Daybreak. Emer'Gen-C provided by Alacer Corp. Lozenges provided by Ricola USA. Mr. Jackman's hair products provided by Rusk and Conair Pro.

SPECIAL THANKS TO Carole Bayer Sager

ORIGINAL AUSTRALIAN PRODUCTION
DIRECTED BY GALE EDWARDS.

---

www.theboyfromoz.com

Original Cast Recording available on Decca Broadway.

SONG CREDITS
"The Lives of Me" (Peter Allen); ©1978 Irving Music, Inc., o/b/o itself and Woolnough Music, Inc. (BMI). "When I Get My Name in Lights" (Peter Allen); ©1989 Woolnough Music (BMI); all rights administered by Warner-Tamerlane Publ. Corp. (BMI). "Love Crazy" (Peter Allen/Adrienne Anderson); ©1976 Irving Music, Inc., o/b/o itself and Woolnough Music, Inc. (BMI). "Waltzing Matilda" (Marie Cowan/A. B. "Banjo" Paterson); ©1936 Allan & Co., ©1941 Carl Fischer, Inc.; all rights assigned to Carl Fischer, LLC. "All I Wanted Was the Dream" (Peter Allen); ©1989 Woolnough Music (BMI); all rights administered by Warner-Tamerlane Publ. Corp. (BMI). "Only an Older Woman" (Peter Allen); ©1989, Woolnough Music (BMI); all rights administered by Warner-Tamerlane Publ. Corp. (BMI). "(Arthur's Theme) Best That You Can Do" (Burt Bacharach/Carole Bayer Sager/Peter Allen/ Christopher Cross); ©1981 Unichappell Music Inc. (BMI), Begonia Melodies, Inc. (BMI), Warner-Tamerlane Publishing Corp. (BMI), Woolnough Music (BMI), Irving Music Inc. (BMI), WB Music Corp. (ASCAP), Pop 'N' Roll Music (ASCAP) and New Hidden Valley Music (ASCAP); all rights on behalf of Begonia Melodies, Inc. (BMI) administered by Unichappell Music Inc. (BMI); all rights on behalf of Woolnough Music (BMI) and Irving Music Inc. (BMI) administered by Warner-Tamerlane Publ. Corp. (BMI); all rights on behalf of Pop 'N' Roll Music (ASCAP) and New Hidden Valley Music (ASCAP) administered by WB Music Corp. (ASCAP). "Don't Wish Too Hard" (Carole Bayer Sager, Peter Allen); ©1977 Irving Music, Inc. o/b/o itself and Woolnough Music, Inc. (BMI) and Begonia

Melodies, Inc. (BMI); all rights on behalf of Begonia Melodies, Inc. (BMI) administered by Warner-Tamerlane Publ. Corp. (BMI). "Come Save Me" (Peter Allen); Woolnough Music, Inc. (BMI);all rights administered by Warner-Tamerlane publishing Corp. (BMI). "The Continental American" (Peter Allen/Carole Bayer Sager); ©1974 Irving Music, Inc., o/b/o itself and Woolnough Music, Inc. (BMI), Alley Music Corp. (BMI), Trio Music, Inc. (BMI). "She Loves to Hear the Music" (Peter Allen/Carole Bayer Sager); used by permission of Alley Music Corp. (BMI), Trio Music Co., Inc. (BMI), Irving Music, Inc., Woolnough Music, Inc. (BMI). "Quiet Please There's a Lady on Stage" (Peter Allen/Carole Bayer Sager); used by permission of Alley Music Corp. (BMI), Trio Music Co., Inc. (BMI), Irving Music, Inc., Woolnough Music, Inc. "I'd Rather Leave While I'm in Love" (Peter Allen/Carole Bayer Sager); ©1976 Irving Music, Inc. o/b/o itself and Woolnough Music, Inc. (BMI) and Begonia Melodies, Inc. (BMI); all rights on behalf of Begonia Melodies, Inc. (BMI) administered by Warner-Tamerlane Publ. Corp. (BMI). "Not the Boy Next Door" (Peter Allen, Dean Pitchford); ©1983 Warner-Tamerlane Publishing Corp. (BMI), Woolnough Music (BMI), Pitchford Music (BMI); all rights administered by Warner-Tamerlane Publ. Corp. (BMI). "Bi-Coastal" (Peter Allen/David Foster/Tom Keane); ©1980 Irving Music, Inc. o/b/o itself, Woolnough Music, Inc. and Foster Frees Music, Inc. (BMI) and Neropub, o/b/o itself, Tomjon and Thunder Music. "If You Were Wondering" (Peter Allen); ©1978 Irving Music, Inc. o/b/o itself and Woolnough Music, Inc. (BMI). "Sure Thing Baby" (Peter Allen); © 1989 Woolnough Music (BMI); all rights administered by Warner-Tamerlane Publ. Corp. (BMI). "Everything Old Is New Again" (Peter Allen/Carole Bayer Sager);©1974 Irving Music, Inc. o/b/o itself and Woolnough Music, Inc (BMI), Alley Music Corp. (BMI), Trio Music Co., Inc. (BMI). "Love Don't Need a Reason" (Peter Allen/Marsha Malamet/Michael Callen); Woolnough Music Inc (BMI), Tops and Bottoms Music (BMI) and Malamution Music/Ensign Music Corp. (BMI); administered by Famous Music; all rights on behalf of Woolnough Music Inc (BMI) administered by Warner-Tamerlane Publ. Corp. (BMI). "I Honestly Love You" (Peter Allen/Jeff Barry); ©1974 (renewed) Irving Music, Inc. o/b/o itself and Jeff Barry International (BMI) & Woolnough Music, Inc.; all rights administered by Warner-Tamerlane Publ. Corp. (BMI). "You and Me (We Wanted It All)" (Peter Allen/Carole Bayer Sager); ©1978 Irving Music, Inc. o/b/o itself and Woolnough Music, Inc. (BMI) and ©Begonia Melodies, Inc. (BMI); all rights on behalf of Begonia Melodies, Inc. (BMI) administered by Warner-Tamerlane Publ. Corp. (BMI). "I Still Call Australia Home" (Peter Allen); ©1980 Rondor Music Australia Pty. Ltd. and Woolnough Music, Inc., administered by Irving Music, Inc. in the U.S and Canada (BMI). "We Don't Cry Out Loud" (Peter Allen/Carole Bayer Sager); ©1976 Irving Music, Inc. o/b/o itself and Woolnough Music, Inc. (BMI) and Begonia Melodies, Inc. (BMI); all rights on behalf of Begonia Melodies, Inc. (BMI) administered by Warner-Tamerlane Publ. Corp. (BMI). "Once Before I Go" (Peter Allen/Dean Pitchford); ©1983 Woolnough Music, Inc. (BMI), Warner-Tamerlane Publishing Corp., Pitchford Music (BMI); all rights administered by Warner-Tamerlane Publishing Corp. "I Go to Rio" (Peter Allen/Adrienne Anderson); ©1976 Irving Music, Inc. o/b/o itself and Woolnough Music, Inc. (BMI). ALL SONGS: ALL RIGHTS RESERVED. USED BY PERMISSION.

Hugh Jackman celebrates winning the 2004 Tony Award as Best Actor in a Musical.

Stephanie Block on the opening day of the Broadway Softball League season in Central Park.

Photos by Aubrey Reuben

Cast members Beth Fowler (center) and Stephanie Block (far right) at the Broadway Softball League opening day, accompanied by players from *Mamma Mia!*, *Fiddler on the Roof*'s Alfred Molina (beard), Susan Egan (short hair, no hat) and *The Producers*' Matthew Broderick (white shirt).

Opening Night Gifts: I gave Hawaiian leis to the cast. Hugh Jackman gave us each a set of gold leather maracas engraved with our names, with hand-painted inscriptions to each of us individually, encased in a Lucite stand about 12 inches tall, with the show's logo on the front. Mine says, "To Beth, with love, Hugh."

Celebrity Visitors: We had Sting, Elvis Costello, Barbara Walters and Shirley MacLaine. Our biggest groupie was Barbara Cook, who came to see the show 15 times, and invited cast members to her home. Ann-Margret came twice. Kaye Ballard told us, "You are so great."

Backstage Rituals: We had a Hawaiian shirt contest that went on for several weeks. Everyone had to wear outrageous Hawaiian shirts backstage. Ninety-nine percent of the best ones came from the stagehands. Semifinalists staged a runway competition, and it was some of the funniest stuff ever seen on the stage of the Imperial. The winner was Carlos, the house electrician.

We also had a team spirit competition. There are five floors of dressing rooms at the Imperial, and the women's ensemble had to climb up to the fifth in high heels and Rockette costumes. So we let each floor compete to show the best team spirit, and my floor won. We wore vintage Hawaiian muumuus and leis and silk flowers.

Also: No one who worked on that show will forget the "Wall of Shame" in the stairwell between the second and third floor of dressing rooms. Everyone brought in their tackiest high school or ballet school pictures. It was really nostalgic. We had a lot of silly pictures up there through the run, and while a lot of ensemble members left during the year, they all left behind their pictures so they'd stay part of that wall.

Next to the wall of shame was a montage of each cast member's resume photo reduction from *Playbill*. Each photo was cut into three parts, eyes, nose and mouth, and when someone didn't have anything better to do, they'd mix and match and make composite pictures. It was fun and people really got into it.

There was also a running gag, a photo posted of a doll being held for ransom.

Correspondent: Beth Fowler, "Marion Woolnough"

PLAYBILL®

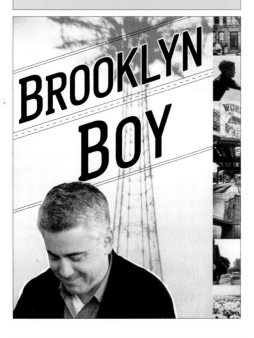

CAST
(in order of appearance)

Eric Weiss	ADAM ARKIN
Manny Weiss	ALLAN MILLER
Ira Zimmer	ARYE GROSS
Nina	POLLY DRAPER
Alison	ARI GRAYNOR
Melanie Fine	MIMI LIEBER
Tyler Shaw	KEVIN ISOLA

Stage Manager: DENISE YANEY

ACT I
Scene I:
Maimonides Hospital,
Brooklyn

Scene II:
The hospital cafeteria

Scene III:
An apartment on
St. Mark's Place, New York

ACT II
Scene IV:
A suite in the Mondrian Hotel, Los Angeles

Scene V:
An office on the Paramount Pictures lot,
Los Angeles

Scene VI:
The Weiss Family apartment on
Ocean Avenue, Brooklyn

BILTMORE THEATRE

MANHATTAN THEATRE CLUB

ARTISTIC DIRECTOR
LYNNE MEADOW

EXECUTIVE PRODUCER
BARRY GROVE

IN ASSOCIATION WITH
SOUTH COAST REPERTORY

PRESENTS

BROOKLYN BOY

BY
DONALD MARGULIES

WITH

ADAM ARKIN   POLLY DRAPER   ARI GRAYNOR
ARYE GROSS   KEVIN ISOLA   MIMI LIEBER   ALLAN MILLER

SCENIC DESIGN
RALPH FUNICELLO

COSTUME DESIGN
JESS GOLDSTEIN

LIGHTING DESIGN
CHRIS PARRY

ORIGINAL MUSIC AND SOUND DESIGN
MICHAEL ROTH

PRODUCTION STAGE MANAGER
ROY HARRIS

DIRECTED BY
DANIEL SULLIVAN

CASTING
**NANCY PICCIONE/
DAVID CAPARELLIOTIS
JOANNE DENAUT**

DIRECTOR OF ARTISTIC OPERATIONS
MANDY GREENFIELD

PRODUCTION MANAGER
RYAN MCMAHON

DIRECTOR OF DEVELOPMENT
JENNIFER ZASLOW

DIRECTOR OF MARKETING
DEBRA A. WAXMAN

PRESS REPRESENTATIVE
BONEAU/BRYAN-BROWN

GENERAL MANAGER
HAROLD WOLPERT

DIRECTOR OF
ARTISTIC DEVELOPMENT
PAIGE EVANS

DIRECTOR OF
ARTISTIC PRODUCTION
MICHAEL BUSH

Brooklyn Boy was commissioned and developed by South Coast Repertory.
Manhattan Theatre Club wishes to express its appreciation to Theatre Development Fund
for its support of this production.

2/3/05

UNDERSTUDIES

For Tyler Shaw: BILL HECK
For Alison: LIESEL MATTHEWS
For Nina/Melanie Fine: CHARLOTTE MAIER
For Eric Weiss/Ira Zimmer: MARK ZEISLER
Standby for Manny Weiss: DAVID LITTLE

Manhattan Theatre Club productions
are made possible in part with public funds
from the New York City Department
of Cultural Affairs and the
New York State Council on the Arts, a state agency.

Adam Arkin and Ari Graynor

Adam Arkin
Eric Weiss

Polly Draper
Nina

Ari Graynor
Alison

Arye Gross
Ira Zimmer

Kevin Isola
Tyler Shaw

Mimi Lieber
Melanie Fine

Allan Miller
Manny Weiss

Donald Margulies
Playwright

Daniel Sullivan
Director

Ralph Funicello
Set Design

Jess Goldstein
Costume Design

Chris Parry
Lighting Design

Lynne Meadow
Artistic Director, Manhattan Theatre Club

Barry Grove
Executive Producer, Manhattan Theatre Club

Photos by Ben Strothmann

Security Officer:
Olanrewaj Ayind

The Crew: Front Row (L-R): Bree Wellwood, Denise Yaney, Sue Poulin, Margiann Flanagan. Middle Row (L-R): Valerie Simmons, Shanna Spinello, Megan Moore, Wendy Wright, Renee Hicks, Kathy White, Teresa Farensbach, Sarah Brodsky. Back Row (L-R): Jeff Dodson, Tim Walters, Lou Shapiro, Allan Miller, Ed Brashear, Michael Growler, Bru Dye, Alex Gutierrez, Stephen "Crash" Burns and Patrick Murray.

MANHATTAN THEATRE CLUB
ADMINISTRATIVE STAFF

Artistic Director ....Lynne Meadow
Executive Producer ....Barry Grove
General Manager ....Harold Wolpert
Director of Artistic Production ....Michael Bush
Director of Artistic Development ....Paige Evans
Director of Artistic Operations ....Mandy Greenfield
Artistic Associate/
Assistant to the Artistic Director...........Amy Gilkes Loe
Artistic Assistants ....William Cusick,Lisa Dozier

Director of Casting ....Nancy Piccione
Casting Director ....David Caparelliotis
Casting Assistant............................Jennifer McCool

Literary Manager ....Emily Shooltz
Play Development Associate/
Sloan Project Manager ....Aaron Leichter
Play Development Assistant....................Lara Mottolo
Director of
Musical Development ....Clifford Lee Johnson III
Director of Writers in Performance ....Steve Lawson

Director of Development ....Jennifer Zaslow
Director, Individual Giving ....Casey Reitz
Director, Planning and Projects ....Blake West
Director, Foundation and
Government Relations ....Josh Jacobson
Manager, Individual Giving ....Allison Goldstein
Senior Associate, Corporate Relations ....Scott Pyne
Senior Development Associate ....Stacey Cloninger
Development Associate ....Belinda Batson,
Development Associate/
Database Coordinator ....Rey Pamatmat
Patrons' Liaison ....Antonello Di Benedetto

Director of Marketing ....Debra A. Waxman
Associate Director of Marketing ....Wendy Hutton
Marketing Associate/
Website Manager ....Ryan M. Klink

Director of Finance &
Administration ....Michael P. Naumann
Business Manager ....Holly Kinney
Business Associate.......................Denise L. Thomas
HR/Payroll Manager ....Paula Reneau
Business Assistant ....Thomas Casazzone
Manager of Systems Operations ....Avishai Cohen
Systems Analyst ....Andrew Dumawal
Associate General Manager ....Seth Shepsle
Company Manager/
NY City Center ....Lindsey T. Brooks
Assistant to the Executive Producer ....Erin Day

Director of Subscriber Services ....Robert Allenberg
Associate Subscriber Services Manager ....Andrew Taylor
Subscriber Services Representatives ....Mark Bowers,
Alva Chinn,
Rebekah Dewald,
Matthew Praet,
Rosanna Consalvo Sarto
Director of Telesales and Telefunding ....George Tetlow
Assistant Manager ....Terrence Burnett

Director of Education ....David Shookhoff
Assistant Director of Education/
Coordinator, Paul A. Kaplan Theatre
Management Program ....Amy Harris
Education Assistants..........................Kayla Cagan,
Jackie McDonnell
MTC Teaching Artists ....Stephanie Alston,
David Auburn, Carl Capotorto,
Chris Ceraso, Charlotte Colavin,

Andy Goldberg, Elise Hernandez,
Jeffrey Joseph, Lou Moreno,
Michaela Murphy, Melissa Murray,
Angela Pietropinto, Carmen Rivera,
Judy Tate, Candido Tirado, Joe White
Theatre Management Interns...............Jeremy Blocker,
Greg Cooper, Nicole Gaignat,
Travis Garner, Andrea Gorzell,
Kel Haney, Tarrah Hirsch,
Meg Keene, Molly Kramer,
Damon Krometis, Jennifer Leeson,
Annie MacRae, Melissa Marano,
Matt Olmos, Jenna Parks,
Aaron Paternoster, Rebecca Sherman,
Carrie Van Deest, Danny Williams
Randy Carrig Casting Intern ....Emily Bohannon
Reception/Studio Manager ....Lauren Snyder

Production Manager ....Ryan McMahon
Associate Production Manager ....Bridget Markov
Assistant Production Manager ....Ian McNaugher

Technical Director ....Bill Mohney
Assistant Technical Director ....Adam Lang
Assistant Technical Director ....Benjamin Lampman
Carpenters ....Brian Corr,
Shayne Izatt,
Nicholas Morales
Scenic Painting Supervisor ....Jenny Stanjeski
Lights and Sound Supervisor ....Willy Corpus
Properties Supervisor ....Scott Laule
Assistant Properties Supervisor ....Arlene Marshall
Props Carpenter............................Peter Grimes
Costume Supervisor ....Erin Hennessy Dean
Assistant Costume Supervisor ....Michelle Sesco

GENERAL PRESS REPRESENTATIVES
BONEAU/BRYAN-BROWN

Chris Boneau   Jim Byk
Aaron Meier

Design Associate ....John Lee Beatty
Script Readers ....Rachel Axler,
Liz Jones,
Talya Klein,
Sadie Foster,
Jeremy Sherber,
Michelle Tattenbaum,
Kathryn Walat,
Ethan Youngerman
Musical Theatre Reader ....Emily King

SERVICES

Accountants ....ERE, LLP
Advertising ....SpotCo/
Drew Hodges, Jim Edwards,
John Lanasa, Aaliytha Davis
Marketing Consultants ....The Marketing Group/
Tanya Grubich, Laura Matalon,
Trish Santini, Bob Bucci,
Erica Schwartz
Corporate Sponsorship ....Amy Willstatter's
Bridge to Hollywood/Broadway, LLC
Market Research ....Audience Research and Analysis/
George Wachtel, Aline Chatmajien
Internet Services ....Artztek LLC
Legal Counsel ....Paul, Weiss, Rifkind,
Wharton and Garrison LLP,
John Breglio, Deborah Hartnett
Real Estate Counsel ....Marcus Attorneys
Labor Counsel ....Harry H. Weintraub/
Glick and Weintraub, P.C.
Special Projects ....Elaine H. Hirsch

Insurance ....DeWitt Stern Group Inc/
Anthony Pittari
Maintenance ....Reliable Cleaning
Production Photographer ....Joan Marcus
Cover Photography ....
Adam Arkin photo by Andrew Eccles;
Brooklyn photos by Micheal McLaughlin
Cover Design ....SpotCo
Theatre Displays ....King Display

FOR MORE INFORMATION VISIT
www.ManhattanTheatreClub.com

PRODUCTION STAFF FOR
BROOKLYN BOY

Company Manager ....Denise Cooper
Production Stage Manager ....Roy Harris
Stage Manager ....Denise Yaney
Assistant Director ....Jeremy Lewit
Assistant Costume Designer ....Stacey Galloway
Assistant Lighting Designer ....John Demous
Assistant Sound Designer ....Cricket S. Myers
Automation Operator ....Stephen "Crash" Burns
Flymen ....Alex Gutierrez, Patrick Murray
Dresser ....Margiann Flanagan
Production Assistant ....Shanna Spinello

SPECIAL THANKS

Montauk Rug and Carpet Corp.,
Command Packaging, Sarah Keener,
P. Sprague, B.C. Keller

CREDITS

Lighting equipment by PRG Lighting.
Sound equipment by Masque Sound.
Scenic elements by Great Lakes Scenic Studios.
Automation by Scenic Technologies.
Natural herbal cough drops courtesy of Ricola USA.

MUSIC CREDIT

"It Happened in Monterey"
by Mabel Wayne and Billy Rose,
©EMI Feist Catalog Inc. (ASCAP).
All rights reserved. Used by permission.

"A Double Life" courtesy of Paramount Pictures.

MANHATTAN THEATRE CLUB/
BILTMORE THEATRE STAFF

Theatre Manager ....Valerie D. Simmons
Assistant House Manager ....Johannah-Joy Magyawe

Box Office Treasurer ....David Dillon
Assistant Box Office Treasurers ....Steven Clopper,
Kim Warner
Head Carpenter ....Chris Wiggins
Head Propertyman ....Timothy Walters
Sound Engineer ....Louis Shapiro
Master Electrician ....Jeff Dodson
Wardrobe Supervisor ....Michael Growler
Apprentices ....Sue Poulin,
Bree Wellwood
Engineers ....Deosarran,
Richardo Deosarran,
Mohd Alamgir Hossain,
Beeram Shiwprsaud
Security...................................OCS Security
Lobby Refreshments ....Sweet Concessions

Opening Night Gifts: Everything was Brooklyn-themed. Mimi Lieber gave a Brooklyn-based game of Monopoly. Polly Draper gave Adam Arkin a copy of *The Magic Mountain*, which is referred to in the play. My parents sent me a poem to the tune of "Danny Boy," titled "Brooklyn Boy." The women got a lot of flowers. Their dressing room looked like the Garden of Eden.

Best Opening Night Telegram: Dana Reeve, who was in the California production, but who had to leave when her husband, Christopher Reeve passed away, sent a great telegram with lots of Yiddish in it.

Celebrity Visitors: Alec Baldwin came to visit the night a woman passed out just before the end of the the show, and he carried her into the lobby. Her husband was a doctor and she turned out to be fine.

Backstage Rituals: Everybody makes sure to say "hi" or "break a leg" to everyone else before each performance.

Favorite Moment: This was my Broadway debut, and the moment before I go on is always a fantastic experience. On the first preview I choked up and had to pull myself together before I made my entrance.

In-Theatre Gathering Place: The women's dressing room.

Off-Site Hangout: Thalia

Snack Food: Every Sunday, the stage management team organizes a brunch. Denise Yaney makes the best damn deviled eggs I ever tasted.

Therapy: Mimi Lieber is the resident MD. She keeps Emergen-C (vitamin C in powder form) to fight winter colds.

Ad-Lib: Ari Graynor has a scene with Adam where they discuss the finer points of Gummi Bears. One night, as she was carrying out her armload of junk food, she accidentally dropped the Gummi bears and when the moment came, all she could find were M&Ms. Instead of saying, "They're soft and smooth like little bits of sea glass," she ad-libbed, "They're round and wonderful and just so chocolate-ly delicious."

Memorable Stage Door Fan Encounter: A man once brought a photo of the cast to be autographed. When I reached out to shake his hand, he grabbed me and gave me a big kiss on the lips.

Directorial Note: Daniel Sullivan has an alter-ego he calls "Broadway Dan," who gives advice on how to get a laugh. When you get a note from Broadway Dan, you may scratch your head over it, but he's always right and you get the laugh.

Correspondent: Kevin Isola, "Tyler Shaw"

Above (L-R) Polly Draper, Mimi Lieber, Adam Arkin, Ari Graynor, Arye Gross at the opening night party at B.B. King's restaurant.

Above left: Kevin Isola. Above center: Opening night visitors Jill Krementz and Kurt Vonnegut. Above right: Playwright Donald Margulies with guest, Cady Huffman.

(L-R): Allan Miller, Adam Arkin and Arye Gross take curtain calls on opening night.

PLAYBILL®

CAST

(in alphabetical order)

A City Weed/Taylor .... KEVIN ANDERSON
A City Weed/
Streetsinger .... CLEAVANT DERRICKS
A City Weed/Brooklyn .... EDEN ESPINOSA
A City Weed/Paradice .... RAMONA KELLER
A City Weed/Faith .... KAREN OLIVO

Place:

A street corner under the Brooklyn Bridge.

Time:

Present.

VOCALISTS

MANOEL FELCIANO,
CAREN LYN MANUEL,
HANEEFAH WOOD

SWINGS

JULIE REIBER, HORACE V. ROGERS

UNDERSTUDIES

For Brooklyn and Faith – CAREN LYN
MANUEL, JULIE REIBER; for Paradice –
HANEEFAH WOOD; for Taylor – MANOEL
FELCIANO; for Streetsinger – HORACE V.
ROGERS.
Dance Captain – JULIE REIBER

PLYMOUTH THEATRE

236 West 45th Street
A Shubert Organization Theatre

Gerald Schoenfeld, *Chairman*   Philip J. Smith, *President*

Robert E. Wankel, *Executive Vice President*

Producers Four   John McDaniel   Jeff Calhoun
Leiter/Levine & Scott Prisand   Jay & Cindy Gutterman Productions

In Association with

Transamerica, Robert G. Bartner, Dallas Summer Musicals Inc,
Rudy Durand, Danny Seraphine, Rick Wolkenberg and Sibling Entertainment

Present

BROOKLYN
The Musical

Book, Music and Lyrics by

Mark Schoenfeld & Barri McPherson

Starring

Kevin Anderson   Cleavant Derricks   Eden Espinosa   Ramona Keller   Karen Olivo

With

Manoel Felciano   Caren Lyn Manuel   Julie Reiber   Horace V. Rogers   Haneefah Wood

Set Design	Costume Design	Lighting Design	Sound Design
Ray Klausen	Tobin Ost	Michael Gilliam	Jonathan Deans
			Peter Hylenski

Associate Director	Music Direction	Music Coordinator
Coy Middlebrook	James Sampliner	John Miller
Press Representative	Marketing	Casting
Boneau/Bryan-Brown	TMG - The Marketing Group	Dave Clemmons Casting
General Management	Production Stage Manager	Technical Supervisor
Ken Denison	Kimberly Russell	TheaterSmith Inc.
WWE		Smitty
Associate Producers	Coordinating Producer	Associate Producer
Feurring/Maffei/Pinsky	Lauren Doll	Ken Denison

Music Supervision, Arrangements & Orchestrations by

John McDaniel

Directed by

Jeff Calhoun

Original version of "Brooklyn" first staged by Stephen Herek and Lori Herek (Producers) and Directed by Stephen Herek.
The producers wish to express their appreciation to Theatre Development Fund for its support of this production.

10/21/04

ORCHESTRA

Conductor/Keyboard 1: James Sampliner

Associate Conductor/Keyboard 2: Daniel Weiss

Guitar 1: John Putnam

Guitar 2: Gary Sieger

Bass: Irio O'Farrill, Jr.

Drums: Shannon Ford

Reeds: Jack Bashkow

Percussion: Roger Squitero

Cello: Clay Ruede

Music Coordinator: John Miller

A THOUGHT FROM THE AUTHORS...

Ain't it funny the things we come to value in this life?

A stone that shines and sparkles can make a young girl

an old man's wife.

I said the right piece of dirt in the right part of town

can make you lord of the land,

And if you happen to be born in just the right home,

You've got the future in the palm of your hands.

But a memory is just a worthless thing.

With every year the price goes down,

Till it's dusted off and sold for what you can get

In America's lost and found.

— *Mark Schoenfeld and Barri McPherson*

Brooklyn: The Musical

MUSICAL NUMBERS

"Heart Behind These Hands" ....The City Weeds
"Christmas Makes Me Cry" ....Faith and Taylor
"Not Sound" ....The City Weeds
"Brooklyn Grew Up" ....Brooklyn and the City Weeds
"Creating Once Upon A Time" ....Brooklyn and Faith
"Once Upon A Time" ....Brooklyn and the City Weeds
"Superlover" ....Paradice and the City Weeds
"Brooklyn In The Blood" ....Paradice, Brooklyn and the City Weeds
"Magic Man" ....Streetsinger and the City Weeds
"Love Was A Song" ....Taylor
"I Never Knew His Name" ....Brooklyn
"The Truth" ....Taylor, Brooklyn and the City Weeds
"Raven" ....Paradice
"Sometimes" ....Taylor and the City Weeds
"Love Me Where I Live" ....Paradice and the City Weeds
"Love Fell Like Rain" ....Brooklyn
"Streetsinger" ....Brooklyn, Streetsinger and the City Weeds
"Heart Behind These Hands" (Reprise) ....The City Weeds

Kevin Anderson
Taylor Collins

Cleavant Derricks
Streetsinger

Eden Espinosa
Brooklyn

Ramona Keller
Paradice

Karen Olivo
Faith

Manoel Felciano
Vocalist

Caren Lyn Manuel
Vocalist

Julie Reiber
Swing/Dance Captain

Horace V. Rogers
Swing

Haneefah Wood
Vocalist

Photo by Joan Marcus

Once Upon a Time: Eden Espinosa, Kevin Anderson, Cleavant Derricks, Ramona Keller and Karen Olivo as The City Weeds.

Mark Schoenfeld and Barri McPherson
Book, Music & Lyrics

Brooklyn: The Musical

Jeff Calhoun
Producer/Director

John McDaniel
Producer/Music Supervisor/Arranger/Orchestrator

Ray Klausen
Set Design

Tobin Ost
Costume Design, Assoc. Set Design

Michael Gilliam
Lighting Design

Jonathan Deans
Sound Design

Peter Hylenski
Sound Design

Coy Middlebrook
Associate Director

James Sampliner
Conductor

John Miller
Music Coordinator

Dave Clemmons
Casting

Ken Denison
General Manager

Christopher C. Smith
Technical Director

Scott Prisand
Producer

Steven Leiter (1947-2005) and Stan Levine
Producers

Jay and Cindy Gutterman
Producers

Rick Wolkenberg
Co-Producer

Charlie Maffei
Associate Producer

Gary Maffei
Associate Producer

Jonathan & Cathy Pinsky
Associate Producers

Lee Morgan
Vocalist

Romelda T. Benjamin
Swing

Sara Schmidt
Vocalist

Shelley Thomas
Vocalist

Will Swenson
Vocalist

Stage Management and Wardrobe
Seated: (L-R) Jennifer Marik (Assistant Stage Manager), Robert Guy (Wardrobe Supervisor) Standing: (L-R) Thom Gates (Stage Manager) and Jessica Worsnop (Dresser).

Box Office
Keith Heigman (Manager) and Vigi Cadunz.

Photos by Ben Strohmann

Brooklyn: The Musical

House Staff
Front Row: (L-R)
Svetlana Pinkhas, Amy Wolk,
Helen Lindberg, Francine
Kramer, Michelle, Lisa Boyd,
Roz Nyman, Carrie Hart and
Bobbi Parker.
Back Row: (L-R)
Kathleen Spock, Jonathan
Flannagan, Seth Sikes, Tony
Massey, Jeanine Buckley,
David M. Conte (House
Manager) and Gregory
Marlow.

Lighting & Sound
(L-R): Andy Catron,
Jim Uphoff,
Simon Matthews.

Photos by Ben Strothmann

Carpentry and Props
(L-R): Tim
McWilliams
(Carpenter),
Trish Avery (Props)
and
Dylan Foley (Props).

Doorman: John Blake.

Brooklyn: The Musical

Clockwise from top left: John McDaniel and guest Maury Yeston on opening night. Early press photo of the cast. Eden Espinosa and Ramona Keller on opening night. Co-author Mark Schoenfeld, director Jeff Calhoun and co-author Barri McPherson at the opening night party. John McDaniel and Jeff Calhoun at "Broadway on Broadway." Hinton Battle and Ben Vereen are guests at opening night party.

Photos by Aubrey Reuben

Memorable Opening Night Telegrams: Good luck messages from *Bombay Dreams, Reckless, Avenue Q* and *Fiddler on the Roof.*

Opening Night Gifts: Backpacks with the show's logo and a heart, dated with the opening night. Metal sculptures from a street person, from Barri and Mark. A framed rendering of the set from the set designer. Renderings of the costumes from the costume designer. A jar of candy from the cast of *Wicked,* because we have Eden in the show. The Brooklyn borough president sent us all cheesecakes.

In-Theatre Gathering Place: Wardrobe. All the swings hang out in there. We've got a microwave, candy and a rest room. We've also plastered the walls with photos of all the cast members, stagehands and Local Ones wearing the lunch lady wig.

Celebrity Visitors: Rosie O'Donnell came backstage and had a fun time, which must have been hard on her, since she was just at this theatre with *Taboo.* Kevin Bacon and Ashford & Simpson were very funny.

Gypsy Robe: Manoel Felciano. The old robe was full, so I was the first to put something on the new one. I made a left sleeve out of a black garbage bag with caution tape and our logo.

Who Played The Most Roles: Karen Olivo. She plays Mom/City Weed/Vietnam/Referee/Painter and she works so hard I have to re-rubber her shoes once a week.

Snack Food: Peanuts double-dipped in chocolate.

Therapy: Tea and water backstage. Blackcurrent pastilles. Entertainer's Secret throat spray.

Mascot: Ramona's fur Beanie Baby stole.

Backstage Rituals: We have a glass peanut that we found when we were doing the show out of town. We keep it in a soapdish and we touch it for luck. When The City Weeds are offstage just before they make their entrance, they all grab hands like a sports team and then all go running onstage together.

Favorite Moment, On Stage Or Off: The "Superlover" number, when Ramona wears the car wash fringe and chip bags on her head.

Heaviest/Hottest Costume: Heaviest costume is the stole of Beanie Babies. It's 15 lbs. and not exactly actor-friendly. But Ramona figures it's worth it. She gets such a great reaction.

Who Wore The Least: Also Ramona, who, when she's not wearing all that, wears a halter and miniskirt.

Also: The Wall of Wigs.

Correspondent: Robert Guy, Wardrobe Supervisor

Caroline, or Change

First Preview: April 13, 2004	Opened: May 2, 2004
Closed: August 29, 2004	22 previews and 136 Performances

PLAYBILL®

CAST

(in order of appearance)

Caroline Thibodeaux .... TONYA PINKINS
The Washing Machine .... CAPATHIA JENKINS
The Radio .... TRACY NICOLE CHAPMAN,
MARVA HICKS,
BRANDI CHAVONNE MASSEY
Noah Gellman .... HARRISON CHAD
The Dryer .... CHUCK COOPER
Grandma Gellman .... ALICE PLAYTEN
Grandpa Gellman .... REATHEL BEAN
Rose Stopnick Gellman .... VEANNE COX
Stuart Gellman .... DAVID COSTABILE
Dotty Moffett .... CHANDRA WILSON
The Moon .... AISHA de HAAS
The Bus .... CHUCK COOPER
Emmie Thibodeaux .... ANIKA NONI ROSE
Jackie Thibodeaux .... LEON G. THOMAS III
Joe Thibodeaux ... MARCUS CARL FRANKLIN
Mr. Stopnick .... LARRY KEITH

STANDBYS

For Caroline Thibodeaux — CHERYL ALEXAN-
DER; for The Washing Machine — LEDISI; for The
Radio — SHANNON ANTALAN, TANESHA
GARY, VANESSA A. JONES, BRANDI
CHAVONNE MASSEY, LEDISI; for Noah
Gellman — SY ADAMOWSKY; for The Dryer —
MILTON CRAIG NEALY; for Grandma Gellman —
SUE GOODMAN; for Grandpa Gellman — JOHN
JELLISON; for Rose Stopnick Gellman — SUE
GOODMAN; for Stuart Gellman — ADAM
HELLER; for Dotty Moffett — VANESSA A.
JONES; for The Moon — VANESSA A. JONES; for

The Bus — MILTON CRAIG NEALY; for Emmie
Thibodeaux — SHANNON ANTALAN; for Jackie
and Joe Thibodeaux — CORWIN TUGGLES; for
Mr. Stopnick — JOHN JELLISON

ORCHESTRA
CONDUCTOR: KIMBERLY GRIGSBY
Associate Conductor: Matthew Sklar
Violins: Paul Woodiel, Christopher Cardona;
Viola: David Creswell; Cello: Anja Wood; Reeds:
Paul Garment, Stephen Wisner; Guitars: Steve
Bargonetti; Bass: Benjamin Franklin Brown;
Keyboards: Matthew Sklar; Percussion: John
Clancy, Shane Shanahan

Music Coordinator: John Miller

EUGENE O'NEILL THEATRE
A JUJAMCYN THEATRE

JAMES H. BINGER   ROCCO LANDESMAN
CHAIRMAN   PRESIDENT

PAUL LIBIN   JACK VIERTEL
PRODUCING DIRECTOR   CREATIVE DIRECTOR

Carole Shorenstein Hays
HBO Films

Jujamcyn Theaters
Freddy DeMann
Scott Rudin   Hendel/Morten/Wiesenfeld   Fox Theatricals/Manocherian/Bergère
Roger Berlind   Clear Channel Entertainment   Joan Cullman
Greg Holland/Scott Nederlander   Margo Lion   Daryl Roth   Zollo/Sine

in association with

The Public Theater

present

Tonya Pinkins
in
CAROLINE, or CHANGE

book and lyrics by

Tony Kushner

music by

Jeanine Tesori

with

Reathel Bean   Harrison Chad   Tracy Nicole Chapman   David Costabile
Veanne Cox   Aisha de Haas   Marcus Carl Franklin   Marva Hicks
Capathia Jenkins   Larry Keith   Brandi Chavonne Massey   Alice Playten
Anika Noni Rose   Leon G. Thomas III   Chandra Wilson

and

Chuck Cooper

scenic design	costume design	lighting design
Riccardo Hernández	Paul Tazewell	Jules Fisher and Peggy Eisenhauer
sound design	hair design	orchestrations
Jon Weston	Jeffrey Frank	Rick Bassett Joseph Joubert Buryl Red
music coordinator		music director
John Miller		Linda Twine
casting	production stage manager	production management
Jordan Thaler/Heidi Griffiths	Rick Steiger	Gene O'Donovan
general press representative	marketing	general management
Boneau/Bryan-Brown	TMG-The Marketing Group	Stuart Thompson Productions

music supervisor and conductor

Kimberly Grigsby

choreography by

Hope Clarke

directed by

George C. Wolfe

The producers would like to thank Helen and Peter Bing for their support of CAROLINE, OR CHANGE.
The producers wish to also express their appreciation to Theatre Development Fund for its support of this production.

8/1/04

Tonya Pinkins as Caroline and Adriane Lenox
(from the Off-Broadway cast) as the Moon.

Caroline, or Change

MUSICAL NUMBERS

This play takes place in Lake Charles, Louisiana, November–December, 1963.

ACT ONE	ACT TWO
Scene 1: Washer/Dryer	Scene 7: Ironing
Scene 2: Cabbage	Scene 8: The Chanukah Party
Scene 3: Long Distance	Scene 9: The Twenty Dollar Bill
Scene 4: Moon Change	Scene 10: Aftermath
Scene 5: Duets	Scene 11: Lot's Wife
Scene 6: The Bleach Cup	Scene 12: How Long Has This Been Going On?
	Epilogue

Ramona Keller, Marva Hicks and Tracy Nicole Chapman as The Radio.

Photo by Michal Daniel

Caroline, or Change

Tonya Pinkins
Caroline Thibodeaux

Reathel Bean
Grandpa Gellman

Harrison Chad
Noah Gellman

Tracy Nicole Chapman
The Radio

Chuck Cooper
The Dryer, The Bus

David Costabile
Stuart Gellman

Veanne Cox
Rose Stopnick Gellman

Aisha De Haas
The Moon

Marcus Carl Franklin
Joe Thibodeaux

Marva Hicks
The Radio

Capathia Jenkins
The Washing Machine

Larry Keith
Mr. Stopnick

Brandi Chavonne Massey
The Radio

Alice Playten
Grandma Gellman

Anika Noni Rose
Emmie Thibodeaux

Leon G. Thomas III
Jackie Thibodeaux

Chandra Wilson
Dotty Moffett

Sy Adamowsky
Standby

Cheryl Alexander
Standby

Shannon Antalan
Standby

Tanesha Gary
Standby The Radio

Sue Goodman
Standby/Rose, Grandma

Adam Heller
Standby/Stuart

John Jellison
Standby/Grandpa, Mr. Stopnik

Vanessa A. Jones
Standby/Dotty, Moon, Radio

Ledisi
Standby/Washing Machine

Milton Craig Nealy
Standby/Dryer, Bus

Corwin Tuggles
Standby/Jackie, Joe

Tony Kushner
Book & Lyrics

Jeanine Tesori
Music

George C. Wolfe
Director

Jules Fisher & Peggy Eisenhauer
Lighting Design

Jeffrey Frank
Hair Design

Joseph Joubert
Orchestrator

Kimberly Grigsby
Music Supervisor & Conductor

John Miller
Music Coordinator

Linda Twine
Music Director

Hope Clarke
Choreography

Heidi Griffiths & Jordan Thaler
Casting

Stuart Thompson
General Manager

ALUMNI

Donald Grody
Standby Grandpa Gellman/Mr. Stopnick

Ramona Keller
The Radio

Adriane Lenox
Standby Caroline

Chevon Rutty
Standby Jackie/Joe Thibodeaux

Photos by Aubrey Reuben

Above left: Anika Noni Rose (with Michael Cerveris) with her 2004 Tony Award. Right: Marva Hicks, Ramona Keller and Tracy Nicole Chapman at "Stars in the Alley."

Curtain call on opening night.

Director George C. Wolfe, composer Jeanine Tesori and lyricist/librettist Tony Kushner arrive at the theatre on opening night.

Leon G. Thomas III holds a window card at the closing-night party.

Opening Night Gift: A day at Exhale spa.
Actor Who Played The Most Roles: Chuck Cooper (The Dryer, The Bus, etc.)
Backstage Rituals: Group prayer at "places."
Favorite In-Theatre Gathering Place: Capathia and Veanne's dressing room.
Off-Site Hangout: Worldwide Plaza and the steps of St. Malachy's Church ("Chuck's Office")
Favorite Snack Food: Pretzels with almond butter. Balance bar (gold).
Favorite Therapy: Water, to keep hydrated.
Orchestra Members Who Played Most Performances Without A Sub: Matt Sklar and Ben Brown.
Sweethearts: Tracy Chapman and Shane Shanahan
Correspondent: Capathia Jenkins, "The Washing Machine"

Above: Chuck Cooper with composer Jeanine Tesori at the closing night party at Rosie O'Grady's.

Below: David Costabile and Veanne Cox.

PLAYBILL®

THE CAST

(in order of appearance)

Velma Kelly	TERRA C. MacLEOD
Roxie Hart	CHARLOTTE D'AMBOISE
Fred Casely	GREGORY BUTLER
Sergeant Fogarty	DAN LoBUONO
Amos Hart	P.J. BENJAMIN
Liz	MICHELLE M. ROBINSON
Annie	ROXANE CARRASCO
June	DONNA MARIE ASBURY
Hunyak	KRISSY RICHMOND
Mona	MICHELLE DeJEAN
Matron "Mama" Morton	ANNE L. NATHAN
Billy Flynn	WAYNE BRADY
Mary Sunshine	R. LOWE
Go-To-Hell Kitty	MICHELLE POTTERF
Harry	SHAWN EMAMJOMEH
Doctor	BERNARD DOTSON
Aaron	MIKE JACKSON
The Judge	BERNARD DOTSON
Bailiff	SHAUN AMYOT
Martin Harrison	JOSH RHODES
Court Clerk	SHAUN AMYOT
The Jury	SHAWN EMAMJOMEH

UNDERSTUDIES

Standby for Roxie Hart and Matron "Mama" Morton—BELLE CALAWAY; For Roxie Hart—BELLE CALAWAY,

☺ AMBASSADOR THEATRE

A Shubert Organization Theatre

Gerald Schoenfeld, *Chairman*   Philip J. Smith, *President*

Robert E. Wankel, *Executive Vice President*

Barry & Fran Weissler
in association with
Kardana/Hart Sharp Entertainment
present

Charlotte d'Amboise   Terra C. MacLeod
P.J. Benjamin

and

Wayne Brady

in

CHICAGO

Lyrics by **Fred Ebb**   Music By **John Kander**   Book by **Fred Ebb & Bob Fosse**

Original Production Directed and Choreographed by **Bob Fosse**

Based on the play by Maurine Dallas Watkins

also starring

Anne L. Nathan   R. Lowe

with

Shaun Amyot   Donna Marie Asbury   Gregory Butler   Belle Calaway
Roxane Carrasco   Michelle DeJean   Bernard Dotson   Shawn Emamjomeh
Gabriela Garcia   Mike Jackson   Gary Kilmer   Dan LoBuono   Jeff Loeffelholz
Sharon Moore   Michelle Potterf   Josh Rhodes   Krissy Richmond
Michelle M. Robinson   Mark Anthony Taylor

Supervising Music Director **Rob Fisher**		Music Director **Leslie Stifelman**
Scenic Design **John Lee Beatty**	Costume Design **William Ivey Long**	Lighting Design **Ken Billington**
Sound Design **Scott Lehrer**	Orchestrations **Ralph Burns**	Dance Music Arrangements **Peter Howard**
Script Adaptation **David Thompson**	Musical Coordinator **Seymour Red Press**	Hair Design **David Brian Brown**
Casting **Howie Cherpakov C.S.A.**	Original Casting **Jay Binder**	
Technical Supervisor **Arthur Siccardi**	Production Stage Manager **Mindy Farbrother**	
Associate Producer **Alecia Parker**	Presented in association with **Clear Channel Entertainment**	
General Manager **B.J. Holt**	Press Representative **The Pete Sanders Group**	

Based on the presentation by City Center's Encores!℠

Choreography by
Ann Reinking
in the style of Bob Fosse

Directed by
Walter Bobbie

Cast Recording on RCA Victor

LIVE BROADWAY   11/11/04

MICHELLE POTTERF, MICHELLE DEJEAN; for Velma Kelly—DONNA MARIE ASBURY, ROXANE CARRASCO; for Billy Flynn—BERNARD DOTSON, DAN LOBUONO; for Amos Hart—SHAUN AMYOT, JOSH RHODES; for Matron "Mama" Morton—BELLE CALAWAY, ROXANE CARRASCO, MICHELLE M. ROBINSON; for Mary Sunshine—J. LOEFFELHOLZ; for Fred Casely—DAN LOBUONO, MARK ANTHONY TAYLOR; for Me and My Baby—GARY KILMER, JOSH RHODES, MARK ANTHONY TAYLOR; For all other roles: GABRIELA GARCIA, GARY KILMER, MARK ANTHONY TAYLOR, SHARON MOORE

Dance Captains:
GREGORY BUTLER, BERNARD DOTSON, GABRIELA GARCIA

TAP DANCE SPECIALTY Performed by
BERNARD DOTSON, SHAUN AMYOT, MIKE JACKSON

ME AND MY BABY SPECIALTY performed by
Shawn Emamjomeh and Dan LoBuono

NOWADAYS WHISTLE performed by
Donna Marie Asbury

Original Choreography for "Hot Honey Rag" by
BOB FOSSE

Chicago

MUSICAL NUMBERS

THE SCENE

Chicago, Illinois. The late 1920s.

ACT I

"All That Jazz"	Velma and Company
"Funny Honey"	Roxie
"Cell Block Tango"	Velma and the Girls
"When You're Good to Mama"	Matron
"Tap Dance"	Roxie, Amos and Boys
"All I Care About"	Billy and Girls
"A Little Bit of Good"	Mary Sunshine
"We Both Reached for the Gun"	Billy, Roxie, Mary Sunshine and Company
"Roxie"	Roxie and Boys
"I Can't Do It Alone"	Velma
"My Own Best Friend"	Roxie and Velma

ACT II

"Entr'acte"	The Band
"I Know a Girl"	Velma
"Me and My Baby"	Roxie and Boys
"Mister Cellophane"	Amos
"When Velma Takes The Stand"	Velma and Boys
"Razzle Dazzle"	Billy and Company
"Class"	Velma and Matron
"Nowadays"	Roxie and Velma
"Hot Honey Rag"	Roxie and Velma
"Finale"	Company

ORCHESTRA

Orchestra Conducted by Leslie Stifelman
Associate Conductor: Jeffrey Saver
Assistant Conductor: Scott Cady
Woodwinds: Seymour Red Press, Jack Stuckey, Richard Centalonza; Trumpets: John Frosk, Darryl Shaw; Trombones: Dave Bargeron, Bruce Bonvissuto; Piano: Scott Cady; Piano & Accordion: Jeffrey Saver; Banjo: Jay Berliner; Bass & Tuba: Ronald Raffio; Violin: Marshall Coid; Drums & Percussion: Ronald Zito

Original cast member Bebe Neuwirth (center) and the dancers of *Chicago*.

Charlotte
D'Amboise
Roxie Hart

Terra C. Macleod
Velma Kelly

Wayne Brady
Billy Flynn

P.J. Benjamin
Amos Hart

Anne L. Nathan
*Matron "Mama"
Morton*

R. Lowe
Mary Sunshine

Shaun Amyot
Bailiff/Court Clerk

Donna Marie
Asbury
June

Gregory Butler
*Fred Casely/
Dance Captain*

Belle Calaway
*Standby Roxie
Hart/Matron
"Mama" Morton*

Chicago

Roxane Carrasco
Annie

Michelle DeJean
Mona

Bernard Dotson
Doctor/
The Judge/
Dance Captain

Shawn Emamjomeh
Harry/The Jury

Gabriela Garcia
Swing/
Dance Captain

Mike Jackson
Aaron

Gary Kilmer
Swing

Dan LoBuono
Sergeant Fogarty

J. Loeffelholz
Understudy Mary
Sunshine

Sharon Moore
Swing

Michelle Potterf
Go-To-Hell Kitty

Josh Rhodes
Martin Harrison

Krissy Richmond
Hunyak

Michelle M.
Robinson
Liz

Mark Anthony
Taylor
Swing

John Kander &
Fred Ebb
Music; Book/Lyrics

Bob Fosse
Book

Walter Bobbie
Director

Ann Reinking
Choreographer

John Lee Beatty
Set Design

William Ivey Long
Costume Designer

Ken Billington
Lighting Designer

Ralph Burns
Orchestrations

Rob Fisher
Supervising Music
Director

Peter Howard
Dance Music
Arranger

David Brian Brown
Wig/Hair Design

Barry & Fran
Weissler
Producers

Morton Swinsky
Producer

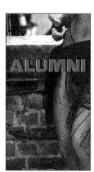
ALUMNI

Brent Barrett
Billy Flynn

R. Bean
Mary Sunshine

Raymond Bokhour
Amos

Wayne Brady
Billy Flynn

Brenda Braxton
Velma Kelly

Christine Brooks
Annie

Paige Davis
Roxie Hart

Bry dn Dowling
Hunyak

Jennifer Mackensie Dunne
Mona

Denis Jones
Doctor

Michael Kubala
Sergeant Fogarty

Mary Ann Lamb
June

John Mineo
Bailiff/Court Clerk

Dana Moore
Hunyak

James Patric Moran
Harry/The Jury

Marti Pellow
Billy Flynn

Greg Reuter
Aaron

Matthew Risch
Sergeant Fogerty

Roz Ryan
Matron "Mama" Morton

D. Sabella-Mills
Mary Sunshine

Solange Sandy
Annie

Tracy Shayne
Roxie Hart

Christopher Sieber
Billy Flynn

Mary Testa
Matron "Mama" Morton

Jennifer West
Hunyak

Carol Woods
Matron "Mama" Morton

Tom Wopat
Billy Flynn

Orchestra
Front Row (L-R): Jay Berliner (Banjo), Jeffrey Saver (Associate Conductor and Piano/Accordion), Leslie Stifelman (Music Director and Conductor), Dave Bargeron, (Trombone),)Marilyn Reynolds (Violin)
Middle Row (L-R): Ronald Zito (Drums), Jay Brandford (Woodwinds), Jack Gayle (Trombone), David Grego (Tuba/Bass), Mort Silver (Woodwinds), Top Row (L-R): Bruce Staelens (Trumpet), Richard Centalonza (Woodwinds), Darryl Shaw (Trumpet)

Regular Players Not Pictured: Seymour Red Press (Contractor/Woodwinds), Scott Cady (Assistant Conductor/Piano), John Frosk (Trumpet), Bruce Bonvissuto (Trombone), Ronald Raffio (Tuba/Bass), Jack Stuckey (Woodwinds), Marshall Coid (Violin)

Photo by Ben Strohmann

Chicago

Stage Managers
Terry Witter and Mindy Farbrother.

Front-of-House Staff
Left Row (from bottom, going up stairs):
Carol Bokun, Pat McElroy, Dorothea Bentley, May Park, Tasha
Allen, Lottie Dennis and Carol Hollenbeck.

Right Row (from bottom, going up stairs):
Marilyn Miller, Sharon Moran, Dion Taylor, Nathaniel Wright,
and Iris Helfand.

Photo by Ben Strothmann

Wardrobe and Hair
(L-R): Jo-Ann Bethell, Kevin Woodworth, Stephen Keough and Kathy Dacey.

Photo by Ben Strohmann

Stage Crew
Front Row (L-R): Dennis Smalls, John Cagney, Vince Jacobi, Robert Jacobi, Eileen MacDonald.
Second Row: Joe Mooneyham, Jimmy Werner, Paula Zwicky, Charlie Grieco.
Third Row: William Nye, Mike Guggino, "Lizard."

STAFF FOR CHICAGO

Presented by special arrangement with
AMERICAN PLAY COMPANY, INC.,
Sheldon Abend, President.

GENERAL MANAGEMENT
B.J. Holt, General Manager
Nina Skriloff, International Manager

PRESS REPRESENTATIVE
THE PETE SANDERS GROUP
Pete Sanders
Jeremy Shaffer
Glenna Freedman   Bill Coyle

Production Stage Manager	Mindy Farbrother
Company Manager	Jolie Gabler
Stage Managers	Terrence J. Witter, Bonnie Panson
General Management Associate	Stephen Spadaro
Associate General Manager	Michael Buchanan
Assistant Director	Jonathan Bernstein
Associate Lighting Designer	John McKernon
Assistant Choreographer	Debra McWaters
Dance Captains	Gregory Butler, Bernard Dotson, Gabriela Garcia
Assistant Set Designers	Eric Renschler, Shelley Barclay
Assistant Costume Designer	Lynn Bowling
Wardrobe Supervisor	Kevin Woodworth
Personal Asst to Mr. Billington	Jon Kusner
Assistant to Mr. Lehrer	Thom Mohrman
Production Carpenter	Joseph Mooneyham
Production Electrician	Luciana Fusco
Front Lite Operator	Michael Guggino
Production Sound Engineer	John Montgomery
Hair Supervisor	Stephen Keough
Production Propman	John Cagney
Dressers	Joann Bethell, Kathy Dacey, Paula Davis,

	Ronald Tagert, Eric Concklin
Banking	Chase Manhattan/Stephanie Dalton
Music Prep	Chelsea Music Services, Inc./ Donald Oliver & Evan Morris
Payroll	Castellana Services, Inc.
Accountants	Rosenberg, Newirth & Kuchner Mark D'Ambrosi
Insurance	Industrial Risk Specialists
Counsel	Seth Gelblum, Loeb & Loeb
Art Design	Spot Design
Advertising	SpotCo/ Drew Hodges, Amelia Heape, Jen McClelland
Education	Students Live!/Amy Weinstein, Laura Sullivan, Allyson Rodriguez
Marketing/Promotions	HHC Marketing/ Hugh Hysell, Michael Redman
Press Intern	Heather Smith
Production Photographer	Carol Rosegg
Merchandising	Dewynters Advertising Inc.
Displays	King Display

NATIONAL ARTISTS MANAGEMENT CO.

Vice President of Worldwide Marketing & Management	Scott A. Moore
Director of Business Affairs	Daniel M. Posener
Director of Casting	Howie Cherpakov
Dramaturg/Creative Consultant	Jack DePalma
Chief Financial Officer	Bob Williams
Accounting	Marian Albarracin
Assistant to Mr. Weissler	Erin Barlow
Assistant to Mrs. Weissler	Brett England
Assistant to the Weisslers	Suzanne Evans
Assistant to Ms. Parker	Emily Dimond
Marketing Manager	Ken Sperr
Receptionist	Michelle Coleman
Messenger	Victor Ruiz
Intern	Peter Ohsiek

SPECIAL THANKS
Additional legal services provided by Jay Goldberg, Esq. and
Michael Berger, Esq. Emer'gen-C super energy booster provided by Alacer Corp. Mr. Brady's tuxedo provided by Brioni.

CREDITS
Lighting equipment by PRG Lighting. Scenery built and painted by Hudson Scenic Studios. Specialty Rigging by United Staging & Rigging. Sound equipment by PRG Audio. Shoulder holster courtesy of DeSantis Holster and Leather Goods Co. Period cameras and flash units by George Fenmore, Inc. Colibri lighters used. Bible courtesy of Chiarelli's Religious Goods, Inc. Black pencils by Dixon-Ticonderoga. Gavel courtesy of The Gavel Co. Thanks to Wolfie. Zippo lighters used. Garcia y Vega cigars used. Hosiery by Donna Karan. Shoes by T.O. Dey. Orthopaedic Consultant, David S. Weiss, M.D.

⑤ THE SHUBERT ORGANIZATION

Gerald Schoenfeld	**Philip J. Smith**
Chairman	President
John W. Kluge	**Lee J. Seidler**
Michael I. Sovern	**Stuart Subotnick**

Irving M. Wall

Robert E. Wankel
Executive Vice President

Peter Entin	**Elliot Greene**
Vice President	Vice President
Theatre Operations	Finance
David Andrews	**John Darby**
Vice President	Vice President
Shubert Ticketing Services	Facilities

House Manager	Patricia Berry

Above: Ryan Lowe performs in the "Gypsy of the Year" sketch. Below: Producers Barry and Fran Weissler welcome Brady to the cast.

Above (L-R): Terra C. MacLeod, Mandie Brady, Wayne Brady, P.J. Benjamin, Charlotte d'Amboise, and D. Sabella-Mills at the party at Justine's for Wayne Brady's debut in *Chicago*. Below: The cast takes bows on Brady's first night.

Holiday Gift: The producers gave us a black nylon laundry bag embroidered with the show's logo.

Celebrity Visitor: Former President Bill Clinton. He set up a receiving line, and went down the line telling everyone they were hot.

"Gypsy Of The Year" Sketch: "Double Diva" by Ryan Lowe, in memory of Fred Ebb.

"Carols For A Cure" Carol: "A Yuletide Duet."

Backstage Rituals: We have "Dollar Friday." Everyone writes their name on a dollar and puts it in a pot, then the one that gets drawn wins the pot.

When Melanie Griffith joined the cast, she would do her vocal warmup on the word "Meow."

We celebrate birthdays religiously, and we wind up having several cakes each month. The person whose birthday it is this time is responsible for buying the next person's cake. I like mine from the Little Pie Company, but Amy's Bread is another of the more popular places.

Favorite Moment: The ensemble number, "All That Jazz" is everyone's favorite, though I personally like "Cell Block Tango," in which I do the "Pop." When either Jennifer Holliday or Carol Woods sang "When You're Good to Mama," they'd blow the audience away.

In-Theatre Gathering Place: The stage manager's office.

Off-Site Hangout: Vintage.

Snack Food: We have a serious, serious candy jar backstage. One of the guys works part-time at a chocolate store in Rockefeller Center and he'll bring huge boxes of things like champagne truffles.

Favorite Therapies: Ricola and Emergen-C.

Memorable Ad-Lib: Wayne Brady was the ad-lib king.

Record Number Of Cellphone Rings: Five.

Strangest Stage Door Fan Encounter: We have a guy who comes to see the show two or three times a month, then comes to the stage door and asks us to sign his program. He says to everyone who comes out, "Are you in the show? Are you in the show?" In nine years I think I've signed his program more than 20 times.

Strangest Press Encounter: We did a spread in City Guide, the tourist publication, where we were all in swimsuits. I'm not sure what that had to do with *Chicago*.

Busiest Day At The Box Office: Every Saturday.

Heaviest/Hottest Costume? Mary Sunshine wears the most clothes. Liz wears a bra with a beaded top and lace pants and a G-string. That's pretty hot.

Who Wore The Least? The Mona character. She wears a bra and panty with a lace unitard.

Catchphrases: "Skidoos" is the name we gave the *Chicago* groupies.

Ghostly Encounters: When we first moved to the Ambassador Theatre we were told there was a ghost in the house, but we haven't experienced anything yet.

Memorable Directorial Note: Walter Bobbie is known for telling all the companies that, to put across the opening number, "All That Jazz," you have to be saying to the audience, "Do you want it? Come and get it! Do you want it? Come and get it!"

Company Legends: One performance where Ann Reinking was doing Roxie, she broke the heel on her shoe and tossed it into the audience. It hit someone in the forehead and we were afraid we'd get sued and the show would close.

Tales From The Put-in: Sandy Duncan took over the role of Roxie Hart, and just days before she opened she was climbing down a ladder in one of her numbers and she broke her ankle.

Melanie Griffith insisted the entire company appear in costume for her put-in rehearsal. When we got there we saw two people sitting out in the audience, and we realized this was going to be a private performance for Antonio Banderas and Chita Rivera.

Understudy Anecdote: I'm understudy for Mama Morton. Jennifer Holliday took over the role for a brief time, but during her first week she was constantly out. I was mortified because everyone was coming to see her.

Sweethearts: Gary and Shawn.

Which Musician Plays The Most Instruments: Our percussionist, Ron Raphael.

Superstition That Turned Out Not To Be True: We all thought that when the movie came out, it would close the show. We were all prepared for it to close. But instead, I think it kicked a couple more years into it.

Company Legend: John Mineo retired last year at age 62. He was our oldest ensemble member.

Correspondent: Michelle Robinson, "Liz"

PLAYBILL®

IAN FLEMING'S
'CHITTY CHITTY BANG BANG'

CAST

Caractacus Potts	RAÚL ESPARZA
Truly Scrumptious	ERIN DILLY
Grandpa Potts	PHILIP BOSCO
Baron Bomburst	MARC KUDISCH
Baroness Bomburst	JAN MAXWELL
Goran	CHIP ZIEN
Boris	ROBERT SELLA
Childcatcher	KEVIN CAHOON
Toymaker	FRANK RAITER
Jeremy Potts	HENRY HODGES
Jemima Potts	ELLEN MARLOW
Coggins/Phillips	DIRK LUMBARD
Lord Scrumptious	KENNETH KANTOR
Sid	KURT VON SCHMITTOU
Violet	ROBYN HURDER
Chicken Farmer	J.B. ADAMS
Toby	MICHAEL HERWITZ
Inventors	JB ADAMS,
	ROBERT CREIGHTON,
	RICK FAUGNO,
	DIRK LUMBARD,
	WILLIAM RYALL,
	KURT VON SCHMITTOU

ENSEMBLE

JB ADAMS, TOLAN AMAN, JULIE BARNES, TROY EDWARD BOWLES, JEFFREY BROADHURST, ROBERT CREIGHTON, ANTONIO D'AMATO, STRUAN ERLENBORN, RICK FAUGNO, ASHLEE FIFE, EMILY FLETCHER, KEARRAN GIOVANNI,

continued on the next page

HILTON THEATRE
A CLEAR CHANNEL THEATRE

DANA BROCCOLI, BARBARA BROCCOLI, MICHAEL G. WILSON, FREDERICK ZOLLO, NICHOLAS PALEOLOGOS, JEFFREY SINE, HARVEY WEINSTEIN, EAST OF DOHENY THEATRICALS and MICHAEL ROSE LIMITED

By Special Arrangement with MGM ON STAGE

present

RAÚL ESPARZA
ERIN DILLY   PHILIP BOSCO

in

IAN FLEMING'S
'CHITTY CHITTY BANG BANG'

Music and Lyrics by
RICHARD M. SHERMAN and ROBERT B. SHERMAN

Adapted for the stage by
JEREMY SAMS

Based on the MGM/United Artists Motion Picture

Also Starring

MARC KUDISCH   JAN MAXWELL

CHIP ZIEN	ROBERT SELLA	KEVIN CAHOON
FRANK RAITER	HENRY HODGES	ELLEN MARLOW

Associate Director	Associate Choreographer	Fight Director
PETER VON MAYRHAUSER	TARA YOUNG	B.H. BARRY

Casting by	Music Coordinator	Additional Material by	Animal Trainer
JIM CARNAHAN, CSA	SAM LUTFIYYA	IVAN MENCHELL	WILLIAM BERLONI

Associate Producer	Production Managers	Press Representative	General Management
FRANK GERO	DAVID BENKEN	BARLOW • HARTMAN	ALAN WASSER
	JAKE BELL		ASSOCIATES

Orchestrations & Dance Arrangements by	Production Musical Supervisor	Musical Director
CHRIS WALKER	ROBERT SCOTT	KRISTEN BLODGETTE

Lighting Designed by	Sound Designed by
MARK HENDERSON	ANDREW BRUCE

Scenery & Costumes Designed by	Musical Staging & Choreography by
ANTHONY WARD	GILLIAN LYNNE

Directed by
ADRIAN NOBLE

LIVE BROADWAY

4/28/05

Ellen Marlow (as Jemima Potts), Raúl Esparza (as Caractacus Potts) & Henry Hodges (as Jeremy Potts) with Chitty.

Photo by Joan Marcus

Chitty Chitty Bang Bang

MUSICAL NUMBERS

The action takes place in England and Vulgaria.

ACT 1

Overture	Orchestra
Prologue	Company
You Two	Caractacus, Jeremy and Jemima
Them Three	Grandpa Potts
Toot Sweets	Caractacus, Truly Scrumptious, Lord Scrumptious and Ensemble
Act English	Boris and Goran
Hushabye Mountain	Caractacus
Come to the Fun Fair	Company
Me Ol' Bamboo	Caractacus and Ensemble
Posh	Grandpa Potts, Jeremy & Jemima
Chitty Chitty Bang Bang	Caractacus, Truly, Jeremy and Jemima
Truly Scrumptious	Jeremy, Jemima and Truly
Chitty Chitty Bang Bang (Nautical Reprise)	Caractacus, Truly, Jeremy and Jemima
Chitty Takes Flight	Company

ACT II

Entre'acte	Orchestra
Vulgarian National Anthem	Company
The Roses of Success	Grandpa Potts and Inventors
Kiddy-Widdy-Winkies	Childcatcher
Teamwork	Caractacus, Toymaker, Truly and Juvenile Ensemble
Chu-Chi Face	Baron and Baroness
The Bombie Samba	Baroness, Baron and Ensemble
Doll on a Music Box/Truly Scrumptious (Reprise)	Truly and Caractacus
Us Two/Chitty Prayer	Jeremy and Jemima
Teamwork (Reprise)	Toymaker and Company
Chitty Flies Home (Finale)	Company

Photo by Joan Marcus

High Chitty, Low Chitty (L-R): Raúl Esparza (Caractacus Potts), Ellen Marlow (Jemima Potts), Philip Bosco (Grandpa Potts), Henry Hodges (Jermemy Potts) and Erin Dilly (Truly Scrumptious) with Chitty Chitty Bang Bang.

Cast Continued

ENSEMBLE (continued)

ROD HARRELSON, BEN HARTLEY, MERRITT TYLER HAWKINS, MICHAEL HERWITZ, ROBYN HURDER, LIBBIE JACOBSON, MATT LOEHR, DIRK LUMBARD, MAYUMI MIGUEL, MALCOLM MORANO, JACLYN NEIDENTHAL, HEATHER PARCELLS, LURIE POSTON, CRAIG RAMSAY, WILLIAM RYALL, ALEX SANCHEZ, BRET SHUFORD, JANELLE VISCOMI, KURT VON SCHMITTOU, EMMA WAHL, BRYNN WILLIAMS

SWINGS

PHILLIP ATTMORE, RICK HILSABECK, JOANNE MANNING, JEFF SIEBERT, JULIE TOLIVAR

UNDERSTUDIES

For Caractacus Potts: RICK HILSABECK, MATT LOEHR, DIRK LUMBARD; for Truly Scrumptious: JULIE BARNES, JULIE TOLIVAR; for Grandpa: JB ADAMS, RICK HILSABECK; for Baron Bomburst: KENNETH KANTOR, KURT VON SCHMITTOU; for Baroness Bomburst: EMILY FLETCHER; for Goran: ROBERT CREIGHTON, RICK FAUGNO; for Boris: DIRK LUMBARD, KURT VON SCHMITTOU; for Childcatcher: WILLIAM RYALL; for Toymaker: JB ADAMS, WILLIAM RYALL; for Jeremy: TOLAN AMAN, STRUAN ERLENBORN; for Jemima: EMMA WAHL, JACLYN NEIDENTHAL, JANELLE VISCOMI

Dance Captain: Joanne Manning
Assistant Dance Captain: Jeff Siebert

ORCHESTRA

Musical Director: Kristen Blodgette

Associate Conductor/Keyboard II: Stan Tucker
Keyboard I: Milton Granger
Violins: Victor Costanzi (Concert Master),
Suzy Perelman
Violin/Viola: Gary Kosloski
Cello: Mairi Dorman-Phaneuf
Bass/Tuba: Patrick Glynn
Reeds: Robert DeBellis, Steven Kenyon,
Salvatore Spicola
Trumpets: Stu Satalof, Joe Burgstaller
French Horn: Jeff Nelsen
Trombones: Marc Donatelle, Charles Gordon
Guitar/Banjo/Mandolin: Justin Quinn
Percussion: Dave Roth
Drum Set: Edward Fast

Music Coordinator: Sam Lutfiyya

Music Copying (US):
Emily Grishman Music Preparation
(Emily Grishman/Katharine Edmonds)

Chitty Chitty Bang Bang

Raúl Esparza
Caractacus Potts

Erin Dilly
Truly Scrumptious

Philip Bosco
Grandpa Potts

Marc Kudisch
Baron Bomburst

Jan Maxwell
Baroness Bomburst

Chip Zien
Goran

Robert Sella
Boris

Kevin Cahoon
Childcatcher

Frank Raiter
Toymaker

Henry Hodges
Jeremy

Ellen Marlow
Jemima

JB Adams
Chicken Farmer/
Inventor/Ensemble

Tolan Aman
Ensemble

Phillip Attmore
Swing

Julie Barnes
Ensemble

Troy Edward
Bowles
Ensemble

Jeffrey Broadhurst
Ensemble

Robert Creighton
Inventor/Ensemble

Antonio D'Amato
Ensemble

Struan Erlenborn
Ensemble

Rick Faugno
Inventor/Ensemble

Ashlee Fife
Ensemble

Emily Fletcher
Ensemble

Kearran Giovanni
Ensemble

Rod Harrelson
Ensemble

Ben Hartley
Ensemble

Merritt Tyler
Hawkins
Ensemble

Michael Herwitz
Toby/Ensemble

Rick Hilsabeck
Swing

Robyn Hurder
Violet/Ensemble

Libbie Jacobson
Ensemble

Kenneth Kantor
Lord Scrumptious/
Ensemble

Matt Loehr
Ensemble

Dirk Lumbard
Coggins/Phillips/
Inventor/Ensemble

Joanne Manning
Dance Captain/
Swing

Mayumi Miguel
Ensemble

Malcolm Morano
Ensemble

Jaclyn Neidenthal
Ensemble

Heather Parcells
Ensemble

Lurie Poston
Ensemble

Craig Ramsay
Ensemble

William Ryall
Inventor/Ensemble

Alex Sanchez
Ensemble

Bret Shuford
Ensemble

Jeff Siebert
*Ass't. Dance Captain
/FightCaptain/Swing*

Julie Tolivar
Swing

Janelle Viscomi
Ensemble

Kurt Von Schmittou
*Sid/Inventor/
Ensemble*

Emma Wahl
Ensemble

Brynn Williams
Ensemble

Ian Fleming
Original Novel

Robert B. and Richard M. Sherman
Composers/Lyricists

Adrian Noble
Director

Gillian Lynne
*Musical Stager and
Choreographer*

Mark Henderson
Lighting Designer

Andrew Bruce
Sound Designer

Kristen Blodgette
Musical Director

Tara Young
*Associate
Choreographer*

B.H. Barry
Fight Director

Jim Carnahan
Casting

William Berloni
Animal Trainer

David Benken
*Production
Manager*

Alan Wasser
General Manager

Nicholas Paleologos &
Frederick Zollo
Producers

Harvey Weinstein
Producer

2004-2005 AWARDS

Drama Desk Award
Featured Actress in a Musical (Jan Maxwell)

Outer Critics Circle Award
Outstanding Set Design (Michael Yeargan)

Photo by Julie Tolivar

Orchestra

Front Row (L-R): Patrick Glynn (Bass/Tuba), Milton Granger (Keyboard I), Gary Kosloski (Violin/Viola).
Second Row (L-R): Stu Satalof (Trumpet), Charles Gordon (Trombone), Joe Burgstaller (Trumpet), Marc Donatelle (Trombone/Euphonium), Victor Costanzi (Violin/Concertmaster).
Third Row (L-R): Robert DeBellis (Reeds), Justin Quinn (Guitar/Banjo/Mandolin), Stan Tucker (Keyboard/Associate Conductor), Steve Kenyon (Woodwinds).
Back Row (L-R): David Roth (Percussion), Suzy Perelman (Violin), Mairi Dorman-Phaneuf (Cello), Jeff Nelsen (French Horn), Edward Fast (Drum Set) and Salvatore Spicola (Reeds).

Chitty Chitty Bang Bang

The "Fantasmagorical" Stage Crew
Front Row (L-R): Guy Wegener (Dog Wrangler), Rob Cox (Dog Wrangler), Jason Wilkosz (Asst. Electrician).
Second Row (L-R): Julienne Schubert-Blechman (Wardrobe), Bob Kwiatkowski (Wardrobe), Laura Ellington (Wardrobe), Danny Paul (Wardrobe), Alice Bee (Wardrobe).
Third Row (L-R): Jenn Molloy (Wardrobe), Gilbert Aleman (Wardrobe), Jaymes Gill (Wardrobe), Jason Heisey (Wardrobe), Phillip Rolfe (Wardrobe).
Back Row (L-R): Chip White (Wardrobe), Angelina Avallone (Makeup), Franc Weinperl (Wardrobe) and Ray Panelli (Wardrobe).

The "More than Spectacular" Front of House Staff
Front Row (L-R): Jeff Dobbins, Delilah Lloydd, Stephanie Carnright, Jeff Metzlar, Pamela Eueton, Lianna Miller, David Loomis, Jamie Morris, Amy Wolk, Dominic Zumbo, Alieke Wijnveldt. Second Row (L-R): John Dancy, Paula Raymond, Vicki Herschman, Eddie Zambrano, Erroll Worthington, Jim Woodworth, Denise Williams, Tony Massey. Third Row (L-R): Matt Blank, Julia Wood, Danielle Tiazio, Trisha Pfister, Kirssy Toribio, Venus Saranbrio, Cherito Golding, Mike Chavez. Fourth Row (L-R): Elizabeth Reardon, Lisa Lopez, Nicole Ellingham, Gonzalo Garcia, Ken Fuller, Kenya Capers, John Wescott, Allison Broder and Michael Garro.

Chitty Chitty Bang Bang

STAFF FOR CHITTY CHITTY BANG BANG

GENERAL MANAGEMENT
ALAN WASSER ASSOCIATES
Alan Wasser   Allan Williams
Connie Yung   Robert Nolan

GENERAL PRESS REPRESENTATION
BARLOW•HARTMAN
Michael Hartman   John Barlow
Carol Fineman   Leslie Baden

COMPANY MANAGER
THOMAS SCHLENK

PRODUCTION STAGE MANAGER
PETER VON MAYRHAUSER

STAGE MANAGER
MICHAEL J. PASSARO

Assistant Stage Managers	Charles Underhill, Seth Sklar-Heyn
Associate Company Manager	Adam J. Miller
Associate Director (UK)	Johanne Davies
Associate Choreographer (UK)	Frank Thompson
Dance Captain	Joanne Manning
Assistant Dance Captain/Fight Captain	Jeff Siebert
Associate Scenic Designer	Paul Weimer
Assistant Scenic Designer	Raul Abrego
Associate Costume Designer (UK)	Christine Rowland
Associate Costume Designers (US)	Patrick Chevillot, Mitchell Bloom
Assistant Costume Designer	Rick Kelly
Associate Lighting Designer	Daniel Walker
Assistant Lighting Designer	Kristina Kloss
Moving Lights Programmer	Stuart Porter
Associate Sound Designer (UK)	Simon Baker
Associate Sound Designer (US)	Mark Menard
Production Management	Jake Bell/ Production Services, Ltd.
Production Technical Supervisor	David Benken
Production Carpenter	Stephen Detmer
Production Electrician	Rick Baxter
Production Property	Timothy Abel
Production Sound	Scott Sanders
Production Wardrobe Supervisor	Rick Kelly
Production Hair and Wig Coordinator	Helen Gregor
Production Hair and Wig Supervisor	Carmel Vargyas
Production Makeup & Prosthetics Designer/Supervisor	Angelina Avallone
Assistant Production Manager	Ana M. Garcia
Production Management Assistant	Jill Johnson
Head Carpenter	Michael Kelly
Assistant Carpenter/Automation	Michael Shepp
Head Electrician	Joe "Fish" Cangelosi
Assistant Electrician	Jason Wilkosz
Assistant Electrician/Pyrotechnician	Norman Ballard
Head Property	Robert Valli

Associate Wardrobe Supervisor	Sarah Schaub
Wardrobe Staff	Gilbert Aleman, Jennifer Barnes, Alice Bee, Julienne Blechman, Gary Biangone, Jane Davis, Christina Foster, Jaymes Gill, Robert Kwiatkowski, Laura Ellington, Jenn Molloy, Ray Panelli, Danny Paul, Phillip Rolfe, Caitley Symons, Franc Weinperl, Chip White
Associate Hair and Wig Supervisor	Thomas Augustine Hewitt
Hair and Wig Stylists	Hazel Higgins, Ryan McWilliams
Assistant Prosthetics Makeup	Joshua Turi
Dialect Coach	Deborah Hecht
Children's Guardians	Bobby Wilson, Vanessa Brown
Tutoring	On Location Education/ Muriel Kester, Teri Flemal
Animal Handlers	Robert Cox, Joanne Genelle
Production Assistants	Jay McLeod, Heather Banta
Assistants to Fight Director	Brad Lemons, Dan Renken
General Management Associates	Thom Mitchell, Lane Marsh, Aaron Lustbader
General Management Office	Jennifer Mudge, Christopher Betz, Jason Hewitt, Ethan Schwartz
Casting Associates	Jeremy Rich, Carrie Gardner
Music Preparation (UK)	Anne Barnard
Synthesizer Programmer	Music Art Technologies, Inc./ Brett Sommer
Legal Counsel	Jay Harris, Esq.
Immigration Counsel	Shannon Such, Esq.
Legal Counsel to EON Productions	David Pope, Esq.
Insurance (US)	Marsh USA, Inc./ Linda Badgett, Yasmine Ramos
Insurance (UK)	Walton & Parkinson/Richard Walton
Banking	JP Morgan Chase & Co.
Accounting	Rosenberg Neuwirth & Kuchner/ Chris Cacace, Annemarie Aguano
Payroll Service	Castellana Services Inc.
Advertising (US)	Serino Coyne/ Sandy Block, Angelo Desimini, Victoria Cairl, Cara Christman
Advertising (UK)	Dewynters Limited
Merchandising	Dewynters Limited/Jim Decker
Production Photographer	Joan Marcus
Publicity Photographer	Andrew Eccles
Study Guide	Peter Royston
Website Coordinator	Jacob Hirzel
Theatre Displays	King Displays, Inc.
Travel/Transportation	Road Rebel Entertainment Touring
Ground Transportation	IBA-STAT Limo/Danny Ibanez
Storage Facility for Publicity Chitty	Bridgehampton Motoring Club
Rehearsal Space	New 42nd Street Studios
Opening Night Coordination	Tobak-Dantchik Events and Promotions/ Suzanne Tobak, Michael Lawrence

CREDITS AND ACKNOWLEDGEMENTS

Scenery fabricated, painted and automated by Hudson Scenic Studio, Inc., Yonkers, NY. Chitty car, automation and effects by Hudson Scenic Studio, Inc. Scenic elements by Adirondack Scenic, Inc., Argyle, NY; F&D Scene Changes Ltd., Calgary, Alberta. Scenic painting and soft goods by Scenic Art Studios, New Windsor, NY. Scenic elements provided by Beyond Imagination, Newburgh, NY. Props provided by Proof Productions, Inc., Beyond Imagination, John Creech Studios. Flying provided by Flying by Foy. Lighting by Fourth Phase/PRG. Sound by Sound Associates. Pyro by Jauchem & Meeh. Interstate hauling by Clark Transfer, Inc. Costumes by Eric Winterling, Inc.; Euroco Costumes; Carelli Costumes, Inc.; Barbara Matera, Ltd.; Seamless Costumes; Werner Russold; By Barak; Jennifer Love Costumes; Studio Rouge; Cego Custom Shirt; Douglas Earl Costumes; and Sarah Persteins. Custom footwear by T.O. Dey, Capezio Theatrical. Hoisery and undergarments by Bra Tenders. Millinery by Rodney Gordon, Inc.; Lynne Mackey Studio; Izquierdo Studios, Ltd.; and FiTA Studios. Custom knitwear by C. C. Wei. Custom medals by Carl W. Lemke Unique Jewelry. Dying and silk screening by Gene Mignola, Inc. Fabric painting by Jeffrey Fender, Robert Funk. Hair by Hugo Royer International, Ltd. Throat lozenges provided by Ricola. Emer'gen-C super energy booster provided by Alacer Group.

The dogs in the show were adopted from the following shelters:
Humane Society of New York; Ahisma Haven Rescue; Humane Society of Central Delaware County, Inc.; Herding Dog Rescue; ASPCA; Closter Animal Welfare Society, Inc.

HILTON THEATRE STAFF

General Manager	Micah Hollingworth
Assistant General Manager	Jorelle Aronovitch
Facility Manager	Kevin DiBetta
House Manager	Jeffrey Dobbins
Box Office Treasurer	Peter Attanasio Jr.
Head Carpenter	James C. Harris
Head Electrician	Art J. Friedlander
Head of Properties	Joseph P. Harris Jr.
Head of Sound	John R. Gibson
Assistant Facility Manager	Jeff Nuzzo
Asst. Box Office Treasurer	Spencer Taustine
Regional Accounting Manager	Patricia Busby O'Shaughnessy
Payroll Administrator	Sharon Payamps
Shipping/Receiving	Dinara Ferreira
Administrative Assistant	Jenny Kirlin

The Company performs, "Toot Sweets"

Photo by Joan Marcus

Above left (L-R): Henry Hodges, Raúl Esparza, Ellen Marlow and Erin Dilly, at the opening night party at the Hilton Hotel. Right: curtain call on opening night.

Photos by Aubrey Reuben

Left: The ensemble gathers on opening night. Right: Animal trainer William Berloni conducts auditions for the canine performers.

Left: Co-composer Robert Sherman arrives at the theatre on opening night with his grandson, Ryan. Right: Co-composer Richard Sherman, with (L-R) Sally Ann Howes, Heather Ripley and Adrian Hall, who played Truly Scrumptious, Jemima and Jeremy in the original film version.

Left: Two Jeremys. Adrian Hall with stage counterpart Henry Hodges. Right: Jan Maxwell and Marc Kudisch arrive at the cast party.

Backstage Rituals: During the overture there the cast performs a chant in the stage-left wings: "Who are we? CCBB!" Followed by "The Pop." Ellen and Henry and I have our own individual handshake.

Favorite Moment: That first flight in the car. Raul says, "The night this doesn't thrill us, something in our souls has died." It's like Space Mountain, it's so much fun. The wall of love that comes at you from the audience is amazing. It's such a fantasy moment for all of us. Chitty beats the heck out of my Ford Focus.

Who Got The Gypsy Robe: Alex Sanchez.

Who Performs The Most Roles: Dirk Lombard has four different tracks, but Rick Hilsabeck, the Swing, covers approximately 79 parts, including the lead roles.

In-Theatre Gathering Place: We have a green room downstairs, but the theatre is enormous. We find ourselves cuddling up in the stairwells up to the stage—as well as in Chip Zien's dressing room.

Favorite Off-Site Hangout: The Hilton Bar. God bless the discount!

Favorite Snack Food: Given the Toot Sweets, there's a lot of candy like Gummi Bears floating around backstage.

Mascot: There are eight dogs in the show, so we have eight mascots—and, of course, Chip Zien.

Favorite Therapy: Lots of physical therapy, pretty much full time. We do most of the show on a raked stage and the ensemble dances their buns off.

Most Memorable Ad Lib: On the second or third preview the entire sound board went out and we had to stop the show for about ten minutes. When the show came back up, Robbie Sella and Chip Zien came out on stage and one of the dogs ran on with them. Chip said, "I think it's the sound designer." And Robbie said, "He'd BETTER run." It brought the house down.

Fastest Costume Change: The boys have 15 seconds to change from the Fun Fair into the "Me Ol' Bamboo" costumes.

Heaviest/Hottest Costumes? All the boys in the Fun Fair have to wear huge clown heads and have to do cartwheels with their bamboo costumes underdressed. I fear for their inner ears.

Who Wore The Least? It's a family show, so we're pretty well buttoned down. There's some minor décolletage in "The Bombie Samba," but that's it.

In-House Parody Lyric: "G's up, ho's down/ Pimp," sung to the song "Posh."

Company In-Jokes: "Gillie juice! She's on the Gillie juice again!"

Sweethearts: Robbie Sella and Chip Zien.

Memorable Directorial Note: "This show is not unlike being children in the bathtub. Remember economy. Don't splash around in the bath."

Correspondent: Erin Dilly, "Truly Scrumptious"

PLAYBILL®

CAST
(in order of appearance)

Dame Edna Everage:
DAME EDNA

Master of the Dame's Musick:
WAYNE BARKER

The Gorgeous Ednaettes:
TERI DiGIANFELICE,
MICHELLE PAMPENA

The Equally Gorgeous TestEdnarones:
RANDY AARON,
GERRARD CARTER

UNDERSTUDIES
For Dame Edna:
MRS. MADGE ALLSOP

Lyrics and Music
Lyrics by Barry Humphries and Wayne Barker
Music by Wayne Barker

THE MUSIC BOX
THE ESTATE OF IRVING BERLIN AND THE SHUBERT ORGANIZATION, OWNERS
239 W. 45th STREET

CREATIVE BATTERY
By arrangement with
HARLEY MEDCALF and BOXJELLYFISH LLC
Presents

A Meditation on Loss and Redemption

Devised and Written by
BARRY HUMPHRIES

Additional Material by
ANDREW ROSS

With
WAYNE BARKER
Master of the Dame's Musick

Featuring
The Gorgeous Ednaettes
TERI DiGIANFELICE   MICHELLE PAMPENA

And the Equally Gorgeous TestEdnarones
RANDY AARON   GERRARD CARTER

Production Design
BRIAN THOMSON, R.O.S.N.S.W.

Lighting Design	Sound Design	Costumes
JANE COX	**DAN SCHEIVERT**	**WILL GOODWIN**
		STEPHEN ADNITT

| Choreography | Production Stage Manager | Production Manager |
| **JASON GILKISON** | **JAMES W. GIBBS** | **PETER FULBRIGHT** |

| Press Representative | Marketing | General Manager | Company Manager |
| **BILL EVANS & ASSOCIATES** | **HHC MARKETING** | **101 PRODUCTIONS, LTD** | **SCOTT WILCOX** |

This lovely program contains no marsupial products.

LIVE BROADWAY

11/21/04

Dame Edna is greeted by her Gorgeous Ednaettes and Equally Gorgeous TestEdnarones.

Photo by David Allen

Dame Edna: Back with a Vengeance!

Dame Edna
*Dame Edna
Everage*

Wayne Barker
*Master of the
Dame's
Musick*

Teri
DiGianfelice
*Gorgeous
Ednaette*

Michelle
Pampena
*Gorgeous
Ednaette*

Randy Aaron
*Equally
Gorgeous
TestEdnarone*

Gerrard Carter
*Equally
Gorgeous
TestEdnarone*

Barry
Humphries
*Deviser and
Writer*

Andrew Ross
*Additional
Material*

Brian Thomson
*Production
Designer*

Jane Cox
*Lighting
Designer*

Jason Gilkison
Choreographer

James W. Gibbs
*Production
Stage Manager*

Ruth Saunders
Stage Manager

STAFF FOR
DAME EDNA: BACK WITH A VENGEANCE!

GENERAL MANAGEMENT
101 PRODUCTIONS, LTD.
Wendy Orshan   Jeffrey M. Wilson
David Auster

COMPANY MANAGER
SCOTT WILCOX
Assistant Company Manager ....Alex Gushin

PRESS REPRESENTATIVE
BILL EVANS & ASSOCIATES
Jim Randolph

PRODUCTION MANAGER
TECH PRODUCTION SERVICES
Peter Fulbright   Mary Duffe
Colleen Houlehen   Lee Martindell

Production Stage Manager ....James W. Gibbs
Stage Manager ....Ruth Saunders
Dance Captain ....Teri DiGianfelice
Musical Arrangements ....Wayne Barker
Associate Scenic Designer ....Nancy Thun
Scenic Design Assistant/ Model Maker ....Nicholas Dare
Photoshop Artist ....Jane Cameron
Associate Lighting Designer ....Josh Epstein
Associate Sound Designer ....Matthew Elie
Production Carpenter ....Douglas Grekin
Assistant Carpenter ....Rich Cocchiara
Production Electrician ....Craig Aves
Assistant Electrician ....Morgan Shevett
Production Props Supervisor ....Tara Hasik
Production Sound Engineer ....Dan Scheivert
Wardrobe Supervisor ....Larry Tarzy
Dame Edna's Dresser ....Judith Badame Scheivert
Dresser ....John Corbo
Hair Stylist to Dame Edna ....Markus Fokken

101 Productions, Ltd. Staff ...Christine Hale, Clark Mims,
   Heidi Neven, Mary Six Rupert, Aaron Slavik
Company Management Interns ....Taylor Shann,
   Amy Stein
101 Productions Intern ....Sara Jane Katz
Legal Counsel .....Franklin, Weinrib, Rudell, and Vassallo/
   Jason Baruch, Esq.
Accountant ....Robert Fried, CPA
Controller ....Joseph Kubala
Advertising ....Serino Coyne/
   Greg Corradetti,
   Diane Niedzialek,
   Ramzi Khalaf
Marketing ....HHC Marketing/
   Hugh Hysell, Michael Redman
Production Photography ....Greg Gorman,
   David Allen
Banking ......City National Bank, Entertainment Division/
   Elizabeth Untiedt,
   Anne McSweeney
Insurance ....DeWitt Stern Group, Inc./
   Peter Shoemaker,
   Jennifer Brown
Domestic Travel ....Pro Travel/
   Silva Jenabian
Immigration ....RAZCo Visas/
   Ron Zeelens
Web Designer for Dame-Edna.com ....David Bruson
Payroll Service ....Castellana Services, Inc.

CREATIVE BATTERY
President and Producer ....Scott Sanders
VP Production & Operations ....Bruce H. Weinstein
Senior Producer & Head of
Creative Development........................Todd Johnson
Creative Development Executive ....Nona Lloyd
Assistant to Mr. Weinstein ....Wendy Walter
Assistant to Mr. Sanders ....Doug Gaeta

TOUR BOOKING AGENT
Steve Levine
International Creative Management

CREDITS
Scenery and flying effects built, painted, electrified and
automated by ShowMotion, Inc., Norwalk, Connecticut.
Automation of scenic elements provided by ShowMotion,
Inc., using the AC2 computerized motion control system.
Dame Edna's costumes constructed by
Will Goodwin Studio.
Additional costumes constructed by
John Schneeman Studio.
Footwear provided by Capezio.
Shoes by LaDuca Shoes NYC.
Conventional and automated lighting system provided by
Scharff Weisberg Lighting LLC.
Properties built by
Island Creative Management LLC and Spoon Group.
Sound equipment by OMNItech Inc.
Trucking provided by Clark Transfer.
Wigs constructed by Richard Mawbey and Wig Specialties.
Gladioli provided by Portafiori.
Grand piano provided by Yamaha.

The producers of Dame Edna: Back with a Vengeance!
would like to thank the following companies
for their generous support:

BANROCK STATION, wine ; BBC VIDEO, Dame Edna
Experience DVDs; BLOOMINGDALE'S, men's clothing;
M*A*C, cosmetics;   MILLENNIUM HOTELS, housing;
PLANTERS, deluxe mixed nuts; POLAROID, cameras and
film; QANTAS, international transportation/stuffed koala
bears; SPANX, undergarments and stockings; TED BAKER
LONDON, suits for the TestEdnarones; YASMENA &
YAZZY BAGS, handbags; LIZA MINNELLI, photos

STAFF FOR THE MUSIC BOX THEATRE
HOUSE MANAGER ....Jonathan Shulman
Box Office Treasurer ....Robert D. Kelly
Assistant Treasurers ....Michael Taustine,
   Timothy Moran, Brendan Berberich
House Carpenter ....Dennis Maher
House Electrician............................F. Lee Iwanski
House Propertyman ....Kim Garnett
Chief of Staff ....Dennis Scanlon
Accountant ....William C. Grother

Barry Humphries (center) with his cast members Randy Aaron, Michelle Pampena, Teri DiGianfelice and Gerrard Carter.

Above Left: Barry Humphries with wife Lizzie at the cast party. Right: Dame Edna takes a curtain call on opening night.

Above: Dame Edna visits Regis Philbin and Kelly Ripa's TV talk show.

At the Sardi's cast party. Left: Barbara Walters, Dame Edna and Joy Behar. Right: Dick Cavett is one of the guests on opening night.

Photos by Aubrey Reuben

Opening Night Notes: People in other shows on our block of 45th Street were our biggest supporters. *Brooklyn* and *Avenue Q* both sent great "Good luck" letters.

Opening Night Gifts: Dame Edna and the producers gave a fantastic robe embroidered with the show's logo. I got a hat from the stage management, and a poster from company management. The stage manager threw a party for us at Sardi's.

Celebrity Visitors: Harrison Ford and Calista Flockhart came. Just to see them in the audience was pretty exciting. We also got Tim Curry, Barbara Walters and the girls from "The View."

"Gypsy Of The Year" Sketch: Edna did a wonderful monologue, similar to what she does in our show. I took part in the opening number, "Ask a Gypsy."

Backstage Rituals: Before half-hour we all warm up together, Edna and the dancers. We do stretches and a vocal warm-up. Then, just before we send Edna off onto the stage, we gather with her so she knows we're together.

Favorite Moment: Watching Edna pick a different woman from the audience each night and somehow make it completely different each night. It's just genius.

In-Theatre Gathering Place: On the stage behind the closed curtain.

Off-Site Hangout: Chelsea Grill. I also stop at McHale's every night. My carpool picks up there.

Snack Food: We're all addicted to Altoids.

Therapy: We all do yoga. Edna is into Alexander stretching technique.

Memorable Ad-lib: Every day there are about 20, usually in the phone-call scene.

Record Number Of Cellphone Rings: Only two, but Edna confiscates the phone and talks to whoever is calling. Also, if Edna sees someone rummaging through their purse during the show, she will take it and try to find out what was so interesting in there.

Strangest Stage Door Fan Encounters: People who come dressed up as Dame Edna.

Heaviest/Hottest Costume: Edna's Empire State Building dress with the taxis and the Statue of Liberty that lights up. It supposedly weighs fifty pounds.

Who Wore The Least: Me.

Sweethearts: Our sound engineer and star dresser are married: Danny and Judy Scheivert.

Also: Edna never misses a performance and neither has anyone else. I've never been in a show where every day everyone loves doing it and is passionate about it. We've become a real tight-knit group. Every day is a new day, and you never know what's going to happen.

Correspondent: Teri DiGianfelice, "Gorgeous Ednaette"

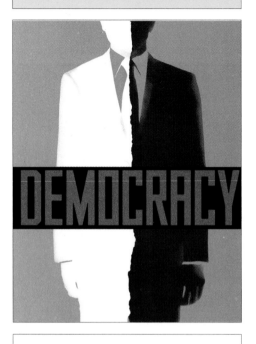

PLAYBILL®

CAST

(in order of appearance)

Günter Guillaume ....RICHARD THOMAS

Arno Kretschmann ....MICHAEL CUMPSTY

Willy Brandt ....JAMES NAUGHTON

Horst Ehmke ....RICHARD MASUR

Reinhard Wilke ....TERRY BEAVER

Ulrich Bauhaus ....JULIAN GAMBLE

Herbert Wehner................ROBERT PROSKY

Helmut Schmidt ....JOHN DOSSETT

Hans-Dietrich Genscher ....JOHN
CHRISTOPHER JONES

Günther Nollau.......................LEE WILKOF

STANDBYS

For Günter Guillaume and Ulrich Bauhaus –
TONY CARLIN; for Horst Ehmke, Reinhard
Wilke and Arno Kretschmann – PAUL O'BRIEN;
for Herbert Wehner, Hans-Dietrich Genscher and
Günther Nollau – MARTIN SHAKAR; for Willy
Brandt and Helmut Schmidt – RAY VIRTA

BROOKS ATKINSON THEATRE
UNDER THE DIRECTION OF JAMES M. NEDERLANDER AND JAMES L. NEDERLANDER

BOYETT OSTAR PRODUCTIONS   NEDERLANDER PRESENTATIONS, INC.
JEAN DOUMANIAN   STEPHANIE P. McCLELLAND   ARIELLE TEPPER
AMY NEDERLANDER   ERIC FALKENSTEIN   ROY FURMAN

present

JAMES NAUGHTON   RICHARD THOMAS
ROBERT PROSKY   MICHAEL CUMPSTY

in

NT THE NATIONAL THEATRE OF GREAT BRITAIN'S

production of

DEMOCRACY

by

MICHAEL FRAYN

with

TERRY BEAVER
JOHN DOSSETT
JULIAN GAMBLE
JOHN CHRISTOPHER JONES
RICHARD MASUR
LEE WILKOF

Set Design	Costume Design	Lighting Design	Sound Design
PETER J. DAVISON	SUE WILLMINGTON	MARK HENDERSON	NEIL ALEXANDER

Casting Director	Press Representative	Marketing
JIM CARNAHAN, CSA	BONEAU/BRYAN BROWN	HHC MARKETING

General Management	Production Stage Manager	Technical Supervisor
101 PRODUCTIONS, LTD.	DAVID HYSLOP	DAVID BENKEN

Directed by

MICHAEL BLAKEMORE

The producers wish to express their appreciation to Theatre Development Fund for its support of this production.

11/13/04

Friends and Secrets: Richard Thomas as Günter Guillaume and Michael Cumpsty as Arno Kretschmann.

Democracy

James Naughton
Willy Brandt

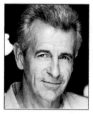
Richard Thomas
Günter Guillaume

Robert Prosky
Herbert Wehner

Michael Cumpsty
Arno Kretschmann

Terry Beaver
Reinhard Wilke

John Dossett
Helmut Schmidt

Julian Gamble
Ulrich Bauhaus

John Christopher Jones
Hans-Dietrich Genscher

Richard Masur
Horst Ehmke

Lee Wilkof
Günther Nollau

Tony Carlin
Standby Guillaume, Bauhaus

Paul O'Brien
Standby Ehmke, Wilke, Kretschmann

Democracy

Martin Shakar
Standby Wehner, Genscher, Nollau

Ray Virta
Standby Brandt, Schmidt

Michael Frayn
Playwright

Michael Blakemore
Director

Peter J. Davidson
Scene Design

Sue Willmington
Costume Design

Mark Henderson
Lighting Design

Jim Carnahan
Casting Director

Hugh Hysell
Marketing

David Benken
Technical Supervisor

Jean Doumanian
Producer

Stephanie P. McClelland
Producer

Arielle Tepper
Producer

Amy Nederlander
Producer

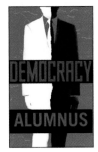

Robert Emmet Lunney
Standby for Arno Kretschmann

A NOTE FROM THE PLAYWRIGHT

The only part of German history that seems to arouse much interest abroad is the Nazi period. The half-century or so which has followed Germany's awakening from that sick dream is thought to be a time of peaceful but dull respectability, with the Federal Republic characterized by nothing much except material prosperity.

To me, I have to say, that material prosperity, that peacefulness, even that supposed dullness, represent an achievement at which I never cease to marvel or to be moved. Federal Germany began life after the Second World War as a grave-yard in which almost every city had been reduced to rubble, and almost every institution and political resource contaminated by complicity in the crimes of National Socialism; yet from this utter desolation its citizens constructed one of the most stable and decent states in Europe, the cornerstone of a peace which has endured now, at least in Western Europe, for nearly 60 years.

In that time the federal government has gone through many crises and scandals. It has survived many revelations that its members or officers had been implicated in the crimes of the past, or were working for East German intelligence, and many alarms when the nationalistic right seemed to be resurgent, or when the electorate seemed to be still nostalgic for past glories. In the last decade the longed-for reunification with East Germany plunged the nation into its most severe and prolonged difficulties yet. But the Federal Republic has worked.

Its success is even more surprising in view of the complexity of German politics. All politics is complex, since it involves the reconciliation of irreconcilable views and interests. This is what the play is about: the complexity of human arrangements and of human beings themselves. In Germany, though, the complexity is multiplied because there is not only a federal government but also one in each of the various Länder (11 of them at the time of the play); because of the existence of a separate East German Communist state, brutally split off by the Iron Curtain; and because every government since the Federal Republic was founded has been a coalition. This coalition has usually been an arrangement between the conservative Christian Democrats and the tiny FDP, the Free Democratic Party (aka the Liberals). In the so-called Grand Coalition of 1966, though, the junior partner of the Christian Democrats became not the FDP but the Social Democratic Party, their principal antagonist, hitherto apparently doomed to serve as the permanent opposition. The elections in the autumn of 1969 transformed the politics of coalition once again, when the SPD picked up enough seats to secure a slim majority in the Bundestag by going into coalition with the FDP. Which is where my play begins.

Is the play fact or fiction? The short answer, as with an earlier play of mine, Copenhagen, is fiction. But once again this fiction does take its rise from the historical record. All the political events referred to are real ones — all the triumphs, scandals and suspicions. The picture of life in the Palais Schaumburg, where the federal Chancellor's office was housed, comes from various recorded accounts, and so does that of life aboard the special train.

The biographies of the protagonists are true to the record, and their personalities are very much those attributed to their real counterparts by observers and historians. I have slightly simplified reality in the case of Arno Kretschmann, Guillaume's controller. At the beginning of his career in the federal Chancellery, Guillaume had other, unknown controllers. ("Arno Kretschmann" was a cover name, and his real identity remains unknown.) All the security aspects of the case that seem hardest to credit, however, (even the farcical conclusion to the hunt for the second son) come from the record.

The oddest aspect of the play, one may think, is the exclusion of the entire female sex. German parliamentary politics at the time, though, was overwhelmingly a man's world; the story of Brandt's government might have been rather different if it hadn't been so closed off from normal demographic reality.

—Michael Frayn

Democracy

Stage Crew
(L-R): Wallace Flores,
Thomas Lavai, Manuel Becker,
Joseph DiPaulo, Joseph Maher,
Deirdre McCrane, Denise Grillo,
Shawn Fertitta, David Hyslop,
James Crayton, David Benken,
Cesar Porto, Kelly Saxon

Photos by Ben Strohmann

Front-Of-House Staff
Front Row seated (L-R):
Brenda Brauer, Barbara Carrellas,
Brenden Imperato, Khadija Dib
Second Row seated (L-R):
Robt Banyai, Rosa Santiago,
Jim Holley, Bill Dillon,
Alex Kanter
Back Row standing (L-R):
Maureen Huff, Robert Brensa,
Timothy Newsome,
Kimberlee Imperato,
Arlene Reilly

Box Office
(L-R):
Bill O'Brien,
Bill Dorso,
Keshave Sattaur

Democracy | Scrapbook

Best Opening Night Telegram: One cast member who prefers to remain nameless received: "A warm hand on your opening."

Opening Night Gift: Each cast member received a personally inscribed copy of director Michael Blakemore's memoir *Arguments With England*.

Celebrity Visitor: Joanne Woodward, who said, "I need a history book!"

Who's Done The Most Shows: Robert Prosky who has done over 200.

Backstage Ritual: Because we spend so much of the show shaking hands on stage, we all put on hand sanitizer to attempt to keep the various viruses from spreading. Not too successfully.

Favorite Moments: (Onstage:) When the Berlin Wall "falls." (Offstage:) When John Dossett visits each cast member in his dressing room before each and every performance.

Gathering Place: The basement, where snacks can be found, and where we have Sunday brunch each week.

Off-Site Hangout: The Edison Hotel Coffee Shop/a.k.a. The Polish Tea Room. Especially Marty Shakar, who claims he came up with the alternate moniker for the place.

Favorite Snack Food: Chris Jones loves chocolate-covered pretzel logs.

Mascot: The visage on our poster, who is referred to as "That *Democracy* Guy."

Memorable Ad-lib: Richard Thomas, rather than saying "My father came home from the war and found my mother in bed with another man," said, "My mother came home from the war and found my father in bed with another man."

Busiest Day At The Box Office: The day after opening.

Memorable Directorial Note: James Naughton was directed to "see if he could generate more heat in his trousers."

Nicknames: Terry Beaver: "Bully Beaver." Richard Masur: "Twinkletoes."

Catchphrase: "Pinch Me."

Ghost Sightings: Julian Gamble thinks he saw Brooks Atkinson sitting in the audience writing a review during our first preview.

Sweethearts: We are all in love with our dresser, Kelly.

Superstitions That Turned Out To Be True: John Christopher Jones uttered the real name of "The Scottish Play" in his dressing room and the next time he was on stage, he forgot all his lines.

Correspondent: Lee Wilkof, "Günther Nollau"

Michael Cumpsty celebrates the reviews.

John Dossett escorts his wife, Michele Pawk, to the opening night cast party.

Curtain call on opening night.

Richard Thomas at the Broadway Flea Market.

The Atkinson marquee with "That *Democracy* Guy."

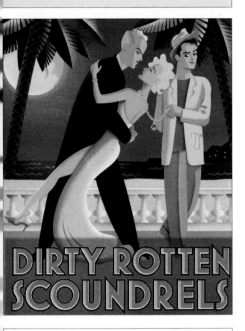

PLAYBILL®

CAST
(in order of appearance)

Andre Thibault	GREGORY JBARA
Lawrence Jameson	JOHN LITHGOW
Muriel Eubanks	JOANNA GLEASON
Freddy Benson	NORBERT LEO BUTZ
Jolene Oakes	SARA GETTELFINGER
Christine Colgate	SHERIE RENE SCOTT

THE ENSEMBLE

TIMOTHY J. ALEX, ROXANE BARLOW,
MATT BAUER, STEPHEN CAMPANELLA,
JOE CASSIDY, JULIE CONNORS, RACHEL
DE BENEDET, LAURA MARIE DUNCAN,
SALLY MAE DUNN, TOM GALANTICH,
JASON GILLMAN, AMY HEGGINS, GRASAN
KINGSBERRY, MICHAEL PATERNOSTRO,
RACHELLE RAK

SWINGS

JEREMY DAVIS, NINA GOLDMAN,
GREG GRAHAM, GINA LAMPARELLA

STANDBYS AND UNDERSTUDIES

Standby for Lawrence Jameson: NICK WYMAN
For Andre Thibault – JOE CASSIDY, MICHAEL
PATERNOSTRO; For Lawrence Jameson – TOM
GALANTICH; For Muriel Eubanks – RACHEL
DE BENEDET, LAURA MARIE DUNCAN;
For Freddy Benson – JOE CASSIDY, JASON
GILLMAN, MICHAEL PATERNOSTRO;

continued on next page

---

⑤ IMPERIAL THEATRE
249 West 45th Street
A Shubert Organization Theatre

Gerald Schoenfeld, *Chairman*   **Philip J. Smith,** *President*

Robert E. Wankel, *Executive Vice President*

THE DIRTY ROTTEN PRODUCERS
MARTY BELL   DAVID BROWN   ALDO SCROFANI   ROY FURMAN   DEDE HARRIS
AMANDA LIPITZ   GREG SMITH   RUTH HENDEL   CHASE MISHKIN   BARRY AND SUSAN TATELMAN
DEBRA BLACK   SHARON KARMAZIN   JOYCE SCHWEICKERT   BERNIE ABRAMS/MICHAEL SPEYER   DAVID BELASCO
BARBARA WHITMAN   WEISSBERGER THEATER GROUP/JAY HARRIS   CHERYL WIESENFELD/JEAN CHEEVER   FLORENZ ZIEGFELD
CLEAR CHANNEL ENTERTAINMENT *and* HARVEY WEINSTEIN

in association with

MGM ON STAGE/DARCIE DENKERT & DEAN STOLBER

and

THE ENTIRE PRUSSIAN ARMY

present

JOHN LITHGOW   NORBERT LEO BUTZ
SHERIE RENE SCOTT

JOANNA GLEASON   GREGORY JBARA

in

DIRTY ROTTEN SCOUNDRELS

Book by
JEFFREY LANE

Music and Lyrics by
DAVID YAZBEK

BASED ON THE FILM "DIRTY ROTTEN SCOUNDRELS"
WRITTEN BY DALE LAUNER AND STANLEY SHAPIRO & PAUL HENNING

Also Starring
SARA GETTELFINGER

TIMOTHY J. ALEX   ROXANE BARLOW   MATT BAUER   STEPHEN CAMPANELLA   JOE CASSIDY
JULIE CONNORS   JEREMY DAVIS   RACHEL DE BENEDET   LAURA MARIE DUNCAN   SALLY MAE DUNN
TOM GALANTICH   JASON GILLMAN   NINA GOLDMAN   GREG GRAHAM   AMY HEGGINS   GRASAN KINGSBERRY
GINA LAMPARELLA   MICHAEL PATERNOSTRO   RACHELLE RAK

Scenic Design	*Costume Design*	*Lighting Design*
DAVID ROCKWELL	GREGG BARNES	KENNETH POSNER

Sound Design	*Casting By*	*Associate Choreographer*
ACME SOUND PARTNERS	BERNARD TELSEY CASTING	DENIS JONES

Orchestrations	*Vocal Music Arrangements*	*Dance Music Arrangements*
HAROLD WHEELER	TED SPERLING DAVID YAZBEK	ZANE MARK

Conductor	*Music Coordinator*	*Technical Supervisor*	*Production Stage Manager*
FRED LASSEN	HOWARD JOINES	CHRISTOPHER SMITH	MICHAEL BRUNNER

Press Representative	*Marketing*	*General Management*
BARLOW•HARTMAN	MARGERY SINGER COMPANY	THE CHARLOTTE WILCOX COMPANY

Executive Producers
MARTY BELL / ALDO SCROFANI

Music Direction and Incidental Music Arrangements by
TED SPERLING

Choreographed by
JERRY MITCHELL

Directed by
JACK O'BRIEN

WORLD PREMIERE AT THE OLD GLOBE THEATRE SAN DIEGO, CALIFORNIA
ARTISTIC DIRECTOR: JACK O'BRIEN / EXECUTIVE DIRECTOR: LOUIS G. SPISTO

4/11/05

2004–2005 AWARDS

TONY AWARD
Leading Actor in a Musical (Norbert Leo Butz)

DRAMA DESK AWARD
Actor in a Musical (Norbert Leo Butz)

DRAMA LEAGUE AWARDS
Distinguished Production of a Musical
Distinguished Performance (Norbert Leo Butz)

OUTER CRITICS CIRCLE AWARD
Actor in a Musical (Norbert Leo Butz)

Dirty Rotten Scoundrels

MUSICAL NUMBERS

ACT ONE

Overture	Orchestra, Ensemble
Give Them What They Want	Lawrence, Andre, Ensemble
What Was a Woman To Do?	Muriel, Women
Great Big Stuff	Freddy, Ensemble
Chimp in a Suit	Andre
Oklahoma?	Jolene, Lawrence, Ensemble
All About Ruprecht	Lawrence, Ruprecht, Jolene
What Was a Woman To Do? (Reprise)	Muriel
Here I Am	Christine, Ensemble
Nothing Is Too Wonderful To Be True	Christine, Freddy
The Miracle (Act I Finale)	Company

ACT TWO

Entr'acte	Orchestra, Ensemble
Rüffhousin' mit Shüffhausen	Freddy, Christine, Dr. Shüffhausen
Like Zis/Like Zat	Andre, Muriel
The More We Dance	Lawrence, Christine, Ensemble
Love Is My Legs	Freddy, Christine, Ensemble
Love Sneaks In	Lawrence
Son of Great Big Stuff	Freddy, Christine
The Reckoning	Lawrence, Freddy, Andre
Dirty Rotten Number	Lawrence, Freddy
Finale	Company

Cast Continued

For Jolene Oakes – JULIE CONNORS, RACHELLE RAK; For Christine Colgate – LAURA MARIE DUNCAN, GINA LAMPARELLA

Dance Captain:
GREG GRAHAM

DIRTY ROTTEN SCOUNDRELS ORCHESTRA
Conductor: Fred Lassen
Associate Conductor: Jan Rosenberg
Assistant Conductor: Howard Joines
Concertmaster: Antoine Silverman

Violins: Michael Nicholas, Claire Chan; Cello: Anja Wood; Woodwinds: Andrew Sterman, Dan Willis, Mark Thrasher; Trumpets: Hollis (Bud) Burridge, Jim Hynes; Trombone: Mike Boschen; Horn: Theresa MacDonnell; Keyboards: Dan Lipton, Jan Rosenberg; Guitar: Erik DellaPenna; Bass: Mike DuClos; Drums: Dean Sharenow; Percussion: Howard Joines.

Music Coordinator: Howard Joines

Music Copying:
Emily Grishman Music Preparation/
Emily Grishman, Katharine Edmonds

Scooter provided by Vespa of Queens, Long Island City.

Give Them What They Want: John Lithgow and Company.

John Lithgow
Lawrence Jameson

Norbert Leo Butz
Freddy

Sherie Rene Scott
Christine Colgate

Joanna Gleason
Muriel Eubanks

Gregory Jbara
Andre Thibault

Sara Gettelfinger
Jolene Oakes

Nick Wyman
Standby for Lawrence Jameson

Timothy J. Alex
Ensemble

Roxane Barlow
Ensemble

Matt Bauer
Ensemble

Stephen Campanella
Ensemble

Joe Cassidy
Ensemble

Julie Connors
Ensemble

Jeremy Davis
Swing

Rachel de Benedet
Ensemble

Laura Marie Duncan
Ensemble

Sally Mae Dunn
Ensemble

Tom Galantich
Ensemble

Jason Gillman
Ensemble

Nina Goldman
Swing

Greg Graham
Dance Captain/ Swing

Amy Heggins
Ensemble

Grasan Kingsberry
Ensemble

Gina Lamparella
Swing

Michael Paternostro
Ensemble

Rachelle Rak
Ensemble

Jeffrey Lane
Book

David Yazbek
Composer/Lyricist

Jack O'Brien
Director

Jerry Mitchell
Choreographer

Ted Sperling
Music Director, Incidental Music Arranger, Co-Vocal Music Arranger

David Rockwell
Scenic Design

Gregg Barnes
Costume Design

Kenneth Posner
Lighting Designer

Bernard Telsey
Casting

Harold Wheeler
Orchestrations

Fred Lassen
Conductor

Howard Joines
Music Coordinator

Christopher C. Smith
Production Manager

Jorge Vargas
Makeup Designer

Margery Singer
Marketing

Charlotte Wilcox
General Manager

Michael Brunner
Production Stage Manager

Daniel S. Rosokoff
Assistant Stage Manager

Dana Williams
Assistant Stage Manager

Marty Bell
Producer/ Executive Producer

David Brown
Producer

Aldo Scrofani
Producer/ Executive Producer

Dede Harris
Producer

Amanda Lipitz
Producer

Ruth Hendel
Producer

Chase Mishkin
Producer

Barbara Whitman
Producer

Sharon Karmazin
Producer

Jay Harris/ WTG
Producer

Harvey Weinstein
Producer

Tom Clark, Mark Menard, and Nevin Steinberg
Sound Design

Andrew Asnes
Ensemble

The More We Dance: Norbert Leo Butz, John Lithgow and Sherie Rene Scott.

Photo by Carol Rosegg

The *Dirty Rotten* Crew

Cast and Crew

Front Row (L-R): Jackie Bayne (Cast), Paul Leggett Chase (Cast), Grasan Kingsberry (Cast), Amy Heggins (Cast), Roxane Barlow (Cast), Matthew Lambert (Company Manager), Dana Williams (Asst. Stage Manager), Dan Rosokoff (Asst. Stage Manager), Jack Scott (Wardrobe), Joby Horrigan (Wardrobe), Jan Rosenberg (Associate Conductor), Fred Lassen (Conductor), Dennis Norwood (Usher).

Second Row (L-R): Julie Connors (Cast), Sally Mae Dunn (Cast), Nina Goldman (Cast), Jeremy Davis (Cast), Sherie Rene Scott (Cast), Michael Brunner (Production Stage Manager), Sonia Rivera (Hair), Margo Lawless (Wardrobe), Michael Kanowlas (Ticket Taker), Marla Karaliolios (Usherette).

Third Row (L-R): Rachelle Rak (Cast), Michael Paternostro (Cast), Jodi Jackson (Hair), Melanie Hansen (Wardrobe), Jessica Scoblick (Wardrobe).

Fourth Row (L-R): Joe Cassio (Cast), Jason Gillman (Cast), Norbert Leo Butz (Cast), Joanna Gleason (Cast), Rhonda Barkow (Physical Therapist), Laura Marie Duncan (Cast), Joe Whitneyer (Hair), Dolly Williams (Wardrobe), Terri Purcell (Wardrobe Supervisor), Peggy Kurz (Wardrobe), Paula Parente (Bartender), Kaylynn Beatrice (Usherette), Frances Barbaretti (Chief Usherette), Fhara Lynch (Usherette).

Fifth Row (L-R): Sara Gettelfinger (Cast), John Lithgow (Cast), Rachel de Benedet (Cast), Tommy Thompson (Propman), Barry Hoff (Wardrobe), Anja Wood (Cello), Tim Young (Bar Manager), Lois Fernandez (Usherette), Greg McDonald (Usher).

Sixth Row (L-R): Chuck Saculla (Cast), Stephen Campanella (Cast), Timothy Alex (Cast), Jerry Marshall (Production Props), Leon Stieb (Carpenter), Michael Berglund (Wardrobe), Tom Bertsch (Wardrobe), Antoine Silverman (Violin, Concertmaster), Kevin Costigan (Usher), Douglas Massell (Usher).

Back Row (L-R): Greg Graham (Cast), Gregory Jbara (Cast), Tom Galantich (Cast), Andrew Agnes (Cast), Justin Sonik (Props), Randy Zaibek (Electrician), Rocco Williams (Moving Light Technician), Eric Gulorry (Follow Spot Light), Dennis Pfeifer (Electrician), Pete Donovan (Deck Electrician), Jay Satterwhite (Property Master), Will Devos (French Horn), Jim Hynes (Trumpet), Michael Huller (Usher), Mark Thrasher (Bassoon, Bass Clarinet, Clarinet, Flute, Baritone Sax), Rex Benincasa (Sub-Percussion), Bud Burridge (Trumpet), Ed Phillips (Ticket Taker) and Tigun Wibisana (Bartender).

STAFF FOR DIRTY ROTTEN SCOUNDRELS

WEST EGG ENTERTAINMENT

Creative Director: Marty Bell

Managing Director: Aldo Scrofani

Creative Associate: J. Max Sullivan

Directors: Marty Bell, Roger Lipitz,
Gary McAvay, Tom Owens, Aldo Scrofani

GENERAL MANAGEMENT
THE CHARLOTTE WILCOX COMPANY

Charlotte W. Wilcox

Matthew W. Krawiec   Kerry L. Parsons

Steve Supeck   Margaret Wilcox   Beth Cochran

GENERAL PRESS RESPREShentATIVE
BARLOW•HARTMAN

Michael Hartman   John Barlow

Rick Miramontez   Jon Dimond

MARKETING

Margery Singer Company

COMPANY MANAGER
Matthew Lambert

Assistant Company Manager
Dina Steinberg

CASTING
BERNARD TELSEY CASTING C.S.A.

Bernie Telsey, Will Cantler, David Vaccari,
Bethany Knox, Craig Burns,
Tiffany Little Canfield, Christine Dall,
Stephanie Yankwitt

PRODUCTION
STAGE MANAGER ....MICHAEL BRUNNER
Stage Manager ....Daniel S. Rosokoff
Assistant Stage Manager ....Dana Williams
Dance Captain ....Greg Graham
Assistant Director ....Benjamin Klein
Associate Scenic Designer ....Richard Jaris
Assistant Scenic Designers ....Larry Gruber,
Todd Ivins,
Rachel Short Janocko,
Daniel Kuchar
Assistant to the Scenic Designer ....Joanie Schlafer
Associate Costume Designer ....Sky Switser
Assistant Costume Designer
at Old Globe...........................Charlotte Deveaux
Associate Lighting Designer ....Philip Rosenberg
Assistant Lighting Designer ....Patricia Nichols
Automated Lighting Programmer ....Timothy F. Rogers
Assistant Sound Designer ....Jeffrey Yoshi Lee
Production Electrician ....Jimmy Fedigan
Production Carpenter ....Gerard Griffin
Production Flyman..............................Jeff Zink
Production Automation Carpenter ...Donald J. Oberpriller
Head Electrician ....Randy Zaibek
Assistant Electrician ....Peter Donovan
Production Sound ....Bob Biasetti
Production Properties ....Jerry Marshall
Assistant Properties ....Steve Woods
Wardrobe Supervisor ....Terri Purcell

Assistant Wardrobe Supervisor ....Joby Horrigan
Star Dresser to Mr. Lithgow ....Patrick Bevilacqua
Dressers ....Tom Bertsch, Mel Hansen,
Barry Hoff, Peggy Kurz,
David Oliver, Jessica Scoblick,
Jack Scott, Dolly Williams
Hair Supervisor ....Sonia Rivera
Assistant Hair Supervisor ....Frederick Waggoner
Hairdresser ....Joseph Whitmeyer
Makeup Designer ....Jorge Vargas
Keyboard Programmer ....Zenox Group, Inc.
Synthesizer Programmer ....James Abbott
Drum Music Arranger ....Dean Sharenow
Additional Musical Arrangements ....Dan Lipton
Music Preparation Service ....Emily Grishman Music
Preparation
Rehearsal Pianist ....Dan Lipton
Assistant to Mr. Lane ....Ryan Mark Weible
Production Assistants ....Gail Eve Malatesta,
Kelly Stillwell
Legal Counsel ....Loeb & Loeb LLP
Seth Gelblum
Accountants ....Rosenberg, Neuwirth, & Kuchner
Mark D'Ambrosi
Jana Jevnikar
Advertising ....SpotCo
Drew Hodges, Jim Edwards,
Tom Greenwald, Jim Aquino,
Lauren Hunter
Website Design ....Damian Bazadona
Press Office Manager ....Bethany Larsen
Press Office Associates ....Dennis Crowley,
Carol Fineman, Wayne Wolfe,
Leslie F. Baden, Mark Pino, Ryan Ratelle,
Miguel Raya, Gerilyn Shur,
Andrew Snyder
Production Photography ....Carol Rosegg
Theatre Displays ....Interboro Sign and Display Corp.
Banking ..................................J.P. Morgan Chase
Stephanie Dalton
Payroll Service ....Castellana Services, Inc.
Group Sales ....Group Sales Box Office, Inc.
Opening Night Coordinators ....Tobak-Dantchik Events
and Promotions/
Suzanne Tobak, Joanna B. Koondel
Merchandise ....Clear Channel
Theatrical Merchandising/
Karen Davidov
Insurance Consultant ....Stockbridge Risk Management
Computer Consultant ....Marion Finkler Taylor
Contracts Consultant ....Elizabeth Schmitt
Travel Services ....Tzell Travel

CREDITS

Scenery and scenic effects built, painted, electrified and automated by Showmotion, Inc., Norwalk, Connecticut. Show control, deck and fly automation effects by Showmotion, Inc., Norwalk, Connecticut, using the AC2 computerized motion control system. Drapery by I. Weiss. Additional scenery construction by the Old Globe Theatre. Costume construction by the Old Globe Theatre, Barbara Matera Limited, Arel Studio and Carelli Costumes. Shoes by LaDuca, J.C. Theatrical & Custom Footwear, T.O. Dey and Capri Shoes. Lighting equipment from PRG Lighting. Sound equipment by Sound Associates. Wigs by the Old Globe Theatre, Ray Marston wig studio - London, and Bob Kelly Wigs. Properties construction by the Old Globe Theatre. Special thanks to Bra*Tenders for hosiery and undergarments.

JEWELRY PROVIDED BY QVC® DESIGNED BY
Kenneth Jay Lane, Nolan Miller and Joan Rivers

MAKEUP PROVIDED BY M·A·C

Drums provided by PEARL.

Pianos provided by BALDWIN PIANO CO.

DIRTY ROTTEN SCOUNDRELS
rehearsed at
the New 42nd Street Studios
and 890 Studios.

SPECIAL THANKS

Louis Spisto,

Sheryl White,

Robert Drake

and the entire staff and board of the Old Globe.

 THE OLD GLOBE
THE OLD GLOBE THEATRE STAFF

Artistic Director: Jack O'Brien

Executive Director: Louis G. Spisto

Artistic Director: Craig Noel

General Manager: Michael G. Murphy

Director of Production: Robert Drake

Director of Marketing & Communications: Dave Henson

Director of Development: Todd Schultz

Director of Finance: Mark Somers

Technical Director: Benjamin Thoron

Costume Director: Stacy Sutton

Properties Director: Neil A. Holmes

 THE SHUBERT ORGANIZATION

Gerald Schoenfeld   **Philip J. Smith**
Chairman   President

John W. Kluge   **Lee J. Seidler**

Michael I. Sovern   **Stuart Subotnick**

Irving M. Wall

Robert E. Wankel
Executive Vice President

Peter Entin   **Elliot Greene**
Vice President   Vice President
Theatre Operations   Finance

David Andrews   **John Darby**
Vice President   Vice President
Shubert Ticketing Services   Facilities

House Manager ....Joseph Pullara

Exterior Metals Maintained by
Remco Maintenance Corporation

Opening night curtain calls (L-R): Tom Galantich, Sara Gettelfinger, Sherie Rene Scott and John Lithgow.

Supportive spouses: (left) Joanna Gleason with husband Chris Sarandon at the opening night party at Copacabana; (right) Gregory Jbara and wife Julie at the party.

Opening Night Gifts: Jackal t-shirts from Sherie Rene Scott, big yellow pencil from me, personalized Beaumont Sur Mer Hotel stationery from Ted Sperling, handsome show-logo-embossed leather scrapbook from Jeffrey Lane and David Yazbek.

Celebrity Visitors: Bette Midler (visited every dressing room), Goldie Hawn and Kurt Russell (did not come backstage but generated lots of buzz with the cast when they were sighted in the house), Florence Henderson, Joan Rivers, Alan Alda, Joyce Dewitt, Jeff Goldblum, Susan Stroman "Your show makes me proud to be in this business."

Who Got The Gypsy Robe: Roxane Barlow, who added a gorgeous hand-beaded show logo with train.

"Easter Bonnet" Sketch: "Spama-Rotten Story" by Greg Graham (*DRS*) and Greg Reuter (*Spamalot*). Frenchmen and Knights face-off á la Sharks and Jets from *West Side Story*.

Actors Who Performed the Most Roles: Rachel de Benedet, Rachelle Rak.

Who Has Done The Most Shows: John Lithgow (19 B'way shows), Roxane Barlow (13 B'way shows).

Favorite Moment: Listening to the audience response to the dog bit in "Here I Am," and the response to the "Bushes of Tex."

Favorite In-Theatre Gathering Place: Stage Manager's office.

Favorite Off-Site Hangout: Chelsea Grill (Hell's Kitchen).

Favorite Snack Food: All M's.

Mascot: Stanley the Stone Marten (ferret).

Favorite Therapy: Physical therapy.

Memorable Ad-lib: With the song already underway, his face white as a ghost, dripping in sweat, Norbert finally got John's attention indicating he forgot to put on his protective underguards for the Schüffhausen number. With the music vamping underneath, John saved the moment by addressing the audience with, "It appears my colleague has forgotten his protective pants...we will proceed with this number as we performed it in rehearsal." John then picked up the pillow from the bed and placed it on Norbert's lap. As it turns out, Norbert still received a laceration on the back of his left hand when the tip of John's bullwhip flexed down and cut him as he held the pillow down.

Cell Phone Rings: Has only happened maybe three times so far in our run. One or two squealing hearing aid distractions.

Strangest Press Encounter: QVC event.

Strangest Stage Door Fan Encounter: "I love your life!," screamed a lone voice from the throng of fans as ensemble members exited from the stage door.

Latest Audience Arrival: One hour late due to the 7 PM curtain on Tuesdays.

Fastest Costume Change: Rachel de Benedet changing from the character 'Lenore' into 'Renee' (26 seconds...full wig and dress change).

Busiest Day at the Box Office: June 6, 2005.

Heaviest/Hottest Costume: Sally Mae Dunn's nun costume.

Who Wore The Least: Rachelle Rak and Amy Heggins.

Orchestra Members Who Played The Most Instruments: Each of the three woodwinds play five instruments in various combinations.

Orchestra Member Who Played The Most Consecutive Perform-ances Without a Sub: Conductor Fred Lassen

Best In-House Parody Lyrics: "Take a look at my back-fat," from "The More We Dance." "This lady is Lenore,/Her husband's ninety four, /He doesn't schtup her anymore," from "Give Them What They Want."

Infamous Directorial Notes: "You're not funny, IT is." "Comedy is an ant farm."

Most Embarrassing Moment: Sherie Rene Scott's dress being tucked up above her underwear exposing her backside at the end of "Here I Am."

Company In-Jokes: Tim Alex dresses up in a towel and nearly makes an entrance every night for "What Is a Woman." There are also shoes of all shapes and sizes showing up in people's dressing rooms, wardrobe pockets, stage props etc.

Nicknames: Casino girls names are "Spooky," "Eugenie," "Sabina." Joe Cassidy as the nun is affectionately referred to by Norbert as "Sister Mary ___." It changes every night.

Catchphrases: "Party On Five" – full company. "Let me be you..." – Jerry Mitchell.

Correspondent: Greg Jbara, "Andre."

Norbert Leo Butz and John Lithgow in rehearsal.

Composer David Yazbek hugs his son Omar on opening night.

Above left: Sherie Rene Scott at rehearsals. Above right: director Jack O'Brien, designer David Rockwell and choreographer Jerry Mitchell at the opening night party.

Photos by Aubrey Reuben

PLAYBILL®

CAST

(in order of appearance)

Father Flynn .... BRÍAN F. O'BYRNE
Sister Aloysius .... CHERRY JONES
Sister James .... HEATHER GOLDENHERSH
Mrs. Muller .... ADRIANE LENOX

Stage Manager:
ELIZABETH MOLONEY

STANDBYS

For Sister James:
NADIA BOWERS

For Mrs. Muller:
CAROLINE STEFANIE CLAY

For Father Flynn:
CHRIS McGARRY

TIME:
Autumn, 1964

PLACE:
St. Nicholas Church School
in the Bronx

WALTER KERR THEATRE
A JUJAMCYN THEATRE
ROCCO LANDESMAN
PRESIDENT

PAUL LIBIN   JACK VIERTEL
PRODUCING DIRECTOR   CREATIVE DIRECTOR

CAROLE SHORENSTEIN HAYS   MTC PRODUCTIONS, INC.
ARTISTIC DIRECTOR   EXECUTIVE PRODUCER
LYNNE MEADOW   BARRY GROVE

ROGER BERLIND   SCOTT RUDIN
PRESENT

CHERRY JONES   BRÍAN F. O'BYRNE

IN

DOUBT
A PARABLE

BY

JOHN PATRICK SHANLEY

WITH

HEATHER GOLDENHERSH   ADRIANE LENOX

SCENIC DESIGN   COSTUME DESIGN   LIGHTING DESIGN   ORIGINAL MUSIC AND SOUND DESIGN
JOHN LEE BEATTY   CATHERINE ZUBER   PAT COLLINS   DAVID VAN TIEGHEM

PRODUCTION STAGE MANAGER   CASTING
CHARLES MEANS   NANCY PICCIONE/DAVID CAPARELLIOTIS

PRODUCTION MANAGEMENT   PRESS REPRESENTATIVE   MARKETING
AURORA PRODUCTIONS   BONEAU/BRYAN-BROWN   TMG–THE MARKETING GROUP

GENERAL MANAGEMENT   EXECUTIVE PRODUCER
STUART THOMPSON PRODUCTIONS/JAMES TRINER   GREG HOLLAND

DIRECTED BY
DOUG HUGHES

ORIGINALLY PRODUCED BY MANHATTAN THEATRE CLUB ON NOVEMBER 23, 2004.
THE PRODUCERS WISH TO EXPRESS THEIR APPRECIATION TO THEATRE DEVELOPMENT FUND FOR ITS SUPPORT OF THIS PRODUCTION.

LIVE BROADWAY   3/31/05

2004-2005 AWARDS

TONY AWARDS
Best Play
Leading Actress in a Play (Cherry Jones)
Featured Actress in a Play (Adriane Lenox)
Director of a Play (Doug Hughes)

OUTER CRITICS CIRCLE AWARDS
Best Play
Leading Actress in a Play (Cherry Jones)
Leading Actor in a Play (Brían F. O'Byrne)
Director of a Play (Doug Hughes)

DRAMA LEAGUE AWARD
Outstanding Production of a Play

PULITZER PRIZE FOR DRAMA 2005

DRAMA CRITICS CIRCLE AWARD
Best Play

DRAMA DESK AWARDS
Best Play
Leading Actress in a Play (Cherry Jones)
Leading Actor in a Play (Brían F. O'Byrne)
Featured Actress in a Play (Adriane Lenox)
Director of a Play (Doug Hughes)

Doubt

Cherry Jones
Sister Aloysius

Brían F. O'Byrne
Father Flynn

Heather Goldenhersh
Sister James

Adriane Lenox
Mrs. Muller

Nadia Bowers
Standby For Sister James

Caroline Stefanie Clay
Standby For Mrs. Muller

Chris McGarry
Standby For Father Flynn

John Patrick Shanley
Playwright

Doug Hughes
Director

John Lee Beatty
Set Design

Catherine Zuber
Costume Design

Pat Collins
Lighting Design

Carole Shorenstein Hays
Producer

Lynne Meadow
Artistic Director, Manhattan Theatre Club

Barry Grove
Executive Producer, Manhattan Theatre Club

Roger Berlind
Producer

Scott Rudin
Producer

Greg Holland
Executive Producer

Cast and Crew

Front Row (L-R): Devon Frett (Security), Adriane Lenox (Mrs. Muller), Brían F. O'Byrne (Father Flynn), Cherry Jones (Sister Aloysius), Heather Goldenhersh (Sister James), T.J. D'Angelo (FOH), Elizabeth Taylor (FOH).
Second Row (L-R): Luis Rivera (FOH), Ronald Laporte (FOH), Lizbeth MacKay (Standby), Adrian Atkinson (FOH).
Third Row (L-R): Patricia Kennedy (FOH), James Gardner (Production Electrician), Caroline Stefanie Clay (Standby), Chris McGarry (Standby), Nadia Bowers (Standby), Charles Means (Production Stage Manager), Rebecca Heroff (Production Props).
Fourth Row (L-R): Deborah Milano (FOH), Laurie Garcia (FOH), Elizabeth Moloney (Stage Manager), Ralph Santos (House Engineer), Brien Brannigan (Production Sound Engineer), Vincent Vallo (House Electrician), Gina Gornik (Dresser)
Back Row (L-R): Bobby Driggers (Company Manager), Eileen Miller (Wardrobe Supervisor), Timothy Bennett (House Props), Danny Braddish (Automation), George Fullum (Production/House Carpenter) and Matt Gurry (FOH).

Photo by Ben Strohmann

Doubt

Photos by Ben Strohmann

Stage Crew
Front Row (L-R): Elizabeth Moloney (Stage Manager), Gina Gornik (Dresser), Eileen Miller (Wardrobe Supervisor), Rebecca Heroff (Production Props), Brien Brannigan (Production Sound Engineer), Charles Means (Production Stage Manager).
Back Row (L-R): Ralph Santos (House Engineer), James Gardner (Production Electrician), George Fullum (Production/House Carpenter), Timothy Bennett (House Props), Danny Braddish (Automation), Vincent Vallo (House Electrician).

Management
Bobby Driggers (Company Manager), Elizabeth Moloney (Stage Manager), Charles Means (Production Stage Manager).

Front-of-House Staff
Back Row (L-R): Dmitri Ponomarev (Doorman), Adrian Atkinson, Matt Gurry, Ronald Laporte, and Luis Rivera.
Middle Row (L-R): Devon Frett (Security), Deborah Milano, Laurie Garcia, Patricia Kennedy.
Front Row (L-R): Brandon Houghton (Ticket Taker), T.J. D'Angelo, Elizabeth Taylor and John Barker (Night Dooman).

Not pictured: Treasurers Stan Shaffer (head), Kathleen Cadunz, Sonia Vasquez, Gail Yerkovich and House Manager Susan Elrod.

Doubt

Staff for DOUBT

GENERAL MANAGEMENT
STUART THOMPSON PRODUCTIONS

Stuart Thompson   James Triner

COMPANY MANAGER
Bobby Driggers

GENERAL PRESS REPRESENTATIVE
BONEAU/BRYAN-BROWN

Chris Boneau   Jim Byk   Aaron Meier   Erika Creagh

PRODUCTION MANAGEMENT
AURORA PRODUCTIONS INC.

Gene O'Donovan

W. Benjamin Heller II   Elise Hanley
Bethany Weinstein

Production Stage Manager	Charles Means
Stage Manager	Elizabeth Moloney
Dialect Coach	Stephen Gabis
Assistant Company Manager	Laura Penney
Assistant Director	Mark Schneider
Associate Set Designer	Eric Renschler
Assistant Set Designer	Yoshinori Tanakura
Associate Lighting Designer	D.M. Wood
Assistant Sound Designer	Walter Trarbach
Production Electrician	James Gardner
Production Props	Rebecca Heroff
Production Sound	Brien Brannigan
Wardrobe Supervisor	Eileen Miller
Dresser	Gina Gornik
Automation	Danny Braddish
Casting Assistant	Jennifer McCool
Production Assistant	Caroline Andersen
Assistant to Mrs. Hays	Kelly Hartgraves
Assistant to Mr. Berlind	Jeffrey Hillock
Assistant to Mr. Rudin	Aaron Janus
Assistant to Mr. Thompson	Caroline Prugh
General Management Assistants	Ryan Smith, John Vennema
Management Intern	Barry Branford, Joel Solari
Banking	Chase Manhattan Bank/ Richard L. Callian, Michele Gibbons
Payroll	Castellana Services, Inc./ Lance Castellana
Accountant	Robert Fried, CPA
Controller	Anne Stewart FitzRoy, CPA
Assistant Controller	Joseph S. Kubala
Insurance	DeWitt Stern Group, Inc./ Jolyon F. Stern, Peter Shoemaker, Anthony L. Pittari
Legal Counsel	Paul, Weiss, Rifkind, Wharton & Garrison/ John F. Breglio, Esq., Rachel Hoover, Esq.
Advertising	SpotCo/Drew Hodges, Jim Edwards, John Lanasa, Aaliytha Davis
Marketing Consultants	The Marketing Group/ Tanya Grubich, Laura Matalon Bob Bucci, Trish Santini, Erica Schwartz
Production Photographer	Joan Marcus
Cover Design by	SpotCo
Cover Photo Illustration by	Marc Yankus

CREDITS
Scenery and automation from Hudson Scenic Studio, Inc.
Lighting equipment supplied by GSD Productions, Inc., West Hempstead, NY.
Sound equipment by Masque Sound.
Doubt rehearsed at Manhattan Theatre Club's Creative Center.
Lozenges by Ricola.

STAFF FOR MANHATTAN THEATRE CLUB

Artistic Director	Lynne Meadow
Executive Producer	Barry Grove
General Manager	Harold Wolpert
Director of Artistic Production	Michael Bush
Director of Artistic Development	Paige Evans
Director of Artistic Operations	Mandy Greenfield
Artistic Associate/Assistant to the Artistic Director	Amy Gilkes Loe
Director of Casting	Nancy Piccione
Casting Director	David Caparelliotis
Director of Development	Jennifer Zaslow
Director of Marketing	Debra Waxman
Director of Finance and Administration	Michael P. Naumann
Associate General Manager	Seth Shepsle
Company Manager/NY City Center	Lindsey T. Brooks
Assistant to the Executive Producer	Erin Day
Director of Subscriber Services	Robert Allenberg
Director of Telesales and Telefunding	George Tetlow
Director of Education	David Shookhoff
Production Manager	Ryan McMahon

JUJAMCYN THEATERS

Rocco Landesman

President

Paul Libin   Jack Viertel

Producing Director   Creative Director

Jerry Zaks

Daniel Adamian   Jennifer Hershey

General Manager   Director of Operations

STAFF FOR THE WALTER KERR THEATRE

Manager	Susan Elrod
Treasurer	Stan Shaffer
Carpenter	George A. Fullum
Propertyman	Timothy Bennet
Electrician	Vincent Valvo, Jr.
Engineer	Ralph Santos

FROM THE PLAYWRIGHT
This play is dedicated to the many orders of Catholic nuns who devoted their lives to serving others in hospitals, schools and retirement homes. Though they have been much maligned and ridiculed, who among us has been so generous?

QUOTES
"The Bad Sleep Well"
— title of an Akira Kurosawa film

"In much wisdom is much grief, and he
that increaseth knowledge, increaseth sorrow."
— Ecclesiastes

"Everything that is hard to attain is
easily assailed by the mob."
— Ptolemy

Celebrating winning the Pulitzer Prize for Drama (L to R): Playwright John Patrick Shanley; actress Cherry Jones; producers Roger Berlind, Lynne Meadow, Carole Shorenstein Hays and Scott Rudin; and director Doug Hughes.

Above left: Caroline Stefanie Clay (L) and Linda Powell at the opening night party. Right: Lynne Meadow and Peter Solomon arrive at the theatre for the first performance.

Arriving at the cast party at the Supper Club, the cast of *Doubt* (L-R): Adriane Lenox, Brían F. O'Byrne, Cherry Jones and Heather Goldenhersh.

Photos by Aubrey Reuben

Opening Night Gifts: Cherry and and I got a pair of foot-tall nun dolls from stage management. They go with a small one I have, named Sister Mary McSqueaky. The producers got us beautiful fountain pens, like the ones Sr. Aloysius refers to in the play. We got engraved leather journals from the director. Cherry and I gave the boys statues of Jesus playing basketball.

Celebrity Visitors: We've had an amazing turnout every night: Robert Redford, Maggie Smith, Meryl Streep, Julia Roberts—Cherry knows, and is loved by, everyone.

Backstage Rituals: Brían says "God bless" to everyone before he goes on stage for the first scene. Brían also takes a Polaroid picture of everyone who comes backstage. If they think Father Flynn is innocent, they hold up a miniature priest doll. If they think Sister Aloysius is right, they hold up a nun doll. If they're not sure, they hold up both. We post these on the wall and we've got quite a collection now. I'm not sure who's ahead.

Favorite Moments: I love hearing Father Flynn crack himself up with his crazy laugh during the basketball scene. I love listening to the applause at the end of Adriane's scene. And I love listening to the major confrontation scene between Sister Aloysius and Father Flynn. The stage manager and I know all the lines by heart and we mouth all the words back and forth as they're doing it.

In-Theatre Gathering Place: Cherry has the biggest and prettiest dressing room, and she's decorated it beautifully. That's where we all gather.

Off-Site Hangout: Angus McIndoe's restaurant. I nicknamed it "The Community Center."

Snack Food: There's always an array of sweets in a candy jar by the coffee table, which we all swear off every day.

Favorite Therapy: Wheatgrass juice every day. Brían claims he's starting to like the taste, but I hate it. We also use Ricolas in an emergency.

Busiest Day At The Box Office: The last week in April 2005 we broke the box office record for the theatre.

Heaviest/Hottest Costume: Cherry and I have those nun habits. Sometimes it gets so hot that Cherry's eyeglasses fog up.

Strange Press Encounters: Reporters keep asking whether we think Father Flynn did it. I tell them it's not so simplistic.

Memorable Directorial Note: "Keep it easy-breezy."

Nicknames: Cherry calls me "Little Sister" and I call her "Big Sister."

Coolest Things About Being In This Show: Winning the Pulitzer. And being in a hit show, period. That's what Brían and Cherry say, and they've had lots of experience!

Also: We call it "The little show that could." The whole experience has felt really smooth, better than you can imagine, like a dream.

Correspondent: Heather Goldenhersh, "Sister James."

PLAYBILL®

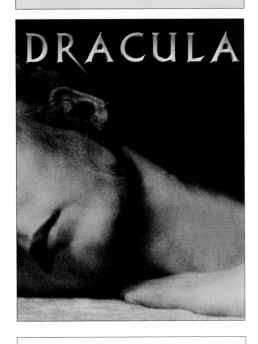

DRACULA

CAST
(in order of appearance)

Jonathan Harker	DARREN RITCHIE
Dracula	TOM HEWITT
Mina Murray	MELISSA ERRICO
First Vampire	MEGAN REINKING
	(at certain performances)
	JENIFER FOOTE
	(at certain performances)
Second Vampire	JENNIFER HUGHES
	(at certain performances)
	ELIZABETH LOYACANO
	(at certain performances)
Third Vampire	PAMELA JORDAN
	(at certain performances)
	MELISSA FAGAN
	(at certain performances)
Renfield	DON STEPHENSON
Jack Seward	SHONN WILEY
Lucy Westenra	KELLI O'HARA
Quincey Morris	BART SHATTO
Arthur Holmwood	CHRIS HOCH
Abraham Van Helsing	STEPHEN MCKINLEY HENDERSON
Child	MICHAEL HERWITZ
	(at certain performances)
	MICHAEL SOLOWAY
	(at certain performances)

ENSEMBLE

MELISSA FAGAN, JENIFER FOOTE,
JENNIFER HUGHES, PAMELA JORDAN,
ELIZABETH LOYACANO,
MEGAN REINKING, GRAHAM ROWAT

⊛ BELASCO THEATRE
111 West 44th Street
A Shubert Organization Theatre

Gerald Schoenfeld, *Chairman*   Philip J. Smith, *President*

Robert E. Wankel, *Executive Vice President*

DODGER STAGE HOLDING and JOOP VAN DEN ENDE
in association with Clear Channel Entertainment

present

Tom Hewitt   Melissa Errico

in

DRACULA
THE MUSICAL

Music by
Frank Wildhorn

Book and Lyrics by
Don Black and Christopher Hampton

also starring

Don Stephenson   Darren Ritchie
Kelli O'Hara   Chris Hoch
Bart Shatto   Shonn Wiley
Stephen McKinley Henderson

Melissa Fagan   Jenifer Foote   Anthony Holds   Jennifer Hughes
Pamela Jordan   Elizabeth Loyacano   Megan Reinking
Graham Rowat   Megan Sikora   Chuck Wagner

Scenic Design	Costume Design	Lighting Design
Heidi Ettinger	Catherine Zuber	Howell Binkley
Sound Design	Aerial Staging	Projection Design
Acme Sound Partners	Rob Besserer	Michael Clark
Orchestrations	Musical Direction and Arrangements	Music Coordinator
Doug Besterman	Constantine Kitsopoulos	John Miller
Makeup Design	Fight Director	Flying by
Angelina Avallone	Steve Rankin	Foy
Production Stage Manager	Technical Supervisor	Casting
Kelly A. Martindale	Don S. Gilmore	Dave Clemmons Casting
Executive Producer	Press Representative	Promotion Services
Dodger Management Group	Boneau/Bryan-Brown	Margery Singer Company

Choreography by
Mindy Cooper

Directed by
Des McAnuff

Originally Produced by La Jolla Playhouse, La Jolla, CA
Des McAnuff, Artistic Director & Terrence Dwyer, Managing Director

12/27/04

STANDBYS AND UNDERSTUDIES

For Dracula: GRAHAM ROWAT; for Mina Murray: ELIZABETH LOYACANO, MEGAN SIKORA; for Jonathan Harker: ANTHONY HOLDS, SHONN WILEY; for Renfield: CHRIS HOCH, GRAHAM ROWAT; for Jack Seward: ANTHONY HOLDS, BART SHATTO; for Lucy Westenra: JENNIFER HUGHES, MEGAN SIKORA; for Quincey Morris: ANTHONY HOLDS; for Arthur Holmwood: ANTHONY HOLDS, BART SHATTO; for Abraham Van Helsing: GRAHAM ROWAT
Standby for Dracula, Van Helsing and Quincey: CHUCK WAGNER

SWINGS
ANTHONY HOLDS, MEGAN SIKORA

Dance Captain
MEGAN SIKORA

ORCHESTRA
CONDUCTOR: CONSTANTINE KITSOPOULOS
Associate Conductor: Ethyl Will
Reeds: Rick Heckman; Cello: Chungsun Kim
Percussion: Barbara Merjan; Key I: Karl Mansfield
Key II: Ethyl Will; Key III: Constantine Kitsopoulos

Music Coordinator: John Miller

Dracula

MUSICAL NUMBERS

TIME AND PLACE:

Transylvania, England and across Europe, aboard the Orient Express a century ago.

ACT ONE

Prelude	Jonathan Harker
"A Quiet Life"	Dracula
"Over Whitby Bay"	Jonathan and Mina Murray
"Forever Young"	First Vampire, Second Vampire and Third Vampire
"Fresh Blood"	Dracula
"The Master's Song"	Renfield and Jack Seward
"How Do You Choose?"	Lucy Westenra, Mina, Quincey Morris, Jack, Arthur Holmwood and Company
"The Mist"	Lucy
"Modern World"	The Company
"A Perfect Life"	Mina
"The Weddings"	The Company
"Prayer for the Dead"	The Company
"Life After Life"	Dracula and Lucy

ACT TWO

"The Heart Is Slow to Learn"	Mina
"The Master's Song" (reprise)	Renfield and Dracula
"If I Could Fly"	Mina
"There's Always a Tomorrow"	Dracula and Mina
"Deep in the Darkest Night"	Van Helsing, Quincey, Arthur, Jack, Jonathan and Mina
"Before the Summer Ends"	Jonathan
"The Longer I Live"	Dracula
"All Is Dark"/"Life After Life" (reprise)	Dracula and Mina
Finale	Dracula and Mina

Tom Hewitt
Dracula

Melissa Errico
Mina Murray

Don Stephenson
Renfield

Darren Ritchie
Jonathan Harker

Kelli O'Hara
Lucy Westenra

Chris Hoch
Arthur Holmwood

Bart Shatto
Quincey Morris

Shonn Wiley
Jack Seward

Stephen McKinley Henderson
Abraham Van Helsing

Melissa Fagan
Third Vampire/ Ensemble

Fresh Blood: Tom Hewitt as Dracula and Melissa Errico as Mina.

Dracula

Jenifer Foote
*First Vampire/
Ensemble*

Anthony Holds
Swing

Jennifer Hughes
*Second Vampire/
Ensemble*

Pamela Jordan
*Third Vampire/
Ensemble*

Elizabeth Loyacano
*Second Vampire/
Ensemble*

Megan Reinking
*First Vampire/
Ensemble*

Graham Rowat
Ensemble

Megan Sikora
*Swing/Dance
Captain*

Chuck Wagner
*Standby for Dracula,
Van Helsing, and
Quincey Morris*

Michael Herwitz
Child

Michael Soloway
Child

Frank Wildhorn
Music

Christopher
Hampton
Book & Lyrics

Des McAnuff
Director

Mindy Cooper
Choreographer

Heidi Ettinger
Scenic Design

Catherine Zuber
Costume Design

Howell Binkley
Lighting Design

Tom Clark, Mark Menard, and Nevin
Steinberg
Sound Design

Doug Besterman
Orchestrations

Constantine
Kitsopoulos
*Musical Direction
& Arrangements*

John Miller
Music Coordinator

Steve Rankin
Fight Director

Dave Clemmons
Casting

Joop van den Ende
Producer

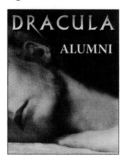
DRACULA ALUMNI

Celina Carvajal
*Second Vampire/
Ensemble*

Tracy Miller
*First Vampire/
Ensemble*

Matthew Nardozzi
Child

Dracula

Doorman: Regan Kimmel

Dressers
(L-R): Cathy Cline, Liam O'Brien and Julienne Schubert-Blechmann

(L-R): Lee Sickels (Carpentry Crew), Dylan Foley (Props Crew), Jennifer Kievit (House Props Crew), Ken Harris (Production Prop Man), Sean Sieger (Assistant Prop Man) and Valarie Lamour (House Props Crew).

Photos by Ben Strothmann

(L-R): Mark Voegale (Foy Carpenter) and Eric "Speed" Smith (Rail Automation Carpenter).

Mike Cornell (Deck Electrician)

(L-R): Lair Paulsen (Hairdresser), Carla Muniz (Hairdresser) and Heather Morris (Hairdresser).

Randy Morrison (Deck Sound)

(L-R): Kelly Rach (Company Management) and Alissa R. Zulvergold (Child Wrangler).

(L-R): Dan Coey (Head Electrician), Randy Morrison (Sound Crew) and Daryl Kral (Sound Operator).

George Dummitt (House Head Carpenter)

Dracula

Front-of-House Staff
Kneeling in front (L-R): Not identifed (Concessions), Naheed Khan (Usherette).
Second Row (L-R): Not identified (Concessions), Daria Cherney (Usherette), Laudi Dennis (Usherette), Eugenia Raines (Usherette), Kathy Powell (Ticket-Taker).
Third Row (L-R): Not identified (Concessions), Dexter Luke (Chief Usher), Daniel Rosario (Usher), Gwen Cowley (Usherette).
Fourth Row (L-R): Kathy Dunn (Usherette), Meaghan McElroy (Usherette), Brad Lewis (Usher), Terry Lynch (Custodian), Not identified (Concessions).

Stage Management
Back Row: (L-R) Brian Meister (Stage Manager), Marti McIntosh (Sub Stage Manager), Mark R. Gordon (Assistant Stage Manager),Front Row: (L-R) Alex Lyu Volckhausen (Assistant Stage Manager) and Kelly Martindale (Production Stage Manager).

Hair and Wig Department
(L-R): Mark Adam Rampmeyer (Wig Supervisor) and Jeff Knaggs (Hair Dresser).

Jeff Lunsford (Deck Automation Carpenter).

(L-R): Pat Kenary (Box Office) and Diane Heatherington (Treasurer).

Staff for DRACULA, THE MUSICAL

EXECUTIVE PRODUCERS
Dodger Management Group

Sally Campbell Morse   Steven H. David

Mimi Intagliata   Bill Schaeffer

Tim Hurley   Staci Levine   Jennifer F. Vaughan

Lee Magadini

GENERAL PRESS REPRESENTATION
Boneau/Bryan-Brown

Adrian Bryan-Brown   Jim Byk

Susanne Tighe   Juliana Hannett

COMPANY MANAGER
Sandra Carlson

Production Stage Manager	Kelly A. Martindale
Stage Manager	Brian Meister
Assistant Stage Managers	Alex Lyu Volckhausen, Mark Gordon
Original Production Stage Manager	Frank Hartenstein
Assistant Director	Daisy Walker
Second Assistant Director	Holly-Anne Ruggiero
Assistant Choreographer	Lillie Kae Stevens
Dance Captain	Megan Sikora
Dialect Coach	Stephen Gabis
Period Movement Consultant	Elizabeth Keen
Assistant Company Manager	Kelly Rach
Fight Captain	Graham Rowat
Child Wrangler	Alissa R. Zulvergold
Special Effects	Chic Silber
Associate Special Effects	Aaron Waitz
Associate Scenic Designer	Luke Cantarella
Assistant Scenic Designers	Larry Gruber, Robert Braun, Mark Erbaugh, Miguel Huidor, Todd Ivins, Ted LeFevre, Rachel Nemec, Todd Potter
Assistant Costume Designers	David Newell, Michael Zecker
Automated Lighting Programmer	Tom Celner
Projection Programmer	Hilary Knox
Associate Lighting Designer	Mark T. Simpson
Assistant Lighting Designer	Patricia Nichols
Assistant Sound Designers	Jeffrey Yoshi Lee, Sten Severson
Assistant Projection Designer	Jason Thompson
Costume Office Staff	T. Michael Hall, Melanie Errico
Production Carpenter	Jim Kane
Deck Automation	Jeff Lunsford
Fly Automation	Eric E. Smith
Foy Automation	James Leonard
Production Electrician	James Fedigan
Head Electrician	Dan Coey
Assistant Electrician	Michael Cornell
Production Sound Engineer	Daryl Kral
Production Prop Man	Kenneth Harris Jr.
Assistant Prop Man	Sean Sieger
Prop Shopper	Tessa Dunning
Wardrobe Supervisor	Lynn Bowling
Wardrobe Department	James Wilcox, Cathy Cline, Virginia Neininger, Liam O'Brien, Nicole Amburg, Susan Checklick
Hair & Makeup Supervisor	Mark Adam Rampmeyer
Hair Department	Wanda Gregory, Eve Morrow, Carla Muniz
Casting Associate	Rachel Hoffman
Casting Assistants	Rye Mullis, Sara Schatz
Assistant to John Miller	Matthew P. Ettinger

Music Assistant to Frank Wildhorn	Nick Cheng
Associate Orchestrator	Kim Schamberg
Music Copying	Anixter Rice Music Service
Synthesizer Programming	Karl Mansfield
Music Production Assistant	John Bauder
Production Assistants	Sarah Bierenbaum, Alyssa Gardner, Mark R. Gordon, Alissa R. Zulvergold
Dramaturg	Allison Horsley
Advertising	Serino Coyne, Inc./ Scott Johnson, Sandy Block, Mindy Gordon
Marketing	Dodger Marketing/ Amy Wigler, Dana Cobb, Mary Farrell, Melissa Fink, Jessica Ludwig, Shanta Mali, Rose Polidoro, Hannah McDonald, Rooney Design
Promotion	Margery Singer Company/ Margery Singer, Janet Lynn
Banking	Commerce Bank/ Barbara von Borstel
Payroll	Castellana Services Inc./ Lance Castellana, Norman Seawell, James Castellana
Accountants	Schall and Ashenfarb, C.P.A.
Finance Director	Paula Maldonado
Finance Office	Joan Mitchell, Celia Botet
Insurance	AON/Albert G. Ruben Insurance Services, Inc./ George Walden, Claudia Kaufman
Counsel	Nan Bases, Esq. Eliott Brown, Esq.
Dodger Special Events	John L. Haber
Travel Arrangements	The "A" Team at Tzell Travel/ Andi Henig
MIS Services	Rivera Technics/ Sam Rivera
Website Design	Media Brand
Website Maintenance	Late August
Production Photographer	Joan Marcus
Theatre Displays	King Displays

STAFF FOR DODGER STAGE HOLDING

Angela Seebaran Assam, Steve Bloom, Celia Botet, Robert Bucci, Amanda Caceres, Piort Candelario, Sandra Carlson, David Carpenter, Dana V. Cobb, Michael Coco, Dianne Cornelison, Michael David, Steven H. David, Robin de Levita, Sara Desitoff, Tracey Diebold, Adorn DuBose, Pablo Estrada, Melissa Estro, Mary Farrell, Melissa Fink, Bessie Ganis, Jose Gaston, Emily Grant, Ron Gubin, John L. Haber, Stephanie Hall, Alexa Harris-Ralff, Barbara Haven, Claire Hayes, Tim Hurley, Mimi Intagliata, Kimberly Kelley, Georgia Kremos, Tina Landau, Staci Levine, Pamela Lloyd, Michael Lonergan, James Elliot Love, Jessica Ludwig, Hannah Macdonald, Lee Magadini, J. Tony Magner, Paula Maldonado, Shanta Mali, Tim McKelvey, Joan Mitchell, Lauren Mitchell, Sally Campbell Morse, Erin Oestreich, Suzy O'Kelly, Cris Petre, Angelo Petronio, L. Glenn Poppleton, Tammy Powell, Kelly Rach, Rainard Rachele, Samuel Rivera, Sarah Rizza, Maureen Rooney, Bill Schaeffer, Ann Schaer, Michael Sinder, Marjorie Singer, Edward Strong, Sean Sullivan, Kyra Svetlovsky, Guy Tanno, Joop van den Ende, Bart van Schriek, Jennifer Vaughan, Dennis Walls, Amy Wigler.

LA JOLLA PLAYHOUSE

Artistic Director	Des McAnuff
Managing Director	Terrence Dwyer
Associate Artistic Director	Shirley Fishman
General Manager	Debby G. Buchholz
Director of Finance	Elizabeth Doran
Director of Institutional Advancement	James Forbes
Associate Director of Development	Melaine Bennett
Director of Communications	Lendre Kearns
Public Relations Manager	Jessica Padilla
Marketing Manager	Gigi Cantin
Director of Education and Outreach	Jeanette Horn

Production Manager	Peter J. Davis
Company Manager	Mandy Lehinger
IT Systems Manager	Todd Sivard
Legal Counsel	F. Richard Pappas, Esq.

Dodger Group Sales	1-877-5DODGER
Exclusive Tour Direction	Dodger Touring, Ltd. L. Glenn Poppleton
Souvenir Merchandise	Theatre Stuff, LLC

CREDITS

Scenery and scenic effects built, painted and automated by Hudson Scenic Studio, Inc., Yonkers, NY.
Lighting equipment from Fourth Phase, NJ.
Sound equipment by ProMix Sound.
Costumes executed by Euroco Costumes, Dodger Costumes Ltd., Carelli Costumes Inc., Parsons-Meares Ltd., Timberlake Studios, La Jolla Playhouse Costume Shop.
Millinery executed by Rodney Gordon, Carelli Costumes Inc., William Crowther.
Period umbrellas and parasols by Barrington Brolly. Docker boots by Fred Longtin Handmade Shoes.
Women's boots by LaDuca Shoes.
Props provided and executed by The Spoon Group, Bograds Fine Furniture, Down Time Productions.
Effects equipment by Sunshine Scenic Studios.
Virtuoso® EXI media server Imagina and Virtuoso® DX2 control console provided by VLPS, Inc.
Wigs by Bob Kelly Wig Creations and Ray Marston Wig Studio Ltd.

SPECIAL THANKS
John Arnone; The Nederlanders

DRACULA TEETH FABRICATED BY
Dr. Marc Beshar, D.M.D., Cosmetic Dentistry.

MAKEUP PROVIDED BY M•A•C COSMETICS.

THE SHUBERT ORGANIZATION, INC.

Gerald Schoenfeld	Philip J. Smith
Chairman	President
John W. Kluge	Lee J. Seidler
Michael I. Sovern	Stuart Subotnick
Irving M. Wall	

Robert E. Wankel
Executive Vice President

Peter Entin	Elliot Greene
Vice President Theatre Operations	Vice President Finance
David Andrews	John Darby
Vice President Shubert Ticketing Services	Vice President Facilities

House Manager	Carol Flemming

Opening Night Telegrams: The best was from an elderly and ailing friend and life-long theater fan Alex Kahn (also known as a cabaret artist/poet in NYC). He wrote, "I give blood every day at the hospital, but the kind you give is to save Broadway. Love, Alex."

Cady Huffman wrote, "Knock 'em dead."

Fran and Barry Weissler wrote, "Finally a role you can really sink your teeth into."

Opening Night Gifts: There were teeth, skeletons, plastic tarantulas and a four-foot vampire doll. I gave Tom Hewitt a 20-inch Gothic candelabrum and I gave Kelli an ornate nouveau-Victorian silver jewelry box inscribed "Lucy." Kelli and her parents cooked a Mexican dinner for the cast, and we ate it in the alley...good Oklahoma hospitality-—really sweet. The producers of the show gave us all these curious objects that resembled sex toys, which you can plug into the wall and they light up and make bubbles inside-—a sort of deep red night-light with "Dracula" written on them. No one was sure what to make of them, but they were fun.

Celebrity Visitors: Billy Crystal went right up to Tom Hewitt and said "Wow! How did you do THAT!!? How did you do this!? How did you disappear/flip/glide/float...!?" He was fascinated with the effects.

Carol Lawrence came into my dressing room and was obsessed with all my hats, and tried them all on!

Who Got The Gypsy Robe: Megan Sikora

Most Roles: Megan Sikora. She covers all the vampire girls and some nights has had to be two people, and that means she played over 14 roles in one night. She is also the Lucy understudy (she went on when Kelli took a personal day in November), and she is the Mina understudy and she is the dance captain! She is definitely our Wonder Woman.

Backstage Rituals: Tracy Miller, one of the vampire girls, does a nightly imitation of Mariah Carey as she comes down the stairs at "places."

The first floor toilet is "The Meaning of Life Loo"; the walls are covered with quotes that people contribute. It's a place to go tinkle and find the meaning of life. During the election we had political cartoons, and quotes from Eugene McCarthy and Oscar Wilde. There are quotes from Emerson, Rilke, Japenese proverbs, etc. Stephen Henderson put up "Use your good and bad luck as your left and right hands." I put up an Anaïs Nin quote.

I always have plants and flowers in my dressing room, and every Tuesday I take a rose and float it in a vase of water and put it outside my room in the hall for everyone to walk by. On Halloween, I built a Gothic shrine of fear for the kids, with garlic, candles, spooky pictures, and candy.

I jump rope on the stage before half-hour

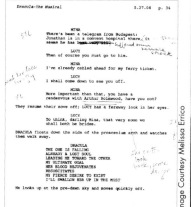

Clockwise from top left: Chuck Wagner in a composite photo with the ghost of David Belasco. Melissa Errico at the opening night cast party. Kelli O'Hara and Tom Hewitt at "Broadway on Broadway" in Times Square. Vampire girls at the opening night cast party. An annotated page from the script. Dressing room on opening night.

while the crew sets up, and they tease me about it.

We call the kids' dressing room the "M&M Room" because the original boys were Matthew and Michael and then we had two Michaels. So the whole place is decorated with M&M designs and empty packages of the candy. It's very festive up there. The little ones have a ritual of singing along with me during "If I Could Fly." They know all my movements and apparently do it full-out while I do. I sometimes think of them upstairs doing it while I am on stage!

Tom Hewitt has a pre-show ritual. We have a statue of a kneeling child holding a skull. As he goes to his first scene, Tom pats the statue on the butt as he goes to his first scene.

Favorite Backstage Moments: Racing from my quick-change after "If I Could Fly." It's an insane 30 seconds.

Favorite Onstage Moments: The best moments are when Kelli and I do a mock Mary Poppins imitation during her waltz "How Do You Choose." We always crack each other up.

For a moment we both sound like Julie Andrews, and we don't know why. Also onstage, the best time is the seduction scene. Tom is grabbing fangs while I swoon after our kiss and while I am trying to not have my boobies fly out of my corset and we are singing post-bite, he is also reaching behind me for the bottle of blood. It is so fast and detailed and important, and Tom and I are such good friends that its nice to execute a sexy moment together while we know it's all about the props!

In-Theatre Gathering Place: The Belasco is really crowded so mostly we all meet in the hallways racing from scene to scene. But off-hours, Darren Ritchie has a TV in his dressing room, which came in especially handy during the famous 2004 World Series. The callboard in the hallway is also a hangout, since there are always interesting letters and messages.

Off-Site Hangout: Red Flame Diner.

Snack Food: With all the corsets and flying harnesses, no one is eating much. There is no room in our clothes!

Mascots: There are vampire toys all over and many bats hang from pipes, some with eyes that light up.

Therapies: I eat Ricolas, Blackcurrent Pastilles and drink Throat-Coat Tea every day. I also have a personal steam inhaler from Vicks that I love. Kelli O'Hara does Pilates in her room every day and I jump rope before the show onstage.

"Carols For A Cure" Carol: "God Rest Ye Merry Gentlemen."

Strange Press Encounters: Everyone wants Tom to bite me in pictures even if we are in street clothes posing in a coffee shop. It's a bit much!

Memorable Stage Door Encounters: I witnessed two women get into an argument over why I killed Dracula. "Why did she have to kill him?" "I think she did what she had to do!" "Was she in a trance?" "Love is a trance!" "No it's not...." I was sort of stunned.

There are always goths and teen-age boys with plastic teeth at the stage door.

Busiest Day At The Box Office: The Saturday night before Halloween.

Heaviest Costumes: My second act wool dress with fur. I hear it's 20 pounds. Tom has a full-length cape he wears when he is upside-down— that must be heavy because it's got metal bars in it so it can open at the end of Act One.

Who Wore The Least: Kelli O'Hara is stripped fully naked at one point, though she is in silhouetted light. I am in a slight slip and do open my bodice downstage on the divan when Dracula is about to bite me. So it depends on which you think is most revealing. Kelli and I do not like to make a big deal out of it. It shows the vulnerability of women in Dracula's power.

Making the press happy: Tom Hewitt chomps Melissa Errico for the cameras on opening night.

Photo by Aubrey Reuben

Who Plays The Most Instruments: Keyboardist Karl Mansfield is the orchestra member with the wildest ride. He invented every sound cue, every music cue, every computerized sound, and he plays keyboards and is an assistant conductor. He spent two workshops and the whole rehearsal process with headphones on, building this show. He is a superhero.

Memorable Directorial Notes: "Don't do anything." Des McAnuff must have said this to everyone at least 50 times. He wanted the play to have a concept of stillness and economy to create suspense. He of course didn't mean it literally. (Or did he?)

Des gave Tom Hewitt a quote that Tom says has driven him mad: "Leave yourself alone."

Nicknames: Chris Hoch calls all the women "My Queen." Darren Ritchie calls Tom Hewitt "Bacon-face" when Tom is dressed as old Dracula in Act One.

Catchphrases: During rehearsals we had a dramaturg, Allison Horsley from La Jolla, worked with us for a week, teaching us extensively about history and vampire lore and the Orient Express and everything about Victorian times. She told us about a university called Nanci University, so we all decided we graduated from there (even though it's not in London and this makes no sense). We became "Team Nanci:" Darren, Melissa, Stephen, Bart, Chris and Shonn. It's the vampire hunter group. We imagine we all had different majors, and Stephen was a professor there. If you say "Team Nanci" at the Belasco, everyone knows the

clan you mean. We are on stage most of Act Two.

Sweethearts: Lynn Bowling, head of wardrobe and Mark Rampmeyer, hair supervisor. They are the heart and soul of keeping us looking good and keeping the machine running. They have to deal with dozens of costumes covered in blood, and get fangs and glow-in-the-dark contact lenses organized. They work non-stop. As does the stage crew since the set is massive. Jeff, who runs the automation, has our lives in his hands, and he is the smartest, most loving man around.

Ghosts: David Belasco does haunt the theater. My dresser Cathy saw him walk into a mirror the other day. She thinks he lives in the mirror on the wall outside my dressing room. One night I forgot my coat and I had turned out the lights in my room. I turned back to get my coat in the dark and someone (David?) turned the small pretty table light on for me to see my way. It was spooky. As I opened the door to leave, as I was walking out, "someone" closed the door behind me. I didn't touch it but watched it move.

Chuck Wagner was David for Halloween. We celebrated David's 150th birthday during previews. We got a cake and sang for him.

I sometimes think I see him in the balcony while I am singing. Or is it the other ghost, the woman with the blue dress? Chuck tells me I resemble her!

Accidents: Once, during tech, the automation of my desk was accidentally set to go nine times as far in the same amount of time. In other words, I suddenly was on a set piece that was going 50 mph. I flew off and so did the furniture. I lightened the moment and said to the crew "Ah, crazy woman driver!"

Later that week, we had the famous flood that delayed our opening. A pipe burst and flooded some of the set and the computers on stage left. The fire department came and, as they walked in and saw the mess, they said "David Belasco strikes again!"

Mistakes on Stage: I stabbed Dracula once and he isn't allowed to die until he can tell that I have done the knife switch (let go the clean one and grab the bloody one). I couldn't find the bloody knife, so after I had stabbed him I had to stare at him to tell him not to die. It felt like forever. Eventually I nodded, "OK, die," and he died.

I'll never forget vampire girl Pamela wearing red curlers during tech, and having to be the ship captain. She was getting ready for a hot date in the real world, and didn't put on her man costume or hide her head! It was so funny to see a dead ship captain hanging from the wheel with this gorgeous woman's body and red curlers.

Correspondent: Melissa Errico, "Mina."

PLAYBILL®

CAST

Tevye's Family

Tevye	HARVEY FIERSTEIN
Golde	ANDREA MARTIN
Tzeitel	SALLY MURPHY
Hodel	LAURA SHOOP
Chava	TRICIA PAOLUCCIO
Shprintze	ALISON WALLA
Bielke	BETSY HOGG

Yente, the Matchmaker .... NANCY OPEL

Papas

Lazar Wolf	DAVID WOHL
Rabbi	YUSEF BULOS
Mordcha	PHILIP HOFFMAN
Avram	MARK LOTITO
Jakov	DAVID ROSSMER
Chaim	BRUCE WINANT

Mamas

Shandel	LORI WILNER
Mirala	ANN VAN CLEAVE
Fredel	RITA HARVEY
Rivka	JOY HERMALYN

Sons

Motel	JOHN CARIANI
Perchik	PAUL ANTHONY STEWART
Mendel	ROBERT WERSINGER

continued on the next page

MINSKOFF THEATRE

UNDER THE DIRECTION OF
JAMES M. NEDERLANDER, JAMES L. NEDERLANDER,
SARA MINSKOFF ALLAN AND THE MINSKOFF FAMILY

JAMES L. NEDERLANDER
STEWART F. LANE/BONNIE COMLEY   HARBOR ENTERTAINMENT
TERRY ALLEN KRAMER   BOB BOYETT/LAWRENCE HOROWITZ   CLEAR CHANNEL ENTERTAINMENT

PRESENT

Harvey Fierstein

in

FIDDLER ON THE ROOF

Based on the Sholom Aleichem stories by special permission of Arnold Perl

Book by	Music by	Lyrics by
Joseph Stein	**Jerry Bock**	**Sheldon Harnick**

Choreography by and Original New York Stage Production Directed by

Jerome Robbins

Originally Produced on the New York Stage by Harold Prince

starring

Andrea Martin

also starring

Christopher Cardona   John Cariani   Patrick Heusinger   Philip Hoffman   Sally Murphy
Tricia Paoluccio   Richard Poe   Laura Shoop   Paul Anthony Stewart   David Wohl
Yusef Bulos   Chris Ghelfi   Betsy Hogg   Mark Lotito   Tom Titone   Alison Walla
David Best   Ward Billeisen   Randy Bobish   Melissa Bohon   Shane Braddock   Enrique Brown   Kristin Carbone
Rachel Coloff   Sean Curley   Rita Harvey   Joy Hermalyn   Keith Kühl   Jeff Lewis   Mark Moreau
Roger Rosen   David Rossmer   Elena Shaddow   Michael Tommer   Francis Toumbakaris   Ann Van Cleave
Robert Wersinger   Lori Wilner   Bruce Winant   Gustavo Wons   Adam Zotovich

and

Nancy Opel

Set Design	Costume Design	Lighting Design	Sound Design
Tom Pye	**Vicki Mortimer**	**Brian MacDevitt**	**Acme Sound Partners**

Hair & Wig Design	Casting by	Music Coordinator	Orchestrations	Additional Orchestrations
David Brian Brown	**Jim Carnahan**	**Michael Keller**	**Don Walker**	**Larry Hochman**

General Manager	Press Agent	Production Manager	Flying Sequences	Production Stage Manager
101 Productions, Ltd.	**Barlow•Hartman**	**Gene O'Donovan**	**ZFX, Inc.**	**Katherine Lee Boyer**

Music Director
Kevin Stites

Musical Staging by
Jonathan Butterell

Directed by

David Leveaux

3/14/05

Wonder of Wonders: Harvey Fierstein (center) as Tevye.

MUSICAL NUMBERS

SETTING

The place: Anatevka, a village in Russia

The time: 1905, on the eve of the revolutionary period

ACT ONE

"Tradition"	Full Company
"Matchmaker"	Tzeitel, Hodel, Chava, Shprintze, Bielke
"If I Were a Rich Man"	Tevye
"Sabbath Prayer"	Family and Villagers
"To Life"	Tevye, Lazar, Village Men
"Miracle of Miracles"	Motel
"Tevye's Dream"	Full Company
"Sunrise, Sunset"	Family and Villagers

ACT TWO

"Now I Have Everything"	Perchik, Hodel
"Do You Love Me?"	Tevye, Golde
"Topsy-Turvy"	Yente, Rivka and Mirala
"Far From the Home I Love"	Hodel
"Chavaleh"	Tevye
"Anatevka"	Family and Villagers

This production is dedicated to our fathers.

Cast Continued

Yussel	MARK MOREAU
Yitzuk	RANDY BOBISH
Label	JEFF LEWIS
Shloime	FRANCIS TOUMBAKARIS

Daughters

Anya	MELISSA BOHON
Surcha	ELENA SHADDOW

Nachum, the Beggar ..... TOM TITONE
Fiddler ..... CHRISTOPHER CARDONA
Boy ..... MICHAEL TOMMER
(Tues. – Sat. eves., Sat. mat.)
Boy ..... SEAN CURLEY
(Wed. and Sun. mats.)
Constable ..... RICHARD POE

Russians

Fyedka	PATRICK HEUSINGER
Sasha	ADAM ZOTOVICH
Vladek	WARD BILLEISEN
Vladimir	KEITH KÜHL
Boris	SHANE BRADDOCK

Grandma Tzeitel ..... ELENA SHADDOW
Fruma Sarah ..... JOY HERMALYN
Bottle Dancers ..... RANDY BOBISH
CHRIS GHELFI, JEFF LEWIS,
FRANCIS TOUMBAKARIS,
ROBERT WERSINGER

SWINGS

KRISTIN CARBONE, RACHEL COLOFF,
MARK MOREAU, ROGER ROSEN,
GUSTAVO WONS

UNDERSTUDIES

For Tevye: PHILIP HOFFMAN, MARK LOTITO; for Golde: ANN VAN CLEAVE, LORI WILNER; for Yente: RACHEL COLOFF, LORI WILNER; for Tzeitel: KRISTIN CARBONE, RITA HARVEY; for Hodel: RITA HARVEY, ELENA SHADDOW; for Chava: MELISSA BOHON, ALISON WALLA; for Shprintze/Bielke: MELISSA BOHON, ELENA SHADDOW; for Motel: JEFF LEWIS, DAVID ROSSMER; for Perchik: DAVID ROSSMER, RANDY BOBISH; for Fyedka: WARD BILLEISEN, SHANE BRADDOCK; for Lazar Wolf: PHILIP HOFFMAN, MARK LOTITO; for Constable: MARK LOTITO, BRUCE WINANT; for Fiddler: DAVID ROSSMER, ENTCHO TODOROV; for Rabbi: TOM TITONE, BRUCE WINANT; for Mendel: RANDY BOBISH, ROGER ROSEN; for Mordcha: TOM TITONE, BRUCE WINANT; for Avram: RANDY BOBISH, TOM TITONE, ROGER ROSEN; for Boy: SEAN CURLEY, DAVID BEST

Photo by Carol Rosegg

Harvey Fierstein and Andrea Martin as Tevye and Golde.

FIDDLER ON THE ROOF ORCHESTRA
Conductor: KEVIN STITES
Associate Conductor: Charles duChateau

Music Coordinator: Michael Keller
Onstage Clarinet Solo: Jonathan Levine

Concertmaster: Martin Agee
Violins: Cenovia Cummins, Conrad Harris, Heidi Stubner, Entcho Todorov
Violas: Debra Shufelt, Maxine Roach
Cellos: Peter Sachon, Charles duChateau
Lead Trumpet: Tim Schadt
Trumpets: Wayne duMaine, Joseph Reardon;
Trombones/Euphonium: Ben Harrington
Flutes: Brian Miller
Oboe: Matthew Dine
Clarinet/Flute: Jonathan Levine
Clarinet/Flute: Martha Hyde
Bassoon: Marc Goldberg
French Horns: Larry DiBello, Peter Schoettler
Drums/Percussion: Billy Miller
Bass: Peter Donovan
Accordion/Celeste: Elaine Lord
Guitar/Mandolin/Lute: Greg Utzig

Harvey Fierstein
Tevye

Andrea Martin
Golde

Nancy Opel
Yente

Yusef Bulos
Rabbi

Christopher Cardona
Fiddler

John Cariani
Motel

Chris Ghelfi
Ensemble

Patrick Heusinger
Fyedka

Philip Hoffman
Mordcha

Betsy Hogg
Bielke

Mark Lotito
Avram

Sally Murphy
Tzeitel

Tricia Paoluccio
Chava

Richard Poe
Constable

Laura Shoop
Hodel

Paul Anthony Stewart
Perchik

Tom Titone
Nachum

Alison Walla
Shprintze

Robert Wersinger
Mendel

David Wohl
Lazar Wolf

David Best
Boy Understudy

Ward Billeisen
Vladek/Russian Dancer

Randy Bobish
Yitzuk/Bottle Dancer

Melissa Bohon
Anya

Shane Braddock
Boris/Russian Dancer

Enrique Brown
Ensemble

Kristin Carbone
Swing

Rachel Coloff
Swing

Sean Curley
Boy Understudy

Rita Harvey
Fredel

Joy Hermalyn
Rivka/Fruma Sarah

Keith Kühl
Vladimir/Russian Dancer

Jeff Lewis
Label/Bottle Dancer

Roger Rosen
Swing

David Rossmer
Jakov

Fiddler On The Roof

Elena Shaddow
Surcha/Grandma

Entcho Todorov
Fiddler Understudy

Michael Tommer
Boy

Francis Toumbakaris
Shloime/Bottle Dancer

Ann Van Cleave
Mirala

Lori Wilner
Shandel

Bruce Winant
Chaim

Gustavo Wons
Swing

Adam Zotovich
Sasha/Russian Dancer

David Leveaux
Director

Joseph Stein
Book

Jerry Bock
Music

Sheldon Harnick
Lyrics

Jerome Robbins
Choreographer/ Original Director

Tom Pye
Scenic Design

Brian MacDevitt
Lighting Design

Tom Clark, Mark Menard, and Nevin Steinberg (Acme Sound Partners)
Sound Design

David Brian Brown
Wig/Hair Design

Michael Keller
Music Coordinator

Kate Wilson Maré
Dialect Coach

Gustavo Zajac
Associate Musical Staging

Jim Carnahan
Casting Director

James L. Nederlander
Producer

Stewart F. Lane and Bonnie Comley
Producers

David Broser and Aaron Harnick
Producers

Terry Allen Kramer
Producer

Alumni

Stephen Lee Anderson
Constable

David Ayers
Fyedka

Enrique Brown
Yussel

Nick Danielson
Fiddler

Molly Ephraim
Bielke

113

Randy Graff
Golde

Ben Hartley
Vladimir/Russian Dancer

Laura Michelle Kelly
Hodel

Gina Lamparella
Swing

Kristin Marks
Swing

Lea Michele
Shprintze

Alfred Molina
Tevye

Craig Ramsay
Boris/Russian Dancer

Jonathan Sharp
Sasha/Russian Dancer

Antoine Silverman
Fiddler Understudy

Haviland Stillwell
Surcha/Grandma Tzeitel

Barbara Tirrell
Shandel

Marsha Waterbury
Mirala

Transfer Students

Dana Lynn Caruso
Fredel

Alphonse Paolillo
Boy Understudy

Paul Anthony Stewart
Perchik

Peter Matthew Smith
Motel

Michael Therriault
Motel

A Blessing on Our House: Andrea Martin and Harvey Fierstein.

Photo by Carol Rosegg

Stage Management
(L-R):Katherine Lee Boyer (Production Stage Manager), Matt Stern (Assistant Stage Manager), Jenny Dewer (Stage Manager)

Electricians, Lighting, Sounds and Props
(L-R): Steve Speer (Assistant House Electrician), Ron Martin (Head Electrician), Matt Lavaia (House Props), Tim Donovan (Spot Operator), Dave Lynch (Spot Operator), Mike Lynch (House Electrician)

Company Management
(L-R): Alex Gushin (Assistant Company Manager), Gregg Arst (Company Manager).

Wardrobe
Front Row (L-R): Hilda Garcia-Suli (Dresser), Wendall Goings (Asst. Wardrobe Supervisor), Dawn Reynolds (Dresser), Timothy Greer (Wardrobe Supervisor)
Back Row (L-R): Theresa Distasi (Dresser), William Hubner (Dresser), James Cavanaugh (Dresser)

Photos by Ben Strothmann

Hair Supervisors
(L-R): Joel Hawkins (Assistant Hair Supervisor), Richard Orton (Hair Supervisor)

Orchestra

Front Row (L-R): Eugene Briskin (Cello), Jonathan Levine (Clarinet), Jeff Nichols (Woodwinds), Kevin Stites (Musical Director), Joe Reardon (Trumpet)
Back Row (L-R): Martin Agee (Violin), Entcho Todorov (Violin), Wayne DuMaine (Trumpet), Ben Herrington (Trombone), Charles duChateau (Cello), Billy Miller (Percussion), Paul Molloy (Guitar), Brian Miller (Flute) and Maxine Roach (Viola).

Photos by Ben Strohmann

Front-of-House Staff

First Row (L-R): Cheryl Bud, Laura Auland, Florence Coulter, Caryl Metner
Second Row (L-R): Chris Quantana (Assistant House Manager), Marion Mooney, Meryl Rosner, Joanne Shannon, Elaine Healy, Jennie Andrea, Nancy Diaz
Third Row (L-R): Linda Rajotte, Mike Diaz and David Vaughn (House Manager).

STAFF FOR **FIDDLER ON THE ROOF**

GENERAL MANAGEMENT
101 PRODUCTIONS, LTD.
Wendy Orshan   Jeffrey M. Wilson
David Auster

COMPANY MANAGER
Gregg Arst

GENERAL PRESS REPRESENTATIVE
BARLOW•HARTMAN
John Barlow   Michael Hartman
Wayne Wolfe   Andrew Snyder

PRODUCTION MANAGEMENT
Aurora Productions, Inc.
Gene O'Donovan
Melissa Mazdra   Tony Menditto
W. Benjamin Heller II

CASTING
Jim Carnahan, CSA
J.V. Mercanti, Associate

Production Stage Manager	Katherine Lee Boyer
Stage Manager	Jenny Dewar
Assistant Stage Manager	Matthew Aaron Stern
Assistant Company Manager	Erica Norgaard

ASSOCIATE MUSICAL STAGING ..GUSTAVO ZAJAC

Assistant Director	Eli Gonda
Choreographic Consultant	Newton Cole
Dance Captain	Roger Rosen
Dialect Coach	Kate Wilson
Associate Scenic Designer	Larry Gruber
First Assistant Scenic Designer	Dawn Robyn Petrilk
Assistant Scenic Designers	John Deegan, Todd Potter, Amy Smith
Assistants to Mr. Pye	Alan Bain, Gaetane Bertol, Daniela Galli, Joanie Schlafer
Associate Costume Designer	Tracy L. Christensen
Assistant Costume Designers	Lynette Mauro, Brian J. Bustos, Amy Clark
Assistant to Ms. Mortimer	Courtney Logan
Costume Intern	Jennifer Fischer
Assistant Lighting Designers	Charles Pennebaker, Anne E. McMills
Moving Light Programmer	David Arch
Assistant to Mr. MacDevitt	Jennifer Schriever
Assistant Sound Designer	Jeffrey Yoshi Lee

MAKEUP DESIGNER ..RANDY HOUSTON MERCER

Production Carpenter	Hank Hale
Assistant Carpenters	Donald Roberts, Erik Yans
Automation	Jason Volpe
Production Electrician	Michael S. LoBue
Head Electrician	Ron L. Martin
Assistant Electrician	Brian Collins
Production Props Supervisor	Robert G. Adams
Assistant Props	Robert H. Brenner
Props Researcher/Purchaser	Kathy Fabian
Assistant Props Researcher	Eliza Brown
Production Sound Supervisor	Scott Sanders
Sound	Brad Gyorgak

Wardrobe Supervisor	Timothy Greer
Assistant Wardrobe Supervisor	Wendall Goings
Mr. Fierstein's Dresser	Charlie Catanese
Dressers	James Cavanaugh, Mark Flesher, Jackie S. Freeman, Hilda Garcia-Suli, Victoria Grecki, William Jones, R.J. Malkmus, Kelly Smith
Hair Supervisor	Richard Orton
Assistant Hair Supervisor	Joel Hawkins
Additional Music Copying	Emily Grishman
Music Preparation/	Katherine Edmonds, Emily Grishman
Incidental Music Arrangements	Kevin Stites
Rehearsal Pianists	Brad Garside, Paul Raiman, Matthew Eisenstein
Production Assistants	Jeff Cureton, Karyn Meek, James Valletti
Assistants to Mr. Lane & Ms. Comley	Jeanine Holiday, Diane Prince
Assistant to Mr. Broser & Mr. Harnick	Lauren Schnipper

HARBOR ENTERTAINMENT THANKS
Josh Kagan,
Barry Funt, Robert Bertsch,
Jeff Ostrow of URL Productions,
Eric Brown, Rufus Collins, Steve Herz

Assistant to Ms. Kramer	Sara Shannon
Assistant to Mr. Boyett	Diane Murphy
Assistant to Dr. Horowitz	Don Schnagl
Legal Counsel	Levine, Plotkin & Menin LLP/ Loren Plotkin, Susan Mindell
Accountant	Rosenberg, Neuwirth & Kushner/ Chris Cacace, Patricia Pedersen
Advertising	Serino-Coyne/ Angelo Desimini, Jennifer Fleckner
Marketing Associate	Leanne Schanzer Promotions, Inc./ Leanne Schanzer, Jennifer Savage, Christine Berrios
101 Productions, Ltd. Staff	Christine Hale, Sara Katz, Clark Mims, Heidi Neven, Mary Six Rupert, Aaron Slavik
Press Associates	Leslie Baden, Dennis Crowley, Jon Dimond, Carol Fineman, Rick Miramontez, Mark Pino, Miguel Raya, Patricia Sewruk
Press Office Manager	Bethany Larsen
Production Photographer	Carol Rosegg
Banking	JP Morgan Chase/ Stephanie Dalton, Michele Gibbons
Insurance	DeWitt Stern, Inc./ Peter Shoemaker, Jennifer Brown
Travel	Altour International, Inc./ Melissa Casal
Housing	Maison International/ Marie Claire Martineau
Children's Tutoring	On Location Education/ Marsha Kobre Anderson, Ph.D.
Children's Guardians	Martin Tommer, Lisa Curley, Angela Best
Immigration	Traffic Control Group, Inc./ David King
Theatre Displays	King Displays, Inc.

Concessions	SFX Theatrical Merchandising/ Larry Turk
Payroll Services	Castellana Services, Inc.
Promotional Merchandising	George Fenmore/ More Merchandising International

CREDITS
Scenery by Hudson Scenic Studio, Inc.
Lighting equipment from Fourth Phase.
Sound equipment from ProMix.
Flying sequences provided by ZFX, Inc.
Costume construction by Tricorne, Barbara Matera, Ltd.,
Carlos Campos and Grace Costume.
Millinery by Lynne Mackey.
Custom footwear by J.C.
Theatrical and handmade shoes by Fred Longtin. Custom
knitwear by Jeff Blumenkrantz and Vanessa Hopkins.
Craftwork for the Dream by Marian J. Hose and Arnold
Levine. Custom dyeing by Gene Mignola and Dye-Namix.
Musician costumes constructed
by Michael-Jon Costumes and Scafati.
Costume distressing and painting by
Martin Izquierdo Studio.
Fruma Sarah costume painted by Hochi Asiatico.
Percussion instruments by Kettles & Co.
Down pillows courtesy of www.downstore.com.
Pottery by Victoria Gold and Francisco Staffanell.
Prop stitchery by Toni Thompson.
Emer'gen-C super energy booster provided by Alacer Corp.
Ricola products used.
Champagne bottles courtesy of Korbel Champagne Cellars.
Additional set and hand props courtesy
of George Fenmore, Inc.
In St. Petersburg, thanks to Alexey Korovin
and the Pine Studio Vendors:
Peter Molchanov, Peter Sirota and Igor Diakov.
Costume designer's thanks to Tara L. Hawkes, Kaufman
Army/Navy, Helen Uffner, Bec Chippendale, Stephen
Merkel, Cosprop and Trouvaille Francaise.
Havdala Candles provided by the
Judaica House, Ltd., Teaneck, NJ.
Light bulbs courtesy of Just Bulbs, the lightbulb store.
Milk products generously donated by Parmalot.

Make-up provided by
M•A•C

FIDDLER ON THE ROOF
rehearsed at New 42nd Street Studios

✷N✷
NEDERLANDER

Chairman	James M. Nederlander
President	James L. Nederlander

Executive Vice President
Nick Scandalios

Vice President Corporate Development Charlene S. Nederlander	Senior Vice President Labor Relations Herschel Waxman
Vice President Jim Boese	Chief Financial Officer Freida Sawyer Belviso

www.nederlander.org

HOUSE STAFF FOR THE MINSKOFF THEATRE

House Manager	David Vaughn
Treasurer	Nicholas Loiacono
Assistant Treasurer	Cheryl Loiacono
House Carpenter	Gary Bender
House Electrician	Michael Lynch
House Propertymaster	Frank Lavaia

Photos by Aubrey Reuben

Above left: director David Leveaux and Tony nominee John Cariani. Above right: Harvey Fierstein takes a curtain call on his opening night as Tevye.

The cast gathers to congratulate the production's first Tevye, Alfred Molina, as his caricature is hung in Sardi's restaurant.

Backstage Ritual: I always practice Bach in the dressing room before the show. I also do this up on the roof before the show begins.

"Gypsy Of The Year" Sketch: "The Circle L'Chaim" by Jonathan Sharp.

"Carols For A Cure" Song: "Auld Lang Syne."

"Easter Bonnet" Sketch: "The Other Side" by Malou Airaudo.

Favorite Therapy: I like to do stretches. Other than that, a nice glass of vodka from the freezer is good therapy.

Best Opening Night Telegram or Note: There are many. The ones from the creators of the show, Jerry Bock, Sheldon Harnick and Joe Stein are the ones I'll treasure most. Jerry is a wonderful man and his music is at the heart of every show.

Funniest Backstage Moment: I was walking in the wings with my fiddle case during one show and, without knowing it, one of the ladies' wigs (which was sitting on a bench) got caught on the end of the case. I put the case in my dressing room and went on with the show. Much later in the show, I went to get the fiddle case and discovered a large clump of hair on the end of it. Apparently the hair department had been looking around frantically for the wig for quite some time.

Favorite Moment In The Show: There are many, but my favorite is dancing with the entire cast onstage at the end of the show.

Correspondent: Nick Danielson, "The Fiddler"

Above: lyricist Sheldon Harnick, librettist Joseph Stein and composer Jerry Bock at the party welcoming Fierstein to the cast.

Above: Harvey Fierstein and Andrea Martin celebrate their opening night as Tevye and Golde. Right: Cast members perform their "Gypsy of the Year" sketch, "The Circle L'Chaim."

PLAYBILL®

CAST

Dancers	Jorge Torres,
	Marcela Durán,
	Guillermina Quiroga,
	Gabriel Ortega, Sandra Bootz,
	Natalia Hills, Francisco Forquera,
	Verónica Gardella, Marcelo Bernadaz,
	Carlos Vera, Laura Marcarie,
	Melina Brufman,
	Claudio González,
	Mariela Franganillo,
	Juan Paulo Horvath, Alejandra Gutty
Singer	Miguel Velázquez
Pianist	Jorge Vernieri

ORCHESTRA

Orchestra Director: Victor Lavallén

Bandoneons—Victor Lavallén, Santos Maggi,
Jorge Trivisonno, Carlos Niesi

Violins—Rodion Boshoer, Abraham Becker

Viola—Alexander Sechkin

Cello—Patricio Villarejo

Bass—Pablo Motta

Piano—Jorge Vernieri

Keyboard—Gustavo Casenave

☺ SAM S. SHUBERT THEATRE

225 West 44th Street
A Shubert Organization Theatre

Gerald Schoenfeld, *Chairman*   Philip J. Smith, *President*

Robert E. Wankel, *Executive Vice President*

Jack Utsick Presents / BACI Worldwide, LLC
Presents

Luis Bravo's
FOREVER TANGO

Orchestra Director
VICTOR LAVALLÉN

Dancers
JORGE TORRES
MARCELA DURÁN & GUILLERMINA QUIROGA
GABRIEL ORTEGA & SANDRA BOOTZ
CARLOS VERA & LAURA MARCARIE
FRANCISCO FORQUERA & NATALIA HILLS
MARCELO BERNADAZ & VERONICA GARDELLA
CLAUDIO GONZALEZ & MELINA BRUFMAN
ALEJANDRA GUTTY & JUAN PAULO HORVATH

Singer
MIGUEL VELAZQUEZ

Musicians
Bandoneons: VICTOR LAVALLÉN   SANTOS MAGGI   JORGE TRIVISONNO   CARLOS NIESI
Violins: RODION BOSHOER ABRAHAM BECKER   Viola: ALEXANDER SECHKIN
Cello: PATRICIO VILLAREJO   Bass: PABLO MOTTA
Piano: JORGE VERNIERI   Keyboard: GUSTAVO CASENAVE

Lighting Design	Costume Design	Sound Design	Hair and Make-Up Design
LUIS BRAVO	**ARGEMIRA AFFONSO**	**MIKE MILLER**	**JEAN LUC DON VITO**

General Manager	Press Representative	Marketing
MARY-EVELYN CARD	**RICHARD KORNBERG & ASSOCIATES** **RICK MIRAMONTEZ**	**RENEE MILLER MUTCHNIK**

Production Manager	Stage Manager
CARLOS DIAZ	**JORGE GONZÁLEZ**

Choreography by
THE DANCERS

Created and Directed by
LUIS BRAVO

7/24/04

Natalia Hills and Francisco Forquera

Photo by Joan Marcus

Forever Tango

MUSICAL NUMBERS

ACT ONE

Preludio del Bandoneón y la Noche	Performed by Sandra Bootz & Gabriel Ortega
Overture	Orchestra
El Suburbio	Company
A Los Amigos	Orchestra
Derecho Viejo	Performed by Francisco Forquera & Natalia Hills
Los Mareados	Performed by Miguel Velázquez
La Mariposa	Performed by Carlos Vera & Laura Marcarie
Comme I'll Faut	Performed by Claudio González & Melina Brufman
Berretín	Orchestra
La Tablada	Performed by Marcelo Bernadaz & Verónica Gardella
Negracha	Performed by Alejandra Gutty & Juan Paulo Horvath
Responso	Orchestra
Oro y Plata *Candombe*	Company

ACT TWO

Vampitango	Performed by Sandra Bootz & Gabriel Ortega
Romance entre el Bandoneón mi Alma	Performed by Jorge Torres & Guillermina Quiroga
Payadora	Orchestra
Quejas de Bandoneón	Performed by Carlos Vera & Laura Marcarie
Gallo Ciego	Performed by Francisco Forquera & Natalia Hills
Zum	Performed by Alejandra Gutty & Juan Paulo Horvath
El Día que me Quieras	Performed by Miguel Velázquez
Tanguera	Performed by Claudio González & Melina Brufman
La Cumparsita	Performed by Francisco Forguera & Natalia Hills
	Alejandra Gutty & Juan Paulo Horvath
	Carlos Vera & Laura Marcarie
Jealousy	Orchestra
Felicia	Performed by Marcelo Bernadaz & Verónica Gardella
Preludio a mi Viejo	Orchestra
Romance del Bandoneón y la Noche	Performed by Sandra Bootz & Gabriel Ortega
A Evaristo Carriego	Performed by Jorge Torres & Marcela Durán
Finale	Company

Luis Bravo
Creator / Director

Photo by Joan Marcus

Melina Brufman and Claudio González

Jack Utsick
Presenter

Gregory Young
Presenter

42nd Street

First Preview: April 4, 2001
Closed: January 2, 2005

Opened: May 2, 2001
31 Previews and 1,524 Performances

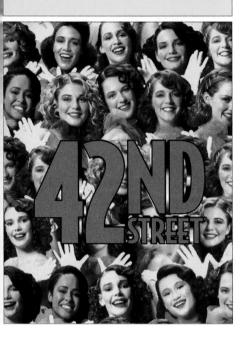

PLAYBILL®

FORD CENTER FOR THE PERFORMING ARTS
A CLEAR CHANNEL THEATRE

Dodger Stage Holding
and Joop van den Ende
present

Patrick Cassidy   Blair Ross

in

42ND STREET

Book by
Michael & Mark
Stewart   Bramble

Music by
Harry
Warren

Lyrics by
Al
Dubin

Based on the novel by Bradford Ropes

Original Direction and Dances by
Gower Champion

also starring

Patti Mariano   Frank Root
David Elder

Chris Clay   Michael Dantuono
Richard Pruitt   Alana Salvatore

Steve Luker
Greg Beck

and

Nadine Isenegger

with

Will Armstrong   Kelli Barclay   Jeremy Benton   Becky Berstler   Graham Bowen
Michael Clowers   Maryam Myika Day   Alexander DeJong   Nikki Della Penta   Angie Everett
Luis Figueroa   Melissa Giattino   Susan Haefner   Brad Hampton   Merritt Tyler Hawkins
Kolina Janneck   Sarah L. Johnson   Jennifer Jones   Angela Kahle   Regan Kays
Dontee Kiehn   Cara Kjellman   Jessica Kostival   Alison Levenberg   Gavin Lodge
Brian J. Marcum   Jennifer Marquardt   Amy Miller   Amy Palomino   Tony Palomino   Wes Pope
Wendy Rosoff   John James Scacchetti   Kelly Sheehan   Kristyn D. Smith   Vanessa Sonon
Erin Stoddard   Jonathan Taylor   Elisa Van Duyne   Erika Vaughn   Mike Warshaw   Merrill West

Scenery Design
Douglas W. Schmidt

Costume Design
Roger Kirk

Lighting Design
Paul Gallo

Sound Design
Peter Fitzgerald

Production Stage Manager
Tripp Phillips

Casting
Jay Binder

Wigs & Hair Design
David H. Lawrence

Musical Adaptation, Arrangements
& Additional Orchestrations

Musical Direction
Todd Ellison

Conductor
Fred Lassen

Donald Johnston

Orchestrations
Philip J. Lang

Music Coordinator
John Miller

Executive Producer
Dodger Management Group

Technical Supervisor
Peter Fulbright

Marketing Consultant
Margery Singer

Press Representative
Boneau/Bryan-Brown

Musical Staging and New Choreography by
Randy Skinner

Directed by
Mark Bramble

The producers wish to express their appreciation to
Theatre Development Fund for its support of this production.

12/14/04

CAST
(in order of appearance)

Andy Lee	CHRIS CLAY
Maggie Jones	PATTI MARIANO
Bert Barry	FRANK ROOT
Mac	STEVE LUKER
Phyllis	ANGELA KAHLE
Lorraine	KELLY SHEEHAN
Diane	MERRITT TYLER HAWKINS
Annie	ALANA SALVATORE
Ethel	SUSAN HAEFNER
Billy Lawlor	DAVID ELDER
Peggy Sawyer	NADINE ISENEGGER
Oscar	GREG BECK
Julian Marsh	PATRICK CASSIDY
Dorothy Brock	BLAIR ROSS
Abner Dillon	RICHARD PRUITT
Dorothy's "Shadow Waltz" Partner	GRAHAM BOWEN
Pat Denning	MICHAEL DANTUONO
Waiters	BRIAN J. MARCUM, BRAD HAMPTON, MIKE WARSHAW
Peggy's "Habit" Dance Partner	MICHAEL CLOWERS
Thugs	STEVE LUKER, GAVIN LODGE
"Dames" Rehearsal Dancers	MICHAEL CLOWERS, BRIAN J. MARCUM, WES POPE, JONATHAN TAYLOR

continued on the next page

Hear the Beat of Dancing Feet: Shirley Jones and son Patrick Cassidy played Dorothy Brock and Julian Marsh for part of the season.

42nd Street

MUSICAL NUMBERS

TIME: 1933

The action takes place in New York City and Philadelphia

ACT ONE

Overture: ....Orchestra

Scene 1:   Stage of the 42nd Street Theatre, New York City
    "Audition" ....Andy Lee and Ensemble
    "Young and Healthy" ....Billy Lawlor and Peggy Sawyer
    "Shadow Waltz" ....Maggie Jones, then Dorothy Brock and Ensemble

Scene 2:   The Gypsy Tea Kettle Restaurant
    "Go Into Your Dance" ....Maggie, Annie, Peggy, Phyllis, Lorraine and Andy

Scene 3:   Stage of the 42nd Street Theatre
    "You're Getting To Be a Habit With Me" ....Dorothy, Billy, Peggy and Ensemble

Scene 4:   Dorothy Brock's Dressing Room

Scene 5:   Stage of the 42nd Street Theatre
    "Getting Out of Town" ....Full Company

Scene 6:   The Arch Street Theatre, Philadelphia
    "Dames" ....Billy and Men
    "Keep Young and Beautiful" ....Maggie, Bert Barry and Girls
    "Dames" (continued) ....Full Company

Scene 7:   Regency Club and Dorothy Brock's Hotel Suite
    "I Only Have Eyes for You" ....Dorothy

Scene 8:   Opening Night of "Pretty Lady" at the Arch Street Theatre, Philadelphia
    "I Only Have Eyes for You" (continued) ....Billy and Girls
    "We're in the Money" ....Annie, Peggy, Lorraine, Phyllis, Billy and Ensemble
    Act One Finale ....Dorothy and Company

ACT TWO

Entr'Acte: ....Orchestra

Scene 1:   A Backstage Corridor at the Arch Street Theatre, Philadelphia ....Fifteen minutes later

Scene 2:   Dressing Rooms at the Arch Street Theatre
    "Sunny Side to Every Situation" ....Annie and Ensemble

Scene 3:   Backstage Corridor at the Arch Street Theatre

Scene 4:   Broad Street Station, Philadelphia
    "Lullaby of Broadway" ....Julian Marsh and Full Company
    "Getting Out of Town" (reprise) ....Bert, Maggie and Company

Scene 5:   Stage of the 42nd Street Theatre, New York City
    Montage ....Julian, Andy, Peggy and Ensemble

Scene 6:   Peggy's Dressing Room
    "About a Quarter to Nine" ....Dorothy and Peggy

Scene 7:   The Opening Night of "Pretty Lady"
    Overture ....Orchestra
    "With Plenty of Money and You" ....Peggy and Men
    "Shuffle Off to Buffalo" ....Bert, Annie, Maggie and Girls
    "42nd Street" ....Peggy, Billy and Ensemble

Scene 8:   Stage of the 42nd Street Theatre
    "42nd Street" (reprise) ....Julian
    Finale ....Full Company

Additional lyrics by Johnny Mercer and Mort Dixon

ORCHESTRA

CONDUCTOR–FRED LASSEN
Associate Conductor–Matthew Sklar
Assistant Conductor–Matt Eisenstein
Woodwinds–Michael Migliore, Ken Hitchcock,
Dave Pietro, Tom Christensen, Roger Rosenberg,
Andrew Drelles, Scott Shachter; Trumpets–Tony
Gorruso, Don Downs, Joe Mosello, Ravi Best;
Trombones–Mark Patterson, Steve Armour, Mike
Christianson; French Horns–Theresa MacDonnell,
Leise Anschuetz, Michael Ishii; Bass–John Arbo;
Guitar–Scott Kuney; Harp–Victoria Drake;
Drums–Tony Tedesco; Percussion–Kory Grossman;
Piano–Matthew Sklar
Music Coordinator–John Miller
Additional Vocal Arrangements–Donald Johnston

Doctor...STEVE LUKER
"42nd Street Ballet" Sailors ...MICHAEL CLOWERS,
    WES POPE
"42nd Street Ballet" Nifties ....DONTEE KIEHN,
    KELLY SHEEHAN
"42nd Street Ballet" Thief .....JONATHAN TAYLOR

ENSEMBLE

WILL ARMSTRONG, BECKY BERSTLER, GRAHAM BOWEN, MICHAEL CLOWERS, MARYAM MYIKA DAY, ALEXANDER DeJONG, NIKKI DELLA PENTA, ANGIE EVERETT, LUIS FIGUEROA, MELISSA GIATTINO, SUSAN HAEFNER, BRAD HAMPTON, MERRITT TYLER HAWKINS, KOLINA JANNECK, SARAH L. JOHNSON, JENNIFER JONES, ANGELA KAHLE, REGAN KAYS, DONTEE KIEHN, JESSICA KOSTIVAL, ALISON LEVENBERG, GAVIN LODGE, BRIAN J. MARCUM, JENNIFER MARQUARDT, AMY MILLER, AMY PALOMINO, WES POPE, WENDY ROSOFF, JOHN JAMES SCACCHETTI, KELLY SHEEHAN, KRISTYN D. SMITH, VANESSA SONON, ERIN STODDARD, JONATHAN TAYLOR, ERIKA VAUGHN, MIKE WARSHAW

Assistant Choreographer/Dance Captain:
KELLI BARCLAY

Assistant Dance Captain:
CARA KJELLMAN

UNDERSTUDIES

For Julian Marsh–MICHAEL DANTUONO, GAVIN LODGE; Dorothy Brock–JESSICA KOSTIVAL, ELISA VAN DUYNE; Peggy Sawyer–VANESSA SONON, ERIN STODDARD; Billy Lawlor–JEREMY BENTON, GAVIN LODGE; Maggie Jones–MELISSA GIATTINO, SUSAN HAEFNER; Bert Barry–STEVE LUKER, JONATHAN TAYLOR; Andy Lee–TONY PALOMINO, JONATHAN TAYLOR; Annie–BECKY BERSTLER, SUSAN HAEFNER; Pat Denning–ALEXANDER DeJONG, GAVIN LODGE; Abner Dillon–MICHAEL DANTUONO, STEVE LUKER; Mac/Thug/Doctor–WILL ARMSTRONG, MIKE WARSHAW; Phyllis–NIKKI DELLA PENTA, ELISA VAN DUYNE; Lorraine–REGAN KAYS, ERIN STODDARD.

SWINGS

KELLI BARCLAY, JEREMY BENTON, CARA KJELLMAN, TONY PALOMINO, ELISA VAN DUYNE, MERRILL WEST; Partial Swings: MELISSA GIATTINO, BRIAN J. MARCUM, JENNIFER MARQUARDT, JOHN JAMES SCACCHETTI, ERIKA VAUGHN

42nd Street

Patrick Cassidy
Julian Marsh

Blair Ross
Dorothy Brock

Nadine Isenegger
Peggy Sawyer

Patti Mariano
Maggie Jones

Frank Root
Bert Barry

David Elder
Billy Lawlor

Chris Clay
Andy Lee

Michael Dantuono
Pat Denning

Richard Pruitt
Abner Dillon

Alana Salvatore
Annie

Steve Luker
Mac/Thug/Doctor

Greg Beck
Oscar

Will Armstrong
Ensemble

Kelli Barclay
*Asst Choreographer/
Dance Captain/
Swing*

Jeremy Benton
Swing

Becky Berstler
Ensemble

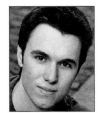
Graham Bowen
Ensemble

Michael Clowers
Ensemble

Maryam Myika Day
Ensemble

Alexander DeJong
Ensemble

Nikki Della Penta
Ensemble

Angie Everett
Ensemble

Luis Figueroa
Ensemble

Melissa Giattino
Ensemble

Susan Haefner
Ethel/Ensemble

Brad Hampton
Waiter/Ensemble

Merritt Tyler Hawkins
Diane/Ensemble

Kolina Janneck
Ensemble

Sarah L. Johnson
Ensemble

Jennifer Jones
Ensemble

Angela Kahle
Phyllis/Ensemble

Regan Kays
Ensemble

Dontee Kiehn
Ensemble

Cara Kjellman
*Asst. Dance
Captain/Swing*

Jessica Kostival
Ensemble

42nd Street

Alison Levenberg
Ensemble

Gavin Lodge
Thug/Ensemble

Brian J. Marcum
Waiter/Ensemble

Jennifer Marquardt
Ensemble

Amy Miller
Ensemble

Amy Palomino
Ensemble

Tony Palomino
Swing

Wes Pope
Ensemble

Wendy Rosoff
Ensemble

John James
Scacchetti
Ensemble

Kelly Sheehan
Lorraine/Ensemble

Kristyn D. Smith
Ensemble

Vanessa Sonon
Ensemble

Erin Stoddard
Ensemble

Jonathan Taylor
Ensemble

Elisa Van Duyne
Swing

Erika Vaughn
Ensemble

Mike Warshaw
Waiter/Ensemble

Merrill West
Swing

Mark Bramble
Director/Co-Author

Randy Skinner
Choreographer

Michael Stewart
Co-Author

Gower Champion
*Director &
Choreographer of
original 42nd Street*

Douglas W.
Schmidt
Scenic Designer

Roger Kirk
Costume Designer

Paul Gallo
Lighting Designer

Ted Ellison
Music Director

Fred Lassen
Conductor

John Miller
Music Coordinator

Joop van den Ende
Producer

42nd Street

42nd Street Alumni

Brad Aspel
Andy Lee

Sara Brians
Assistant Dance Captain/Swing

Cindy Shadel
Ensemble

Celina Carvajal
Annie

Kristen Gaetz
Phyllis/Ensemble

Shirley Jones
Dorothy Brock

Amy F. Karlein
Ensemble

Todd Lattimore
Swing

Sarah McLellan
Swing

Darin Phelps
Ensemble

Megan Schenk
Phyllis/Ensemble

Jennifer Leigh Schwerer
Diane/Ensemble

Eric Sciotto
Waiter/Ensemble

Dorothy Stanley
Standby for Dorothy Brock and Maggie Jones

Will Taylor
Ensemble

Josh Walden
Swing

Kevin B. Worley
Ensemble

Ericka Yang
Ethel/Ensemble

Front-of-House Staff
Front Row (L-R): Vicki Herschman, Shirley Dean, Denise Williams, Jeffrey Dabbins.
2nd Row (L-R): Merchandising Gal, Merchandising Guy, Sokima Moultrie, Kirssy Toribio, Eric Nieves.
3rd Row (L-R): Merchandising Gal, Nicole Murphy, Mario Scott, Delilah Lloyd, Algema Toribo, Orlando Ortiz.
Back Row (L-R): Michael Gough, Ryan Tschetter, James Dittami, Eddie Zambrano, Mike Chavez and Juan Thompson.

42nd Street

Hair, Makeup and Wig Department
Front Row (L-R): Sakie Onozawa, Gay Bosker
Middle Row (L-R): Samantha Birchett, Amanda Duffy, Kim Schriver
Back Row (L-R): Joshua First, John Jack Curtin, Jennifer Mooney, Paula Schaffer (Asst. Hair Supervisor).
Not Pictured: Mark Adam Rampmeyer (Production Hair and Make-Up Supervisor)

Wardrobe Department
Front Row, Far Right (L-R): Jane Davis, Pat Sullivan.
Second Row (L-R): Teri Pruitt, Dawn Marcoccia, Gary Seibert, Jerry Winslow, Amelia Haywood, Alexis Vazquez. Third Row (L-R): Marisa LeRette, Theresa DiStasi, Cheryl Widner, Del Miskie, Jennifer Barnes. Fourth Row (L-R): Paul Soule, Michael Michalski, Tony Wilkes, Jeri Grieco, Jeff Johnson, Lori Elwell, Mark Jones, Rhonda Clark, Meredith Benson and Tina Clifton.

Box Office Staff
(L-R):
Michelle Smith,
Spencer Taustine,
Peter Attanasio, Jr.,
Shari Teitelbaum

Electricians
Front Row (L-R): Art Friedlander, Roy Franks, Jamie Crayton (Asst. Electrician, Moving Light Technician).
Back Row (L-R): Jeff Werner, Tom Burke and Thomas Lawrey (Head Electrician).

Sound Department
(L-R): John Gibson, Kurt Fischer, Ed Chapman (Sound Engineer), and John Carlotto.
Not Pictured: Valerie L. Spradling (Production Sound Engineer)

42nd Street

Prop Department
(L-R): Tommy Coles, Jr. (Props Supervisor), Joseph P. Harris, Jr,
Harold Abott, Evan Canary (Propertyman)
Not pictured: Robert G. Adams (Production Prop Supervisor)

Stage Crew
Front Row (L-R): Joe Hennesy, John Gentile (Fly Automation),
James Harris, Mike Fedigan.
Back Row (L-R): John Weingarten, Mike Beetham (Production Carpenter),
Chris Keene, Sean Jones (Deck Automation).

Orchestra
First Row (L-R): Joe Mosello (Trumpet), Chris Costanzi
(French Horn), Mark Vanderpool (Bass), Dan Downes
(Trumpet), Leise Anschuetz (French Horn), Mike
Christensen (Trombone).
Second Row (L-R): Scott Newman (Drums), Keith
O'Quinn (Trombone), Tony Gorruso (Trumpet), Fred
Lassen (Conductor), Alden Banta (Woodwinds),
Elaine Bert (Trumpet), Mike Ishii (French Horn), Dan
Willis (Woodwinds).
Third Row(L-R): Scott Kuney (Guitar), Emily Mitchell
(Harp), Dave Phillips (Bass), Kory Grossman
(Percussion), Steve Armour (Trombone), Walt
Weiskopf (Woodwinds), Jimmy Cozter (Woodwinds),
Sal Spicola (Woodwinds), Dave Pietro (Woodwinds),
Matt Sklar (Piano), Terry Cook (Woodwinds).

Photos by Ben Strohmann

Stage and Company Managers
Back Row (L-R): Kelly Rach (ACM), B.J. Forman (SM), Patty Lyons (SM), Janet Friedman (SM)
Front Row (L-R): Tripp Phillips (PSM), Kim Kelley (CM).

Doorman
Bill Blackstock

STAFF FOR 42ND STREET

EXECUTIVE PRODUCERS
DODGER MANAGEMENT GROUP
Sally Campbell Morse, Steven H. David
Mimi Intagliata, Bill Schaeffer
Tim Hurley, Staci Levine, Jennifer F. Vaughan,
Lee Magadini

GENERAL PRESS REPRESENTATION
BONEAU/BRYAN-BROWN
Adrian Bryan-Brown, Susanne Tighe
Amy Jacobs, Erika Creagh

COMPANY MANAGER .... KIMBERLY KELLEY

Production Stage Manager .... Tripp Phillips
Stage Manager .... Patty Lyons
Assistant Stage Managers ..... B.J. Forman, Janet Friedman
Original Company Manager .... Sandra Carlson
Assistant Company Manager .... Kelly Rach
Company Management Assistant ...... Alissa R. Zulvergold
Technical Supervision by
Tech Production Services, Inc. .... Peter Fulbright,
   Elliot Bertoni, Mary Duffe, Rich Cocchiara
Company Management Interns .... Kevin Neveloff,
   Alana Karpoff, Beverly Baker, Toby Cohen
Associate Scenic Designer .... Chad Owens
Assistants to the Scenic Designer .... Robert J. Braun,
   Robert John Andrusko, Robert Bissinger,
   Yank Frances, Jesse Poleshuck
Associate Costume Designer .... Nancy A. Palmatier
Costume Design Assistants .... Angela Kahler,
   Jennifer Halpern, Johann A. Stegmeir
Associate Lighting Designer .... Philip S. Rosenberg
Assistant Lighting Designers .... Daniel Ordower,
   Jason Lyons
Assistant to Mr.Gallo .... John Viesta
Associate Sound Designer .... Janet Smith
Assistant Director .... Valerie Gardner Rives
Dance Captain .... Kelli Barclay
Assistant Dance Captain .... Cara Kjellman
Historical Research .... Megan Bramble
Production Carpenter .... Michael Beetham
Deck Automation .... Sean Jones
Fly Automation .... John Gentile
Production Electrician .... Jonathan Lawson
Head Electrician .... Thomas Lawrey
Automated Lighting Programmer .... David Arch
Asst. Electrician/Moving Light Technician .. Jamie Crayton
Production Prop Supervisor .... Robert G. Adams
Prop Supervisor .... Thomas Cole, Jr.
Propertyman .... Evan Canary
Production Sound Engineer .... Valerie L. Spradling
Sound Engineer .... Ed Chapman
Production Hair & Make-Up
Supervisor .... Mark Adam Rampmeyer
Hair Supervisor .... Renee Kelly
Assistant Hair Supervisor .... Paula Schaffer
Production Wardrobe Supervisor .... Kenn Hamilton
Wardrobe Supervisor .... Amelia Haywood
Assistant Wardrobe Supervisors .... Jeri Grieco,
   Michael Michalski
Casting Associates .... Jack Bowdan, C.S.A., Mark Brandon,
   Laura Stanczyk, Sarah Prosser
Music Preparation Supervisors .... Miller Music Service,
   Peter R. Miller, Supervisor
Rehearsal Pianist .... Craig Baldwin
Production Assistants .... Adam John Hunter,
   Alex Lyu Volckhausen
Assistant to John Miller .... David Obele
Banking .... Morgan Guaranty Trust Co.
Payroll .... Castellana Services, Inc/
   Lance Castellana, Norman Seawell, James Castellana
Accountants .... Schall and Ashenfarb, C.P.A.
Finance Director .... Paula Maldonado
Finance Office .... Joan Mitchell, Celia Botet
Insurance .. AON/Albert G. Ruben Insurance Services,Inc./
   George Walden, Claudia Kaufman
Counsel .... Nan Bases, Esq.
Advertising .... Serino Coyne Inc.:
   Sandy Block, Jordon Garcia,
   Mindy Gordon, Scott Johnson

Production Photographer .... Joan Marcus
Marketing .... Dodger Marketing:
   Robert Bucci, Dana Vokolek Cobb,
   Mary Farrell, Melissa Fink,
   Jessica Ludwig, Shanta Mali,
   Amy Wigler, Rooney Design
42nd Street Creative Design .... Echo Advertising
Dodger Special Events .... John L. Haber
MIS Services .... Rivera Technics: Sam Rivera
Theatre Displays .... King Displays
Physical Therapy .... Performing Arts Physical Therapy

STAFF FOR DODGER STAGE HOLDING
Angela Seebaran Assam, Steve Bloom, Celia Botet,
Robert Bucci, Amanda Caceres, Piort Candelario,
Sandra Carlson, David Carpenter, Dana V. Cobb,
Michael Coco, Dianne Cornelison, Michael David,
Steven H. David, Robin de Levita, Sara Desitoff,
Tracey Diebold, Adorn DuBose, Pablo Estrada,
Melissa Estro, Mary Farrell, Melissa Fink, Bessie Ganis, Jose
Gaston, Nathan Gehan, Emily Grant, Ron Gubin, John L.
Haber, Stephanie Hall, Alexa Harris-Ralff,
Barbara Haven, Claire Hayes, Tim Hurley, Mimi Intagliata,
Kimberly Kelley, Georgia Kremos, Tina Landau,
Staci Levine, Pamela Lloyd, Michael Lonergan,
James Elliot Love, Jessica Ludwig, Hannah MacDonald,
Lee Magadini, J. Tony Magner, Paula Maldonado,
Shanta Mali, Tim McKelvey, Joan Mitchell,
Lauren Mitchell, Sally Campbell Morse, Erin Oestreich,
Suzy O'Kelly, Cris Petre, Angelo Petronio,
L. Glenn Poppleton, Tammy Powell, Kelly Rach,
Rainard Rachele, Samuel Rivera, Sarah Rizza,
Maureen Rooney, Bill Schaeffer, Ann Schaer,
Michael Sinder, Marjorie Singer, Edward Strong,
Sean Sullivan, Kyra Svetlovsky, Guy Tanno,
Joop van den Ende, Bart van Schriek,
Jennifer Vaughan, Dennis Walls, Amy Wigler.

STAGE HOLDING New York, Inc.
Tony Adams, Steven Bloom,
Robin de Levita, Erin Oestreich

DODGER GROUP SALES 1-877-5-DODGER

Souvenir Merchandise ..Theatre Stuff, Inc. 718-729-1744
Exclusive Tour Direction .... Dodger Touring, Ltd.,
   L. Glenn Poppleton, 212-768-8705

42nd Street is presented by arrangement with
Tams-Witmark Music Library, Inc.,
560 Lexington Avenue, New York, New York 10022.

The stage version of *42nd Street* is based upon the motion
picture *42nd Street* owned by Turner Entertainment Co. and
distributed by Warner Bros.

The use of all songs is by arrangement with Warner Bros.,
the owner of music publishers' rights.

Scenery constructed by Entolo/Scenic Technologies,
a division of Production Resource Group L.L.C., New
Windsor, NY; Hudson Scenic Studio, Inc.; Showman
Fabricators, Inc., Brooklyn, NY; Center Line Studios, Inc;
Showmotion, Inc., Norwalk, CT; Tait Towers; scenic paint-
ing by Scenic Arts Studio; soft goods by I. Weiss and Sons.
Show control and scenic motion control featuring Stage
Command Systems by Entolo/Scenic Technologies, and
Showmotion, Inc., using the AC2 computerized motion
control system designed and built by Showmotion, Inc.
Lighting equipment provided by WESTSUN Show Systems
(US) Inc., VARI*LITE New York and Main Light
Industries, Inc. Automated pianos/specialty props by Prism
Production Services. Sound equipment by Sound Associates,
Inc. Needlework props by Toni Thompson. Cough drops
courtesy of Ricola. Period Cogi Images
provided by the Numismatic Guarantee Corporation.

Costumes executed by Barbara Matera, Ltd.;
Carelli Costumes, Inc.; Dodger Costumes Ltd.; Saint Laurie
Merchant Tailors, New York City; Tricorne New York; Eric
Winterling Costumes. Poppies and irises made by Parsons
Meares, Ltd. Millinery by Lynne Mackey Studio and
Rodney Gordon. Custom dance shoes by Capezio's
Professional Store; T.O.Dey; Menkes Theatrical Shoes.
Selected foundations by Bra Tenders. Wigs executed by Bob

Kelly. Make-up provided by M.A.C.
Make-up consultant: Angela Johnson.

SPECIAL THANKS TO
William Craver, Sargent L. Aborn, Dale Davis.

FORD CENTER FOR THE PERFORMING ARTS
General Manager .... Micah Hollingworth
Assistant General Manager .... Heather Hamilton
Facility Manager .... Kevin DiBetta
House Manager .... Jeffrey Dobbins
Box Office Treasurer .... Peter Attanasio Jr.
Head Carpenter .... James C. Harris
Head Electrician .... Art J. Friedlander
Head of Properties .... Joseph P. Harris, Jr.
Head of Sound .... John R. Gibson
Asst.Box Office Treasurer .... Spencer Taustine
Regional Accounting Manager .... Patricia Busby
Payroll Administrator .... Sharon Payamps
Shipping/Receiving .... Dinara Ferreira
Administrative Assistant .... Jenny Kirlin

CLEAR CHANNEL ENTERTAINMENT —
THEATRICAL
Executive Vice President,
Clear Channel Entertainment .... Miles Wilkin
CEO, Clear Channel Entertainment,
Theatrical North America .... Scott Zeiger
President and COO,
Theatrical North America .... Steve Winton
Executive Vice President .... Lauren Reid
President of Merchandise .... Larry Turk
Senior Vice President of Presenting .... Susan Krajsa
Senior Vice President
of Strategic Marketing .... Bradley Broecker
Senior Vice President of Production .... Jennifer Costello
Senior Vice President of Production .... Carl Pasbjerg
Senior Vice President of Family .... Joanna Hagan
Senior Vice President of Sales .... Courtney Pierce
CFO and Vice President of Finance ...... Lynn Blandford
Vice President of Business Affairs .... David Lazar
Vice President of Business Affairs .... Debra Peltz
Vice President of Operations .... Dan Swartz
Vice President of Marketing .... Jennifer DeLange
Vice President of Sponsorship & Marketing ... Eric Joseph
Vice President of Publishing/
Show People Magazine .... Hailey Lustig

CLEAR CHANNEL ENTERTAINMENT —
THEATRE MANAGEMENT GROUP
President .... David Anderson
Senior Vice President & COO .... Drew Murphy
Senior Vice President of Development .... Denise Perry
National Director of Operations .... Susan Thorman
Executive Assistant .... Rachel Avery
Development and Operations Associate ..... Michael Forte
Operations Associate .... Alex Scott

NATIONAL STAFF:
Ronald Andrew, Cynthia Argo, John Ballard,
David Bartlett, Steve Boulay, Mike Brand,
Chris Brockmeyer, Leslie Broecker, Philip Brohn,
Stacey Burns, Melanie Callison, Nicole Champagne,
Rob Cheatham, Marks Chowning, Carolyn Christensen,
Cameron Cobb, Joan Cochran, Wendy Connor,
Margaret Daniel, Vincent DeFranco, Jamilla Deria,
Greg Dyrsten, Elin Eggertsdottir, Steven Ehrenberg,
Nicholas Falzon, Mary Ann Farrell, Sharnice Fludd,
Matt Garrity, Tiffani Gavin, Ryan Gilbert,
Suzanne Goldensohn, Kelli Houston, DeVida Jenkins, Sheri
Johnson, Erich Jungwirth, Amy Kessler,
Jill Keyishian, Melissa Klein, Tony McLean,
Erin McMurrough, Robin Mishik-Jett, Chante Moore,
Barrett Newman, Kimberly Nieves, Stephanie Parker,
Gil Parkin, Jane Podgurski, John Poland, Marissa Poe,
Rebecca Reyes, Kurt Rodeghiero, Scott Rowen,
Lauren Serebrenik, Maggie Seidel, Jim Sheeley,
Sara Skolick, Alison Spiriti, Andrea Sweeney,
Amy Taylor, Lindsay Weintraub,
Kristen Whitmore, Matt Wolf, Kyle Young

www.cc.com and www.clearchannel.com

Exciting Celebrity Visitor: Harry Connick, Jr. He addressed me in a thank-you letter to the company with a P.S., saying, "Tenor Man, take it easy with the flips and the high notes... I don't need any more competition."

Favorite Moment: Hearing the audience reaction during "We're in the Money" when I would hold the handstand. Also the audience's excited applause when the opening curtain would rise to show what looked like hundreds of tapping feet.

In-Theatre Gathering Place: My dressing room, better known as "The Hamptons."

Off-Site Hangout: Tony's on 43rd between Sixth and Broadway.

Favorite Snack Foods: Egg salad sandwich before every show.

Favorite Therapy: Dimming the lights and opening out my twin sofa bed with soft music between shows in my dressing room.

Who Got The Gypsy Robe: Brad Aspel.

"Gypsy Of The Year" Sketch: "The Last 'Hurrah'" by Alison Levenberg, Patti Mariano, Frank Root and Vanessa Sonon.

"Easter Bonnet" Sketch: "Funny, Fast Flawless" (2004) by Fred Lassen and Todd Lattimore.

"Carols For A Cure" Carol: "Up on the Housetop."

Strangest Press Encounter: Our event in the makeup department of Macy's for probably 10 employees and no customers.

Heaviest/Hottest Costume: The costumes for "We're in the Money," which are probably 15 or 20 pounds.

Who Played The Most Parts: Steve Luker, who played Mac, Doc and Thug.

Who Wore The Least: The ensemble ladies in "Young and Healthy."

Sweethearts: Chris Clay and Keirsten Kupiec; Chris Clay and Starlight; Michael Warshaw and Celina Carvajal.

Correspondent: David Elder, "Billy Lawlor."

Photos (clockwise from upper left): Scenes from backstage, captured by cast member Chris Clay: An actress hurries down a hallway. Gavin Lodge leaps in his dressing room. Another actress has a refreshing beverage. A pair of dancers in chocolate and strawberry chalk stripes. An actress indulges in some fine reading material. David Elder puts on his makeup.

Photos by Chris Clay

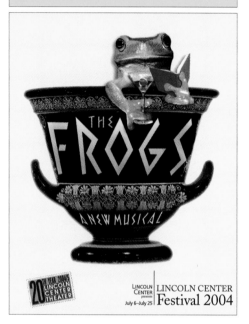

PLAYBILL®

20 LINCOLN CENTER THEATER

LINCOLN CENTER presents July 6–July 25 | LINCOLN CENTER Festival 2004

CAST

Dionysos	NATHAN LANE
Xanthias	ROGER BART
Herakles	BURKE MOSES
Charon/Aeakos	JOHN BYNER
Pluto	PETER BARTLETT
George Bernard Shaw	DANIEL DAVIS
William Shakespeare	MICHAEL SIBERRY

A Greek Chorus,
A Splash of Frogs,
A Revel of Dionysians .... RYAN L. BALL,
BRYN DOWLING,
REBECCA EICHENBERGER,
MEG GILLENTINE,
PIA C. GLENN,
TYLER HANES,
FRANCESCA HARPER,
ROD HARRELSON,
JESSICA HOWARD,
NAOMI KAKUK,
KENWAY HON WAI K. KUA,
LUKE LONGACRE,
DAVID LOWENSTEIN,
KATHY VOYTKO,
STEVE WILSON,
JAY BRIAN WINNICK

Fire Belly Bouncing Frogs .... RYAN L. BALL,
LUKE LONGACRE

Three Graces .... MEG GILLENTINE,
JESSICA HOWARD,
NAOMI KAKUK

continued on next page

LINCOLN CENTER THEATER AT THE VIVIAN BEAUMONT

under the direction of
André Bishop and **Bernard Gersten**
in association with
Bob Boyett
presents

THE FROGS
A New Musical

a comedy written in 405 b.c. by
Aristophanes

freely adapted by
Burt Shevelove

even more freely adapted by
Nathan Lane

music & lyrics
Stephen Sondheim

with (in alphabetical order)

Ryan L. Ball   Peter Bartlett   James Brown III   John Byner   Daniel Davis
Bryn Dowling   Rebecca Eichenberger   Meg Gillentine   Eric Michael Gillett
Pia C. Glenn   Timothy Gulan   Tyler Hanes   Francesca Harper   Rod Harrelson
Jessica Howard   Naomi Kakuk   Chris Kattan   Kenway Hon Wai K. Kua
Nathan Lane   Luke Longacre   David Lowenstein   Joanne Manning   Burke Moses
Mia Price   Michael Siberry   Kathy Voytko   Steve Wilson   Jay Brian Winnick

set design	costume design	lighting design	sound design
Giles Cadle	William Ivey Long	Kenneth Posner	Scott Lehrer

dance music arrangements	aerial design	special effects	puppet design
Glen Kelly	AntiGravity®	Gregory Meeh	Martin P. Robinson

casting	associate director &choreographer	stage manager	musical theater associate producer
Tara Rubin Casting	Tara Young	Thom Widmann	Ira Weitzman

general manager	production manager	director of development	director of marketing	general press agent
Adam Siegel	Jeff Hamlin	Hattie K. Jutagir	Andrew Flatt	Philip Rinaldi

orchestrations
Jonathan Tunick

musical direction
Paul Gemignani

direction &choreography
Susan Stroman

Sponsored by **Mr. and Mrs. Benjamin M. Rosen**.
The Frogs is presented as part of the 2004 Lincoln Center Festival.
Leadership support from The Peter Jay Sharp Foundation.
Major support from The Shen Family Foundation,
The New York Community Trust - Mary P. Oenslager Foundation Fund and Perry and Marty Granoff.
Generous support from AT&T.
Special thanks to The Harold and Mimi Steinberg Charitable Trust for supporting new American plays at LCT.
American Airlines is the official airline of Lincoln Center Theater.
Merrill Lynch is a 2004 LCT Season Sponsor.

6/22/04

We're the Frogs: Dionysos (Nathan Lane, front bottom) is beset by the amphibians of the title.

The Frogs

MUSICAL NUMBERS

SETTING
The time is the present.
The place is Ancient Greece.

ACT I

Prologue:　Onstage at the Vivian Beaumont
　　Invocation and Instructions to the Audience ....1st Actor, 2nd Actor, Greek Chorus

Scene 1:　Ancient Greece
　　"I Love to Travel" ....Dionysos, Xanthias, Greek Chorus

Scene 2:　The House of Herakles
　　"Dress Big" ....Herakles, Dionysos, Xanthias

Scene 3:　The Banks of the River Styx
　　"I Love to Travel" ....Dionysos, Xanthias
　　"All Aboard" ....Charon

Scene 4:　On the River Styx
　　"Ariadne" ....Dionysos
　　"The Frogs" ....Dionysos, A Splash of Frogs, Fire Belly Bouncing Frogs

ACT II

Scene 1:　On the River Styx

Scene 2:　On the Shore of Hades

Scene 3:　A Myrtle Grove in Hades
　　Hymn to Dionysos ....3 Graces, Dionysians, Dionysos, Xanthias

Scene 4:　Outside the Palace of Pluto

Scene 5:　The Palace of Pluto
　　"Hades" ....Pluto & The Hellraisers
　　"It's Only a Play" ....Greek Chorus

Scene 6:　Outside the Palace of Pluto

Scene 7:　Outside the Palace of Pluto
　　"Shaw" ....Dionysos, Shaw, Shavians
　　"All Aboard" ....Charon
　　"Fear No More" (from Shakespeare's Cymbeline.) ....Shakespeare

Scene 8:　Return From Hades
　　Hymn to Dionysos ....Greek Chorus
　　Final Instructions to the Audience ....Dionysos and Company

Cast Continued

Handmaiden Charisma ....BRYN DOWLING
Virilla, the Amazon ....PIA C. GLENN
Ariadne ....KATHY VOYTKO
Pluto's Hellraisers ....BRYN DOWLING,
　　　　　　　　　　　MEG GILLENTINE,
　　　　　　　　　　FRANCESCA HARPER,
　　　　　　　　　　JESSICA HOWARD,
　　　　　　　　　　NAOMI KAKUK
Shavians ....REBECCA EICHENBERGER,
　　　　　　　　　　MEG GILLENTINE,
　　　　　　　　　　TYLER HANES,
　　　　　　　　　　FRANCESCA HARPER,
　　　　　　　　　　DAVID LOWENSTEIN,
　　　　　　　　　　JAY BRIAN WINNICK
Assistant Stage Managers ....
　　　　　　　SCOTT TAYLOR ROLLISON,
　　　　　　　SARAH MARIE ELLIOT

SWINGS

JAMES BROWN III, ERIC MICHAEL GILLETT,
TIMOTHY GULAN, JOANNE MANNING,
MIA PRICE

UNDERSTUDIES

For Dionysos – TIMOTHY GULAN, JAY BRIAN
WINNICK; for Xanthias – TIMOTHY GULAN, JAY
BRIAN WINNICK; for Herakles – RYAN L. BALL,
STEVE WILSON; for Charon/Aeakos – DAVID
LOWENSTEIN, JAY BRIAN WINNICK; for Pluto –
ERIC MICHAEL GILLETT, TIMOTHY GULAN; for
George Bernard Shaw – ERIC MICHAEL GILLETT,
STEVE WILSON; for William Shakespeare – ERIC
MICHAEL GILLETT, STEVE WILSON; for Ariadne –
MEG GILLENTINE, MIA PRICE; for Virilla, the
Amazon – MEG GILLENTINE, FRANCESCA HARP-
ER; for Handmaiden Charisma – MEG GILLENTINE,
MIA PRICE

THE ORCHESTRA
CONDUCTOR: PAUL GEMIGNANI
Assoc. Conductor: ANNBRITT duCHATEAU
Assistant Conductor: THAD WHEELER
Concertmistress - MARILYN REYNOLDS;
Violin - MINEKO YAJIMA; Viola - RICHARD BRICE;
Cello - DEBORAH SEPE; First Clarinet - LES SCOTT;
Second Clarinet - ERIC WEIDMAN; First Bassoon -
TOM SEFCOVIC; Second Bassoon - GILI SHARETT;
First Trumpet - DOMINIC DERASSE; Second Trumpet
- PHIL GRANGER; First Trombone - RICHARD
CLARK; Second Trombone - MIKE BOSCHEN; Bass
Trombone - DEAN PLANK; Piano - ANNBRITT
duCHATEAU; Harp - JENNIFER HOULT; Bass -
JOHN BEAL; Drums and Percussion - PAUL PIZZUTI;
Percussion - THAD WHEELER.

Photo by Paul Kolnik

Battle of Wits: Dionysos (Nathan Lane, on raised chair) watches a contest between William Shakespeare (Michael Siberry, center) and George Bernard Shaw (Daniel Davis, right).

The Frogs

Ryan L. Ball
Ensemble

Roger Bart
Xanthias

Peter Bartlett
Pluto

James Brown III
Dance Captain/
Swing

John Byner
Charon/Aeakos

Daniel Davis
George Bernard
Shaw

Bryn Dowling
Handmaiden
Charisma/Ensemble

Rebecca
Eichenberger
Ensemble

Meg Gillentine
Ensemble

Eric Michael Gillett
Swing

Pia C. Glenn
Virilla The
Amazon/Ensemble

Timothy Gulan
Swing

Tyler Hanes
Ensemble

Francesca Harper
Ensemble

Rod Harrelson
Ensemble

Jessica Howard
Ensemble

Naomi Kakuk
Ensemble

Kenway Hon Wai
K. Kua
Ensemble

Nathan Lane
Dionysos/
Co-Adaptor

Luke Longacre
Ensemble

David Lowenstein
Ensemble

Joanne Manning
Dance Captain/
Swing

Burke Moses
Herakles

Mia Price
Swing

Michael Siberry
William
Shakespeare

Kathy Voytko
Ariadne/Ensemble

Steve Wilson
Ensemble

Jay Brian Winnick
Ensemble

Stephen Sondheim
Music/Lyrics

Susan Stroman
Director/
Choreographer

William Ivey Long
Costumes

Kenneth Posner
Lighting Design

Paul Gemignani
Musical Direction

Jonathan Tunick
Orchestrations

Tara Young
Associate Director
and Choreographer

Thom Widmann
Stage Manager

Scott Bishop
Assistant Director

The Frogs

ADMINISTRATIVE STAFF

GENERAL MANAGER ....ADAM SIEGEL
Assistant General Manager ....Melanie Weinraub
General Management Assistant ....Beth Dembrow
Facilities Manager ....Alex Mustelier
Assistant Facilities Manager ....Michael Assalone

GENERAL PRESS AGENT ....PHILIP RINALDI
Press Associate ....Barbara Carroll

PRODUCTION MANAGER ....JEFF HAMLIN
Associate Production Manager ....Paul Smithyman

DIRECTOR OF DEVELOPMENT ....HATTIE K.
JUTAGIR
Associate Director of Development ....Rachel Norton
Manager of Special Events and
Young Patron Program ....Karin Schall
Grants Writer ....Neal Brilliant
Coordinator, Patron Program ....Sheilaja Rao
Development Associate ....Chris Chrzanowski
Assistant to the Director of Development .....Betsy Tucker

DIRECTOR OF FINANCE ....DAVID S. BROWN
Controller ....Susan Knox
Systems Manager ....John N. Yen
Finance Assistant ....Kellie Kroyer

DIRECTOR OF MARKETING ....ANDREW FLATT
Marketing Associate..........................Denis Guerin
Marketing Assistant ....Elizabeth Kandel

DIRECTOR OF EDUCATION ....KATI KOERNER
Associate Director of Education ....Dionne O'Dell

Assistant to the Executive Producer ......Barbara Hourigan
Office Assistant ....Kenneth Collins
Messenger ....Esau Burgess
Reception ....Andrew Elsesser, Daryl Watson

ARTISTIC STAFF

ASSOCIATE DIRECTORS ......GRACIELA DANIELE,
NICHOLAS HYTNER,
SUSAN STROMAN,
DANIEL SULLIVAN

DRAMATURG and DIRECTOR,
LCT DIRECTORS LAB ....ANNE CATTANEO

CASTING DIRECTOR ....DANIEL SWEE, C.S.A

MUSICAL THEATER
ASSOCIATE PRODUCER ....IRA WEITZMAN

Artistic Administrator ....Julia Judge
Casting Associate ....Kristin McTigue

IN LOVING MEMORY OF
GERALD GUTIERREZ
Associate Director 1991–2003

HOUSE STAFF

HOUSE MANAGER ....RHEBA FLEGELMAN
Production Carpenter ....Walter Murphy

Production Electrician ....Patrick Merryman
Production Propertyman ....Karl Rausenberger
Production Flyman ....William Nagle
House Technician ....Bill Burke
Chief Usher ................................M.L. Pollock
Box Office Treasurer ....Fred Bonis
Assistant Treasurer ....Robert A. Belkin

SPECIAL SERVICES

Advertising ....Serino-Coyne/
Jim Russek, Brad Lapin
Principal Poster Artist ....James McMullan
Counsel ....Peter L. Felcher, Esq.;
Charles H. Googe, Esq.;
and Rachel Hoover, Esq. of
Paul, Weiss, Rifkind, Wharton & Garrison
Immigration Counsel ....Theodore Ruthizer, Esq.;
Mark D. Koestler, Esq.
of Bryan Cave LLP
Auditor ....Douglas Burack, C.P.A.
Lutz & Carr, L.L.P.
Insurance ....Jennifer Brown of
DeWitt Stern Group
Photographer ....Paul Kolnik
Travel ....Tygon Tours
Consulting Architect ....Hugh Hardy,
Hardy Holzman Pfeiffer Associates
Construction Manager ....Yorke Construction
Payroll Service.................Castellana Services, Inc.

STAFF FOR THE FROGS
COMPANY MANAGER ....MATTHEW MARKOFF
Assistant Company Manager ....Josh Lowenthal
Assistant Director ....Scott Bishop
Assistant to Mr. Sondheim ....Steven Clar
Assistants to Mr. Lane ....Andrea Wolfson,
Sam Wasson
Dance Captains ....James Brown III, Joanne Manning
Assistant Set Designer ....Robert John Andrusko
Associate Costume Designer ....Tom Beall
Production Wardrobe Supervisor ....Doug Petitjean
Personal Assistants to
William Ivey Long ....Rachel Attridge,
Donald Sanders
Make-Up Designer ....Melissa Silver
Associate Lighting Designer ....Ben Stanton
Automated Lighting Programmer ....Timothy F. Rogers
Assistant to Kenneth Posner ....Paul Hackenmueller
Assistant Sound Designer ....Anthony Smolenski
Associate Musical Director ....Annbritt duChateau
Rehearsal Pianists ....Glen Kelly, Shawn Gough
Rehearsal Percussionist ....Paul Pizzuti
Music Copyist ....Emily Grishman Music Preparation/
Katharine Edmonds,
Emily Grishman
Special Effects Associate ....Patrick Boyd
Props Supervisor ....Harlan Silverstein
Assistant Props Supervisor ....Terry Marek
Production Soundman ....Marc Salzberg
Light Board Operator ....Bruce Rubin
Automated Light Technician ....Frank Linn
Deck Automation ....John Weingart
Aerial Automation ....Kevin McNeill
Pyrotechnician ....Joe Pizzuto
Followspot Operators ....Matt Altman, Nick Irons,
Georgia Liszt, Jeff Ward
Flymen ....Juan Bustamante, John Howie,
Scott Poitras
Deck Carpenters ....Mike Corbett,
Pat O'Connor,
Ray Skillin
Deck Sound ....Stephanie Vetter, Larry White
Deck Electricians ....Tim Altman, Josh Rich
Propmen ....Mark Dignam,

Scott Jackson,
John Ross
Wardrobe Supervisor ....Sheri Maher
Dressers ....Kenneth Brown,
Maura Clifford,
Shawnique Hill,
Lizz Hirons,
Mark Mathews,
Eileen Miller,
Herbert Ouellette,
Elizabeth Strader
Stitcher/Swing Dresser ....Lara Anderson
Production Stitcher ....Melanie Olbrych
Wig Supervisor ....Larry Boyette
Hair ....Vanessa Anderson,
Gail McGuire
Assistant Hair................................Joel Hawkins
Production Assistants ....Rachel A. Wolff,
Chad Lewis,
Matthew Melchiorre
Production Intern ....Kirsten Lane
Dialect Coach ....Stephen Gabis
Casting Associates ....Dunja Vitolic, Eric Woodall
Casting Assistants ....Laura Schutzel,
Mona Slomsky

WIG AND HAIR DESIGN
Paul Huntley

AERIAL DESIGN ....ANTIGRAVITY®
Director...............................Christopher Harrison
General Manager ....Alexander Schlempp
Aerial Consultants: ....Jared Burke,
Mam Smith,
Brendan O'Neil
Rigging Consultant: ....Scott Sloan

SPECIAL THANKS
Bill Hoffman

SPECIAL THANKS TO
SELIM ZILKHA AND LAETITIA WINERY.

CREDITS
Scenic fabrication, show control and scenic motion
control featuring stage command systems® by
Scenic Technologies, a division of
Production Resource Group, L.L.C., New Windsor, NY.
Scenery fabricated by
Showman Fabricators, LIC, New York.
Costumes by Carelli Costumes, Jennifer Love Costumes,
TriCorne, Timberlake Studios, Inc., and Euro Co.
Special thanks to tdf Costume Collection.
Lighting equipment from Fourth Phase.
Sound equipment by Masque Sound.
Audience cyc photograph by John Labriola.
Makeup provided by M•A•C.
Cough drops courtesy of Ricola.

Excerpt from "You Did It" from My Fair Lady.
Music by Frederick Loewe. Lyrics by Alan Jay Lerner
©1956; (Renewed) Frederick Loewe and Alan Jay Lerner
All rights administered by Chappell & Co., Inc.

Plaza Frogs Soundscape by Guy Sherman's Aural Fixation.

Photo by Aubrey Reuben

(L-R) Roger Bart, Michael Siberry, John Byner, Susan Stroman, Burke Moses, Nathan Lane, Daniel Davis and Peter Bartlett at the opening night party at Tavern on the Green.

Opening Night Gifts: We got many things on a frog theme from Tiffany and Baccarat, and, from Stephen Sondheim, a jigsaw puzzle made out of the logo from the show with each recipient's initials.

Who Got The Gypsy Robe: I did! I added a frog hood, like the ones worn in the frog number, but I added a laurel-wreath crown to give it a little more Greek significance and everyone signed one of the leaves.

Who Played The Most Roles: Bryn Dowling. She played a handmaiden and lyre babe, and whenever someone had a couple of extra lines they went to Bryn.

Backstage Rituals: My two closest friends in show, Kathy Voytko and Rebecca Eichenberger, after our first big entrance as a Greek chorus singing "I Love To Travel," would gather in my dressing room and eat grapes—like the Greeks!

Memorable Ad Lib: One night when a joke didn't land, Nathan turned to the cast and said, "Aw, fuck 'em, we're having a good time."

Cell Phone Rings: Even though there's a joke about cell phones in the opening number, we still had rings three or four times during the run, usually during Shaw's big speech from *St. Joan*. It made us want to jump up and strangle them.

Best In-House Parody Lyric: Steve Wilson, who played a guard in the ensemble, wrote these new lyrics to "Ariadne" for opening night:

What a lark it has been
What a marvelous crusade
We should pause and admire
The statement we've made.

We'll be here every night
It will fill us with joy
We'll take pills for the pain
And remember how lucky we are
To be actors and artists and friends
Break a leg
Time to unleash the dogs
And be Frogs!

Happy openin'
Happy openin'
Happy openin'

Favorite Moment: When the Graces slid down those long bolts of silk.

Snack Food: Grapes.

Favorite Therapy: The calf-stretcher in the hallway.

Busiest Day At The Box Office: It was the day the tickets went on sale. We were very encouraged.

Memorable Audience Encounter: We got a letter from a 13-year-old who said he loved the show, then went on to offer his notes on how to make the show better: "Shorten the numbers, cut some of the contest," etc. This kid is going to be the next David Merrick!

Nicknames: Everybody got a ghetto name. Mine was "DeeLo," which turned into "DeeLocious." Tyler Hanes became "TT." Nathan was "NayNay."

Catchphrases: A lot of lines cut from show became catchphrases: "It's all coming together like a well-made play!"

Sweethearts: Meg Gillentine and Chris Kattan met on this show.

Superstition That Turned Out To Be True: Someone said the title of the Scottish Play, and the next day they posted the closing notice.

Also: The most memorable thing for us in the ensemble was being involved in a new Stephen Sondheim musical. Seeing him get up and sing new songs no one had heard before—our jaws just dropped on the floor. We pinched ourselves and wondered if it was really happening. A big piece of the puzzle of the dream of my career was to be in that room.

Correspondent: David Lowenstein, Ensemble

PLAYBILL®

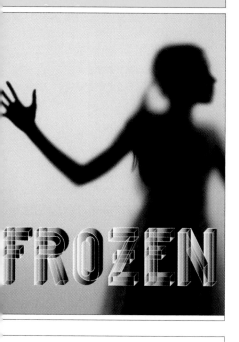

CAST
(in order of appearance)

Agnetha .... LAILA ROBINS
Nancy .... SWOOSIE KURTZ
Ralph .... BRÍAN F. O'BYRNE
Guard .... SAM KITCHIN

UNDERSTUDIES

For Ralph/Guard – DREW McVETY
For Nancy/Agnetha – PIPPA PEARTHREE

CIRCLE IN THE SQUARE
UNDER THE DIRECTION OF THEODORE MANN and PAUL LIBIN

MCC THEATER
ROBERT LUPONE, BERNARD TELSEY, Artistic Directors
WILLIAM CANTLER, Associate Artistic Director JOHN G. SCHULTZ, Executive Director

HAROLD NEWMAN ZOLLO/PALEOLOGOS & JEFFREYSINE ROY GABAY
LORIE COWEN LEVY & BETH SMITH PEGGY HILL THOMPSON H.ROGERS
SWINSKY/FILERMAN/HENDEL SIRKIN/MILLS/BALDASSARE DARREN BAGERT
present

SWOOSIE KURTZ   BRÍAN F. O'BYRNE   LAILA ROBINS
in the MCC THEATER production of

FROZEN

by BRYONY LAVERY

and featuring
SAM KITCHIN

Set Design	Costume Design	Lighting Design
HUGH LANDWEHR	CATHERINE ZUBER	CLIFTON TAYLOR
Orig. Music & Sound Design	Fight Direction	Casting
DAVID VAN TIEGHEM	RICK SORDELET	BERNARD TELSEY CASTING
Make-up & Tattoo Design	Production Manager	Press Representative
ANGELINA AVALLONE	B.D. WHITE	BONEAU/BRYAN-BROWN
Dialect Coach	Marketing	Production Stage Manager
STEPHEN GABIS	TMG–THE MARKETINGGROUP	NEIL KRASNOW
General Manager		Associate Producers
ROY GABAY		EDMUND & MARY FUSCO RUSS LYSTER

Directed by DOUG HUGHES

The Producers wish to express their appreciation to Theatre Development Fund for its support of this production.

7/1/04

Swoosie Kurtz as the bereaved mother.

Laila Robins and Brían F. O'Byrne as researcher and child-murderer.

Photos by Dixie Sheridan

Frozen

 Swoosie Kurtz
Nancy

 Brian F. O'Byrne
Ralph

 Laila Robins
Agnetha

 Sam Kitchin
Guard

 Drew McVety
Understudy for Ralph/Guard

 Pippa Pearthree
Understudy for Nancy/Agnetha

 Bryony Lavery
Playwright

 Jim Baldassare
Producer

 Darren Bagert
Producer

 Doug Hughes
Director

 Catherine Zuber
Costume Design

 Clifton Taylor
Lighting Designer

 Bernard Telsey
Casting

 Rick Sordelet
Fight Direction

 Stephen Gabis
Dialect Coach

 James FitzSimmons
Production Stage Manager

 Neil Krasnow
Production Stage Manager

 David Hilder
Assistant Director

 Frederick Zollo / Nicholas Paleologos
Producer / Producer

 Roy Gabay
Producer/ General Manager

 Peggy Hill
Producer

 Thompson H. Rogers
Producer

 Mort Swinsky
Producer

 Michael Filerman
Producer

 Ruth Hendel
Producer

 Spring Sirkin
Producer

STAFF FOR FROZEN

GENERAL PRESS REPRESENTATIVE
Boneau/Bryan-Brown
Chris Boneau Adriana Douzos

GENERAL MANAGEMENT
Roy Gabay Theatrical Production & Management
Cheryl Dennis, Steven DeLuca,
Susan Vargo, Daniel Kuney

CASTING
BERNARD TELSEY CASTING, C.S.A.
Bernie Telsey, Will Cantler, David Vaccari,
Bethany Berg, Craig Burns, Tiffany Little Canfield,
Christine Dall, Margaret Santa Maria

PRODUCTION STAGE MANAGER
Neil Krasnow

Company Manager ....Kim Sellon
Assistant Stage Manager ....Elizabeth Moloney
Associate Sound Designer ....Jill B. C. Du Boff
Assistant Director...............................David Hilder
Assistant Set Designer ....Timothy R. Mackabee
Assistant Costume Designer ....David Newell
Assistant Lighting Designers ...Steve O'Shea, Eric Cornwell
Research ....Mark Schneider
Hanging Effects Designer ....Paul Rubin/ZFX
Production Sound Engineer ....Robert S. Lindsay
Production Carpenter ....Robert Gordon
Production Props ....Sal Caruso
Light Programmer ....Hillary Knox
Wardrobe Supervisor ....Jennifer Lyons
Wardrobe ....Deidra Herrold
Makeup and Tattoo Design ....Angelina Avallone
Dialect Coach ....Stephen Gabis
TalkBack Moderators ....Kara Manning, Josh Hecht
Attorneys ....Brooks & Distler Attorneys/
Marsha S. Brooks and Tom Distler
Insurance ....Williams & Williams Inc.
Production Photography ....Joan Marcus
Original Photography ....Jonathan De Villiers and
Dixie Sheridan
Original Art Direction and Design ....Helicopter
Accounting....................Rosenberg, Neuwirth & Kuchner/
Mark D'Ambrosi
Advertising ....SpotCo/
Drew Hodges, Jim Edwards,
Kim Smarsh, Lesley Anne Stone

Press Intern ....Rick Hayashi
Marketing....................TMG The Marketing Group
Scenery Built by ....Center Line Studios, Inc.,
Cornwall, NY
Scenic Artist ....Diane Fargo
Lighting Equipment ....Fourth Phase
Sound Equipment ....One Dream Sound
Payroll Service ....Castellana Services, Inc.

MCC THEATER STAFF

Artistic Directors ....Robert LuPone and Bernard Telsey
Associate Artistic Director ....William Cantler
Executive Director ....John G. Schultz
General Manager ....Barbara L. Auld
Literary Manager ....Stephen Willems
Director of Development ....John W. Fichtel
Ticketing & Marketing Manager ....Anne M. Love
Director of Education and Outreach ....Katie Miller
Office Manager ....Eric Bornemann
Asst. Literary Manager...........................Josh Hecht
Resident Director ....Doug Hughes
Youth Company Director ....Stephen DiMenna
Youth Playwrights Mentor...................Brooke Berman
Development Assistant ....Laura von Holt
Education Assistant ....Catherine Ward
Playwrights' Coal. Coord. ....Mark Schultz &
Josh Hecht
Web Design ....Dave Auld
Literary Interns .... Kate Farrington, Laurel Pinson
Marketing Intern ....Amanda Marikar
Education and Outreach Intern ......John Michael Diresta
General Office Intern ....Meredith Dillard

MCC THEATER ADMINISTRATIVE OFFICES
145 West 28th Street, 8th Floor, NY, NY 10001
tel: 212-727-7722 fax: 212-727-7780
subscription line: 212-727-7765
E-mail: mcc@mcctheater.org

BOARD OF DIRECTORS
Dianne Barclay, Brian Duffy, Jill Furman, Judith Garson,
Marjorie Kalins, Lorie Cowen Levy, Robert LuPone,
Harold Newman, Susan Raanan, Steven Rappaport,
Barbara Shulman, Melissa Talarico, Bernard Telsey

SPECIAL THANKS
Brian Abbott, Hope Albrecht, Brian Burdelle, Jan Cantler,
Tess Carse and John Gould Rubin, Classic Stage Company,
Ramona Collier, Bob Cuccioli, Eneil De La Pena,
Amy Fiore, James P. FitzSimmons, Barbara Shulman,

J.C. Hansen, Nancy Harrington, Tony Hauser, Mark
Hoegel, Lynn Fusco Hughes, Ildiko Juhasz, Eric Krebs,
Virginia LuPone, Anne Marino, Melanie Montes, Johnny
M. Mooi, The Royal National Theatre, Mike Rafael and
Ticket Central, Steve Schaeffer,Jodi Sweetbaum, Jessica
Franks at Scharff Weisberg, Aliza Licht at Donna Karan
New York, Samantha Sopin at Kenneth Cole, Catherine
Hickland at Cats Cosmetics. Paul Margolin at Marc
Bouwer. Lotion provided by Purell.
Cough drops provided by Ricola.

Frozen rehearsed at the New 42nd Street Studios

MCC Theater is a member of the New York
(A.R.T./New York) Alliance of Resident Theatres.

Frozen supports The National Center for Missing and
Exploited Children.
www.missingkids.com

CIRCLE IN THE SQUARE THEATRE
Thespian Theatre, Inc.
Under the direction of
Theodore Mann and Paul Libin

House Manager ....Richard D. Berg
Head Carpenter ....Robert Gordon
Head Electrician ....Stewart Wagner
Prop Master ....Owen E. Parmele
Sound Board Operator ....Robert S. Lindsay
Box Office Treasurer ....Ilene Towell
Finance ....Susan Frankel
Assistant to Paul Libin ....Patricia Michael
Assistant to Theodore Mann ....Holly Ricciuti
Administrative Assistant ....Joey Stocks

CIRCLE IN THE SQUARE THEATRE SCHOOL
Staff
President ....Paul Libin
Artistic Director............................Theodore Mann
Theatre School Director ....E. Colin O'Leary
Administrative Assistant ....Jonathan Kronenberger
Administrative Assistant ....David Pleva
Arts Education/Development ....Jonathan Mann
Development Associate ....Holly Ricciuti

Curtain call at the opening night at Circle in the Square Theatre (L-R): Sam Kitchin, Laila Robins, Swoosie Kurtz and Brían F. O'Byrne.

Laila Robins (L) and Swoosie Kurtz at "Broadway's Stars in the Alley."

Photos by Aubrey Reuben

Aidan Quinn and Swoosie Kurtz at the opening night party.

Playwright Bryony Lavery at the cast party.

Laila Robins, Swoosie Kurtz, Brían F. O'Byrne.

Costume designer Catherine Zuber on opening night.

Barnard Hughes with son Doug Hughes (director of *Frozen*), daughter Laura Hughes and wife Helen Stenborg at the opening night party.

PLAYBILL®

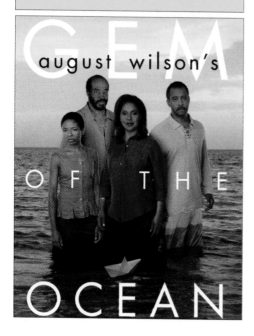

august wilson's
GEM
OF THE
OCEAN

CAST
(in order of appearance)

Eli .... EUGENE LEE
Citizen Barlow .... JOHN EARL JELKS
Aunt Ester .... PHYLICIA RASHAD
Black Mary .... LISAGAY HAMILTON
Rutherford Selig .... RAYNOR SCHEINE
Solly Two Kings .... ANTHONY CHISHOLM
Caesar .... RUBEN SANTIAGO-HUDSON

SETTING

1904 • the Hill District • Pittsburgh, Pennsylvania
in the parlor of Aunt Ester's home at
1839 Wylie Avenue

STANDBYS

For Eli and Solly Two Kings: RON CEPHAS
JONES; For Citizen Barlow and Caesar: BILLY
EUGENE JONES; For Aunt Ester: EBONY
JO-ANN: For Black Mary: HEATHER ALICIA
SIMMS; For Rutherford Selig: TUCK MILLIGAN

PRODUCTION HISTORY

August Wilson's *Gem of the Ocean* had its world
premiere at the **Goodman Theatre**, Chicago, IL,
in April 2003 and at the **Mark Taper Forum**, Los
Angeles, CA, in July 2003, directed by Marion
McClinton. Immediately prior to its New York
engagement, the play was presented at the
Huntington Theatre Company, Boston, MA,
where it was directed by Kenny Leon.

WALTER KERR THEATRE
A JUJAMCYN THEATRE

JAMES H. BINGER
CHAIRMAN

ROCCO LANDESMAN
PRESIDENT

PAUL LIBIN
PRODUCING DIRECTOR

JACK VIERTEL
CREATIVE DIRECTOR

CAROLE SHORENSTEIN HAYS and JUJAMCYN THEATERS
present

PHYLICIA
RASHAD

RUBEN
SANTIAGO-HUDSON

LISAGAY
HAMILTON

ANTHONY
CHISHOLM

august wilson's
GEM OF THE OCEAN

with

EUGENE LEE   RAYNOR SCHEINE

and introducing

JOHN EARL JELKS
as Citizen Barlow

set design	costume design	lighting design	sound design
DAVID GALLO	CONSTANZA ROMERO	DONALD HOLDER	DAN MOSES SCHREIER

fight director	dramaturg	casting	production supervisor	production stage manager
J. ALLEN SUDDETH	TODD KREIDLER	HARRIET BASS	NEIL A. MAZZELLA/ GENE O'DONOVAN	NARDA E. ALCORN

press representation	general management	associate producer
BARLOW•HARTMAN	STUART THOMPSON PRODUCTIONS/ JAMES TRINER	ROBERT G. BARTNER

original music composition and vocal arrangements
KATHRYN BOSTIC

directed by
kenny leon

August Wilson's *Gem of the Ocean* had its world premiere at the Goodman Theatre and the Mark Taper Forum.
It was presented at the Huntington Theatre Company in October 2004.

The producers wish to express their appreciation to Theatre Development Fund for its support of this production.

LIVE
BROADWAY

12/6/04

Phylicia Rashad and LisaGay Hamilton.

Gem of the Ocean

Phylicia Rashad
Aunt Ester

LisaGay Hamilton
Black Mary

Anthony Chisholm
Solly Two Kings

John Earl Jelks
Citizen Barlow

Eugene Lee
Eli

Raynor Scheine
Rutherford Selig

Ebony Jo-Ann
*Standby for
Aunt Ester*

Billy Eugene Jones
*Standby for Citizen
Barlow and Caesar*

Ron Cephas Jones
*Standby for Solly
Two Kings and Eli*

Tuck Milligan
*Standby for
Rutherford Selig*

Heather Alicia
Simms
*Standby for
Black Mary*

Kenny Leon
Director

David Gallo
Scenic Designer

Constanza Romero
Costume Designer

Donald Holder
Lighting Designer

Dan Moses Schreier
Sound Designer

J. Allen Suddeth
Fight Director

Carole Shorenstein
Hays
Producer

Stuart Thompson
General Manager

Derrick Sanders
Assistant Director

PRODUCTION STAFF FOR
AUGUST WILSON'S GEM OF THE OCEAN

JUJAMCYN THEATERS
James H. Binger, Chairman
Rocco Landesman, President
Paul Libin, Producing Director
Jack Viertel, Creative Director
Jerry Zaks, Resident Director
Daniel Adamian, General Manager
Jennifer Hershey, Director of Operations
Meredith Villatore, Chief Financial Officer
Nicole Kastrinos, Associate Creative Director

GENERAL MANAGEMENT
STUART THOMPSON PRODUCTIONS
Stuart Thompson   James Triner

GENERAL PRESS REPRESENTATIVE
BARLOW HARTMAN
Michael Hartman John Barlow
Carol Fineman Leslie Baden

TECHNICAL SUPERVISOR
Neil A. Mazzella

PRODUCTION MANAGEMENT
Aurora Productions, Inc.
Gene O'Donovan
W. Benjamin Heller II   Michelle McDaniel
Bethany Weinstein

COMPANY MANAGER
CHRIS MOREY

Production Stage Manager	Narda E. Alcorn
Stage Manager	Neveen Mahmoud
Assistant to Mr. Wilson	Dena Levitin
Assistant Director	Derrick Sanders
General Management Associate	Caroline Prugh
General Management Assistant	Ryan Smith
Associate Scenic Designers	Charlie Smith
	Robert John Andrusko
Assistant Scenic Designers	Emily Beck
	Asaki Oda, Blair Mielnick
Assistant Costume Designer	Mary Ann D. Smith

Associate Lighting Designer	Vivien Leone
Assistant Lighting Designers	Hilary Manners, Michelle Habeck, Carolyn Wong
Associate Sound Design	David Bullard
Assistant Sound Design	Tony Smolenski
Wardrobe Supervisor	Eileen L. Miller
Hair & Wig Supervisor	Brenda O'Brien
Dressers	Cleon D. Byerly, Aissatou Parks
Production Assistant	Annette Verga-Lagier
Accounting	Robert Fried CPA, Sarah Galbraith
Advertising	SpotCo/Drew Hodges, Jim Edwards, John Lanasa, Aaliytha Davis
Audience Development	Donna Walker-Kuhne
Banking	J.P. Morgan Chase/Michelle Gibbons
Casting Associate	Eileen Duffy
Insurance	Marsh Inc./Yasmine Ramos
Web Design/Internet Marketing	Situation Marketing/ Damian Bazadona, Ian Bennett
Marketing and Audience Development.	Walker International Communications Group, Inc
Legal	Paul, Weiss, Rifkind, Wharton & Garrison LLP/ John F. Breglio, Esq., Jason Cooper, Esq.
Local Transportation	I.B.A. Limousine/Danny Ibanez and Excel Limousine/Mike Petrone
Payroll Services	Castellana Services Inc.
Production Photographer	Carol Rosegg
Theater Displays	King Displays
Travel Agent	Tzell Travel/Andi Henig, Marta Anicic
Voice Coach	Kate Maré

CREDITS
Scenery by Hudson Scenic Studio, Yonkers NY.
Lighting equipment supplied by GSD Productions Inc., West Hempstead, NY.
Sound by Masque Sound & Recording Corp., East Rutherford, NJ.

WWW.GEMOFTHEOCEAN.COM

STAFF FOR THE WALTER KERR THEATRE

Manager	Susan Elrod
Treasurer	Stan Shaffer
Carpenter	George A. Fullum
Propertyman	Timothy Bennet
Electrician	Vincent Valvo, Jr.
Engineer	Ralph Santos

Opening Night Telegram: We got a "break a leg" from the cast of the *Lion King* tour, who we got to know during our tryout in Boston.

Opening Night Gifts: The producers gave us the "two pennies" in a Lucite cube, dated 1904 (the time of the play) and 2004, so we could "pay our passage," like it says in the script. Carol Shorenstein Hays gave me an African justice stick so I could keep order.

Celebrity Visitors: Cicely Tyson came backstage and said "I'm trying to find enough strength to stand up after taking this incredible journey." Geoffrey Holder, said it was masterful. Angela Bassett and Courtney Vance came back and said it was one of the most powerful experiences they ever had.

Backstage Rituals: Before the show, at five minutes, we form a prayer circle, which we started when we were in Boston. Some nights it's just humming. Some nights there is moaning and someone launches into a sermon. We get very emotional about it.

Favorite Moment: Each night I find myself enraptured with a different favorite moment. It depends on the journey that night

In-Theatre Gathering Place: Right off-stage.

Favorite Off-Site Hangout: La Maseria, the little Italian restaurant next door.

Snack Foods: Nuts and fresh-brewed tea. The house manager keeps a big candy jar down in the basement by the prop room, and every day it always magically re-fills.

Favorite Therapy: I box at the gym five days a week, and do aerobics and cardio.

Record number of Cell Phone Rings: Five.

Memorable Ad-lib: One night when LisaGay was telling off Aunt Ester, she said, "Tuck in the corners of the chicken" instead of "the corners of the sheet."

Strangest Stage Door Fan Encounter: One guy walked up to me and asked if I would sign a photo of myself that he'd downloaded. When I said yes, he proceeded to pull out 11 more. A week later he came back with ten! I never refused a photo in my life, but I could tell he was selling them, so I said, "I'll sign two." He looked like he was ready to slap me, if he'd been big enough.

Ghostly Encounters: I sometimes feel a cold breeze go by even when no door is open. I mentioned it to my dresser and he said, "That's the ghost of Walter Kerr!"

Nicknames: Phylicia calls LisaGay "Sassy Mae."

Catchphrases: Eugene Lee always says, "Don't get none on you!" and does Michael Jackson's "hee-hee."

Also: I'll always remember the determination of this cast to see this thing through, through all the adversity, with producers taking money out, and journalists writing that we should close. We got through it all by going into our prayer circle and coming out with a positive take on what we had to do. This play is important, not only to American theatre, but to American history.

Correspondent: Ruben Santiago-Hudson, "Caesar."

Left: Playwright August Wilson (center) arrives on opening night with daughter Sakina and Cassandra Ramirez. Right: The cast takes bows at the first performance.

Photos by Aubrey Reuben

(L-R): Star Phylicia Rashad arrives on opening night. Co-producer Carole Shorenstein Hays. Opening night guest Angela Bassett.

Director Kenny Leon arrives at the opening.

Below: Yoko Ono in the first-night crowd.

Ruby Dee and Ossie Davis on the red carpet opening night.

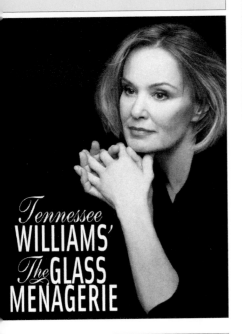

PLAYBILL®

Tennessee
WILLIAMS'
The **GLASS**
MENAGERIE

CAST

Amanda Wingfield .... JESSICA LANGE

Tom Wingfield .... CHRISTIAN SLATER

Laura Wingfield .... SARAH PAULSON

The Gentleman Caller .... JOSH LUCAS

TIME:

Now and the Past

UNDERSTUDIES

For Amanda Wingfield:
JENNIFER HARMON

For Tom Wingfield and The Gentleman Caller:
JOEY COLLINS

For Laura Wingfield:
CHEYENNE CASEBIER

⊛ ETHEL BARRYMORE THEATRE

243 West 47th Street
A Shubert Organization Theatre

Gerald Schoenfeld, *Chairman*   Philip J. Smith, *President*

Robert E. Wankel, *Executive Vice President*

BILL KENWRIGHT
presents

JESSICA LANGE

JOSH LUCAS   SARAH PAULSON
and
CHRISTIAN SLATER
in

Tennessee **WILLIAMS'**
The **GLASS**
MENAGERIE

Scenic & Costume Design   Lighting Design
TOM PYE   **NATASHA KATZ**

Sound Design   Hair/Wig Design   Music Composed by
JON WESTON   **DAVID BRIAN BROWN**   **DAN MOSES SCHREIER**

Technical Supervisor   Casting   Production Stage Manager
LARRY MORLEY   **PAT McCORKLE, C.S.A./**   **BONNIE L. BECKER**
                    BONNIE GRISAN

Press   General Manager
PHILIP RINALDI PUBLICITY   **RICHARDS/CLIMAN, INC.**

Directed by
DAVID LEVEAUX

The Glass Menagerie is presented by special arrangement with The University of the South, Sewanee, Tennessee.
The Producer wishes to express his appreciation to Theatre Development Fund for its support of this production.

LIVE BROADWAY   3/22/05

Rise and Shine: Jessica Lange as Amanda and Christian Slater as Tom.

Photo by Paul Kolnik

Jessica Lange
Amanda Wingfield

Christian Slater
Tom Wingfield

Sarah Paulson
Laura Wingfield

Josh Lucas
The Gentleman Caller

Cheyenne Casebier
Understudy for Laura Wingfield

Joey Collins
Understudy for Tom Wingfield and The Gentleman Caller

Jennifer Harmon
Understudy for Amanda Wingfield

Tennessee Williams
Playwright

David Leveaux
Director

Tom Pye
Set & Costume Design

Natasha Katz
Lighting Design

Jon Weston
Sound Design

David Brian Brown
Hair/Wig Design

Dan Moses Schreier
Original Music

Kate Maré
Dialect Coach

Photo by Ben Strohmann

The Crew
(L-R): Jim Bey (Sound Engineer), Manny Diaz (House Electrician), Catherine Osborne (Dresser), Victor Verdejo (House Carpenter), Tree Sarvay (Dresser), Dan Landon (House Manager), Cristel Murdock (Dresser), Diana Sikes (Hair Supervisor) and Philip Feller (House Props).

The Glass Menagerie

Staff for THE GLASS MENAGERIE

GENERAL MANAGEMENT
RICHARDS/CLIMAN, INC.
David R. Richards   Tamar Climan

COMPANY MANAGER
Kimberly Kelley

GENERAL PRESS REPRESENTATIVE
PHILIP RINALDI PUBLICITY
Philip Rinaldi   Barbara Carroll

Production Stage Manager	**Bonnie L. Becker**
Stage Manager	**J. Philip Bassett**
Assistant Director	Eli Gonda
Assistant Set Design	Larry Gruber
Associate Costume Design	Brian J. Bustos
Assistant to Mr. Pye	James Humphrey
Associate Lighting Designers	Josh Epstein, Kristina Kloss
Associate Sound Designer	Jason Strangfeld
Production Electrician	James Fedigan
Production Propertyman	Emiliano Pares
Production Sound	Charles Grieco
Sound Engineer	Jim Bey
House Carpenter	Victor Verdejo
House Electrician	Manny Diaz
House Propertyman	Philip Feller
Dialect Coach	Kate Maré
Wardrobe Supervisor	Rob Bevenger
Dressers	Christel Murdock, Shaun A. J. Ozminski, Tree Sarvay
Hair Supervisor	Diana Sikes
Makeup Consultant	Angelina Avallone
Magic Consultant	Doug McKenzie
Medical Consultant	Anthony Cardillo, M.D.
General Management Assistants	Laura Kaufmann, Melissa Mazdra
Advertising	The Eliran Murphy Group, Jon Bierman
Artwork Photo	Gasper Tringale, Tringale/Meo Reps
Logo & Design	Frank "Fraver" Verlizzo
Marketing	Hugh Hysell Communications
Accountant	Anne Stewart Fitzroy, CPA Robert Fried, CPA
Banking	JPMorgan Chase Bank, Richard Callian, Michelle Gibbons
Insurance	DeWitt Stern Group, Anthony Pittari
Payroll Services	CSI, Lance Castellana
Opening Night Coordinator	Lisa Seidman
Theatre Displays	King Displays, Wayne Sapper
Cop on the Block	Officer Don Lennon

CREDITS
Scenery constructed by Showman Fabricators.
Women's dressmaking by Tricorne, Inc.
Men's tailoring by Barbara Matera, Ltd.
Hats by Lynne Mackey Studio.
Shoes by The Moulded Shoe, Inc.
Custom orthotic caliper by Marian J. Hose.
Custom knitwear by CC Wei.
Lighting equipment from PRG Lighting.
Sound equipment from PRG Audio.
Newspapers reprinted with permission of the St. Louis Post-Dispatch, 2005.
Glass figurines by Bob Carson – The Glass Menagerie, Corning, NY.
Rosebud matches by Diamond Brands, Inc.
Zippo lighters used (courtesy of George Fenmore, Inc.).
Wig built by Ray Marston Wig Studio, Ltd.
Hair products by Redken on Fifth Avenue.

MUSIC CREDITS
"Smoke Rings" by Ned Washington and Gene Gifford; EMI Publishing; recorded by Glen Gray & The Casa Orchestra.
"Stardust" by Hoagy Carmichael and Mitchell Parish; EMI Publishing, Peer Music; recorded by Vince Giordano & His Nighthawks Orchestra; Sony Music.
"Riverboat Shuffle" by Hoagy Carmichael, Mitchell Parish, Irving Mills, Dick Voynow; EMI Publishing, Peer Music; recorded by Vince Giordano & His Nighthawks Orchestra; Circle Music.
"My Twilight Dream" by Eddy Duchin and Lee Sherwood; EMI Publishing; recorded by Eddy Duchin and His Orchestra; Tony Leonard, vocal.
"Always" music and lyrics by Irving Berlin; this selection is used by special arrangement with The Rodgers and Hammerstein Organization, on behalf of the Estate of Irving Berlin 1065 Avenue of the Americas, Suite 2400, New York, New York 10018; recorded by Billie Eckstein and Sarah Vaughan; Universal Music Enterprises.
"Who Loves You" by Fred Coots, Benny Davis; Benny Davis Music; Toy Town Tunes Inc.; recorded by Billie Holiday with Teddy Wilson and His Orchestra; Sony Music.
"I'm Confessin' That I Love You" by Don Dougherty, Al J. Neiburg, Ellis Reynolds; Bourne Co.; recorded by Guy Lombardo & His Royal Canadians; ASV Music.
"Stars in My Eyes" by Dorothy Fields and Fritz Kreisler; Warner Chappell; recorded by The Victor Silvester Orchestra. "Nocturne Op 32 #2 in A-Flat" by Frederick Chopin; recorded by Evgeny Kissin; RCA.
"Sunburst" by Bob Chester; Universal; recorded by Bob Chester and His Orchestra.
"Piano Sonata in F Major, K. 280: II Adagio" by Wolfgang Amadeus Mozart; recorded by Alicia de Larrocha.

FOR BILL KENWRIGHT LTD.

Managing Director	Bill Kenwright
Finance Director	Guy Williams
Associate Producers (Theatre)	Tom Siracusa, Julius Green, Simon Meadon
Associate Producer (BKL New York)	Dante Di Loreto
Marketing Manager	Steve Potts
Production Manager	David Stothard
Head of Touring	Jamie Clark
Production Executive	Sheila Formoy
Assistant Marketing Manager	Sarah Swanson
Production Assistants	David Bingham, Zoe Caldwell
Marketing Assistant	Amy Taylor
Systems Co-Coordinator (Marketing)	John Collings
Systems Co-Coordinator (Office)	Patrick Crichton-Stewart
Management Accountant	Halyna Dyszkant
Senior Accountant	Margaret Frame
Cost Accountant	Kit Liu
Pay Controller	Lesley-Anne Williams
PA to Bill Kenwright	Emma Tyson
Management PA	Geraldine Mackey
Receptionist	Lesley Pryer
Legal & Business Affairs	Simon Meadon
Theatre Consultant	Rod H. Coton

THE SHUBERT ORGANIZATION, INC.

Gerald Schoenfeld	Philip J. Smith
Chairman	President
John W. Kluge	Lee J. Seidler
Michael I. Sovern	Stuart Subotnick
Irving M. Wall	

Robert E. Wankel
Executive Vice President

Peter Entin	Elliot Greene
Vice President Theatre Operations	Vice President Finance
David Andrews	John Darby
Vice President Shubert Ticketing Services	Vice President Facilities

Opening Night Gifts: The stage managers got little bottles of white wine and then used Photoshop to make custom labels with references to things in the play. There was an image of blue roses, and it said it was dandelion wine from the Paradise Dance Hall. Also, Eli Gonda made us amazing photo books that documented all five weeks of rehearsal in photographs.

Celebrity Visitor: Meryl Streep came backstage and said our production was beautiful. If I had known she was in the audience, I probably wouldn't have been able to go onstage.

"Easter Bonnet": I was one of the judges.

Who Has Done The Most Shows: Jessica and Christian; they're tied at two each.

Backstage Rituals: The three actors who play the Wingfield family get down on our knees in a circle each night and say a prayer, or just talk about the show—something to get us excited. Then, just before we go on stage, we do a little dance we call "The Wingfield Shuffle."

Favorite Moment During Each Performance: Sometimes I go backstage during scene five and check my e-mail.

In-Theatre Gathering Place: The outside fire escape where everybody has a cigarette after the show.

Off-Site Hangout: Angus McIndoe's, if we go as a group.

Snack Food: Manny, who runs the sound board, keeps watermelon, oranges and other fruit, plus a bowl of chocolates.

Mascot: We have lots of glass unicorns backstage, but I have a little glass penguin that I carry with me around the theatre.

Favorite Therapy: Vocalzones lozenges

Memorable Ad-Lib: When Josh Lucas comes on, he's supposed to say "Where shall I set the candles?," and later asks me, "Would you like some gum?" One night he came in and said, "Where should I set the gum?"

Record Number Of Cell Phone Rings: Four. Much worse, though, are the coughers.

Strange Press Encounter: A photo shoot Christian Slater and I had to do with Amy Arbus. She wanted us to recreate key moments from our scenes, but without our props. It was bizarre.

Strange Stage Door Fan Encounters: I've begun to notice how a lot of people have really dirty hands.

Nicknames: Jessica Lange calls me "Freckles," and I call her "Freckles' Mom."

Coolest Thing About Being In This Show: Working with those people and just being employed.

Correspondent: Sarah Paulson, "Laura Wingfield"

Cherry Jones, left, joins members of the onstage Wingfield Family, Sarah Paulson, Christian Slater and Jessica Lange, for the cast party at Bryant Park Grill.

Left: Sam Shepard grins at wife Jessica Lange's opening night: Right: Lange with director David Leveaux.

Left: "Gentleman Caller" Josh Lucas with Christian Slater arrive at the party. Right: The cast takes bows on opening night.

Photos by Aubrey Reuben

PLAYBILL®

CAST
(in order of appearance)

Shelly Levene ....ALAN ALDA
John Williamson ....FREDERICK WELLER
Dave Moss ....GORDON CLAPP
George Aaronow...............JEFFREY TAMBOR
Richard Roma ....LIEV SCHREIBER
James Lingk............................TOM WOPAT
Baylen ....JORDAN LAGE

STANDBYS

For Messrs. Schreiber and Weller:
JORDAN LAGE
For Messrs. Alda and Tambor:
JACK DAVIDSON
For Messrs. Wopat, Clapp and Lage:
JAY PATTERSON

ROYALE THEATRE
242 West 45th Street
A Shubert Organization Theatre

Gerald Schoenfeld, *Chairman*   Philip J. Smith, *President*

Robert E. Wankel, *Executive Vice President*

JEFFREY RICHARDS   JERRY FRANKEL   JAM THEATRICALS
BOYETT OSTAR PRODUCTIONS   RONALD FRANKEL   PHILIP LACERTE
STEPHANIE P. MCCLELLAND/CJM PROD.   BARRY WEISBORD   ZENDOG PRODUCTIONS
in association with
HERBERT GOLDSMITH PRODUCTIONS
by special arrangement with THE ROUNDABOUT THEATRE COMPANY
Todd Haimes, Artistic Director
Ellen Richard, Managing Director
Julia C. Levy, Executive Director, External Affairs

present

ALAN ALDA   LIEV SCHREIBER
FREDERICK WELLER TOM WOPAT GORDON CLAPP
and JEFFREY TAMBOR

in

GLENGARRY GLENROSS

by DAVID MAMET

also with
JORDAN LAGE

Set By	Costumes By	Lighting By
SANTO LOQUASTO	LAURA BAUER	KENNETH POSNER

Casting by	Production Stage Manager	Company Manager
BERNARD TELSEY CASTING	WILLIAM JOSEPH BARNES	BRUCE KLINGER

Press Representative	General Management	Technical Supervision
IRENE GANDY	ALBERT POLAND	NEIL A. MAZZELLA

Directed by
JOE MANTELLO

4/30/05

2004-2005 AWARDS

TONY AWARDS:
Best Revival of a Play
Featured Actor in a Play (Liev Schreiber)

DRAMA DESK AWARDS:
Outstanding Ensemble Performance
Outstanding Set Design of a Play (Santo Loquasto)

Glengarry Glen Ross

Alan Alda
Shelly Levene

Liev Schreiber
Richard Roma

Jeffrey Tambor
George Aaronow

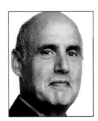

Frederick Weller
John Williamson

Tom Wopat
James Lingk

Gordon Clapp
Dave Moss

Jordan Lage
Baylen

Jack Davidson
*Standby for
Levene, Aaronow*

Jay Patterson
*Standby for Moss,
Lingk, Baylen*

David Mamet
Playwright

Joe Mantello
Director

Santo Loquasto
Set Design

Laura Bauer
Costume Design

Kenneth Posner
Lighting Design

Bernard Telsey
Casting

Neil A. Mazzella
*Technical
Supervision*

Albert Poland
General Manager

Jeffrey Richards
Producer

Jerry Frankel
Producer

Stephanie P.
McClelland
Producer

Jane Bergère
Producer

Jay and Cindy Gutterman
Producers

Morton Swinsky
Producer

Glengarry Glen Ross

Backstage Crew
Front Row (L-R): Kimberly Baird (Dresser), Mike VanPraagh, Eddie Ruggiero, William Joseph Barnes (Production Stage Manager).
Seated at Tables (L-R): Jim Fossi (Production Carpenter), Jessica Worsnop (Dresser), Danny Carpio, Robert Guy (Wardrobe Supervisor), Herbert Messing, Brien Brannigan.
Standing (L-R): Jill Cordle (Stage Manager), Abe Morrison (Production Properties), Scott Shamenek (Dresser), Jerry Klein, Kevin Keene and Brad Robertson (Head Electrician).

Photos by Ben Strohmann

Front-of-House Staff
Sitting (L-R): William Mitchell, Eva Laskow, Christian Borcan, Al Peay, Timithy Meyers, John Minore.
Standing (L-R): Patanne McEvoy, Al Nazario, Sean Cutler and Monssor Saidi.

Staff for GLENGARRY GLEN ROSS

GENERAL MANAGEMENT
ALBERT POLAND

COMPANY MANAGER
BRUCE KLINGER

PRESS REPRESENTATIVE
JEFFREY RICHARDS ASSOCIATES

IRENE GANDY

Alana Karpoff, Eric Sanders, Adam Farabee

CASTING
BERNARD TELSEY CASTING, C.S.A.

Bernie Telsey, Will Cantler, David Vaccari,

Bethany Knox, Craig Burns,

Tiffany Little Canfield, Christine Dall,

Stephanie Yankwitt

PRODUCTION STAGE MANAGER	WILLIAM JOSEPH BARNES
TECHNICAL SUPERVISOR	NEIL A. MAZZELLA
Stage Manager	Jill Cordle
Assistant Director	Paul Dobie
Associate Set Designer	Antje Ellermann
Assistants to Mr. Loquasto	Michael Byrnes, Wilson Chin
Associate Costume Designer	Bobby Tilley
Assistant Lighting Designer	Aaron Spivey
Dialect Coach	Sam Chwat
Assistant to Mr. Poland	Michael Gesele
Production Assistant	Annette Verga-Lagier
Production Carpenter	Jim Fossi
Production Electrician	Jimmy Maloney
Head Electrician	Brad Robertson
Production Properties	Abe Morrison
Wardrobe Supervisor	Robert Guy
Dressers	Kimberly Baird, Scott Shamenek, Jessica Worsnop
Personal Assistants to Mr. Alda	Jean Chemay, Montana Dodel
Personal Assistant to Mr. Schreiber	Lauren Barnhart
Production Photographer	Scott Landis
Banking	J.P. Morgan Chase
Accountant	Kenneth D. Glatzer, CPA
Insurance	DeWitt Stern Group/ Peter Shoemaker, Anthony Pittari, Stan Levine

Legal Counsel	Nan Bases, Esq.
Opening Night Coordination	Tobak-Dantchik Events and Promotions/ Cathy Dantchik, Joanna B. Koondel
Advertising	SPOTCO/ Drew Hodges, Jim Edwards, Jim Aquino, Lauren Hunter
Merchandising	Jay and Cindy Gutterman Productions, LLC
Payroll Services	Castellana Services Inc.
Mascots	Lottie and Skye

CREDITS
Scenery constructed by Hudson Scenic Studio Inc.

Lighting equipment from PRG Lighting.

Costumes executed by John Kristiansen New York, Inc.

Office dressing by Men of Steel, PA, Bergen Office Furniture and Jim DiMarco of Advance Paper Recycling.

Brochure by Glenn Lloyd.

Thomas D. Wright, Esq. – Florida real estate prop consultant.

Selected hand props by George Fenmore and Spoon Group.

Flameproofing by Turning Star.

Glengarry Glen Ross rehearsed at Manhattan Theatre Club's Creative Center.

House Manager	William Mitchell

Exterior Metals Maintained by
Remco Maintenance Corporation.

 THE SHUBERT ORGANIZATION, INC.

Gerald Schoenfeld	**Philip J. Smith**
Chairman	President
John W. Kluge	Lee J. Seidler
Michael I. Sovern	Stuart Subotnick

Irving M. Wall

Robert E. Wankel
Executive Vice President

Peter Entin	Elliot Greene
Vice President	Vice President
Theatre Operations	Finance
David Andrews	John Darby
Vice President	Vice President
Shubert Ticketing Services	Facilities

Photos by Aubrey Reuben

Above left: Alan Alda grins on opening night. Right: Arriving at Sardi's for the cast party: Tom Wopat, Liev Schreiber, Jeffrey Tambor, Frederick Weller, Gordon Clapp and Alan Alda.

Rebecca Pidgeon and husband David Mamet at Sardi's.

Above: Director Joe Mantello.

Left: Co-star Liev Schreiber with girlfriend Natane Boudreau.

Right: First-nighters Sutton Foster and Christian Borle.

Below: "Saturday Night Live" cast members Fred Armisen, Rachel Dratch, Tina Fey arrive at opening.

Below left: Producer Jeffrey Richards with Penny Fuller and Joe Hardy.

Best Opening Night Telegram Or Note: From the company of *Who's Afraid of Virginia Woolf?*: "Look. We're telling you ... We're telling you... We're telling you. Happy fucking opening."
From John Bolton of *Spamalot*: "Break a leg, Glen. Loved you in *Fatal Attraction*."
Opening Night Gifts: *Glengarry* action figures made by Fred Weller. St. Lucy (patron saint of salesmen) medals, sets of steak knives, silver money clips, key rings, business card cases.
Celebrity Visitor: David Mamet on opening night: It was the first time he had seen this production and he told us it was "stupendous."
Backstage Rituals: Running lines in the dressing room before each performance. Liev Schreiber saying, "Fuck you" to the stage managers before his Act I entrance.
Favorite In-Theatre Gathering Place: The trap room in the basement where we had our Passover seder.
Favorite Snack Food: Biscotti and honey wheat pretzels. Both bought in bulk from Costco.
Favorite Therapy: Ricola, Emergen-C.
Most Memorable Ad-Lib: Actually a quote from Alan Alda during a note session: "Can you help me out there because I'm just filling in with franticosity."
Memorable Directorial Note: "I'm nobody's poodle."
Coolest Thing About Being In The Show: The Drama Desk Ensemble Award
Correspondent: William Barnes, Production Stage Manager

PLAYBILL®

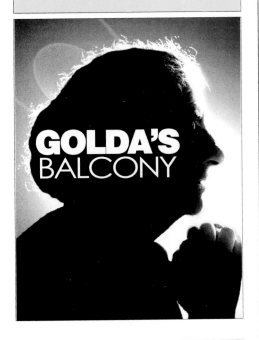

CAST

Golda Meir .... TOVAH FELDSHUH

THE HELEN HAYES THEATRE

MARTIN MARKINSON   DONALD TICK

MANHATTAN ENSEMBLE THEATER (DAVID FISHELSON, PRODUCER)
ROY GABAY   RANDALL L. WREGHITT   JERRY & CINDY BENJAMIN
CHERYL & PHILIP MILSTEIN   JEROME L. STERN   DAVID & SYLVIA STEINER
present

TOVAH FELDSHUH
in
GOLDA'S BALCONY

A new play by
WILLIAM GIBSON

Set Design	Costume Design	Lighting Design	Sound Design & Additional Music
Anna Louizos	Jess Goldstein	Howell Binkley	Mark Bennett

Projection Design	Wig Design	Golda Meir Makeup	Properties Artisan
Batwin & Robin Productions	Paul Huntley	John Caglione, Jr.	Kathy Fabian

Wardrobe Supervisor	Dramaturg	Assistant Director	Production Associate
Trevor McGinness	Aaron Leichter	Nell Balaban	Tara Goode

Production Stage Manager	Production Management	Company Manager
Charles M. Turner III	Gene O'Donovan	Cheryl Dennis

General Manager	Press Representation	Advertising & Marketing
Roy Gabay Productions	Richard Kornberg & Associates	Manhattan Ensemble Theater
	Rick Miramontez	

Associate Producers
LYNNE PEYSER   STEPHEN HERMAN   ZEV GUBER
DEDE HARRIS/RUTH HENDEL/SHARON KARMAZIN/MORTON SWINSKY
JAMES E. SPARNON   SANDRA GARNER

Directed by
SCOTT SCHWARTZ

Originally produced by Shakespeare & Company, Lenox, MA   www.goldasbalcony.com

9/1/04

Sunrise, Sunset: Left and above: Tovah Feldshuh as Golda Meir.

Golda's Balcony

Tovah Feldshuh
Golda Meir

William Gibson
Playwright

Scott Schwartz
Director

Anna Louizos
Set Design

Jess Goldstein
Costume Design

Howell Binkley
Lighting Design

Mark Bennett
*Sound/Additional
Music*

Paul Huntley
Wig Design

Roy Gabay
*Producer/General
Manager*

Randall L. Wreghitt
Producer

Jerry & Cindy Benjamin
Producers

Sharon Karmazin
Associate Producer

Dede Harris
Associate Producer

Ruth Hendel
Associate Producer

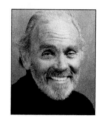

Morton Swinsky
Associate Producer

STAFF FOR GOLDA'S BALCONY

GENERAL MANAGEMENT
Roy Gabay Theatrical Production & Management
Cheryl Dennis, Steven DeLuca,
Susan Vargo, Daniel Kuney

PRESS REPRESENTATIVE
Richard Kornberg & Associates
Rick Miramontez
Don Summa, Tom D'Ambrosio,
Carrie Friedman

COMPANY MANAGER
Cheryl Dennis

PRODUCTION SUPERVISION
Aurora Productions Inc
Gene O'Donovan, Melissa Mazdra,
W. Benjamin Heller II

Production Stage Manager ....Charles M. Turner III
Assistant Director ....Nell Balaban
Associate Sound Designers ....Robert Etter, Rob Kaplowitz
Associate Lighting Designer ....Rob White
Associate Set Designer ....Todd Potter
Assistant Set Designers ....Donyale Werle, Heather Dunbar
Backdrop Photo ....Donyale Werle
Assistant Costume Designer ....Trevor McGinness
Moving Light/Projection Programmer ...Timothy F. Rogers
Associate Projection Designer ....Eric Suquet
Production Carpenter ....Ron Moody
Production Electrician ....Joseph Beck
Production Propertyman ....Roger Keller
Wardrobe Supervisor.....................Trevor McGinness
Asst. to Ms. Feldshuh.............................Tara Good
Production Sound Engineer ....Robert Etter
Production Photographer ....Aaron Epstein

Accountant ....Elliot Aronstam/Robert Fried
Banking............................Chase Manhattan Bank
Insurance ....DeWitt Stern Group Inc
Legal ......Paul, Weiss, Rifkind, Wharton & Garrison LLP/
Olivier Sultan, John Breglio
Theatre Display................................King Display
Car Service ....I.B.A. Luxury Sedan Service/ Danny Ibanez
Security..................Full Security, Inc./Joseph Nicolosi
Payroll Services.....................Castellana Services, Inc.
Opening Night Coordination ....Tobak-Dantchik
Events & Promotions/
Cathy Dantchik, Joanna B. Koondel

STAFF FOR MANHATTAN ENSEMBLE THEATER
David Fishelson ....Producer
James Sparnon ....Producing Director
Sandra Garner..........................Managing Director
Rachel Colbert ....Director of Development
Kevin Gillespie ....Creative Director
Jordan Horowitz ....Marketing Director
Margo Brooks ....Business Manager
Elizabeth Bojsza ....Literary Manager

WWW.GOLDASBALCONY.COM

CREDITS
Scenery supplied by Showman Fabricators.
Lighting equipment supplied by GSD Productions, Inc.
Sound equipment supplied by Masque Sound.
Projection rentals supplied by Scharff-Weissberg.
Costume construction by John Kristiansen New York.

SPECIAL THANKS
The Meir/Rahabi Families, Shimon Peres, Elie Wiesel,
Ambassador Dan Gillerman, Simcha Dinitz, General Ben
Adan, Malcolm Hoenlein, James and Merryl Tisch,
Abraham H. Foxman, Rabbi Jerome Epstein,
Gloria Cohen, June Walker, Ruth B Hurwitz, Ira

Pittelman, Jean Fox, Lucille Rubin, Patti Kenner, Helaine
Lender Travel, Geoffrey Weill, Avi Rosenthal, Max and
Tybie Taglin, Tim Monich, Harold Shapiro, Howard Adler,
Gershon Priewer and The Gallery of Wearable Art.

THE HELEN HAYES THEATRE
owned and operated by
MARTIN MARKINSON and DONALD TICK
General Manager ....Susan S. Myerberg
Associate General Manager ....Elizabeth Jurist

STAFF FOR THE HELEN HAYES THEATRE
HOUSE MANAGER ....Alan R. Markinson
Treasurer ....David Heveran
Assistant Treasurers ......Michael A. Lynch, Manuel Rivera
Head Carpenter ....Ron Mooney
Head Electrician ....Joseph Beck
Head Propertyman ....Roger Keller
Engineer/Maintenance ....Hector Angulo
Head Usher ....John Biancamano
Stage Door ....Fernando Sepulveda, Robert Seymour
Accountant.....................Chen-Win Hsu, CPA., P.C.

HELEN HAYES THEATRE RESTORATION 2003
Electrics ....Barbaro Electric Co. Inc., Joseph Barbaro
Roof and Exterior Waterproofing .....United Construction
Weatherproofing Co. Inc.
Interior Theatre Painting ....Allstate Painting Inc./
Nicholas Palmieri
Interior Wall Colors and Detail ....Anna Louizos &
Jenny Stanjeski
Nosing and Carpet Repairs ...Alliance Carpet & Tile Inc.,
Marcus Bailey,
Popular Carpet Distributors, Inc.
Exterior Facade and Mezzanine ....Sebastian Carbajal
Ladder Cages ....Koenig Iron Works, Inc.
Consultant ....Dave Fishelson
Special Thanks ...Hector Angulo, Erinn Tobin, Robert Rea

Tovah Feldshuh (third from L) in costume as Golda Meir, with (L to R) son Garson Brandon, daughter Amanda Claire, and husband Andrew Harris Levy backstage after the closing performance.

Above: Director Scott Schwartz, Feldshuh and producer David Fishelson at the closing night party.

Director Scott Schwartz (left) is congratulated by his father, composer Stephen Schwartz at the show's 400th performance.

Feldshuh at a party celebrating the show's becoming the longest running one-woman show, at Angus McIndoe restaurant.

The Cast and Crew:
Clockwise from center bottom: Kim Sellon (Company Manager), Tara Good (Assistant to Ms. Feldshuh), Bob Etter (Sound Op), Roger Keller (Deck Props), Ron "Moonman" Mooney (Deck Carp), Tovah Feldshuh (in costume as Golda Meir), Charles M. Turner III (Production Stage Manager), Trevor McGinness (Costumes & Wardrobe Manager), Joe "More Cowbell" Beck (Light Board).

Photo by Ben Strohmann

PLAYBILL®

the
GOOD
BODY

⑤ BOOTH THEATRE

222 West 45th Street
A Shubert Organization Theatre

Gerald Schoenfeld, *Chairman*   **Philip J. Smith,** *President*

Robert E. Wankel, *Executive Vice President*

HARRIET NEWMAN LEVE
THE ARACA GROUP   EAST OF DOHENY
In Association with AMERICAN CONSERVATORY THEATRE

Present

Eve Ensler

the
GOOD
BODY

Set Design	Costume Design	Lighting Design	Original Music & Sound Design
ROBERT BRILL	SUSAN HILFERTY	KEVIN ADAMS	DAVID VAN TIEGHEM

Video Design	Co-Sound Design
WENDALL K. HARRINGTON	JILL BC Du BOFF

Production Supervisor	Production Stage Manager	Company Manager	Press Representative
DREW SICCARDI	ARABELLA POWELL	JULIE CROSBY	THE PUBLICITY OFFICE

General Management	Marketing	Associate Producers
THE ARACA GROUP	THE ARACA GROUP	CLINT BOND, JR.
LEVE PRODUCTIONS		EDWARD NELSON
		ALLISON PROUTY
		LAURA WAGNER

Directed by

PETER ASKIN

11/15/04

Eve Ensler
*Playwright/
Performer*

Peter Askin
Director

Robert Brill
Set Design

Susan Hilferty
Costume Designer

Harriet Newman
Leve
Producer

Body Issues: Playwright and star Eve Ensler.

Photo by Joan Marcus

The Good Body

STAFF FOR THE GOOD BODY

GENERAL MANAGEMENT
MARKETING/MERCHANDISING
THE ARACA GROUP

Matthew Rego   Michael Rego   Hank Unger

Edward Nelson   Clint Bond, Jr.

James M. Pellechi, Jr.   Daniel J. Pardes

Kirsten Berkman   Julie Monahan   Marisa Seachrest

Audra Ewing   Zachary Lezberg   Chet Unger

Carol Fox Prescott   Karen Davidov

GENERAL MANAGEMENT
LEVE PRODUCTIONS

Harriet Newman Leve   Laura Wagner   Ron Nicynski

GENERAL PRESS REPRESENTATIVE
THE PUBLICITY OFFICE

Bob Fennell   Marc Thibodeau   Michael Borowski

TECHNICAL SUPERVISOR
Drew Siccardi

COMPANY MANAGER
Julie Crosby, Ph.D.

Production Stage Manager	**Arabella Powell**
Stage Manager	**Elisa Guthertz**
Assistant Scenic Designers	Dustin O'Neill, Jenny Sawyers
Assistant Costume Designer	Maiko Matsushima
Assistant Lighting Designer	Elizabeth Gaines
Assistant Video Designer	Zak Borovay
Production Electrician	Jimmy Maloney
Production Sound Engineer	Robert S. Lindsay
Wardrobe Supervisor	Herb Ouellette
Dramaturg	Priya Parmar
Movement Consultant	Lisa Leguillou
Performance Consultant	Carol Fox Prescott
Associate Production Electrician	Joe "Fish" Cangelosi
Front Light Operator	Christopher Ryan
Video Programmer	Paul Vershbow
Cinematographer	Hope Hall
Image Researchers	Miranda Hardy, Mary Recine
Assistant to Ms. Ensler	Tony Montenieri
Development Associate to Mr. Askin	Kristin Kopp
Producing Associate to Ms. Leve	Ron Nicynski
Araca Opening Night Associate	Jayna Neagle
Araca Interns	Anthony Francavilla, Amanda Long, Brittany Rostron, Aaron Schwartzbord, Liz Zimmerman
Banking	JPMorgan Chase/ Richard Callian, Michelle Gibbons
Payroll	CSI/Lance Castellana
Accountant	Robert Fried, CPA
Controller	Julie Monahan
Insurance	Marsh USA Inc./Yasmine Ramos
Legal Counsel	Schreck, Rose & Dapello, LLP

Advertising	SpotCo Drew Hodges, Jim Edwards, Tom McCann, Kim Smarsh
Website Designer	Daniel J. Pardes
Promotional Outreach	Jennifer Fruzzetti, Erin Ortman, Kris Todd
Travel	Road Rebel Travel/ Carolyn Peachey
Local Transportation	I.B.A.-Limousine/ Danny Ibanez
Production Photographer	Joan Marcus
Opening Night Coordinator	Tobak-Dantchik Events & Promotions/ Joanna B. Koondel, Cathy Dantchik
Theatre Displays	King Display, Inc./ Wayne Sapper

DIALECT COACH
DEBORAH HECHT

CREDITS

Set constructed by Atlas Scenic Studio,
with additional scenery provided by
Hudson Scenic Studio, Inc.
Prop fabrication by Rose Brand Inc., Paragon Inc.
Lighting equipment supplied by
GSD Productions, Inc., West Hempstead, NY.
Video projection system provided by
Scharff Weisberg Inc.
Sound equipment by
Sound Associates, Inc.
Costumes constructed at
Eric Winterling, Inc.

OPENING NIGHT SPONSORSHIP
generously provided by
EILEEN FISHER

American Conservatory Theater
is under the direction of
Carey Perloff, Artistic Director, and
Heather Kitchen, Managing Director.

A percentage of all profits from the Broadway engagement
will support V-Day,
a nonprofit movement that funds grassroots groups
working to stop violence against women and girls
and helping those who are survivors of violence.

Selected Moving Images
provided courtesy of
HBO.

Select moving images originally directed by
Pratibha Parmar.

Select footage provided by NBC News Archives.

For more information about this production
or for merchandise visit:
www.thegoodbody.org

IMAGE CREDITS

Selected glamour photography by Peter Cunningham,
with clothes styled by Sarah Parlow
and hair/makeup by Jan Pedis.

Additional images provided by
Dinesh Khanna, Roy Morsch Photography, Photofest,
Ajit Mookerjee, Sveva Costa Sanseverino, Hope Hall,
Paula Allen, Zachary Borovay and Peter Cunningham.

Ms. Ensler would like to acknowledge:

Ilene Smith, Gary Sunshine, Nancy Rose, George Lane,
Charlotte Sheedy, Paula Allen, Nicoletta Billi, Rada Boric,
Sil Reynolds, Kim Rosen, Rade Serbedzija, Lenka Udovicki
& Ulysses Theatre Company and V-Day.

Special thanks to Ariel Orr Jordan.

The Producers give special thanks to
V-Day, Carol Kaplan, David Stone,
Nancy Rose, Koethi Zan and George Lane.

The Designers thank
Garth Hemphill, Joan Raymond,
David Ferdinand, Shelly Schwartz
and Sportsplex (New Windsor).

THE SHUBERT ORGANIZATION, INC.

Gerald Schoenfeld	Philip J. Smith
Chairman	President
John W. Kluge	Lee J. Seidler
Michael I. Sovern	Stuart Subotnick

Irving M. Wall

Robert E. Wankel
Executive Vice President

Peter Entin	Elliot Greene
Vice President Theatre Operations	Vice President Finance
David Andrews	John Darby
Vice President Shubert Ticketing Services	Vice President Facilities

STAFF FOR THE BOOTH THEATRE

House Manager	Laurel Ann Wilson
Head Carpenter	Tommy Manoy
Head Electrician	Ronnie Burns, Sr.
Prop Master	James Keane
Flyman	Joe Manoy

Photos by Aubrey Reuben

Above (L-R): Ariel Jordan, Kerry Washington, Eve Ensler, Julia Stiles, Jane Fonda and Sally Field at the opening night party at Gustavino's.

Above left: Hazelle Goodman bares her belly for Eve Ensler on opening night.

Photo by Ernio Hernandez

The show's marquee at the Booth Theatre.

Guest Marisa Tomei on the red carpet.

Director Peter Askin at the opening night party.

Opening Night Gifts: Most of the gifts were references to things in the script. Eve got the crew guys exercise balls like she uses in the show. The producers and agents got Ben & Jerry's ice cream, like she eats at the end of the show. Designers got ice cream bowls and a gift basket with things like chocolate sauce.

Celebrity Visitors: Two of the most memorable on opening night were Annie Lennox of Eurythmics, who is one of Eve's idols, and Wangari Maathai, the Nobel Peace Prize winner..

Who Plays The Most Roles: Eve plays ten named characters, plus herself.

Backstage Rituals: Eve does a dance warmup with her iPod to get herself pumped and ready to go. She always likes to drink a doppio macchiato, which we call her "Fuel."

Favorite Moment: The final moment of the show, when Eve eats the ice cream. It was slightly different at every performance.

In-Theatre Gathering Place: Eve's dressing room.

Off-Site Hangouts: Angus McIndoe's and Orzo.

Favorite Snack Food: Peanut M&Ms, which started with her in *The Vagina Monologues*.

Mascot: A tree.

Favorite Therapies: "Fuel," Ricolas, Throat-Coat Tea, and Eve gets a massage at least once a week.

Memorable Press Encounter: When Eve went on Jane Pauley's show and she served the entire audience ice cream.

Memorable Stage Door Fan Encounter: A girl from Vassar, who had done *The Vagina Monologues* to benefit rape crisis centers and shelters for women, came to see the show, but missed her train and didn't get there until after the late-seating break. So she waited out in the 15-degree cold just so she could meet Eve. Eve was very touched.

Who Wore The Least: Eve, when she shows off her tummy.

In-House Joke: Eve doesn't have an understudy, but we've all seen the show so many times, we always say that if anything happens, any of us could throw on the black bob and go onstage.

Catchphrases: "Love your tree!" If any of us ever made reference to our bodies, like "I don't feel so great" or "This shirt is too small on me," Eve would say, "Love your tree!"

Superstition That Turned Out To Be True: We have perfected a system and try never to change it. Whenever we do, even if, for example, Eve's "Fuel" isn't from Starbucks, something goes wrong.

Also: The whole process of watching the show go from script to workshop to out-of-town and to Broadway, was an amazing experience, like free therapy.

Correspondent: Tony Montenieri, Assistant to Eve Ensler

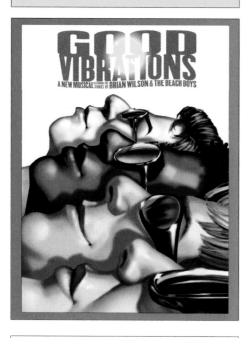

PLAYBILL®

EUGENE O'NEILL THEATRE
A JUJAMCYN THEATRE

JAMES H. BINGER
CHAIRMAN

ROCCO LANDESMAN
PRESIDENT

PAUL LIBIN
PRODUCING DIRECTOR

JACK VIERTEL
CREATIVE DIRECTOR

NCJ Productions/Michael Watt and Dodger Theatricals
With
SEL & GFO   TheatreDreams/Shamrock Partners   Stage Holding/Joop van den Ende

present

GOOD VIBRATIONS

A New Musical

Music and Lyrics
**Brian Wilson and
The Beach Boys**

Book
Richard Dresser

with

Sebastian Arcelus   Tracee Beazer   Tituss Burgess   Heath Calvert
Janet Dacal   Tom Deckman   Carlos L. Encinias   Sarah Glendening
Milena Govich   Amanda Kloots   David Larsen   John Jeffrey Martin
Vasthy Mompoint   Steve Morgan   Jesse Nager   Joe Paparella
Kate Reinders   David Reiser   Krysta Rodriguez   Jackie Seiden
Allison Spratt   Brandon Wardell   Jessica-Snow Wilson

Scenic Design
Heidi Ettinger

Costume Design
Jess Goldstein

Lighting Design
Brian MacDevitt/Jason Lyons

Sound Design
Tom Morse

Projection Design
Elaine J. McCarthy

Wig and Hair Design
Charles LaPointe

Musical Supervision and Arrangements
David Holcenberg

Orchestrations
Steve Margoshes

Musical Director
Susan Draus

Dance Arrangements
Henry Aronson/Jeff Kazee

Musical Consultant
Van Dyke Parks

Music Coordinator
John Miller

Casting
Tara Rubin Casting

Production Stage Manager
Peter Wolf

Technical Supervisor
Teckeneally, Inc.

Press Representative
Boneau/Bryan-Brown

Promotions
HHC Marketing

Marketing
Dodger Marketing

Executive Producer
**Dodger Management Group
Sally Campbell Morse**

Associate Producers
**William J. Kenney
Silverman Partners**

Directed and Choreographed by
John Carrafa

Originally Presented by
New York Stage and Film and The Powerhouse Theater at Vassar – July 2004

2/2/05

CAST
(in order of appearance)

Surfer Guys	HEATH CALVERT, JOHN JEFFREY MARTIN, JESSE NAGER, JOE PAPARELLA, DAVID REISER
Bobby	DAVID LARSEN
Bikini Girl	AMANDA KLOOTS
Marcella	JESSICA-SNOW WILSON
Caroline	KATE REINDERS
Dave	BRANDON WARDELL
Eddie	TITUSS BURGESS
Class President/ Giggles Manager	TOM DECKMAN
Rhonda	MILENA GOVICH
Country Dude	JOHN JEFFREY MARTIN
Cowboy	HEATH CALVERT
Jan	SEBASTIAN ARCELUS
Dean	DAVID REISER
Deirdre	JACKIE SEIDEN
Wendy	TRACEE BEAZER
Randy	JOE PAPARELLA

Ensemble:
(High School Kids, Chili Dog Kids,
Giggles Girls, Beach Kids)
SEBASTIAN ARCELUS, TRACEE BEAZER,
HEATH CALVERT, JANET DACAL, TOM
DECKMAN, SARAH GLENDENING,
MILENA GOVICH, AMANDA KLOOTS,
JOHN JEFFREY MARTIN, JESSE NAGER, JOE
PAPARELLA, DAVID REISER,
JACKIE SEIDEN, ALLISON SPRATT

continued on the next page

Surfin' USA: Sebastian Arcelus and Company.

Good Vibrations

MUSICAL NUMBERS

ACT ONE

"Our Prayer" ....Surfer Guys
"Fun, Fun, Fun" ....Bobby, Company
"Karate" ....High School Kids
"Keep an Eye on Summer" ....Surfer Guys
"Wouldn't It Be Nice" .... Eddie, Marcella, Surfer Guys
"In My Room" ....Caroline, Marcella, High School Kids
"I Get Around" ....Dave, Bobby, Eddie, Surfer Guys
"When I Grow Up to Be a Man" ....Caroline, Bobby, David, Eddie, Marcella, High School Kids
"Breakaway" ....Bobby, Dave, Eddie, Surfer Guys
"Don't Worry Baby" ....Caroline, Bobby, High School Kids
"Surf City" ....Dave, Bobby, Eddie, Caroline, Surfer Guys
"Shutdown" ....Bobby, Caroline, Dave, Eddie, Surfer Guys
"Be True to Your School" ....Country Dude, Chili Dog Kids
"Car Crazy Cutie" ....Bobby, Dave, Eddie, Surfer Guys
"Warmth of the Sun" ....Marcella, Caroline, Giggles Girls
"Pet Sounds" ....Instrumental
"Surfin' USA" ....Jan, Dean, Beach Kids
"Dance, Dance, Dance" ....Caroline, Jan, Beach Kids

ACT TWO

"California Girls" ....Jan, Dean, Beach Kids
"Help Me, Rhonda" ....Eddie, Bobby, Dave, Beach Guys
"Stoked" ....Beach Guys
"Surfer Girl" ....Bobby, Beach Guys
"Darlin'" ....Jan, Caroline, Beach Kids
"Your Imagination" ....Caroline, Marcella
"Caroline, No" ....Bobby
"All Summer Long" ....Beach Kids
"I Just Wasn't Made for These Times" ....Dave, Bobby, Eddie
"Wouldn't It Be Nice" (Reprise) ....Eddie, Marcella, Surfer Guys
"Sail on Sailor" ....Eddie, Dean, Beach Kids
"Sloop John B" ....Jan, Dave, Beach Kids
"Friends" ....Surfer Guys
"Good Vibrations" ....Bobby, Company
"God Only Knows" ....Bobby, Caroline, Company
Finale ....The Company

Cast Continued

UNDERSTUDIES
For Bobby: STEVE MORGAN; for Dave: JOHN
JEFFREY MARTIN, DAVID REISER; for Eddie: JESSE
NAGER; for Caroline: SARAH GLENDENING,
KRYSTA RODRIGUEZ; for Marcella: TRACEE
BEAZER, KRYSTA RODRIGUEZ; for Jan: CARLOS L.
ENCINIAS, DAVID REISER; for Class President/
Giggles Manager: CARLOS L. ENCINIAS, JESSE
NAGER; for Rhonda: JACKIE SEIDEN, ALLISON
SPRATT; for Bikini Girl: VASTHY MOMPOINT,
KRYSTA RODRIGUEZ; for Country Dude: CARLOS
L. ENCINIAS, STEVE MORGAN; for Cowboy:
CARLOS L. ENCINIAS, STEVE MORGAN; for Dean:
CARLOS L. ENCINIAS, STEVE MORGAN; for
Randy: CARLOS L. ENCINIAS, JESSE NAGER

SWINGS
CARLOS L. ENCINIAS, STEVE MORGAN,
VASTHY MOMPOINT, KRYSTA RODRIGUEZ

Dance Captain: CARLOS L. ENCINIAS

ORCHESTRA
MUSIC DIRECTOR/
CONDUCTOR: SUSAN DRAUS
Music Supervisor: David Holcenberg
Associate Conductor: Henry Aronson
Guitars: Chris Biesterfeldt, Larry Saltzman
Keyboards: Susan Draus, Henry Aronson
Bass: John Arbo
Drums: Frank Pagano
Percussion: Bill Hayes
Accordion: Henry Aronson
Reeds: Matt Hong
Music Coordinator: John Miller

Stage and Company Managers
(L-R): Peter Wolf (Production Stage
Manager), Karen Moore (Stage Manager),
Brian Bogin (Assistant Stage Manager),
Doug Rodgers (Company Manager)

Photo by Ben Strothmann

Good Vibrations

Sebastian Arcelus
Jan, Ensemble

Tracee Beazer
Wendy, Ensemble

Tituss Burgess
Eddie

Heath Calvert
Cowboy, Surfer Guy, Ensemble

Janet Dacal
Ensemble

Tom Deckman
Class President, Giggles Manager, Ensemble

Carlos L. Encinias
Swing

Sarah Glendening
Ensemble

Milena Govich
Rhonda, Ensemble

Amanda Kloots
Bikini Girl, Ensemble

David Larsen
Bobby

John Jeffrey Martin
Country Dude, Surfer Guy, Ensemble

Vasthy Mompoint
Swing

Steve Morgan
Swing

Jesse Nager
Surfer Guy, Ensemble

Joe Paparella
Randy, Surfer Guy, Ensemble

Kate Reinders
Caroline

David Reiser
Dean, Surfer Guy

Krysta Rodriguez
Swing

Jackie Seiden
Deirdre, Ensemble

Allison Spratt
Ensemble

Brandon Wardell
Dave

Jessica-Snow Wilson
Marcella

Brian Wilson & The Beach Boys
Music and Lyrics

Richard Dresser
Book

John Carrafa
Director/ Choreographer

Heidi Ettinger
Set Design

Jess Goldstein
Costume Designer

Brian MacDevitt
Lighting Design

Henry Aronson
Dance Arranger/ Associate Conductor

John Miller
Music Coordinator

Tara Rubin
Casting

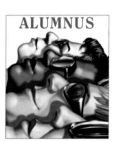
ALUMNUS
Chad Kimball
Randy, Surfer Guy, Ensemble

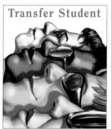
Transfer Student

Beth Curry
Rhonda, Ensemble

158

Good Vibrations

Hair (L-R): Janelle Leone and Amy Neswald.

Carpenters (L-R): David Cohen, Clark Middleton and John Taccone.

Photos by Ben Strothmann

Wardrobe
(L-R): Seated:
Nanette Golia and
Missy Skop.

Behind:
Melanie McClintock,
Lisa Preston,
David Mills,
Maria Fusco,
Margo Lawless and
Shana Skop.

Not pictured:
Linda Zimmerman and
Dawn Reynolds.

Doorman
Kevin Wallace

Sound
(L-R);
Andy Funk,
Emile Lafargue
and Tucker
Howard.

159

Good Vibrations

Running Crew
Front (L-R):
David Holliman,
Todd D'Aiuto,
James Shea,
Richard Mortell,
Brian Dawson;

Back (L-R):
Emile Lafargue,
Andy Funk and
Michelle Gutierrez

House Staff
Top Row (L-R):
Lorraine Wheeler, Charlotte Brauer,
Verna Hobson, Hal Goldberg
and Arthur Van Salisbury.

Center Row (L-R):
Rosemary Roman, Adrian Atkinson,
Christine Ehren, Tammy Powell; and
Carmella Galante.

Bottom Row (L-R):
Byron Vargas, Irene Vincent,
John Dapolito and Raya Konyk.

Orchestra
Back Row: (L-R): Chris Biesterfeldt,
(Guitar), Larry Saltzman (Guitar),
Frank Pagano (Drums),
Susan Draus (Keyboards and
Conductor)

Front Row: (L-R): Henry Aronson
(Keyboards, Accordion and Associate
Conductor), Matt Hong (Reeds), and
Bill Hayes (Percussion)

Good Vibrations

STAFF FOR GOOD VIBRATIONS

EXECUTIVE PRODUCERS

Dodger Management Group

Sally Campbell Morse   Steven H. David

Mimi Intagliata

Staci Levine   Jennifer F. Vaughan

GENERAL MANAGER

Steven H. David

GENERAL PRESS REPRESENTATION

Boneau/Bryan-Brown

Adrian Bryan-Brown   Susanne Tighe

Heath Schwartz

COMPANY MANAGER

Doug Rogers/Sandra Carlson

Production Stage Manager	Peter Wolf
Stage Manager	Karen Moore
Assistant Stage Manager	Brian Bogin
Associate Director	Seth Sklar-Heyn
Associate Choreographer	Tyce Diorio
Assistant Choreographer	Jodi Melnick
Fight Captain	Steve Morgan
Assistant Company Manager	Tim Hurley
Associate Scenic Designer	Larry Gruber
Assistant Scenic Designer	Gaetane Bertol, Daniela Galli, Rachel Janocko, Heesoo Kim, Ed Pisoni, Thomas Sarr
Associate Costume Designer	Alejo Vietti
Assistant Costume Designer	China Lee
Assistant to Mr. Goldstein	Elizabeth Flauto
Associate Lighting Designer	Mark T. Simpson
Assistant Lighting Designer	Jennifer Schriever
Assistant Sound Designer	Susan Ash
Projection Designer Assistant	Jake Pinholster
Automated Lighting Programmer	David Arch
Sound Board Programmer	Mac Kerr
Projection Programmer	Hillary Knox
Production Carpenter	David M. Cohen
Deck Automation	Clark Middleton
Production Electrician	Richard Mortell
Assistant Electrician	Brian Dawson
Production Sound Engineer	Tucker Howard
Production Property Master	Ray Lutz
Assistant Property Master	Reggie Vessie
Prop Shopper	Ron Groomes
Wardrobe Supervisor	Nanette Golia
Assistant Wardrobe Supervisor	Shana Skop
Dressers	Maria Fusco, Melanie McClintock, David Mills, Linda Zimmerman
Hair Supervisor	Amy Neswald
Assistant Hair Supervisor	Janelle Leone
Casting Associates	Dunya Vitolic, Eric Woodall
Casting Associates	Mona Slomsky, Laura Schutzel
Assistant to John Miller	Matthew Ettinger
Music Copying	Paul Holderbaum/Chelsea Music Services
Synthesizer Programming	Henry Aronson
Production Assistants	Jennifer Cox, Rachel McCutchen
Advertising	Serino Coyne, Inc./ Sandy Block, Scott Johnson, Jordan Garcia, Mindy Gordon
Marketing	Dodger Marketing/ Amy Wigler, Dana Cobb, Melissa Fink, Jessica Ludwig, Shanta Mali, Rose Polidoro
Promotions	HHC Marketing/ Hugh Hysell, Michael Redman, Jillian Boeni, Adam Jay, Matt Sicoli
Banking	Commerce Bank/Barbara von Borstel
Payroll	Castellana Services Inc./ Lance Castellana, Norman Seawell, James Castellana
Accountants	Schall and Ashenfarb, C.P.A.
Finance Director	Paula Maldonado
Finance Office	Joan Mitchell, Celia Botet
Insurance	AON/Albert G. Ruben Insurance Services, Inc./ George Walden, Claudia Kaufman

Counsel	Nan Bases, Esq.
Dodger Special Events	John L. Haber
Dance Assistants	Cherice Barton, Larry Keigwin, Jodi Melnick
Dance Research	Rebecca Katz
Travel Arrangements	The "A" Team at Tzell Travel/ Andi Henig
MIS Services	Rivera Technics/Sam Rivera
Website Design	Serino Coyne, Inc.
Website Maintenance	Late August Design
SSDC Observer	Casey Hushion
Production Photographers	Joan Marcus, Carol Rosegg
Theatre Displays	King Displays

DODGERS

Dodger Theatricals

Marney Andersen, Angela Seebaran Assam, Celia Botet, Piort Candelario, Sandra Carlson, Dana V. Cobb, Michael Coco, Dianne Cornelison, Michael David, Steven H. David, Tracey Diebold, Matthew Downey, Melissa Estro, Melissa Fink, Bessie Ganis, Emily Grant, Ron Gubin, Claire Hayes, Tim Hurley, Mimi Intagliata, Kimberly Kelley, Tina Landau, Staci Levine, Pamela Lloyd, James Elliot Love, Jessica Ludwig, Tony Magner, Paula Maldonado, Shanta Mali, Tim McKelvey, Joan Mitchell, Lauren Mitchell, Sally Campbell Morse, Suzy O'Kelly, Angelo Petronio, L. Glenn Poppleton, Tammy Powell, Kelly Rach, Rainard Rachele, Samuel Rivera, Sarah Rizza, Doug Rodgers, Maureen Rooney, Michael Sinder, Marjorie Singer, Edward Strong, Sean Sullivan, Kyra Svetlovsky, Jennifer Vaughan, Dennis Walls, Amy Wigler, Alissa Zulvergold

STAGE HOLDING

Board of Directors

Joop van den Ende, Bart van Schriek, Robin de Levita, Caspar Gerwe, Maik Klokow

Stage Holding New York

Steven Bloom, Orin Oestreich

CREDITS

Scenery, show control and automation by ShowMotion, Inc. Norwalk, CT, using the AC2 computerized motion control system. Conventional and automated lighting system provided by Scharff Weisberg Lighting LLC. Sound equipment by Sound Associates. Video projection system provided by Scharff Weisberg, Inc. Costumes executed by Jennifer Love Costumes, Carelli Costumes Inc., Dodger Costumes Ltd. Wigs by Watson Associates. Props by The Spoon Group and Tom Carroll Scenery. Rehearsed at The New 42nd Street Studios. Onstage guitars provided by Taylor Guitars.

www.goodvibrationsonbroadway.com

SONG CREDITS

"All Summer Long" (Brian Wilson, Mike Love); ©1964, 1992 Irving Music, Inc. (BMI). "Be True to Your School" (Brian Wilson, Mike Love); ©1963, 1991 Irving Music, Inc. (BMI). "Breakaway" (Brian Wilson, Murray Wilson); ©1975 Brother Publishing Company (BMI). "California Girls" (Brian Wilson, Mike Love); ©1965, 1993 Irving Music, Inc. (BMI). "Car Crazy Cutie" (Brian Wilson, Roger Christian);©1964, 1992 Irving Music (BMI) and Careers-BMG Music Publishing (BMI); used by kind permission from Irving Music, Inc. and BMG Music Publishing Inc. "Caroline, No" (Brian Wilson, Tony Asher); ©1966, 1994 Irving Music, Inc. (BMI). "Catch a Wave" (Brian Wilson, Mike Love); ©1963, 1991 Irving Music, Inc. (BMI). "Dance, Dance, Dance" (Brian Wilson, Carl Wilson, Mike Love); ©1964, 1992 Irving Music, Inc. (BMI). (Brian Wilson, Mike Love); ©1968, 1996 Irving Music, Inc. (BMI). "Do It Again" (Brian Wilson, Mike Love); ©1968, 1996 Irving Music, Inc. (BMI). "Don't Worry Baby" (Brian Wilson, Roger Christian); ©1964, 1992 Irving Music (BMI) and Careers-BMG Music Publishing (BMI); used by kind permission from Irving Music, Inc. and BMG Music Publishing Inc. "Friends" (Brian Wilson, Carl Wilson, Dennis Wilson, Al Jardine); ©1968, 1996 Irving Music, Inc. (BMI). "Fun, Fun, Fun" (Brian Wilson, Mike Love); ©1964, 1992 Irving Music, Inc.

(BMI). "God Only Knows" (Brian Wilson, Tony Asher); ©1966, 1994 Irving Music, Inc. (BMI). "Good Vibrations" (Brian Wilson, Mike Love); ©1966, 1994 Irving Music, Inc. (BMI). "Help Me Rhonda" (Brian Wilson, Mike Love); ©1965, 1993 Irving Music, Inc. (BMI). "I Get Around" (Brian Wilson, Mike Love); ©1964, 1992 Irving Music, Inc. (BMI). "I Just Wasn't Made for These Times" (Brian Wilson, Tony Asher); ©1966, 1994 Irving Music, Inc. (BMI). "In My Room" (Brian Wilson, Gary Usher); ©1964, 1992 Irving Music, Inc. (BMI). "Karate" (Carl Wilson); ©1964 Guild Music (BMI). "Keep an Eye on Summer" (Brian Wilson, Bob Norman); published by Screen Gems-EMI Music Inc. (BMI). "Let's Go Away for Awhile" (Brian Wilson); ©1966, 1994 Irving Music, Inc. (BMI). "Little Deuce Coupe" (Brian Wilson, Roger Christian); ©1963, 1991 Irving Music, Inc. (BMI) and Careers-BMG Music Publishing (BMI); used by kind permission from Irving Music, Inc. and BMG Music Publishing Inc. "Little Honda" (Wilson/Love); Irving Music (1964). "Our Prayer" (Brian Wilson) ©1968, 1996 Irving Music, Inc. (BMI). "Pet Sounds" (Brian Wilson); ©1966, 1994 Irving Music, Inc. (BMI). "Sail On, Sailor" (Brian Wilson, Ray Kennedy, John F. Rieley III, Tandyn Almer, Van Dyke Parks); ©1973 Brother Publishing Company (BMI). "Sloop John B" (Brian Wilson); ©1966 New Executive Music (BMI). "Shut Down" (Brian Wilson, Roger Christian); ©1963, 1991 Irving Music, Inc. (BMI) and Careers-BMG Music Publishing (BMI); used by kind permission from Irving Music, Inc. and BMG Music Publishing Inc. "Stoked" (Brian Wilson); ©1964, 1992 Irving Music, Inc. (BMI). "Surf City" (Jan Berry, Brian Wilson); published by Screen Gems-EMI Music Inc. (BMI). "Surfer Girl" (Brian Wilson); ©1962 Guild Music (BMI). "Surfin' Safari" (Brian Wilson, Mike Love); ©1962 Guild Music (BMI). "Surfin' U.S.A." (Chuck Berry);©1963 Arc Music Corp. (renewed) Arc Music Corp.and Isalee Music; used by permission, all rights reserved, international copyright secured. "Warmth of the Sun" (Brian Wilson, Mike Love); ©1964, 1992 Irving Music, Inc. (BMI). "Wendy" (Brian Wilson, Mike Love); ©1964 Irving Music, Inc. (BMI). "When I Grow Up (To Be a Man)" (Brian Wilson, Mike Love); ©1964, 1992 Irving Music, Inc. (BMI). "Wouldn't It Be Nice" (Brian Wilson, Tony Asher, Mike Love); ©1966, 1994 Irving Music, Inc. (BMI). "Your Imagination" (Brian Wilson, Joseph Thomas, Steve Dahl, Jim Peterik); ©1998 New Executive Music (BMI)/On The Fox Music (BMI)/Jim Peterik Music (ASCAP) (administered by On The Fox Music)

SPECIAL THANKS

Capitol Records; Tommy Hilfiger U.S.A., Inc.; Steve Rankin; Meredith Miller; Andrea White; Erica; and all those who participated in the readings and NYSAF production.

JUJAMCYN THEATERS

ROCCO LANDESMAN
President

PAUL LIBIN
Producing Director

JACK VIERTEL
Creative Director

JERRY ZAKS

DANIEL ADAMIAN
General Manager

JENNIFER HERSHEY
Director of Operations

STAFF FOR EUGENE O'NEILL THEATRE

Manager	Hal Goldberg
Treasurer	Dean Gardner
Carpenter	Donald Robinson
Propertyman	Christopher Beck
Electrician	Todd D'Aiuto

Opening Night Gifts: Beach towels, bathrobes, Martini glasses, and lots of libations!

Most Exciting Celebrity Visitor: Brian Wilson

Who Got the Gypsy Robe and What They Put On It: Milena Govich: She took the back panel and added the backside of a sun-bather whose bikini bottom says "Good Vibrations" on it. The entire cast signed it.

"Easter Bonnet" Sketch: "Some Chick in a Bikini and Her Busted Beach Kids."

Backstage Ritual: Group prayer, stage right, usually beautifully led by Tituss Burgess.

Favorite Moment During Each Performance: Beach Balls!!

Favorite In-Theatre Gathering Place: On the stage, just before curtain.

Favorite Off-Site Hangout: Thalia.

Favorite Snack Food: Peanut M&M's.

Favorite Therapies: Lots of crunches & cardio at NYSC, protein smoothies from Mid-City gym, and anything from Starbuck.

Record Number of Cell Phone Rings During a Performance: Our show is so loud that we never hear them!

Heaviest/Hottest Costume: The sadly missed alien costume worn by Tom Deckman.

Who Wore the Least: That's a tough call—EVERYONE wears a bathing suit!

Strange Press Encounter: The stealth documentary crew that showed up around every corner for about a week.

Most memorable Ad-lib: Caroline: "Something, something, something...."

Nicknames: Juppet, Boo-Bop, Peaches, Big 'Un.

Catchphrases: "Get it!," "Hot!," "Good Libations!"

Sweethearts: Kate & Sebastian.

Memorable Directorial Note: Just rock out!; "Surfin' USA"— No it's..., or wait... no, it's..., or it's...."

Also: Through all of the trials and frustrations in the process of putting up *Good Vibrations*, this has proved to be one of the most dedicated, patient, loving, and supportive casts that I've had the privilege to be a part of.

Correspondent: Milena Govich, "Rhonda"

California Girls: Milena Govich, Janet Dacal, Sarah Glendening, Allison Spratt, Jackie Seiden, Tracee Beazer, Amanda Kloots, David Reiser. Background: Heath Calvert and Tom Deckman.

Photo courtesy Milena Govich

Director John Carrafa at rehearsal.

Photo by Aubrey Reuben

The cast celebrates as Milena Govich (center) gets The Gypsy Robe backstage just before the curtain rises on opening night.

Photo courtesy Milena Govich

(L-R) Allison Spratt, Kate Reinders, Jessica-Snow Wilson, Jackie Seiden at the party for "Good Vibrations" at Dodger Stages.

Photo by Aubrey Reuben

Amanda Kloots, Kate Reinders and David Larsen in rehearsals.

Photo by Aubrey Reuben

PLAYBILL®

NEIL SIMON THEATRE

UNDER THE DIRECTION OF JAMES M. NEDERLANDER AND JAMES L. NEDERLANDER

Margo Lion   Adam Epstein   The Baruch · Viertel · Routh · Frankel Group
James D. Stern/Douglas L. Meyer   Rick Steiner/Frederic H. Mayerson
SEL & GFO   New Line Cinema
In Association With
Clear Channel Entertainment   A. Gordon/E. McAllister
D. Harris/M. Swinsky   J. & B. Osher
Present

HAIRSPRAY

Book By
Mark O'Donnell
Thomas Meehan

Music By
Marc Shaiman

Lyrics By
Scott Wittman
Marc Shaiman

Based upon the New Line Cinema film written and directed by John Waters

Starring
Carly Jibson   **Bruce Vilanch**

Also Starring
Jordan Ballard   Richard H. Blake   Jim J. Bullock   Mary Bond Davis
Jonathan Dokuchitz   Chester Gregory II   Julie Halston   Blake Hammond
Tracy Miller   Nia Imani Soyemi   Barbara Walsh
and
Todd Susman

With
Joe Abraham   Cameron Adams   Gretchen Bieber   Lindsay Nicole Chambers   Eric L. Christian   Michael Cunio
Shannon Durig   Leslie Goddard   Becky Gulsvig   Carla J. Hargrove   Tyrick Wiltez Jones   Leslie Kritzer
Abdul Latif   Rusty Mowery   CJay Hardy Philip   Nicole Powell   Andrew Rannells   Terita R. Redd
Todd Michel Smith   Bryan West   Tommar Wilson   Candice Marie Woods

Scenery Designed by
David Rockwell

Costumes Designed by
William Ivey Long

Lighting Designed by
Kenneth Posner

Sound Designed by
Steve C. Kennedy

Casting by
Bernard Telsey Casting

Wigs & Hair Designed by
Paul Huntley

Production Stage Manager
Frank Lombardi

Associate Director
Matt Lenz

Associate Choreographer
Michele Lynch

Orchestrations by
Harold Wheeler

Music Direction by
Lon Hoyt

Arrangements by
Marc Shaiman

Music Coordinator
John Miller

General Management
Richard Frankel Productions
Laura Green

Technical Supervisor
**Tech Production
Services, Inc.**

Press Representative
Richard Kornberg
Don Summa

Associate Producers
**Rhoda Mayerson
The Aspen Group
Daniel C. Staton**

Choreography by
Jerry Mitchell

Direction by
Jack O'Brien

The world premiere of "HAIRSPRAY" was produced with the 5th Avenue Theatre in Seattle, Washington David Armstrong, Producing Artistic Director; Marilynn Sheldon, Managing Director
The producers wish to express their appreciation to Theatre Development Fund for its support of this production.
ORIGINAL BROADWAY CAST RECORDING ON SONY CLASSICAL

LIVE BROADWAY

5/9/05

CAST
(in order of appearance)

Tracy Turnblad	CARLY JIBSON
Corny Collins	JONATHAN DOKUCHITZ
Amber Von Tussle	JORDAN BALLARD
Brad	MICHAEL CUNIO
Tammy	LINDSAY NICOLE CHAMBERS
Fender	ANDREW RANNELLS
Brenda	CAMERON ADAMS
Sketch	BRYAN WEST
Shelley	LESLIE KRITZER
IQ	TODD MICHEL SMITH
Lou Ann	BECKY GULSVIG
Link Larkin	RICHARD H. BLAKE
Prudy Pingleton	JULIE HALSTON
Edna Turnblad	BRUCE VILANCH
Penny Pingleton	TRACY MILLER
Velma Von Tussle	BARBARA WALSH
Harriman F. Spritzer	JIM J. BULLOCK
Wilbur Turnblad	TODD SUSMAN
Principal	JIM J. BULLOCK
Seaweed J. Stubbs	CHESTER GREGORY II
Duane	TYRICK WILTEZ JONES
Gilbert	ERIC L. CHRISTIAN
Lorraine	TERITA R. REDD
Thad	TOMMAR WILSON
The Dynamites	CARLA J. HARGROVE, NICOLE POWELL, CANDICE MARIE WOODS
Mr. Pinky	JIM J. BULLOCK
Gym Teacher	JULIE HALSTON

continued on the next page

Mama, I'm A Big Girl Now: Bruce Vilanch, Carly Jibson and the cast.

Photo by Paul Kolnik

Hairspray

MUSICAL NUMBERS

Baltimore, 1962

Act One

Prologue: "Good Morning Baltimore" ....Tracy & Company

Scene 1:   TV Station WZZT & Turnblad Home

"The Nicest Kids in Town" ....Corny Collins & Council Members

Scene 2:   At the Vanities

"Mama, I'm a Big Girl Now" ....Edna & Tracy, Velma & Amber, Penny & Prudy

Scene 3:   TV Station WZZT

"I Can Hear the Bells" ....Tracy

"(The Legend of) Miss Baltimore Crabs" ....Velma & Council Members

Scene 4:   Detention

Scene 5:   Patterson Park High School Gymnasium

"The Madison" ....Corny & Company

Scene 6:   WZZT & Turnblad Home

"The Nicest Kids in Town" (Reprise) ....Corny & Council Members

"It Takes Two" ....Link & Tracy

Scene 7:   Turnblad Home and Streets of Baltimore

"Welcome to the '60s" ....Tracy, Edna, The Dynamites & Company

Scene 8:   Patterson Park Playground

"Run and Tell That" ....Seaweed

Scene 9:   Motormouth Maybelle's Record Shop

"Run and Tell That" ....Seaweed, Little Inez & Company

"Big, Blonde & Beautiful" ....Motormouth, Little Inez, Tracy, Edna, Wilbur

Act Two

Scene 1:   Baltimore Women's House of Detention

"The Big Dollhouse" ....Women

"Good Morning Baltimore" (Reprise) ....Tracy

Scene 2:   The Har-De-Har Hut

"Timeless to Me" ....Wilbur & Edna

Scene 3:   Tracy's Jail Cell & Penny's Bedroom

"Without Love" ....Link, Tracy, Seaweed, Penny

Scene 4:   Motormouth Maybelle's Record Shop

"I Know Where I've Been" ....Motormouth & Company

Scene 5:   The Baltimore Eventorium

"Hairspray" ....Corny & Council Members

"Cooties" ....Amber & Council Members

"You Can't Stop the Beat" ....Tracy, Link, Penny, Seaweed,
Edna, Wilbur, Motormouth & Company

Cast Continued

Little Inez ....NIA IMANI SOYEMI

Motormouth Maybelle ....MARY BOND DAVIS

Matron ....JULIE HALSTON

Guard ....JIM J. BULLOCK

Denizens of Baltimore ....CAMERON ADAMS
JIM J. BULLOCK
LINDSAY NICOLE CHAMBERS
ERIC L. CHRISTIAN, MICHAEL CUNIO
BECKY GULSVIG, JULIE HALSTON
CARLA J. HARGROVE
TYRICK WILTEZ JONES, LESLIE KRITZER
NICOLE POWELL
ANDREW RANNELLS, TERITA R. REDD, TODD
MICHAEL SMITH
BRYAN WEST, TOMMAR WILSON
CANDICE MARIE WOOD

Dance Captain ....**Rusty Mowery**

Assistant Dance Captain ....**C. Jay Hardy Philip**

Swings

Joe Abraham, Gretchen Bieber, Leslie Goddard, Abdu
Latif, Rusty Mowery, C. Jay Hardy Philip

Understudies

Understudy for Tracy Turnblad — SHANNON DURIG
LESLIE KRITZER; for Edna Turnblad— Jim J. Bullock
BLAKE HAMMOND; for Wilbur Turnblad — Jim J.
Bullock, BLAKE HAMMOND; for Velma Von Tussle —
JULIE HALSTON, LESLIE KRITZER, LIZ LARSEN
for Amber Von Tussle — CAMERON ADAMS, BECKY
GULSVIG; for Motormouth Maybelle — CARLA J.
HARGROVE, C. JAY HARDY PHILIP, TERITA R.
REDD; for Seaweed — eric l. christian, TOMMAR
WILSON; for Link Larkin — BRYAN WEST, ANDREW
RANNELLS; for Corny Collins — MICHAEL CUNIO
RUSTY MOWERY, ANDREW RANNELLS; for Penny
Pingleton — LINDSAY NICOLE CHAMBERS
BECKY GULSVIG; for Little Inez — CJAY HARDY
PHILIP, CANDICE MARIE WOODS; for
Spritzer/Principal/Mr. Pinky/Guard — BLAKE HAM-
MOND, ANDREW RANNELLS; for Prudy, Gym
Teacher, Matron — LINDSAY NICOLE CHAMBERS
LESLIE KRITZER, LIZ LARSEN; for Dynamites — C.
JAY HARDY PHILIP, TERITA R. REDD, TOMMAR
WILSON.

Hairspray

Bruce Vilanch
Edna Turnblad

Carly Jibson
Tracy Turnblad

Todd Susman
Wilbur Turnblad

Jordan Ballard
Amber Von Tussle

Richard H. Blake
Link Larkin

Jim J. Bullock
Harriman F.
Spritzer, Principal,
Mr. Pinky, Guard

Mary Bond Davis
Motormouth
Maybelle

Jonathan Dokuchitz
Corny Collins

Chester Gregory II
Seaweed

Julie Halston
Prudy Pingleton/
Gym Teacher/
Matron

Blake Hammond
u/s Harriman F.
Spritzer, Principal,
Mr. Pinky, Guard

Tracy Miller
Penny Pingleton

Nia Imani Soyemi
Little Inez

Barbara Walsh
Velma Von Tussle

Joe Abraham
Swing

Cameron Adams
Brenda

Gretchen Bieber
Swing

Lindsay Nicole
Chambers
Tammy

Eric L. Christian
Gilbert

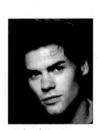
Michael Cunio
Brad

Shannon Durig
Understudy Tracy

Leslie Goddard
Swing

Becky Gulsvig
Lou Ann

Carla J. Hargrove
Dynamite

Tyrick Wiltez Jones
Duane

Hairspray

Leslie Kritzer
Shelley

Liz Larsen
*u/s Velma Von Tussle,
Prudy Pingleton, Gym
Teacher/Matron*

Abdul Latif
Swing

Rusty Mowery
*Swing/Production
Dance Supervisor/
Dance Captain*

C. Jay Hardy Philip
*Swing/Assistant
Dance Captain*

Nicole Powell
Dynamite

Andrew Rannells
Fender

Terita R. Redd
Lorraine

Todd Michel Smith
IQ

Bryan West
Sketch

Tommar Wilson
Thad

Candice Marie
Woods
Dynamite

Mark O'Donnell
Book

Thomas Meehan
Book

Marc Shaiman
*Music & Lyrics/
Arrangements*

Scott Wittman
Lyrics

Jack O'Brien
Director

Jerry Mitchell
Choreographer

David Rockwell
Scenic Designer

William Ivey Long
Costume

Kenneth Posner
Lighting Designer

Paul Huntley
Wig & Hair Design

John Waters
Consultant

Bernard Telsey
Casting

Harold Wheeler
Orchestrations

Lon Hoyt
Music Director

John Miller
Music Coordinator

Michele Lynch
*Associate
Choreographer*

Margo Lion
Producer

Rick Steiner
Producer

Frederic H.
Mayerson
Producer

Allan S. Gordon
Producer

Elan V. McAllister
Producer

Dede Harris
Producer

Morton Swinsky
Producer

John and Bonnie Osher
Producer

Daniel C. Staton
Associate Producer

Rhoda Mayerson
Associate Producer

Shoshana Bean
Understudy Velma Von Tussle, Prudy Pingleton, Gym Teacher/Matron

Tracee Beazer
Dynamites

Joshua Bergasse
Swing

Amanda DeFreitas
Dynamite

Katrina Dideriksen
Tracy understudy

Tracy Jai Edwards
Amber Von Tussle

Jennie Ford
Swing

Jennifer Gambatese
Penny Pingleton

Greg Graham
IQ

Kevin Hale
Duane

John Hill
Fender

Jackie Hoffman
Prudy Pingleton, Gym Teacher/ Matron

Hollie Howard
Tammy

Judine
Dynamite

Michelle Kittrell
Brenda/Dance Captain

Serge Kushnier
Sketch

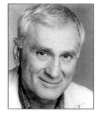

Dick Latessa
Wilbur Turnblad

Kathleen Leonard
Lou Ann

Michael Longoria
Swing

Aja Maria
Little Inez

John Jeffrey Martin
Fender

Michael McKean
Edna Turnblad

Rashad Naylor
Thad

Sabrina Reitman
Little Inez

Chandra Lee Schwartz
Lou Ann

Peter Scolari
Wilbur Turnblad

Peter Matthew Smith
Brad

Shayna Steele
Dynamite

Brooke Tansley
Penny Pingleton

Joel Vig
Harriman F. Spritzer/Principal/ Mr. Pinky/Guard

Crew
Back Row (on towers) (L-R): Mike Bennett, Ben Horrigan, Tom Green, Michael Bogden, Istvan "Ish" Tamas
Front Row (L-R): Ron Cucos, Art Lutz, Mike Pilipski, Brian Munroe, John J. Kelly, Brent Oakley, Brian Davis, Lorena Sullivan, Scott Mecionis, Stephen Vessa and James Mosaphir

Stage Management
(L-R): Marisha Ploski (Stage Manager), Frank Lombardi (Production Stage Manager), Jason Brouillard (Assistant Stage Manager).

Wardrobe and Hair Departments
Back Row (L-R): Tanya Guercy, Anna Rivera, Stephanie Barnes, Joe Armon, Johnny Roberson, Frank Sancineto, James Mosaphir, Alex Bartlett, Vangeli Kaseluris
Middle Row (L-R): Jodi Jackson, Kate McAleer, Kay Gowenlock, Meghan Carsella, Sara Foster, Mindy Eng
Front Row: Laura Horner

Front of House Staff
Front Row (L-R): Theresa Sachse, Jessica Mroz, Michelle Smith, Evelyn Olivero, Jane Publik, Wambui Bahati
Middle Row (L-R): Mary Ellen Palermo, Michelle Schechter, Dana Diaz, Angel Diaz, Frances Banyai, Annette Luyando, Adrianne Watson, Cecelia Luna, Julie Blondia
Back Row (L-R): Mayda Quintana, Christopher Langdon, Susie Martin, Irene Vincent, Jose Lopez, Dawn Edmonds, Josh Reid, Marc Needleman and Victor Irving

Photos by Ben Strohmann

Hairspray

STAFF FOR HAIRSPRAY

GENERAL MANAGEMENT
RICHARD FRANKEL PRODUCTIONS
Richard Frankel Marc Routh
Laura Green Rod Kaats
Jo Porter Joe Watson

COMPANY MANAGER
Marc Borsak

Associate Company Manager ....Aliza Wassner

GENERAL PRESS REPRESENTATIVE
RICHARD KORNBERG & ASSOCIATES
Richard Kornberg   Don Summa
Tom D'Ambrosio   Carrie Friedman

CASTING
BERNARD TELSEY CASTING C.S.A.
Bernie Telsey   Will Cantler   David Vaccari
Bethany Berg   Craig Burns
Tiffany Little Canfield   Christine Dall
Stephanie Yankwitt

PRODUCTION STAGE MANAGER ....Frank Lombardi
Stage Manager ....Marisha Ploski
Assistant Stage Manager ....Jason Brouillard
Associate Director ....Matt Lenz
Associate Choreographer ....Michele Lynch
Production Dance Supervisor ....Rusty Mowery
Technical Supervision ....Tech Production Services, Inc./
Peter Fulbright, Elliot Bertoni,
Mary Duffe, Colleen Houlehen,
Jarid Sumner, Michael Altbaum
Associate Set Designer ....Richard Jaris
Assistant Set Designers ....Emily Beck,
Robert Bissinger, Ted LeFevre
Associate to David Rockwell ....Barry Richards
Assistants to David Rockwell ....Michael Dereskewicz,
Joanie Schlafer
Associate Costume Designer ....Martha Bromelmeier
Assistant Costume Designer ....Laura Oppenheimer
Assistants to William Ivey Long .....Melissa-Anne Blizzard,
Donald Sanders
Automated Light Programmer ....Paul J. Sonnleitner
Associate Lighting Designer ....Philip Rosenberg
Assistant Lighting Designer ....Paul Miller
Associate Sound Designer ....John Shivers
Associate Wig and Hair Designer ....Amy Solomon

Make-Up Design by ....Randy Houston Mercer

Supervising Production Carpenter ....Ken Fieldhouse
Head Carpenter ....Brian Monroe
Assistant Carpenters ....Brian Davis, Ben Horrigan
Supervising Production Electrician ....Michael Lo Bue

Head Electrician ....Brent Oakley
Assistant Electrician ....Jessica Morton
Head Sound Engineer ....Andrew Keister
Assistant Sound Engineer ....Dave Dignazio
Deck Sound ....Art Lutz
Head Property Master ....Michael Pilipski
Assistant Property Master ....Lorena Sullivan
Wardrobe Supervisor ....Michael Sancineto
Assistant Wardrobe Supervisor ....Meghan Carsella
Star Dressers ....Kay Gowenlock, Joseph Phillip Armon
Dressers ....Alex Bartlett, Mindy Eng, Larry Foster,
Laura Horner, Liz Goodrum, Tanya Guercy,
Kate McAleer, Vangeli Kaseluris
Hair and Makeup Supervisor ....Jon Jordan
Assistant Hair Supervisor ....William Graham
Hair Assistants ....Stephanie Barnes, Lee Brock,
Isabelle Decauwert, Jodi Jackson,
Mark Manalanasan, John Roberson
Music Coordinator ....John Miller
Associate Conductor ....Keith Cotton
Drummer ....Clint DeGanon
Assistant Music Coordinator ....Matthew Ettinger,
Chuck Butler
Electronic Music System ....Music Arts Technologies,
Design and Programming   Jim Harp, Brett Sommer
Rehearsal Pianist ....Edward Rabin
Producing Assoc. to Ms. Lion ....Lily Hung
Asst. to Mr. Baruch ....Sonja Soper
Asst. to Mr. Viertel ....Tania Senewiratne
Associate Producer/
Adam Epstein Productions ....Lynn Shaw
Asst. to Mr. Steiner ....Kathy Wall
Asst. to Mr. Stern ....Leah Callaghan, Shira Sergant
Management Assistant ....Kevin Meyers
Juvenile Actors' Guardian ....Anna Rivera
Production Assistants ....Sharon DelPilar,
Travis Milliken, Noah Pollock,
Daniel Kelly
Press Interns ....Alyssa Hart, Jillian Lawrence
Advertising ....Serino Coyne, Inc./ Nancy Coyne,
Greg Coradetti, Joaquin Esteva,
Christina M. Prospero
Promotions/Marketing .....TMG - The Marketing Group/
Tanya Grubich, Laura Matalon
Photographer ....Paul Kolnik
Web Designer ....Simma Park
Theatre Displays ....King Displays
Insurance ....Marsh USA Inc., Margery Boyar
Legal Counsel ....Patricia Crown, Coblence & Warner
Banking ....Chase Manhattan Bank,
Richard Callian, Michael Friel
Payroll Service ....Castellana Services, Inc.
Accounting ....Lutz & Carr
Travel Agency ....JMC Travel
Concessions ....Rick Steiner Productions
New York Rehearsals ....The New 42nd Street Studios
New York Opening Night Coordinator .....Tobak-Danthik
Events and Promotions,
Suzanne Tobak, Jennifer Falik

EXCLUSIVE TOUR DIRECTION:
On the Road

RICHARD FRANKEL PRODUCTIONS STAFF
Finance Director ....Ann Caprio
Assistant to Mr. Frankel ....Heidi Schading

Assistant to Mr. Routh ....Michael Sag
Assistant to Ms. Green ....Adam M. Muller
Assistant Finance Director ....Liz Hines
Information Technology Manager ....Roddy Pimentel
Accounting Assistant ....Elsie Jamin-Maguire
National Sales and Marketing Director .....Ronni Mandell
Director of Business Affairs ....Carter McGowan
Director of Tour Management ....Simma Levine
Marketing Assistant ....Jocelyn Laporte
Booking Assistant ....ElizBeth Anne Jones
Office Manager ....Lori Steiger-Perry
Office Assistant ....Stephanie Kennedy
Receptionist ....Mandy Shuker
Interns ....Fran Acuna, Danny Bergold,
Alex Edwards, Lev Gartman,
Brian Luskey, Megan Lyle,
Lauren Pokras, Robert Scherzer,
Samantha Weber, Jim Woodward

CREDITS AND ACKNOWLEDGEMENTS

Scenery and scenic effects built, painted, electrified and
automated by Showmotion, Inc., Norwalk, Ct.
Scenery automation by Showmotion, Inc., using the
Autocue Computerized Motion Control System.
Lighting equipment from Fourth Phase, New Jersey. Sound
equipment by Sound Associates, Inc.
Specialty props by Prism Production Services, Rahway, NJ.
Costumes built by Euro Co Costumes Inc., Jennifer Love
Costumes, Scafati Incorporated, Schneeman Studios,
Tricorne New York City and Timberlake Studios, Inc.
Custom shoes by LaDuca Shoes NYC.
Champagne provided by Veuve Clicquot.
Lite Brite Wall engineered, constructed
and electrified by Showmotion, Inc.
Soft goods by Rosebrand Textiles, Inc.
Scenic painting by Scenic Art Studios. Hair Curtain Main
Drape by I. Weiss and Sons, Inc.

NEDERLANDER

Chairman ....**James M. Nederlander**
President ....**James L. Nederlander**

Executive Vice President
Nick Scandalios

Vice President	Senior Vice President
Corporate Development	Labor Relations
Charlene S. Nederlander	Herschel Waxman

| Vice President | Chief Financial Officer |
| Jim Boese | Freida Sawyer Belviso |

www.nederlander.org

STAFF FOR THE NEIL SIMON THEATRE
Theatre Manager ....Victor Irving
Treasurer ....Richard Aubrey
Associate Treasurer ....Eddie Waxman
House Carpenter ....Thomas Green
Flyman ....Douglas McNeill
House Electrician ....James Travers, Sr.
House Propman ....Scott Mecionis
House Engineer ....John Astras

Above left: Mark O'Donnell, Scott Wittman (kneeling) Jerry Mitchell, Jack O'Brien, Margo Lion, Tom Meehan, David Rockwell, Tom Viertel with the cake celebrating the 1,000th performance at the Neil Simon Theatre. Above right: Jackie Hoffman and John Waters.

Michael McKean (center) takes a curtain call at the special Actors' Fund concert performance of *Hair* at the New Amsterdam Theatre.

Kathy Brier.

Librettists Thomas Meehan and Mark O'Donnell.

Opening Night Gifts: When we walked in on opening night, it was like Christmas morning. David Rockwell who designed the sets, gave us a lunch pail he designed that was very period, filled with different *Hairspray* stuff. We got all kinds of memorabilia from the show, including cans of Ultra-Clutch hairspray.

Celebrity Visitors: Everybody's come to see the show. Perhaps the most memorable is when George Bush Sr. and Barbara Bush came around the time of the Republican convention. We were definitely not on the list of recommended shows for convention-goers. But George and Barbara came anyway. Mrs. Von Tussel has a line about how manipulating the judicial system just to win an election is un-American. When she said it, the audience went bonkers. But George and Barbara were great sports about it. They came backstage afterward and took pictures with us.

Best Fan Letter: We got a great letter from a Roman Catholic priest who had been transferred to New York from a small-town parish and was having a difficult time here. We read it out loud at our pre-show prayer circle. Here's a quote: "From the opening number, my spirits were lifted. The show brought me back to a time of joy and happiness. I sat there saying, 'I did that dance move. And I did that dance.' At the intermission I was crying. I just wanted to be dancing and singing with all of you on stage. I was just so happy and my sense of feeling down was gone."

Who Got The Gypsy Robe: Judine Richard. She added a *Hairspray* face from the poster.

"Gypsy Of The Year" Sketch: "Broadway Squares" by Bruce Vilanch (Joan Rivers made an appearance in it!)

"Carols For A Cure" Carol: "Hello Christmas."

"Easter Bonnet" Sketch: "Let Me Fall"

Which Actor Performed The Most Roles in the Show: Julie Halston plays four roles.

Who Has Done The Most Shows: Judine Richard had the most in the ensemble, but actually Dick Latessa has been in every Broadway show ever!

Backstage Rituals: Right before the top of the show, we usually do a little prayer circle. It's not extremely religious, but people do thank God for all the blessings we have, being in our show and on Broadway. If somebody is not feeling well or is having personal problems, we try to send good energy their way. It gets us revved up to do the show in the right, positive place.

Favorite Moment During Each Performance: It used to be Jackie Hoffman's spot. Her character, Penny Pingleton, comes on from the audience, and every performance something different would come out of her mouth. When she'd see little kids, she'd say, "Oh, hi, isn't that sweet?" Or, "What's the matter, couldn't your parents get tickets for *The Lion King*?" When the McGreevey scandal was breaking she had a field day with that. Stage management actually kept a log of all the things she said. Her line is supposed to be just five or six words, but on her final performance it turned into a ten-minute bit, including singing "Somewhere" from *West Side Story* at the top of her voice.

In-Theatre Gathering Place: The star dressing room has a little anteroom, which Harvey decorated with a couch. Harvey would take pictures backstage and hang them on the wall. It built up so quickly it now covers every inch of the anteroom wall. It's really amazing and very creative. It's also a good running history of the show.

Off-Site Hangout: The Palm.

Favorite Snack Food: Lime Tostito chips, Zingers.

Mascot: When we were trying out in Seattle we stayed at a hotel and used to play poker in the lobby. One day we found a little wooden duckie, which people in the cast took a shine to. It somehow found its way into someone's bag, and now lives backstage at the Neil Simon Theatre. We named it Squat the Wooden Duck and it makes the rounds of dressing rooms.

Favorite Therapy: A physical therapist comes in every week from Performing Arts Physical Therapy. The therapist always knows everything going on on Broadway. Sometimes he knows what's happening on Broadway before we do.

Most Memorable Ad Lib: You never really knew what was going to come out of Harvey Fierstein's mouth or Bruce Vilanch's mouth. But there was one Sunday matinee when the light board crashed just before "Welcome to the '60s." Harvey and Marissa happened to be onstage together, and they just sat on the edge of the stage and did a mother-daughter shtick for ten minutes until the board was fixed. It was hilarious and it was brilliant. I remember one line: "I feel like Judy and Liza!"

Record Number Of Cell Phone Rings During A Performance: Never more than one, that I remember. At the top of the show, we announce that the "The Corny Collins Show" took place in 1962, a time before the invention of cells phones and pages. That gets most people to turn them off.

Memorable Stage Door Fan Encounter: A couple of people have seen the show more than 100 times, and every time they come they want something signed.

Heaviest/Hottest Costume: This has got to be Edna. He wears a fat suit and wig and everything.

Who Wore The Least: During "Big Doll House" some of the chorus is dressed as ladies of the night, and they've got some skin showing.

Catchphrase: "Oh Shaka Khan!" It was started by Marc Shaiman and the original company, and it's kind of hung on.

Also: The guys of the ensemble organized our

Michael McKean (center) and Hairspray cast members at the "Broadway on Broadway" event in Times Square.

Above: (L-R) Tracy Jai Edwards, composer Marc Shaiman, Peter Scolari at a farewell party for four members of the cast at Azalea restaurant.

Right: Mary Bond Davis and Carly Jibson at Azalea.

own parody of a reality TV show, which we called "Dressing Room Survivor." Serge Kushnier videotaped it. We did eight episodes, and one guy got voted off each week. It was hilarious. John Hill wound up winning. We screened it at the theatre and most of the cast came to watch.

Correspondent: Todd Michel Smith, "I.Q."

PLAYBILL

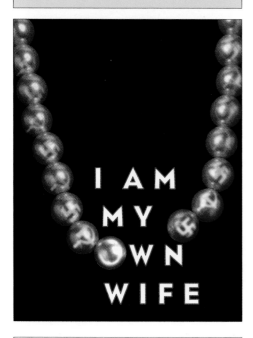

CAST

Charlotte von Mahlsdorf, et al.
JEFFERSON MAYS

ACT ONE

Phonographs

ACT TWO

Clocks

Playwrights Horizons, Inc. New York City,
produced the World Premiere of *I Am My Own Wife*
Off-Broadway 2003.

This play was written with support from
Playwrights Horizons, made possible by funds
granted to the author through a program sponsored by
Amblin Entertainment, Inc.

A workshop of *I Am My Own Wife* was presented by
La Jolla Playhouse,
Des McAnuff, Artistic Director &
Terrence Dwyer, Managing Director.

This play was developed in part with the support of the
Sundance Theatre Laboratory.

A workshop of *I Am My Own Wife* was presented
by About Face Theatre, Chicago
(Eric Rosen, Artistic Director), in association with the
Museum of Contemporary Art.

The producers wish to thank
Tectonic Theater Project
for their aid in the development of this play.

The producers wish to express
their appreciation to
Theatre Development Fund
for its support of this production.

LYCEUM THEATRE

A Shubert Organization Theatre
Gerald Schoenfeld, Chairman   Philip J. Smith, President
Robert E. Wankel, Executive Vice President

DELPHI PRODUCTIONS
in association with
PLAYWRIGHTS HORIZONS
present

I AM MY OWN WIFE

by
DOUG WRIGHT

starring
JEFFERSON MAYS

scenic design	lighting design	costume design	sound design
DEREK McLANE	**DAVID LANDER**	**JANICE PYTEL**	**ANDRE J. PLUESS**

production stage manager
NANCY HARRINGTON

production supervisor
ARTHUR SICCARDI

general manager
NIKO COMPANIES, LTD.

press representative
**RICHARD KORNBERG
AND ASSOCIATES**

directed by
MOISÉS KAUFMAN

9/1/04

A NOTE FROM THE PLAYWRIGHT

I Am My Own Wife draws upon several sources: transcribed interviews I conducted with its subject, Charlotte von Mahlsdorf, from our initial meeting in August of 1992 until January 1994; letters we exchanged until her death in 2002; newspaper accounts of her life in the public record; her Stasi file; and my own personal, sometimes selective remembrances of our encounters. I have also taken the customary liberties of the dramatist: editing for clarity, condensing several pivotal characters into one utilitarian one and imagining some scenes I only heard recounted, while inventing others for narrative continuity.
– *Doug Wright*

Consultant/Translator ....Jeffrey Schneider,
Vassar College

Jefferson Mays in character as Charlotte von Mahlsdorf in *I Am My Own Wife*.

Celebrity Visitor: Siegfried (of Siegfried and Roy), who said, "Do Americans understand this? Do they get it?"

Who Played The Most Characters: Jefferson Mays played every character (38).

Backstage Rituals: Jefferson would have a cup of coffee or tea each night before he went onstage.

Favorite Off-Site Hangout: Home.

Favorite Therapy: Ricola, Throat-Coat Tea, humidifier.

Record Number Of Cell Phone Rings: Nine.

Strangest Press Encounter: One reporter made the statement to Jefferson, "I was shocked you won the Tony and even more shocked that you're not gay."

Sweethearts: My wife and I.

Superstitions: The Lyceum is an old theatre, and I'm sure it's haunted. Strange things would happen. Things would move from one place to another and no one knew how. We all used to get strange feelings back there, but no one I know saw anything beyond that.

Correspondent: James Lawson, Company Manager

Jefferson Mays
Charlotte von Mahlsdorf

Doug Wright
Playwright

Moisés Kaufman
Director

Derek McLane
Scenic Designer

Thea Bradshaw Gillies
Assistant Stage Manager

Charlene & Anthony Marshall
Producers

PRODUCTION STAFF FOR
I AM MY OWN WIFE

GENERAL MANAGEMENT
NIKO COMPANIES
Manny Kladitis   David Cole
Steve Marquard, Comptroller

PRESS REPRESENTATION
RICHARD KORNBERG & ASSOCIATES
Richard Kornberg   Don Summa
Tom D'Ambrosio   Carrie Friedman   Rick Miramontez

COMPANY MANAGER
James Lawson

Production Stage Manager	Nancy Harrington
Stage Manager	Thea Bradshaw Gillies
Artistic Consultant	Susan Lyons
Assistant Scenic Designer	Shoko Kambara
Assistant Lighting Designer	Ted Sullivan
Associate Sound Designer	Josh Bender-Dubiel
House Carpenter	Adam Braunstein
Production Electrician	Richie Mortell
House Electrician	William K. Rowland
Production Sound	Tony Polemeni
Production Props	Mike Pilipski
House Props	Steve McDonald
Wardrobe Supervisor	Christel Murdock
Assistant to Mr. Richenthal	Judy Insel
Production Assts.	Jeremy Lewit, Carol Sullivan
Advertising	Spotco/ Drew Hodges, Jim Edwards, Jim Aquino, Lauren Hunter
Marketing	The Karpel Group/ Craig Karpel, Billy Zavelson
Opening Night Coordination	Tobak-Dantchik Events &

	Promotions/ Joanna B. Koondel, Cathy Dantchik
Accountant	Elliott Aranstam/Robert Fried
Legal Service	Franklin, Weinrib, Rudell & Vasallo
Insurance	Marsh USA, Inc./Elda Luisi
Banking	JP Morgan Chase/Mary Ann Viafore
Payroll Services	Checks & Balances, Inc., Burton Greenhouse, Ed Greenhouse

PLAYWRIGHTS HORIZONS STAFF

Artistic Director	**Time Sanford**
Managing Director	**Lelsie Marcus**
General Manager	**William Russo**
Literary Manager	Lisa Timmel
Casting Director	James Calleri
Production Manager	Christopher Boll
Director of Development	Jill Garland
Controller	Daniel C. Smith
Director of Marketing	Eric Winick
Director of Ticket Central	Mike Rafael
Director of Playwrights Horizons Theatre School	Helen R. Cook

PLAYWRIGHTS HORIZONS
BOARD OF DIRECTORS
Judith O. Rubin, Chairman; Lawrence B. Buttenweiser, Vice Chairman; Mikael Salovaara, Vice Chairman; Herbert A. Morey, Treasurer; Marjorie G. Rosen, Secretary; Andre Bishop, David Caplan, Geoffrey G. Clark, Jane Epstein, Ethan Geto, Robert W. Jones, Leslie Marcus, Robert Moss, Kathleen O'Grady, Michael Patsalos-Fox, Robert Rimsky, Tim Sanford, Joseph S. Steinberg, Paul A. Travis, Alan Wasser, Rachel Wilder, Jide J. Zeitlin

CREDITS
Scenery by Atlas Scenic. Lighting equipment by Fourth Phase. Sound equipment by One Dream Sound. Props by Custom Craftsmen, Decco Studio, Anything but Costumes, Paper Mill Playhouse, Purchase College, Dong Hwan Kim, Paul Eric Pape. Natural herb cough drops courtesy of Ricola USA, Inc.

SPECIAL THANKS
Jung Griffin and Ellen Pilipski

 THE SHUBERT ORGANIZATION INC.

Gerald Schoenfeld   Philip J. Smith
Chairman   President

John W. Kluge   Lee J. Seidler

Michael I. Sovern   Stuart Subotnick

Irving M. Wall

Robert E. Wankel
Executive Vice President

Peter Entin   Elliot Greene
Vice President   Vice President
Theatre Operations   Finance

David Andrews   John Darby
Vice President   Vice President
Shubert Ticketing Services   Facilities

House Manager	Joann Swanson

PLAYBILL®

JACKIE MASON
freshly squeezed
JUST ONE JEW TALKING!

THE HELEN HAYES THEATRE

MARTIN MARKINSON   **DONALD TICK**

Jyll Rosenfeld, Jon Stoll and James Scibelli
present

JACKIE MASON
freshly squeezed

Lighting Design by   Sound Design by
Paul Miller   **Peter Hylenski**

General Press Representative   Marketing   Advertising
Larry Weinberg   **Keith Hurd**   **Echo Advertising**

General Management   Production Stage Manager   Company Manager
Theatre Production Group   **Don Myers**   **G. Eric Muratalla**

Written and Directed by
Jackie Mason

3/23/05

STAFF FOR
JACKIE MASON: FRESHLY SQUEEZED;
JUST ONE JEW TALKING

GENERAL MANAGEMENT
THEATRE PRODUCTION GROUP

Frank P. Scardino
in association with
Joseph P. Harris

COMPANY MANAGER
G. ERIC MURATALLA

GENERAL PRESS REPRESENTATIVE
LARRY WEINBERG

PRODUCTION STAGE MANAGER
Don Myers

Production Carpenter ....Ron Mooney
Production Electrician ....Joe Beck
Production Prop ....Roger Keller
Sound Engineer ....Bob Etter
Assistant to General Manager ....Tegan Meyer
Assistant to Jyll Rosenfeld ....Melissa Flores
Assistant to Jon Stoll ....Susan Christopher
Advertising ..Echo Advertising/Barry Avrich, Tracy Chang
Marketing ....Keith Hurd
Insurance ....C&S International
Insurance Brokers, Inc./
Debra Kozee
Legal Counsel ....Raoul Lionel Felder
Accounting ....Rosenberg, Neuwirth & Kuchner/
Michele Gugliero
Payroll Services ....Castellana Services, Inc
Banking..................................Commerce Bank/
Barbara von Borstel,
Ashley Elezi
Web-Site Design ....Sarah
DiSanti

CREDITS

Lighting equipment provided by
PRG Lighting.
Sound equipment provided by
PRG Audio.
Soft goods Rosebrand, Inc.
Company boards and sliders by
King Displays.

THE HELEN HAYES THEATRE
owned and operated by
MARTIN MARKINSON
and DONALD TICK

General Manager
Susan S. Myerberg

Associate General Manger
Jeffrey T. Hughes

STAFF FOR THE
HELEN HAYES THEATRE

House Manager
Alan R. Markinson

Treasurer:
David Heveran

Assistant Treasurers:
Michael A. Lynch, Manuel Rivera

Head Carpenter ....Ron Mooney
Head Electrician ....Joseph Beck
Head Propertyman ....Roger Keller
Engineer/Maintenance ....Hector Angulo
Head Usher ....John Biancamano
Stage Door ....Vincent Kwasnicki,
Robert Seymour
Accountant ....Chen-Win Hsu

Jackie Mason: Freshly Squeezed

The Crew
Back Row (L-R): Roger Keller, Jessica Bailey, Olivia Goode, John Biancamano, Don Myers, Joe Beck, Michael Lynch, Bobby Seymour.
Middle Row (L-R): Gary Stocker, David Heveran, Eric Muratalla, Shannon Taylor, Berdine Vaval, Hirendra Joshi.
Front Row (L-R): Ron Mooney, Jyll Rosenfeld, Jackie Mason and Linda Maley-Biancamano.

Larry Weinberg
General Press Rep

Alan Markinson
House Manager

Keith Hurd
Marketing

Raoul Lionel Felder
Legal Counsel

Jackie Mason

Photo by Bill Milne

Opening Night Gifts: Big flower pots.
Celebrity Visitor: Jerry Seinfeld, who's always worshipful. He always gives me the same speech: "I never imagined someone could create all new material every time I see him. How do you do it?"
Backstage Rituals: I'm not one who gets nervous or jumps around or dances or sweats a lot. I got no tricks or misgivings or nervousness or gyrations.
Favorite In-Theatre Gathering Place: I just sit like an old Jew by the coffee table.
Favorite Off-Site Hangout: When I want a real meal, Da Tommaso. When I go in for light fruit or a snack, I go to the Polish Tea Room (The Edison Café).
Favorite Snack Food: They always have some kind of diet cookie because I have a manager obsessed with dieting. She has concern and feeling for me. If she sees a non-diet cookie, it's like if you were to see a guy with a pistol about to shoot you.
Favorite Therapy: I work very hard in preparing jokes for the show. I tape the jokes and try them out every day in clubs all over the country, trying to perfect them to a level of delicacy and perfection to have the ultimately most perfect show I could create. With all the honing and polishing, by the time I come to Broadway I'm comfortable that the jokes are landing and popping in as lovely a way as I could possibly achieve. I'm like a fighter who's ready to jump into the ring because I could beat anybody. I could kill any audience. Some actors are afraid. All fears come from basic psychological insecurities. But it has nothing to do with the occasion. Why would a guy who is fifty or sixty or seventy and been doing this all his life possibly be afraid of an audience? No matter what you do, even if you bomb, they're not going to kill you. They're not going to chase you out of the theatre. They're not going to hire Mafia people to come after you. Chances are, you're safer on that stage than any Jew in town.
Record Number Of Cell Phone Rings: When it happens, it's never more than once.
Strange Stage Door Fan Encounters: All kinds of meshugoyim come to my stage door with strange complaints and requests. And now, phones they bring. "I've known you thirty years—could you say hello to my mother?" "I don't like you much myself, but my sister-in-law is a big fan. She'd love to hear your voice."
Two weeks ago a woman comes to the stage door and says, "I have a sister, but my sister can't stand you. Something about you gets her sick, gets her nauseous. Something about the sound of your voice, it just makes her physically ill. She just can't stand the severe Jewishness of you, even though she herself is Jewish....So could you say hello?" And she hands me a phone! So I say, "Don't you have any respect for your sister! Why would you want her to speak to someone who makes her sick?" And the woman says, "I want to prove to her you're a nice person. She would get such a kick!" I said, "Positively not!" I told her to drop *dead* with her telephone.
They all have stories. "My father's been in the hospital three weeks with a bad foot. Could you go visit him for a few minutes? Just drop by and say a few words. What, you don't have the decency to go visit my sick father in the hospital even though he saw two of your shows eleven years ago? It's not far—only in Boston!"
Correspondent: Jackie Mason

PLAYBILL®

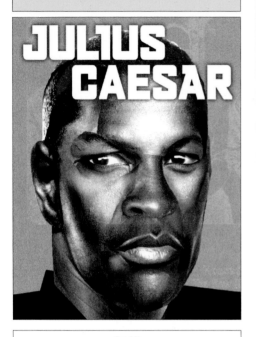

JULIUS CAESAR

CAST
(in order of appearance)

Soothsayer ....STEPHEN LEE ANDERSON
Marcus Brutus ....DENZEL WASHINGTON
Portia.................................JESSICA HECHT
Artemidora ......JACQUELINE ANTARAMIAN
Flavius ....JOHN DOUGLAS THOMPSON
Marullus ....HENRY WORONICZ
Carpenter ....HOWARD W. OVERSHOWN
Cobbler................................KEITH DAVIS
Guards to Caesar ....MARK
MINEART,
DAN MORAN
Mark Antony ....EAMONN WALKER
Julius Caesar ....WILLIAM SADLER
Calpurnia ....TAMARA TUNIE
Casca ....JACK WILLIS
Decius Brutus.....................PATRICK PAGE
Cassius ....COLM FEORE
Cicero ....DAVID CROMWELL
Cinna.............................RICHARD TOPOL
Metellus Cimber ....PETER JAY
FERNANDEZ
Trebonius ....HENRY WORONICZ
Lucius ....MAURICE JONES
Servant to Caesar ....SETH FISHER
Popilius Lena ....JASON MANUEL
OLAZÁBAL
Servant to Mark Antony ....ED ONIPEDE
BLUNT
Servant to Octavius Caesar ....QUENTIN
MARÉ

cast continued on next page

⑤ BELASCO THEATRE
111 West 44th Street
A Shubert Organization Theatre

Gerald Schoenfeld, *Chairman*   Philip J. Smith, *President*

Robert E. Wankel, *Executive Vice President*

Carole Shorenstein Hays   Freddy DeMann

present

Denzel Washington

in

JULIUS CAESAR

by
William Shakespeare

with

Colm Feore   Jessica Hecht   William Sadler   Tamara Tunie   Eamonn Walker   Jack Willis

Stephen Lee Anderson   Jacqueline Antaramian   Kelly AuCoin   Ed Onipede Blunt   David Cromwell   Keith Davis
Peter Jay Fernandez   Seth Fisher   Effie Johnson   Maurice Jones   Ty Jones   Aaron Krohn   Quentin Maré
Christopher McHale   Mark Mineart   Dan Moran   Jason Manuel Olazábal   Howard W. Overshown   Patrick Page
Kurt Rhoads   John Douglas Thompson   Richard Topol   Henry Woronicz

Set Design	Costume Design	Lighting Design	Original Music and Sound Design
Ralph Funicello	Jess Goldstein	Mimi Jordan Sherin	Dan Moses Schreier

Fight Director	Special Effects Design	Wig and Hair Design	Make-up Design
Robin H. McFarquhar	Gregory Meeh	Charles Lapointe	Angelina Avallone

Dramaturge	Vocal Consultant	Production Management	Production Stage Manager
Dakin Matthews	Elizabeth Smith	Aurora Productions	Lisa Dawn Cave

Casting	Marketing	Press Representative	Company Manager	General Management
Daniel Swee C.S.A.	Eric Schnall	Boneau/Bryan-Brown	Edward Nelson	Stuart Thompson Productions/ James Triner

Executive Producers
Pilar DeMann   Greg Holland

Directed by
Daniel Sullivan

LIVE
BROADWAY

4/3/04

Warning Caesar: (L-R): Dan Moran, Jacqueline Antaramian, Denzel Washington, William Sadler and Mark Mineart.

Julius Caesar

UNDERSTUDIES

Denzel Washington
Marcus Brutus

Colm Feore
Cassius

Jessica Hecht
Portia

William Sadler
Julius Caesar

Tamara Tunie
Calpurnia

Eamonn Walker
Mark Antony

Jack Willis
Casca

Stephen Lee
Anderson
*Soothsayer,
Titinius, Ensemble*

Jacqueline
Antaramian
*Artemidora,
Understudy
Portia/Calpurnia*

Kelly Aucoin
*Octavius Caesar,
Ensemble*

Ed Onipede Blunt
*Servant To Mark
Antony, Cato,
Ensemble*

David Cromwell
*Cinna The Poet,
Cicero, Ensemble*

Keith Davis
*Cobbler, Pindarus,
Ensemble*

Peter Jay Fernandez
*Lucilius, Metellus
Cimber, Ensemble
Understudy Brutus*

Seth Fisher
*Servant To Caesar,
First Soldier,
Ensemble*

Effie Johnson
*Ensemble,
Understudy
Artemidora*

Maurice Jones
Lucius, Ensemble

Ty Jones
*Ensemble,
Understudy Mark
Antony, Octavius
Caesar*

Aaron Krohn
*Ensemble
Understudy Lucius,
Cato*

Quentin Maré
*Clitus, Servant To
Octavius Caesar,
Messenger,
Understudy
Marullus Trebonius*

Julius Caesar

Christopher McHale
*Second Soldier,
Ensemble, u/s Decuis
Brutus, Metllus
Cimber, Lepidus*

Mark Mineart
*Guard To Caesar,
Ensemble, Fight
Captain*

Dan Moran
*Guards To Caesar,
Voluminus,
Ensemble, u/s
Cobbler, Pindarus*

Jason Manuel
Olazábal
*Popilius Lena,
Ensemble*

Howard W.
Overshown
*Carpenter,
Dardanius, Ens.*

Patrick Page
*Decius Brutus.
Messala,
Ensemble, u/s
Cassius*

Kurt Rhoads
*Ensemble,
u/s Cicero, Decius
Brutus, Marullus*

John Douglas
Thompson
Flavius, Ensemble

Richard Topol
*Cinna, Lepidus,
Ensemble, u/s
Casca*

Henry Woronicz
*Marullus, Trebonius,
Ensemble
u/s Julius Caesar*

Daniel Sullivan
Director

Ralph Funicello
Set Designer

Jess Goldstein
Costume Designer

Mimi Jordan Sherin
Lighting Designer

Dan Moses Schreier
*Original Music and
Sound Design*

Robin H.
McFarquhar
Fight Direction

Elizabeth Smith
Vocal Consultant

Stuart Thompson
General Manager

Greg Holland
Executive Producer

Carole Shorenstein
Hays
Producer

Photo by Ben Strohmann

**The Crew and
Front-of-House Staff**
Front Row (kneeling, L-R): Kathleen Dunn,
Selena Nelson, Daniel Rosario, Tasha Allen,
Tadese Bartholomew, Gwendolyn Coley,
Mindy Lutz, Meaghan McElroy.

Second Row (L-R): Devlani James,
Eugenia Raines, Derek Moreno, Nancy
Ronan, Sakie Onazawa, Jen Kievit,
Kathleen Powell, Susan Goulet.

Third Row (L-R): Eric "Speed" Smith,
Lisa Dawn Cave, Brian Meister, Jenny
Montgomery, Rick Dal Curtivo, Mia Neal,
Jared Beasley, Scott McLelland.

Back Row (L-R): Davis Duffield, Charles
Loesche, Curtis Croome, Kevin Bertolacci,
Lee J. Austin, Amanda Ezell, Mike LoBue,
George Dummitt, Joe Moritz, Dexter L. Luke.

Julius Caesar

Above left: Tamara Tunie at the cast party. Above right: Curtain calls on opening night.

Left: William Sadler arrives on opening night.

Right: Phylicia Rashad and Samuel L. Jackson are among celebrity guests.

Best Opening Night Note: The cast of *Spamalot* sent over a note wishing us good luck on opening night, signed by everyone. One of the actors wrote, "Et tu? Et three—they're small!"

Opening Night Gifts: Producers gave us a copy of the script. (I wasn't sure what exactly they meant by that….) My wife hunted down some imitation Roman coins, which I gave out.

Most Exciting Celebrity Visitors: When we heard that Paul Newman and Joanne Woodward were in the audience halfway through the first act, we had actors with decades of experience peeking out from the wings like junior high schoolers. Afterward, they came backstage and were as gracious as can be.

Who Has Done The Most Shows: David Cromwell or Peter Jay Fernandez.

Special Backstage Rituals: Jack Willis (who plays Casca) and I share a dressing room. While we're getting dressed, from half-hour call to fifteen-minutes, we put on a piece of Argentinian jazz/klezmer music and the two of us dance.

Favorite Moment: My personal favorite moment happens in the massage scene where Calpurnia talks me into staying home from the Senate. But then Decius Brutus talks me into going after all. I sit there in a white bathrobe in the middle of a wonderful tug o' war.

Memorable Ad-Lib: One night the wheels on the massage table didn't lock and I started rolling toward the audience. I man-aged to stop it and I found myself saying, "Caesar is not going to stay home today!"

Most Embarrassing Moment: That happened in my damn nude scene. I'm supposed to get off the massage table, drop the towel, take two steps and put on the big white bathrobe. One night, I grabbed the bathrobe, but it wouldn't close all the way. It seemed that when they washed and dried it, it shrunk. It felt like doll clothes. I somehow managed to stretch it across my front and tie it, but I had to keep my legs crossed the rest of the scene.

Favorite In-Theatre Gathering Place: The Green Room, which also serves as the laundry room, the shower room and the espresso bar.

Favorite Off-Site Hangout: Restaurant Un Deux Trois, which is right next door to the Belasco. José, the owner, did a very clever thing. The night of the first preview, he invited the entire cast and crew over for food and drinks on him. He created a clubhouse for us, and it just stuck. We have a table behind the bar where every night a great contingent of the cast ends up.

Favorite Therapy: Eamonn Walker has created a kind of tea that has honey and raw grated ginger and I don't know what all else. I only know that everybody wants Eamonn's Throat Concoction all the time. That, and freshly pulled espresso.

Memorable Stage Door Fan Encounters: A little Russian guy appeared at the stage door one day wanting us to sign some pic-tures of the show. But we could tell from looking at them that he had shot us with his cell phone camera from the audience, and printed them out! That's illegal, so we refused to sign.

One of the coolest things that's ever happened to me also happened at the stage door. There's always an enormous crowd waiting for Denzel, spilling off the sidewalk in both directions. He always takes the time to autograph everyone's *Playbill*. One night I stepped out and didn't think anyone would notice me. But four hundred people shouted in unison, "Hail, Caesar!"

Ghostly Encounters: I don't think anybody has seen the ghost of David Belasco, but we've had a lot of mischief going on with lighting instruments: lamps blowing up and lights flickering on and off in the wings for no reason at all.

Coolest Thing About Being In This Show: There are many: Working with Denzel Washington is high on the list. Dan Sullivan is up there. But maybe the coolest thing is getting the chance to do Shakespeare on Broadway at the beautiful old 1907 Belasco Theatre. It's a rare and wonderful thing. I'll tell you a story. The first day of rehearsal, I got to the theatre an hour early, but I didn't go in. I walked around on the street for an hour. Why? Because I didn't want it to start. I knew that the minute it started, the clock would be ticking. And one day it would be over.

Correspondent: William Sadler, "Julius Caesar."

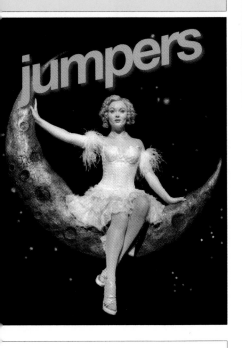

PLAYBILL®

CAST

(in order of appearance)

Dorothy	ESSIE DAVIS
Secretary	ELIZA LUMLEY
Crouch	JOHN ROGAN
George	SIMON RUSSELL BEALE
Archie	NICKY HENSON
Bones	NICHOLAS WOODESON
Jumper	MICHAEL ARNOLD
Jumper	ANDREW ASNES
Jumper	CLARK SCOTT CARMICHAEL
Jumper	TOM HILDEBRAND
Jumper (Greystoke)	MICHAEL HOLLICK
Jumper	DON JOHANSON
Jumper	JOSEPH P. McDONNELL
Jumper (McFee)	HILLEL MELTZER

STANDBYS

For George - JOHN CURLESS; for Dorothy and Secretary – CRISTA MOORE; for Archie – TONY CARLIN; for Bones and Crouch – JULIAN GAMBLE; Jumper Swings – KARL CHRISTIAN, AARON VEXLER

Simon Russell Beale is appearing with the permission of Actors' Equity Association.

Essie Davis, Nicky Henson, Eliza Lumley and John Rogan are appearing with the permission of Actors' Equity Association pursuant to an exchange program between American Equity and British Equity.

⇒N⇐ BROOKS ATKINSON THEATRE
UNDER THE DIRECTION OF JAMES M. NEDERLANDER AND JAMES L. NEDERLANDER

BOYETT OSTAR PRODUCTIONS   NEDERLANDER PRESENTATIONS INC.
FREDDY DeMANN   JEAN DOUMANIAN   STEPHANIE McCLELLAND   ARIELLE TEPPER
present
NT THE NATIONAL THEATRE OF GREAT BRITAIN'S
production of

jumpers
Tom Stoppard

Director	DAVID LEVEAUX
Set Designer	VICKI MORTIMER
Costume Designer	NICKY GILLIBRAND
Lighting Designer	PAULE CONSTABLE
Music	CORIN BUCKERIDGE
Choreographer	AIDAN TREAYS
Sound Designer	JOHN LEONARD FOR AURA
Video Designers	DICK STRAKER & SVEN ORTEL FOR MESMER
US Casting	JIM CARNAHAN, CSA
Music Coordinator	MICHAEL KELLER
Conductor	TIM WEIL
General Management	101 PRODUCTIONS, LTD
Press Representative	BONEAU/BRYAN-BROWN
Marketing	HHC MARKETING
Technical Supervisor	DAVID BENKEN
Production Stage Manager	ARTHUR GAFFIN

Cast

SIMON RUSSELL BEALE
ESSIE DAVIS
NICKY HENSON
ELIZA LUMLEY
JOHN ROGAN
NICHOLAS WOODESON

MICHAEL ARNOLD   ANDREW ASNES   CLARK SCOTT CARMICHAEL   KARL CHRISTIAN
TOM HILDEBRAND   MICHAEL HOLLICK   DON JOHANSON
JOSEPH P. McDONNELL   HILLEL MELTZER   AARON VEXLER

6/28/04

JUMPERS TRIO

CONDUCTOR/KEYBOARD: TIM WEIL

Drums: James Saporito

Bass: Dick Sarpola

Music Coordinator: Michael Keller

Simon Russell Beale gains inspiration in Tom Stoppard's *Jumpers*.

Photo by Hugo Glendinning

Jumpers

Simon Russell Beale
George

Essie Davis
Dorothy

Nicky Henson
Archie

Eliza Lumley
Secretary

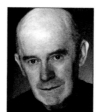
John Rogan
Crouch

Nicholas Woodeson
Bones

Michael Arnold
Jumper

Andrew Asnes
Jumper

Clark Scott Carmichael
Jumper

Karl Christian
Swing

Tom Hildebrand
Jumper

Michael Hollick
Jumper/Greystoke

Don Johanson
Jumper

Joseph P. McDonnell
Jumper

Hillel Meltzer
Jumper/McFee

Aaron Vexler
Swing

Tony Carlin
Standby Archie

John Curless
Standby George

Julian Gamble
Standby Bones & Crouch

Crista Moore
Standby Dorothy & Secretary

Tom Stoppard
Playwright

David Leveaux
Director

Paule Constable
Lighting Design

Corin Buckeridge
Music

John Leonard
Sound Design

Jim Carnahan
U.S. Casting

Michael Keller
Music Coordinator

David Benken
Technical Supervisor

Matt Wilde
Associate Director

Jean Doumanian
Producer

Stephanie McClelland
Producer

Arielle Tepper
Producer

Jumpers

To learn more about upcoming productions, please visit our website at www.NTNY.org

Playwright Tom Stoppard arrives at the theatre on opening night with Glenn Close.

Essie Davis and Eliza Lumley arrive at Radio City Music Hall for the 2004 Tony Awards.

Director David Leveaux at the opening night party at Tavern on the Green.

Spamalot co-author Eric Idle with *Jumpers* cast member Nicky Henson.

Cast member Nicholas Woodeson.

Simon Russell Beale and Essie Davis at the opening night party.

Curtain call on opening night.

PLAYBILL®

✦N✦ MARQUIS THEATRE

UNDER THE DIRECTION OF JAMES M. NEDERLANDER AND JAMES L. NEDERLANDER

JAMES L. NEDERLANDER   CLEAR CHANNEL ENTERTAINMENT
KENNETH GREENBLATT   TERRY ALLEN KRAMER   MARTIN RICHARDS
present

ROBERT GOULET   GARY BEACH
in

LA CAGE AUX FOLLES

Music and Lyrics by   Book by
JERRY HERMAN   **HARVEY FIERSTEIN**

Based on the play 'La Cage Aux Folles' by Jean Poiret

also starring
GAVIN CREEL   ANGELA GAYLOR   RUTH WILLIAMSON
MICHAEL MULHEREN   LINDA BALGORD   JOHN SHUMAN   MICHAEL BENJAMIN WASHINGTON

ADRIAN BAILEY   BRYAN BATT   PAUL CANAAN   JOEY DUDDING   MERWIN FOARD   CHRISTOPHER FREEMAN   PATTY GOBLE   DALE HENSLEY
JOHN HILLNER   LEAH HOROWITZ   CLARK JOHNSEN   PAUL MCGILL   BRAD MUSGROVE   ERIC OTTE   NATHAN PECK   ANDY PELLICK
T. OLIVER REID   JERMAINE R. REMBERT   DOROTHY STANLEY   ERIC STRETCH   CHARLIE SUTTON   WILL TAYLOR   JOSH WALDEN   EMMA ZAKS

Set Design   Costume Design   Lighting Design   Sound Design
SCOTT PASK   **WILLIAM IVEY LONG**   **DONALD HOLDER**   **PETER FITZGERALD**

Hair & Wig Design   Casting by   Production Managers
PAUL HUNTLEY   **JIM CARNAHAN, CSA**   **ARTHUR SICCARDI**
PATRICK SULLIVAN

Original Orchestrations   Additional Orchestrations   Dance Music Arrangements   Music Coordinator
JIM TYLER   **LARRY BLANK**   **DAVID KRANE**   **MICHAEL KELLER**

General Manager   Press Representative   Production Supervisor   Associate Producers
101 PRODUCTIONS, LTD.   **BARLOW•HARTMAN**   **STEVEN BECKLER**   **TGA ENTERTAINMENT**
LENI SENDER
BOB CUILLO
KATHI GLIST

Music Director
PATRICK VACCARIELLO

5/1/05

CAST
(in order of appearance)

Georges .... ROBERT GOULET

"Les Cagelles"

Chantal	T. OLIVER REID
Monique	CHRISTOPHER FREEMAN
Dermah/Slaveboy	ERIC OTTE
Nicole	NATHAN PECK
Hanna	BRAD MUSGROVE
Mercedes	JOSH WALDEN
Bitelle	JOEY DUDDING
Lo Singh	JERMAINE R. REMBERT
Odette	CHARLIE SUTTON
Angelique/White Bird	ANDY PELLICK
Phaedra	WILL TAYLOR
Clo-Clo	PAUL CANAAN
Francis	JOHN SHUMAN
Jacob	MICHAEL BENJAMIN WASHINGTON
Albin	GARY BEACH
Jean-Michel	GAVIN CREEL
Anne	ANGELA GAYLOR
Jacqueline	RUTH WILLIAMSON

St. Tropez Townspeople

M. Renaud	MERWIN FOARD
Mme. Renaud	DOROTHY STANLEY
Paulette	EMMA ZAKS
Hercule	JOEY DUDDING
Etienne	JOHN HILLNER
Fisherman	DALE HENSLEY

continued on the next page

2004-2005 AWARDS

TONY AWARD
Choreography (Jerry Mitchell)

OUTER CRITICS CIRCLE AWARDS
Revival of a Musical
Choreography (Jerry Mitchell)

DRAMA DESK AWARDS
Revival of a Musical
Choreography (Jerry Mitchell)

DRAMA LEAGUE AWARD
Revival of a Musical

La Cage aux Folles

MUSICAL NUMBERS

TIME: Summer
PLACE: St. Tropez, France

ACT I
Overture .... Orchestra
"We Are What We Are" .... Les Cagelles
"A Little More Mascara" .... Albin and Friends
"With Anne on My Arm" .... Jean-Michel and Georges
"With You on My Arm" (Reprise) .... Georges and Albin
"The Promenade" .... Townspeople
"Song on the Sand" .... Georges
"La Cage aux Folles" .... Albin and Les Cagelles
"I Am What I Am" .... Albin

ACT II
Entr'acte .... Orchestra
"Song on the Sand" (Reprise) .... Georges and Albin
"Masculinity" .... Georges, Albin and Townspeople
"Look Over There" .... Georges
"Cocktail Counterpoint" .... Georges, Dindon, Mme. Dindon, Jacob, Jean-Michel and Anne
"The Best of Times" .... Albin, Jacqueline and Patrons
"Look Over There" (Reprise) .... Jean-Michel
Grand Finale .... Full Company

Cast Continued

Colette .... PATTY GOBLE
Fisherman .... ADRIAN BAILEY
Edouard Dindon .... MICHAEL MULHEREN
Mme. Dindon .... LINDA BALGORD

SWINGS
CLARK JOHNSEN, PAUL MCGILL,
ERIC STRETCH, LEAH HOROWITZ
STANDBY
BRYAN BATT

DANCE CAPTAIN: Nathan Peck
ASSISTANT DANCE CAPTAIN: Charlie Sutton

UNDERSTUDIES
For Albin: BRYAN BATT, DALE HENSLEY; for
Georges: DALE HENSLEY, JOHN HILLNER; for
Jean-Michel: JOEY DUDDING, WILL TAYLOR; for
Anne: LEAH HOROWITZ, EMMA ZAKS; for
Jacqueline: PATTY GOBLE, DOROTHY STANLEY;
for Edouard Dindon: MERWIN FOARD, JOHN
HILLNER; for Mme. Dindon: PATTY GOBLE,
DOROTHY STANLEY; for Francis: ADRIAN
BAILEY, JOHN HILLNER; for Jacob: ADRIAN
BAILEY, T. OLIVER REID.

LA CAGE AUX FOLLES Orchestra
CONDUCTOR: PATRICK VACCARIELLO
Associate Conductor: Jim Laev
Concertmaster: Paul Woodiel; Violins: Mary Whitaker,
Victor Heifets, Dana Ianculovici; Cellos: Peter Prosser,
Vivian Israel; Lead Trumpet: Jeff Kievit;
Trumpets: Trevor Neumann, Earl Gardner;
Trombones: Michael Seltzer, Randy Andos;
French Horn: Roger Wendt; Reeds: Ted Nash, Ben
Kono, David Young, Ron Jannelli; Drums: Ron Tierno;
Percussion: Dan McMillan; Bass: Bill Sloat;
Keyboard 1: Jim Laev; Keyboard 2: Maggie Torre;
Guitar/Banjo: JJ McGeehan

Music Coordinator: Michael Keller
Music Copying: Kaye-Houston Music/
Annie Kaye and Doug Houston

Photo by Carol Rosegg

Zaza Appears: Gary Beach as Zaza/Albin.

La Cage aux Folles

 **Robert Goulet**
Georges

 **Gary Beach**
Albin

 **Gavin Creel**
Jean-Michel

 **Angela Gaylor**
Anne

 **Ruth Williamson**
Jacqueline

 **Michael Mulheren**
Edouard Dindon

 **Linda Balgord**
Mme. Dindon

 **John Shuman**
Francis

 **Michael Benjamin Washington**
Jacob

 **Adrian Bailey**
Fisherman

 **Bryan Batt**
Standby Albin

 **Paul Canaan**
Clo-Clo

 **Joey Dudding**
Bitelle, Hercule

 **Merwin Foard**
M. Renaud

 **Christopher Freeman**
Monique

 **Patty Goble**
Colette

 **Dale Hensley**
Fisherman

 **John Hillner**
Etienne

 **Leah Horowitz**
Swing

 **Clark Johnsen**
Swing

 **Paul McGill**
Swing

 **Brad Musgrove**
Hanna

 **Eric Otte**
Dermah/Slaveboy

 **Nathan Peck**
Nicole

 **Andy Pellick**
Angelique

 **T. Oliver Reid**
Chantal

 **Jermaine R. Rembert**
Lo Singh

 **Dorothy Stanley**
Mme. Renaud

 **Eric Stretch**
Swing

 **Charlie Sutton**
Odette

 **Will Taylor**
Phaedra

 **Josh Walden**
Mercedes

 **Emma Zaks**
Paulette

 **Jerry Herman**
Composer/Lyricist

 **Harvey Fierstein**
Book

La Cage aux Folles

Jerry Zaks
Director

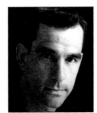
Jerry Mitchell
Choreographer

Scott Pask
Set Design

William Ivey Long
Costume Design

Donald Holder
Lighting Design

Paul Huntley
Hair & Wig Design

Patrick Vaccariello
Music Director

Larry Blank
Additional Orchestrations

Michael Keller
Music Coordinator

Jim Carnahan
Casting

Steven Beckler
Production Supervisor

Marc Bruni
Associate Director

Robert Tatad
Assistant Choreographer

James L. Nederlander
Producer

Kenneth D. Greenblatt
Producer

Terry Allen Kramer
Producer

Daniel Davis
Georges

Michael Benjamin Washington as Jacob.

Photo by Carol Rosegg

La Cage aux Folles

STAFF FOR LA CAGE AUX FOLLES

GENERAL MANAGEMENT
101 PRODUCTIONS, LTD.
Wendy Orshan   Jeffrey M. Wilson
David Auster

COMPANY MANAGER
Penelope Daulton

GENERAL PRESS REPRESENTATIVE
BARLOW HARTMAN
Michael Hartman   John Barlow
Wayne Wolfe   Andrew Snyder

PRODUCTION MANAGER
Arthur Siccardi
Patrick Sullivan

CASTING
JIM CARNAHAN CASTING
Jim Carnahan, CSA
Mele Nagler   J.V. Mercanti
Carrie Gardner   Kate Schwabe   Stephen Kopel

Production Stage Manager	**David Hyslop**
Stage Manager	**Michael Pule**
Assistant Stage Manager	**Travis Milliken**
Associate Company Manager	Janice Jacobson
Associate Director	Marc Bruni
Assistant Choreographer	Robert Tatad
Associate Scenic Designer	Orit Jacoby Carroll
First Assistant Scenic Designer	Emily Jean Beck
Assistant Scenic Designers	Tobin Ost, Brian Russman, Erik Flatmo, Lauren Alvarez, Reiko Fuseya, Tal Goldin
Assistant to Scott Pask	Matthew Shultz
Associate Costume Designers	Tom Beall, Martha Bromelmeier
Shoppers	Rachel Attridge, Matthew Pachtman, Sarah Sophia Turner
Assistant to Mr. Long	Donald Sanders
Associate Lighting Designer	Karen Spahn
Assistant Lighting Designers	Hilary Manners, Michael Berelson
Associate Lighting Designer/ Automated Lights	Warren Flynn
Assistant Sound Designer	Janet Smith
Sound Programmer	Erich Bechtel
Sound Design Consultant	Domoni Sack
Synthesizer Programmer	Bruce Samuels
Makeup Designer	Melissa Silver
Special Makeup Design	Mykel Renner
Special Effects	Chic Silber
Special Effects Associate	Aaron Waitz
Vocal Arrangements	Don Pippin
Production Carpenter	Patrick Sullivan
Assistant Carpenters	Kenneth Harris, Chad Heulitt, Brian Hutchinson
Production Electrician	James Fedigan
Head Electrician	Jon Mark Davidson

Assistant Electrician	Brian Aman
Production Props Supervisor	Joseph Harris, Jr.
Head Props	Laura McGarty
Assistant Props	Richard Anderson
Production Sound Supervisor	Valerie Spradling
Wardrobe Supervisor	Nancy Schaefer
Assistant Wardrobe Supervisor	Edmund Harrison
Mr. Goulet's Dresser	Talbott Dowst
Mr. Beach's Dresser	Geoffrey Polischuk
Dressers	Mark Caine, Dana Fucarino, Susan Gomez, Lizz Hirons, Franklin Hollenbeck, Greg Holtz, Jeff McGovney, Rodd Sovar, Janet Turner, Ricky Yates
Wig, Hair & Makeup Supervisor	Edward J. Wilson
Assistant Hair Supervisor	Vanessa Anderson
Hair Dressers	Chris Calabrese, Steven Kirkham, Lair Paulson
Production Assistants	Emma Casale-Katzman, Chad Lewis, Alex Libby, Chris McGriff

CLEAR CHANNEL ENTERTAINMENT — THEATRICAL
Miles C. Wilkin, Scott Zeiger, Steve Winton, David Anderson, Lauren Reid, Lynn Blandford, Bradley Broecker, Jennifer Costello, Jennifer DeLange, Joanna Hagan, Eric Joseph, Susan Krajsa, David Lazar, Hailey Lustig, Drew Murphy, Carl Pasbjerg, Debra Peltz, Denise Perry, Courtney Pierce, Alison Spiriti, Dan Swartz

For La Cage aux Folles:
Executive Producer	Jennifer Costello
Marketing Directors	Jennifer DeLange, Carolyn Christensen

Production Executives	Dan Gallaghe, Mrchael Milton for The Producer Circle Co
Assistant to Ms. Krame	Sara Shannon
Legal Counsel	Levine, Plotkin, & Menin LLP/ Loren Plotkin, Susan Mindell
Accountant	Rosenberg, Neuwirth, & Kushner, Chris Cacace, Anne Marie Aguanno
Advertising	SPOTCO/ Drew Hodges, Jim Edwards, John Lanasa, Aaliytha Davis
Illustration	Robert De Michiell
Marketing	Clear Channel Entertainment-Theatrical
101 Productions, Ltd. Staff	Christine Hale, Clark Mims, Heidi Neven, Mary Six Rupert, Aaron Slavik
101 Productions, Ltd. Interns	Sara Katz, Andrea Mayer
Press Office Manager	Bethany Larsen
Press Office Associates	Leslie F. Baden, Dennis Crowley, Jon Dimond, Carol Fineman, Rick Miramontez, Mark Pino, Ryan Ratelle, Miguel Raya, Gerilyn Shur
Production Photographer	Carol Rosegg
Banking	JP Morgan Chase/ Stephanie Dalton, Michele Gibbons
Insurance	DeWitt Stern, Inc./ Jennifer Brown
Housing	Maison International/ Marie Claire Martineau
Tutoring	On Location Education

Physical Therapy	PT Plus, P.C.
Theatre Displays	King Displays, Inc.
Concessions	SFX Theatrical Merchandising/ Larry Turk
Payroll Services	Castellana Services, Inc.
Website Design/Online Marketing	Situation Marketing/ Damian Bazadona, Ian Bennett

CREDITS
Scenery and automation by Hudson Scenic Studio, Inc.
Lighting by Hudson Sound & Light, LLC.
Sound equipment from Sound Associates.
Drapery and soft LED drop by I. Weiss, New York.
Sculpture by Nino Novellino of Costume Armour, Inc.
Effects equipment by Sunshine Scenic Studios.
Chez Jacqueline photographs by Carol Rosegg.
Costumes executed by Tricorne, Inc.; Carelli Costumes, Inc.; Euro Co Costumes.(com); Fur & Furgery; Jennifer Love Costumes; Scafati, Inc.; Schneeman Studio, Limited.
Millinery by Carelli Costumes, Inc.
Custom fabric dyeing by Gene Mignola, Inc.
Feathers by American Plume and Fancy Feather.
Shoes by T.O. Dey, J.C. Theatrical and LaDuca Shoes NYC.
Undergarments and hosiery provided by Bra*Tenders.
Properties built by the Spoon Group.
Bicycle courtesy of Rivendell Bicycle Works.
Cough drops courtesy of Ricola USA, Inc.
Salon services provided by Avalon Salon and Day Spa.

Makeup provided by M.A.C.

LA CAGE AUX FOLLES
rehearsed at New 42nd Street Studios.

SPECIAL THANKS
Millennium Hotel 44th Street

NEDERLANDER

Chairman	**James M. Nederlander**
President	**James L. Nederlander**

Executive Vice President
Nick Scandalios

Vice President Corporate Development Charlene S. Nederlander	Senior Vice President Labor Relations Herschel Waxman
Vice President Jim Boese	Chief Financial Officer Freida Sawyer Belviso

www.nederlander.org

STAFF FOR THE MARQUIS THEATRE
Manager	David Calhoun
Associate Manager	Ava Probst
Treasurer	Rick Waxman
Assistant Treasurer	John Rooney
Carpenter	Joseph P. Valentino
Electrician	James Mayo
Property Man	Roland Weigel

Best Opening Night Note: My sisters sent me a note that said, "Don't fuck up." When I was in *The Boy From Oz* with Hugh Jackman, he and I would say it to each other just before we went on stage, instead of saying "Break a leg" or "merde."

Opening Night Gifts: Choreographer Jerry Mitchell gave us all hooded sweatshirts. Harvey Fierstein and Jerry Herman gave us overnight bags with the show's logo on them. Marty Richards and the producers gave us Dom Perignon, nice chocolates and assorted other goodies.

Most Exciting Celebrity Visitor: Rod Stewart came and posed at intermission with all the Cagelles—and they all had equally ridiculous hair.

Who Got The Gypsy Robe: Merwin Foard. When we passed it on to the next show, *Dirty Rotten Scoundrels*, the Cagelles all went over to present it in person.

"Easter Bonnet" Sketch: "It's All in the Heel" by Jim Laev, Josh Walden and Steve Beckler.

Who Has Done The Most Shows: Adrian Bailey, who's done 13.

Backstage Rituals: A lot of stretching, a lot of pain and a lot of moaning from the Cagelles. Also, every Saturday night after half-hour, Gavin Creel and the stage manager play loud, funky dance music and start dancing in the hall like idiots. I don't know how it started, but it's a lot of fun.

Favorite Moment During Each Performance: That's got to be the can-can section of the song "La Cage aux Folles," where the Cagelles are getting thrown around and doing amazing splits and getting tossed over the passarelle. I used to watch it every night from the wings and it is amazing.

In-Theatre Gathering Place: The green room, which is up the first flight of stairs by the men's ensemble dressing room. We've got everything in there: a TV left over from *Thoroughly Modern Millie*, vending machines, etc. Linda Balgord re-covered all the couches. I contributed a hand-held massage thing. You can walk in there any time and see people watching TV, people eating and people doing stretches with their legs wrapped around themselves like a pretzel.

Favorite Off-Site Hangout: The Cagelles frequent two or three of the gay clubs in the theatre district. We mainly get take-out from Daniela on Eighth Avenue between shows.

Favorite Snack Food: Anything brought in by Adrian Bailey. He's a bit of an insomniac and so he bakes and brings in fantastic cookies, dozens at a time, and

Above: Opening night curtain call for the principals. From left: Michael Mulheren, Linda Balgord, Angela Gaylor, Gavin Creel, Daniel Davis, Gary Beach, Michael Benjamin Washington, Ruth Williamson and John Shuman.

The marquee of the Marquis.

Above: Choreographer Jerry Mitchell with composer Jerry Herman and director Jerry Zaks. Left, costume designer William Ivey Long with colleague Willa Kim.

"Les Cagelles" in street clothes for the opening night party at the Marquis Theatre.

"Les Cagelles" take their bow on opening night.

Photos by Aubrey Reuben

Left: Will Taylor and Michael Mulheren. Right: Gavin Creel, Gary Beach, Daniel Davis and librettist Harvey Fierstein.

Above left: Harvey Fierstein and composer/lyricist Jerry Herman.

Right: Gavin Creel and Angela Gaylor.

cakes, or turkey chili or chili bean soup. It's gotten to the point where we organized a kitty to help him pay for it all.

Favorite Therapy: Physical therapy is twice a week and very popular.

Memorable Ad-Lib: One day, going into the last scene, sets weren't working. Gary Beach was standing on the stage waiting for the sets to come on and the lights to go up, and finally he made a wisecrack to the audience, "We'll be with you shortly." Angela Gaylor, who plays the daughter, was still laughing when the lights came up.

Record Number Of Cellphone Rings: One or two. But I wish the theatre owners would spend a few bucks and put in cloaks.

Strangest Press Encounter: A guy from one of the alternate lifestyle papers was complimenting me on how good I looked in a dress with my hairy back. It was just not right!

Strangest Stage Door Fan Encounter: A lot of Stage Door Johnnies in their 50s wait there for the Cagelles to come out.

Who Wears The Heaviest/Hottest Costume: Gary Beach wears a black beaded dress under his robe for "Mascara" and it's all rigged.

Who Wears The Least: The Cagelles, of course. In the opening number all 12 guys are wearing hose and dance belts—and that's it. They have furs wrapped around them, but it's supposed to give the illusion that they're nude underneath.

Most Embarrassing Moment: Nothing embarrasses the Cagelles. In the opening scene when they're wearing the furs that are supposed to be covering their butts, they sometimes let them "slip." They're flirting with the audience.

Best In-House Parody Lyrics: As we're walking off stage to the play-out, which is the title song, the Cagelles sing the lyrics as Bob Dylan.

Memorable Directorial Notes: Jerry Zaks has a lot of them. When someone makes a suggestion, he'll listen very carefully, then say, "That's a great idea—don't do it." He's also known for giving you an odd piece of directing, then saying, "Trust me on this, it will get a laugh."

Company Legends: Cindy Adams wrote in her column that Donald Trump was going to be replacing me as Dindon. It was the strangest thing I ever read.

Catchphrases: In the scene where Georges calls his ex-wife Sibyl "a big fat pig," the Cagelles sing, "Sibyl is a pig a big fat pig, oink oink oink oink oink oink! Snort snort!"

Correspondent: Michael Mulheren, "Edouard Dindon"

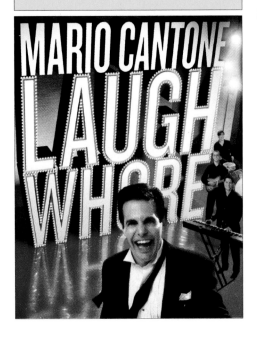

PLAYBILL®

MARIO CANTONE
LAUGH WHORE

MUSICAL NUMBERS

ACT I
"La Vita"

"A Jim Morrison Christmas"

"I Ain't Finished Yet"

ACT II
"Nevertheless"

"My Name Is Gumm"

"Laugh Whore"

BAND
Band Leader:
Tom Kitt

Keyboards:
Tom Kitt

Bass:
Dan Grennes

Drums:
Damien Bassman

Guitar:
Michael Aarons

---

⑧ CORT THEATRE
138 West 48th Street
A Shubert Organization Theatre

Gerald Schoenfeld, *Chairman*   Philip J. Smith, *President*

Robert E. Wankel, *Executive Vice President*

Showtime Networks
presents

MARIO CANTONE
LAUGH WHORE

Written by
Mario Cantone

Original Music by
Jerry Dixon

Additional Music by
Mario Cantone & Harold Lubin

Original Lyrics by
Mario Cantone, Jerry Dixon & Harold Lubin

Set Design by
Robert Brill

Sound Design by
Tony Meola

Lighting Design by
Jules Fisher & Peggy Eisenhauer

Music Director & Orchestrator
Tom Kitt

Arrangements
Jerry Dixon & Tom Kitt

Production Manager
Aurora Productions

Production Stage Manager
William Joseph Barnes

Marketing
HHC Marketing

Press
Pete Sanders Group

Musical Staging
Lisa Leguillou

General Manager
Roy Gabay

Produced in Association with
Jonathan Burkhart

Directed by
Joe Mantello

LIVE BROADWAY   10/24/04

Mario Cantone

Laugh Whore

Mario Cantone
Laugh Whore

Harold Lubin
Co-Lyricist

Joe Mantello
Director

Robert Brill
Set Design

Tony Meola
Sound Designer

Jules Fisher &
Peggy Eisenhauer
Lighting Designers

Tom Kitt
Musical Director/
Arranger,
Conductor/
Pianist

William Joseph
Barnes
Production Stage
Manager

Jon Krause
Stage Manager

Rochelle Joseph
Stylist

Jonathan Burkhart
Associate
Producer

Jay Larkin/
Showtime
Producer

Staff for LAUGH WHORE

GENERAL MANAGEMENT
ROY GABAY THEATRICAL
PRODUCTION & MANAGEMENT
Cheryl Dennis, Noah Goldsmith, Daniel Kuney,
Kim Sellon, Cori Silberman

COMPANY MANAGER
Bruce Klinger

PRESS REPRESENTATIVE
PETE SANDERS GROUP
Pete Sanders/Jim Mannino
Glenna Freedman, Jeremy Shaffer, Bill Coyle

PRODUCTION MANAGEMENT
AURORA PRODUCTIONS, INC.
Gene O'Donovan,
W. Benjamin Heller II, Michele McDaniel,
Bethany Weinstein

Production Stage Manager	William Barnes
Stage Manager	Jon Krause
Assistant Director	Jerry Dixon
Assistant Scenic Designer	Jenny Sawyers
Assistant to Mr. Brill	Dustin O'Neill
Assistant Lighting Designers	Scott Davis, Pamela Kupper
Automated Lighting Programmer	Matt Hudson
Assistant Sound Designer	Ryan Powers
Production Carpenter	Ed Diaz
Production Electrician	Jon Lawson
Production Sound Supervisor	John Dory
Wardrobe Supervisor	Joe Hickey
Synthesizer Programmer	Jim Abbott
Additional Movement	Lisa Leguillou
Assistant to Mr. Cantone	Akwasi Taha

Assistant to Mr. Mantello	Jeffery Self
Production Assistant	Dave Solomon
Legal Counsel	Loeb & Loeb LLP/ Seth Gelblum, Richard Garmise
Accountant	Rosenberg, Neuwirth, & Kushner CPAs/ Mark A. D'Ambrosi, Jana Jevnikar
Advertising	SpotCo/ Drew Hodges, Jim Edwards, Ilene Rosen, Jimmy McNicholas
Marketing	HHC Marketing/ Hugh Hysell, Jillian Boeni, Cate Wilson
Press Intern	Heather Smith
Banking	JPMorgan Chase/ Richard L. Callian, Michele Gibbons
Insurance	DeWitt Stern Group/ Jolyon Stern, Peter Shoemaker
Theatre Displays	King Displays, Inc.
Payroll Services	Castellana Services, Inc.
Concessions	Clear Channel Entertainment

CREDITS
Scenery by Atlas Scenic Studios, Inc.
Lighting equipment from PRG Lighting.
Sound equipment from PRG Sound.
Stylist for Mr. Cantone and the Band: Rochelle Joseph.

SPECIAL THANKS
To Hugo Boss for providing the wardrobe for
Mr. Cantone and the Tom Kitt Band; Christine Healey
for Mr. Cantone and the band's grooming.

MUSIC CREDITS
"Believe" composed by Paul Barry, Steve Torch and Brian
Higgins, Right Bank Music, Inc. (ASCAP). Warner Chappell
Music LTD and Xenomania Music (NS)
administered by WB Music Corp. All rights reserved.
Used by permission.

"Do You Hear What I Hear" composed by Gloria Shayne and
Noel Regney ©1962 (renewed), Jewel Music Publishing
Company, Inc. (ASCAP). All rights reserved.
International copyright secured.

"Frosty the Snowman" composed by Steve Nelson and Jack
Rollins © 1950 (renewed), Chappell & Co. (ASCAP).
All rights reserved.

"Nevertheless (I'm in Love With You)" composed by Bert
Kalmar and Harry Ruby ©1931 (renewed), Chappell & Co.
Inc.(ASCAP) and Harry Ruby Music Co. (ASCAP). All rights
reserved. Performed by Debbie Gravitte.
By permission Varese Sarabande.

"Proud Mary" composed by John C. Fogarty.
Used by permission of Jondora Music/Fantasy, Inc. (BMI).

"La Vita" composed by Bruno Canfora, Norman Newell and
Antonio Amurri. By permission of EMI Miller Catalogue, Inc.
(ASCAP), Edizioni Curci.

Ⓣ THE SHUBERT ORGANIZATION, INC.

Gerald Schoenfeld	**Philip J. Smith**
Chairman	President
John W. Kluge	Lee J. Seidler
Michael I. Sovern	Stuart Subotnick
Irving M. Wall	

Robert E. Wankel
Executive Vice President

Peter Entin	**Elliot Greene**
Vice President	Vice President
Theatre Operations	Finance
David Andrews	**John Darby**
Vice President	Vice President
Shubert Ticketing Services	Facilities

CORT THEATRE
House Manager .... Joseph Traina

Opening Night Gifts: Handmade ceramic bowls and tea sets for most of the company. For some on the periphery of the company, wooden sake carafes with cups, or hand-crafted incense plates.

Backstage Rituals: My dresser Joe Hickey and I play Birdie and Margo Channing in *All About Eve.* I also sometimes trot out my Joan Crawford.

Favorite Moment: The *Vagina Monologues* stuff. The audience shouts out names and Mario acts out different vaginas.

In-Theatre Gathering Place: Mario's dressing room, where we have tea, chat, read the news and bust each other's chops.

Off-Site Hangouts: Mario goes home. The crew goes to Apizz in the Lower East Side.

Snack Food: Dark chocolate. See's brand candy.

Favorite Therapies: Yoga, tea with a dash of honey.

Most Memorable Ad-Lib: This ad-lib came out of a true story. One night, toward the end of the run, I was doing the bit about my parents, who were not the most happy couple. I told how I once said, "Dad, thank you for accepting my lifestyle." And he said, "Thanks for accepting mine." In my mind I thought, "Touché!" and I said it out loud, and the audience loved it.

Record Number Of Cellphone Rings: Only one on any single night. But I go at them and say, "This is not a musical! I can break the fourth wall and attack!" And I do. But then I feel bad.

Memorable Press Encounter: I do phoners while sitting in bed, like Agnes Moorehead.

Memorable Fan Encounter: One old lady, laughing so hard her face was wet, grabbed the house manager's arm and said, "You should have told us it was going to be this funny, I would have worn my Depends!"

Busiest Day At The Box Office: A week into the run.

Nicknames: I call my band Tom Kitt and the Can-Tones. They're all straight boys, so sometimes I call them Tom Kitt and the Pussy Hounds. My dresser I call Birdie and every character ever abused in any camp movie.

Catchphrases: Everybody gets called a Whore. We are the company of Whores.

Superstitions: When we were putting together the show, we were going on a premise that Mario would not appeal to women over 55. We were wrong. We get the typical demographic: Women and straight couples.

Also: My dressing room was so tiny, it was like living in Barbie's Townhouse. "Where's Skipper?"

Correspondents: Star Mario Cantone and producer Jonathan Burkhart

Clockwise from top left: Mario Cantone celebrates on opening night. The marquee of the Cort. Julie Halston and Charles Busch. Cantone's opening night curtain call. Christine Taylor and Ben Stiller at the cast party. LaChanze and Derek Fordjour. Lee Tergesen and Christopher Meloni arrive at the party.

PLAYBILL®

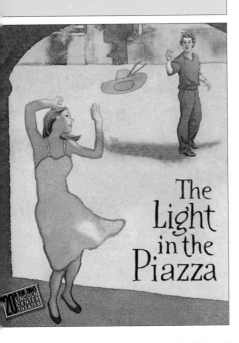

The Light in the Piazza

20 LINCOLN CENTER THEATER

LINCOLN CENTER THEATER AT THE VIVIAN BEAUMONT

under the direction of
André Bishop and Bernard Gersten
presents

The Light in the Piazza

book
Craig Lucas

music and lyrics
Adam Guettel

based on the novel by Elizabeth Spencer

with (in alphabetical order)

Glenn Seven Allen   Michael Berresse   Sarah Uriarte Berry   David Bonanno
David Burnham   Victoria Clark   Patti Cohenour   Beau Gravitte   Laura Griffith
Mark Harelik   Prudence Wright Holmes   Jennifer Hughes   Felicity LaFortune
Catherine LaValle   Michel Moinot   Matthew Morrison   Kelli O'Hara   Joseph Siravo

sets
Michael Yeargan

costumes
Catherine Zuber

lighting
Christopher Akerlind

sound
ACME Sound Partners

orchestrations
Ted Sperling and Adam Guettel

additional orchestrations
Bruce Coughlin

casting
Janet Foster

stage manager
Thom Widmann

general press agent
Philip Rinaldi

musical theater
associate producer
Ira Weitzman

general
manager
Adam Siegel

production
manager
Jeff Hamlin

director of
development
Hattie K. Jutagir

director of
marketing
Linda Mason Ross

music direction
Ted Sperling

musical staging
Jonathan Butterell

direction
Bartlett Sher

Questa produzione di "The Light in the Piazza" é dedicata alla memoria di Andrew Heiskell.
Durante la sua vita anche lui ha emesso una luce propria.
LCT thanks the Blanchette Hooker Rockefeller Fund for its outstanding support.
Major support is provided by The Shen Family Foundation and generous support by The New York Community Trust –
Mary P. Oenslager Foundation Fund and the Henry Nias Foundation.
LCT gratefully acknowledges an extraordinary gift from the Estate of Edith K. Ehrman.
Special thanks to The Harold and Mimi Steinberg Charitable Trust for supporting new American plays at LCT.

American Airlines is the official airline of Lincoln Center Theater.
Merrill Lynch is a 2005 LCT Season Sponsor.

The World Premiere of "The Light in the Piazza" was produced by the Intiman Theatre, Seattle, Washington; Bartlett Sher, Artistic Director,
Laura Penn, Managing Director; and the Goodman Theatre, Chicago, Illinois; Robert Falls, Artistic Director, Roche Schulfer, Executive Director.
Developed with the Assistance of the Sundance Institute Theatre Laboratory.
Produced by arrangement with Turner Entertainment Co, Owner of the original motion picture "Light in the Piazza."

4/18/05

CAST

(in order of appearance)

Margaret Johnson ....VICTORIA CLARK

Clara Johnson, her daughter .....KELLI O'HARA

Fabrizio Naccarelli ....MATTHEW
MORRISON

Signor Naccarelli,
Fabrizio's father ....MARK HARELIK

Giuseppe Naccarelli,
Fabrizio's brother ....MICHAEL BERRESSE

Franca Naccarelli,
Giuseppe's wife........SARAH URIARTE BERRY

Signora Naccarelli,
Fabrizio's mother ....PATTI COHENOUR

Roy Johnson,
Margaret's husband ....BEAU GRAVITTE

Tour Guide..............FELICITY LaFORTUNE

Priest ....JOSEPH SIRAVO

Ensemble ....DAVID BONANNO,
DAVID BURNHAM,
LAURA GRIFFITH,
PRUDENCE WRIGHT HOLMES,
JENNIFER HUGHES,
FELICITY LaFORTUNE,
MICHEL MOINOT,
JOSEPH SIRAVO

continued on the next page

2004-2005 AWARDS

Tony Awards
Leading Actress in a Musical (Victoria Clark)
Original Score Written for the Theatre (Adam Guettel)
Scenic Design of a Musical (Michael Yeargan)
Lighting Design of a Musical (Christopher Akerlind)
Costume Design of a Musical (Catherine Zuber)
Orchestrations (Ted Sperling, Adam Guettel and Bruce Coughlin)

Drama Desk Awards
Actress in a Musical (Victoria Clark)
Music (Adam Guettel)
Orchestrations (Ted Sperling, Adam Guettel and Bruce Coughlin)
Scenic Design of a Musical (Michael Yeargan)
Lighting Design (Christopher Akerlind)

Outer Critics Circle Awards
Actress in a Musical (Victoria Clark)
Lighting Design (Christopher Akerlind)

The Light in the Piazza

MUSICAL NUMBERS

TIME AND PLACE

The Light in the Piazza takes place in Florence and Rome in the summer of 1953, with occasional side trips to America.

ACT ONE

Overture

Statues and Stories ....Margaret and Clara

The Beauty Is ....Clara

Il Mondo Era Vuoto ....Fabrizio

Passeggiata ....Fabrizio and Clara

The Joy You Feel ....Franca

Dividing Day ....Margaret

Hysteria ....Clara and Margaret

Say It Somehow ....Clara and Fabrizio

ACT TWO

Aiutami ....The Naccarelli Family

The Light in the Piazza ....Clara

Octet ....Company

Tirade ....Clara

Octet (Reprise) ....Company

The Beauty Is (Reprise) ....Margaret

Let's Walk ....Signor Naccarelli and Margaret

Love to Me ....Fabrizio

Fable ....Margaret

Cast Continued

Assistant Stage Manager
CLAUDIA LYNCH

Swings
GLENN SEVEN ALLEN,
CATHERINE LaVALLE

UNDERSTUDIES

For Margaret—PATTI COHENOUR; for Clara—JENNIFER HUGHES; for Fabrizio— DAVID BURNHAM; for Signor Naccarelli and Roy Johnson—JOSEPH SIRAVO; for Signora Naccarelli—FELICITY LaFORTUNE; for Giuseppe—DAVID BONANNO; for Franca— LAURA GRIFFITH; for Tour Guide—CATHERINE LaVALLE; for Priest—GLENN SEVEN ALLEN.

ORCHESTRA
Conductor
TED SPERLING

Associate Conductor, Piano, Celesta:
DAN RIDDLE

Violins:
CHRISTIAN HEBEL (Concertmaster)
MATTHEW LEHMANN
SYLVIA D'AVANZO
JAMES TSAO
LISA MATRICARDI
KATHERINE LIVOLSI-STERN

Celli:
PETER SACHON, ARIANE LALLEMAND

Harp:
VICTORIA DRAKE

Bass:
BRIAN CASSIER

Clarinet/English Horn/Oboe:
RICHARD HECKMAN

Bassoon:
GILI SHARETT

Percussion:
WILLARD MILLER

Guitar/Mandolin:
ANDREW SCHWARTZ

Music Coordinator:
SEYMOUR RED PRESS

Photo by Liz Lauren

Mark Harelik and Victoria Clark in *The Light in the Piazza*.

The Light in the Piazza

Glenn Seven Allen
Swing

Michael Berresse
Giuseppe Naccarelli

Sarah Uriarte Berry
Franca Naccarelli

David Bonanno
Ensemble

David Burnham
Ensemble

Victoria Clark
Margaret Johnson

Patti Cohenour
Signora Naccarelli

Beau Gravitte
Roy Johnson

Laura Griffith
Ensemble

Mark Harelik
Signor Naccarelli

Prudence Wright Holmes
Ensemble

Jennifer Hughes
Ensemble

Felicity LaFortune
Tour Guide, Ensemble

Catherine LaValle
Swing

Michel Moinot
Ensemble

Matthew Morrison
Fabrizio Naccarelli

Kelli O'Hara
Clara Johnson

Joseph Siravo
Priest, Ensemble

Craig Lucas
Book

Adam Guettel
Music and Lyrics, Orchestrations

Bartlett Sher
Director

Ted Sperling
Orchestrations, Musical Direction

Michael Yeargan
Sets

Catherine Zuber
Costumes

Christopher Akerlind
Lighting

Bruce Coughlin
Additional Orchestrations

Janet Foster
Casting

The Light in the Piazza

Hair and Wig Department
(L-R): Alice Ramos (Hair Assistant), Lazaro Arencibia (Hair Supervisor) and Wesley Cagle (Hair Assistant). Not pictured: Jun Kim (Hair Assistant)

Electricians, Carpenters, Sound and Props
Front Row (L-R): Fred Bredenbach, John Howie, Rudy Wood, Juan Bustrumantic, Ray Skillin, Nick Irons and Gary Simon.
Back Row (L-R): Scott Jackson, John Ross, Linda Heard, Karl Rausenberger (Production Propertyman), Walt Murphy (Production Carpenter), Matt Altman, Jeff Ward, Patrick Merryman (Production Engineer), Bruce Rubin (Light Board Operator), Marc Salzberg (Production Soundman) and Frank Linn.
Not Pictured: Mark Dignam.

Wardrobe
(L-R): Tony Hoffman (Dresser), Cathy Cline (Dresser), Pat Sullivan (Dresser), Lynn Bowling (Wardrobe Supervisor) and Kimberly Mark-Sirota (Dresser).
Not pictured: Virginia Neininger (Dresser), Liam O'Brien (Dresser) and James Wilcox (Dresser).

Box Office
Bob Belkin, Marc Friedenreich and Fred Bonis.

Front of House Staff
Front Row (L-R): Donna Zurich, Patricia Jenkins, Susan Lehman, Matt Barnaba, Denise Bergen, Jodie Gigliobianco, Officer Steve Spear
Second Row (L-R): Barbara Zavilowicz, Lydia Tchornobai, Farida Asencio, Margareta Shakridge, Margie Blair, Gine Chen, Brett Stasiewicz, Leah Scott
Third Row (L-R): Roberto Debarros, Jeff Goldstein, Rheba Flegleman, Patricia Dodd, Christina Owen, Lindley Lee
Back Row (L-R): Judith Fanelli, Eleanor Rooks and Nick Andors

Stage Managers
Thom Widmann, Claudia Lynch, Matthew Melchiorre

The Light in the Piazza

LINCOLN CENTER THEATER

ANDRÉ BISHOP   BERNARD GERSTEN
ARTISTIC DIRECTOR   EXECUTIVE PRODUCER

ADMINISTRATIVE STAFF

GENERAL MANAGER ....ADAM SIEGEL
Associate General Manager ....Melanie Weinraub
General Management Assistant ....Beth Dembrow
Facilities Manager ....Alex Mustelier
Assistant Facilities Manager ....Michael Assalone

GENERAL PRESS AGENT ....PHILIP RINALDI
Press Associate ....Barbara Carroll

PRODUCTION MANAGER ....JEFF HAMLIN
Associate Production Manager ....Chris Akins

DIRECTOR OF
DEVELOPMENT ....HATTIE K. JUTAGIR
Associate Director of Development ....Rachel Norton
Manager of Special Events and
Young Patron Program ....Karin Schall
Grants Writer ....Neal Brilliant
Coordinator, Patron Program ....Sheilaja Rao
Development Associate ....Chris Chrzanowski
Assistant to the
Director of Development ....Betsy Tucker

DIRECTOR OF FINANCE ....DAVID S. BROWN
Controller ....Susan Knox
Systems Manager ....John N. Yen
Finance Assistant ....Kellie Kroyer

DIRECTOR OF MARKETING ....Linda Mason Ross
Marketing Associate...........................Denis Guerin
Marketing Assistant ....Elizabeth Kandel

DIRECTOR OF EDUCATION ....KATI KOERNER
Associate Director of Education ....Dionne O'Dell
Assistant to the Executive Producer ......Barbara Hourigan
Office Assistant ....Kenneth Collins
Messenger ....Esau Burgess
Reception ....Andrew Elsesser, Daryl Watson

ARTISTIC STAFF

ASSOCIATE DIRECTORS ......GRACIELA DANIELE,
NICHOLAS HYTNER,
SUSAN STROMAN,
DANIEL SULLIVAN

DRAMATURG and DIRECTOR,
LCT DIRECTORS LAB ....ANNE CATTANEO

CASTING DIRECTOR ....DANIEL SWEE, C.S.A.

MUSICAL THEATER ASSOCIATE
PRODUCER...........................IRA WEITZMAN

Artistic Administrator ....Julia Judge
Casting Associate ....Kristin McTigue

IN LOVING MEMORY OF
GERALD GUTIERREZ
ASSOCIATE DIRECTOR 1991-2003

HOUSE STAFF

HOUSE MANAGER ....RHEBA FLEGELMAN
Production Carpenter ....Walter Murphy
Production Electrician ....Patrick Merryman
Production Propertyman ....Karl Rausenberger
Production Flyman ....William Nagle
House Technician ....Bill Burke
Chief Usher ..................................M.L. Pollock
Box Office Treasurer ....Fred Bonis
Assistant Treasurer ....Robert A. Belkin

SPECIAL SERVICES

Advertising ....Serino-Coyne/
Jim Russek, Brad Lapin
Principal Poster Artist ....James McMullan
Poster Art for *The Light in the Piazza* .....James McMullan

Counsel ....Peter L. Felcher,
Esq.;
Charles H. Googe, Esq.;
and Rachel Hoover, Esq. of
Paul, Weiss, Rifkind, Wharton & Garrison

Immigration Counsel ....Theodore Ruthizer, Esq.;
Mark D. Koestler, Esq.
of Kramer, Levin, Naftalis & Frankel LLP

Auditor ....Douglas Burack, C.P.A.

Insurance ....Jennifer Brown of
DeWitt Stern Group

Photographer ....Joan Marcus

Travel ....Tygon Tours

Web Design and Development ......Four Eyes Productions

Consulting Architect ....Hugh
Hardy,
Hardy Holzman Pfeiffer Associates
Construction Manager ....Yorke Construction

Payroll Service......................Castellana Services, Inc.

STAFF FOR **THE LIGHT IN THE PIAZZA**

COMPANY MANAGER ....Matthew Markoff
Associate Company Manager ....Josh Lowenthal
Assistant Director ....Sarna Lapine
Assistant to Mr. Lucas ....Troy Miller

Dance Captain ....Laura Griffith

Assistant Set Designer ....Mikiko Suzuki
Assistant Costume Designers ....David Newell,
Michael Zecker
Assistant Lighting Designer ....Michael J. Spadaro
Assistant Sound Designer ....Jeffrey Yoshi Lee
Associate Orchestrator ....Bruce Coughlin

Rehearsal Pianist ....Adam Ben-David
Music Copyist ....Emily Grishman Music Preparation/
Emily Grishman,
Katharine Edmonds

Dialect Coach ....Ralph Zito

Props ....Christopher Schneider
Production Soundman ....Marc Salzberg
Light Board Operator ....Bruce Rubin
Moving Light Programmer ....Victor Seastone

Wardrobe Supervisor ....Lynn Bowling
Dressers ....Cathy Cline,
Kimberly Mark-Sirota,
Virginia Neininger,
Liam O'Brien,
Pat Sullivan,
James Wilcox
Hair and Wig Designer ....Jerry Altenburg
Make-up Designer ....Angelina Avallone
Hair Supervisor ....Lazaro Arencibia
Hair Assistants ....Jun Kim, Alice Ramos

Production Assistants ....Andrew Einhorn,
Matthew Melchiorre,
Melanie T. Morgan

Italian translation for "Il Mondo Era Vuoto"
by Judith Blazer.

L.A. Casting Consultant ....Julia Flores

CREDITS

Show control and scenic motion control featuring stage
command systems by Scenic Technologies, a division of
Production Resource Group, LLC, New Windsor, NY.
Scenery fabrication by
PRG Scenic Technologies, a division of Production
Resource Group, LLC, New Windsor, NY.
Men's costumes executed by
Tim McKelvey, Angels the Costumier and Vos Savant, Inc.
Women's costumes by Parson-Meares, Ltd.
and Euro Co. Costumes.
Millinery by Hugh Hanson for Carelli Costumes Inc.
Shoes by LaDuca Shoes NYC.
Lighting equipment from PRG Lighting.
Sound equipment by Sound Associates.
Piano by Steinway & Sons.
Natural herb cough drops courtesy of Ricola USA, Inc.

MR. GUETTEL WOULD LIKE TO THANK THE FOLLOWING PEOPLE:

Loy Arcenas, Judith Blazer, Ted Chapin, Mary Cleere
Haran, Alison Cochrill, Stephanie Coen, Eric Ebbenga,
Michael Feinstein, Peter Franklin, Father John Fraser,
Pat Graney, Michael Greif, John Guare, Robert Hurwitz,
Celia Keenan-Bolger, Tina Landau, Arthur Laurents,
Marcella Lorca, John McDermott, Steven Pasquale,
Stephen Sondheim, Alfred Uhry, and Wayne Wilcox.

Lobby refreshments by
Sweet Concession

SUNDANCE INSTITUTE

Developed with the assistance of the
Sundance Institute Theatre Laboratory

Photos by Aubrey Reuben

(L-R): Matthew Morrison, Kelli O'Hara, composer Adam Guettel, Sarah Uriarte Berry and Michael Berresse at the opening night party at Tavern on the Green.

At the opening night party (L-R): Debbie Gravitte, director Bartlett Sher, and leading lady Victoria Clark (doing an interview).

Michael Berresse and Beau Gravitte.

Patti Cohenour on opening night.

Backstage Opening Night Gift: Adam Guettel and Craig Lucas gave us autographed antique Baedeker guidebooks like the one Victoria uses in the show.

Celebrity Visitor: Meryl Streep. She cried, which was nice.

Who Got The Gypsy Robe: Laura Griffith

Most Roles: Myself and David Bonanno double as priests, hookers and townspeople.

Backstage Rituals: All through rehearsals and opening week, we would do a group massage and yoga, which was Musical Stager Jonathan Butterell's idea. It really helped us focus. Now, everyone has their own ritual. Mark Harelik has soup and sushi before every performance. Michael Berresse lays on the floor of his dressing room and listens to Sicilian peasant songs to get himself in the mood. At five minutes to curtain, David Bonanno and I do 25 push-ups and gargle with mouthwash. Patti Cohenour looks in the mirror and speaks every one of her lines. Matthew Morrison, looks in the mirror as well, and visualizes his character. Just before Kelli O'Hara makes her entrance, she punches John Howie in the arm. As we all pass each other backstage before each show, we always say, "Good show" to each other.

Therapy: David Bonanno is a massage therapist; he has a sign-up list to give massages in our dressing room on matinee days. We have a song in the show called "Passeggiata," so we've nicknamed these sessions "Massaggiata."

Cell Phone Rings: One came at the absolute worst moment. There is a pause of about 20 seconds going into the kiss, and a cell started ringing. The owner let it go four rings, and instead of turning it off, she answered it and went outside. The audience was shooting daggers at her, and so was the cast.

Fastest Costume Change: Matthew Morrison and Kelli O'Hara have a ten-second change in Act I.

Busiest Day At The Box Office: The day after the Tony nominations were announced.

Most Embarrassing Moments: David Bonanno has to make a quick entrance up a flight of stairs carrying a telephone at a really tense moment. One night he tripped and went down on all fours. Victoria Clark said, "Are you all right?" But only his pride was wounded.

We also had a lot of trouble with the moment where Kelli throws a glass of water on Sarah Uriarte Berry. During previews she would sometimes miss, and for three performances water kept splashing all over the people in the first row. Finally they changed the blocking. In that same scene, Kelli is supposed to run into a tea cart, knocking silverware on the ground. One night a fork flew into the audience and landed on a man's lap. Kelli went up to him during curtain calls and apologized.

Company In-Joke: "It didn't ring!"

Nicknames: Matthew Morrison is "Matty Fresh." We call Prudence Wright Holmes "P-Train."

Coolest Things About Being In This Show: Being on Broadway, being at Lincoln Center and being associated with a show that has such prestige. Craig and Adam were trying to do something of value, which is really nice.

Correspondent: David Burnham, "Nino the Bike Boy," Ensemble, "Fabrizio" cover.

PLAYBILL®

THE LION KING
BROADWAY'S AWARD-WINNING BEST MUSICAL

DISNEP
PRESENTS

THE LION KING

Music & Lyrics by
ELTON JOHN & TIM RICE

Additional Music & Lyrics by
LEBO M, MARK MANCINA, JAY RIFKIN, JULIE TAYMOR, HANS ZIMMER

Book by
ROGER ALLERS & IRENE MECCHI

Starring
DEREK SMITH   ALTON FITZGERALD WHITE   TSHIDI MANYE
JEFF BINDER   TOM ALAN ROBBINS   DANNY RUTIGLIANO
JOSH TOWER   KISSY SIMMONS
BENJAMIN STERLING CANNON   BONITA J. HAMILTON   ENRIQUE SEGURA
KAILANI M. COBA   AARON D. CONLEY   ZIPPORAH G. GATLING   JARRELL J. SINGLETON

KYLE R. BANKS   JOHN E. BRADY   KYLIN BRADY   CAMILLE M. BROWN   LaTRISA A. COLEMAN
E. CLAYTON CORNELIOUS   GABRIEL A. CROOM   BOBBY DAYE   GARLAND DAYS   LINDIWE DLAMINI
BONGI DUMA   JEAN MICHELLE GRIER   MICHAEL ALEXANDER HENRY   TONY JAMES
DENNIS JOHNSTON   CORNELIUS JONES, JR.   KESWA   GREGORY A. KING   JACK KOENIG
RON KUNENE   LISA LEWIS   NIKKI LONG   SHERYL McCALLUM   IAN VINCENT McGINNIS
RAY MERCER   JENNIFER HARRISON NEWMAN   ANGELICA EDWARDS PATTERSON
MPUME SIKAKANE   KEENA SMITH   SOPHIA N. STEPHENS   RYAN BROOKE TAYLOR   TORYA
STEVEN EVAN WASHINGTON   REMA WEBB   KENNY REDELL WILLIAMS   FRANK WRIGHT II

Adapted from the screenplay by
IRENE MECCHI & JONATHAN ROBERTS & LINDA WOOLVERTON

Produced by
PETER SCHNEIDER & THOMAS SCHUMACHER

Scenic Design RICHARD HUDSON	*Costume Design* JULIE TAYMOR	*Lighting Design* DONALD HOLDER	*Mask & Puppet Design* JULIE TAYMOR & MICHAEL CURRY
Hair & Makeup Design MICHAEL WARD	*Casting* BINDER CASTING/ MARK BRANDON	*Associate Director* ANTHONY LYN	*Production Dance Supervisor* MAREY GRIFFITH
Associate Producers TODD LACY AUBREY LYNCH II	*Technical Director* DAVID BENKEN	*Production Stage Manager* JIMMIE LEE SMITH	*Production Supervisor* DOC ZORTHIAN
Music Director KARL JURMAN	*Associate Music Producer* ROBERT ELHAI	*Music Coordinator* MICHAEL KELLER	*Press Representative* BONEAU/ BRYAN-BROWN
Music Produced for the Stage & Additional Score by MARK MANCINA	*Additional Vocal Score, Vocal Arrangements & Choral Director* LEBO M		*Orchestrators* ROBERT ELHAI DAVID METZGER BRUCE FOWLER

Choreography by
GARTH FAGAN

Directed by
JULIE TAYMOR

5/9/05

CAST
(in order of appearance)

Rafiki ....TSHIDI MANYE
Mufasa ....ALTON FITZGERALD WHITE
Sarabi...................JEAN MICHELLE GRIER
Zazu ....JEFF BINDER
Scar....................................DEREK SMITH
Young Simba..........JARRELL J. SINGLETON
(At certain performances)
Young Simba................AARON D. CONLEY
(At certain performances)
Young Nala....................KAILANI M. COBA
(At certain performances)
Young Nala............ZIPPORAH G. GATLING
(At certain performances)
Shenzi ....BONITA J. HAMILTON
Banzai ......BENJAMIN STERLING CANNON
Ed ....ENRIQUE SEGURA
Timon ....DANNY RUTIGLIANO
Pumbaa ....TOM ALAN ROBBINS
Simba ....JOSH TOWER
Nala ....KISSY SIMMONS
Ensemble Singers ....KYLE R. BANKS,
E. CLAYTON CORNELIOUS,
BOBBY DAYE, LINDIWE DLAMINI,
BONGI DUMA, JEAN MICHELLE GRIER,
MICHAEL ALEXANDER HENRY,
KESWA, RON KUNENE,
SHERYL McCALLUM,
MPUME SIKAKANE,
REMA WEBB,
KENNY REDELL WILLIAMS

continued on the next page

Photo by Joan Marcus

The Lion King

MUSICAL NUMBERS

ACT ONE

Scene 1	Pride Rock	
	"Circle of Life" with "Nants' Ingonyama"	Rafiki, Ensemble
Scene 2	Scar's Cave	
Scene 3	Rafiki's Tree	
Scene 4	The Pridelands	
	"The Morning Report"	Zazu, Young Simba, Mufasa
Scene 5	Scar's Cave	
Scene 6	The Pridelands	
	"I Just Can't Wait to Be King"	Young Simba, Young Nala, Zazu, Ensemble
Scene 7	Elephant Graveyard	
	"Chow Down"	Shenzi, Banzai, Ed
Scene 8	Under the Stars	
	"They Live in You"	Mufasa, Ensemble
Scene 9	Elephant Graveyard	
	"Be Prepared"	Scar, Shenzi, Banzai, Ed, Ensemble
Scene 10	The Gorge	
Scene 11	Pride Rock	
	"Be Prepared" (Reprise)	Scar, Ensemble
Scene 12	Rafiki's Tree	
Scene 13	The Desert/The Jungle	
	"Hakuna Matata"	Timon, Pumbaa, Young Simba, Simba, Ensemble

ACT TWO

Entr'acte	"One by One"	Ensemble
Scene 1	Scar's Cave	
	"The Madness of King Scar"	Scar, Zazu, Banzai, Shenzi, Ed, Nala
Scene 2	The Pridelands	
	"Shadowland"	Nala, Rafiki, Ensemble
Scene 3	The Jungle	
Scene 4	Under the Stars	
	"Endless Night"	Simba, Ensemble
Scene 5	Rafiki's Tree	
Scene 6	The Jungle	
	"Can You Feel the Love Tonight"	Timon, Pumbaa, Simba, Nala, Ensemble
	"He Lives in You" (Reprise)	Rafiki, Simba, Ensemble
Scene 7	Pride Rock	
	"King of Pride Rock"/"Circle of Life" (Reprise)	Ensemble

Cast Continued

Ensemble Dancers ....KYLIN BRADY, CAMILLE M. BROWN, LaTRISA A. COLEMAN, GABRIEL A. CROOM, GREGORY A. KING, LISA LEWIS, NIKKI LONG, IAN VINCENT McGINNIS, RAY MERCER, KEENA SMITH, RYAN BROOKE TAYLOR, STEVEN EVAN WASHINGTON

SWINGS

GARLAND DAYS, TONY JAMES, DENNIS JOHNSTON, CORNELIUS JONES, JR., JENNIFER HARRISON NEWMAN, ANGELICA EDWARDS PATTERSON, SOPHIA N. STEPHENS, TORYA, FRANK WRIGHT II

UNDERSTUDIES

Rafiki: SHERYL McCALLUM, MPUME SIKAKANE, REMA WEBB; Mufasa: LESLIE ELLIARD, MICHAEL ALEXANDER HENRY; Sarabi: CAMILLE M. BROWN, SHERYL McCALLUM; Zazu: JOHN E. BRADY, ENRIQUE SEGURA; Scar: JEFF BINDER, JACK KOENIG; Shenzi: ANGELICA EDWARDS PATTERSON, SOPHIA N. STEPHENS, REMA WEBB; Banzai: E. CLAYTON CORNELIOUS, GARLAND DAYS, CORNELIUS JONES, JR.; KENNY REDELL WILLIAMS; Ed: DENNIS JOHNSTON, CORNELIUS JONES JR., FRANK WRIGHT II; Timon: JOHN E. BRADY, ENRIQUE SEGURA; Pumbaa: JOHN E. BRADY, JACK KOENIG; Simba: E. CLAYTON CORNELIOUS, BOBBY DAYE, DENNIS JOHNSTON, CORNELIUS JONES, JR.; Nala: KYLIN BRADY, SOPHIA N. STEPHENS, REMA WEBB

DANCE CAPTAINS: GARLAND DAYS, TORYA

SPECIALTIES

Circle Of Life Vocals: E. CLAYTON CORNELIOU, BONGI DUMA; Mouse Shadow Puppet: BOBB DAYE; Ant Hill Lady: LaTRISA A. COLEMAN Guinea Fowl: RYAN BROOKE TAYLOR; Buzzard Pol GREGORY A. KING; Gazelle Wheel: KEEN SMITH; Butterflies: KEENA SMITH; Gazell STEVEN EVAN WASHINGTON; Lioness Cha Vocal: E. CLAYTON CORNELIOUS; Acrobat Trickster: RAY MERCER; Stilt Giraffe Cross: GABRIE A. CROOM; Giraffe Shadow Puppets: STEVEN EVA WASHINGTON, KENNY REDELL WILLIAM Cheetah: LaTRISA A. COLEMAN; Scar Shado Puppets: RYAN BROOKE TAYLOR, STEVEN EVA WASHINGTON, KENNY REDELL WILLIAM Simba Shadow Puppets: GREGORY A. KING, IA VINCENT McGINNIS, RAY MERCER; One By On Vocal: BONGI DUMA, KESWA; One By One Dance E. CLAYTON CORNELIOUS, BONGI DUMA RON KUNENE; Fireflies: CAMILLE M. BROWN Pumbaa Pole Puppet: KENNY REDELL WILLIAM Nala Pole Puppet: LISA LEWIS; Floor Dancer LaTRISA A. COLEMAN, RYAN BROOKE TAYLOR Flying Dancers: GABRIEL A. CROOM, LISA LEWIS KEENA SMITH, STEVEN EVAN WASHINGTON Lioness/Hyena Shadow Puppets: LINDIWE DLAMIN KESWA, SHERYL McCALLUM, MPUM SIKAKANE, REMA WEBB

Keswa and Mpume Sikakane
are appearing with the permission of
Actors' Equity Association.

ORCHESTRA

CONDUCTOR: KARL JURMAN

Keyboard Synthesizer/Associate Conductor: Cherie Rosen; Drums/Assistant Conductor: Tommy Igoe; Percussion/Assistant Conductor: Rolando Morales-Matos; Synthesizers: Ted Baker, Paul Ascenzo; Wood Flute Soloist/Flute/Piccolo: David Weiss; Concertmaster: Francisca Mendoza; Violins: Krystof Witek, Avril Brown; Violin/Viola: Ralph Farris; Cellos: Eliana Mendoza, Bruce Wang; Flute/Clarinet/Bass Clarinet: Bob Keller; French Horns: Alexandra Cook, Katie Dennis, Jeff Scott; Trombone: Rock Ciccarone; Bass Trombone/Tuba: George Flynn; Upright and Electric Basses: Tom Barney; Guitar: Kevin Kuhn; Mallets/Percussion: Valerie Dee Naranjo, Tom Brett; Percussion: Junior "Gabu" Wedderburn; Music Coordinator: Michael Keller

The Lion King

 Derek Smith
Scar

 Alton Fitzgerald White
Mufasa

 Tshidi Manye
Rafiki

 Jeff Binder
Zazu

 Tom Alan Robbins
Pumbaa

 Danny Rutigliano
Timon

 Josh Tower
Simba

 Kissy Simmons
Nala

 Benjamin Sterling Cannon
Banzai

 Bonita J. Hamilton
Shenzi

 Enrique Segura
Ed

 Kailani M. Coba
Young Nala

 Aaron D. Conley
Young Simba

 Zipporah G. Gatling
Young Nala

 Jarrell J. Singleton
Young Simba

 Kyle R. Banks
Ensemble

 John E. Brady
Standby Timon, Pumbaa, Zazu

 Kylin Brady
Ensemble

 Camille M. Brown
Ensemble

 LaTrisa A. Coleman
Ensemble

 E. Clayton Cornelious
Ensemble

 Gabriel A. Croom
Ensemble

 Bobby Daye
Ensemble

 Garland Days
Swing, Dance Captain

 Lindiwe Dlamini
Ensemble

 Bongi Duma
Ensemble

 Jean Michelle Grier
Ensemble/Sarabi

 Michael Alexander Henry
Ensemble

 Tony James
Swing

 Dennis Johnston
Swing

 Cornelius Jones, Jr.
Swing

 Keswa
Ensemble

 Gregory A. King
Ensemble

 Jack Koenig
Standby for Scar and Pumbaa

 Ron Kunene
Ensemble

Lisa Lewis
Ensemble

Nikki Long
Ensemble

Sheryl McCallum
Ensemble

Ian Vincent
McGinnis
Ensemble

Ray Mercer
Ensemble

Jennifer Harrison
Newman
Swing

Angelica Edwards
Patterson
Swing

Mpume Sikakane
Ensemble

Keena Smith
Ensemble

Sophia N. Stephens
Swing

Ryan Brooke Taylor
*Ensemble, Fight
Captain*

Torya
*Swing, Dance
Captain*

Steven Evan
Washington
Ensemble

Rema Webb
Ensemble

Kenny Redell
Williams
Ensemble

Frank Wright II
Swing

Elton John
Music

Tim Rice
Lyrics

Julie Taymor
*Director, Costume
Design, Mask/Puppet
Co-Design, Addl. Lyrics*

Garth Fagan
Choreographer

Donald Holder
Lighting Design

Michael Curry
*Mask & Puppet
Design*

Anthony Lyn
Associate Director

Karl Jurman
*Music Director/
Conductor*

Brian Hill
Resident Director

Robert Elhai
*Associate Music
Producer,
Orchestrator*

Michael Keller
Music Coordinator

THE LION KING
ALUMNI

Christian Anthony
Young Nala

Adrian Bailey
Ensemble

Alexio K. Barbozo
Young Simba

Iresol Cardona
Ensemble

Ahnjel Chavonne
Swing

Rodrick Covington
Banzai

The Lion King

Robert Scott Daye
Ensemble

Michelle Dorant
Ensemble

C. Ross Edwards
Swing

Leslie Elliard
Ensemble

Danny Fetter
Young Simba

Ramon Flowers
Ensemble

Tony Freeman
Zazu

Rajonie Hammond
Young Simba

Rod Harrelson
Ensemble

Charles Holt
Ensemble

Timothy Hunter
Ensemble

Meena T. Jahi
Sarabi, Ensemble

Dennis Johnston
Swing

LaMae
Ensemble

Dennis Lue
Swing

Sydney McNeal
Young Nala

Nhlanhla "Lucky"
Ngema
Ensemble

Clifton Oliver
Simba

Patrick Page
Scar

Robyn Payne
Sarabi

Cinda RamSeur
Ensemble

Natalie Ridley
Ensemble

Marlayna Syms
Shenzi

Jeremiah Tatum
Ensemble

Price Waldman
*Standby for Scar,
Pumbaa, Zazu,
Timon*

Shonte Walker
Ensemble

Nayo K. Wallace
Sarabi, Ensemble

Thom Christopher
Warren
*Standby Scar,
Pumbaa, Zazu, Timon*

Leonard
Wooldridge
Ensemble

Zulu-Lava
Ensemble

The *Lion King* Crew

Photo by Ben Strothmann

Front Row (L-R): Steve Stackle, Jazmine Dugall, Svetlana Avelore, Naomi Genece, Caitlin White, Brandon D'Orlando, Afton Boggiano.

Second Row (L-R): Sara Jablon, April Fernandez-Taylor, Tiffany Edleblute, Shirley Roy, Eddie Rospigliosi, Kjeld Andersen, Kristin Newhouse, Donna Doiron.

Third Row (L-R): Aldo "Butch" Servilio, Scott Stauffer, Kevin Strohmeyer, Fudie Carriocia, Victoria Epstein, Mike Phillips, James Maloney.

Fourth Row (L-R): Douglas Graf, Marie Renee Foucher, Edward M. Greenberg, Bo Metzler, Ray King, Dylan Trotto, Drew Siccardi, Elizabeth Cohen.

Fifth Row (L-R): Gail Luna, Joseph P. Garvey, Dave Tisue, Ilya Vett, Edmond Rodriguez, Douglas Hamilton, Cassandra Mucha.

Sixth Row (L-R): Dacia West, Lorna Reed, Nicole Kureshi, Carla Dawson, Kelli Bragdon, Debbie Vogel, Elise Gainer, Mark Houston.

Seventh Row (L-R): Michael Gilbert, Cassin Espy, Christian Bradford, Michelle Dunn, Michael Jackson, Craig Kilander, Alison Wadsworth, Niki White.

Eighth Row (L-R): Nicholas Kjos, Tania Velez, Jason Blanche, Natalie Ellis, Alyssa Northrop, Kristine Baker, Kyle Pickles, Walter Weiner.

Ninth Row (L-R): Dawn Bentley, Holly Seiger, Guy Bentley, Unidentified, Jonathan Hanson, John Loiacono, Dana Amendola, Keith Guralchuk.

Tenth Row (L-R): Sean Strohmeyer, George Zegarsky, Michael P. Corbett, Angela Johnson, Jimmy Maher, Kirk Bender, Adrian Bou, Sylvia Brown, Herlinda Moncada.

STAFF FOR THE LION KING WORLDWIDE

Associate Producer ....Todd Lacy
Associate Producer ....Aubrey Lynch II
Associate Director ....Anthony Lyn
Production Dance Supervisor ....Marey Griffith
Production Manager ....Anne Quart
Production Supervisor ....Doc Zorthian
Supervising Resident Director ....John Stefaniuk
Dance Supervisor ....Celise Hicks
Associate Music Supervisor ....Jay Alger
Associate Scenic Designer ....Peter Eastman
Associate Costume Designer ....Mary Nemecek Peterson
Associate Mask & Puppet Designer ....Louis Troisi
Associate Sound Designer ....John Shivers
Associate Hair & Makeup Designer ....Carole Hancock
Associate Lighting Designer ....Jeanne Koenig
Assistant Lighting Designer ....Marty Vreeland
Automated Lighting Programmer ....Aland Henderson
Casting Associate ....Kevin Kennison
Production Coordinator ....Jane Abramson
Management Assistants........... Suyin Chan, Tara Engler

GENERAL PRESS REPRESENTATIVES
BONEAU/BRYAN-BROWN

Chris Boneau   Jackie Green   Matt Polk   Aaron Meier

STAFF FOR THE LION KING NEW YORK

COMPANY MANAGER.....................**DAVE EHLE**
Production Stage Manager ....Jimmie Lee Smith
Resident Director ....Brian Hill
Resident Dance Supervisor ....Ruthlyn Salomons
Musical Director/Conductor ....Karl Jurman

Stage Managers ....**Victoria Epstein, Gail P. Luna,**
Kristin Newhouse, Ron Vodicka
Assistant Company Manager ....Laura Eichholz
Fight Captain ....Ryan Brooke Taylor
Assistant Choreographers ....Norwood J. Pennewell,
Natalie Rogers
Fight Consultant ....Rick Sordelet
South African Dialect Coach ....Ron Kunene
Casting Associates ....Jack Bowdan, C.S.A.,
Megan Larche, Leah Alter, Sarah Prosser
Show Accountant ....Alma LaMarr
Corporate Counsel ....Michael Rosenfeld
Physical Therapy ....Neuro Tour Physical Therapy,
Emelie Vulcain
Consulting Orthopedist ....Philip A. Bauman, M.D.
Child Guardian ....Niki White
Executive Travel ....Robert Arnao, Patt McRory
Production Travel ....Jill Citron
Advertising ....Serino/Coyne Inc.

Production Carpenter ....Drew Siccardi
Assistant Carpenters ....Michael P. Corbett,
Mike Phillips, Michael Trotto
Automation Carpenters .....Steve Stackle, George Zegarsky
Carpenters ....Kirk Bender, Fudie Carriocia,
Ray King, Jimmy Maher,
Mike Rahilly, Aldo "Butch" Servilio,
Dylan Trotto
Production Flyman ....Brad Ingram
Production Electrician ....James Maloney
Key Spot Operator ....Joseph P. Garvey
Board Operator ....Edward M. Greenberg
Automated Lighting Technician ....Sean Strohmeyer
Production Electricians ....Gregory Dunkin,
Douglas Graf, Joe Lynch,
Al Manganaro, Kevin Strohmeyer
Production Propman ....Victor Amerling
Assistant Propman ....Tim Abel
Props ....Joe Bivone, Bo Metzler
Production Sound Engineer ....Scott Stauffer

Assistant Sound Engineer ....Marie Renee Foucher
Sound Assistant ....Bill Romanello
Production Wardrobe Supervisor ....Kjeld Andersen
Assistant Wardrobe Supervisor ....Cynthia Boardman
Puppet Supervisor ....Pamela Pierzina
Puppet Dayworkers ....Islah Abdul-Rahiim, Ilya Vett
Mask/Puppet Studio ....Jeff Curry
Dressers ....Meredith Chase-Boyd, Elizabeth Cline,
Andy Cook, Donna Doiron, Joelyn Draut,
April Fernandez-Taylor, Michelle Gore,
Kimberly Greenberg, Douglas Hamilton,
Mark Houston, Sara Jablon,
Mark Lauer, Michelle Palladino,
Sheila Little Terrell, Dave Tisue,
Gregory Young, Walter Weiner
Stitcher ....Janeth Iverson
Production Hair Supervisor ....Craig Kilander
Assistant Hair Supervisor ....Alison Wadsworth
Production Makeup Supervisor ....Elizabeth Cohen
Assistant Makeup Supervisor ....Angela Johnson
Makeup Artist ....Milagros Medina-Cerdeira

Music Development ....Nick Glennie-Smith
Music Preparation ....Donald Oliver and Evan Morris/
Chelsea Music Service, Inc.
Synthesizer Programmer ....Ted Baker
Orchestral Synthesizer Programmer ......Christopher Ward
Electronic Drum Programmer ....Tommy Igoe
Addt'l Percussion Arrangements ....Valerie Dee Naranjo
Music Assistant ....Elizabeth J. Falcone
Personal Assistant to Elton John ....Bob Halley
Assistant to Tim Rice ....Eileen Heinink
Assistants to Mark Mancina ..Chuck Choi, Kevin Mayfield

Associate Scenic Designer ....Jonathan Fensom
Assistant Scenic Designer ....Michael Fagin
Lighting Design Assistant ....Karen Spahn
Automated Lighting Tracker ....Lara Bohon
Projection Designer ....Geoff Puckett
Projection Art ....Caterina Bertolotto
Assistant Sound Designer ....Kai Harada
Assistant Costume Designer ....Tracy Dorman
Stunt Consultant ....Peter Moore
Children's Tutoring ....On Location Education
Production Photography ....Joan Marcus,
Marc Bryan-Brown
Associate Producer 1996–1998 ....Donald Frantz
Project Manager 1996–1998 ....Nina Essman
Associate Producer 1998–2002 ....Ken Denison
Associate Producer 2000-2003 ....Pam Young
Original Music Director ....Joseph Church

Disney's THE LION KING is a registered trademark
owned by The Walt Disney Company and used under
special license by Disney Theatrical Productions, Ltd.

Cover Art Design © Disney.

DISNEY THEATRICAL PRODUCTIONS

President...............................Thomas Schumacher
Senior Vice President & General Manager ......Alan Levey
Senior Vice President,
Managing Director & CFO ....David Schrader

General Management

Vice President, International ....Ron Kollen
Vice President, Operations.................Dana Amendola
Vice President, Labor Relations ....Allan Frost
Director, Human Resources ....June Heindel
Director, Domestic Touring ....Michele Gold
Manager, Labor Relations ....Stephanie Cheek
Manager, Information Systems ....Scott Benedict
Senior Computer Support Analyst ....Kevin McGuire

Production

Executive Music Producer ....Chris Montan
Senior Vice President, Creative Affairs .....Michele Steckler
Vice President, Creative Affairs ....Greg Gunter
Vice President, Physical Production ....John Tiggeloven

Purchasing Manager ....Joseph Doughney
Staff Associate Director ....Jeff Lee
Staff Associate Producer ....Florie Seery
Staff Associate Designer ....Dennis W. Moyes
Staff Associate Dramaturg ....Ken Cerniglia

Marketing

Vice President ....Heather Epple
Vice President, Domestic Touring ....Jack Eldon
Director, New York ....Andrew Flatt
Manager, New York ....Michele Holland
Manager, New York ....Leslie Barrett
Manager ....Joel Hile

Sales

Vice President, Ticketing ....Jerome Kane
Manager, Group Sales ....Jacob Lloyd Kimbro
Assistant Manager, Group Sales & Marketing ......Juil Kim

Business and Legal Affairs

Vice President ....Jonathan Olson
Vice President ....Robbin Kelley
Director ....Harry S. Gold
Attorney ....Seth Stuhl
Paralegal/Contract Administration ....Colleen Lober

Finance

Director ....Joe McClafferty
Manager, Finance ....Justin Gee
Manager, Production Accounting ....Bill Hussey
Senior Business Planner ....Jason Fletcher
Senior Analyst ....Amir Feder
Production Accountants ....Jamie Cousins,
Alma LaMarr, Barbara Toben
Analyst ....Ronnie Cooper

Controllership

Director, Accounting ....Leena Mathews
Manager, Accounting ....Erica McShane
Senior Analyst ....Stephanie Badie
Analyst ....Adrineh Ghoukassian

Administrative Staff

Elliot Altman, Amy Andrews, Alice Baeza, Jennifer Baker,
Antonia Barba, Gregory Bonsignore, Anne Calamease,
Tiffany Casanova, Karl Chmielewski, Matthew Cronin,
Carl Flanigan, Dayle Gruet, Jonathan Hanson, Jay
Hollenback, Connie Jasper, Janine McGuire, Sarah Norris,
Jeff Parvin, Giovanna Primak, Roberta Risafi, Susan Rubio,
Kisha Santiago, Christian Trimmer

Disney Theatrical Productions
1450 Broadway • New York, NY 10018
mail@disneytheatrical.com

BUENA VISTA THEATRICAL MERCHANDISE, L.L.C.

Vice President ....Steven Downing
Manager ....John F. Agati
Operations Manager ....Shawn Baker
Assistant Manager, Inventory ....Suzanne Jakel
Buyer..Suzanne Araneo
Retail Supervisor ....Mark Nathman
Merchandising Assistant ....Ed Pisapia
On-site Retail Manager ....Katie Thompson
On-site Assistant Retail Manager ....Eddie Rospigliosi

STAFF FOR THE NEW AMSTERDAM THEATRE

Theatre Manager ....John Liacono
Guest Services Manager ....Keith Guralchuk
Box Office Treasurer ....Helen Cullen
Assistant Treasurer ....Harry Jaffie
Coordinator, Special Events ....Amy Andrews
Chief Engineer ....Frank Gibbons
Engineers ....John Burke, Dan Milan
Security Supervisor ....Richard Gonzalez
Head Usher ....Susan Linder
Lobby Refreshments ....Sweet Concessions
Special Thanks ....Harry Grossman, Lynn Beckemeyer,
Amy Bawden, Nancy Holland

Left: Cast members celebrate winning Best Bonnet Design (by Ilya Vett, Walter Weiner and Camille Brown) at the annual "Easter Bonnet" competition. Right: Company member Kissy Simmons takes part in "Broadway on Broadway."

Memorable Anniversary Gifts: The best one was a sweatshirt with the title in a university kind of logo. Also, *Lion King* umbrellas.

Most Exciting Celebrity Visitor: Poet Maya Angelou came backstage one night and a group of people wanted to get in a photo with her. Someone started getting on their knees to be in the front of the shot, but Miss Angelou said, "No, no, baby, never get down on your knees."

"Gypsy Of The Year" Sketch: "Driven" by Cornelius Jones Jr. and Frank Wright II.

"Carols For A Cure" Carol: "Holiday Lament (The Fruitcake Song)."

"Easter Bonnet" Sketch: "What Is Peace?" conceived and directed by Josh Tower (with help from Camille Brown and Lisa Lewis), composed by Frank Wright II. Winner: Best Bonnet Design, 2005.

Backstage Rituals: A group of us warm up on stage in close proximity just before the show. It's our chance to touch base and talk. Then comes the opening of the show, "The Circle of Life," which is so awe-inspiring. It's like a spiritual awakening every night.

Favorite Moments: When the Grassheads come up from the elevator, and then the Mufasa mask comes together to create the apparition.

Mascots: Upstage, behind the scrim are five or six photos of the great Ziegfeld dancers who appeared on this stage. They're visible only to the actors, and they remind us of the history of our theatre.

Favorite In-Theatre Gathering Place: Our green room is usually taken over by the orchestra, and by people napping. The fifth floor men's ensemble singing room is the place where we have birthdays and other celebrations.

Favorite Off-Site Hangout: It's split. Some go to the Above Bar at the Hilton (50 percent off for union members!). The rest go to Jack's on 40th Street.

Favorite Snack Food: Everybody has something different. There's also a bowl of candy in the stage manager's office, with miniature Kit-Kats and Snickers and Jolly Ranchers—but no gum! Everybody coming down the stairs grabs one or two pieces of candy at some point.

Favorite Therapies: We have a physical therapist and a lot of people warm up on the ballet bar, or do Pilates or jump rope. My favorite thing is to go up to the eighth floor to the abandoned theatre, the New Amsterdam Roof, and jump rope in that huge dilapidated space where it's totally quiet.

Record Number Of Cell Phone Rings: The strangest ones come from the crew in the wings. That's happened at least three times that I can remember.

Memorable Stage Door Fan Encounter: A fan drew my name on his back in a heart. He pulled up his shirt and showed it to me.

Musician Who Plays The Most Instruments: Our flutist, Bob Keller, who plays 17 different wind instruments.

Strangest Press Encounter: People ask, "Can you say your lines as Simba," even when I'm in my street clothes. I find that really weird.

Heaviest/Hottest Costume: We have a lot of heavy and hot costumes. Our current Zazu sweats off his makeup by intermission. Scar has two 15-pound motors on his hips and leather jodhpurs. The Pumbaa puppet weighs about 40 pounds, so that's probably the heaviest.

Who Wore The Least: My counterpart, Little Simba, and I.

Catchphrases: "Heybo," a Zulu greeting or exclamation.

Sweethearts Within The Company: I met my fiancée, Jennifer Newman, on the *Lion King* tour, and she's now in the New York company. One of our ensemble dancers and stage managers are getting married. A former Banzai and former dancer had twins not long ago.

Company Legends: It's always amazing when Julie Taymor comes to the theatre.

Memorable Directorial Note: "What is doing nothing that's full of something?"

Ghosts: The ghost of a former Ziegfeld girl, Olive Thomas, is very active. Stuff happens all the time. Things disappear and no one can find them. Some nights everything goes wrong, like there are gremlins in the works. We just say, "Olive is at play."

Also: I think that people will say that this was one of our most inspired years.

Correspondent: Josh Tower, "Simba"

PLAYBILL®

CAST
(in order of appearance)

Chiffon ....DeQUINA MOORE
Crystal ....TRISHA JEFFREY
Ronnette....................CARLA J. HARGROVE
Mushnik ....ROB BARTLETT
Audrey ....JESSICA-SNOW WILSON
Seymour ....JOEY FATONE
Derelicts,
Skid Row Occupants .....ANTHONY ASBURY,
                       BILL REMINGTON,
                 MARTIN P. ROBINSON,
          MICHAEL-LEON WOOLEY,
                       MATT VOGEL

Orin, Bernstein, Luce,
Snip and Everyone Else ....ROBERT EVAN
The Voice of Audrey II ....MICHAEL-LEON
                              WOOLEY

Audrey II (Manipulation),
Dentist's Patient ....MARTIN P. ROBINSON,
                    ANTHONY ASBURY,
                    BILL REMINGTON,
                       MATT VOGEL

UNDERSTUDIES

For Chiffon, Crystal, Ronnette – DANA DAWSON;
For Mushnik – RAY DeMATTIS; For the Voice of
Audrey II – MICHAEL A. SHEPPERD; For
Seymour and Orin, et al. – JONATHAN RAYSON

Prologue Voice ....DON MORROW

VIRGINIA THEATRE
A JUJAMCYN THEATRE

JAMES H. BINGER   ROCCO LANDESMAN
CHAIRMAN   PRESIDENT

PAUL LIBIN   JACK VIERTEL
PRODUCING DIRECTOR   CREATIVE DIRECTOR

Marc Routh   Richard Frankel   Tom Viertel   Steven Baruch
James D. Stern   Douglas L. Meyer
Rick Steiner/John & Bonnie Osher   Simone Genatt Haft
in association with
Frederic H. Mayerson   Amy Danis/Mark Johannes
present

Joey Fatone
in

LITTLE SHOP OF HORRORS

Book and Lyrics by   Music By
Howard Ashman   **Alan Menken**
Based on the Film by **Roger Corman**, Screenplay by **Charles Griffith**

with

Jessica-Snow Wilson
Robert Evan   Michael-Leon Wooley
Carla J. Hargrove   Trisha Jeffrey   DeQuina Moore
Martin P. Robinson   Anthony Asbury   Bill Remington   Matt Vogel
and
Rob Bartlett

Set Design   Costume Design   Lighting Design   Sound Design
Scott Pask   **William Ivey Long**   **Donald Holder**   **T. Richard Fitzgerald**

Puppet Design   Wig & Hair Design   Make-Up Design   Casting
The Jim Henson Company   **Robert-Charles Vallance**   **Angelina Avallone**   **Bernard Telsey Casting**
Martin P. Robinson

Music Director   Original Vocal Arrangements   Music Coordinator
Henry Aronson   **Robert Billig**   **John Miller**

General Management   Production Stage Manager   Production Management   Press Representative
Richard Frankel Productions   **Karen Armstrong**   **Juniper Street Productions**   **Barlow•Hartman**
Jo Porter

Associate Producers
HoriPro/Tokyo Broadcasting System   Clear Channel Entertainment   Endgame Entertainment
Zemiro   M. Swinsky/M. Fuchs   Judy Marinoff Cohn   Rhoda Mayerson

Music Supervision and New Arrangements   Orchestrations
Michael Kosarin   **Danny Troob**

Choreographer
Kathleen Marshall

Director
Jerry Zaks

Originally Produced by the WPA Theatre (Kyle Renick, Producing Director)
Originally Produced at the Orpheum Theatre, NYC, by the WPA Theatre, David Geffen, Cameron Mackintosh and the Shubert Organization.
Piano courtesy of Yamaha
The producers wish to express their appreciation to Theatre Development Fund for its support of this production.

8/2/04

Don't Feed the Plant: Carla J. Hargrove, DeQuina Moore, Trisha Jeffrey as the chorus.

Photo by Paul Kolnik

Little Shop of Horrors

MUSICAL NUMBERS

ACT I

"Little Shop of Horrors" ....Chiffon, Crystal, Ronnette
"Downtown (Skid Row)" ....Company
"Da-Doo" ....Seymour, Chiffon, Crystal, Ronnette
"Grow for Me" ....Seymour
"Ya Never Know" ....Mushnik, Seymour, Chiffon, Crystal, Ronnette
"Somewhere That's Green" ....Audrey
"Closed for Renovation" ....Mushnik, Seymour, Audrey
"Dentist!" ....Orin, Chiffon, Crystal, Ronnette
"Mushnik and Son" ....Mushnik, Seymour
"Git It" ....Seymour, Audrey II, Chiffon, Crystal, Ronnette
"Now (It's Just the Gas)" ....Orin, Seymour

ACT II

"Call Back in the Morning" ....Audrey, Seymour
"Suddenly Seymour" ....Seymour, Audrey, Chiffon, Crystal, Ronnette
"Suppertime" ....Audrey II, Chiffon, Crystal, Ronnette
"The Meek Shall Inherit" ....Seymour, Chiffon, Crystal, Ronnette, Bernstein, Luce, Snip
"Sominex"/"Suppertime" (Reprise) ....Audrey, Audrey II
"Somewhere That's Green" (Reprise) ....Audrey
Finale: "Don't Feed the Plants" ....Company

Photo by Paul Kolnik

Kerry Butler and Hunter Foster as Audrey and Seymour.

LITTLE SHOP OF HORRORS ORCHESTRA

CONDUCTOR:
HENRY ARONSON

Associate Conductor:
John Samorian

Keyboards:
Henry Aronson, John Samorian

Guitars/Mandolin:
John Benthal

Bass:
Steve Gelfand

Drums:
Rich Mercurio

Percussion:
David Yee

Trumpets:
Tony Kadleck, Dave Spier

Woodwinds:
Tom Murray, Matt Hong

Music Coordinator – John Miller

A developmental production of
LITTLE SHOP OF HORRORS
was presented at the Actors' Playhouse at the
Miracle Theatre, Coral Gables, Florida

Executive Producing Director: Barbara S. Stein
Artistic Director: David Arisco

www.littleshopofhorrors.com

Joey Fatone
*Seymour
Krelbourn*

Jessica-Snow
Wilsow
Audrey

Robert Evan
*Orin Scrivello
D.D.S., et al.*

Rob Bartlett
Mushnik

Michael-Leon Wooley
*The Voice of
Audrey II*

Carla J. Hargrove
Ronnette

Trisha Jeffrey
Crystal

DeQuina Moore
Chiffon

Martin P. Robinson
*Puppet Design/
Puppeteer*

Anthony Asbury
Puppeteer

Bill Remington
Puppeteer

Matt Vogel
Puppeteer

Little Shop of Horrors

Dana Dawson
Understudy Chiffon, Crystal, Ronnette

Ray DeMattis
Understudy Mushnik

Jonathan Rayson
Understudy Seymour and Orin, et. al.

Michael A. Shepperd
Understudy Voice of Audrey II

Howard Ashman (1950-1991)
Book and Lyrics

Alan Menken
Music

Jerry Zaks
Director

Kathleen Marshall
Choreographer

Michael Kosarin
Music Supervision & New Arrangements

Scott Pask
Set Design

William Ivey Long
Costume Designer

Donald Holder
Lighting Design

Carl Casella
Sound Design

Bernard Telsey
Casting

Henry Aronson
Music Director

Robert Billig
Original Vocal Arrangements

John Miller
Music Coordinator

Juniper Street Productions: Guy Kwan, John Paull, Hillary Blanken, Kevin Broomell, Ana-Rose Greene
Technical Supervisors

Marc Bruni
Assistant Director

Vince Pesce
Associate Choreographer

Rick Steiner
Producer

John and Bonnie Osher
Producer

Frederic H. Mayerson
Producer

Amy Danis/Mark Johannes
Producer

Morton Swinsky
Associate Producer

Michael Fuchs
Associate Producer

Rhoda Mayerson
Associate Producer

Kerry Butler
Audrey

Ta'Rea Campbell
Understudy

Nikki Renée Daniels
Understudy

Hunter Foster
Seymour

Michael James Leslie
Voice of Audrey II

Darren Ritchie
Orin Scrivello D.D.S.

Douglas Sills
Orin Scrivello D.D.S.

Staff for LITTLE SHOP OF HORRORS

GENERAL MANAGEMENT
RICHARD FRANKEL PRODUCTIONS
Richard Frankel   Marc Routh
Jo Porter   Laura Green
Rod Kaats   Joe Watson

COMPANY MANAGER
Sammy Ledbetter

Associate Company Manager
Grant A. Rice

GENERAL PRESS REPRESENTATIVE
BARLOW•HARTMAN
John Barlow   Michael Hartman
Jeremy Shaffer

CASTING
BERNARD TELSEY CASTING, C.S.A.
Bernie Telsey   Will Cantler   David Vaccari
Bethany Berg   Craig Burns
Tiffany Little Canfield   Christine Todino

Production Stage Manager .... Karen Armstrong
Stage Manager .... Adam John Hunter
Assistant Stage Manager .... Claudia Lynch
Associate Choreographer .... Vince Pesce
Assistant Director .... Marc Bruni
Dance Captain .... Carla J. Hargrove

Production Managers .... Hillary Blanken,
John H. Paull, III
Production Management Associates .... Guy Kwan,
Kevin Broomell
Associate Set Designer .... Orit Jacoby Carroll
Assistant Set Designers .... Tobin Ost,
Nicholas Keslake,
Heesoo Kim,
Matt Schultz
Associate Costume Designer .... Tom Beall
Assistant Costume Designers .... Patrick Chevillot,
Paul Spadone
Assistant to Mr. Long .... David Castellano
Automated Light Programmers .... Aland Henderson,
William McLachlan
Associate Lighting Designer .... Vivien Leone
Assistant Lighting Designers .... Michael Jones,
Carolyn Wong
Associate Sound Designers .... Carl Casella,
Domonic Sack

Supervising Production Carpenter .... Walter Murphy
Head Carpenter .... Jack Anderson
Production Flyman .... Geoff Vaughn
Automation Carpenter .... Bill Partello
Supervising Production Electrician .... Jonathan Lawson
Head Electrician .... Craig Aves
Assistant Electrician .... Morgan Shevett
Production Sound Engineer .... Wallace Flores

Supervising Production Property Master .. Joseph Harris, Jr.
Head Property Master .... Christopher Pantuso
Assistant Property Master .... Geoffrey Friedlander
Wardrobe Supervisor .... Lorraine Borek
Dressers .... Alice Bee, Mark Flesher,
Jeannie Naughton, David Oliver
Hair Design Assistant .... Wendy Parson
Hair & Makeup Supervisor .... Gary Arave
Hair & Makeup Assistant .... Frederick C. Waggoner

Assistant to John Miller .... David Obele
Associate Conductor .... John Samorian
Synthesizer Programming .... Henry Aronson

Original Orchestrations .... Robby Merkin
Production Pianist .... Georgia Stitt
Rehearsal Drummer .... Rich Mercurio
Music Preparation .... Miller Music Services/
Peter Miller

AUDREY II CULTIVATION TEAM
Project Manager .... Emily Lawson
Technical Operator .... Geoffrey Friedlander
Fabricators .... Andrew Benepe, Andrea Detwiler,
Victoria Ellis, Eric Engelhardt,
Cathy McCullough, Anney McKilligan,
Paul Rice, Sara Schmidt-Boldon,
Ilya Vatt, James Vogel

Asst. to Mr. Baruch .... Sonja Soper
Asst. to Mr. Viertel .... Tania Senewiratne
Asst. to Mr. Steiner .... Kathy Wall
Asst. to Mr. Stern .... Shira Sergant
Asst. to Ms. Genatt .... Ari Wishkoff
Management Assistant .... David Redman Scott
Production Assistants .... Justin Scribner,
Erica Tuchman
Production Intern .... Billy Rosen

Press Assistant .... Dayle Gruet
Press Intern .... Jim Nash
Advertising .... Serino Coyne, Inc./
Sandy Block,
Scott Johnson,
Jennifer Fleckner
Promotions/Marketing ..... TMG - The Marketing Group/
Tanya Grubich, Martha Foster,
Johanna Lindsay
Additional Marketing Services .... Leanne Schanzer
Promotions, Inc./
Leanne Schanzer,
Christine Berrios
Production Photography .... Paul Kolnik, Joan Marcus
Additional Photography .... Richard Mitchell
Web Designer .... Simma Park
Theatre Displays .... King Displays

Physical Therapist .... Sean Gallagher,
Performing Arts Physical Therapy
Insurance .... Marsh USA Inc.
Legal Counsel .... Patricia Crown, Esq.,
Coblence & Warner
Banking .... Chase Manhattan Bank/
Michele Gibbons, Richard Callian
Payroll Service .... Castellana Services, Inc.
Accounting .... FK Partners, LLP
Travel Agency .... JMC Travel
Merchandising .... Rick Steiner Productions
New York Rehearsals .... Roundabout Rehearsal Studios,
Ford Center for the Performing Arts
Opening Night Coordinator .... Tobak-Dantchik Events
and Promotions/
Suzanne Tobak, Jeffry Gray

For Touring Information, contact
On the Road
(212) 302-5559
Director of Booking .... Siobhan O'Neill
Director of Tour Management .... Simma Levine
Booking Coordinator .... ElizBeth Jones

LITTLE SHOP OF HORRORS
was originally
Directed by Howard Ashman
with
Musical Staging by Edie Cowan

CREDITS AND ACKNOWLEDGEMENTS
Scenery and scenic effects built, painted, electrified and
automated by Showmotion, Inc., Norwalk, CT.
Flower shop, deck and additional scenery built,
painted and electrified by Scenic Technologies.
Show control and scenic motion control featuring stage
command systems by Scenic Technologies, a division of
Production Resource Group, LLC, New Windsor, NY.
Scenery painted by Scenic Art Studios.
Lighting equipment from Fourth Phase, New Jersey.
Sound equipment by Sound Associates, Inc.
Specialty props by Prism Production Services,
Rahway, NJ, and Beyond Imagination.
Audrey II mechanization provided by Scenic Technologies.
Dental equipment provided by Baystate Dental,
Springfield, Mass. Prosthetic design by Louie Zakarian.
Costumes built by Euroco Costumes, John Schneeman
Costumes, Jennifer Love Costumes, Scafati Uniforms,
Cego Shirtmakers. Wigs by The Broadway Wig Company.
Lozenges provided by Ricola, Inc.
Makeup provided by M.A.C.
Emer'gen-C provided by Alacer Corp.

RICHARD FRANKEL PRODUCTIONS STAFF
Finance Director .... Ann Caprio
Director of Business Affairs .... Carter Anne McGowan
Assistant to Mr. Frankel .... Anthony Taccetta
Assistant to Mr. Routh .... Michael Sag
Assistant to Ms. Porter .... Rebecca Budd
Assistant Finance Director .... Liz Hines
Accounting Assistant .... Elsie Jamin-Maguire
National Director of Marketing and Sales ... Ronni Mandell
Marketing Assistant .... Sarah Versprille
Office Manager .... Lori Steiger-Perry
Office Assistant .... Katie Pugh
IT Manager .... Roddy Pimentel
Receptionists .... Alana Conti, Stephanie Kennedy
Interns .... Ron Nicynski, Jennifer Baker,
Colleen Sherry, Jay Pucciarelli,
Myriah Perkins, Lauren Krupka,
Alec Walker, Patrick Kirkland,
David Scott, Emily Powell,
Kgomotso Mpyane

SPECIAL THANKS
The producers wish to express their thanks to
Sarah Gillespie, William Lauch, Fred Gallo,
John Sochocky, Javier Chacin, Chris Jahn,
Jessica Pagan, Kimberly Collins,
Heidi Schading, Denise Grillo, Michelle Habeck,
Carl Wasisanen, S. Magnus Porter

JUJAMCYN THEATERS

JAMES H. BINGER   ROCCO LANDESMAN
Chairman   President

PAUL LIBIN   JACK VIERTEL
Producing Director   Creative Director

JERRY ZAKS

DANIEL ADAMIAN   JENNIFER HERSHEY
General Manager   Director of Operations

STAFF FOR THE VIRGINIA THEATRE
Manager .... Matt Fox
Treasurer .... Nick Russo
Assistant Manager .... Lauren Bean
Carpenter .... Dan Dour
Propertyman .... Scott Mulrain
Electrician .... Donald Beck
Engineer .... Vladimir Belenky

Memorable Telegram: The opening night telegram from Ellen Greene, the original Audrey, wishing us well

Memorable Opening Night Gifts: The creative staff gave literally dozens of gifts. Most memorable: a numbered lithograph of all the principals, and a papyrus-like sheet of music given by the show's composer, Alan Menken.

Celebrity Visitors: Justin Timberlake of 'N Sync. Ray Romano came onstage and greeted the cast. Mary Wilson of The Supremes came backstage and took a picture with the Urchins, DeQuina Moore, Trisha Jeffrey and Carla Hargrove, who mimic The Supremes in one of the pivotal moments in Act II.

"Easter Bonnet" Sketch (2004): Rob Bartlett and Hunter Foster wrote a send-up of James Lipton interviewing Audrey II.

Backstage Rituals: Prayer Circle before the show, led by either Kerry Butler, Carla Hargrove or DeQuina Moore. Virtually every company member attended.

Favorite Moments: Onstage: When the audience realized that the actors who had been eaten by Audrey II were blooming out of pods. And when the Audrey II went out into the audience over their heads. Offstage: Assistant stage manager Adam Hunter saying "Cinco minutos" instead of "Five minutes."

In-Theatre Gathering Place: The theatre was very small so the only place everyone could gather was the basement. There, cast, crew, and musicians assembled and laughed continually.

Off-Site Hangout: Café Cielo

Snack Food: Candy, candy, candy!

Mascot: Marty Robinson's live rooster.

Therapy: Ricola

Memorable Ad-lib: The night Rob Bartlett forgot to bring the radio onstage for "You Never Know" and he and the urchins pretended to listen through a door.

Strangest Stage Door Fan Encounter: A fan who came to the stage door dressed as Audrey, who was NOT a woman!!

Heaviest/Hottest Costume? Hands down: Doug Sills as Orin et al.

Who Wore the Least? Kerry Butler

Catchphrases: "Shing-a-Ling." "There He Go." "What did Ta'Rea say?"

Memorable Directorial Note: "If you are totally listening and clearly putting the ball in the other actor's court, you will sometimes forget your next line. Of course, I don't want you to forget your lines!"

Company Legends: Rob Bartlett, who played Mushnik and was the most generous person of anyone in the company. Karen Armstrong, PSM, who ran one of the best ships that most of the actors had ever witnessed. DeQuina Moore, who had a brilliant way of getting laughs out of her body movements. Hunter Foster for just being himself.

Correspondents: Michael James Leslie, understudy, "Audrey II," and Ray DeMattis, understudy "Mushnik."

(L-R:) Hunter Foster, Kerry Butler, Rob Bartlett, Douglas Sills at the opening night party at Tavern on the Green.

Director Jerry Zaks on opening night.

Michelle Castro helps welcome Joey Fatone to the cast as Seymour.

DeQuina Moore, Carla J. Hargrove and Trisha Jeffrey at the "Stars in the Alley" event.

PLAYBILL®

LITTLE WOMEN
the musical

♩ VIRGINIA THEATRE
A JUJAMCYN THEATRE
ROCCO LANDESMAN
PRESIDENT

PAUL LIBIN   JACK VIERTEL
PRODUCING DIRECTOR   CREATIVE DIRECTOR

Randall L. Wreghitt   Dani Davis   Ken Gentry   Chase Mishkin
Jack Utsick   Ruben Brache   Lisa Vioni
Jana Robbins   Addiss/Duke Associates
in association with
John & Danita Thomas, Thomas Keegan, Scott Freiman,
and Theatre Previews at Duke
present

Sutton Foster

in

LITTLE WOMEN
the musical

Book By   Music By   Lyrics By
Allan Knee   **Jason Howland**   **Mindi Dickstein**

also starring
Maureen McGovern as Marmee

with

Janet Carroll   Danny Gurwin   John Hickok   Amy McAlexander
Megan McGinnis   Jenny Powers   Robert Stattel   Jim Weitzer
Julie Foldesi   Chris Gunn   Anne Kanengeiser   Larissa Shukis   Andrew Varela

Set Design **Derek McLane**	Costume Design **Catherine Zuber**	Lighting Design **Kenneth Posner**	Sound Design **Peter Hylenski**
Music Director/Conductor and Additional Arrangements **Andrew Wilder**	Orchestrations **Kim Scharnberg**	Vocal Arrangements **Lance Horne**	Music Coordinator **John Miller**
Technical Supervisor **Larry Morley** **William J. Craven**	Associate Director **Darcy Evans**	Hair & Wig Design **Lazaro Arencibia**	Production Supervisor **Beverley Randolph**
Casting **Barry Moss, CSA** **Bob Kale**	Press Representative **The Pete Sanders Group**	Marketing **The Marketing Group**	General Management **Richards/Climan, Inc.**

Choreographed by
Michael Lichtefeld

Directed by
Susan H. Schulman

Based on the novel LITTLE WOMEN by Louisa May Alcott
And based on the play originally commissioned and produced by Theatreworks/USA

The producers wish to express their appreciation
to the Theatre Development Fund for their support of this production.

LIVE BROADWAY

1/21/0.

CAST

Professor Bhaer .... JOHN HICKOK
Jo .... SUTTON FOSTER
Amy .... AMY McALEXANDER
Meg .... JENNY POWERS
Beth .... MEGAN McGINNIS
Marmee .... MAUREEN McGOVERN
Mr. Laurence .... ROBERT STATTEL
Laurie .... DANNY GURWIN
Aunt March .... JANET CARROLL
Mr. Brooke .... JIM WEITZER
Mrs. Kirk .... JANET CARROLL

"Operatic Tragedy" Players

Clarissa .... JENNY POWERS
Braxton .... JIM WEITZER
Rodrigo .... DANNY GURWIN
The Hag .... MAUREEN McGOVERN
The Troll .... AMY McALEXANDER
The Knight .... ROBERT STATTEL
Rodrigo Too .... MEGAN McGINNIS

STANDBYS

For Jo — JULIE FOLDESI, LARISSA SHUKIS;
for Marmee/The Hag, Aunt March/Mrs. Kirk —
ANNE KANENGEISER; for Beth/Rodrigo Too,
Meg/Clarissa — JULIE FOLDESI, LARISSA
SHUKIS; for Amy/The Troll — LARISSA
SHUKIS; for Mr. Brooke/Braxton — CHRIS
GUNN, ANDREW VARELA; for Laurie/Rodrigo
— CHRIS GUNN; for Professor Bhaer, Mr.
Laurence/The Knight — ANDREW VARELA

The cast of *Little Women.*

Little Women

MUSICAL NUMBERS

THE SCENE

Concord, Massachusetts and New York City

Christmas, 1863 – Spring, 1867

ACT ONE

Scene One:

Summer 1865, Mrs. Kirk's boarding house; Christmas 1863, the attic, the March parlor

"An Operatic Tragedy" .... Jo, Clarissa, Braxton, Rodrigo, Professor Bhaer

"Better" .... Jo

"Our Finest Dreams" .... Jo, Beth, Meg, Amy

"Here Alone" .... Marmee

Scene Two :

Early winter 1864, Aunt March's house

"Could You?" .... Aunt March, Jo

Scene Three:

Winter 1864, the March parlor, Annie Moffat's ball

"I'd Be Delighted" .... Marmee, Meg, Jo, Beth

"Take a Chance on Me" .... Laurie

"Better" (Reprise) .... Jo

Scene Four:

Late winter 1864, the March parlor

"Off to Massachusetts" .... Beth, Mr. Laurence

"Five Forever" .... Jo, Laurie, Beth, Meg, Amy

Scene Five:

Early spring 1865, outside the March house

"More Than I Am" .... John Brooke, Meg

Scene Six:

Late spring 1865, the attic

"Astonishing" .... Jo

ACT TWO

Scene One:

Early summer 1866, Mrs. Kirk's boarding house

"The Weekly Volcano Press" .... Company

Scene Two:

Summer 1866, the March parlor; late summer 1866, Mrs. Kirk's boarding house

"Off to Massachusetts" (Reprise) .... Beth, Mr. Laurence

"How I Am" .... Professor Bhaer

Scene Three:

Fall 1866; Falmouth, Cape Cod

"Some Things Are Meant to Be" .... Beth, Jo

Scene Four:

Winter 1867, the March parlor, the attic

"The Most Amazing Thing" .... Laurie, Amy

"Days of Plenty" .... Marmee

"The Fire Within Me" .... Jo

Scene Five:

Spring 1867, outside the March house

"Small Umbrella in the Rain" .... Professor Bhaer, Jo

LITTLE WOMEN ORCHESTRA

Conductor – Andrew Wilder
Associate Conductor/Piano – Robert Meffe

Reeds – Lawrence Feldman, Lynne Cohen;
Trumpet – Tony Kadleck;
Trombone – Mark Lusk; Horn – Russell Rizner;
Percussion – James F. Saporito;
Piano – Robert Meffe;
Violin – Eric DeGioia, Karl Kawahara;
Viola – Liuh-Wen Ting;
Cello – Ted Mook;
Bass – Richard Sarpola

Sutton Foster
Jo

Maureen McGovern
Marmee

Janet Carroll
Aunt March

Danny Gurwin
Laurie

John Hickok
Professor Bhaer

Amy McAlexander
Amy

Megan McGinnis
Beth

Jenny Powers
Meg

Little Women

Robert Stattel
Mr. Laurence

Jim Weitzer
Mr. Brooke

Julie Foldesi
Standby for Jo, Beth, Meg

Chris Gunn
Standby for Laurie, Mr. Brooke

Anne Kanengeiser
Standby for Marmee, Aunt March/Mrs. Kirk

Larissa Shukis
Standby for Beth, Meg, Amy

Andrew Varela
Standby for Prof. Bhaer, Mr. Brooke, Mr. Laurence

Allan Knee
Book

Jason Howland
Music

Mindi Dickstein
Lyrics

Susan H. Schulman
Director

Michael Lichtefeld
Choreographer

Derek McLane
Scenic Design

Catherine Zuber
Costume Design

Kenneth Posner
Lighting Design

Peter Hylenski
Sound Design

Andrew Wilder
Music Director/ Conductor

Kim Scharnberg
Orchestrations

John Miller
Music Coordinator

Lance Horne
Vocal Arrangements

Barry Moss
Casting

Bob Kale
Casting

Randall L. Wreghitt
Producer

Dani Davis
Producer

Ken Gentry
Producer

Chase Mishkin
Producer

Jack Utsick
Producer

Ruben Brache
Producer

Lisa Vioni
Producer

Jana Robbins
Producer

Pat Addiss
Addiss/Duke Associates
Producer

Heather Duke
Addiss/Duke Associates
Producer

Danita Thomas
Co-Producer

John Thomas
Co-Producer

Thomas Keegan
Co-Producer

Transfer Student

Jim Stanek
Standby for Laurie, Mr. Brooke, Professor Bhaer

Little Women

Hair: Theodora Katsoulogiannakis and Mary Elizabeth Micari.

Wardrobe: Seated (L-R): Deborah Black, Susan Checklick, Leslie Thompson. Standing (L-R): Julien Havard, Karen L. Eifert, Leo Namba.

Stage Managers (L-R): Joe Bowerman, Beverley Randolph and Scott Taylor Rollison.

Photos by Ben Strothmann

Carpentry: William J. Craven and Tokuda Moody
Not Pictured: Peter Wright and Dan Dour.

Musical Director: Andrew Wilder

Box Office (L-R): Nick Russo, Matt Fox (House Manager) and Kevin Dublynn. (Not Pictured: Jim Matty)

Little Women

Front of House
Back Row (L-R): Amy Marquez, Robert Fowler, Don Schatzberg, Irene Vincent, Barbara Kagan
Middle Row (L-R): Saime Hodzic, Mike Cali, Stephanie Zurich, Gail Worthman, Michelle Fleury.
Front Row (L-R): Sally Lettieri, Winnie Sekulo, Rose Balsamo, Susie Spillane, Anne Cavanaugh.

Photo by Ben Strohmann

Props
(L-R): Eric Castaldo, Heidi Brown, John Thomson

(Not Pictured: Scott Mulrain)

Electrics Dept:

Standing (L-R): Dave Shepard, Chris Beck, Don Beck, Dorion Fuchs.

Seated (L-R): Greg Cap, Sean Fedigan, Michael Lyons, Dan Hochstine (Sound).

Little Women

STAFF FOR **LITTLE WOMEN**

GENERAL MANAGEMENT
RICHARDS/CLIMAN, INC.
David R. Richards   Tamar Climan

COMPANY MANAGER
Amy Merlino

PRESS REPRESENTATIVE
THE PETE SANDERS GROUP
Pete Sanders   Glenna Freedman   Jeremy Shaffer

Production Supervisor	**Beverley Randolph**
Stage Manager	Scott Taylor Rollison
Assistant Stage Manager/Dance Captain	Joe Bowerman
Assistant Company Manager	Janice Anderson
Associate Choreographer	Joe Bowerman
Assistant Set Designers	Michael Todd Potter, Shoko Kambara, Court Watson, Michael Auszura, Amy Gilbert, Amy Smith
Assistant Costume Designers	David Newell, Michael Zecker, T. Michael Hall
Associate Lighting Designer	Paul Miller
Associate Lighting Designer/Programmer	Timothy F. Rogers
Assistant Lighting Designers	Aaron Spivey, Chris Akins
Assistant Sound Designer	Tony Smolenski
Head Carpenter	William J. Craven
Automation	Tokuda Moody
Production Electrician	Neil McShane
Head Electrician	Gregory D. Cap
Assistant Electrician	Susan Goulet
Production Properties Supervisor	Heidi L. Brown
Assistant Properties Supervisor	Eric Castaldo
Production Sound	Dan Hochstine
Wardrobe Supervisor	Karen L. Eifert
Hair Supervisor	Theodora Katsoulogiannakis
Assistant Hair Supervisor	Mary Elizabeth Micari
Dresser to Ms. Foster	Julien Havard
Dressers	Debbie Black, Susan Checklick, Leo Namba, Leslie Thompson
Assistant to Mr. Gentry	Blake Hannon
Production Assistants	Pamela Brusoski, Melanie T. Morgan, James Valletti
Assistants to the General Manager	Laura Kaufmann, Melissa Mazdra
Press Associate	Bill Coyle
Dialect Coach	Deborah Hecht
Assistant to John Miller	Charles Butler
Music Copyist	Anixter Rice Music/ Russ Anixter, Don Rice
Banking	Chase Manhattan Bank/ Richard L. Callian, Michele Gibbons
Payroll	Castellana Services, Inc./ Lance Castellana
Accountants	Fried and Kowgios CPAs, LLP Elliott Aronstam
Insurance	DeWitt Stern Group, Inc./ Anthony Pittari
Legal	Franklin, Weinrib, Rudell, & Vassallo, P.C./ Elliott H. Brown, Daniel M. Wasser, Jonathan A. Lonner
Advertising	Eliran Murphy Group/ Richard Robertson, Jeff Matisoff
Logo Artwork	Frank "Fraver" Verlizzo

Marketing	The Marketing Group/ Tanya Grubich, Laura Matalon, Trish Santini, Lesley Alpert, Johanna Lindsay
Student Marketing	Students Live!
Merchandising	CCE Theatrical Merchandising/ Larry Turk
Production Photographer	Joan Marcus
Additional Photography	Paul Kolnik
Theatre Displays	King Display
Website Design & Management	www.purpleducks.com/ Maggie Monty, Mary Jo Place

CREDITS
Set construction by F&D Scenic Changes.
Show control and scenic motion control
featuring stage command systems® by Scenic Technologies,
a division of Production Resource Group, LLC, New Windsor, NY.
Additional scenic elements by Scenic Arts. Lighting equipment by PRG Lighting.
Sound equipment by PRG Audio.
Costumes by Dawson Tailors, Euro Co Costumes, John Kristiansen,
Goodspeed Musicals, Carelli Costumes, Bruce Mailla, Centre Stage, Kelly Kohen.
Hand knits by Karen L. Eifert and Carmel Zuber. Makeup by MAC.
Rehearsed at Roundabout Rehearsal Studios.
Natural herb cough drops courtesy of Ricola, Inc.
Emer'gen-C super energy booster provided by Alacer Corp.

SPECIAL THANKS

Avalon Salon, Bill Conner, Noah Cornman, Kurt Deutsch, Karen Elliott,
Heidi Ettinger, Bruce Robert Harris, Scott and Chloe Hatcher, Jason Juenker,
Maggie Kuypers, Peter Miller, Patti Morris, Jan Ohye, Bill Paul,
Jill Prince, Alice Ramos, Rhonda Schaller, Bill Stein,
Jan Turnquist, Gerald Schoenfeld.

The producers would like to extend a special thanks to all of
the actors, crew members, assistants, interns, investors,
volunteers, colleagues, friends
and more who have helped us bring
Little Women The Musical to Broadway.
WE NEVER COULD HAVE DONE IT WITHOUT YOU!

READ THE MODERN LIBRARY BROADWAY EDITION
BY RANDOM HOUSE.

www.littlewomenonbroadway.com

JUJAMCYN THEATERS

ROCCO LANDESMAN
President

PAUL LIBIN
Producing Director

JACK VIERTEL
Creative Director

JERRY ZAKS

DANIEL ADAMIAN
General Manager

JENNIFER HERSHEY
Director of Operations

STAFF FOR THE VIRGINIA THEATRE

Manager	Matt Fox
Treasurer	Nick Russo
Assistant Manager	Lauren Bean
Carpenter	Dan Dour
Propertyman	Scott Mulrain
Electrician	Donald Beck
Engineer	Vladimir Belenky

The March family: (L-R) Amy McAlexander, Sutton Foster, Maureen McGovern, Jenny Powers and Megan McGinnis at McGovern's cabaret act at Le Jazz Au Bar.

Librettist Allan Knee shows off his namesake on opening night.

Curtain calls on opening night.

The cast rehearses at Roundabout Rehearsal Studios.

Opening Night Memory: It was an important opening night for me because it was my first Broadway opening in the original cast of a new musical. I had had a mini opening night when I replaced Linda Ronstadt in *Pirates of Penzance*, and I was out with an injury the opening week of *3 Penny Opera*, so, come hell or high water, I was making this opening! We had heavy snow, as it turned out, and my date wound up being diverted to Dulles and missed it. But otherwise it was one of those transcendant nights. After a week under the microscope by critics, we said, "Tonight is for us!" And it really was a celebration.

Memorable Opening Night Gift: Director Susan Schulman found a vintage illustration from one of the first editions of the book *Little Women*. It shows Marmee consoling Jo while Beth is dying. She framed it, and it made me cry.

Celebrity Visitors: Marian Seldes and Elizabeth Franz were most gracious. Both were incredibly supportive of my performance, which means a lot to me.

"Easter Bonnet" Sketch: "March Girls Gone Wild!" by Danny Gurwin and Jim Weitzer.

Backstage Rituals: Sutton Foster has "Bagel Sunday" every week, and brings bagels and cream cheese for everyone before the Sunday performance. I like to get to the theatre very early and do vocal warm-ups and stretches. It helps to make the outside world disappear. When I was in *Nine* with Raul Julia, the cast always gathered for "circle" before each performance. We don't do that here. However, once, our producer, Dani Davis, gathered us into a circle for a ritual that she always did when she attended Duke University as a student in the theatre department. We, one by one, squeezed each other's hand to send the energy around the circle. At the end she asked us to make a wish. Our collective wish was for the "theatre gods" to grant us a long, happy and healthy run.

Favorite Moment: The "Days of Plenty" song in which Marmee talks to Jo and Jo decides to go on. The whole scene is so beautifully written.

Favorite In-Theatre Gathering Place: Way up on the fifth floor of the theatre is an oddly shaped little room with a slanting ceiling, which we've taken to calling "Jo's Attic." We have cast meetings and birthday parties up there.

Off-Site Hangout: Arriba! Arriba! and Giovanni's.

Snack Foods: On this show we're all major chocoholics. I sometimes bring in homemade chocolates, which I label "From Marmee's Kitchen." Personally, I'm addicted to Starbucks' Chai Tea with soymilk.

Therapies: Yoga and meditation. Janet Carroll (our Aunt March) and I have Reiki degrees.

Memorable Ad Libs: I have been known to render an unusual line or lyric on occasion. We've come to call these "Marmeeisms."

After learning several versions of "Here Alone," one night, instead of singing "Counting days/praying for news," out of my mouth came "Praying for rain." Don't ask me why. Poltergeists, I assume! As I left the stage, some of the crew were doing a rain dance!

Record Number Of Cell Phone Rings: Only one so far. But once during my cabaret show at the Algonquin, a man sitting right next to the stage took a call and carried on a conversation through the whole first song. Afterward I said to him, "You better be a doctor!"

Ghostly Encounter: My dressing room door makes a strange sound like it's talking to you, but only the first time it's opened each day. I have Liam Neeson's old dressing room. I wonder if it talked to him as well?

Heaviest/Hottest Costume: Not only do the women have to wear these big dresses, but we are also sometimes underdressed with another costume for the scenes where we act out Jo's stories. For instance, when I'm playing the Hag, I've still got my whole Marmee costume underneath.

Fan Encounters: One of the things I love about this show is the fact that grandmothers will come with their daughters and granddaughters, and they all bring their special copies of the book to be signed.

Correspondent: Maureen McGovern, "Marmee"

PLAYBILL

CAST
(in order of speaking)

Sophie Sheridan ....SARA KRAMER
Ali ....REBECCA KASPER
Lisa ....KEISHA T. FRASER
Tanya ....JUDY McLANE
Rosie ....LIZ McCARTNEY
Donna Sheridan ....CAROLEE CARMELLO
Sky ....AARON STATON
Pepper ....BEN GETTINGER
Eddie ....ALBERT GUERZON
Harry Bright ....DAVID BEACH
Bill Austin ....MARK L. MONTGOMERY
Sam Carmichael ....DANIEL McDONALD
Father
Alexandrios ....BRYAN SCOTT JOHNSON

THE ENSEMBLE
MEREDITH AKINS
BRENT BLACK
ISAAC CALPITO
MEGHANN DREYFUSS
SAMANTHA EGGERS
SHAKIEM EVANS
KURT ANDREW HANSEN
BRYAN SCOTT JOHNSON
CAROL LINNEA JOHNSON
CORINNE MELANÇON
MEGAN OSTERHAUS
JOI DANIELLE PRICE
SANDY ROSENBERG

continued on the next page

CADILLAC ⊕ WINTER GARDEN THEATRE ♿

1634 Broadway
A Shubert Organization Theatre

Gerald Schoenfeld, *Chairman*   Philip J. Smith , *President*

Robert E. Wankel, *Executive Vice President*

JUDY CRAYMER, RICHARD EAST AND BJÖRN ULVAEUS
FOR LITTLESTAR IN ASSOCIATION WITH UNIVERSAL

PRESENT

MAMMA MIA!

MUSIC AND LYRICS BY

BENNY ANDERSSON
BJÖRN ULVAEUS

AND SOME SONGS WITH STIG ANDERSON

BOOK BY CATHERINE JOHNSON

PRODUCTION DESIGNED BY
MARK THOMPSON

LIGHTING DESIGNED BY
HOWARD HARRISON

SOUND DESIGNED BY
ANDREW BRUCE &
BOBBY AITKEN

MUSICAL SUPERVISOR, ADDITIONAL MATERIAL
& ARRANGEMENTS
MARTIN KOCH

CHOREOGRAPHY
ANTHONY VAN LAAST

DIRECTED BY
PHYLLIDA LLOYD

5/2/05

The Dynamos: Judy McLane, Liz McCartney and Carolee Carmello.

Photo by Ben Strothmann

THE SETTING
On a Greek Island, a wedding is about to take place...

PROLOGUE
Three months before the wedding

ACT ONE
The day before the wedding

ACT TWO
The day of the wedding

MUSICAL NUMBERS
(in alphabetical order)
"Chiquitita"
"Dancing Queen"
"Does Your Mother Know"
"Gimme! Gimme! Gimme!"
"Honey, Honey"
"I Do, I Do, I Do, I Do, I Do"
"I Have A Dream"
"Knowing Me, Knowing You"
"Lay All Your Love on Me"
"Mamma Mia"
"Money, Money, Money"
"One of Us"
"Our Last Summer"
"Slipping Through My Fingers"
"S.O.S."
"Super Trouper"
"Take a Chance on Me"
"Thank You For the Music"
"The Name of the Game"
"The Winner Takes It All"
"Under Attack"
"Voulez-Vous"

Cast Continued

ENSEMBLE (continued)
PATRICK SARB
RYAN-MICHAEL SHAW
BRITT SHUBOW

UNDERSTUDIES

For Sophie Sheridan – Meghann Dreyfuss, Britt Shubow
for Ali – Samantha Eggers, Joi Danielle Price; for Lisa –
Meredith Akins, Britt Shubow; for Tanya – Carol Linnea
Johnson, Corinne Melançon; for Rosie – Corinne
Melançon, Sandy Rosenberg; for Donna Sheridan –
Carol Linnea Johnson, Corinne Melançon; for Sky –
Ryan Sander, Patrick Sarb; for Pepper – Isaac Calpito,
Ryan-Michael Shaw; for Eddie – Shakiem Evans,
Matthew Farver; for Harry Bright – Kurt Andrew
Hansen, Bryan Scott Johnson; for Bill Austin – Brent
Black, Kurt Andrew Hansen, Bryan Scott Johnson; for
Sam Carmichael – Brent Black, Kurt Andrew Hansen;
for Father Alexandrios – Brent Black, Matthew Farver,
Kurt Andrew Hansen

SWINGS
LANENE CHARTERS
JOANNA CHOZEN
MATTHEW FARVER
RYAN SANDER

DANCE CAPTAIN
JANET ROTHERMEL

THE BAND

Music Director/Conductor/Keyboard 1:
ROB PREUSS
Associate Music Director/Keyboard 3:
STEVE MARZULLO
Keyboard 2:
SUE ANSCHUTZ
Keyboard 4:
MYLES CHASE
Guitar 1:
DOUG QUINN
Guitar 2:
JEFF CAMPBELL
Bass:
PAUL ADAMY
Drums:
RAY MARCHICA
Percussion:
DAVID NYBERG

Music Coordinator:
MICHAEL KELLER
Synthesizer Programmer:
NICHOLAS GILPIN

(L-R): Judy McLane, Carolee Carmello and Liz McCartney

Photo by Joan Marcus

Mamma Mia!

Carolee Carmello
Donna Sheridan

Sara Kramer
Sophie Sheridan

Liz McCartney
Rosie

Judy McLane
Tanya

Daniel McDonald
Sam Carmichael

David Beach
Harry Bright

Mark L. Montgomery
Bill Austin

Aaron Staton
Sky

Keisha T. Fraser
Lisa

Rebecca Kasper
Ali

Ben Gettinger
Pepper

Albert Guerzon
Eddie

Meredith Akins
Ensemble

Brent Black
Ensemble

Isaac Calpito
Ensemble

Lanene Charters
Swing

Joanna Chozen
Swing

Meghann Dreyfuss
Ensemble

Samantha Eggers
Ensemble

Shakiem Evans
Ensemble

Matthew Farver
Swing

Kurt Andrew Hansen
Ensemble

Bryan Scott Johnson
*Father Alexandrios,
Ensemble*

Carol Linnea Johnson
Ensemble

Corinne Melançon
Ensemble

Megan Osterhaus
Ensemble

Joi Danielle Price
Ensemble

Sandy Rosenberg
Ensemble

Janet Rothermel
Dance Captain

Patrick Sarb
Ensemble

Ryan Sander
Swing

Ryan-Michael Shaw
Ensemble

Britt Shubow
Ensemble,

Tom Capps
*Production
Supervisor*

Björn Ulvaeus
Music & Lyrics

Mamma Mia!

Benny Andersson
Music & Lyrics

Catherine Johnson
Book

Phyllida Lloyd
Director

Anthony Van Laast
Choreographer

Mark Thompson
Production Designer

Howard Harrison
Lighting Designer

Andrew Bruce
Sound Designer

Bobby Aitken
Sound Designer

Martin Koch
Musical Supervisor; Additional Material; Arrangements Musical Supervisor

Nichola Treherne
Associate Choreographer

Martha Banta
Resident Director

Tara Rubin Casting
Casting

David Grindrod
Casting Consultant

Judy Craymer
Producer

Richard East
Producer

ALUMNI

Tamara Bernier
Tanya

Jerad Bortz
Swing

Christopher Carl
Ensemble

Tony Carlin
Ensemble

Bill Carmichael
Father Alexandrios, Ensemble

Carlos L. Encinias
Ensemble

Jenny Fellner
Sophie

Harriett D. Foy
Rosie

Tom Galantich
Ensemble

Jon-Erik Goldberg
Swing

Somer Lee Graham
Ensemble

Lori Hammel
Ensemble

John Hillner
Sam Carmichael

Dee Hoty
Donna

Adam LeFevre
Bill Austin

Joe Machota
Sky

Tyler Maynard
Swing

Jesse Nager
Ensemble

Chris Prinzo
Pepper

Summer Rognlie
Ensemble

Michael Benjamin Washington
Eddie

Jason Weston
Pepper

Michael Winther
Harry

Leah Zepel
Ensemble

224

Crew
Top Row (L-R): Frank Lofgren, Aarne Lofgren, Glenn Russo, Mai-Linh De Virgilio, Greg Chabay, Dennis Wiener, John Maloney, Richie McQuail
Middle Row (L-R): Chris Nass, Reggie Carter, Gregory Martin, Pat Sullivan, Craig Cassidy, Richie Carney
Front Row (L-R): Art Soyk, George Huckins, Don Lawrence, Andy Sather

Wardrobe and Hair Departments
Standing (L-R): Vickey Walker, Josh Marquette, Carey Bertini, Crisy Richmond, Jessica Boyd, Jim Collum
Seated (L-R): Lauren Kievit, Elvia Pineda, Irene L. Bunis, Eric Anthony Pregent, I. Wang

House Staff & Security
Standing (L-R): Michael Bosch, Malcolm Perry, John Mitchell
Seated (L-R): Patricia Zwicker, Dottie Arney, Mendy Levine (House Manager), Sherry McIntyre, Vinnie Macaluso, Carol Kennedy, Michael Cleary, Rosa Pesante

Band
(L-R): Ray Marchica, Myles Chase, Sue Anschutz, David Nyberg, Paul Adamy, Rob Preuss, Jeff Campbell

Stage & Company Management
(L-R): Rina Saltzman (Company Manager), Dean R. Greer (SM), Sherry Cohen (SM), Liza Garcia (Asst. Co. Manager), Andrew Fenton (PSM)

Mamma Mia!

226

Photos by Aubrey Reuben

John Hillner and Dee Hoty (fourth and fifth from left) and fellow cast members take part in "Broadway on Broadway."

Left and above: Scenes from "Red State Ready," the *Mamma Mia!* sketch in the 2004 "Gypsy of the Year" competition.

Ensemble members take to the field in Central Park as part of the *Mamma Mia!* softball team.

Dee Hoty and John Hillner at "Broadway on Broadway" in Times Square.

Opening Night Gifts: On my first performance as Sophie, Judy Craymer, and Björn Ulvaeus gave me a bouquet of flowers and bottle of champagne—which I couldn't drink because I'm only 18!

"Gypsy Of The Year" Sketch: "Red State Ready," by David Beach.

"Carols For A Cure" Carol: "Shalom Rav"

"Easter Bonnet" Sketch: "*Mamma Mia!*: A Blank Page" by David Beach.

Who Performed The Most Roles: The most actual speaking roles are done by Summer Rognlie, who covers the three Dynamos.

Backstage Ritual: A group of us goes on stage behind the curtain during the overture and, when the music halts for a second, we do a group clap.

Favorite Moment: When the curtain goes up and it's just me on the stage, I get an overwhelming, great feeling.

In-Theatre Gathering Place: We've been gravitating to Eric and Mark's dressing room (they play Sky and Bill). They sometimes put on hip-hop music and have a little dance party.

Off-Site Hangout: Stella on 50th Street.

Therapy: We ran out of Ricolas one day and people were going insane. It was like a famine.

Snack Food: There's always food backstage on a table by the stage manager's office. Holidays and birthdays are like a street fair.

Mascot: Stage manager Andy Fenton. He's a character and we love him. He makes funny announcements over the speakers, he gives people little nicknames, and he's always making funny comments in a British accent. He adds a lot of life, and is a big part of why working on this show is so much fun.

Embarrassing Moment: I was backstage waiting for my cue from Harry (David Beach), but I couldn't hear what was going on on the stage. Suddenly I heard silence, and I realized I missed it. I thought, "Oh shoot!," and ran on.

Record Number Of Cell Phone Rings: Two during the time I have been present. Once, in a very quiet and tense moment, I was in the middle of asking the biggest question in the show, and suddenly a cell phone goes off. Obnoxious!

Memorable Stage Door Fan Encounter: We had a big school group, maybe 30 or 40 screaming 12-year-olds at the stage door. Sky and I came out together. They were literally screaming "Oh my God!" and wanted to hug us. Security had to put up barricades.

Heaviest/Hottest Costume: During the nightmare scene, the Ensemble wears some very interesting getups. At one point Sky, my fiancé, comes in wearing a wedding dress.

Who Wore The Least: In one number, the ensemble boys and Sky are wearing pretty much nothing but Speedos.

In-House Parody Lyrics: Instead of, "You are the dancing queen," we sometimes sing "Jew are the dancing queen." (I'm Jewish.)

Correspondent: Sara Kramer, "Sophie"

PLAYBILL®

⑤ SAM S. SHUBERT THEATRE
225 West 44th Street
A Shubert Organization Theatre

Gerald Schoenfeld, *Chairman*   Philip J. Smith, *President*

Robert E. Wankel, *Executive Vice President*

Boyett Ostar Productions   The Shubert Organization
Arielle Tepper   Stephanie McClelland/Lawrence Horowitz   Elan V. McAllister/Allan S. Gordon
Independent Presenters Network   Roy Furman   GRS Associates
Jam Theatricals   TGA Entertainment   Clear Channel Entertainment

present

Monty Python's
SPAMALOT

Book & Lyrics by   Music by
Eric Idle   John Du Prez & Eric Idle

A new musical lovingly *ripped off from the motion picture*
"Monty Python and the Holy Grail"

starring
David Hyde Pierce   Tim Curry   Hank Azaria

also starring
Christopher Sieber
Michael McGrath   Steve Rosen   Christian Borle

with
John Bolton   Brad Bradley   Thomas Cannizzaro   Kevin Covert
Jennifer Frankel   Lisa Gajda   Jenny Hill   Emily Hsu
James Ludwig   Abbey O'Brien   Ariel Reid   Pamela Remler
Greg Reuter   Brian Shepard   Rick Spaans   Scott Taylor   Darlene Wilson

and
Sara Ramirez

Set & Costume Design by **Tim Hatley**	Lighting Design by **Hugh Vanstone**

Sound Design by **Acme Sound Partners**	Hair & Wig Design by **David Brian Brown**	Special Effects Design by **Gregory Meeh**	Projection Design by **Elaine J. McCarthy**
Music Director/Vocal Arrangements **Todd Ellison**	Orchestrations by **Larry Hochman**	Music Arrangements by **Glen Kelly**	Music Coordinator **Michael Keller**
Casting by **Tara Rubin Casting**	Associate Director **Peter Lawrence**	Associate Choreographer **Darlene Wilson**	Production Management **Gene O'Donovan**
General Management **101 Productions, Ltd.**	Press Representative **Boneau/Bryan-Brown**	Marketing **HHC Marketing**	Associate Producers **Randi Grossman** **Tisch/Avnet Financial**

Choreography by
Casey Nicholaw

Directed by
Mike Nichols

LIVE
BROADWAY

3/17/05

CAST OF CHARACTERS
(in order of appearance)

Historian, Not Dead Fred,
French Guard, Minstrel,
Prince Herbert .... CHRISTIAN BORLE
Mayor, Patsy, Guard 2 ... MICHAEL McGRATH
King Arthur .... TIM CURRY
Sir Robin, Guard 1,
Brother Maynard .... DAVID HYDE PIERCE
Sir Lancelot, The French Taunter,
Knight of Ni,
Tim the Enchanter .... HANK AZARIA
Sir Dennis Galahad,
The Black Knight, Prince Herbert's Father
.... CHRISTOPHER SIEBER
Dennis' Mother,
Sir Bedevere, Concorde .... STEVE ROSEN
The Lady of the Lake .... SARA RAMIREZ
Sir Not Appearing .... KEVIN COVERT
God .... JOHN CLEESE
French Guards ...... THOMAS CANNIZZARO,
                                        GREG REUTER
Minstrels .... BRAD BRADLEY,
                                        EMILY HSU,
                                        GREG REUTER
Sir Bors .... BRAD BRADLEY

ENSEMBLE
BRAD BRADLEY, THOMAS CANNIZZARO,
KEVIN COVERT, JENNIFER FRANKEL,
continued on next page

2004-2005 AWARDS

TONY AWARDS
Best Musical
Direction of a Musical (Mike Nichols)
Featured Actress in a Musical (Sara Ramirez)

DRAMA DESK AWARDS
Outstanding Musical
Lyrics (Eric Idle)

DRAMA DESK AWARDS: (cont'd)
Costume Design (Tim Hatley)

OUTER CRITICS CIRCLE AWARDS
Best Musical
Direction of a Musical (Mike Nichols)
Featured Actress in a Musical (Sara Ramirez)
Costume Design (Tim Hatley)

Monty Python's Spamalot

MUSICAL NUMBERS

ACT I

Overture

Scene 1: The Mighty Portcullis

Scene 2: Moose Village
"Fisch Schlapping Song" ....Historian, Mayor, Villagers

Scene 3: Mud Castle
"King Arthur's Song" ....King Arthur, Patsy

Scene 4: Plague Village
"I Am Not Dead Yet" ....Not Dead Fred, Lance, Robin and Bodies

Scene 5: Mud Village

Scene 6: The Lady of the Lake and The Laker Girls
"Come With Me" ....King Arthur, Lady of the Lake and Laker Girls
"The Song That Goes Like This" ....Sir Galahad and Lady of the Lake

Scene 7: The Knights
"All for One" ....King Arthur, Patsy, Sir Robin, Sir Lancelot,
Sir Galahad and Sir Bedevere

Scene 8: Camelot
"Knights of the Round Table" ....Lady of the Lake, King Arthur, Patsy,
Sir Robin, Sir Lancelot, Sir Galahad,
Sir Bedevere and The Camelot Dancers
"The Song That Goes Like This (Reprise)" ....Lady of the Lake

Scene 9: The Feet of God

Scene 10: Find Your Grail
"Find Your Grail" ....Lady of the Lake, King Arthur, Patsy, Sir Robin,
Sir Lancelot, Sir Galahad, Sir Bedevere,
Knights and Grail Girls

Scene 11: The French Castle
"Run Away" ....French Taunters, King Arthur, Patsy, Sir Robin,
Sir Lancelot, Sir Galahad, Sir Bedevere,
French Guards and French Citizens

ACT II

Scene 1: The Mighty Portcullis

Scene 2: A Very Expensive Forest
"Always Look on the Bright Side of Life" ....Patsy, King Arthur, Knights and
The Knights of Ni

Scene 3: Sir Robin and His Minstrels
"Brave Sir Robin" ....Sir Robin and Minstrels

Scene 4: The Black Knight

Scene 5: Another Part of the Very Expensive Forest
"You Won't Succeed on Broadway" ....Sir Robin and Ensemble

Scene 6: A Hole in the Universe
"The Diva's Lament" ....Lady of the Lake

Scene 7: Prince Herbert's Chamber
"Where Are You?" ....Prince Herbert
"Here Are You" ....Prince Herbert
"His Name Is Lancelot" ....Sir Lancelot, Prince Herbert and Ensemble

Scene 8: Yet Another Part of the Very Expensive Forest
"I'm All Alone" ....King Arthur, Patsy and Knights
"The Song That Goes Like This (Reprise)" ....Lady of the Lake and King Arthur

Scene 9: The Killer Rabbit
"The Holy Grail" ....King Arthur, Patsy, Sir Robin, Sir Lancelot,
Sir Galahad, Sir Bedevere and Knights

Finale
"Find Your Grail Finale - Medley" ....The Company

---

Cast Continued

ENSEMBLE (continued)
LISA GAJDA, JENNY HILL, EMILY HSU, ABBEY
O'BRIEN, ARIEL REID, GREG REUTER,
BRIAN SHEPARD, SCOTT TAYLOR

STANDBYS
JOHN BOLTON, JAMES LUDWIG,
DARLENE WILSON

SWINGS
PAMELA REMLER, RICK SPAANS

DANCE CAPTAINS
PAMELA REMLER, SCOTT TAYLOR

SPAMALOT ORCHESTRA
Conductor: TODD ELLISON
Associate Conductor: ETHYL WILL
Concertmaster: Ann Labin
Violins: Maura Giannini, Ming Yeh
Viola: Richard Brice
Cello: Diane Barere
Reeds: Ken Dybisz, Alden Banta
Lead Trumpet: John Chudoba
Trumpet: Anthony Gorruso
Trombone: Mark Patterson
French Horn: Zohar Schondorf
Keyboard 1: Ethyl Will
Keyboard 2: Antony Geralis
Guitars: Scott Kuney
Bass: Dave Kuhn
Drums: Sean McDaniel
Percussion: Dave Mancuso

Music Coordinator: Michael Keller
Music Copying: Emily Grishman Music Preparation/
Emily Grishman, Katherine Edmonds

Greg Reuter, Brad Bradley and David Hyde
Pierce in the "Brave Sir Robin" scene.

Monty Python's Spamalot

David Hyde Pierce
*Sir Robin, Guard 1,
Brother Maynard*

Tim Curry
King Arthur

Hank Azaria
*Sir Lancelot, The
French Taunter,
Knight of Ni, Tim the
Enchanter*

Christopher Sieber
*Sir Dennis Galahad,
The Black Knight,
Prince Herbert's Father*

Michael McGrath
*Mayor, Patsy,
Guard 2*

Steve Rosen
*Dennis's Mother,
Sir Bedevere,
Concorde*

Christian Borle
*Historian, Not Dead
Fred, French Guard,
Minstrel, Prince
Herbert*

Sara Ramirez
*The Lady of the
Lake*

John Bolton
*Standby for Arthur,
Lancelot, Galahad,
Robin, Bedevere*

Brad Bradley
*Minstrel,
Sir Bors,
Ensemble*

Thomas Cannizzaro
*French Guard,
Ensemble*

John Cleese
God

Kevin Covert
*Sir Not Appearing,
Ensemble*

Jennifer Frankel
Ensemble

Lisa Gajda
Ensemble

Jenny Hill
Ensemble

Emily Hsu
*Minstrel,
Ensemble*

James Ludwig
*Standby for Robin,
Bedevere, Patsy,
Historian, Not Dead Fred,
Prince Herbert, Lancelot*

Abbey O'Brien
Ensemble

Ariel Reid
Ensemble

Pamela Remler
*Swing, Dance
Captain*

Greg Reuter
*French Guard,
Minstrel, Ensemble*

Brian Shepard
Ensemble

Rick Spaans
Swing

Scott Taylor
*Ensemble,
Dance Captain*

Darlene Wilson
*Standby for Lady of
the Lake/Assoc.
Choreographer*

Eric Idle
*Book, Lyrics and
Music*

John Du Prez
Composer

Mike Nichols
Director

Casey Nicholaw
Choreography

Tim Hatley
*Set and Costume
Design*

Hugh Vanstone
Lighting Design

Tom Clark, Mark Menard, Nevin Steinberg
Sound Design

David Brian Brown
Wig & Hair Design

Monty Python's Spamalot

Larry Hochman
Orchestrations

Michael Keller
Music Coordinator

Tara Rubin
Casting

Arielle Tepper
Producer

Stephanie P.
McClelland
Producer

Elan V. McAllister
Producer

Allan S. Gordon
Producer

Mahlon Kruse
Stage Manager

Jim Woolley
Stage Manager

Rachel A. Wolff
Assistant Stage Manager

Todd Ellison
Musical Director

Photos by Ben Strohmann

Photo by Joan Marcus

They Eat Ham and Jam and Spam a Lot: David Hyde Pierce as Sir Robin (holding the Vicious Chicken of Bristol), Hank Azaria as Sir Lancelot, Christopher Sieber as Sir Dennis Galahad, Steve Rosen as Sir Bedevere and Tim Curry as King Arthur.

Monty Python's Spamalot

STAFF FOR SPAMALOT

GENERAL MANAGEMENT
101 PRODUCTIONS, LTD.
Wendy Orshan Jeffrey M. Wilson
David Auster

COMPANY MANAGER
Elie Landau

GENERAL PRESS REPRESENTATIVE
BONEAU/BRYAN-BROWN
Adrian Bryan-Brown Jackie Green
Aaron Meier

CASTING
TARA RUBIN CASTING
Tara Rubin
Dunja Vitolic Eric Woodall
Laura Schutzel Mona Slomsky

PRODUCTION MANAGEMENT
AURORA PRODUCTIONS, INC.
Gene O'Donovan Elise Hanley
W. Benjamin Heller II Bethany Weinstein

Fight Director ....David DeBesse

Make-Up Designer ....Joseph A. Campayno

Production Stage Manager ....**Peter Lawrence**
Stage Manager ....**Mahlon Kruse**
Stage Managers ....**Jim Woolley, Rachel Wolff**
Assistant Company Manager ....Nathan Gehan
Dance Captains ....Pamela Remler, Scott Taylor
Fight Captain ....Greg Reuter
Assistant to Mike Nichols ....Jane Levy
Associate Scenic Designer ....Paul Weimer
Assistant Scenic Designers ....Raul Abrego, Derek Stenborg
UK Assistant Designer ....Andy Edwards
Associate Costume Designer ....Scott Traugott
Costume Associate ....Ilona Somogyi
Assistant Costume Designers ....Cory Ching,
Robert J. Martin
Costume Assistant ....Jessica Wegener
Magic Consultant ....Marshall Magoon
Puppetry Consultant........................Michael Curry
Associate Lighting Designer ....Philip S. Rosenberg
Assistant Lighting Designer ....John Viesta
Moving Light Programmer ....Laura Frank
Assistant Sound Designer ....Sten Severson
Associate Special Effects Designer ....Vivien Leone
Associate Projection Designer ....Gareth Smith
Assistant Projection Designers ....Ariel Sachter-Zeltzer,
Jake Pinholster
Projection Programmers ....Randy Briggs,
Paul Vershbow
Projection Illustrator ....Juliann E. Kroboth
Production Carpenter ....Michael Martinez
Assistant Carpenters................Gus Poitras, Bill Partello
Production Electrician ....Michael S. LoBue
Head Electrician ....Michael Hyman
Assistant Electricians ....Adam Biscow,
Karen Zitnick, Brian Collins
Production Props Supervisor ....Will Sweeney
Assistant Props ....James Cariot
Props Shopper ....Maggie Kuypers
Production Sound Supervisor ....Bones Malone
Assistant Sound ....Mike Wojchik
Wardrobe Supervisor ....Kenn Hamilton
Assistant Wardrobe Supervisor ....Sonya Wysocki
Dressers ....Robert Condon, Lori Elwell,
Joe Godwin, Amelia Haywood,
Jeffrey Johnson, Shannon McDowell,
Jean Marie Naughton, Emily Petrolle,

Keith Shaw, Paul Soule
Hair Supervisor ....Larry Boyette
Assistant Hair Supervisor ....Gary Arave
Hairdressers ....Jeff Knaggs, Eve Morrow
Vocal Coach ....Kate Wilson
Rehearsal Pianists ....Glen Kelly, Ethyl Will,
Antony Geralis
Rehearsal Drummer ....Sean McDaniel
Production Associate ....Lisa Gilbar
Production Assistants ....Chad Lewis,
Mary Kathryn Flynt
Assistant to Mr. Haber ....Theresa Pisanelli
Assistant to Mr. Boyett ....Diane Murphy
Assistant to Messrs. Granat & Traxler ....Katrine Heintz
Legal Counsel ....Lazarus & Harris LLP/
Scott Lazarus, Esq.
Robert C. Harris, Esq.
Accountant ....Rosenberg, Neuwirth, &
Kuchner, CPAs/
Christopher Cacace
Comptroller ....Jana Jevnikar
Advertising ....Serino Coyne/
Thomas Mygatt, Victoria Cairl
Marketing ....HHC Marketing,
Hugh Hysell, Jillian Boeni,
Adam Jay, Michael Redman
Assistant to the
General Managers ....Christine Hale
101 Productions, Ltd. Staff ....Aaron Slavik,
Clark Mims, Heidi Neven,
Mary-Six Rupert, Karl Baudendistel
101 Productions, Ltd. Interns ....Sara Katz,
Andrea Mayer
Press Associates ....Chris Boneau, Jim Byk,
Brandi Cornwell, Jackie Green,
Matt Polk, Susanne Tighe
Press Assistants ....Erika Creagh, Adriana Douzos,
Juliana Hannett, Hector Hernandez,
Jessica Johnson, Kevin Jones,
Eric Louie, Joe Perrotta,
Linnae Petruzzelli, Heath Schwartz
Banking ....City National Bank/Anne McSweeney
Insurance ....DeWitt Stern, Inc./Jennifer Brown
Travel ....Altour International, Inc./Melissa Casal
Housing ....Road Rebel Entertainment Touring,
Alison Muffitt
Opening Night Coordinator ....Tobak-Dantchik/
Suzanne Tobak, Michael Lawrence
Physical Therapy ....PhysioArts/Jennifer Green
Orthopedist ....David S. Weiss, M.D.
Immigration ....Traffic Control Group, Inc./
David King
Theatre Displays ....King Displays, Inc.
Merchandising ....Max Merchandising, LLC/
Shopalot, LLC
Merchandise Manager ....David Eck
Production Photographer ....Joan Marcus
Payroll Services ....Castellana Services, Inc.

Finnish program by Michael Palin.

www.MontyPythonsSpamalot.com

CREDITS
Scenery and scenic automation by Hudson Scenic Studio, Inc. Additional scenery by Scenic Art Studios, Inc., Chicago Scenic Studios, Hawkeye Scenic Studios. Lighting equipment from Fourth Phase. Sound equipment from PRG Audio. Costumes executed by Barbara Matera Ltd.; Carelli Costumes; Euro Co. Costumes; Parsons-Meares, Ltd.; Tricorne, Inc. Additional costumes by Costume Armour, Inc., John Kristiansen; Western Costumes. Shoes by T.O. Dey; LaDuca Productions, Ltd.; Capri Shoes; Capezio. Millinery by Lynne Mackey Studio, Rodney Gordon. Hair by Ray Marston Wig Studio Ltd., Bob Kelly Wig Creations. Selected makeup furnished by M•A•C. Props by The Spoon

Group LLC; The Rabbit's Choice; Cigar Box Studios, Inc.; Costume Armour, Inc.; Jerard Studio; Gilbert Center; Margaret Cusack; Elizabeth Debbout; Erin Edmister; George Fenmore. Some specialty props and costumes furnished by Museum Replicas Inc. Piano from Ortigara's Musicville, Inc. Video projection system provided by Scharff-Weisberg, Inc. Video projection services by Vermillion Border Productions. Flying by Foy. Black Knight illusion executed by Entertainment Design & Fabrication. Spam cam and film furnished by Polaroid. Lozenges by Ricola.

SPAM® is a registered trademark of
Hormel Foods LLC.

Air travel consideration furnished by Orbitz®.

Housing consideration in NYC furnished by
Millennium Broadway, 145 W. 44th St., NYC.
Diarmaid O'Sullivan, Bernadette D'Arcy

All songs published by Rutsongs Music & Ocean Music Ltd., ©2004. All Rights Reserved, except songs from *Monty Python & the Holy Grail*, published by EMI/Python (Monty) Pictures as follows: "Finland," music and lyrics by Michael Palin; "Knights of the Round Table," music by Neil Innes, lyrics by Graham Chapman and John Cleese; "Brave Sir Robin," music by Neil Innes, lyrics by Eric Idle; and "Always Look on the Bright Side of Life," music and lyrics by Eric Idle from *Life of Brian*, published by Python (Monty) Pictures.

SPAMALOT
rehearsed at New 42nd Street Studios

SPECIAL THANKS
Bill Link, Devin Burgess,
Veronica DeMartini, John Malakoff

Original cast recording coming soon from
Decca Broadway.

THE SHUBERT ORGANIZATION, INC.

Gerald Schoenfeld
Chairman

Philip J. Smith
President

John W. Kluge

Lee J. Seidler

Michael I. Sovern

Stuart Subotnick

Irving M. Wall

Robert E. Wankel
Executive Vice President

Peter Entin
Vice President
Theatre Operations

Elliot Greene
Vice President
Finance

David Andrews
Vice President
Shubert Ticketing Services

John Darby
Vice President
Facilities

House Manager ....Brian Gaynair

Above: Members of the original Monty Python team link arms in Shubert Alley on opening night: (L - R): Michael Palin, Terry Jones, Eric Idle, Terry Gilliam and John Cleese.

Opening night curtain calls (L - R): David Hyde Pierce, Michael Palin, Hank Azaria, Mike Nichols, Tim Curry, Eric Idle and composer John Du Prez.

Opening Night Gifts: Robes, umbrella, compass, mini sword, fleece jacket.
Most Exciting Celebrity Visitor: Robin Williams. He said he wants to be in the movie.
"Easter Bonnet" Sketch: "Spama-Rotten Story" by Greg Graham and Greg Reuter.
Favorite In-Theatre Gathering Place: Men's Ensemble dressing room.
Favorite Off-Site Hangout: Angus McIndoe's.
Favorite Therapy: PhysioArts Therapy comes to the theatre twice a week.
Strangest Press Encounter: This survey (hee-hee).
Latest Audience Arrival: Intermission. Tuesday night shows begin at 7 p.m., and people sometimes think it's 8.
Fastest Costume Change: The Minstrel: 30 seconds.
Memorable Directorial Note: "Kill Babies" (meaning, get rid of safe and favorite moments).
Company In-Joke: "Shooters."
Correspondent: Brad Bradley, "Sir Bors"

Above: Members of the men's ensemble in kilts at the cast party.

Left: Eric Idle, Tim Curry, David Hyde Pierce and Hank Azaria arrive at the cast party.

Above: Leading lady Sara Ramirez arrives at the opening night cast party at Roseland.

Above: The men's ensemble backstage just before curtain on opening night.

Below: Composer Frank Wildhorn and Pamela Jordan join the first night crowd.

Above: Taking curtain calls on opening night: Christopher Sieber, Hank Azaria, David Hyde Pierce and Tim Curry.

Above left: Christopher Sieber and Christian Borle on opening night. Above right: director Mike Nichols chows down on a Spam sandwich as a stunt on the day the Shubert Theatre opened its box office.

234

PLAYBILL®

CAST

Eddie	JOHN SELYA
Brenda	ELIZABETH PARKINSON
Tony	DESMOND RICHARDSON
Judy	ASHLEY TUTTLE
James	BENJAMIN G. BOWMAN
Sergeant O'Leary/Drill Sergeant	SCOTT WISE
Piano/Lead Vocals	MICHAEL CAVANAUGH

THE ENSEMBLE

MICHAEL BALDERRAMA,
ALEXANDER BRADY, MELISSA DOWNEY,
PASCALE FAYE, PHILIP GARDNER,
TIGER MARTINA, JILL NICKLAUS,
RIKA OKAMOTO, JUSTIN PECK,
KARINE PLANTADIT-BAGEOT

SWINGS

TED BANFALVI, TIMOTHY W. BISH,
STUART CAPPS, IAN CARNEY,
CAROLYN DOHERTY, MARTY LAWSON,
BRIAN LETENDRE, LORIN LATARRO,
MARC MANN, MABEL MODRONO,
ERIC OTTO, MEG PAUL,
LAWRENCE RABSON, DAVIS ROBERTSON,
JESSICA WALKER

Dance Supervisor:
STACY CADDELL

continued on next page

RICHARD RODGERS THEATRE

UNDER THE DIRECTION OF JAMES M. NEDERLANDER AND JAMES L. NEDERLANDER

James L. Nederlander
Hal Luftig   Scott E. Nederlander   Terry Allen Kramer
Clear Channel Entertainment   Emanuel Azenberg
present

MOVIN' OUT
a new musical

Conceived by
Twyla Tharp

Music and Lyrics by
Billy Joel

starring

John Selya   Elizabeth Parkinson   Desmond Richardson
Ashley Tuttle
Scott Wise   Benjamin G. Bowman

and

Michael Cavanaugh

with

Michael Balderrama   Ted Banfalvi   Timothy W. Bish   Alexander Brady   Stuart Capps
Ian Carney   Carolyn Doherty   Melissa Downey   Pascale Faye   Philip Gardner
Henry Haid   Lorin Latarro   Marty Lawson   Brian Letendre   Marc Mann   Tiger Martina
Mabel Modrono   Jill Nicklaus   Rika Okamoto   Eric Otto   Meg Paul   Justin Peck
Karine Plantadit-Bageot   Wade Preston   Lawrence Rabson   Davis Robertson   Jessica Walker

Scenic Design	Costume Design	Lighting Design
Santo Loquasto	**Suzy Benzinger**	**Donald Holder**

Sound Design
Brian Ruggles
Peter J. Fitzgerald

Additional Musical Arrangements
and Orchestrations
Stuart Malina

Hair Design	Synthesizer Programmer	Music Coordinator	Musical Consultant
Paul Huntley	**David Rosenthal**	**John Miller**	**Tommy Byrnes**

Assistant Choreographer/ Assistant Director	Production Associate	Technical Supervision	Casting
Scott Wise	**Jesse Huot**	**Brian Lynch**	**Jay Binder Casting** **Sarah Prosser**

Press Representative	Marketing	Production Stage Manager	General Manager
Barlow • Hartman	**TMG** **The Marketing Group**	**Kim Vernace**	**Abbie M. Strassler**

Musical Continuity and Supervision
Stuart Malina

Directed and Choreographed by
Twyla Tharp

LIVE BROADWAY

3/21/05

Just the Way You Are: Ashley Tuttle, Ian Carney and the Ensemble.

Movin' Out

MUSICAL NUMBERS

ACT I

Overture: "It's Still Rock and Roll to Me" ....The Company

Scene 1: Brenda and Eddie Split
"Scenes from an Italian Restaurant" ....Brenda, Eddie, Tony, James,
Judy, Sergeant O'Leary and Ensemble

Scene 2: Tony Moves Out
"Movin' Out (Anthony's Song)" ....Tony, Eddie, James and Sergeant O'Leary

Scene 3: James and Judy Are Forever
"Reverie (Villa D'Este)/Just the Way You Are" ....James, Judy and Ensemble

Scene 4: Brenda Is Back
"For the Longest Time/Uptown Girl" ....Brenda, Eddie, Tony and Ensemble

Scene 5: Tony and Brenda Get Together
"This Night" ....Tony, Brenda and Ensemble

Scene 6: Eddie Knows
"Summer, Highland Falls" ....Eddie, Brenda, Tony and Ensemble

Scene 7: Off to War
"Waltz #1 (Nunley's Carousel)" ....Tony, Eddie, James, Drill Sergeant and Ensemble

Scene 8: The Sky Falls
"We Didn't Start the Fire" ....Judy, Brenda, James, Tony, Eddie and Ensemble

Scene 9: Two Bars: Hicksville/Saigon
"She's Got a Way" ....Tony, Brenda and Ensemble

Scene 10: Coming Home
"The Stranger" ....Judy and Ensemble
"Elegy (The Great Peconic)" ....Judy, Brenda, Tony, Eddie,
Drill Sergeant and Ensemble

ACT II

Scene 1: Vets Cast Out
"Invention in C Minor" ....Eddie and Ensemble

Scene 2: Eddie Rages
"Angry Young Man" ....Eddie and Ensemble

Scene 3: Tony Disconnects
"Big Shot" ....Tony, Brenda and Ensemble

Scene 4: A Contest of Pain
"Big Man on Mulberry Street" ....Tony, Brenda and Ensemble

Scene 5: Eddie Gets High
"Captain Jack" ....Eddie and Ensemble

Scene 6: Eddie Reaches Out
"Innocent Man" ....Eddie and Ensemble

Scene 7: Eddie's Nightmares
"Pressure" ....Judy, Eddie and Ensemble

Scene 8: Eddie's Journey Back
"Goodnight Saigon" ....Eddie, Judy, James, Tony and Ensemble

Scene 9: Brenda's Lost Dreams
"Air (Dublinesque)" ....Brenda

Scene 10: Tony and Brenda Reconcile
"Shameless" ....Brenda and Tony

Scene 11: Judy Releases Eddie
"James" ....Judy and Eddie

Scene 12: Eddie Attains Grace
"River of Dreams/Keeping the Faith/
Only the Good Die Young" ....Eddie and Ensemble

Scene 13: The Reunion Begins
"I've Loved These Days" ....Tony, Brenda, Eddie and Ensemble

Scene 14: Reunion/Finale
"Scenes From an Italian Restaurant (Reprise)" ....The Company

---

Cast Continued

Dance Captains:
IAN CARNEY and MEG PAUL.

WEDNESDAY MATINEE & SATURDAY MATINEE

Eddie ....TED BANFALV[

Brenda ....KARINE PLANTADIT-BAGEO[

Tony ....IAN CARNE[

Judy ....MABEL MODRON[

James ....ERIC OTT[

Sergeant O'Leary/Drill Sergeant ....SCOTT WIS[

Piano/Lead Vocals ....WADE PRESTO[

UNDERSTUDIES

For Eddie – Ted Banfalvi, Marty Lawson, Lawren[
Rabson; For Brenda – Carolyn Doherty, Lorin Latar[
Meg Paul, Karine Plantadit-Bageot; For Tony – Micha[
Balderrama, Stuart Capps, Ian Carney, Lawrence Rabso[
For Judy – Melissa Downey, Meg Paul, Mabel Modron[
For James – Alex Brady, Stuart Capps, Eric Otto; Fo[
Sergeant O'Leary/Drill Sergeant – Michael Balderram[
Ted Banfalvi, Stuart Capps, Ian Carney, Philip Gardne[
For Piano/Lead Vocals – Wade Preston, Henry Haid.

THE MOVIN' OUT BAND

Piano/Lead Vocals:
MICHAEL CAVANAUGH

Leader/Guitar:
TOMMY BYRNES

Keyboard:
WADE PRESTON

Lead Guitar:
DENNIS DELGAUDIO

Bass:
GREG SMITH

Drums:
CHUCK BÜRGI

Lead Sax/Percussion:
JOHN SCARPULLA

Sax:
SCOTT KREITZER

Trumpet:
BARRY DANIELIAN

Trombone/Whistler/Vocals:
KEVIN OSBORNE

Music Coordinator:
John Miller

Movin' Out

John Selya
Eddie

Elizabeth Parkinson
Brenda

Desmond Richardson
Tony

Ashley Tuttle
Judy

Scott Wise
*Sgt. O'Leary/Drill
Sgt./Asst. Director
& Choreographer*

Benjamin G.
Bowman
James

Michael
Cavanaugh
Piano/Lead Vocals

Michael
Balderrama
Ensemble

Ted Banfalvi
Swing

Timothy W. Bish
Ensemble

Alexander Brady
Ensemble

Stuart Capps
Swing

Ian Carney
*Swing/
Dance Captain*

Carolyn Doherty
Swing

Melissa Downey
Ensemble

Pascale Faye
Ensemble

Philip Gardner
Ensemble

Henry Haid
*Understudy
Piano/Lead Vocals*

Lorin Latarro
Swing

Marty Lawson
Swing

Brian Letendre
Swing

Marc Mann
Swing

Tiger Martina
Ensemble

Mabel Modrono
Swing

Jill Nicklaus
Ensemble

Rika Okamoto
Ensemble

Eric Otto
Swing

Meg Paul
*Swing/Dance
Captain*

Karine Plantadit-
Bageot
Ensemble

Justin Peck
Ensemble

Wade Preston
*Synthesizer,
Piano/Lead Vocals
at certain
performances*

Lawrence Rabson
Swing

Davis Robertson
Swing

Jessica Walker
Swing

Twyla Tharp
*Conception,
Choreography,
Direction*

Billy Joel
Music & Lyrics

Santo Loquasto
Scenic Design

Suzy Benzinger
Costume Design

Donald Holder
Lighting Design

Paul Huntley
Hair Designer

John Miller
Music Coordinator

Kim Vernace
*Production Stage
Manager*

Gregory Victor
*Assistant Stage
Manager*

James L.
Nederlander
Producer

Hal Luftig
Producer

Terry Allen Kramer
Producer

Emanuel Azenberg
Executive Producer

The Band
Back Row (L-R): Barry Danielian (Trumpet), Dennis Delgaudio (Lead Guitar/Vocals), Wade Preston
(Synthesizer, and Piano/Lead Vocals at certain performances), Tommy Byrnes (Guitar/Vocals/Musical
Director), John Scarpulla (Lead Sax/Percussion/Contractor), Chuck Bürgi (Drums), Kevin Osborne
(Trombone/Vocals/Whistler) and Greg Smith (Bass/Vocals).
In front of Wade Preston: Scott Kreitzer (Sax). Very Front: Michael Cavanaugh (Piano/Lead Vocals).

Todd Eric Allen
Swing

Aliane Baquerot
Swing

Christopher Body
Swing

Ron de Jesus
Ensemble

Kurt Froman
Swing

Lisa Gajda
Ensemble

Darren Holden
Piano/Lead Vocals

Nancy Lemenager
Brenda

Matt Loehr
Swing

Keith Roberts
Tony

Rasta Thomas
Eddie

Ron Todorowski
Eddie

Mark Arvin
(1964–2004)

Uptown Girl: Elizabeth Parkinson, as Brenda, with the Ensemble.

STAFF FOR MOVIN' OUT

GENERAL MANAGER
ABBIE M. STRASSLER

COMPANY MANAGER
SEAN FREE

PRODUCTION ASSOCIATE
GINGER MONTEL

PRESS REPRESENTATIVE
BARLOW•HARTMAN

Michael Hartman John Barlow
Carol R. Fineman Leslie Baden

CASTING
JAY BINDER CASTING

Jay Binder C.S.A., Jack Bowdan C.S.A.,
Mark Brandon, Laura Stanczyk,
Sarah Prosser

DANCE SUPERVISOR
Stacy Caddell

Production Stage Manager	**Kim Vernace**
Stage Manager	**Joshua Halperin**
Assistant Stage Manager	**Gregory Victor**
Associate Company Manager	Shelley Ott
Assistant Director/Choreographer	Scott Wise
Dance Captains	Ian Carney, Meg Paul

Associate Set Designer	David Swayze
Associate Costume Designer	Rory Powers
Associate Lighting Designers	Jeanne Koenig, Karen Spahn
First Assistant Lighting Designer	Michelle Habeck
Assistant Lighting Designers	Hilary Manners, Traci Klainer, Thomas Hague
Associate Lighting Design/ Automated Lighting	Aland Henderson
Associate Hair Designer	Amy Solomon

Assistant Set Designer	Emily Beck
Assistant Costume Designer	Mitchell Bloom
Assistant Sound Designer	Janet Smith
Assistant Musical Supervisor	David Rosenthal
Sound Effects	Randy Hansen
Technical Supervision	Theatretech, Inc./Brian Lynch
Production Carpenter	Michael Connors
Head Carpenter	Joe Ippolito
Flyman	Angelo Grasso
Automation	Duke Wilson, Sean Hughes
Production Electrician	Jack Culver
Front Light Operator	Mike Van Nest
Moving Light Operator	Bruce Liebenow
Production Properties	George Wagner
Head Props	Augie Mericola
Production Sound Engineer	Dan Tramontozzi
Production Monitor Engineer	Craig Van Tassel
Wardrobe Supervisor	Linda Lee
Asst. Wardrobe Supervisor	Angie Simpson Phillips
Dressers	Betty Gillispie, Janet Netzke, Jennifer Griggs, Timothy Hanlon, Nicholas Staub, Russell Easley, Lara Greene, Shannon Koger, Tracey Boone
Stitcher	Alicia Aballi
Laundry	Ruth Goya
Production Hair Supervisor	Carole Morales
Hair Dressers	Natasha Steinhagen, Marion Geist
Music Copying	John Leonard
Assistant to Mr. Miller	Matthew P. Ettinger
Assistant to Mr. Joel	Stepanie Rosenzweig
Production Assistants	Megan Durden, Victor Lukas, Tessa Peterson
Research/Historian	Gregory Victor
Drill Instruction	Stephan Wolfert
Company Orthopedist	Dr. Philip Bauman
Company Physical Therapists	Physio Arts, PLLC
Company Massage Therapist	Russ Beasley
Makeup Design	M•A•C Cosmetics/ Patrick Eichler
Banking	JPMorgan Chase/ Richard Callian
Payroll	Castellana Services, Inc./ Lance Castellana
Assistant to Mr. Luftig	Shannon R. Morrison
Accountants	Fried and Kowgios CPAs, LLP, Robert Fried, CPA, Sarah Galbraith
Insurance	MARSH USA, Inc./ Anthony Catanzoro
Legal Counsel	Lazarus & Harris LLP/ Scott R. Lazarus, Esq., Robert C. Harris, Esq., David H. Friedlander, Esq.
Immigration Counsel	Shannon K. Such, Attorney At Law
Press Office Manager	Bethany Larsen
Advertising	Serino Coyne, Inc./ Angelo Desimini, Diane Niedzialek
Marketing	TMG The Marketing Group/ Tanya Grubich, Laura Matalon, Trish Santini, Bob Bucci, Erica Lynn Schwartz
Education Program	Students Live!/Amy Weinstein, Laura Sullivan, Marcie Sturiale
Production Photographer	Joan Marcus
Onstage Merchandising	George Fenmore/ More Merchandising International
Souvenir Merchandising	Clear Channel Entertainment/ Larry Turk
Theater Displays	King Displays, Inc.
Group Sales	Nederlander Group Sales
Travel Agency	Tzell Travel/The "A" Team
Opening Night Coordination	Tobak-Dantchik Events & Promotions/ Suzanne Tobak, Jeffry Gray

Classical pieces performed by
Stuart Malina.
Classical pieces recorded and produced by
David Rosenthal.

CREDITS

Scenery and Automation by Hudson Scenic Studio, Inc.
Lighting equipment by GSD.
Sound equipment by Sound Associates, Inc.
Costumes executed by D. Barak Stribling, Carelli
Costumes, Euroco Costumes, Schneeman Studios,
Seamless Costumes, Donna Langman Studio, Barbara
Matera Ltd. and Tricorne New York City, Fabric painting
and aging by Jeffrey Fender and Dean Batten, Custom
footwear by La Duca, JC Theatrical and T.O. Dey.
Wigs by Paul Huntley.
Makeup provided by M•A•C.
Rehearsed at the New 42nd Street Studios.
Clearances provided by Wendy Cohen.
Military surplus items provided by
S-4 Military Surplus Hackensack, NJ.
Military uniforms by Jim Korn/
Kaufman's Army Navy Surplus.
Natural herb cough drops courtesy of Ricola USA, Inc.

SPECIAL THANKS

Elizabeth Nehls, Terence Dale, Matt Stern,
Jim Corona, Jesse Huot,
Sony Music Studios (Mike Negri & Daphne Walter),
Prism Production Services, David O'Brien, Erica Schwartz,
Kurzweil/Jeff Allen, American Ballet Theatre, City Center,
Dana Calanan, Cameron Roberts, Larry Moss, Claire
Mercuri, Teddy Krause, Lee Eastman and Ed London.

BAND CREDITS

Mr. Bürgi uses Tama drums,
Paiste cymbals and Pro-Mark drumsticks.
Mr. Smith uses Hartke amplification,
GMP 5-string basses and Fender basses.
Mr. DelGaudio uses pedal boards from Pedalboards.com.
Mr. Scarpulla uses Vandoren reeds distributed by
J. D'addario & Co., SKB cases and Kiwi wind products.
Mr. Byrnes uses Gibson guitars, Marshall amplifiers
and B'Aquisto strings.
Mr. Danielian uses Calicchio trumpets and
custom mouthpieces by GR Technologies.
Support provided by Yamaha Artist Services.
Piano custom built by Young Chang America.

Yamaha is the official piano of the
Nederlander Organization.

Drumheads courtesy of Evans Drumheads.

MUSIC CREDITS

All compositions written by Billy Joel
and published by Impulsive Music (ASCAP)
and Joelsongs (BMI).

Original cast recording available on SONY CLASSICAL

NEDERLANDER

Chairman	**James M. Nederlander**
President	**James M. Nederlander**

Executive Vice President
Nick Scandalios

Vice President • Corporate Development Charlene S. Nederlander	Senior Vice President • Labor Relations Herschel Waxman
Vice President Jim Boese	Chief Financial Officer Freida Sawyer Belviso

www.nederlander.org

HOUSE STAFF FOR
THE RICHARD RODGERS THEATRE

House Manager	Timothy Pettolina
Box Office Treasurer	Fred Santore, Jr.
Assistant Treasurer	Daniel Nitopi
Electrician	Steve Carver
Carpenter	Kevin Camus
Propertymaster	Steve DeVerna
Engineer	Sean Quinn

Theatre insurance provided by Emar Group.

Celebrity Visitor: Shirley MacLaine came and held court with the cast on the stage.

Rituals: Because it's such a busy dance show, most people arrive an hour early and do warmups and stretching on the stage. It becomes our social hour.

"Carols For A Cure" Carol: "Dance of the Sugar Punk Fairy."

"Easter Bonnet" Sketch: "Voices of Wings" by Ron DeJesus, Hans Zimmer and Lisa Gerrard. Winner: Best Bonnet Presentation.

Favorite Moment: "River of Dreams," the big number at the end of the show that goes into "Only the Good Die Young," because the whole company gets to really cut loose, and the audience goes a little crazy. It's always a fun thing to look forward to.

Therapy: We have ten hours of physical therapy each week, and ten hours of massage therapy.

In-Theatre Gathering Place: The PT room on the sixth floor. It has a massage table and a couch with pillows, and there's always tranquil music playing. It's the favorite hangout for the swings and anyone not on stage.

Off-site Hangout: McHale's.

Snacks: Most of the dancers eat very healthy stuff, but my assistant has a drawer full of chocolate and sometimes, when there's a lull, people will come into the office and head straight for the chocolate drawer. I also keep a bowl of Tootsie Pops.

Memorable Ad-Libs: Every once in a while, during "River of Dreams," John Selya will break the fourth wall and touch the hand of someone sitting in the front row.

Mascot: James Montana Wise, the new baby of cast members Elizabeth Parkinson and Scott Wise.

Record Number Of Cell Phone Rings: Two.

Heaviest/Hottest Costume: John Selya dances "River" in a pair of grey sweatpants.

Who Wore The Least: In one number Liz Parkinson wears very short, jean hot pants with a bronze coated bra.

Memorable Press Encounter: This was unusual, but a lot of fun. The luggage retailer Dooney and Bourke shot an entire catalog with our company.

Memorable Directorial Note: From Twyla Tharp: "Learn the counts—and then forget about them."

Musician Who Plays The Most Instruments: John Scarpulla, who plays two saxes and a variety of percussion instruments.

Also: It's always great when Billy Joel stops by and jumps in with the band. It's exciting for the cast and for the audience.

Correspondent: Kim Vernace, Production Stage Manager

Above left: Composer Billy Joel plays two tunes following the two-year anniversary performance of *Movin' Out*. Above right: The cast takes a curtain call after that performance.

Daughter Alexa, Billy Joel and wife Katie Lee arrive at the 2004 Tony Awards.

Keith Roberts and Michael Cavanaugh at the Second Anniversary show.

Cast members Elizabeth Parkinson and Scott Wise with their month-old baby, James.

Stage Manager Gregory Victor (L) and producer James M. Nederlander (R) accept a Community Service Award from Tim Glover, representing Chapter 82 of the Vietnam Veterans of America.

Producers Jimmy Nederlander (L) and Nick Scandalios (R) at the anniversary show.

PLAYBILL®

®ROYALE THEATRE

242 West 45th Street
A Shubert Organization Theatre

Gerald Schoenfeld, *Chairman* Philip J. Smith, *President*

Robert E. Wankel, *Executive Vice President*

FOX THEATRICALS HARBOR ENTERTAINMENT
EAST OF DOHENY THE ARACA GROUP TERRY SCHNUCK
AMANDA DUBOIS RUTH HENDEL HAL GOLDBERG WIESENFELD/MEYER

present

EDIE FALCO **BRENDA BLETHYN**
in

'night, Mother

By

MARSHA NORMAN

Set Design by	Costume Design by	Lighting Design by	Sound Design by
NEIL PATEL	MICHAEL KRASS	BRIAN MacDEVITT	DAN MOSES SCHREIER

Wig Designer	Production Stage Manager	Production Manager
PAUL HUNTLEY	JAMES HARKER	KAI BROTHERS

Casting	Press Representatives	Marketing	General Manager
JIM CARNAHAN, C.S.A.	BONEAU/ BRYAN-BROWN	THE ARACA GROUP	ROY GABAY

Directed by

MICHAEL MAYER

11/14/04

CAST
(in order of appearance)

Thelma Cates ....BRENDA BLETHYN
Jessie Cates ....EDIE FALCO

TIME:
Tonight

PLACE:
The home where Mama and Jessie live

STANDBYS
For Thelma Cates:
BARBARA EDA-YOUNG

For Jessie Cates:
JULIA GIBSON

Left: Edie Falco. Above: Falco and Brenda Blethyn.

Brenda Blethyn
Thelma Cates

Edie Falco
Jessie Cates

Barbara Eda-Young
Standby for Thelma Cates

Julia Gibson
Standby for Jessie Cates

Marsha Norman
Playwright

Michael Mayer
Director

Neil Patel
Scene Design

Brian MacDevitt
Lighting Design

Marsha Moses Schreier
Dan Moses Schreier
Sound Design

Paul Huntley
Wig Design

James Harker
Production Stage Manager

Jim Carnahan
Casting

Roy Gabay
General Manager

David Broser and Aaron Harnick/
Harbor Entertainment
Producers

Terry E. Schnuck
Producer

Ruth Hendel
Producer

Hal Goldberg
Producer

Box Office: Karen Coscia, Brian Good

Doorman: Jerry Klein

Electric: Stewart Wagner, Herb Messing

Wardrobe: Kimberly Prentice, Kay Grunder

Front: Stewart Wagner (Sound)
Back: Heather Cousens, Jim Harker (Stage Managers)

Props: Fred Ricci

Front of House Staff:
Front Row: Deanna Sorenson, Martha Rodriguez, Al Nazario, Sean Cutler, Raisa Ramos (porter), Eva Frances, Billy Mitchell

Back Row: John Minore, Roxanne Gayol, Greg Marlow, Patanne McEvoy

Photos by Ben Strothmann

'night, Mother

Memorable Opening Night Gifts: A Tiffany keychain with a charm of a Hostess SnoBall, from Edie Falco.

Celebrity Visitor: Kathy Bates (from the original cast). Edie and Brenda were so surprised.

Backstage Ritual: Brenda reaching for God or salvation upstage of the show drop at "places."

Mascot: Edie's dog, Marley.

Favorite Moment: Marley's photo is attached to the stage right prop table, and Edie touches it when she's briefly offstage during the show.

In-Theatre Gathering Place: The stage manager's office. Sometimes we have cookies. Mostly good personalities and lively conversation.

Off-site Hangout: Joe Allen's

Favorite Snack Food: Dog biscuits for Marley. It's the only snack food in almost every room! She makes a tour of the backstage stopping where she knows people will give her biscuits.

Favorite Therapy: Message therapist Jay Zimmerman visits between shows.

Who Wore the Least: Marley, when she's running around backstage looking for food.

Memorable Directorial Note: This was a dialect note given by director Michael Mayer, mainly for Brenda: "'Fuzzy-Wuzzy was a bear/Fuzzy-Wuzzy had no hair.' Say it every day."

Also: During rehearsals, as an exercise, Michael Mayer would ask Brenda to describe the experience and sensation of whatever sweets we had around, in as fine a detail as possible. She would give explicit descriptions of the taste experience. It was quite extraordinary.

Correspondent: PSM Heather Cousens

Top left: Brenda Blethyn and Edie Falco rehearse. Top right: Royale marquee. Center: Blethyn, playwright Marsha Norman, director Michael Mayer and Falco at the opening night cast party at Tavern on the Green. Bottom left: Opening night well-wishers Brooke Shields, Roger Rees and Sherie Rene Scott. Bottom right: A toast from Anne Pitoniak, Gerald Schoenfeld and Barbara Barrie.

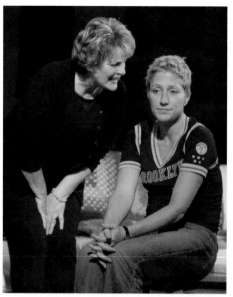

PLAYBILL®

on golden pond

CAST
(in order of appearance)

Norman Thayer, Jr. ....JAMES EARL JONES
Ethel Thayer ....LESLIE UGGAMS
Charlie Martin ....CRAIG BOCKHORN
Chelsea Thayer Wayne ....LINDA POWELL
Billy Ray ....ALEXANDER MITCHELL
Bill Ray ....PETER FRANCIS JAMES

TIME
The Present

PLACE
The Thayers' summer home
on Golden Pond in Maine

STANDBYS

For Norman – CHARLES TURNER
for Ethel – PETRONIA PALEY
for Chelsea – OPAL ALLADIN
for Bill and Charlie – CORNELL WOMACK
for Billy – RYDELL ROLLINS

⑤ CORT THEATRE
138 West 48th Street
A Shubert Organization Theatre

Gerald Schoenfeld, *Chairman*   Philip J. Smith, *President*

Robert E. Wankel, *Executive Vice President*

Jeffrey Finn
Arlene Scanlan
Stuart Thompson

present

JAMES EARL JONES   LESLIE UGGAMS

in

on golden pond

by

Ernest Thompson

with

Linda Powell   Peter Francis James
Craig Bockhorn   Alexander Mitchell

Scenic Design	Costume Design	Lighting Design	Original Music and Sound Design
Ray Klausen	Jane Greenwood	Brian Nason	Dan Moses Schreier

Technical Supervisor	Production Stage Manager
Christopher C. Smith/Smitty	Kelley Kirkpatrick

Press Representative	Marketing	Casting
The Publicity Office	TMG The Marketing Group	Stuart Howard/Amy Schecter/ Paul Hardt

General Management	Associate Producers
Stuart Thompson Productions/ James Triner	Magnesium.com, Inc./ Neal Edelsen/Andy Sawyer

Directed by
Leonard Foglia

The Producers wish to express their appreciation to Theatre Development Fund for its support of this production.

4/7/05

James Earl Jones and Leslie Uggams in *On Golden Pond.*

Photo by Joan Marcus

James Earl Jones
Norman Thayer, Jr

Leslie Uggams
Ethel Thayer

Linda Powell
*Chelsea Thayer
Wayne*

Peter Francis James
Bill Ray

Craig Bockhorn
Charlie Martin

Alexander Mitchell
Billy Ray

Charles Turner
*Standby for
Norman*

Petronia Paley
Standby for Ethel

Opal Alladin
*Standby for
Chelsea*

Cornell Womack
*Standby for Bill
And Charlie*

Rydell Rollins
*Standby for Billy
Ray*

Ernest Thompson
Playwright

Leonard Foglia
Director

Ray Klausen
Scenic Designer

Jane Greenwood
Costume Designer

Brian Nason
Lighting Designer

Dan Moses Schreier
*Original Music and
Sound Designer*

Theatersmith, Inc.
Christopher C. Smith,
Technical Supervisor

Stuart Thompson
Producer

Arlene Scanlan
Producer

Jeffrey Finn
Producer

Standbys
(L-R): Cornell
Womack,
Rydell Rollins,
Petronia Paley
and Charles
Turner.
Not pictured:
Opel Alladin.

Photo by Ben Strohmann

On Golden Pond

Backstage Crew
(L-R): Hair & Make-Up Supervisor Grantley A. McIntyre, Press Agent Michael S. Borowski, Production Sound Man Thomas B. Grasso, Production Electrician James Fedigan, Original Production Prop Supervisor Emiliano Pares, Stage Manager Marti McIntosh, Dresser (To Ms. Uggams) Valerie Gladstone, Technical Supervisor Christopher "Smitty" C. Smith, Current Production Prop Supervisor Dylan Foley, Wardrobe Supervisor Kathryn B. Guida and Production Stage Manager Kelley Kirkpatrick

Photo by Ben Strothmann

Photos by Aubrey Reuben

Above (L-R): Director Leonard Foglia, James Earl Jones, Leslie Uggams and playwright Ernest Thompson at a press conference at The New 42nd Street Studios.

Linda Powell and her father, former Secretary of State Colin Powell, at the opening night party at the Blue Fin.

James Earl Jones, Craig Bockhorn and Leslie Uggams.

Best Opening Night Telegram or Note: "Give 'em Hell," from playwright Ernest Thompson.

Opening Night Gifts: From James Earl Jones, a loon call. From the producers, a plush loon that makes a loon call.

Most Exciting Celebrity Visitor And What They Said: Michael Ealy: "Keep on going, man."

Actor Who Performed The Most Roles: Standby Cornell Womack (Bill and Charlie).

Actor Who Has Done The Most Shows: In D.C., Wilmington and now New York, Linda Powell, Craig Bockhorn and myself have so far not missed a show (knock wood!).

Favorite Moment During Each Performance: When I curse!

Favorite In-Theatre Gathering Place: My dressing room. Leslie's dressing room is also a popular hangout spot for everybody.

Favorite Off-Site Hangout: The movies for the kids. Langdon's for the adults.

Favorite Snack Food: Cinnamon Pretzels. Smitty, our nighttime stage doorman, also keeps the stage manager's office stocked with chocolate and other great snacks.

Mascot: Rydell Rollins (my understudy).

Favorite Therapy: Ricola.

Record Number Of Cellphone Rings During A Performance: Two.

Strangest Press Encounters: Wherever James Earl Jones and Leslie Uggams go (even when it's unannounced), they are mobbed by fans with pictures to sign. We never know just how they find them!

Strangest Stage Door Fan Encounter: A fan followed me to the parking garage.

Fastest Costume Change: Leslie Uggams.

Busiest Day At The Box Office: The day after we opened to a rave in the *Times*.

Most Embarrassing Moment: I slid and fell during the show (my shoes were slippery).

Company Legends: James Earl Jones, Leslie Uggams, Linda Powell.

Nicknames: "Cool Breeze."

Correspondent: Alexander Mitchell, "Billy Ray"

Well-wishers on opening night, Far left: Audra McDonald and Michael Cerveris.

Immediate left: Brian Stokes Mitchell and wife Allyson on opening night.

PLAYBILL®

PACIFIC OVERTURES

CAST

Reciter .... B.D. WONG

Observer, Officer, Warrior,
British Admiral, ... EVAN D'ANGELES

Samurai, Thief, Soothsayer,
Storyteller .. JOSEPH ANTHONY FORONDA

Tamate .... YOKO FUMOTO

Shogun's Mother, Old Man ..... ALVIN Y. F. ING

Noble .... FRED ISOZAKI

Madam, Dutch Admiral .... FRANCIS JUE

Officer, American Admiral,
Sailor .... DARREN LEE

Merchant, Commodore Perry,
Lord of South, Sailor .... HOON LEE

Kayama .... MICHAEL K. LEE

Councilor, Priest, Emperor Priest ..... MING LEE

Observer, Shogun's Companion,
Boy, Noble, Sailor .... TELLY LEUNG

Manjiro .... PAOLO MONTALBAN

Councilor, Grandmother .... ALAN MURAOKA

Kanagawa Girl, Daughter ... MAYUMI OMAGARI

Priest, Kanagawa Girl,
French Admiral .... DANIEL JAY PARK

Shogun's Wife,
Kanagawa Girl ... HAZEL ANNE RAYMUNDO

Lord Abe .... SAB SHIMONO

Son, Shogun's Wife's Servant,
Kanagawa Girl .... YUKA TAKARA

continued on the next page

STUDIO 54

ROUNDABOUT THEATRE COMPANY

TODD HAIMES, Artistic Director
ELLEN RICHARD, Managing Director
JULIA C. LEVY, Executive Director, External Affairs

in association with GORGEOUS ENTERTAINMENT

Presents

B.D. Wong

in

PACIFIC OVERTURES

Music and Lyrics by Stephen Sondheim

Book by John Weidman

Additional material by Hugh Wheeler

Eric Bondoc   Evan D'Angeles   Rick Edinger   Joseph Anthony Foronda   Yoko Fumoto
Alvin Y. F. Ing   Fred Isozaki   Francis Jue   Darren Lee   Hoon Lee   Michael K. Lee   Ming Lee
Telly Leung   Orville Mendoza   Paolo Montalban   Alan Muraoka   Mayumi Omagari   Daniel Jay Park
Hazel Anne Raymundo   Sab Shimono   Yuka Takara   Kim Varhola   Scott Watanabe

Set and Mask Design by Rumi Matsui	*Costume Design by* Junko Koshino	*Lighting Design by* Brian MacDevitt	*Sound Design by* Dan Moses Schreier
Production Stage Manager Arthur Gaffin	*Casting by* Jim Carnahan, C.S.A.	*Technical Supervisor* Steve Beers	*Executive Producer* Sydney Beers
Founding Director Gene Feist	*Associate Artistic Director* Scott Ellis	*Press Representative* Boneau/Bryan-Brown	*Director of Marketing* David B. Steffen

Orchestrations by Jonathan Tunick

Musical Direction by Paul Gemignani

Directed and Choreographed by Amon Miyamoto

Based on an October 2000 production directed by Amon Miyamoto at the New National Theatre, Tokyo, Japan (Tamiya Kuiyama, Artistic Director).

Original Broadway Production Directed by Harold Prince

Major support for Roundabout's Musical Theatre Fund provided by The Kaplen Foundation

Special assistance for *Pacific Overtures* provided by The Japan Foundation

Major support for *Pacific Overtures* provided by
CANON U.S.A., INC.   The Mitsui USA Foundation   Toyota

Official Airlines
American Airlines   Japan Airlines

12/20/04

A Million Miles From Stepney Green: Sailors serenade a Japanese girl with the song "Pretty Lady."

Photo by Joan Marcus

Pacific Overtures

MUSICAL NUMBERS

PLACE AND TIME: Japan, 1853-Present

ACT I

The Advantages of Floating in the Middle of the Sea ....Reciter and Company
There Is No Other Way ....Observers
Four Black Dragons ....Fisherman, Thief, Reciter and Company
Chrysanthemum Tea ....Shogun, Shogun's Mother, Shogun's Wife, Soothsayer,
　　　　　　　　　　　　　　Priests, Shogun's Companion, Physician, Shogun's Wife's Servant
Poems ....Kayama and Manjiro
Welcome to Kanagawa ....Madam and Girls
Someone in a Tree ....Old Man, Reciter, Boy, Warrior
Lion Dance ....Company

ACT II

Please Hello! ....Lord Abe; Reciter; American, British,
　　　　　　　　　　　　　　　　　　　　　　　Dutch, Russian and French Admirals
A Bowler Hat ....Kayama
Pretty Lady ....Sailors
Next ....Reciter and Company

Cast Continued

Fisherman, Physician,
Older Swordsman, Russian Admiral,
Samurai Bodyguard ....SCOTT WATANABE
Townspeople,
Officers, Priests, Samurai ....COMPANY

UNDERSTUDIES

For Reciter: JOSEPH ANTHONY FORONDA; for
Manjiro: DARREN LEE; for Lord Abe: MING LEE; for
Kayama: TELLY LEUNG; for Observer, Officer,
Warrior, British Admiral: HOON LEE, RICK
EDINGER; for Samurai, Thief, Soothsayer, Storyteller:
HOON LEE, FRED ISOZAKI; for Shogun's Mother,
Old Man: MING LEE, RICK EDINGER; for Noble,
Officer, American Admiral, Sailor, Councilor, Priest,
Emperor Priest, Kanagawa Girl, French Admiral: ERIC
BONDOC; for Madam, Dutch Admiral: ALAN
MURAOKA; for Merchant, Commodore Perry, Lord of
the South, Sailor, Councilor, Grandmother: RICK
EDINGER; for Observer, Shogun's Companion, Boy,
Noble, Sailor: ERIC BONDOC; for Sailor: DANIEL
JAY PARK; for Fisherman, Physician, Older Swordsman,
Russian Admiral: FRED ISOZAKI, RICK EDINGER;
for Tamate, Kanagawa Girls, Daughter, Shogun's Wife,
Son, Shogun's Wife's Servant: KIM VARHOLA

SWINGS

Eric Bondoc, Rick Edinger,
Orville Mendoza, Kim Varhola

Associate Choreographer/Dance Captain:
Darren Lee

Assistant Dance Captain:
Mayumi Omagari

Production Stage Manager ....ARTHUR GAFFIN
Stage Managers ....KENNETH J. MCGEE
　　　　　　　　　　　　　　　JUSTIN SCRIBNER

ORCHESTRA

MUSICAL DIRECTOR: PAUL GEMIGNANI

Woodwinds: Dennis Anderson

Cello: Deborah Assael

Keyboard #1: Paul Ford

Keyboard #2/Associate Conductor: Mark Mitchell

Violin/Viola: Suzanne Ornstein

Percussion #1: Paul Pizzuti

Percussion #2: Thad Wheeler

B.D. Wong (front) leads the cast in singing "The Advantages of Floating in the Middle of the Sea."

Photo by Joan Marcus

Pacific Overtures

B.D. Wong
Reciter

Eric Bondoc
Swing

Evan D'Angeles
Observer, Officer, Warrior, British Admiral

Rick Edinger
Swing

Joseph Anthony Foronda
Samurai, Thief, Soothsayer, Storyteller

Yoko Fumoto
Tamate

Alvin Y. F. Ing
Shogun's Mother, Old Man

Fred Isozaki
Noble

Francis Jue
Madam, Dutch Admiral

Darren Lee
Assoc.Choreo., Dance Capt./Officer, Amer. Admiral, Sailor

Hoon Lee
Merchant, Commodore Perry, Lord Of South, Sailor

Michael K. Lee
Kayama

Ming Lee
Second Councilor, Emperor, Priest

Telly Leung
Observer, Shogun's Companion, Boy, Noble, Sailor

Orville Mendoza
Swing

Paolo Montalban
Manjiro

Alan Muraoka
Third Councilor, Grandmother

Mayumi Omagari
Kanagawa Girl, Daughter/Assistant Dance Captain

Daniel Jay Park
Priest, Kanagawa Girl, French Admiral

Hazel Anne Raymundo
Shogun's Wife, Kanagawa Girl

Sab Shimono
Lord Abe

Yuka Takara
Son, Shogun's Wife's Servant, Kanagawa Girl

Kim Varhola
Swing

Scott Watanabe
Fisherman, Physician, Older Swordsman, Russian Admiral, Samurai Bodyguard

Stephen Sondheim
Music and Lyrics

John Weidman
Book

Amon Miyamoto
Director and Choreographer

Paul Gemignani
Musical Director

Rumi Matsui
Set and Mask Design

Junko Koshino
Costume Designer

Brian MacDevitt
Lighting Design

Dan Moses Schreier
Sound Design

Jonathan Tunick
Orchestrations

Jim Carnahan
Casting

Gene Feist
Founding Director Roundabout Theatre Company

Todd Haimes,
Artistic Director, Roundabout Theatre Company

ALUMNUS

Michael J. Bulatao
Swing

Stage and Company Management
(L-R): Justin Scribner (Stage Manager),
Artie Gaffin (Production Stage Manager),
Kenny McGee, (Stage Manager); and
(being held) Nichole Larson (Company Manager)

Sound and Electric
Top Row (L-R): George Carleton, Josh Weitzman,
and Jocelyn Pammy Smith.
Bottom Row (L-R): Dorion Fuchs, Jenny
Montgomery, John Wooding and David Bullard.
Not pictured: Greg Peeler, Sue Pelkofer and
Francis Elers.

Photo by Ben Strohmann

Box Office
(L-R): Krystin MacRitchie and Steve Howe

House Staff
Top Row (L-R): Jen, Nicky and Jason
Middle Row (L-R): Elicia, Victor, Lauren, Linda and Omar.
Bottom Row (L-R): Anthony, Connie, Jack, Mary Ann, Jonathan and Ralph.

Wardrobe and Hair
Clockwise from top left: Nadine Hettel, Jay Woods, Susan Cook, Kurt Kielmann, Nellie LaPorte, Daryl Terry, Linda McAllister, Kim Baird and Andrea Gonzalez.
Not pictured: Laisi Rogovin, Amanda Scott and Chevy Cavalier.

Props
Scott Crawford, Jean Scheller and Larry Jennino

Not pictured: Dan Mendeloff

Photos by Ben Strothmann

Pacific Overtures

Carpenters
(L-R): Peter Ruen, Al Steiner, Paul Ashton, Steve Jones, Dan Hoffman, Elisa Kuhar and Erin Delaney.
Not pictured: Billy Lombardi.

Photo by Ben Strohmann

The Pacific Overtures Crew:
Top Row (L-R): Dorion Fuchs, John Wooding, Jocelyn Pammy Smith, Josh Weitzman, Peter Ruen, Al Steiner, Paul Ashton, Steve Jones, Dan Hoffman, Erin Delaney and Elisa Kuhar.
Middle Row: Justin Scribner, Jenny Montgomery, Kurt Kielmann, Jean Scheller, Jay Woods, Nadine Hettel, Nellie LaPorte, Linda McAllister and Susan Cook.
Bottom Row: Kenny McGee, Artie Gaffin, Kim Baird, Andrea Gonzalez, Scott Crawford, Larry Jennino and Daryl Terry.

Pacific Overtures

ROUNDABOUT THEATRE COMPANY STAFF
Artistic Director .... **TODD HAIMES**
Managing Director .... **ELLEN RICHARD**
Executive Director, ... **JULIA C. LEVY**
External Affairs
Associate Artistic Director .... **SCOTT ELLIS**

ARTISTIC STAFF
Director of Artistic Development/
Director of Casting .... **Jim Carnahan**
Artistic Consultant .... Robyn Goodman
Resident Director .... Michael Mayer
Associate Artists .... Scott Elliott, Bill Irwin,
Joe Mantello, Mark Brokaw
Consulting Dramaturg .... Jerry Patch
Artistic Associate .... Samantha Barrie
Casting Director .... Mele Nagler
Senior Casting Associate .... Jeremy Rich
Casting Associate .... Carrie Gardner
Casting Assistant .... Kate Schwabe
Casting Intern .... Stephen Kopel
Artistic Intern .... Rachel Holmes

EDUCATION STAFF
Education Director .... **Megan Kirkpatrick**
Director of Instruction and
Curriculum Development .... Renee Flemings
Education Program Associate .... Lindsay Erb
Education Dramaturg .... Ted Sod
Teaching Artists .... William Addis,
Tony Angelini,
Philip Alexander,
Cynthia Babak, Victor Barbella,
Brigitte Barnett-Loftis, Caitlin Barton,
Joe Basile, Bonnie Brady, LaTonya Borsay,
Mike Carnahan, Joe Clancy, Melissa Denton,
Stephen DiMenna, Joe Doran, Alvin Eng,
Tony Freeman, Jonathan Goldstein,
Susan Hamburger, Karla Hendrick,
Sarah Iams, Jim Jack, Alvin Keith,
Jeannine Lally-Jones, Padraic Lillis,
Mark Lonergan, Erin McCready,
Andrew Ondrecjak, Marilyn Pasekoff,
Laura Poe, Drew Sachs, Anna Saggese,
David Sinkus, Olivia Tsang, Jennifer Varbalow,
Leese Walker, Eric Wallach, Corey Warren,
Ryan Weible, Diana Whitten,
Gail Winar, Kirche Zeile
Education Assistant .... Cassidy Jones
Education Interns .... Fumiko Eda, Tommy Marr

ADMINISTRATIVE STAFF
General Manager .... **Sydney Beers**
General Counsel .... Laura O'Neill
Associate Managing Director .... Greg Backstrom
Associate General Managers .... Don-Scott Cooper,
Jean Haring
Office Operations Manager .... Bonnie Berens
Human Resources Manager .... Stephen Deutsch
Network Systems Manager .... Jeff Goodman
Facilities Manager .... Timothy Santillo
Manager of Corporate & Party Rentals .... Jetaun Dobbs
MIS Associate .... Lloyd Alvarez
MIS Assistant .... Anthony Foti
Receptionists .... Jennifer Decoteau, Andre Forston,
Carolyn Miller, Elisa Papa
Messenger .... Robert Weisser
Management Interns .... Andrew Jones,
Izumi Asakawa, Noriko Nakajima

FINANCE STAFF
Controller .... **Susan Neiman**
Assistant Controller .... John LaBarbera
Accounts Payable Administrator .... Frank Surdi
Customer Service Coordinator .... Trina Cox
Business Office Associate .... David Solomon
Business Assistant .... Yonit Kafka
Business Intern .... Chelsea Glickfield

DEVELOPMENT STAFF
DIRECTOR OF DEVELOPMENT .... **Jeffry Lawson**
Director, Institutional Giving .... Julie K. D'Andrea
Director, Individual Giving .... Julia Lazarus
Director, Special Events .... Steve Schaeffer
Manager, Donor Information Systems ...... Tina Mae Bishko
Associate, External Affairs .... Stacey L. Morris

Annual Giving Associate .... Justin P. Steensma
Special Events Associate .... Elaina Grillo
Institutional Giving Assistant .... Kristen Bolibruch
Patron Services Assistant .... Barbara Dente
Development Associate .... Adam Gwon
Development Assistant .... Stephenie L. Overton
Development Interns .... Sara Schmidtchen,
Robert Weinstein, Brigid Ducey

MARKETING STAFF
Director of Marketing .... **David B. Steffen**
Marketing/Publications Manager .... Tim McCanna
Marketing Associate .... Sunil Ayyagari
Marketing Assistant .... Rebecca Ballon
Marketing Intern .... Alexis Goldberg
Website Consultant .... Keith Powell Beyland
Director of Telesales Special Promotions .... **Tony Baksa**
Telesales Manager .... Anton Borissov
Telesales Office Coordinator .... J.W. Griffin

TICKET SERVICES STAFF
DIRECTOR OF SALES OPERATIONS .... Jim Seggelink
Ticket Services Manager .... Ellen Holt
Subscription Manager .... Charlie Garbowski
Box Office Managers .... Edward P. Osborne,
Jaime Perlman, Jessica Bowser
Group Sales Manager .... Jeff Monteith
Assistant Box Office Managers .... Paul Caspary,
Steve Howe, Megan Young
Assistant Ticket Services Managers .... Robert Kane,
Kris Todd, David Meglino
Assistant to the Director of .... Nancy Mulliner
Sales Operations
Ticket Services .... Paola Arinci, Solangel Bido,
Andrew Clements, Johanna Comanzo,
Sean Crews, Barbara Dente, Nisha Dhruna,
Lindsay Ericson, Scott Falkowski,
Catherine Fitzpatrick, Steven Gottlieb,
Julie Hilimire, Talia Krispel,
Alexander LaFrance, Krystin MacRitchie,
Robert Morgan, Carlos Morris,
Nicole Nicholson, Shannon Paige,
Hillary Parker, Julie Sherwood,
Heather Siebert, Monté Smock,
Melissa Snyder, Catherine Sorensen,
Lillian Soto, Justin Sweeney,
Greg Thorson, Ryan Weible
Ticket Services Intern .... Joel Solari

SERVICES
Counsel .... Jeremy Nussbaum,
Cowan, Liebowitz & Latman, P.C.
Counsel .... Rosenberg & Estis
Counsel .... Rubin and Feldman, P.C.
Counsel .... Cleary, Gottlieb, Steen & Hamilton
Counsel ...... Harry H. Weintraub/Glick and Weintraub, P.C.
Immigration Counsel .... Mark D. Koestler and
Theodore Ruthizer
House Physicians .... Dr. Theodore Tyberg,
Dr. Lawrence Katz
House Dentist .... Neil Kanner, D.M.D.
Insurance .... Marsh USA Inc.
Accountant .... Brody, Weiss,
Zucarelli & Urbanek CPAs, P.C.
Advertising .... Eliran Murphy Group/Denise Ganjou
Events Photography .... Anita and Steve Shevett
Production Photographer .... Joan Marcus
Press Assistant .... Erika Creagh
Theatre Displays .... King Displays, Wayne Sapper

BONEAU/BRYAN-BROWN
GENERAL PRESS REPRESENTATIVES
Adrian Bryan-Brown   Matt Polk
Jessica Johnson   Joe Perrotta

Credits for PACIFIC OVERTURES
EXECUTIVE PRODUCER .... Sydney Beers
Company Manager .... Nichole Larson
Production Stage Manager .... Arthur Gaffin
Stage Managers .... Kenneth J. McGee, Justin Scribner
Dramaturg to the Director .... Mariko Kojima
Assistant Director .... Scott Smith
Associate Choreographer .... Darren Lee
Fight Direction .... based on original Fight Choreography
by Akinori Tani
Fight Director .... Kazuki Takase

Assistant to the Fight Director .... Yoshihisa Kuwayama
Costume Associate Designer .... Maiko Matsushima
Associate Lighting Designer .... Anne E. McMills
Assistant Lighting Designer .... Rachel Eichorn
Assistant to Brian MacDevitt .... Patrick Johnston
Associate Sound Designer .... David Bullard
House Head Electrics .... Josh Weitzman
Production Head Electrics ..... Josh Weitzman, John Wooding
Follow Spot Operators .... Sue Pelkofer, Dorian Fuchs
House Head Carpentry .... Dan Hoffman
Production Head Carpentry .... Dan Hoffman
Carpentry Running Crew .... Erin Delaney, Steve Jones,
Billy Lombardi, Peter Ruen, Al Steiner
Production Head Properties .... Lawrence Jennino
Properties Running Crew .... Jean Scheller, Dan Mendeloff
Moving Light Programmer .... David Arch
Production Sound Engineer .... Francis Elers
Assistant Sound Engineer .... Jenny Scheer Montgomery
Production Properties .... Denise J. Grillo
Assistant Production Properties .... Kevin Crawford
Japanese Props Coordinator .... Miyuki Fujinami
Props .... Fujinami Properties Co., Ltd.,
Backstage, Inc., Tokyo, Japan
Wardrobe Supervisor .... Nadine Hettel
Dressers .... Kimberly Baird,
Susan Cook, Andrea Gonzales,
Kurt Kielmann, Laisann S. Rogovin, Jay Woods
Hair Supervisor .... Manuela LaPorte
Assistant Hair .... Daryl Terry
Production Assistants .... Brendan Clifford, Sara Sahin
Japanese Costumes by .... Nihon Engeki Isho, Inc.,
Tokyo, Japan
Western Costumes by ...... Junko Koshino, Inc., Tokyo, Japan
New York Costume Shop .... Eric Winterling, Inc.
Wigs by .... Yamada Katsura, Inc., Tokyo, Japan
Masks and Specialty Wigs .... Elizabeth Flauto,
Brad L. Scoggins, Billie Jo Fisher,
Stafani Mitchell
Music Copying .... Emily Grishman Music Preparation/
Katharine Edmonds, Emily Grishman
Music Instruments .... Okadayafuse Co., Ltd.
Percussion Instruments .... Ayers Percussion, Inc.,
Carroll Musical Instruments
Sound Equipment .... Provided by Sound Associates
Lighting Equipment .... Provided by PRG Lighting
Scenery provided by .... Atlas Scenic Studios,

Showman Fabricators, Aquarium Design Computer Motion
Control
and Automation of Scenery and Rigging by
Hyde Power Systems

SHOWTRAK* Computer Motion Control for
Scenery and Rigging

Admiral Perry Puppet .... Brad L. Scoggins

OFFICIAL SUPPORT PROVIDED BY
Japan External Trade Organization,
Japanese Ministry of Foreign Affairs,
Japanese Chamber of Commerce of New York,
Nippon Club and New National Theatre, Tokyo

Emer'Gen-C Super Provided by
Alacer Corp
Energy BoosterCough Drops Provided by
Ricola U.S.A.

STUDIO 54 THEATRE STAFF
House Manager .... LaConya Robinson
Assistant House Managers .... Jack Watanachaiyot,
House Staff .... Matt Bailey, Jeffrey Collado,
Onercida Concepcion, Linda Edwards,
Jason Fernandez, Greg Hall,
William Klemm, Jen Kneeland,
Kate Longosky, Johnathan Martinez,
Dana McCaw, Roger Motter,
Jason Ostrowski, Lauren Parker, Dario Puccini
Security .... Gotham Security
Maintenance .... Ralph Mohan, Maman Garba
Refreshments and Merchandising .... Studio 54 Promotions

Pacific Overtures

Opening Night Telegram Or Note: We got good-luck wishes from *La Cage*, *Avenue Q*, *Mamma Mia!*, *Brooklyn* and other shows. That was very nice.

Opening Night Gifts: Bonnie Panson of *Chicago* sent over a bag of cookies and candy. We each got a framed poster of the show, and a photo of the whole company in a silver frame. Sondheim gave everyone a jigsaw puzzle that turned out to be the show's logo, but at the top was your initials.

Who Got The Gypsy Robe: Darren Lee. We added a kimono sleeve with origami.

Actor Who Performed The Most Roles: Darren Lee, who did eight.

Backstage Rituals: We had the theatre blessed by Shinto priests who sat around an altar, drank sake and said prayers. It turned out to be similar to the scene in the show where we sing, "The priest exalts the rice." After the Gypsy Robe ceremony, we all passed around cups of sake.

Every Saturday night the women organize a dance party at 15-minute call in the female ensemble room. There's an island in Japan called Shikoku, so we all call it "Club Shikoku," and we just have a great time dancing for 10 minutes, then go out and do the show.

Favorite Moment During Each Performance: At the end of the discovery of Tamate's death, Michael Lee goes all the way upstage. The women, who are just offstage getting ready to do "Welcome to Kanagawa," put themselves in obscene or pornographic poses to try to make Michael laugh. The audience definitely never gets to see this!

In-Theatre Gathering Place: Club Shikoku

Off-Site Hangouts: We go to Vintage, Flute and Mee's noodle shop, though we also had a party for the director at Yakitori Totto. B.D. Wong goes there.

Snack Food: Cream puffs from Beard Papa's. This cast likes all kinds of food. Sometimes we have potluck, a combination of noodles and all kinds of Asian food—plus pizza.

Therapy: We have physical therapy twice a week, organized by the producers, because we do a lot of running around on a raked stage.

Memorable Ad-lib: We have screens on the set that get different covers with different images to suggest different scenes. At one performance the pivoting of the screens caused one of the covers to come off and fall on the stage. B.D. was quite far downstage, but when he heard the thud, he screamed, "Ouch!"

Cell Phone Rings: We haven't had a huge problem with them, but we have had trouble with fire alarms going off

Left: Director Amon Miyamoto welcomes his father to opening night. Right: B.D. Wong takes his bow at opening night curtain calls.

Left: Recording the cast album. Right: Librettist John Weidman and composer Stephen Sondheim at the opening night party.

during performances. The smoke from the bomb scene sometimes sets them off.

Memorable Press Encounter: We had a lot of Asian press covering this show. The Japanese press surrounded our director Amon Miyamoto, who was the first Japanese to direct a Broadway musical. Once we had 20 press people from Japan come in during rehearsal and wanted to take pictures of us posing as if we were in an office looking at a bogus calendar. We just said, "Uh-huh...."

Busiest Day At The Box Office: The best week was post-Christmas to New Year.

Heaviest/Hottest Costume: The Commodore Perry costume, which covers the entire head.

Who Wore The Least: Yoko Fumoto has the fewest costume changes.

Orchestra Member Who Played the Most Instruments: Percussionist Paul Pizzuti. He has one of the hardest tracks, with so many accents throughout the script, plus playing traditional Japanese instruments. He's our MVP.

Best In-House Parody Lyric: When we rehearse "Four Black Dragons" we say, "Four black drag queens."

Memorable Directorial Note: During the Hiroshima moment at the end of the show, Amon was talking about the need to see the true pain and horror of being burnt throughout their bodies, but then he added, "Of course, you have to make it look pretty on stage."

Nicknames: We call our director, Amon Miyamoto, "Amonski" or "Amonele" (like in Yiddish). He said he prefers "Amonski."

Catchphrases: "The Rice!" When we sign letters, we sign it "The Rice!" Also, before we go on stage, we say, "Katsuto-ine" ("I hope you win" in Japanese).

Sweethearts: One of the women in the company, Hazel Anne Raymundo, announced she's pregnant.

Also: It's interesting how much knitting goes on backstage, especially among the men—and that includes the straight boys in the cast.

Also: The cast has a huge appreciation for the chance to work together. It means a great deal for them as Asian American actors.

Correspondents: PSM Artie Gaffin, ASMs Kenny McGee and Justin Scribner.

PLAYBILL®

CAST

The Phantom of the Opera ....HUGH PANARO
Christine Daaé ....SANDRA JOSEPH
Christine Daaé ....JULIE HANSON
(Wed. Eve. & Sat. Mat. Performances)
Raoul, Vicomte de Chagny ....JOHN CUDIA
Carlotta Giudicelli.......ANNE RUNOLFSSON
Monsieur André.....GEORGE LEE ANDREWS
Monsieur Firmin ....JEFF KELLER
Madame Giry ....MARILYN CASKEY
Ubaldo Piangi ....LARRY WAYNE MORBITT
Meg Giry ....HEATHER McFADDEN
Monsieur Reyer/Hairdresser ("Il Muto") ....
RICHARD POOLE
Auctioneer ....CARRINGTON VILMONT
Jeweler (Il Muto).............DAVID GASCHEN
Monsieur Lefèvre/Firechief ......TIM JEROME
Joseph Buquet ....RICHARD WARREN PUGH
Don Attilio ("Il Muto") ....GREGORY
EMANUEL RAHMING
Passarino ....CARRINGTON VILMONT
("Don Juan Triumphant")
Slave Master ("Hannibal") ....JACK HAYES
(Mon. thru Wed.)
Slave Master ("Hannibal") ...DANIEL RYCHLEC
(Thurs. thru Sat.)
Solo Dancer ("Il Muto") ....DANIEL RYCHLEC
(Mon. thru Wed.)
Solo Dancer ("Il Muto") ....JACK HAYES
(Thurs. thru Sat.)
Page ("Don Juan Triumphant") ....KRIS KOOP
Porter/Fireman ....JOHN WASINIAK

continued on the next page

MAJESTIC THEATRE
247 West 44th Street
A Shubert Organization Theatre

Gerald Schoenfeld, *Chairman*   **Philip J. Smith,** *President*

Robert E. Wankel, *Executive Vice President*

CAMERON MACKINTOSH and
THE REALLY USEFUL THEATRE COMPANY, INC.
present

The PHANTOM of the OPERA.

starring

HUGH PANARO
SANDRA JOSEPH
JOHN CUDIA

JEFF KELLER   GEORGE LEE ANDREWS   ANNE RUNOLFSSON
MARILYN CASKEY   LARRY WAYNE MORBITT   HEATHER McFADDEN

At certain performances
JULIE HANSON
plays the role of "Christine"

Music by
ANDREW LLOYD WEBBER

Lyrics by CHARLES HART

Additional lyrics by RICHARD STILGOE

Book by RICHARD STILGOE & ANDREW LLOYD WEBBER
Based on the novel 'Le Fantôme de L'Opéra' by GASTON LEROUX

Production Design by MARIA BJÖRNSON   Lighting by ANDREW BRIDGE
Sound by MARTIN LEVAN   Musical Supervision & Direction DAVID CADDICK
Musical Director DAVID LAI   Production Supervisor PETER von MAYRHAUSER
Orchestrations by DAVID CULLEN & ANDREW LLOYD WEBBER
Casting by TARA RUBIN CASTING   Original Casting by JOHNSON-LIFF ASSOCIATES
General Management ALAN WASSER

Musical Staging & Choreography by GILLIAN LYNNE

Directed by HAROLD PRINCE

1/17/05

Angel of Music: Hugh Panaro and Julie Hanson as The Phantom and Christine.

Photo by Joan Marcus

The Phantom of the Opera

MUSICAL NUMBERS

PROLOGUE
The stage of the Paris Opéra House, 1911

OVERTURE

ACT ONE—PARIS 1881

Scene 1: The dress rehearsal of "Hannibal"
"Think of Me" ....Carlotta, Christine, Raoul

Scene 2: After the Gala
"Angel of Music" ....Christine and Meg

Scene 3: Christine's dressing room
"Little Lotte/The Mirror" (Angel of Music) ....Raoul, Christine, Phantom

Scene 4: The Labyrinth underground
"The Phantom of the Opera" ....Phantom and Christine

Scene 5: Beyond the lake
"The Music of the Night" ....Phantom

Scene 6: Beyond the lake, the next morning
"I Remember/Stranger Than You Dreamt It" ....Christine and Phantom

Scene 7: Backstage
"Magical Lasso" ....Buquet, Meg, Madame Giry and Ballet Girls

Scene 8: The Managers' office
"Notes/Prima Donna" ....Firmin, André, Raoul, Carlotta, Giry, Meg,
Piangi and Phantom

Scene 9: A performance of "Il Muto"
"Poor Fool, He Makes Me Laugh" ....Carlotta and Company

Scene 10: The roof of the Opéra House
"Why Have You Brought Me Here/Raoul, I've Been There" ...Raoul and Christine
"All I Ask of You" ....Raoul and Christine
"All I Ask of You" (Reprise) ....Phantom

ENTR'ACTE

ACT TWO — SIX MONTHS LATER

Scene 1: The staircase of the Opéra House, New Year's Eve
"Masquerade/Why So Silent" ....Full Company

Scene 2: Backstage

Scene 3: The Managers' office
"Notes/Twisted Every Way" ....André, Firmin, Carlotta, Piangi, Raoul,
Christine, Giry and Phantom

Scene 4: A rehearsal for "Don Juan Triumphant"

Scene 5: A graveyard in Peros
"Wishing You Were Somehow Here Again" ....Christine
"Wandering Child/Bravo, Bravo" ....Phantom, Christine and Raoul

Scene 6: The Opéra House stage before the Premiere

Scene 7: "Don Juan Triumphant"
"The Point of No Return" ....Phantom and Christine

Scene 8: The Labyrinth underground
"Down Once More/Track Down This Murderer" ....Full Company

Scene 9: Beyond the Lake

Cast Continued

Spanish Lady ....SALLY WILLIAMS

Wardrobe Mistress/Confidante ("Il Muto") ......MARY LEIGH STAH

Princess ("Hannibal") ....SUSAN OWEN

Madame Firmin ....MELODY RUBIE

Innkeeper's Wife ...WREN MARIE HARRINGTON ("Don Juan Triumphant")

Marksman ....MICHAEL SHAWN LEWIS

The Ballet Chorus of the Opéra Populaire ....
POLLY BAIRD
SABRA LEWIS
GIANNA LOUNGWAY
JESSICA RADETSKY
CARLY BLAKE SEBOUHIAN
DIANNA WARREN

Ballet Swing
EMILY ADONNA

Swings
SCOTT MIKITA
JAMES ROMICK,
JANET SAIA

UNDERSTUDIES

For the Phantom—JOHN CUDIA, DAVID GASCHEN, JAMES ROMICK, JEFF KELLER; for Christine—KRIS KOOP, SUSAN OWEN; for Raoul— JAMES ROMICK, MICHAEL SHAWN LEWIS CARRINGTON VILMONT; for Firmin—RICHARD WARREN PUGH, TIM JEROME, GREGORY EMANUEL RAHMING, JAMES ROMICK; for André—SCOTT MIKITA, RICHARD POOLE JAMES ROMICK; for Carlotta—WREN MARIE HARRINGTON, KRIS KOOP, MELODY RUBIE JANET SAIA; for Mme. Giry—KRIS KOOP, JANET SAIA, SALLY WILLIAMS; for Piangi—DAVID GASCHEN, RICHARD WARREN PUGH, JOHN WASINIAK; for Meg Giry—POLLY BAIRD, SABRA LEWIS, CARLY BLAKE SEBOUHIAN; for Slavemaster—DANIEL RYCHLEC; for Solo Dancer ("Il Muto")—JACK HAYES

Dance Captain:
Harriet Clark
Assistant Dance Captain:
Heather McFadden

The Phantom of the Opera

Conductors
David Caddick
Kristen Blodgette
David Lai
Tim Stella
Norman Weiss

THE PHANTOM OF THE OPERA
ORCHESTRA:

Violins:
Joyce Hammann (Concert Master)
Jan Mullen
Alvin E. Rogers
Gayle Dixon
Kurt Coble
Karen Milne

Violas:
Stephanie Fricker
Veronica Salas

Cellos:
Jeanne LeBlanc
Ted Ackerman

Bass:
Melissa Slocum

Harp:
Henry Fanelli

Flute:
Sheryl Henze

Flute/Clarinet:
Ed Matthew

Oboe:
Melanie Feld

Clarinet:
Matthew Goodman

Bassoon:
Atsuko Sato

Trumpets:
Lowell Hershey, Francis Bonny

Bass Trombone:
William Whitaker

French Horns:
Daniel Culpepper
David Smith
Peter Reit

Percussion:
Eric Cohen, Jan Hagiwara

Keyboards:
Tim Stella
Norman Weiss

Hugh Panaro
*The Phantom of
the Opera*

Sandra Joseph
Christine Daaé

John Cudia
*Raoul, Vicomte de
Chagny*

Jeff Keller
Monsieur Firmin

George Lee
Andrews
Monsieur André

Anne Runolfsson
Carlotta Giudicelli

Marilyn Caskey
Madame Giry

Larry Wayne
Morbitt
Ubaldo Piangi

Heather McFadden
Meg Giry

Julie Hanson
*Christine Daaé
at certain
performances*

Emily Adonna
Ballet Chorus

Polly Baird
Ballet Chorus

Harriet Clark
*Dance
Captain/Swing*

David Gaschen
Jeweler

Wren Marie
Harrington
Innkeeper's Wife

Jack Hayes
*Slave Master/
Solo Dancer*

Matthew R. Jones
Swing

Tim Jerome
*Monsieur LeFèvre/
Firechief*

Kris Koop
Page

Michael Shawn
Lewis
Marksman

The Phantom of the Opera

Sabra Lewis
Ballet Chorus

Gianna Loungway
Ballet Chorus

Scott Mikita
Swing

Susan Owen
Princess

Richard Poole
*Monsieur Reyer/
Hairdresser*

Richard Warren Pugh
Joseph Buquet

Jessica Radetsky
Ballet Chorus

Gregory Emanuel
Rahming
Don Attilio

James Romick
Swing

Melody Rubie
Madame Firmin

Daniel Rychlec
*Solo Dancer/
Slave Master*

Janet Saia
Swing

Carly Blake
Sebouhian
Ballet Chorus

Mary Leigh Stahl
*Wardrobe Mistress/
Confidante*

Carrington Vilmont
*Auctioneer/
Passarino*

Dianna Warren
Ballet Chorus

John Wasiniak
Porter/Fireman

Sally Williams
Spanish Lady

Anne Runolfsson
and Larry Wayne
Morbitt in a scene
from the show-with-
in-a-show,
Hannibal.

Photo by Joan Marcus

The Phantom of the Opera

Andrew Lloyd
Webber
*Composer/Book/
Co-Orchestrator*

Harold Prince
Director

Charles Hart
Lyrics

Richard Stilgoe
*Book and
Additional Lyrics*

Gillian Lynne
*Musical Staging
And Choreography*

Maria Björnson
*(1949-2002)
Production Design*

Andrew Bridge
Lighting Designer

Martin Levan
Sound Designer

David Caddick
*Musical Supervision
and Direction*

Kristen Blodgette
*Associate Musical
Supervisor*

David Cullen
Co-Orchestrator

Ruth Mitchell
*(1919-2000)
Assistant to
Mr. Prince*

Denny Berry
*Production Dance
Supervisor*

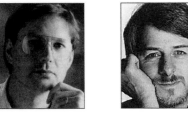

Craig Jacobs
*Production Stage
Manager*

David Lai
Musical Director

Vincent Liff and Geoffrey Johnson
Original Casting

Alan Wasser
General Manager

Cameron
MacKintosh
Producer

ALUMNI

Stephen R.
Buntrock
Swing

Marie
Danvers
*Alternate
Christine
Daaé*

Kara Klein
Meg Giry

Howard
McGillin
*The Phantom
of the Opera*

Ken Kantor
*Monsieur
Lefevre/
Firechief*

Eric Otte
Slave Master

Julie Schmidt
*Carlotta
Giudicelli*

Erin Stewart
*Innkeeper's
Wife*

Kenneth H.
Waller
*Monsieur
Lefevre/
Firechief*

Jim Weitzer
Marksman

Sharon
Wheatley
Swing

The *Phantom of the Opera* Crew

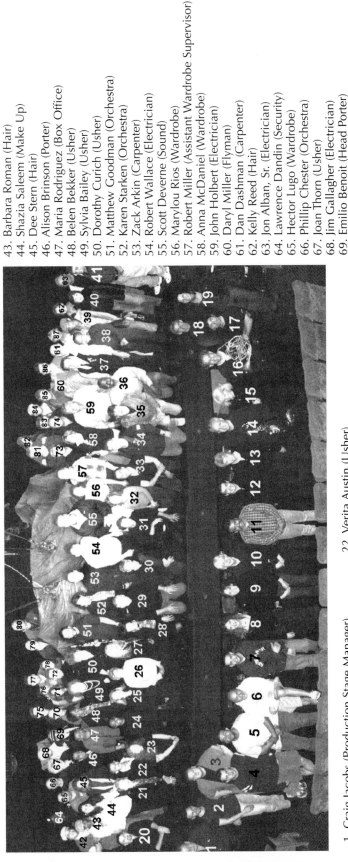

1. Craig Jacobs (Production Stage Manager)
2. Michael Borowski (Press Agent)
3. Spencer Bell (Assistant Props)
4. Frank Billings (Electrician)
5. Tony Robinson (Props)
6. Terrence Doherty (Dresser)
7. Jonathan Deverna (Props)
8. Kathy Halvorson (Orchestra)
9. Harriet Clark (Swing/Dance Captain)
10. Lowell Hershey (Orchestra)
11. Raoul Sanchez (Automation)
12. Neil Albstein (Production Assistant)
13. Bethe Ward (Stage Manager)
14. Bill Whitaker (Orchestra)
15. Theresa Norris (Orchestra)
16. Peter Reit (Orchestra)
17. Giancarlo Cottignoli (Carpenter)
18. Brendan Smith (Assistant Stage Manager)
19. Janet Saia (Swing)
20. Chris Brandon (Concessions Manager)
21. Deanna Sorenson (Usher)
22. Verita Austin (Usher)
23. Denise Reich (Usher)
24. Giovanni LaDuke (Usher)
25. Cynthia Carlin (Usher)
26. Margie Marchioni (Wardrobe)
27. Lucia Cappelletti (Usher)
28. Lucianna Lenihan (Chief Usher)
29. Fred Smith (Carpenter)
30. Karen Milne (Orchestra)
31. Craig Evans (Props)
32. Angie Finn (Wardrobe)
33. J.C. Sheets (Wardrobe)
34. Dan Gilloon (House Carpenter)
35. Eddie Griff (Electrician)
36. Ron Blakley (Costumes)
37. Ron Razz (Concessions)
38. Erna Dias (Costumes)
39. Charise Champion (Hair)
40. Eileen Casey (Wardrobe)
41. Russell Tiberio (Carpenter)
42. Lisa Renay Harris (Hair)
43. Barbara Roman (Hair)
44. Shazia Saleem (Make Up)
45. Dee Stern (Hair)
46. Alison Brinson (Porter)
47. Maria Rodriguez (Box Office)
48. Belen Bekker (Usher)
49. Sylvia Bailey (Usher)
50. Dorothy Curich (Usher)
51. Matthew Goodman (Orchestra)
52. Karen Starken (Orchestra)
53. Zack Arkin (Carpenter)
54. Robert Wallace (Electrician)
55. Scott Deverne (Sound)
56. Marylou Rios (Wardrobe)
57. Robert Miller (Assistant Wardrobe Supervisor)
58. Anna McDaniel (Wardrobe)
59. John Holbert (Electrician)
60. Daryl Miller (Flyman)
61. Dan Dashman (Carpenter)
62. Kelly Reed (Hair)
63. Jon Alban, Sr. (Electrician)
64. Lawrence Dandin (Security)
65. Hector Lugo (Wardrobe)
66. Phillip Chester (Orchestra)
67. Joan Thorn (Usher)
68. Jim Gallagher (Electrician)
69. Emilio Benoit (Head Porter)
70. Joe Grillman (Carpenter)
71. Annette Lovece (Wardrobe)
72. Mike Girman (Automation)
73. Scott Westervelt (Wardrobe Supervisor)
74. Francis Bonny (Orchestra)
75. Matt Mezick (Head Props)
76. Antoinette Martinez (Wardrobe)
77. Tim Higgins (House Prop Head)
78. Sarah Hench (Wardrobe)
79. Peter McIven (Wardrobe)
80. Alan Lampel (Head Electrician)
81. Jack Farmer (Carpenter)
82. Kristina Miller (Carpenter)
83. Jason Strangfeld (Sound)
84. Jeff Blackwood (Hair Supervisor)
85. Steve Thornburg (Wardrobe)
86. Michael Jacobs (Wardrobe)
87. Rose Mary Taylor (Wardrobe)

The Phantom of the Opera

Staff for THE PHANTOM OF THE OPERA

GENERAL MANAGER
ALAN WASSER

GENERAL PRESS REPRESENTATLVE
THE PUBLICITY OFFICE
Marc Thibodeau   Bob Fennell
Michael S. Borowski

ASSISTANT TO MR. PRINCE
RUTH MITCHELL

PRODUCTION SUPERVISOR
PETER von MAYRHAUSER

PRODUCTION DANCE SUPERVISOR
DENNY BERRY

ASSOCIATE MUSICAL SUPERVISOR
KRISTEN BLODGETTE

Associate General Manager ....Allan Williams
Technical Production Managers ....John H. Paull III,
Jake Bell
Company Manager ....Robert Nolan
Production Stage Manager ....Craig Jacobs
Stage Managers ....Bethe Ward,
Brendan Smith

U.S. DESIGN STAFF
Associate Scenic Designer ....Dana Kenn
Associate Costume Designer ....Mary Fleming
Associate Lighting Designer ....Debra Dumas
Assistant Sound Designer ....Jon Weston
Assistants to the Scenic Designer ....Paul Kelly,
Paul Weimer,
Steven Saklad
Assistants to the Costume Designer ......David Robinson,
Marcy Froehlich
Assistant to theLighting Designer ....Vivien Leone
Assistants to the Sound Designer ....Jon Weston,
James M. Bay,
Joan Curcio

U.K. DESIGN STAFF
Production Technical Consultant .Martyn Hayes Associates
Associate Scenic Designer ....Jonathan Allen
Associate Costume Designer ....Sue Willmington
Associate Lighting Designer ....Howard Eaton
Automation Consultant ....Michael Barnet
Draperies Consultant ....Peter Everett
Sculptures Consultant ....Stephen Pyle
Sound Consultant ....Ralph Colhns

Assistant to Gillian Lynne ....Naomi Sorkin
Associate Manager ....Thom Mitchell
Assistant Company Manager ....Steve Greer
Casting Associate ....Ron LaRosa
Dance Captain ....Harriet Clark
Production Carpenter ....Joseph Patria
Production Electrician ....Robert Fehribach
Production Propertyman ....Timothy Abel
Production Sound Operator ....Steve Kennedy
Production Wig Supervisor ....Leone Gagliardi
Production Make-up Supervisor ....Thelma Pollard
Make-up Assistant ....Pearleta N. Price
Head Carpenter ....Russell Tiberio III
Automation Carpenters ....Santos Sanchez,
Michael Girman
Assistant Carpenter ....Giancarlo Cottignoli
Flyman ....Daryl Miller
Head Electrician ....Alan Lampel
Assistant Electrician ...............................J.R. Beket
Head Props ....Marvin Crosland
Asst. Props./Boat Captain ....Joe Caruso
Sound Operator ....Jason Strangfeld
Assistant Wardrobe Supervisors ....Scott Westervelt,

Robert Strong Miller
Hair Supervisor ....Jeff Blackwood
Hairdressers ....Jeffrey Blackwood,
Charise Champion,
Lisa Harrell,
Elizabeth Martinelli,
Barbara Roman
Production Costume Design Assistant ...Cynthia Hamilton
Production Sound Design Assistant ....Larry Spurgeon

Associate Conductor ....Tim Stella
Assistant Conductor ....Norman Weiss
Musical Preparation Supervisor (U.S.) ....Chelsea Music
Service, Inc
Mathilde Pincus/Victor Jarowey
Synthesizer Consultant ....Brett Sommer
Music Technologies Inc.

Assistants to the General Manager. ....Jenny Bates,
Christopher Betz, Jason Hewitt,
Temah Higgins, Jake Hirzel,
Bill Miller, Jennifer Mudge,
Eric Orton,   Steven Schnepp
Lighting Intern ....Wendy Bodzin

Legal Counsel ....S. Jean Ward/
Frankfurt Garbus Kurnit Klein & Selz, P.C.
Legal Advisor to The Really Useful Company ....Brooks &
Distler/
Marsha Brooks
Accounting ....Rosenberg, Neuwirth and Kutchner/
Chris Cacace
General Manager, Harold Prince Organization ..Arlene R.
Caruso
Logo Design and Graphics ....Dewynters Plc
London
Merchandising ....Dewynters Advertising Inc.
Advertising ....Serino Coyne Inc.,
Greg Corradetti, Rebecca Russell,
Denise Geiger
Marketing/Promotions ....Hugh Hysell Communications /
Hugh Hysell,
Michael Redman, Adam Jay
Press Intern ....Jaclyn DeGiorgio
Displays ....King Displays, Wayne Sapper
Insurance (U.S.) ....J & H Marsh & McLennan, Inc.
Robert A. Boyar
Insurance (U.K.) ....Walton & Parkinson Limited
Richard Walton
Banking ....Morgan Guaranty Trust Company
Travel Agent ....Gloria & Associates Travel
Customs Broker (U.S.) ..T.L. Customs House Brokers, Inc.
Customs Broker (U.K.) ....Theatours, Ltd.
Payroll Service ....Castellana Services, Inc.

Original Production Photographer ....Clive Barda
Additional Photography ....Joan Marcus
Bob Marshak, Peter Cunningham
House Manager ....Peter Kulok

Special thanks to
McNABB & ASSOCIATES
Jim McNabb

CREDITS AND ACKNOWLEDGMENTS
Scenic construction and boat automation by
Hudson Scenic Studios.
Scenery automation by Jeremiah J. Harris Associates,
Inc./East Coast Theatre Supply, Inc.
Scenery painted by Nolan Scenery Studios.
Set and hand properties by
McHugh Rollins Associates, Inc.
Sculptural elements by Costume Armour.
"Opera Ball" newell post statues and elephant by
Nino Novellino of Costume Armour.
Proscenium sculptures by Stephen Pyle.
Draperies by I. Weiss and Sons, Inc.
Soft goods provided by Quartet Theatrical Draperies.
Safety systems by Foy Lighting equipment
and special lighting effects by Four Star Lighting, Inc.

Sound equipment and technical service provided by
Masque Sound and Recording Corp.
Special effects designed and executed by
Theatre Magic, Inc., Richard Huggins, President.
Costumes executed by Barbara Matera, Ltd.
Costumes for "Hannibal" and "Masquerade"
executed by Parsons/Meares, Ltd.
Men's costumes by Vincent Costumes, Inc.
Costume crafts for "Hannibal" and "Masquerade"
by Janet Harper and Frederick Nihda.
Fabric painting by Mary Macy.
Additional costumes by Carelli Costumes, Inc.
Costume accessories by Barak Stribllng.
Hats by Woody Shelp.
Millinery and masks by Rodney Gordon.
Footwear by Sharlot Battin of Montana Leatherworks, Ltd.
Shoes by JC Theatrical and Costume Footwear & Taffy's N.Y.
Jewelry by Miriam Haskell Jewels.
Eyeglasses by H.L. Purdy.
Wigs by The Wig Party.
Garcia y Vega cigars used.
Makeup consultant Kris Evans.
Emer'gen-C super energy booster provided by Alacer Corp.

Champagne courtesy of
The Seagram Classics Wine Company

Furs by Christie Bros.

Shoes supplied by Peter Fox Limlted

"The Phantom" character make-up created and
designed by Christopher Tucker

Magic Consultant—Paul Daniels

Costumes laundered in Whirlpool equipment

CAMERON MACKINTOSH, INC.
Joint Managing Directors ....Nicholas Allott &
Matthew Dalco
Production Associate ....Shidan Majidi

THE REALLY USEFUL COMPANY INC.
Public Relations ....BROWN LLOYD JAMES/
PETER BROWN

THE REALLY USEFUL GROUP LIMITED
Directors ....THE LORD LLOYD-WEBBER
WILLIAM TAYLOR
JONATHAN HULL
JONATHAN WHEELDON

⑤ THE SHUBERT ORGANIZATION, INC.

Gerald Schoenfeld	Philip J. Smith
Chairman	President
John W. Kluge	Lee J. Seidler
Michael I. Sovern	Stuart Subotnick
Irving M. Wall	

Robert E. Wankel
Executive Vice President

Peter Entin	Elliot Greene
Vice President	Vice President
Theatre Operations	Finance
David Andrews	John Darby
Vice President	Vice President
Shubert Ticketing Services	Facilities

Exterior Metals Maintained by
Remco Maintenance Corporation.

The Phantom of the Opera | Scrapbook

Curtain call at the 17th anniversary performance at the Majestic Theatre, January 26, 2005. Right: Jeff Keller ("Monsieur Firmin") and George Lee Andrews ("Monsieur André") at the 17th anniversary party.

Memorable Fan Letters: The proposals of marriage and all kinds of other intimacies from *Phantom* fans around the world...even we understudies get a fair share of international wooing. I'm already blissfully married to Steve Ouellette, Asst. House Manager at the Gershwin.

Memorable Anniversary Gift: After attending a performance, Nicolas Cage and his new bride, Alice, sent three cases of Dom Perignon Champagne, a basket of luscious baked goods and an elegant floral arrangement to the cast, in thanks for a wonderful night. The champagne was served on stage several weeks later in celebration of the 17th anniversary of the show's Broadway run. I played the role of Carlotta on the night the Cages attended, so the bubbly in my glass tasted especially sweet.

Celebrity Visitor: The amazing Carol Burnett, on the arm of our director, Hal Prince, in the hour prior to our first performance after the devastation of September 11, 2001. Outside, the acrid smell of burning jet fuel filled the air. And inside that night, there were no stars in the room and there were no chorus people and no understudies. We were all just human beings in the midst of a tragedy, and desperate to summon the courage to fulfill every stage-actor's pledge: "The show must go on." Everybody hugged everybody, and we all clung to each other for dear life. Following our performance that night, Howard McGillin, after beautifully playing the role of the Phantom, led the company and the audience in singing a most emotional "God Bless America"...a powerful memory none of us will ever forget.

Backstage Rituals: #1) During his first 17 years with the show, Kenneth Waller present-ed fellow original-cast-mate Mary Leigh Stahl with a cookie (usually homemade by his wife, a former Phantom castmember, Linda Poser) or other some other sweet in the Stage Left quick-change room, every matinee performance, right before the "Fireman Scene," in which he played the lead Fireman.

#2) Since I've been in the show, I've initiated a ritual whereupon every woman who wears gloves in the Sitzprobe scene removes them in time to swat Raoul on the rear end as she exits into the SL quick change room, at every performance. Some of our dressers get an extra swat in, for good luck.

"Easter Bonnet"/"Gypsy": Richard Poole, Broadway veteran, has an uncanny knack for unearthing *Phantom* spoofs from every possible source. For "Gypsy" 2004, Richard staged "The Phrogdom of the Opera," a *Phantom* spoof featuring Kermit the Frog in the role of the Phantom, Miss Piggy as Pigtine Daae, etc. Thirteen cast and crew members donned Muppet costumes and brought the skit to life.

In between the "Gypsy" and the "Easter Bonnet" competitions, the *Phantom* company raised more than $40,000 in Tsunami Relief Funds over a two-week period.

For the "Easter Bonnet" competition in 2005, we focused our energy on fund-raising, dedicating our effort to the fond memory of our darling Barbara-Mae Phillips, Stage Manager and longtime BC/EFA supporter, who passed away in December after a brief but furious battle with cancer. By the end of the six-week period we had nearly a quarter of a million in donations. The *Phantom of the Opera* company took first place in the fund-raising category in its 18th year on Broadway, besting new shows with bigger houses. We thank our angel, Barbara-Mae, for showing us the way.

Favorite Moment: The brilliant opening sequence, when the Auctioneer "lights" the chandelier and causes an explosion which begins the journey of our play.

In-Theatre Gathering Place: The Majestic theatre features several: **#1)** The couch in the Phantom's dressing room is a favorite hangout for the residents of the Stage Right dressing rooms pre-show. **#2)** The Stage Right quick-change room hosts a number of different groups throughout the evening, including the entire ballet corps who sit on the floor on individual mats to help keep their costumes clean. **#3)** The Stage Manager's office also serves as a meeting place throughout the performance. Not only is that where the GOOD candy is, but the Internet provides us a chance to scope out real estate that we can't afford unless the show runs ANOTHER 18 years, and dream vacations that we only get to dream of booking. **#4)** "Naked Lady Landing" is another gathering place, but only when costume changes are taking place, hence the name.

Off-Site Hangout: Angus McIndoe, right across the street from our marquee. Barbara-Mae Phillips often held court there, surrounded by her many famous and infamous friends. Angus himself hosted BMP's post-memorial bash, and he served her favorite treats from the bar and from the menu, including one food item that Barbara-Mae had pestered him to make since the moment she set foot in the place: Buffalo Chicken Wings. Though the wings are still not on the menu, on the day of Barbara-Mae's memorial, Angus served the best tasting Buffalo Chicken Wings in the world.

Favorite Snack Foods: Let's approach this by category:

Ballet corps: Pretzels, chocolate.

Principals: Chocolate, any caffeine source, and surprisingly, hard boiled eggs.

Ensemble: Girl Scout cookies, chocolate, anything from Amy's Bread.

Crew: Kristina Miller's hot wings, hot wings, hot wings.

Orchestra: Anything home-made, but especially Norman Weiss's Blondies.

Understudies: Krispy Kreme donuts. At the put-in for any understudy, it is rather an expectation that a generous assortment of Krispy Kreme donuts will be served, paid for and delivered by the understudy in question. I once suggested substituting veggies for donuts and have since been shunned by the entire *Phantom* company.

Mascot: Kermit the Frog puppet, formerly the property of our darling Barbara-Mae Phillips. Kermit is rather worse for wear, and accompanied BMP to the "calling desk" at every performance in her tenure. Kermit is now enshrined in the Stage Manager's office, wearing a necklace of beads that have torn off of the ballerinas' *Hannibal* costumes as though they were Mardi Gras beads.

Favorite Therapy: Emergen-C (for energy and germ fighting—we've got a lot of people kissing other people in this show). Either chocolate or Jolly Rancher hard candy serve as an immediate Emergen-C chaser.

Memorable Ad-Libs: RAOUL: Should Have Been: "So, it is to be war between us. But this time, my clever friend, the disaster will be YOURS!"

Ad-lib Was: (RAOUL turned to face the audience, shaking his fists and screaming, "AAUUGGHH" for the entire duration of what would have been the speech.)

AUCTIONEER: Should Have Been: "Perhaps we may frighten away the ghost of so many years ago with a little illumination, gentlemen?"

Ad-Lib Was: "Ladies and Gentlemen, *The Phantom of the Opera!*"

MSSR. FIRMIN: Should Have Been: (In a note from the Phantom) "Gentlemen, I have now sent you several notes of the most amiable nature...."

Ad-Lib Was: (because actor was handed wrong note) "Uhhhhh, I...can't read this!"

MME. GIRY: Should Have Been: "Let her sing for you, monsieur. She has been well taught."

Ad-Lib Was: "Let her sing for you, monsieur. She has been well FED."

Memorable Stage Door Fan Encounter: A group called OGRE (Opera Ghost, Return to England) lobbied for Michael Crawford to return to London.

Heaviest/Hottest Costume: Carlotta makes her initial entrance in the heaviest costume in the show, weighing approximately 50-55 lbs. Christine wears a 40-lb. wedding dress at the end of the show. The Phantom wears the hottest costume in "Masquerade."

Who Wears The Least: The Slave Master, in the Hannibal scene.

Catchphrase: "Oh my God, the Stars!" (a choreography reference).

Sweethearts: Rebecca Eichenberger and Victor Amerling met and married while at *Phantom* on Broadway; Scott Mikita and Sarah Pfisterer, Gary Mauer and Beth Southard, Kate Wray and John Keither, and many, many others either met here, were already married here, loved here.... But the biggest contribution this show has made in the sweetheart department is in the generation of babies! So many *Phantom* babies have been born in the original Broadway run, that the company made a skit out of parading the kiddies on stage at a BC/EFA event, while singing the tune, "Make Our Garden Grow." We later reprised the song (not the skit) on "The Rosie O'Donnell Show," post-9/11.

Ghostly Encounters: The appearance of Barbara-Mae Phillips every time we walk around a corner and used to see her there. We really miss our Barbara-Mae. Also, sometimes, an actor will climb to the top of the small landing on the stage right side of the travelator and THINK they are carrying on a full conversation with an actor or crew member who is actually elsewhere in the building. We offer no explanation, but it happens all the time.

Memorable Directorial Notes: #1) From Hal Prince to George Lee Andrews and Jeff Keller, original company members, long in the roles of the Managers: "You're indicating again...I give them this note every five years or so...."

#2) From Craig Jacobs to any and all of us, on any occasion: "ACT BETTER."

#3) From Gillian Lynne to the entire cast about our physical carriage onstage: "Nipples firing, darlings. I need your nipples firing!"

Understudy Anecdote: I am very proud to be the first person to ever get to cover the roles of Christine, Carlotta and Mme. Giry simultaneously. I have appeared in all three roles during a two-plus week period this past year. On an especially fateful December I had to run to the seventh floor (where my dressing room is) to get my makeup, bra, tights, and other essentials when I went on for Christine three performances in a row. The problem was that I returned my makeup, etc. to the seventh floor following each of the performances, because we all believed that the "real" Christine would be back to perform the following show. By the time we got to performance #3, I had had it. I now keep my makeup, bra, tights, and other essentials in a cabinet outside the Hair Room in the basement of the theatre.

Superstitions: I've broken both of my feet at least once, but that's when I was touring in Lord Andrew's other gi-normous hit, *Cats.* Because of this, my mother- and sister-in-law, Allison and Sherri, refused to tell me to "Break a Leg" when I opened in *Phantom,* nor when I debuted in any of the roles I cover. They, and innumerable others, have now adopted my original pre-show wish to all cast, crew and orchestra: "Don't Suck." And yes, it is my own original backstage greeting. I started saying it to cast-mates at my teeny-tiny junior high school in Pennsylvania, and that was before most of the people who claim this phrase as their own were born. "Don't Suck" belongs to me!

Correspondent: Kris Koop Ouellette, Understudy for "Christine," "Carlotta" and "Mme. Giry."

Ballet chorus members (L-R) Dianna Warren, Polly Baird and Gianna Loungway.

The late Barbara-Mae Phillips (center) in 2002, celebrating the 6000th performance with Craig Jacobs and Bethe Ward.

Julie Hanson (Christine) and Heather McFadden (Meg Giry) at the 17th anniversary party.

Wren Marie Harrington (Carlotta) and Gregory Emanuel Rahming (Buquet).

A scene from the "Gypsy of the Year" sketch, "The Phrogdom of the Opera."

Photos by Aubrey Reuben

PLAYBILL

THE PILLOWMAN

⊗ BOOTH THEATRE

222 West 45th Street
A Shubert Organization Theatre

Gerald Schoenfeld, *Chairman*   **Philip J. Smith,** *President*

Robert E. Wankel, *Executive Vice President*

Boyett Ostar Productions   Robert Fox
Arielle Tepper   Stephanie P. McClelland   Debra Black   Dede Harris/Morton Swinsky
Roy Furman/Jon Avnet in association with Joyce Schweickert

present

BILLY CRUDUP   JEFF GOLDBLUM
ŽELJKO IVANEK   MICHAEL STUHLBARG

in

NT The National Theatre of Great Britain's
production of

THE PILLOWMAN

by MARTIN McDONAGH

with

JESSE SHANE BRONSTEIN   KATE GLEASON   RICK HOLMES
TED KŌCH   MADELEINE MARTIN   COLBY MINIFIE   VIRGINIA LOUISE SMITH

Scenic/Costume Designer
SCOTT PASK

Lighting Design
BRIAN MacDEVITT

Sound Design
PAUL ARDITTI

Music by
PADDY CUNNEEN

Casting
JIM CARNAHAN

Press Representative
BARLOW•HARTMAN

Marketing
HHC MARKETING

Production Manager
ARTHUR SICCARDI

General Management
NINA LANNAN ASSOCIATES

Fight Director
J. STEVEN WHITE

Production Stage Manager
JAMES HARKER

Directed by
JOHN CROWLEY

Special thanks to British Airways for their generous support of the National Theatre on Broadway.

4/10/05

CAST
(in order of appearance)

Tupolski ....JEFF GOLDBLUM
Katurian ....BILLY CRUDUP
Ariel ....ŽELJKO IVANEK
Michal ....MICHAEL STUHLBARG
Father ....TED KŌCH
Mother ....VIRGINIA LOUISE SMITH
Boy ....JESSE SHANE BRONSTEIN
Girl ....MADELEINE MARTIN
Man ....RICK HOLMES

UNDERSTUDIES

For Tupolski and Ariel:
TED KŌCH

for Katurian, Michal and Father:
RICK HOLMES

for Mother:
KATE GLEASON

for Boy and Girl:
COLBY MINIFIE.

2004-2005 AWARDS

DRAMA CRITICS CIRCLE AWARD
Best Foreign Play

TONY AWARDS
Scenic Design of a Play (Scott Pask),
Lighting Design of a Play
(Brian MacDevitt).

OUTER CRITICS CIRCLE AWARD
Featured Actor in a Play
(Jeff Goldblum).

DRAMA DESK AWARD
Featured Actor in a Play
(Michael Stuhlbarg).

Photo by Joan Marcus

Billy Crudup, Željko Ivanek and Jeff Goldblum in
the interrogation scene.

Billy Crudup
Katurian

Jeff Goldblum
Tupolski

Zeljko Ivanek
Ariel

Michael Stuhlbarg
Michal

Ted Koch
*Father/Standby for
Tupolski and Ariel*

Virginia Louise
Smith
Mother

Jesse Shane
Bronstein
Boy

Madeleine Martin
Girl

Rick Holmes
*Blind Man/Standby
for Katurian and
Michal*

Kate Gleason
*Standby For
Mother*

Colby Minifie
*Standby for Boy
and Girl*

Martin McDonagh
Playwright

John Crowley
Director

Scott Pask
*Scenic & Costume
Designer*

Brian MacDevitt
Lighting Designer

Jim Carnahan
Casting

J. Steven White
Fight Director

Arielle Tepper
Producer

Stephanie P.
McClelland
Producer

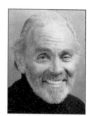

Morton Swinsky
Producer

Jon Avnet
Producer

The Pillowman

Photos by Ben Strothmann

Stage Management
Thea Gillies and Jim Harker.

Stage Crew
First Row (L-R): Chris Cronin (Associate Sound Designer), Amanda Tramontozzi ("Back Stage Guardian"), Kelly Kinsella (Dresser),
Second Row (L-R): Jimmy Keane (House Props), Denise Grillo (Prop Sub), Kathleen Gallagher (Production Wardrobe Supervisor), Jessica Chaney (Dresser).
Third Row (L-R): Brian GF McGarity (Head Electrician), Ronnie Burns (House Electrician), Thea Bradshaw Gillies (1st Asst. Stage Manager), Patrick Shea (Production Carpenter), Leone Gagliardi (Hair Supervisor), James Harker (Production Stage Manager).

Wardrobe: Kelly Kindella, Jessica Chaney and Kathleen Gallagher.

Hair: Leone Gagliardi and Tom Denier, Jr.

Front of House Staff
Front Row (L-R): Ralph Jett, Chrissy Collins, Theresa Aceves, Laurel Ann Wilson (House Manager) and Bernadette Bokun.
Back Row (L-R): Jorge Colon, Vincent Whittaker, Jaime Wilhelm, Marjorie Glover, Dara Cohen and Tim Wilhelm.

Box Office
Vincent Whittaker and Edward Whittaker.
Not Pictured: Marshall Colbrunner, Rianna Bryceland, Head Usher Katherine Coscia and Nirmala Sharma.

PRODUCTION STAFF FOR **THE PILLOWMAN**

GENERAL MANAGER
NINA LANNAN ASSOCIATES

Associate General Manager	MAGGIE EDELMAN
Company Manager	LESLIE A. GLASSBURN

GENERAL PRESS REPRESENTATIVE
BARLOW•HARTMAN PUBLIC RELATIONS

John Barlow	Michael Hartman
Dennis Crowley	Ryan Ratelle

CASTING

Jim Carnahan Casting

Carrie Gardner, Mele Nagler, CSA

JV Mercanti, Kate Schwabe,

Stephen Kopel

Production Stage Manager	James Harker
Stage Manager	Thea Bradshaw Gillies
Assistant Director	Todd Lundquist
Associate Scenic Designers	Orit Jacoby Carroll, Nancy Thun
Scenic Design Assistant	Tobin Ost
Associate Costume Designer (US)	Brian Russman
Associate Costume Designer (UK)	Irene Bohan
Associate Lighting Designer	Jason Lyons
Assistant Lighting Designer	Rachel Eichorn
Associate Sound Designer	Christopher Cronin
Makeup Design	Angelina Avallone
Hair Supervisor	Leone Gagliardi
Production Carpenter	Patrick Shea
Production Electrician	Michael Pitzer
Head Electrician	Brian G. F. McGarity
Production Sound	Christopher Cronin
Production Properties	Joe Redmond
Fight Captain	Rick Holmes
Production Wardrobe Supervisor	Kathleen Gallagher
Dressers	Jessica Chaney, Kelly Kinsella
Makeup Supervisor	Tom Denier, Jr.
Production Assistant	Bethany Russell
Lighting Intern	Ali Cruso
Assistants to Mr. Boyett	Diane Murphy, Tom Alberg
Assistant to Mr. Haber	Theresa Pisanelli
Advertising	SpotCo/Drew Hodges, Jim Edwards, Jim Aquino, Lauren Hunter
Marketing	HCC Marketing/ Hugh Hysell, Adam Jay, Michael Redman, Jillian Boeni, Matt Sicoli, Amananda Marcus, Caitlin Strype, Jason Zammit
Production Photographer	Joan Marcus
Production Web Design	Situation Marketing/ Damian Bazadona
NTNY Web Design	Dotmeta
Accounting	Fried & Kowgios CPA's LLP, Robert Fried, CPA
Controller	Anne Stewart FitzRoy, CPA

Legal Counsel	Lazarus & Harris, LLP/ Scott Lazarus, Esq., Robert Harris, Esq., David Friedlander, Esq.
Immigration Counsel	Kramer Levin Naftalis & Frankel LLP, Mark D. Koestler
General Management Associates	Kristy Bronder, Ethan Brown, Jon Ferrari, Katherine McNamee
Press Office Manager	Bethany Larsen
Press Associates	Leslie Baden, Jon Dimond, Carol Fineman, Rick Miramontez, Mark Pino, Miguel Raya, Gerilyn Shur, Andy Snyder, Wayne Wolf
Insurance	Yasmine Ramos, MARSH USA, Inc.
Banking	JP Morgan Chase
Payroll	Castellana Services, Inc.
Merchandising	Max Merchandising
Travel Agent	Andi Henig, Tzell Travel
Children's Tutoring	On-Location Education
Children's Teacher	Meryl Finger
Children's Wrangler	Bridget Walders
Sign Language Consultant	Jackie Roth

NATIONAL THEATRE, LONDON

Chairman of the NT Board	Sir Hayden Phillips
Director	Nicholas Hytner
Executive Director	Nick Starr
Assistant Producer	Tim Levy

CREDITS

Scenery constructed and painted by Hudson Scenic Studio, Inc.
Lighting and sound equipment from PRG.
UK properties constructed by the National Theatre of Great Britain.
Costumes by Barbara Matera Ltd., Tricorne Inc., Arel Studio.
Costume painting by Hochi Asiatico.

 THE SHUBERT ORGANIZATION, INC.

Gerald Schoenfeld	Philip J. Smith
Chairman	President
John W. Kluge	Lee J. Seidler
Michael I. Sovern	Stuart Subotnick

Irving M. Wall

Robert E. Wankel
Executive Vice President

Peter Entin	Elliot Greene
Vice President Theatre Operations	Vice President Finance
David Andrews	John Darby
Vice President Shubert Ticketing Services	Vice President Facilities

Custom shirts by Allmeier.
Wigs by The Wig Party.
Smoking accessories by Nat Sherman.
Rehearsed at Roundabout Rehearsal Studio.

SPECIAL THANKS

National Theatre: Katrina Gilroy, James Manley, Jason Barnes, Alison Rankin, David Milling, Nic Haffenden; Jo Nield, Suzie Fairchild and the American Associates

House Manager	Laurel A. Wilson

Opening Night Gifts: Severed toes in a black velvet bag, *Pillowman* pillows, pig cookies, pillowman hats and pig-piggy banks.

Celebrity Visitor: John Lithgow said "Welcome to the union! May I have your autograph?"

Who Performed The Most Roles: Madeleine Martin who plays three roles, Katurian's brother as a child, the little Jesus child and the little mute girl.

Who Has Done The Most Shows: Michael Stuhlbarg, who has done more than 17.

Backstage Rituals: Jeff Goldblum sings outside his window and rehearses the whole play before he goes on. Zeljko Ivanek at half hour call goes on stage and works his vocal scales. Michael Stuhlbarg becomes his character as he dresses in his costume. Billy Crudup rehearses his lines constantly. He is on stage the whole show and really never gets a break.

Favorite In-Theatre Gathering Place: My room! We had the Easter party there, and that's where the party starts before the show.

Favorite Off-Site Hangout: Angus Steakhouse.

Favorite Snack Food: Pretzels and Twizzlers.

Mascot: The Pillowman, the man-pillow. Really.

Favorite Therapy: Ricoolaaaa!!

Record Number of Cell Phone Rings: One. People are too scared to interrupt us!

Fastest Costume Change: Me! I can't keep my fans waiting.

Busiest Day at the Box Office: Every night is a busy night for us.

Heaviest/Hottest Costume: Jeff Goldblum with that gun at his side.

Memorable Directorial Note: At the end of a rehearsal, John Crowley would say, "Good Man."

Embarrassing Moment: During a rehearsal I accidentally lost my axe and it fell down to the stage from the plank.

Company In-Joke: "Knock knock—that's there—interrupting cow—interrupting c...–moo."

Catch Phrase: "Owa taggo siam." ("Oh what a goose I am.")

Coolest Thing About Being in This Show: Meeting other famous people.

Also: During the scene with the writer and the writer's brother (the scene I'm in) a man started breathing heavily and everyone told him to be quiet. Then people started calling out "call an ambulance." So the show had to completely stop and then ambulances came. Afterward, we just started the show right were we left off. Everyone thought it was an asthma attack but it was a heart attack. Thank God he turned out all right.

Correspondent: Jesse Shane Bronstein, "Boy"

At the opening party at Osteria Stella (L-R) Jeff Goldblum, Zeljko Ivanek, director John Crowley, Michael Stuhlbarg, Billy Crudup, and playwright Martin McDonagh.

Photos by Aubrey Reuben

Billy Crudup being interviewed at the opening night party.

Jeff Goldblum and Catherine Wreford on opening night.

(L-R): Zeljko Ivanek and Michael Stuhlbarg at Osteria Stella.

Madeleine Martin at the cast party.

PLAYBILL®

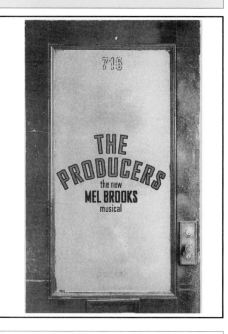

CAST
(in order of appearance)

The Usherettes	MELISSA RAE MAHON, JENNIFER SMITH
Max Bialystock	RICHARD KIND
Leo Bloom	ALAN RUCK
Hold-me Touch-me	MADELEINE DOHERTY
Mr. Marks	KEVIN LIGON
Franz Liebkind	JOHN TREACY EGAN
Carmen Ghia	BROOKS ASHMANSKAS
Roger DeBris	JONATHAN FREEMAN
Bryan	PETER MARINOS
Kevin	KEVIN LIGON
Scott	JIM BORSTELMANN
Shirley	KATHY FITZGERALD
Ulla	ANGIE SCHWORER
Lick-me Bite-me	JENNIFER SMITH
Kiss-me Feel-me	KATHY FITZGERALD
Jack Lepidus	PETER MARINOS
Donald Dinsmore	JIM BORSTELMANN
Jason Green	KEVIN LIGON
Lead Tenor	ERIC GUNHUS
Sergeant	KEVIN LIGON
O'Rourke	MIKE McGOWAN
O'Riley	CHRIS HOLLY
O'Houllihan	ROBERT H. FOWLER
Guard	JIM BORSTELMANN
Bailiff	MIKE McGOWAN
Judge	PETER MARINOS
Foreman of Jury	KATHY FITZGERALD
Trustee	KEVIN LIGON

cast continued on next page

♪ ST. JAMES THEATRE
A JUJAMCYN THEATRE
ROCCO LANDESMAN
PRESIDENT

PAUL LIBIN
PRODUCING DIRECTOR

JACK VIERTEL
CREATIVE DIRECTOR

Rocco Landesman   Clear Channel Entertainment   The Frankel • Baruch • Viertel • Routh Group
Bob and Harvey Weinstein   Rick Steiner   Robert F.X. Sillerman   Mel Brooks
In Association with James D. Stern/Douglas Meyer

present

Richard Kind   Alan Ruck

in

THE PRODUCERS

the new
Mel Brooks
musical

Book by Mel Brooks and Thomas Meehan   Music and Lyrics by Mel Brooks
and by Special Arrangement with StudioCanal

also starring

Brooks Ashmanskas   John Treacy Egan   Jonathan Freeman   Angie Schworer

With

Madeleine Doherty   Kathy Fitzgerald   Eric Gunhus
Kevin Ligon   Peter Marinos   Jennifer Smith

Jim Borstelmann   Angie C. Creighton   Robert H. Fowler   Justin Greer   Kimberly Hester   Chris Holly
Shauna Hoskin   Kimberly Catherine Jones   Renée Klapmeyer   Melissa Rae Mahon   Mike McGowan
Liz McKendry   Jessica Perrizo   Jason Patrick Sands   Patrick Wetzel   Courtney Young

Scenery Designed by	Costumes Designed by	Lighting Designed by
Robin Wagner	William Ivey Long	Peter Kaczorowski

Sound Designed by	Casting by	Original Casting by
Steve C. Kennedy	Tara Rubin Casting	Johnson-Liff Associates

Associate Director	Associate Choreographer	Wigs & Hair Designed by
Steven Zweigbaum	Warren Carlyle	Paul Huntley

Music Direction and Vocal Arrangements by	Orchestrations by	Music Coordinator
Patrick S. Brady	Doug Besterman	John Miller

General Management	Technical Supervisor	Press Representative	Associate Producers
Richard Frankel Productions Laura Green	Juniper Street Productions	Barlow • Hartman	Frederic H. and Rhoda Mayerson Jennifer Costello

Musical Arrangements and Supervision by
Glen Kelly

Direction and Choreography by
Susan Stroman

LIVE
BROADWAY

Grammy Award-winning Original Broadway Cast Recording Available On Sony Classical

3/7/05

That Face: Richard Kind (Bialystock), Angie Schworer (Ulla) and Alan Ruck (Bloom).

The Producers

MUSICAL NUMBERS

ACT ONE
New York, 1959

Scene 1: Shubert Alley
"Opening Night" ....The Ensemble
"The King of Broadway" ....Max & Ensemble

Scene 2: Max's Office, June 16, 1959
"We Can Do It" ....Max & Leo

Scene 3: The Chambers Street Offices of Whitehall and Marks
"I Wanna Be A Producer" ....Leo & The Accountants

Scene 4: Max's Office
"We Can Do It" (Reprise) ....Max & Leo

Scene 5: Max's Office Early the Following Morning

Scene 6: The Rooftop of a Greenwich Village Apartment Building
"In Old Bavaria" ....Franz
"Der Guten Tag Hop Clop" ....Franz, Max, Leo

Scene 7: The Living Room of Renowned Theatrical Director Roger Debris' Elegant Upper East Side Townhouse on a Sunny Tuesday Afternoon in June
"Keep It Gay" ....Roger, Carmen, Bryan, Kevin,
Scott, Shirley, Max, Leo

Scene 8: Max's Office
"When You Got It, Flaunt It" ....Ulla

Scene 9: Little Old Lady Land
"Along Came Bialy" ....Max, Little Old Ladies
"Act One Finale" ....Max, Leo, Franz, Ulla, Roger, Carmen,
Bryan, Kevin, Scott, Shirley, Ensemble

ACT TWO

Scene 1: Max's Office, late morning, a few weeks later
"That Face" ....Leo, Ulla, Max

Scene 2: The Bare Stage of a Broadway Theatre
"Haben Sie Gehoert Das Deutsche Band?" ....Jason, Franz

Scene 3: Shubert Alley
"Opening Night" (Reprise) ....The Usherettes
"You Never Say 'Good Luck' On Opening Night" ....Roger, Max, Carmen, Franz, Leo

Scene 4: The Stage of The Shubert Theatre
"Springtime For Hitler" ....Lead Tenor, Roger, Ulla, Ensemble

Scene 5: Max's Office, later that night
"Where Did We Go Right?" ....Max, Leo

Scene 6: The Holding Cell of a New York Courthouse, ten days later.
"Betrayed" ....Max

Scene 7: A New York Courtroom
"'Til Him" ....Leo, Max

Scene 8: Sing Sing
"Prisoners Of Love" ....The Convicts

Scene 9: The Stage of The Shubert Theatre
"Prisoners Of Love" (continued) ....Roger, Ulla, The Ensemble

Scene 10: Shubert Alley
"Prisoners of Love (Reprise): Leo and Max" ....Leo, Max

Curtain Call
"Goodbye!" ....The Company

Cast Continued

THE ENSEMBLE
Jim Borstelmann, Madeleine Doherty,
Kathy Fitzgerald, Robert H. Fowler,
Eric Gunhus, Kimberly Hester, Chris
Holly, Shauna Hoskin, Kimberly Catherine Jones,
Renée Klapmeyer, Kevin Ligon, Melissa Rae Mahon,
Peter Marinos, Mike McGowan, Jessica Perrizo,
Jennifer Smith

SWINGS
Angie C. Creighton, Justin Greer, Liz McKendry,
Jason Patrick Sands, Patrick Wetzel, Courtney Young

UNDERSTUDIES
MAX BIALYSTOCK: John Treacy Egan, Kevin Ligon;
LEO BLOOM: Brooks Ashmanskas, Justin Greer, Patrick
Wetzel; FRANZ LIEBKIND: Jim Borstelmann, Kevin
Ligon, Patrick Wetzel; CARMEN GHIA: Justin Greer,
Patrick Wetzel; ROGER DE BRIS: Jim Borstelmann,
John Treacy Egan, Kevin Ligon; ULLA: Renée Klapmeyer,
Melissa Rae Mahon.

ORCHESTRA
CONDUCTOR: PATRICK S. BRADY

Associate Conductor: PHIL RENO

Woodwinds:
Vincent Della Rocca, Steven J. Greenfield, Jay
Hassler, Alva F. Hunt, Frank Santagata

Trumpets:
David Rogers, Nick Marchione, Frank Greene

Tenor Trombones:
Dan Levine, Tim Sessions

Bass Trombone:
Chris Olness

French Horn:
Nancy Billman

Concert Master:
Rick Dolan

Violins:
Ashley D. Horne, Louise Owen,
Karen M. Karlsrud, Helen Kim

Cello:
Laura Bontrager

Harp:
Anna Reinersman

String Bass:
Robert Renino

Drums:
Larry Lelli

Percussion:
Benjamin Herman

Keyboard:
Phil Reno

Music Coordinator: JOHN MILLER
Additional Orchestrations: LARRY BLANK

The Producers

Richard Kind
Max Bialystock

Alan Ruck
Leo Bloom

Brooks Ashmanskas
Carmen Ghia

John Treacy Egan
Franz Liebkind

Jonathan Freeman
Roger DeBris

Angie Schworer
Ulla

Madeleine Doherty
Hold-Me Touch-Me

Kathy Fitzgerald
Shirley, Kiss-me Feel-me, Foreman of Jury

Eric Gunhus
Lead Tenor

Kevin Ligon
Mr. Marks, Kevin, Jason Green, Sergeant, Trustee

Peter Marinos
Bryan, Jack Lepidus, Judge

Jennifer Smith
Usherette, Lick-Me Bite-Me

Jim Borstelmann
Blind Violinist, Scott, Donald Dinsmore, Guard

Angie C. Creighton
Swing

Robert H. Fowler
O'Houllihan

Justin Greer
Swing

Kimberly Hester
Ensemble

Chris Holly
O'Riley

Shauna Hoskin
Ensemble

Kimberly Catherine Jones
Ensemble

Renée Klapmeyer
Ensemble

Melissa Rae Mahon
Usherette

Mike McGowan
O'Rourke, Bailiff

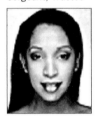
Liz McKendry
Swing

Jessica Perrizo
Dance Captain, Ensemble

Jason Patrick Sands
Swing

Patrick Wetzel
Swing

Courtney Young
Resident Choreographer, Swing

Mel Brooks
Book, Composer & Lyricist, Producer

Thomas Meehan
Book

Susan Stroman
Director/ Choreographer

Robin Wagner
Set Design

William Ivey Long
Costume Designer

Peter Kaczorowski
Lighting Designer

The Producers

Johnson-Liff Associates/Tara Rubin
Casting

Paul Huntley
Wig and Hair Design

Doug Besterman
Orchestrations

John Miller
Music Coordinator

Richard Frankel
General Manager

Juniper Street Productions
Guy Kwan, John Paull, Hillary Blanken,
Kevin Broomell, Ana-Rose Greene
Technical Supervisors

Rocco Landesman
Producer

Harvey and Bob Weinstein
Producers

Rick Steiner
Producer

Robert F.X.
Sillerman
Producer

Frederic H.
Mayerson
Associate Producer

Rhoda Mayerson
Associate Producer

Roger Bart
Leo Bloom

Gary Beach
Roger DeBris

Justin Bohon
O'Riley

Jennifer Clippinger
Usherette

Hunter Foster
Leo Bloom

Adrienne Gibbons
Swing

James Gray
O'Rourke/Bailiff

Stacey Todd Holt
Swing

Brad Musgrove
Carmen Ghia

Brad Oscar
Max Bialystock

Larry Raben
Swing

Lisa Rothauser
Hold-Me Touch-Me

Jenny-Lynn Suckling
Ensemble

Tracy Terstriep
Ensemble

The Producers

Staff for THE PRODUCERS

GENERAL MANAGEMENT
RICHARD FRANKEL PRODUCTIONS
Richard Frankel,
Marc Routh, Laura Green,
Rod Kaats, Jo Porter, Joe Watson

COMPANY MANAGER
Kathy Lowe
Associate Company Manager . . . . .Jackie Newman

GENERAL PRESS REPRESENTATIVE
BARLOW • HARTMAN
John Barlow   Michael Hartman
Rick Miramontez   Jon Dimond

CASTING
TARA RUBIN CASTING
Tara Rubin
Dunja Vitolic, Eric Woodall,
Laura Schutzel, Mona Slomsky

Production Stage Manager . . . . .Steven Zweigbaum
Stage Manager . . . . .Ira Mont
Assistant Stage Managers . . . . .Alexis
Shorter,
Casey Aileen Rafter, Julia P. Jones
Associate Choreographer . . . . .Warren Carlyle
Assistant Director . . . . .Scott Bishop
Assistant Choreographer . . . . .Lisa Shriver
Resident Choreographer . . . . .Courtney Young
Dance Captain . . . . .Jessica Perrizo
Technical Supervisor . . . . .Juniper Street Productions
Hillary Blanken, John H. Paul III
Associates . . . . .Kevin Broomell,
Lonnie Goertz, Guy Kwan
Associate Set Designer . . . . .David Peterson
Assistant Set Designers . . . . .Atkin Pace, Thomas Peter
Sarr
Associate Costume Designer . . . . .Martha Bromelmeier
Assistant Costume Designer . . . . .Tom Beall
Assistants to William Ivey Long . . . . .Laura
Oppenheimer,
Heather Bair
Automated Light Programmer . . . . .Josh Weitzman
First Assistant Lighting Designer . . . . .Paul Miller
Assistant Lighting Designers . . . . .Mick Addison Smith,
Philip S. Rosenberg
Associate Sound Designer . . . . .John Shivers
Supervising Production Carpenter . . . . .Joe Patria
Head Carpenter . . . . .Jack Cennamo
Assistant Carpenters . . . . .Michael Cennamo,
Christopher Morcone, Guy Patria,
Richard Patria
Supervising Production Electrician . . . . .Rick Baxter
Head Electrician . . . . .Joe Pearson
Assistant Electrician . . . . .Tom Ferguson
Head Sound Engineer . . . . .David Gotwald
Assistant Sound Engineer . . . . .Scott Silvian
Supervising Property Master . . . . .Laura Koch
Wardrobe Supervisor . . . . .Douglas C. Petitjean
Assistant Wardrobe Supervisor . . . . .Dede LaBarre
Mr. Kind's Dresser . . . . .Terry Lavada
Mr. Ruck's Dresser .Scotty Cain
Dressers . . . . .Laura Beattie,
Dennis Birchall, Jessica Dermody, Ron Fleming,
Susie Ghebresillassie, Constance Holpern,
Jessica Minczeski, Shannon Munn,
John Rinaldi, Roy Seiler, Sunny Vedrine
Wig Supervisor . . . . .Michele Rutter
Assistant Wig Supervisor . . . . .Ron Mack
Wig Stylists . . . . .Leah Bosworth,
Judith Farley Haugh, Shanah-Ann Kendall

MAKE UP DESIGN . . . . . .RANDY HOUSTON MERCER

Music Coordinator .John Miller
Assistant Music Coordinator . . . . .Todd Cutrona

Assistant to Mr. Miller . . . . .Matthew P. Ettinger
Associate Conductor .Philip Reno
Synthesizer Programming . . . . .Music Arts Technologies/
Brett Sommer
Rehearsal Drummer . . . . .Cubby O'Brien
Music Preparation . . . . .Miller Music Services
Additional Orchestrations . . . . .Larry Blank
Make-up Consultant . . . . .Melissa Silver
Physical Therapy Services . . . . .PhysioArts
Associate to Mr. Brooks . . . . .Leah Zappy
Assistant to Mr. Brooks . . . . .Lale Arpaci
Asst. to Mr. Landesman . . . . .Nicole Kastrinos
Assts. to Mr. Sillerman . . . . .Gini Smythe,
Matthew Morse, Manuela Perea
Asst. to Mr. Steiner . . . . .Kathy Wall
Asst. to Mr. Stern . . . . .Debbie Bisno, Leah Callaghan
Asst. to Mr. Baruch . . . . .Sonja Soper
Asst. to Mr. Viertel . . . . .Tania Senewiratne
Management Assistant . . . . .Kevin Meyers
Production Assistants . . . . .Kate Sullivan,
Donald Fried, Erin J. Riggs,
Leah Richardson, Sharon Del Pilar
Advertising . . . . .Serino Coyne, Inc., Nancy Coyne,
Sandy Block, Thomas Mygatt,
Brad Lapin, Jennifer Richman
Promotions/Marketing . . . . .The Marketing Group
Photographers . . . . .Paul Kolnik, Norman Jean Roy
Theatre Displays .King Displays
Insurance . . . . .Marsh USA Inc., Margery Boyar
Legal Counsel . . . . .Elliott Brown, Jason Baruch,
Franklin Weinrib,
Rudell & Vassallo, P.C.,
Alan U. Schwartz,
Manatt, Phelps & Phillips, LLP
Banking .Chase Manhattan Bank,
Stephanie Daulton, Michelle Gibbons
Payroll Service . . . . .Castellana Service, Inc.
Accounting . . . . .Lutz & Carr
Travel Agencies . . . . .JMC Travel,
Navigant International
Exclusive Tour Direction . . . . .On The Road,
The Booking Group
On-Stage Merchandising . . . . .George Fenmore/
More Merchandising International
Concessions . . . . .Clear Channel Entertainment,
Theatrical Merchandising
New York Rehearsals . . . . .The New 42nd Street Studios
Opening Night Coordinator . . . . .Tobak-Dantchik
Events and Promotions/
Suzanne Tobak, Jennifer Falik, Rebakah Sale

RICHARD FRANKEL PRODUCTIONS STAFF
Finance Director . . . . .Ann Caprio
Assistant to Mr. Frankel . . . . .Anthony Taccetta
Assistant to Mr. Routh . . . . .Michael Sag
Assistant to Ms. Green . . . . .Adam M. Muller
Assistant Finance Director . . . . .Liz Hines
Information Technology Manager . . . . .Roddy Pimentel
Management Assistant . . . . .Heidi Schading
Accounting Assistant . . . . .Elsie Jamin-Maguire
National Sales and Marketing Director . . . . . .Ronni Mandell
Director of Business Affairs . . . . .Carter McGowan
Booking Director . . . . .Siobhan O'Neill
Director of Tour Management . . . . .Simma Levine
Marketing Assistant . . . . .Jocelyn Laporte
Booking Assistant . . . . .ElizBeth Anne Jones
Office Manager . . . . .Lori Steiger-Perry
Office Assistant . . . . .Stephanie Kennedy
Receptionist . . . . .D'Arcy
Drollinger,
Alec Walker
Interns . . . . .Fran Acuna, Danny Bergold,
Alia Rose Connor, Alex Edwards,
Lev Gartman, Megan Lyle,
Lauren Pokras, John Retsios,
Robert Scherzer, Samantha Weber

CLEAR CHANNEL ENTERTAINMENT —
THEATRICAL

Miles C. Wilkin, Scott Zeiger, Steve Winton,
David Anderson, Lauren Reid, Lynn Blandford, Bradley
Broecker, Jennifer Costello,
Jennifer DeLange, Joanna Hagan, Eric Joseph,
Susan Krajsa, David Lazar, Hailey Lustig,
Drew Murphy, Debra Peltz, Denise Perry,
Courtney Pierce, Alison Spiriti, Dan Swartz

MAKE-UP COURTESY OF MAC COSMETICS

CREDITS AND ACKNOWLEDGEMENTS
Scenery and scenic effects built, painted, electrified and
automated by Showmotion, Inc., Norwalk, Ct.;
Scenery fabrication by Entolo/Scenic Technologies,
a division of Production Resource Group, L.L.C., New
Windsor, NY; Additional scenery built by Hudson Scenic
Studios; Scenery automation by Showmotion, Inc.,
using the Autocue Computerized Motion Control System;
Show control and scenic motion control featuring Stage
Command Systems by Entolo, a division of Production
Resource Group, L.L.C., New Windsor, NY; Soft goods by I.
Weiss, New York; Water fountain effect by Waltzing Waters;
Stormtrooper puppets designed and fabricated by Eoin Sprott;
Tanks and pigeon puppets designed and fabricated by Jerard
Studio; Lighting equipment from Fourth Phase New Jersey;
Sound equipment from ProMix

Costumes by Euro Co., Timberlake Studios, Inc.,
Tricorne New York City, Jennifer Love Costumes

Tailoring by Scafatti Custom Tailors; Shoes by LaDuca Shoes
NYC, T.O. Dey; Hosiery provided by Hue

Specialty props fabricated by Prism Production Services,
Rahway, N.J.; Max's office furniture, the script stacks and
Roger's furniture by the Rabbit's Choice; Assorted hand props
by Jennie Marino, Moon Boot Prod.; Vintage lighting fixture
courtesy of Four Star Lighting; MP40 Schmeissers machine
guns by Costume Armour; Walkers through J & J Medical
Supplies, Teaneck, NJ; Champagne by Mumm's; Krylon spray
paint by Siperstein's Paints;

Custom shirts by Cego; Millinery by Rodney Gordon and
Henry Ewoskio; Showgirl specialty costumes by
Martin Adams; Set poster art by Jim Miller;
Lozenges provided by Ricola, Inc.;
Parker jotter pens courtesy of the Parker Corporation.

MUSIC CREDITS
Words and Music by Mel Brooks.
Songs published by Mel Brooks Music, except for
"Have You Ever Heard the German Band," "Springtime for
Hitler" and "Prisoners of Love," published by
Legation Music Corp.

JUJAMCYN THEATERS

ROCCO LANDESMAN
President

PAUL LIBIN   JACK VIERTEL
Producing Director   Creative Director

JERRY ZAKS

DANIEL ADAMIAN   JENNIFER HERSHEY
General Manager   Director of Operations

STAFF FOR THE ST. JAMES THEATRE
Manager . . . . .Daniel Adamian
Treasurer . . . . .Vincent Sclafani
Carpenter . . . . .Timothy McDonough
Propertyman .Barnett Epstein
Electrician . . . . .Albert Sayers
Engineer . . . . .James Higgins

The Producers

Photos by Ben Strohmann

Front-of-House Staff

Back Row: Scott Rippe

Middle Row (L-R): Leonard Baron, Jim Barry, Michelle Cairol, Donna Vanderlinden, Catherine Junior, Hal Goldberg, Cynthia Lopiano, Heather Jewels.

Front Row (L-R): Erica Engstrom, Tyzok Wharton and Christine Ehren.

Box Office
(L-R): Vinny Sclafani, Jeff Nevin and Vinny Siniscalchi.

Wardrobe and Wig Department

Kneeling/Sitting (L-R): Roy Seiler, Dennis Birchall, Terry LaVada, Julie Alderfer, Mary Kay Yezerski, Ron Mack.

Front Standing Row (L-R): Connie Holperin, Dede LaBarre, Michele Rutter, Jessica Dermody.

Back Row (L-R): Judith Haugh, Douglas Petitjean, Laura Beattie, Susie Ghebresillassie, Jessica Minczeski, Shanah Kendall, Scotty Cain, Misty Fernandez and Ron Fleming.

Stage Management
(L-R): Steven Zweigbaum, Alexis Shorter and Ira Mont.

Electricians, Props Department, Lighting and Carpentry

Front Row (L-R): Al Sayers, Joe Pearson, Steve Pugliesi, Laura Koch, Jack Cennamo, Bob Miller, Jim Devins and Tom Ferguson.

Back Row (L-R): Tom Galinski, Tim McDonough Jr., Todd D'Aiuto and Joe Caputo.

279

Backstage Ritual: When the stage manager calls places, we all go to the stage, even the principals who aren't in the first number, and mill around on the stage behind the closed curtain and say hello. When the overture begins we stand behind the Shubert Theatre set. It's our way of coming together as a company.

Catchphrase: "Not you."

Who Got The Gypsy Robe: Jennifer Smith

Easter Bonnet Skit: "La Dame Orange" by Jennifer Smith and Louiguy.

"Carols For A Cure" Carol: "A Christmas Carol."

In-Theatre Gathering Place: The big prop room offstage left. Every Sunday we have brunch with bagels and cream cheese before the matinee.

Off-Site Hangout: The company goes to Angus McIndoe right next door to the theatre. I like Joe Allen.

Therapies: Throat stuff: Ricola, Throat-Coat Tea, Thayer's Slippery Elm Lozenges, Luden's Wild Cherry Throat Drops. And yoga.

Snacks: Sugars! Chocolate, Snickers, York Peppermint Patties and, in the fall, all kinds of trick-or-treat candy.

Strange Audience Encounter: A cute little Italian man with a moustache and goatee kept appearing at the stage door trying to get me to take some papers he was carrying. I thought they were religious pamphlets or something. One night I took them, and it turned out he had written a play and he wanted to meet Mel Brooks. Two nights later he showed up again, only this time he had shaved off the left side of his moustache and goatee and said he had more plays. I told him he should get an agent. It was slightly strange.

Memorable Ad-lib: The night Nathan Lane and Matthew Broderick came back in the show, Nathan worked in a remark about President Bush. But it turned out we had Laura Bush and her daughters in the audience, so it wasn't the funniest moment.

Record Number Of Phone Rings: Two.

Heaviest Costumes: The chorus girls who wear the crazy German costumes in "Springtime for Hitler": the ones with giant pretzels, beer steins and sausages for hats.

Who Wore The Least: Coincidentally, the same girls in the same costumes.

Celebrity Visitor: Dave Wannstedt, coach of the Miami Dolphins. We talked about the similarities of sports and theatre, like we both have to perform eight times a week.

Also: In an upper floor hallway the stage managers have been putting up the full-page ads from the *Times* from throughout the run. There's the first ad with Nathan Lane and Matthew Broderick, the Tony nominations, the Tony wins, and Weber and I coming in. They have every ad and every window card. Now that we've been running four years, that hallway is like a walk back in time.

Correspondent: Brad Oscar, "Max Bialystock"

Left: Matthew Broderick, Angie Schworer and Alan Ruck. Right: Brad Oscar models the Gypsy Robe in the annual "Gypsy of the Year" opening number.

Left: Cast members celebrate the arrival of new leads Richard Kind and Alan Ruck at Angus McIndoe restaurant. Right: Chorus girls surround Hunter Foster at the "Broadway on Broadway" event.

Left: Matthew Broderick and Alec Baldwin participate in opening day of the Broadway Softball League. *The Producers* will go on to win the championship for the third time in four years. Right: Ruck and Kind get some tips from the master: composer/librettist Mel Brooks.

PLAYBILL®

A RAISIN IN THE SUN
by Lorraine Hansberry

CAST

(in order of appearance)

Ruth Younger .... AUDRA McDONALD
Travis Younger ...... ALEXANDER MITCHELL
Walter Lee Younger .... SEAN COMBS
Beneatha Younger .... SANAA LATHAN
Lena Younger .... PHYLICIA RASHAD
Joseph Asagai .... TEAGLE F. BOUGERE
George Murchison .... FRANK HARTS
Karl Lindner .... DAVID AARON BAKER
Bobo .... BILL NUNN
Moving Men .... LAWRENCE BALLARD,
BILLY EUGENE JONES

UNDERSTUDIES

For Walter Lee — BILLY EUGENE JONES; for
Bobo — BILLY EUGENE JONES, CYRUS
FARMER; for Ruth and Beneatha — HEATHER
ALICIA SIMMS; for Lena — GRETA OGLESBY;
for Lindner — MARTIN KILDARE; for Asagai
and George — LAWRENCE BALLARD, CYRUS
FARMER; for Travis — AARON PANNELL; for
Moving Men — CYRUS FARMER.

SETTING

Chicago's Southside in the 1950s

⊛ ROYALE THEATRE

242 West 45th Street
A Shubert Organization Theatre

Gerald Schoenfeld, *Chairman*   Philip J. Smith, *President*

Robert E. Wankel, *Executive Vice President*

David Binder

Vivek J. Tiwary   Susan Batson

Carl Rumbaugh   Ruth Hendel   Jayne Baron Sherman   Dede Harris

Arielle Tepper   *in association with*
Barbara Whitman   Cynthia Stroum

present

Sean Combs
Audra McDonald
Phylicia Rashad
Sanaa Lathan

in

a play by

Lorraine Hansberry

David Aaron Baker   Lawrence Ballard   Teagle F. Bougere
Frank Harts   Billy Eugene Jones   Alexander Mitchell

and

Bill Nunn

set design	costume design	lighting design
Thomas Lynch	Paul Tazewell	Brian MacDevitt

sound design	composer	casting
T. Richard Fitzgerald	Dwight Andrews	James Calleri, C.S.A.

production management	associate producer/marketing director	associate producers	production stage manager
Gene O'Donovan	Eric Schnall	Brian Savelson Hal Goldberg	Michael Brunner

press	company manager	general management
The Publicity Office	G. Eric Muratalla	Robert Cole Productions Lisa M. Poyer

directed by

Kenny Leon

5/3/04

A Dream Deferred: Audra McDonald and Sean Combs as Ruth and Walter Lee Younger.

Sean Combs
Walter Lee Younger

Audra McDonald
Ruth Younger

Phylicia Rashad
Lena Younger

Sanaa Lathan
Beneatha Younger

David Aaron Baker
Karl Lindner

Lawrence Ballard
*Moving Man/
Understudy*

Teagle F. Bougere
Joseph Asagai

Frank Harts
George Murchiso

Billy Eugene Jones
*Moving Man/
Understudy*

Alexander Mitchell
Travis Younger

Bill Nunn
Bobo

Cyrus Farmer
Understudy

Martin Kildare
Understudy

Greta Oglesby
Understudy

Aaron Pannell
Understudy

Heather Alicia
Simms
Understudy

Lorraine Hansberry
Playwright

Kenny Leon
Director

Thomas Lynch
Scenic Designer

Brian MacDevitt
Lighting Designer

Dwight Andrews
Composer

James Calleri
Casting

Patdro Harris
Choreographer

Kate Wilson
*Dialect & Vocal
Coach*

David Binder
Producer

Susan Batson
Producer

Carl Rumbaugh
Producer

Ruth Hendel
Producer

Jayne Baron
Sherman
Producer

Dede Harris
Producer

Arielle Tepper
Producer

Barbara
Whitman
Producer

Cynthia Stroum
Producer

Eric Schnall
*Assoc.
Producer/
Marketing Dir.*

Brian Savelson
*Associate
Producer*

Hal Goldberg
*Associate
Producer*

A Raisin in the Sun

Photo by Joan Marcus

Alexander Mitchell, Audra McDonald and Phylicia Rashad.

Photos by Aubrey Reuben

Above left: Sanaa Lathan and Sean "P. Diddy" Combs arrive at Radio City Music Hall for the 2004 Tony Awards. Right: Audra McDonald wins her fourth Tony.

Phylicia Rashad enters the Tony press room with her newly won 2004 Tony as Best Actress in a Play.

John Lithgow with Sean Combs at Radio City.

Carol Channing and Audra McDonald at the 2004 Tony Awards.

Best Opening Night Opening Night Gift: First issue of Spider-man.

Most Exciting Celebrity Visitor: Denzel Washington, who told me, "You did great." There were always lots of celebrities, with at least five or six huge stars at any given show, and they'd all come backstage afterwards.

Actor Who Performed The Most Roles in This Show: Heather Alicia Simms

Who Has Done The Most Shows: Phylicia Rashad

Special Backstage Ritual: Holding hands and praying.

Favorite Moment During Each Performance (On Stage Or Off): Playing checkers with the dressers.

Favorite In-Theatre Gathering Place: The Royale basement for brunch and birthdays.

Favorite Snack Food: French fries.

Favorite Therapy: Ricola

Record Number Of Cell Phone Rings: At least ten.

Stage Door Fan Encounter: A man from Africa asked for my autograph. He was very excited and didn't speak any English. The stage door was wild with huge crowds after every show.

Latest Audience Arrival: Forty minutes.

Fastest Costume Change: Phylicia Rashad

Busiest Day At The Box Office: Every day! People started lining up every day at 6 AM.

Memorable Directorial Note: "Stay loud."

Most Embarrassing Moment: I slammed into a closed door and fell!

Company Legends: Phylicia Rashad, Audra McDonald, Sean Combs.

Superstition That Turned Out To Be True: Whistling in the theatre.

Correspondent: Alexander Mitchell, "Travis"

(L-R): Idina Menzel, Hugh Jackman, Phylicia Rashad and Jefferson Mays hold their Tonys.

PLAYBILL®

BILTMORE THEATRE

MANHATTAN THEATRE CLUB

Artistic Director
LYNNE MEADOW

Executive Producer
BARRY GROVE

and

SECOND STAGE THEATRE

Artistic Director
CAROLE ROTHMAN

Executive Director
TIMOTHY J. McCLIMON

Present

Reckless

by

CRAIG LUCAS

with

CARSON ELROD   OLGA MEREDIZ   DEBRA MONK
MICHAEL O'KEEFE   MARY-LOUISE PARKER
ROSIE PEREZ   THOMAS SADOSKI

Set Design
ALLEN MOYER

Costume Design
MICHAEL KRASS

Lighting Design
CHRISTOPHER AKERLIND

Original Music and Sound Design
DAVID VAN TIEGHEM

Production Stage Manager
JAMES FITZSIMMONS

Directed by

MARK BROKAW

Casting
**NANCY PICCIONE/
DAVID CAPARELLIOTIS
TARA RUBIN**

*Director of
Artistic Operations*
MANDY GREENFIELD

Production Manager
RYAN McMAHON

Director of Development
JENNIFER ZASLOW

Director of Marketing
DEBRA A. WAXMAN

Press Representative
BONEAU/BRYAN-BROWN

General Manager
HAROLD WOLPERT

*Director of
Artistic Development*
PAIGE EVANS

*Director of
Artistic Production*
MICHAEL BUSH

MANHATTAN THEATRE CLUB WISHES TO EXPRESS ITS APPRECIATION TO THEATRE DEVELOPMENT FUND FOR ITS SUPPORT OF THIS PRODUCTION.

12/6/04

CAST
(in order of appearance)

Rachel .... MARY-LOUISE PARKER
Tom .... THOMAS SADOSKI
Lloyd .... MICHAEL O'KEEFE
Pooty .... ROSIE PEREZ
Roy .... CARSON ELROD
Trish .... OLGA MEREDIZ
Doctors One through Six .... DEBRA MONK
Tim Timko .... CARSON ELROD
Talk Show Host .... CARSON ELROD
Sue .... ROSIE PEREZ
Man in Ski Mask .... THOMAS SADOSKI
Woman Patient .... OLGA MEREDIZ
Tom Junior .... THOMAS SADOSKI

Fight Director – RICK SORDELET
Stage Manager – JILL CORDLE

UNDERSTUDIES

For Rachel, Pooty/Sue – JENNIFER MUDGE;
For Trish, Woman Patient, Doctors One through
Six – MARGO SKINNER; For Tom, Lloyd, Roy,
Tim Timko, Talk Show Host, Man in Ski Mask,
Tom Junior – CURTIS MARK WILLIAMS

Olga Merediz and Mary-Louise Parker in *Reckless.*

Photo by Joan Marcus

Carson Elrod
Roy/Tim Timko/
Talk Show Host

Olga Merediz
Trish/Woman
Patient

Debra Monk
Doctors One
through Six

Michael O'Keefe
Lloyd

Mary-Louise Parker
Rachel

Rosie Perez
Pooty/Sue

Thomas Sadoski
Tom/Tom Jr./Man
In Ski Mask

Craig Lucas
Playwright

Mark Brokaw
Director

Allen Moyer
Set Design

Christopher
Akerlind
Lighting Design

Lynne Meadow
Artistic Director,
Manhattan Theatre
Club

Barry Grove
Exec. Producer,
Manhattan Theatre
Club

Photo by Ben Strohmann

The Biltmore Theatre Crew
Bottom Row (L-R): Alexis Kanfer—Wigs; Steven Clopper—Asst. Box Office Treasurer; Johannah-Joy Magyawe—Asst. House Manager; Shanna Spinello—Production Asst.; Margiann Flanagan—Dresser; Stephen "Crash" Burns—Flyman; Caroline Andersen—Production Asst.; Denise Cooper—Company Manager; Patrick Murray—Flyman.
Middle Row (L-R): Wendy Wright—Usher; Kathleen White—Usher; Jill Cordle—Stage Manager; Renee Hicks—Ticket Taker; David Dillon—Box Office Treasurer; Barry Hoff—Dresser; Michael Growler—Wardrobe Supervisor; Sue Poulin—Apprentice.
Top Row (L-R): Sarah Brodsky—Usher; Edward Brashear—Usher; Bruce Dye—Usher; Louis Shapiro—Sound Engineer; Tim Walters—Head Propertyman; James FitzSimmons—Production Stage Manager; Obadiah Savage—Apprentice; Ted Rounsaville—Asst. House Manager; Jeff Dodson—Master Electrician; Chris Wiggins—Head Carpenter.
Not Pictured: Valerie Simmons (Biltmore Theatre Manager).

MANHATTAN THEATRE CLUB ADMINISTRATIVE STAFF

Artistic Director ....Lynne Meadow
Executive Producer ....Barry Grove
General Manager ....Harold Wolpert
Director of Artistic Production ....Michael Bush
Director of Artistic Development ....Paige Evans
Director of Artistic Operations ....Mandy Greenfield
Artistic Associate/
Asst. to the Artistic Director ....Amy Gilkes Loe
Artistic Assistants..............William Cusick, Lisa Dozier
Director of Casting ....Nancy Piccione
Casting Director ....David Caparelliotis
Casting Assistant...........................Jennifer McCool
Literary Manager ....Emily Shooltz
Play Development Associate/
Sloan Project Manager ....Aaron Leichter
Play Development Assistant..................Lara Mottolo
Director of Musical
Development ....Clifford Lee Johnson III
Director of Writers in Performance ....Steve Lawson
Director of Development ....Jennifer Zaslow
Director, Corporate Relations ....Lauren Rabin
Director, Individual Giving ....Casey Reitz
Director, Planning and Projects ....Blake West
Director, Foundation and
Government Relations ....Josh Jacobson
Manager, Individual Giving ....Allison Goldstein
Senior Associate, Corporate Relations ....Scott Pyne
Development Associates ....Belinda Batson,
Stacey Cloninger
Development Associate/
Database Coordinator ....Rey Pamatmat
Patrons' Liaison ....Antonello Di Benedetto
Director of Marketing ....Debra A. Waxman
Associate Director of Marketing ....Wendy Hutton
Marketing Associate/Website Manager ......Ryan M. Klink
Director of Finance &
Administration ....Michael P. Naumann
Business Manager ....Holly Kinney
Business Associate ....Denise Thomas
HR/Payroll Manager ....Paula Reneau
Business Assistant ....Thomas Casazzone
Manager of Systems Operations ....Avishai Cohen
Systems Analyst ....Andrew Dumawal
Associate General Manager ....Seth Shepsle
Company Manager/NY City Center ....Lindsey T. Brooks
Assistant to the Executive Producer ....Erin Day
Director of Subscriber Services ....Robert Allenberg
Associate Subscriber Services Manager ......Andrew Taylor
Company Representatives ....Channon Booth,
Susan Jordan White
Subscriber Services Representatives ....Alva Chinn,
Matthew Praet,
Rosanna Consalvo Sarto
Director of Telesales and Telefunding ....George Tetlow
Assistant Manager ....Terrence Burnett
Director of Education....................David Shookhoff
Asst. Director of Education/
Coordinator, Paul A. Kaplan
Theatre Management Program ....Jamie Beth Schindler
Education Assistants ....Kayla Cagan, Jackie McDonnell
MTC Teaching Artists ....Stephanie Alston,
David Auburn, Carl Capotorto,
Chris Ceraso, Charlotte Colavin,
Andy Goldberg, Elise Hernandez,
Jeffrey Joseph, Lou Moreno,
Michaela Murphy, Melissa Murray,
Angela Pietropinto, Carmen Rivera,
Judy Tate, Candido Tirado,
Joe White
Paul A. Kaplan Theatre Management
Interns ....Emily Bohannon,
Mark Bowers, Steven (Tevy) Bradley,
David Carson, Greg Cooper,
Nicole Gaignat, Kel Haney,
Tarrah Hirsch, Molly Kramer,
Jennifer Leeson, Annie MacRae,
Jenna Parks, Aaron Paternoster,
Joshua Randall, Rebecca Sherman,
Shanna Spinello, Meagan Swiney,
Danny Williams

Randy Carrig Casting Intern ....Rosemary Rodriguez
Reception/Studio Manager ....Lauren Snyder
Production Manager ....Ryan McMahon
Associate Production Manager ....Bridget Markov
Assistant Production Manager ....Ian McNaugher
Technical Director ....Bill Mohney
Assistant Technical Director ....Adam Lang
Assistant Technical Director ....Benjamin Lampman
Assistant Technical Director ....Brian Morrill
Carpenters ....Brian Corr, Shayne Izatt,
Nicholas Morales
Scenic Painting Supervisor ....Pamela Lenau
Lights and Sound Supervisor ....Willy Corpus
Properties Supervisor ....Scott Laule
Assistant Properties Supervisor ....Arlene Marshall
Props Carpenter..............................Peter Grimes
Costume Supervisor ....Erin Hennessy Dean
Assistant Costume Supervisor ....Michelle Sesco

GENERAL PRESS REPRESENTATIVES
BONEAU/BRYAN-BROWN
Chris Boneau   Jim Byk
Aaron Meier

Design Associate ....John Lee Beatty
Script Readers ....Liz Jones, Talya Klein
Sadie Foster, Michelle Tattenbaum,
Kathryn Walat, Ethan Youngerman
Musical Theatre Reader ....Emily King

SERVICES
Accountants ....ERE, LLP
Advertising ....SpotCo/
Drew Hodges, Jim Edwards,
John Lanasa, Aaliytha Davis
Marketing Consultants ....The Marketing Group/
Tanya Grubich, Laura Matalon,
Trish Santini, Bob Bucci
Corporate Sponsorship ....Amy Willstatter's Bridge to
Hollywood/Broadway, LLC
Market Research ....Audience Research and Analysis/
George Wachtel, Aline Chatmajien
Internet Services ....Artztek LLC
Legal Counsel ....Paul, Weiss, Rifkind,
Wharton and Garrison LLP,
John Breglio, Deborah Hartnett
Real Estate Counsel ....Marcus Attorneys
Labor Counsel ....Harry H. Weintraub/
Glick and Weintraub, P.C.
Special Projects ....Elaine H. Hirsch
Insurance ....DeWitt Stern Group Inc/
Anthony Pittari
Maintenance ....Reliable Cleaning
Production Photographer ....Joan Marcus
Cover Photography ....Chris Buck
Cover Design ....SpotCo
Theatre Displays ....King Display

For more information visit
www.ManhattanTheatreClub.com

SECOND STAGE THEATRE STAFF
Artistic Director ....Carole Rothman
Executive Director ....Timothy J. McClimon

ADMINISTRATIVE
General Manager ....C. Barrack Evans
Management Associate ....Daniel A. Finney
Business Associate ....Charlotte Han
Administrative Manager ....John Mackessy
Director of Development ....Sarah Bordy
Manager of Individual Giving ....Glenn Alan Stiskal
Manager of Institutional Giving ....Heather Janoff
Database Administrator ....Brooke Belott
Director of Marketing ....David Henderson
Associate Director of Marketing ....Melissa Skinner
Marketing Assistant ....Emily Africano
Ticket Services Manager ....Kathleen Grace
Assistant Box Office Treasurer ....Emily Africano
Box Office Assistants ....Jason Schmidt, Emily Wilbur
Business Affairs ....Andrew Farber

ARTISTIC
Associate Artistic Director ....Christopher Burney
Literary Manager ....Elizabeth Bennett
Playwright in Residence ....Roberto Aguirre-Sacasa

PRODUCTION
Production Manager ....Jeff Wild
Technical Directors ....Robert G. Mahon, III;
Dominic Housiaux
Facilities Coordinator ....Chris Meade
House Manager ....Stephanie Wallis
Front of House Staff ....Emily Africano, Sara Bathum,
Jess McLeod, Fredda Tone, John Webb
Building Maintenance ....Brian Engram

PRODUCTION STAFF FOR RECKLESS
Company Manager ....Denise Cooper
Production Stage Manager ....James FitzSimmons
Stage Manager ....Jill Cordle
Assistant Director ....Hilary Adams
Playwright Assistant ....Marc Parees
Assistant Set Designer ....Warren Karp
Assistant Costume Designer ....Tracy Christensen
Assistant Lighting Designer ....Justin Townsend
Associate Sound Designer ....Jill B.C. Du Boff
Wigs ....Paul Huntley
Hair/Wig Supervisor ....Alexis Kanfer
Sign Language Consultant ....Lewis Merkin
Flymen ....Stephen "Crash" Burns, Patrick Murray
Dressers ....Barry Hoff, Margiann Flanagan
Costume Assistant ....Jessica Barrios
Costume Intern ....Ruby Randig
Production Assistants ....Caroline Andersen,
Sarah Duncan, Chad Lewis,
Christine Zinno

"I'll Be Home for Chistmas" by Kim Gannon, Walter Kent
and Buck Ram. Worldwide rights administered by Gannon
& Kent Music Co. (ASCAP). Used by permission.
All rights reserved.

"Christmas Song" by Mel Torme and Bob Wells. Used by
permission of Edwin H. Morris & Company. A division of
MPL Publishing, Inc.

SPECIAL THANKS
Atlas Scenic Studio, Ltd.

CREDITS
Lighting equipment by Fourth Phase.
Sound equipment by Masque Sound.
Costume construction by Scafati Tailoring
and Timberlake Studios, Inc.
Specialty costumes and crafts by Sarah Laux.
Costume rental from Odds Costumes.
Millinery by Arnold Levine.
Natural herbal cough drops courtesy of Ricola.

MANHATTAN THEATRE CLUB/
BILTMORE THEATRE STAFF
Theatre Manager ....Valerie D. Simmons
Assistant House Manager ....Johannah-Joy Magyawe
Box Office Treasurer ....David Dillon
Assistant Box Office Treasurers.............Steven Clopper,
Kim Warner
Head Carpenter ....Chris Wiggins
Head Propertyman ....Timothy Walters
Sound Engineer ....Louis Shapiro
Master Electrician ....Jeff Dodson
Wardrobe Supervisor ....Michael Growler
Apprentices ....Sue Poulin, Obadiah Savage
Engineers ....Deosarran, Richardo Deosarran,
Mohd Alamgir Hossain,
Beeram Shiwprsaud
Security ....OCS Security
Lobby Refreshments ....Sweet Concessions

Best Opening Night Telegram: "Don't fuck up," from the company of *Brooklyn: The Musical*.

Memorable Opening Night Gifts: Craig Lucas gave antique Christmas cards. Mary-Louise Parker gave gingerbread Christmas trees and lots and lots of chocolate.

Celebrity Visitors: Paul Newman and Joanne Woodward. They didn't come backstage but sent a lovely note saying they enjoyed the production.

"Gypsy Of The Year" Sketch: We didn't do a sketch, but we raised money through a curtain-call appeal by Rosie Perez and Debra Monk. Deb addressed the audience in her nun costume.

Backstage Rituals: We have an ongoing solitaire game going on at the prop table throughout the show. Rosie starts it and other people finish it as they come and go.

Favorite Moment: Jill's favorite moment of business is during the game show sequence, which requires some tricky choreography backstage. There's also the final curtain when we celebrate that everyone's made it through alive.

Favorite In-Theatre Gathering Place: The stage manager's office, which has a running supply of sugar, or the dressing room shared by Deb Monk, Rosie Perez and Olga Merediz.

Favorite Off-Site Hangout: The crew goes to the Bull Moose Saloon. Each cast member does their own thing. If we go out together, it's usually to Joe Allens.

Snack Foods: York Peppermint Patties, Reese's peanut butter cups and Tootsie Rolls. Any sugar in this company goes fast! We also drink a healthy amount of Starbucks and we set up our own cappuccino maker.

Mascot: Sue Poulin, our props person.

Favorite Therapy: Ricola, yoga, meditation. Rosie Perez sings Broadway show tunes backstage

Record Number Of Cellphone Rings During A Performance: Five or six.

Heaviest/Hottest Costume? Deb Monk has a chicken suit with flippers for the feet. She also has to do some very fast costume changes in Act II with lots and lots of wigs.

Also: The cast, stage crew and front-of-house staff sometimes would gather in the lower lobby to watch movies on the big flat-screen TV.

Correspondents: James FitzSimmons and Jill Cordle, Stage Managers

Thomas Sadoski and Mary-Louise Parker.

Above: Debra Monk.

Below: Mary-Louise Parker in costume.

Right: The marquee of the Biltmore Theatre.

Below right: Parker with playwright Craig Lucas.

PLAYBILL®

 **∋N∈ NEDERLANDER THEATRE**

UNDER THE DIRECTION OF
JAMES M. NEDERLANDER AND JAMES L. NEDERLANDER

Jeffrey Seller   Kevin McCollum   Allan S. Gordon
and New York Theatre Workshop

present

RENT

Book, Music and Lyrics by
Jonathan Larson

Karmine Alers   Matt Caplan   Frenchie Davis   D'Monroe
Danielle Lee Greaves   Colin Hanlon   Sala Iwamatsu
Marcus Paul James   Justin Johnston   Kelly Karbacz
Caren Lyn Manuel   Destan Owens   Enrico Rodriguez
Nick Sanchez   Cary Shields   Owen Johnston II   Catrice Joseph
Diana Kaarina   Philip Dorian McAdoo   Dominique Roy   Jay Wilkison

Set Design	Costume Design	Lighting Design	Sound Design
Paul Clay	Angela Wendt	Blake Burba	Kurt Fischer

Original Concept/Additional Lyrics	Musical Arrangements	Dramaturg
Billy Aronson	Steve Skinner	Lynn M. Thomson

Casting	Publicity
Bernard Telsey Casting	Richard Kornberg/Don Summa

Music Director	Production Stage Manager
Boko Suzuki	John Vivian

General Manager	Technical Supervision
John Corker	Unitech Productions, Inc.

Music Supervision and Additional Arrangements	Choreography
Tim Weil	Marlies Yearby

Director
Michael Greif

Original cast recording available on DreamWorks Records' CD's and cassettes

LIVE
BROADWAY

5/2/05

CAST
(in order of appearance)

Roger Davis ....CARY SHIELDS
Mark Cohen ....MATT CAPLAN
Tom Collins ....DESTAN OWENS
Benjamin Coffin III ....D'MONROE
Joanne Jefferson .....DANIELLE LEE GREAVES
Angel Schunard ....JUSTIN JOHNSTON
Mimi Marquez ....KARMINE ALERS
Maureen Johnson ....KELLY KARBACZ
Mark's Mom
and Others ....CAREN LYN MANUEL
Christmas Caroler, Mr. Jefferson,
a Pastor, and Others.....MARCUS PAUL JAMES
Mrs. Jefferson, Woman with bags,
and Others ....FRENCHIE DAVIS
Gordon, the Man,
Mr. Grey, and others ....COLIN HANLON
Steve, man with squeegee,
a waiter, and others ....ENRICO RODRIGUEZ
Paul, a Cop, and Others ....NICK SANCHEZ
Alexi Darling, Roger's mom,
and others ....SALA IWAMATSU

UNDERSTUDIES

For Roger: COLIN HANLON, OWEN
JOHNSTON II, JAY WILKISON; for Mark:
COLIN HANLON, JAY WILKISON; for Tom
Collins: MARCUS PAUL JAMES, PHILIP
DORIAN McADOO;

continued on the next page

One Song Glory: The cast of *Rent*.

Photo by Joan Marcus

Rent

MUSICAL NUMBERS

ACT ONE

"Tune Up/Voice Mail #1" .... Mark, Roger, Mrs. Cohen, Collins, Benny
"Rent" .... The Company
"You Okay Honey?" .... Angel, Collins
"One Song Glory" .... Roger
"Light My Candle" .... Roger, Mimi
"Voice Mail #2" .... Mr. & Mrs. Jefferson
"Today 4 U" .... Angel
"You'll See" .... Benny, Mark, Collins, Roger, Angel
"Tango: Maureen" .... Mark, Joanne
"Life Support" .... Paul, Gordon, The Company
"Out Tonight" .... Mimi
"Another Day" .... Roger, Mimi, The Company
"Will I?" .... Steve, The Company
"On the Street" .... The Company
"Santa Fe" .... Collins and The Company
"I'll Cover You" .... Angel, Collins
"We're Okay" .... Joanne
"Christmas Bells" .... The Company
"Over the Moon" .... Maureen
"La Vie Boheme/I Should Tell You" .... The Company

ACT TWO

"Seasons of Love" .... The Company
"Happy New Year/Voice Mail #3" .... Mimi, Roger, Mark, Maureen, Joanne,
Collins, Angel, Mrs. Cohen, Alexi Darling, Benny, The man
"Take Me or Leave Me" .... Maureen, Joanne
"Without You" .... Roger, Mimi
"Voice Mail #4" .... Alexi Darling
"Contact" .... The Company
"I'll Cover You: Reprise" .... Collins, The Company
"Halloween" .... Mark
"Goodbye, Love" .... Mark, Mimi, Roger, Maureen, Joanne, Collins, Benny
"What You Own" .... Pastor, Mark, Collins, Benny, Roger
"Voice Mail #5" .... Roger's Mom, Mimi's Mom, Mr. Jefferson, Mrs. Cohen
"Your Eyes/Finale" .... Roger, The Company

Crew
(Starting from the bottom of the stairs and then moving left to right): Mike Angelina, Sonny Curry, Elena Mavoides, Terrence Cummiskey, Ray Rosaly, Willie Fiqueroa, Junesse Cartegna, Kyle Luker, Trish Ryan, Zeff Blacer, Iris Cortes, Jaoquin Quintana and Lee Bonacci.

Photo by Ben Strohmann

Rent

Karmine Alers
Mimi

Mayumi Ando
Ensemble

Matt Caplan
Mark

Merle Dandrige
Joanne

Frenchie Davis
Ensemble

D'Monroe
Benny

Marcus Paul James
Ensemble

Justin Johnston
Angel

Kelly Karbacz
Maureen

Joshua Kobak
Ensemble

Destan Owens
Collins

Caren Lyn Manuel
Ensemble

Enrico Rodriguez
Ensemble

Nick Sanchez
Ensemble

Cary Shields
Roger

Owen Johnston II
Understudy

Catrice Joseph
Understudy

Diana Kaarina
Understudy

Philip Dorian McAdoo
Understudy

Dominique Roy
Understudy

Jonathan Larson
Book, Music, Lyrics

Michael Greif
Director

David Santana
Wig, Hair and Make-up Designer

Bernard Telsey
Casting

Jeffrey Seller
Producer

Kevin McCollum
Producer

Allan S. Gordon
Producer

Sebastian Arcelus
Swing

Maggie Benjamin
Maureen Johnson

Melanie Brown
Mimi Marquez

Shaun Earl
Paul, a Cop, and others

Mark Richard Ford
Tom Collins

Danielle Lee
Greaves
Joanne

Rent

Stu James
Benjamin Coffin III

Kendra Kassebaum
Mark's mom and others

Kristen Lee Kelly
Mark's mom and others

Joshua Kobak
Gordon, the man, Mr. Grey, and others

Jeremy Kushnier
Roger Davis

Drew Lachey
Mark Cohen

Todd E. Pettiford
Christmas caroler, Mr. Jefferson, a pastor, and others

Jai Rodriguez
Angel Schunard

Andy Señor
Angel Schunard

Krystal L. Washington
Mimi Marquez

Haneefah Wood
Swing

The Band
(L-R):
Jeff Potter,
John Korba,
Boko Suzuki,
Steve Mack,
Bob Baxmeyer

Sound and Electricians
(L-R):
Richie Beck (Electrician),
Charles Peek (Electrician),
Brian Ronan (Sound),
Eric Carney (Sound),
Alain Van Achte (Sound),
Steve Clem (Electrician),
Holli Shevett (Electrician)

Photos by Ben Strothmann

Rent

Wardrobe
(L-R):
Paula Inocent,
Lisa Zinni,
Roberta Christy,
Tammy Kopko

**Hair & Wig
Department**
David Santana
and Leslie Ziegler

Carpentry and Props
(L-R):
Billy Wright, Jr.,
Billy Wright,
Joe Ferreri, Jr.,
Jan Marasek,
Terry Armstrong

(Not Pictured: Joe Ferreri, Sr.)

Photos by Ben Strothmann

Rent

Doorman
Joe Domingo

Box Office
(L-R): Gary Kenny and Mike Hughes

Engineer
Tony Ferrao

Stage and Company Management
Ken McGee (Assistant Stage Manager), Gay Merwin (Substitute Stage Manager),
John Vivian (Production Stage Manager), Nick Kaledin (Company Manager), Crystal Huntington (Stage Manager)

Photos by Ben Strohmann

Rent

Above: Colin Hanlon, Enrico Rodriguez, Kendra Kassebaum and Jeremy Kushnier at a welcoming party for Drew Lachey at Hotel 41. Right: Caren Lyn Manuel performs "Womyn in Three" at "Gypsy of the Year."

Memorable Fan Letter: We get the deepest fan mail. One 16-year-old girl wrote us an incredible letter saying she had attempted suicide twice, but after her parents had sent her to *Rent*, it completely changed her perspective. She didn't want to end her life anymore. It gave her some bit of hope.

Anniversary Gifts: When the show first opened it was such a success they gave $5000 checks to every actor, including my sister, Yassmin Alers, who was the original understudy for Mimi and Maureen. Now, we get small gifts each Christmas. One year we got robes; another year we got wallets; another year we got candles.

"Gypsy Of The Year" Sketch: "Womyn in Three" by Caren Lyn Manuel.

"Carols For A Cure" Carol: "What Child Is This?"

Backstage Rituals: There is a wooden plaque with Jonathan Larson's picture and name right above the sign-in sheet. Everyone has to pass it on the way to places. Everyone rubs Jonathan's name for luck just before we go on stage. I have my own personal ritual, too. Just before I go on to do "Out Tonight," I have a moment with Jonathan. I say, "Thank you for writing this and for believing in me. This one's for you." And then the music starts.

Favorite Moment: During "Will I," there is a moment where everyone is on stage at once, all at different places. It's such a pensive, thoughtful moment, a moment when you can think about your character, but also about yourself.

In-Theatre Gathering Places: For most of us, it's the Green Room. There's also the hair room, where the boys like to play poker.

Favorite Off-Site Hangout: We get together at Bar 41, which is right next to the theatre. They recognize us and give us half-off on drinks.

Favorite Snack Foods: When we need a sugar rush, we dig into a big candy jar in the stage management office. They have Reese's peanut butter cups, Tootsie Rolls, Butterfingers and all kinds of things.

Favorite Therapy: Emergen-C and Herbal Resistance liquid. We call it "The wellness formula."

Memorable Ad-Libs: Sherie Rene Scott had a great one. When she was playing Maureen she blanked during the performance piece and just said, "Oh f— me up the a–." She got a note from stage management saying: "Don't ever say that again," but it was so in-character the audience just went along with it.

Jacques Smith had just come back from vacation when he blanked during the fight scene. He didn't try to make anything up. All he could say was, "I'm losing my mind!"

Cellphone Rings: I don't think we've ever had more than one or two, but they always seem to happen during the quiet, beautiful songs.

Strangest Stage Door Fan Encounter: We had one guy who snuck in with a group and went and sat in one of the girls' dressing rooms. Everyone thought he was with someone else, but finally the stage manager had to go up there and say, "You have to leave." He didn't hurt anyone, but it certainly was strange.

Busiest Day At The Box Office: In the early days of the run, of course, people would line up outside for hours. Some would bring tents and hook up small TV sets to car batteries. Throughout the run, New Year's Eve has routinely been the biggest. When Joey Fatone joined the cast, we had a couple of days when it was crazy, like a rock concert.

Heaviest/Hottest Costume: Angel wears three layers during "Today for You."

Who Wore The Least: Mayumi Ando, who wears a pink, fuzzy bra.

Catchphrases: We picked up something from *The Color Purple* that we always say to each other. There's a scene where Celie tells Mister, "Everything you ever done to me, already been done to you." She holds up three fingers to him when she says it. Well, we used that whenever we wanted to say, "I'm going to get you back for that." Now we just hold up the three fingers, and everybody knows what that means.

Sweethearts: We've had a lot of backstage romances. The most famous is Taye Diggs and Idina Menzel, who met here and got married. There was also Cristina Fadale and Chad Richardson, and Mayumi Ando and Cary Shields. We've had some pretty dramatic breakups too!

Famous Directorial Note: Michael Greif loves to use the word "goosh" as in, "You've got to go goosh," and we're supposed to understand what that means from his body language.

Company Legends: Taye Diggs used to run through the building naked right before places. He'd open the door to the girls' dressing room and show his beautiful naked body.

Right after one of the terrorist attacks, Manley Pope heard a loud pop coming from outside the theatre during the opening number, and he ran right off the stage to the stage manager.

Tales From The Put-In: Erica Munoz was going on for Mimi and had a series of disasters. During her rehearsal with Norbert Leo Butz, the candle set her hair on fire. Then, in the same scene, she brought her head up suddenly and cracked Norbert's tooth. Then, that night, in the performance, when she was coming out of the door to do "Out Tonight," she fell over the bar and nearly fell to the stage. She had to hang on and then climb back up onto the platform. This all happened in a single day.

Musician Who Plays The Most Instruments: Boko Suzuki, plays keyboard, bass and guitar.

Correspondent: Karmine Alers, "Mimi."

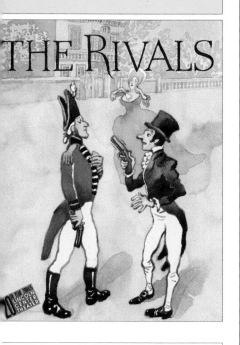

PLAYBILL®

THE RIVALS

CAST

(in order of speaking)

Fag, ...JAMES URBANIAK
servant to Captain Absolute

Thomas ....HERB FOSTER

Lucy, maid to Lydia ....KEIRA NAUGHTON

Lydia Languish ....EMILY BERGL

Julia Melville ....CARRIE PRESTON

Mrs. Malaprop, aunt to Lydia ....DANA IVEY

Sir Anthony Absolute ......RICHARD EASTON

Captain Jack Absolute,........MATT LETSCHER
his son

Faulkland, ...JIM TRUE-FROST
friend to Jack Absolute

Bob Acres, ...JEREMY SHAMOS
a country gentleman

Errand Boy..........................P.J. VERHOEST

Sir Lucius O'Trigger, ...BRIAN MURRAY
an Irishman

David, servant to Acres ....DAVID MANIS

Footmen ....DAVID FURR,
MALCOLM INGRAM,
JIM STANEK,
DAVID CHRISTOPHER WELLS

Time: 1775

Place: Bath, England

*"...I will only tell you, in brief, yet in truth, —
It looks a City of Palaces — a Town of Hills, & a
Hill of Towns." —Fanny Burney, 20 August, 1791*

Assistant Stage Manager ......CLAUDIA LYNCH

LINCOLN CENTER THEATER AT THE VIVIAN BEAUMONT

under the direction of
André Bishop and **Bernard Gersten**
presents

THE RIVALS

by **Richard Brinsley Sheridan**

with (in alphabetical order)

Emily Bergl   Barbara Caruso   Richard Easton   Herb Foster

David Furr   Malcolm Ingram   Dana Ivey   Matt Letscher

David Manis   Brian Murray   Keira Naughton   Laura Odeh

Carrie Preston   Jeremy Shamos   Jim Stanek   Jim True-Frost

James Urbaniak   P.J. Verhoest   David Christopher Wells   Sarah Zimmerman

Sets **John Lee Beatty**   Costumes **Jess Goldstein**   Lighting **Peter Kaczorowski**

Original Music **Robert Waldman**   Sound **Scott Stauffer**

Choreography **Seán Curran**

Stage Manager **Michael McGoff**   Casting **Daniel Swee**   Dramaturg **Anne Cattaneo**

Director of Development **Hattie K. Jutagir**   Director of Marketing **Andrew Flatt**

General Manager **Adam Siegel**   Production Manager **Jeff Hamlin**   General Press Agent **Philip Rinaldi**

Directed by **Mark Lamos**

THE RIVALS is supported by a major grant from The Andrew W. Mellon Foundation.

This production is made possible by a special fund for LCT established by The Peter Jay Sharp Foundation.

Thanks to The Hess Foundation and Norma Hess.

Thanks to the Theatre Development Fund for its support of THE RIVALS.

American Airlines is the official airline of Lincoln Center Theater.

Merrill Lynch is a 2004 LCT Season Sponsor.

12/15/04

UNDERSTUDIES

For Fag - JIM STANEK, DAVID CHRISTOPHER WELLS; for Captain Jack Absolute, Errand Boy – DAVID FURR; for Lydia Languish, Lucy - SARAH ZIMMERMAN; for Julia Melville, Lucy, Errand Boy - LAURA ODEH; for Mrs. Malaprop - BARBARA CARUSO; for Sir Anthony Absolute, Sir Lucius O'Trigger, Thomas - MALCOLM INGRAM; for Sir Lucius O'Trigger – DAVID MANIS; for Faulkland – DAVID CHRISTOPHER WELLS; for Bob Acres, David – JIM STANEK; for Footmen - DAVID FURR, LAURA ODEH, SARAH ZIMMERMAN.

Richard Easton (left) and Matt Letscher.

Emily Bergl
Lydia Languish

Barbara Caruso
Understudy

Richard Easton
*Sir Anthony
Absolute*

Herb Foster
Thomas

David Furr
Footman

Malcolm Ingram
Footman

Dana Ivey
Mrs. Malaprop

Matt Letscher
*Captain Jack
Absolute*

David Manis
*David,
Understudy*

Brian Murray
Sir Lucius O'Trigger

Keira Naughton
Lucy

Laura Odeh
Understudy

Carrie Preston
Julia

Jeremy Shamos
Bob Acres

Jim Stanek
Footman

Jim True-Frost
Faulkland

James Urbaniak
Fag

P.J. Verhoest
Errand Boy

David Christopher
Wells
Footman

Sarah Zimmerman
Understudy

Richard Brinsley
Sheridan
Playwright

Mark Lamos
Director

John Lee Beatty
Sets

Jess Goldstein
Costumes

Peter Kaczorowski
Lighting

Seán Curran
Choreography

Elizabeth Smith
Dialect Coach

The Rivals

LINCOLN CENTER THEATER

ANDRÉ BISHOP   BERNARD GERSTEN

ARTISTIC DIRECTOR   EXECUTIVE PRODUCER

ADMINISTRATIVE STAFF

GENERAL MANAGER ....ADAM SIEGEL
Assistant General Manager ....Melanie Weinraub
General Management Assistant ....Beth Dembrow
Facilities Manager ....Alex Mustelier
Assistant Facilities Manager ....Michael Assalone

GENERAL PRESS AGENT ....PHILIP RINALDI
Press Associate ....Barbara Carroll

PRODUCTION MANAGER ....JEFF HAMLIN
Associate Production Manager ....Paul Smithyman

DIRECTOR OF DEVELOPMENT ....HATTIE K. JUTAGIR
Associate Director of Development ....Rachel Norton
Manager of Special Events and Young Patron Program ....Karin Schall
Grants Writer ....Neal Brilliant
Coordinator, Patron Program ....Sheilaja Rao
Development Associate ....Chris Chrzanowski
Assistant to the Director of Development ....Betsy Tucker

DIRECTOR OF FINANCE.............................DAVID S. BROWN
Controller ....Susan Knox
Systems Manager ....John N. Yen
Finance Assistant ....Kellie Kroyer

DIRECTOR OF MARKETING ....ANDREW FLATT
Marketing Associate ....Denis Guerin
Marketing Assistant ....Elizabeth Kandel

DIRECTOR OF EDUCATION ....KATI KOERNER
Associate Director of Education ....Dionne O'Dell
Assistant to the Executive Producer ....Barbara Hourigan
Office Assistant ....Kenneth Collins
Messenger ....Esau Burgess
Reception ....Andrew Elsesser, Daryl Watson

ARTISTIC STAFF

ASSOCIATE DIRECTORS ....GRACIELA DANIELE,
NICHOLAS HYTNER,
SUSAN STROMAN,
DANIEL SULLIVAN

DRAMATURG and DIRECTOR, LCT DIRECTORS LAB ......ANNE CATTANEO

CASTING DIRECTOR ....DANIEL SWEE, CSA

MUSICAL THEATER ASSOCIATE PRODUCER ....IRA WEITZMAN

Artistic Administrator ....Julia Judge
Casting Associate ....Kristin McTigue

In Loving Memory of
GERALD GUTIERREZ
Associate Director 1991-2003

HOUSE STAFF

HOUSE MANAGER...RHEBA FLEGELMAN
Production Carpenter ....Walter Murphy
Production Electrician ....Patrick Merryman
Production Propertyman ....Karl Rausenberger
Production Flyman ....William Nagle
House Technician ....Bill Burke
Chief Usher...M.L. Pollock
Box Office Treasurer ....Fred Bonis
Assistant Treasurer ....Robert A. Belkin

SPECIAL SERVICES

Advertising ....Serino-Coyne/Jim Russek
Brad Lapin, Sue Wozny

Principal Poster Artist ....James McMullan
Poster Art for The Rivals...James McMullan
Counsel ....Peter L. Felcher, Esq.;
Charles H. Googe, Esq.;
and Rachel Hoover, Esq. of
Paul, Weiss, Rifkind, Wharton & Garrison
Immigration Counsel ....Theodore Ruthizer, Esq.;
Mark D. Koestler, Esq.
of Kramer, Levin, Naftalis & Frankel LLP
Auditor ....Douglas Burack, C.P.A.
Lutz & Carr, L.L.P.
Insurance ....Jennifer Brown of
DeWitt Stern Group
Photographer ....Joan Marcus
Travel ....Tygon Tours
Consulting Architect ....Hugh Hardy,
Hardy Holzman Pfeiffer Associates
Construction Manager ....Yorke Construction
Payroll Service ....Castellana Services, Inc.

STAFF FOR THE RIVALS

COMPANY MANAGER ....Matthew Markoff
Associate Company Manager ....Josh Lowenthal
Assistant Director...Evan Cabnet
Dance Captain ....Sarah Zimmerman
Associate Set Designer ....Eric Renschler
Assistant Set Designer..Yoshi Tanokura
Assistant Costume Designer ....Anne Kenney
Associate Lighting Designer ....Mick A. Smith
Assistant Lighting Designer ....Chris Akins
Associate Sound Designer ....Josh Bender-Dubiel
Props Coordinator ....Christopher Schneider
Light Board Operator ....Bruce Rubin
Production Soundman ....Marc Salzberg
Period Movement Coach ....Thomas Baird
Make-up Designer ....Angelina Avallone
Wardrobe Supervisor ....Lynn Bowling
Hair Supervisor ....Lazaro Arencibia
Hair Assistants ....Jun Kim, Alice Ramos
Dressers ....Danny Paul, Sarah Schaub,
Michael Woll
Child Guardian ....Robert Wilson
Child's Tutor ....On Location Education
Production Assistant ....Jen Nelson

MUSIC COMPOSED AND ARRANGED BY
Robert Waldman.

Recorded at Scott Lehrer Studios.

Musicians:
Belinda Whitney - Violin; Richard Locker - Cello; Brian Miller - Flute;
Lynne Cohen - Oboe; Wayne du Maine - Trumpet;
Theresa MacDonnell - French horn;
Joe Thaikin - Harpsichord;

John Miller - Contractor

Wig Designer ....Charles LaPointe
Dialect Coach ....Elizabeth Smith

CREDITS

Scenery built by Center Line Studios, Inc. Cornwall, New York.
Paint by Scenic Arts.
Scenery fabrication by Scenic Technologies,
a division of Production Resource Group, LLC., New Windsor, NY.
Show control and scenic motion control featuring stage command systems by Scenic
Technologies, a division of Production Resource Group, LLC., New Windsor, NY.
Lighting equipment from PRG Lighting.
Costumes and millinery by Carelli Costumes, Inc.
Shoes and boots by Fred Longtin. Sound Equipment by Masque Sound.
Wigs by Watson Associates.
Natural herb cough drops courtesy of Ricola USA, Inc.

LOBBY REFRESHMENTS BY SWEET CONCESSIONS

Photos by Aubrey Reuben

Above left: Carrie Preston at the opening night party at Avery Fisher Hall. Above right: Richard Easton, Brian Murray and Dana Ivey.

Cast members at the opening night party (L-R): David Manis, P. J. Verhoest and Emily Bergl.

Backstage Hobby: One thing that took huge amounts of time: knitting. Sometimes six people were doing it at once.

Favorite Backstage Gathering Place: The hallway where there was a big table and we always had a jigsaw puzzle going. There were people who never seemed to want to leave that area.

Favorite Off-Site Hangout: The new O'Neal's on the east side of Broadway.

Memorable Ad-Lib: Twice during the run we had two people in the cast who got sick and had to be replaced by their understudies in the middle of a show. One night, Matt Letscher, who played Jack Absolute, was looking a little green in one scene. Jeremy Shamos, who played Bob Acres, had the line, "I have business with Sir Anthony. I have to be off." And Matt ad-libbed, "I think I'll go with you!," and he barely made it off stage before he was spectacularly sick. There was a five-minute pause, and David Furr put on the costume and took over. He went on to great success.

Inside Jokes: I made an elaborate backstage video called *I Was a Teen-age Dead Male Playwright*, that purported to show what would happen if Richard Brinsley Sheridan found out we were reviving his play, came to see our production, and compared it to the original. It had a lot of jokes about our show. Everyone took part, including Bernie Gersten, who played a cheapskate producer. It was like *Spinal Tap* for *The Rivals*.

Correspondent: David Manis, "David, Servant to Acres"

Left: Lincoln Center Theater leaders André Bishop and Bernard Gersten. Center: Matt Lenscher on the Lincoln Center promenade. Right: Director Mark Lamos.

PLAYBILL®

Billy Crystal
*Playwright/
Performer*

Des McAnuff
Director

Alan Zweibel
Additional Material

Janice Crystal
Producer

⑧ BROADHURST THEATRE

235 West 44th Street
A Shubert Organization Theatre

Gerald Schoenfeld, *Chairman*   **Philip J. Smith,** *President*

Robert E. Wankel, *Executive Vice President*

Janice Crystal, Larry Magid
and **Face Productions**

Present

BILLY CRYSTAL

700 Sundays

Written by

Billy Crystal

Additional material by	Scenic Design	Lighting Design	Production Design
Alan Zweibel	**David F. Weiner**	**David Lee Cuthbert**	**Michael Clark**

Sound Design	Clothing Stylist	Technical Supervisor	Production Stage Manager
Steve Canyon Kennedy John Shivers	**David C. Woolard**	**Don Gilmore-DSG Entertainment**	**Lurie Horns Pfeffer**

General Manager	Company Manager	Press Representative
Niko Companies, Ltd	**Brig Berney**	**Barlow • Hartman**

Directed By

Des McAnuff

700 SUNDAYS was originally produced by the La Jolla Playhouse
Des McAnuff, Artistic Director & Terrence Dwyer, Managing Director

Presented in association with Clear Channel Entertainment

12/5/04

Photo by Carol Rosegg

Billy Crystal recalls his childhood.

2004-2005 AWARDS

TONY AWARD
Special Event

DRAMA DESK AWARD
Solo Performance (Billy Crystal)

OUTER CRITICS CIRCLE AWARD
Solo Performance (Billy Crystal)

Photo by Ben Strothmann

Backstage Crew and Cast
Front Row (L-R): Ron Vitelli (House Properties), Lurie Horns Pfeffer (Production Stage Manager), Robert Thurber (Stage Manager), Steve Abbott (Follow Spot Operator), Billy Crystal (Star), Janice Crystal (Producer), Charlie DeVerna (House Electrician), Hugh Barnett (House Manager), Phil Lojo (Production Sound Engineer) and Scott DeVerna (Electrician).
Back Row (L-R): Brig Berney (Company Manager), Bill Staples (Spot Operator), Dan Novi (Follow Spot Operator), Brian McGarty (House Carpenter), Jonathan Cohen (Deck Sound), Brian Bullard (House Flyman) and Marcie Olivi (Wardrobe Supervisor).

Photo by Ben Strothmann

Front-of-House Staff
Front Row (L-R): Marie Gonzales, Rose Ann Cipriano, Saviel Almonte (kneeling) and Marie Mangelli.
Standing (L-R): Henry Bathea, Carmen Rodriguez, Lashone Cleveland, Latoya Sewell, Hugh Lynch, Karen Diaz, and Hugh Barnett (House Manager).

700 Sundays

Staff for 700 SUNDAYS

GENERAL MANAGEMENT
NIKO COMPANIES, LTD.
Manny Kladitis
David Cole   James Lawson
Maia Sutton   Walter Shepherd

COMPANY MANAGER
Brig Berney

GENERAL PRESS REPRESENTATIVE
BARLOW•HARTMAN
Michael Hartman   John Barlow
Carol Fineman   Leslie Baden

Production Stage Manager ....Lurie Horns Pfeffer
Stage Manager ....Donald Fried
Production Assistant ....Sarah Kirby
Assistant to the Director ....Holly-Anne Ruggiero
Associate Scenic Designer ....Christopher T. Borreson
Associate Lighting Designer ....Patricia Nichols
Associate Sound Designers ....Chris Luessman,
                                         Walter Trarbach
House Carpenter ....Brian McGarty
House Properties ....Ron Vitelli
House Electrician ....Charlie DeVerna
House Flyman ....Brian Bullard
Production Electrician ....John Michael Pitzer, Jr.
Assistant Production Electrician ....Shannon January
Follow Spot Operators ....Steve Abbott, Jr.;
                                         Dan Novi
Production Sound Engineer ....Phillip Lojo
Deck Sound ....Jonathan Cohen
Wardrobe Supervisor ....Marcie Olivi
Video Coordinator ....Chris Luessman
Projection Programmer ....Paul Vershbow
Properties Supervisor ....Emiliano Pares
Assistant to Mr. Crystal ....Carol Sidlow
Assistant to Mr. Magid ....Carrie Cunningham
Assistant to Mr. McAnuff ....Jim Roderick
Legal Counsel ....Franklin, Weinrib, Rudell & Vasallo
                   Elliott Brown, Daniel Wasser
Accountant ....Rosenberg, Neuwirth, & Kuchner CPAs
                   Mark A. D'Ambrosi, Sandra Lattanzio,
                   Jana Jevnikar
Advertising ....Serino Coyne Inc.
                   Nancy Coyne, Angelo Desimini,
                   Sandy Block, Ben Downing
Marketing ....Clear Channel Marketing
                   Jennifer DeLange, Carolyn Christensen
Groups Sales ....Clear Channel Group Sales
                   Nicholas Falzon
Souvenir Merchandise ....Clear Channel Theatrical/
                   Larry Turk
Opening Night Coordinators ....Tobak-Dantchik
                   Suzanne Tobak, Joanna Koondel
Banking ....JP Morgan Chase
                   Mary Ann Viafore
Insurance ....Tanenbaum Harber of FL, LLC
                   Carol Bressi-Cilona
Theatre Displays ....King Displays, Inc.
Payroll Services ....Castellana Services, Inc.

CREDITS
Scenery by PRG Scenic Technologies.
Lighting equipment from Fourth Phase.
Sound equipment by Masque Sound.
Projection equipment from Scharff Weisberg.
Mr. Crystal's gym equipment provided by Gym Source.

Security provided by RL Security, Inc.

SPECIAL THANKS
American Express, The New York Yankees,
The New York Times, UPS, Carl Pasbjerg, Eric Joseph,
David Steinberg, Steve Tennenbaum, Bob Shepard

The photo of Billy Crystal on the cover
of the PLAYBILL® is by Nigel Parry/CPi.

CLEAR CHANNEL ENTERTAINMENT –
THEATRICAL
Brian Becker, Miles C. Wilkin, Scott Zeiger, Steve Winton,
David Anderson, Lauren Reid, Lynn Blandford,
Bradley Broecker, Jennifer Costello, Jennifer DeLange,
Joanna Hagan, Eric Joseph, Susan Krajsa, David Lazar,
Hailey Lustig, Drew Murphy, Carl Pasbjerg, Debra Peltz,
Denise Perry, Courtney Pierce, Alison Spiriti, Dan Swartz

700 SUNDAYS CREDITS

MUSIC CREDITS
"The Alley Cat" written by Frank Bjorn.
Used by permission of Music Sales Group.
All rights reserved. Used by permission.

"American Collection Theme" (John Williams).
© Marjer Publishing (BMI).
All rights on behalf of Marjer Publishing (BMI).
Administered by Warner-Tamerlane Publishing Corp.
(BMI). All rights reserved. Used by permission.

"Baby Won't You Please Come Home"
written by Charles Warfield and Clarence Williams.
All rights owned or administered by Universal-MCA Music
Publishing, a division of Universal Studios, Inc. and Great
Standard's Music c/o The Songwriters Guild.
Used by permission.

"Butterfly's Day Out" by Mark O'Connor. ©
Mark O'Connor Musik International (administered by
MCS Music America, Inc.). All rights reserved.
Used by permission,

"Candy" by Alex Kramer, Joan Whitney and Mack David.
© 1944 by Bourne Co. and PolyGram International Pub.
Copyright renewed. All rights reserved.
International copyright secured, ASCAP.

"Cute" instrumental (Neal Hefti). © 1958 (renewed)
WB Music Corp. All rights reserved. Used by permission.

"It's a Lovely Day," "My Walking Stick," "Steppin' Out
With My Baby" and "They Say It's Wonderful":
music and lyrics by Irving Berlin.
These selections are used by special arrangement with

The Rodgers and Hammerstein Organization,
on behalf of the Estate of Irving Berlin, 1065 Avenue of
the Americas, Suite 2400, New York, New York 10018.
All rights reserved.

"Love Is Just Around the Corner" written by Leo
Robin/Louis Gensler. Published by Famous Music
Corporation (ASCAP). Used by permission.
All rights reserved.

"Memories of You" written by Eubie Blake and Andy
Razaf. Used by permission of Shapiro, Bernstein & Co.,
Inc. and Razaf Music, c/o The Songwriters Guild. All
rights reserved. International copyright secured.

"Muskrat Ramble" written by Edward Ory.
Used by permission of Slick Tongue Ory Music care of
Bughouse, a division of Bug Music, Inc. All rights reserved.
Used by permission.

"On the Sunny Side of the Street"
written by Dorothy Fields and Jimmy McHugh.
Used by permission of Shapiro, Bernstein & Co., Inc. and
Cotton Club Publishing c/o EMI Music Publishing.
All rights reserved. International copyright secured.

"One B" written by Edgar A. Meyer.
Used by permission of Hendon Music, Inc.
All rights reserved. Used by permission.

"Someone to Watch Over Me"
(George Gershwin, Ira Gershwin).© 1926 (renewed),
WB MUSIC CORP. (ASCAP).
All rights reserved. Used by permission.

"Sunrise, Sunset" music by Jerry Bock, lyrics by Sheldon
Harnick. This selection is used by special arrangement with
Jerry Bock Enterprises and with R&H Music, on behalf of
Mayerling Productions Ltd.

"Vocalise" written by Sergei Rachmaninoff.
Used by permission of Boosey and Hawkes, Inc.
All rights reserved. Used by permission.

"Wrap Your Troubles in Dreams (And Dream Your
Troubles Away)" written by Harry Barris, Ted Kochler, and
Billy Moll. Used by permission of Shapiro, Bernstein &
Co., Inc. and the Fred Ahlert Music Corporation.
All rights reserved. International copyright secured.

"You Always Hurt the One You Love" written by Doris
Fisher and Allan Roberts. All rights owned or administered
by Universal-MCA Music Publishing, a division of
Universal Studios, Inc. and Doris Fisher Music
Corporation. Used by permission.

Incidental music performed by Stephen "Hoops" Snyder
(piano), Ken Dow (bass), and Kevin Dow (drums).

VIDEO CREDITS
Shane courtesy of Paramount Pictures.
Jazz dance film provided by
Mark Cantor/ Celluloid Improvisations Film Archive.

Opening Night Gifts: Billy gave us black wool show jackets with the logo on the breast pocket; also real Louisville Slugger baseball bats engraved with the logo and the opening date.

Celebrity Visitors: Oprah Winfrey and Jerry Seinfeld came backstage together and were waiting for Billy in the green room. Seinfeld asked, "What's Billy doing right now?" I said he was changing. Oprah said, "You know—the things people do after shows." Seinfeld said, "No, I don't know. I don't wear makeup and I wear my own clothes. When I'm done, I just put on my coat and go home." He was being honest.

Backstage Rituals: We have brunch every Saturday before the matinee. Billy also listens to a lot of jazz CDs in his dressing room. His family founded Commodore records, a jazz label, and a lot of great music from that time is always coming from that dressing room. Also, if a Yankees game is on cable, he's always watching that.

Snack Foods: Billy eats a lot of healthy food and vitamin drinks. One of our producers brings boxes of Italian butter cookies, so we eat a lot of those.

Therapies: He does a very strenuous physical warmup. We have gym equipment in the basement, and he does stretches, treadmill and Exercycle to get his blood pumping for the show.

Favorite Moment: The section where he talks about sitting with Henry Kissinger and Donald Trump and watching President Bush at the third game of the 2001 World Series. It's unbelievably funny.

Memorable Ad Lib: In the same scene, he's supposed to say, "The president and his Secret Service people left Mr. Steinbrenner's box." Instead of "Secret Service," one night he said, "Social Security" and it got a laugh, I guess because Social Security has been in the news so much. Billy recovered and said, "Well, I guess the president could take those people, too." The audience roared.

In-Theatre Gathering Place: We have our brunches on a big table in the middle of the basement under the stage.

Off-Site Hangout: Billy goes to Angus McIndoe's, which is very convenient. Some of the crew goes to Carmine's.

Record Number Of Cell Phone Rings: The followspot operator keeps a running tally, and one night he recorded 23. This, despite the fact that we begin the show with an announcement from former Yankee announcer Bob Shepard telling people to turn them off. One night, Billy gave a curtain speech thanking the audience, and telling the person whose phone kept ringing that they could shove it up their a**! It got in the papers.

Company In-Jokes: PSM Lurie Horns Pfeffer sometimes forgets half-hour call, so she'll come on the loudspeaker and give a 23-minute call, or a 19-minute call.

Catchphrase: "Time to practice the bat cracks!"

Correspondent: Brig Berney, Company Manager.

Photos by Aubrey Reuben

Photos by Ernio Hernandez

Clockwise from top left: Billy Crystal with wife/producer Janice at the opening night party at Tavern on the Green. Crystal takes his curtain call opening night. Director Des McAnuff. Other arrivals on opening night: New York Yankees Manager Joe Torre and wife. Stanley Tucci and Tovah Feldshuh, Robin Williams. At left: the marquee of the Broadhurst Theatre.

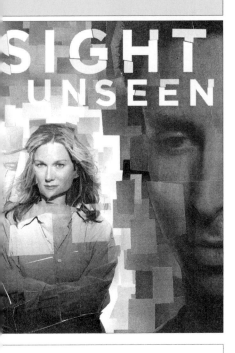

PLAYBILL®

SIGHT UNSEEN

CAST
(in order of appearance)

Nick ....BYRON JENNINGS
Jonathan Waxman.............BEN SHENKMAN
Patricia..............................LAURA LINNEY
Grete ....ANA REEDER

SCENES

Act I

Scene 1: A cold farmhouse in Norfolk, England. 1991.
Scene 2: An art gallery in London. Four days later.
Scene 3: The farmhouse. An hour before the start of Scene 1.
Scene 4: A bedroom in Brooklyn. Fifteen years earlier.

Act II

Scene 5: The farmhouse. A few hours after the end of Scene 1.
Scene 6: The art gallery. Continued from the end of Scene 2.
Scene 7: The farmhouse. A few hours after the end of Scene 5.
Scene 8: A painting studio in an art college. New York State. Seventeen years earlier.

Stage Manager ....Denise Yaney

UNDERSTUDIES

For Jonathan Waxman – J. ANTHONY CRANE
For Nick – PAUL DeBOY
For Patricia/Grete – LAURIE WILLIAMS and KATE FORBES

MANHATTAN THEATRE CLUB AT THE BILTMORE THEATRE

ARTISTIC DIRECTOR
LYNNE MEADOW

EXECUTIVE PRODUCER
BARRY GROVE

PRESENTS

SIGHT UNSEEN

BY

DONALD MARGULIES

WITH

BYRON JENNINGS
ANA REEDER

LAURA LINNEY
BEN SHENKMAN

SET DESIGN
DOUGLAS W. SCHMIDT

COSTUME DESIGN
JESS GOLDSTEIN

LIGHTING DESIGN
PAT COLLINS

ORIGINAL MUSIC AND SOUND DESIGN
JOHN GROMADA

PRODUCTION STAGE MANAGER
ROY HARRIS

DIRECTED BY

DANIEL SULLIVAN

CASTING
**NANCY PICCIONE/
DAVID CAPARELLIOTIS**

PRESS REPRESENTATIVE
BONEAU/BRYAN-BROWN

PRODUCTION MANAGER/
DIRECTOR OF CAPITAL PROJECTS
MICHAEL R. MOODY

DIRECTOR OF DEVELOPMENT
ANDREW D. HAMINGSON

DIRECTOR OF MARKETING
DEBRA A. WAXMAN

GENERAL MANAGER
HAROLD WOLPERT

DIRECTOR OF ARTISTIC DEVELOPMENT
PAIGE EVANS

SIGHT UNSEEN WAS COMMISSIONED AND ORIGINALLY PRODUCED BY SOUTH COAST REPERTORY.

MANHATTAN THEATRE CLUB WISHES TO EXPRESS ITS APPRECIATION TO THEATRE DEVELOPMENT FUND FOR ITS SUPPORT OF THIS PRODUCTION.

5/25/04

Laura Linney, Byron Jennings and Ben Shenkman.

Photo by Joan Marcus

Byron Jennings
Nick

Laura Linney
Patricia

Ana Reeder
Grete

Ben Shenkman
Jonathan Waxman

Donald Margulies
Playwright

Daniel Sullivan
Director

Douglas W. Schmidt
Set Design

Jess Goldstein
Costume Design

Pat Collins
Lighting Design

John Gromada
*Original Music/
Sound Design*

Lynne Meadow
*Artistic Director,
Manhattan Theatre
Club*

Barry Grove
*Executive Producer,
Manhattan Theatre
Club*

Ben Shenkman and Ana Reeder.

Photo by Joan Marcus

Sight Unseen

Who Played the Most Performances: Of the four principals—Laura Linney, Ben Shenkman, Byron Jennings and Ana Reeder—the first three did all 91 performances. Because of her stepfather's death, Ana had to be away the final week. Her standby, Laurie Williams, made her Broadway debut and played the final seven performances.

Backstage Rituals: Before we moved into the Biltmore, the company had a very strong feeling that we wanted to rid the theatre of the bad vibes that were there from the first two productions earlier in the season. The day we moved into the theatre, Laura brought fresh sage. We lit it, and with her as the leader, we ran through the entire theatre, backstage, orchestra, mezzanine, dressing rooms, and the basement. The theatre was filled with the burning scent of sage, so we scourged the entire space. We then opened to great reviews and we extended the production for two extra weeks. We hope Manhattan Theatre Club's gorgeous space that ensures three new American plays on Broadway each season will continue to be bad-vibe free.

Stage management had a nightly ritual with Ms. Linney. I would call half-hour seated at my calling desk. Laura would come by, we would put two fingers together and say, "Light switch." She would walk a few feet close to the stage where my assistant Denise Yaney stood. They would put two thumbs together, say "Thumbs up," then put two fingers together and say with great ferocity, "Light switch." "Light switch" was the catchword because, at the final dress rehearsal, Laura had forgotten to turn off a lamp.

Favorite Offstage Moment: My favorite moment at each performance was the following: Ms. Linney would exit having just slugged Mr. Shenkman at the end of the first act. Our production assistant, Greg Covert, and one of our props people, Sue Poulin, would greet her in a new guise at every show: Once they were dancers doing pirouettes. Once they were dressed in backup costumes as other characters in the play. Once they had a trail of Jelly Bellies, which they illuminated with their flashlights. No one remembers exactly how this ritual began, but many people gathered at every show to see what new idea would arise.

Favorite Onstage Moment: Two favorites (these are my own, from watching the show each night): Watching Ben's face, in the first few minutes of the play when he is facing his former lover's husband of eight

Backstage on opening night (L-R): Laura Linney, Byron Jennings, director Daniel Sullivan (holdi his opening night gift from the cast), Ben Shenkman and Ana Reeder.

years and she is out buying a lamb roast. The look of panic, terror and pain as he looked longingly and yearningly at the door, wondering if she would return. My other favorite moment is in the next-to-last scene of the play. Patricia (Laura) has just relinquished a painting done of her by Jonathan (Ben). Her husband (Byron) has sold it to her former lover for a huge amount of money. As her husband leaves, she says very simply, "Soon," letting him know she's going back up to bed. That "soon" was different every single one of the 91 performances. It always had pain, yearning, resignation, hope, fear and dread, among many others, but always in a different combination. A superb moment from a gifted actress.

In-Theatre Gathering Place: One of our favorites was the green room in the basement, most often on Sundays before the matinee, where we had some of the best brunches on Broadway. There were deviled eggs and sometimes quiche from Denise Yaney, cheese spread from electrician Jeff Dodson, coffee cake from prop man Tim Walters, and various other delights from Greg Covert, the actors, and front-of-house personnel.

Off-Site Hangout: Joe Allen's, a slight edge over Angus McIndoe's.

Snack Food: Anything chocolate! However, a close runner-up would be Jelly Bellies or jelly beans. A thirty-dollar pack of jelly beans would be gone in two days. (Do you

know how many jelly beans thirty dollars can buy?)

Memorable Ad-Lib: The most memorable one came from Ben Shenkman. Over several days the Biltmore had been having trouble with fire alarms. During the final scene of the play, which takes place in a college campus art class, the fire alarm went off several times, then stopped. "Class is finally over," Ben said. The audience thought it was part of the play.

Cellphone Rings: Six, even after an announcement at the top of the show and a reminder at the top of the second act. However, the day following one of our most horrible evenings of cellphone hell, we got a beautiful vase of flowers, with the following note: "Dear Cast of *Sight Unseen*, please accept this bouquet and an apology for the inexcusable disruption of the beautiful performance last night caused by my cell phone. A Chastened Theatregoer."

Nicknames: Mr. Shenkman was sometimes lovingly called "Shenky." (We were never sure if he liked it or not, but he took it with great aplomb.) Ms. Reeder was called, "The Girly-Girl." And Laura was occasionally referred to as, "That Linney Woman."

Also: This was a glorious experience for all concerned: a great play given a transcendent production with four stunning performances.

Correspondent: Roy Harris, Production Stage Manager

PLAYBILL

CAST

(in order of speaking)

Simon Able ....BRONSON PINCHOT
Sly's Servants ....JEREMY HOLLINGWORTH,
MacINTYRE DIXON,
LINDA HALASKA
Foxwell J. Sly ....RICHARD KIND
Lawyer Craven ....JASON KRAVITS
Jethro Crouch ....RICHARD LIBERTINI
Abner Truckle ....BOB DISHY
Miss Fancy ....CAROL KANE
Mrs. Truckle ....RACHEL YORK
Crouch's Servant ....JASON MA
Captain Crouch ....NICK WYMAN
The Chief of Police ....LARRY STORCH
1st Policeman ....ROBERT LaVELLE
2nd Policeman/Bailiff ....GORDON JOSEPH
WEISS
3rd Policeman ....JEFF TALBOTT
Court Clerk ....PROFESSOR IRWIN COREY
The Judge ....RICHARD KIND

UNDERSTUDIES

For Foxwell J. Sly/The Judge – NICK WYMAN; for
Simon Able – JEREMY HOLLINGWORTH; for
Abner Truckle – MacINTYRE DIXON, LARRY
STORCH, GORDON JOSEPH WEISS; for Jethro
Crouch – MacINTYRE DIXON, PROFESSOR
IRWIN COREY; for Mrs. Truckle and Miss Fancy
- LINDA HALASKA; for Captain Crouch –
ROBERT LaVELLE; for Lawyer Craven – JERE-
MY HOLLINGWORTH, GORDON JOSEPH
WEISS; for Chief of Police – GORDON JOSEPH
WEISS; for Court Clerk – MacINTYRE DIXON;
for the Policemen – JEFF TALBOTT, JASON MA;
for the Bailiff and the Servants – JEFF TALBOTT.

---

⑤ ETHEL BARRYMORE THEATRE

243 West 47th Street
A Shubert Organization Theatre

Gerald Schoenfeld, *Chairman*   **Philip J. Smith,** *President*

Robert E. Wankel, *Executive Vice President*

Julian Schlossberg   Roy Furman   Ben Sprecher
Michael Gardner Jim Fantaci Cheryl Lachowicz Christine Duncan and Nelle Nugent
by arrangement with Andrew Braunsberg

present

Richard Kind   Bronson Pinchot
Bob Dishy   Richard Libertini   Jason Kravits
Rachel York   and   Carol Kane

in

"SLY FOX"

by

Larry Gelbart

with

Professor Irwin Corey   Nick Wyman

MacIntyre Dixon   Linda Halaska   Jeremy Hollingworth
Robert LaVelle   Jason Ma   Jeff Talbott   Gordon Joseph Weiss

and

Larry Storch

Scenic Design	Costume Design	Lighting Design	Sound Design
George Jenkins	Albert Wolsky	Phil Monat	T. Richard Fitzgerald
Jesse Poleshuck			Carl Casella

Wigs By	Casting	Technical Supervision
Paul Huntley	Stuart Howard & Amy Schecter, CSA	Teckeneally, Inc.

Marketing	Fight Staging	Associate Producers
TMG—The Marketing Group	B.H. Barry	Aaron Levy, Jill Furman
		Debra Black, Peter May

Production Stage Manager	Press Representative	General Manager
Marybeth Abel	The Publicity Office	Peter Bogyo

Directed By

Arthur Penn

The Producers wish to thank Theatre Development Fund for its support of this production.

8/23/04

SETTING

San Francisco, one day in the late 1800s

ACT ONE

Scene 1: Sly's Bedroom
Scene 2: Truckle's Living Room
Scene 3: Crouch's Office
Scene 4: Sly's Bedroom

ACT TWO

Scene 1: A Jail Cell
Scene 2: The Courtroom
Scene 3: Sly's Bedroom

Photo by Carol Rosegg

From His Deathbed: Elizabeth Berkley and Richard
Dreyfuss from the opening night cast.

Richard Kind
Foxwell J. Sly/
The Judge

Bronson Pinchot
Simon Able
(prev: Lawyer Craven)

Bob Dishy
Abner Truckle

Richard Libertini
Jethro Crouch

Jason Kravits
Lawyer Craven

Rachel York
Mrs. Truckle
(prev: Miss Fancy)

Carol Kane
Miss Fancy

Professor Irwin
Corey
Court Clerk

Nick Wyman
Captain Crouch

Larry Storch
Chief of Police

MacIntyre Dixon
Second Servant

Linda Halaska
Third Servant

Jeremy Hollingworth
First Servant

Robert LaVelle
First Policeman

Jason Ma
Crouch's Servant

Jeff Talbott
Third Policeman

Gordon Joseph Weiss
Second
Policeman/Bailiff/
Fight Captain

Larry Gelbart
Author

Arthur Penn
Director

Carl Casella
Sound Designer

Paul Huntley
Wigs

B.H. Barry
Fight Director

Peter Bogyo
General Manager

Julian Schlossberg
Producer

Ben Sprecher
Producer

Michael Gardner
Producer

'SLY FOX'
ALUMNI

Charles Antalosky
Second Servant

René Auberjonois
Jethro Crouch

Richard Dreyfuss
Foxwell J. Sly/The
Judge

Elizabeth Berkley
Lauren
Mrs. Truckle

Peter Scolari
Chief of Police

Eric Stoltz
Simon Able

Sly Fox

STAFF FOR SLY FOX

GENERAL MANAGER
PETER BOGYO

GENERAL PRESS REPRESENTATIVE
THE PUBLICITY OFFICE

Bob Fennell   Marc Thibodeau

Michael S. Borowski

COMPANY MANAGER
Laura Heller

TECHNICAL SUPERVISION
Teckeneally, Inc.

Ken Keneally

CASTLE HILL PRODUCTIONS
Chairman	Julian Schlossberg
Asst to Mr. Schlossberg	Ruth Better

THE SPRECHER ORGANIZATION
Chairman	Ben Sprecher
General Manager/Theatre Operations	Mary Miller
General Manager/Production	Peter Bogyo
Assistant to General Manager	Rebecca Frick
Production Associate	Nicole Newton
Technical Director	Rob Conover

THE FOXBORO COMPANY, INC
President	Nelle Nugent
SVP Creative Affairs	Kenneth Teaton
Assistant	Michael Casieri
Legal Counsel	Lazarus & Harris LLP, David H. Friedlander, Esq. Sidney Feinberg, Esq.

PRODUCTION STAGE MANAGER	Marybeth Abel
Stage Manager	Bryan Landrine
Assistant to Mr. Furman	Eileen Corrigan
Assistant to Michael Gardner	Marsha Rosenberg
Production Assistant	Cyrille Blackburn
Assistant to the Director	Jessica Brickman
Assistant Set Designer	Frank McCullough
Associate Costume Designer	MaryAnn D. Smith
Assistant Lighting Designer	John Tees III
2nd Assistant Lighting Designer	George Gountas
Production Properties Master	George Wagner
Production Carpenter	Patrick Shea
Assistant Carpenter	Rob Presley
Production Electrician	Richard Mortell
Properties Master	Abraham Morrison
Wardrobe Supervisor	Kathy Guida
Mr. Kind's Dresser	Susan Gomez
Dresser	Kate McAleer
Hair Supervisor	Marty Kopulsky
Production Legal Counsel	Fitelson, Lasky, Aslan & Couture/ Floria V. Lasky, Esq.
Insurance	DeWitt Stern/Peter Shoemaker
Accountant	Robert Fried, CPA
Controller	Anne Stewart FitzRoy
Advertising	Serino Coyne/Thomas Mygatt
Press Interns	Nicole Grillos, Alexa Shaughnessy
Casting Associate	Paul Hardt
Logo Artwork	Chava Ben-Amos
Production Photography	Carol Rosegg
Theatre Displays	BAM Signs, Inc./ Adam Miller

Opening Night Coordination	Tobak-Dantchik Events & Promotions/ Suzanne Tobak, Michael P. Lawrence
Banking	JP Morgan Chase/Keith D. Simpson
Marketing	TMG Marketing
Barter Marketing	Barter Luxury, Inc./Robert Esposito
Payroll Service	CSI, Castellana Services Inc.
Car Service	Broadway Trans, Inc./ Ralph Taliercio
Rehearsal Space	Manhattan Theatre Club
Pre-Show Announcement	Don LaFontaine
Merchandising	George Fenmore/ More Merchandising International

CREDITS

Scenery built and painted by F&D Scene Changes Ltd., Calgary, Alberta. Computer motion control and automation of scenery and rigging by Feller Precision, Inc. SHOWTRAK® computer motion control for scenery and rigging. Lighting equipment supplied by GSD Productions, Inc., West Hempstead, NY. Sound equipment from Sound Associates, Inc. Costumes constructed by Eric Winterling, Inc. Millinery by Lynne Mackey Studio. Additional costumes by Western Costume Co. Mr. Dreyfuss' boots by Montana Leatherworks. Shirts by Anto Shirts. Original oil paintings provided by Robert Waltsak, The Woodworker Shop, Wayne, NJ. Pewterware courtesy of Wilton Armetale. Cristal d'Arques crystal drinkware used. Bedlinens by Martex. Cane, smoking supplies and accessories courtesy of Nat Sherman International. Matches by Diamond Brands, Inc. Silver pieces courtesy of Oneida Silversmiths Ltd. Witness chair provided by Blatt Billiards, NYC. Coins courtesy of Educational Coin, Hewitt, NJ. Treasure chest items provided by New York Galleries, New York, NY. Theatrical prop styling and consultation provided by George Wagner, Proper Decorum Inc., Kinnelon, NJ. Additional period and hand props courtesy of George Fenmore, Inc. Study guide and educational program by Peter Royston/GUIDEWRITE in conjunction with the Museum of Comic and Cartoon Art.

MUSIC CREDITS

"Shady Grove," Traditional (arr. by Ricky Skaggs); Heartbound Sounds, Inc. (ASCAP); courtesy of Skaggs Family Records, Inc.

SPECIAL THANKS

Peter Parkin, Don LaFontaine, William P. Miller, Wylie Griffin, Susan Fulginiti.

THE SHUBERT ORGANIZATION, INC.

Gerald Schoenfeld	Philip J. Smith
Chairman	President
John W. Kluge	Lee J. Seidler
Michael I. Sovern	Stuart Subotnick

Irving M. Wall

Robert E. Wankel

Executive Vice President

Peter Entin	Elliot Greene
Vice President Theatre Operations	Vice President Finance
David Andrews	John Darby
Vice President Shubert Ticketing Services	Vice President Facilities

STAFF FOR THE ETHEL BARRYMORE
House Manager	Dan Landon

Playwright Larry Gelbart on opening night.

(L-R): Eric Stoltz, Richard Dreyfuss and, Bronson Pinchot at the opening night party at Tavern on the Green.

Elizabeth Berkley takes part in the "Stars in the Alley" event.

Above left: Rachel York on the show's softball team. Center: Bows on opening night. Right: Irwin Corey and his grandson, Amedeo Corey, at the opening night party.

Opening Night: Larry Gelbart, an old-fashioned gentleman of the theatre, gave the three women in the cast enormous potted flowering shrubs. The men got wonderful handwritten notes.

Favorite Moment: The Act II courtroom scene. It never played exactly the same way twice, and we'd find ourselves saying, "What's going to happen in the courtroom tonight?"

Nicknames: The show's cast fell into two groups of players. There were ten principals and then there were seven smaller roles. This group came to be known as "The Lilliputians," because we were surrounded by giants. Bob Dishy was "The Dish." Eric Stoltz was "The Captain." Richard Dreyfuss was "Mr. Theatre." Other nicknames came and went, but Peter Scolari was the most faithful in using them.

Backstage Rituals: The circle at five minutes. This started in Boston. Richard Dreyfuss liked to see each performer before the play started. We'd talk about what had happened that day, and laugh together. This tradition continued through the run.

Before every show, Eric "The Captain" Stoltz would get on the loudspeaker and say: "Go big team *Sly Fox*! Go big team!"

In-Theatre Hangout: Eric Stoltz's dressing room has a living room and he generously offered it to the company as a stage manager's office and green room.

Favorite Off-Site Hangout: People would go to Sardi's or McHale's, but generally didn't do all that much socializing.

Snack Foods: Company manager Laura Heller was known for her biscotti. I liked to bake brownies or cake for people's birthdays, but everyone was concerned about carbs. I once brought in something yummy and Elizabeth Berkley would only eat a crumb. After that, I called her Elizabeth "one-bite" Berkley.

Favorite Therapy: Réne Auberjonois could time his Act II cough drop so it would dissolve just before his first line. The cast wondered if the accumulation of Ricola wrappers in his coat pocket had a therapeutic purpose as well.

Celebrity Visitor: One night, a woman stood between me and the stage door. I said "Excuse me" to get past, and the

woman said "Of course." And that's when I noticed it was Lauren Bacall.

Actor Who Performed The Most Roles: Definitely that was me. I was the busiest guy in the building. Some nights I would play my own role, plus two or three of the characters I was covering. They were: 1st Policeman, 2nd Policeman, Bailiff, Crouch's Servant, Sly's Servant.

Who Has Done The Most Shows on Broadway: Not sure, but hair supervisor Marty Kopulsky has tattoos on his legs with the logos of shows that have been important to him, from *Dreamgirls* to *Sly Fox*.

Fastest Costume Change: Richard Dreyfuss played two characters. Once, his costume got stuck in a door. Another time, he came on without part of his ensemble and went back to get it.

Also: After the reviews were in, the cast started to play. It was like being on "The Carol Burnett Show," trying to make each other laugh. Bronson was always the first to say something directly to the audience.

Correspondent: Jeff Talbott, "3rd Policeman"

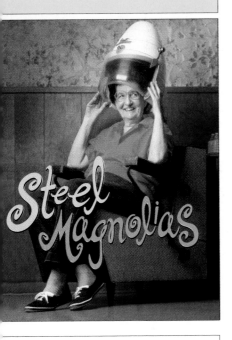

PLAYBILL®

CAST
(in order of appearance)

Truvy ....DELTA BURKE
Annelle ....LILY RABE
Clairee ....FRANCES STERNHAGEN
Shelby ....REBECCA GAYHEART
M'Lynn ....CHRISTINE EBERSOLE
Ouiser ....MARSHA MASON

Time: 1987
Place: Chinquapin, Louisiana

ACT ONE
Scene 1: April
Scene 2: December

ACT TWO
Scene 1: June, 18 months later
Scene 2: November

STANDBYS
PATRICIA KILGARRIFF
GINIFER KING
SALLY MAYES

⑧LYCEUM THEATRE
A Shubert Organization Theatre
Gerald Schoenfeld, Chairman   Philip J. Smith, President
Robert E. Wankel, Executive Vice President

Roy Gabay   Robyn Goodman

Danzansky Partners Ergo Entertainment Ruth Hendel Sharon Karmazin

Susan Dietz/Ina Meibach Michael Galvis/Billy Huddleston Elsa Daspin Suisman/Martha R. Gasparian

present

| Delta Burke | Christine Ebersole | Rebecca Gayheart | Marsha Mason | Lily Rabe | Frances Sternhagen |

in

Steel Magnolias

By Robert Harling

Set Design by	Costume Design by	Lighting Design by
Anna Louizos	David Murin	Howell Binkley

Sound Design by	Hair Design & Supervision by	Production Stage Manager
Ken Travis	Bobby H. Grayson	James FitzSimmons

Press Representative	Casting by	Dialect Coach
Boneau/Bryan-Brown	Bernard Telsey Casting	Stephen Gabis

Props Coordinator	Production Manager	General Manager	Associate Producers
Kathy Fabian	Showman Fabricators, Inc.	Roy Gabay	Stephen Kocis
			Bill Goodman

Directed by
Jason Moore

Originally produced by the WPA Theatre, New York City, 1987
(Kyle Renick, Artistic Director)

The producers wish to thank Theatre Development Fund for their support of this production.

LIVE BROADWAY

4/4/04

Frances Sternhagen and Delta Burke.

Photo by Joan Marcus

Delta Burke
Truvy

Christine Ebersole
M'Lynn

Rebecca Gayheart
Shelby

Marsha Mason
Ouiser

Lily Rabe
Annelle

Frances Sternhagen
Clairee

Patricia Kilgarriff
Standby

Ginifer King
Standby

Robert Harling
Playwright

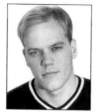
Jason Moore
Director

Anna Louizos
Set Design

David Murin
Costume Design

Howell Binkley
Lighting Design

Bernard Telsey
Casting

Jen Bender
Assistant Director

Roy Gabay
Producer/General Manager

Robyn Goodman
Producer

Ruth Hendel
Producer

Sharon Karmazin
Producer

(L-R) Rebecca Gayheart as Shelby, Delta Burke as Truvy, Lily Rabe as Annelle and Christine Ebersole as M'Lynn.

Photo by Joan Marcus

Steel Magnolias

Backstage Crew
(L-R): Leah Nelson, William Rowland, Gerry Stein, Steve Loehle, Neil Krasnow, Adam Braunstein, Kim Prentice, James FitzSimmons (Production Stage Manager and Yearbook Correspondent), Kay Grunder and Nancy Lawson.

Front of House
Front Row (L-R): Lorraine Bellaflores, Merida Colon (Chief Usher), Chip Jorgensen (Head Treasurer) and Joann Swanson (House Manager).
Middle Row (L-R): Kevin Pinzon, Susan Houghton, Elsie Grosvenor and Sonia Moreno.
Top Row (L-R): Saviel Almonte, Robert De Jesus and Nicole McIntyre.

Hair Department
Susan Corrado (Assistant Hair) and Bobby H. Grayson (Hair Designer/Supervisor).

Steel Magnolias

STAFF FOR STEEL MAGNOLIAS

GENERAL MANAGEMENT
ROY GABAY THEATRICAL
PRODUCTION & MANAGEMENT
Cheryl Dennis, Daniel Kuney,
Shawn Murphy, Cori Silberman

GENERAL PRESS REPRESENTATION
BONEAU/BRYAN-BROWN
Chris Boneau   Susanne Tighe
Heath Schwartz

COMPANY MANAGER
CHERYL DENNIS

CASTING
BERNARD TELSEY CASTING, C.S.A.
Bernie Telsey, Will Cantler, David Vaccari,
Bethany Knox, Craig Burns,
Tiffany Little Canfield, Christine Dall,
Stephanie Yankwitt

PRODUCTION SUPERVISION
SHOWMAN FABRICATORS, INC.
Production Strategies
Kai Brothers, Jason Block

PRODUCTION STAGE MANAGER
James FitzSimmons

Stage Manager	Neil Krasnow
Assistant Director	Jen Bender
Associate Set Designer	Donyale Werle
Set Design Assistants	Michael Carnahan, Heather Dunbar
Assistant Costume Designer	Leslie Fuhs Allen
Associate Lighting Designer	Aaron Copp
Assistant Sound Designer	Shannon Slaton
Production Sound Operator	Gerry Stein
On Stage Styling Instruction	Bobby H. Grayson
Assistant Wig Design	Inga Thrasher
Assistant Hair Supervisor	Susan Corrado
Production Carpenter	Chris Wiggins
Production Electrician	Graeme McDonnell
Production Props	Steven Loehle
Props Assistants	Carrie S. Hash, Carrie Mossman
Wardrobe Supervisor	Kay Grunder
Dressers	Nancy Lawson, Kim Prentice
Production Assistants	Amy Birnbaum, Cyrille Blackburn
Assistant to Aged in Wood	Josh Fiedler
Press Representative Staff	Adrian Bryan-Brown,
	Jim Byk, Brandi Cornwell,
	Erika Creagh, Adriana Douzos,
	Jackie Green, Juliana Hannett,
	Hector Hernandez, Jessica Johnson,
	Kevin Jones, Eric Louie,
	Aaron Meier, Joe Perrotta,
	Linnae Petruzzelli, Matt Polk
Accountant	Fried & Kowgios CPAs LLP/Robert Fried, CPA
Controller	Elliott Aronstam
Banking	JPMorgan Chase
Insurance	DeWitt Stern Group Inc
Legal	John Silberman & Associate/ Karen Levinson

Advertising	Serino Coyne, Inc./
	Greg Corradetti, Joaquin Esteva
	Ruth Rosenberg, Sue Wozny
Production Photographer	Joan Marcus
Theatre Displays	King Displays
Car Service	I.B.A. Luxury Sedan Service/Danny Ibanez
Rehearsal Studios	Playwrights Horizons
Payroll Services	Castellana Services, Inc.
On Stage Merchandising	George Fenmore, Inc.
Opening Night Coordination	Toback-Dantchik Events & Promotion

CREDITS

Scenery supplied by SMI Showmotion.
Lighting equipment supplied by PRG Lighting.
Sound equipment supplied by Masque Sound.
Costume construction by The Costume Lab.
Wig construction by Ray's Marston and Victoria Wood.
Beauty parlor equipment by Veeco Manufacturing, Inc., David S.S. Davis.
Additional period props courtesy of George Fenmore, Inc.
Hair care products and styling tools provided by ConairPro and Rusk.
Makeup provided By M·A·C.
Manicure products provided by OPI Products, Inc.
Ms. Gayheart's jeans provided by Joe's Jeans.
Some of Ms. Ebersole's wardrobe provided by Talbots.
Salon decor and hair accessories by Ray's Beauty Supply.
Skincare products used in the show are provided by Murad.
Children's bath and body products provided by Circle of Friends.
Natural herb cough drops courtesy of Ricola USA, Inc.

Playbill cover photo by Lee Crum.

www.steelmagnoliasbroadway.com

SPECIAL THANKS

Midge Lucas (Painter), Elizabeth Payne (Crafts and Painting),
Kevin Mark Harris (Tailor), Virginia Johnson (Draper), Ray Beauty Supply,
Catherine Small, Anne Guay, Erin Eagleton, John Kilgore, Michael Pilibski,
Robin Santos, Trattoria Dopo Teatro, Playwrights Horizons Costume Shop

 THE SHUBERT ORGANIZATION, INC.

Gerald Schoenfeld Chairman	**Philip J. Smith** President
John W. Kluge	**Lee J. Seidler**
Michael I. Sovern	**Stuart Subotnick**

Irving M. Wall

Robert E. Wankel
Executive Vice President

Peter Entin Vice President Theatre Operations	**Elliot Greene** Vice President Finance
David Andrews Vice President Shubert Ticketing Services	**John Darby** Vice President Facilities

House Manager	Joann Swanson

Memorable Opening Night Gifts: Everyone got gift certificates to Bloomingdale's because there is a line in the show about how "you can't go through there without getting made up." There's also a line about "Bleeding Armadillo Cake," so I baked everyone Bleeding Armadillo Cookies.

"Easter Bonnet" Sketch: "Steel Magnolias" by James FitzSimmons and Neil Krasnow, with help from wardrobe, props and hair. It was a big group effort.

Who Has Done The Most Shows: Frannie Sternhagen. This is her sixth show at the Lyceum alone!

Ritual: Frannie does a dance backstage when the pre-show music starts.

In-Theatre Gathering Place: The Lyceum has a huge backstage area for a playhouse, so everyone has their own space. We do have the most luxurious quick-change booth on Broadway. It's got pink silk bunting and pink curtains.

Snack Food: Anything chocolate.

Therapies: Red Bull, Diet Coke, Snickers and Throat-Coat Tea. I keep all of these very well stocked.

Memorable Ad-Lib: One night an audience member loudly shushed another audience member during one of Delta's speeches, and she stopped and asked, "Was that shush for me?" The audience went wild.

Strangest Press Encounter: We had a big group press day and so many reporters asked Delta about her wig, she finally took it off and let someone try it on.

Strangest Stage Door Fan Encounters: This show has some diehard fans. We get a lot of, "Oh, I didn't know they made the movie into a play!" One day, when we were collecting for BC/EFA, one woman said, "I will give you a check for $1,000 if my daughter can talk to Delta Burke. She looks just like her." And you know something? She did!

Heaviest/Hottest Costumes: Delta's wigs and Lily Rabe's pregnancy.

Embarrassing Moment: Rebecca Gayheart has a line, "I have just discovered the early stages of crow's feet." During rehearsal she had to ask what crow's feet were. She didn't know! The maturer women were all like, "Just wait...."

Nickname: Our props person, Leah Nelson, is known as "Peppermint Girl."

Catchphrases: "The Alka-Seltzer will be at the calling station." "Welcome to Mr. Toad's wild ride."

Also: We call ourselves "The Red State Show."

The front row is very close to the stage. You can get hit with water from the sink, get orange juice spilled on you, or have Rebecca spit a peppermint in your lap.

We're like *Rocky Horror*. People know the show so well, they say the lines along with us, and laugh at the jokes before we say them.

Correspondent: Production Stage Manager James FitzSimmons

Photos by Aubrey Reuben

Above Left: John Demsey, President of MAC and Rebecca Gayheart at the opening night party at Tavern on the Green. Right: Director Jason Moore and stepmother Rhonda Moore.

Playwright Robert Harling, flanked by Rebecca Gayheart and Delta Burke, take curtain calls on opening night.

Above Left: Frances Sternhagen and Delta Burke perform a skit in the "Easter Bonnet" competition. Right: Marsha Mason on opening night.

PLAYBILL®

A Streetcar Named Desire

CAST

A Negro Woman ....WANDA L. HOUSTON
Eunice Hubbell ....KRISTINE NIELSEN
Stanley Kowalski ....JOHN C. REILLY
Harold Mitchell (Mitch) ....CHRIS BAUER
Stella Kowalski ....AMY RYAN
Blanche DuBois .....NATASHA RICHARDSON
Steve Hubbell ....SCOTT SOWERS
Pablo Gonzales ....FRANK PANDO
A Young Collector ....WILL TOALE
A Mexican Woman ....TERESA YENQUE
A Doctor ....JOHN CARTER
A Nurse ....BARBARA SIMS
Street People ...JOHN CARTER, WILL TOALE,
　　TERESA YENQUE, ALFREDO NARCISO,
　　STARLA BENFORD, FRANK PANDO

New Orleans, 1947

UNDERSTUDIES/STANDBYS

For Blanche and Stella – ANGELA PIERCE
For Stanley and Mitch – CHARLES BORLAND
For Eunice, Negro Woman, Mexican Woman and
Nurse – STARLA BENFORD
For Steve and Doctor –
ROBERT EMMET LUNNEY
For Pablo and Collector – ALFREDO NARCISO

Production Stage Manager – JANE GREY
Stage Manager – PHILIP CUSACK

STUDIO 54

ROUNDABOUT THEATRE COMPANY

TODD HAIMES, Artistic Director
ELLEN RICHARD, Managing Director
JULIA C. LEVY, Executive Director, External Affairs

Presents

Natasha Richardson　John C. Reilly

in

Tennessee Williams'

A Streetcar Named Desire

with

Amy Ryan　Chris Bauer

Starla Benford　Kate Buddeke　John Carter　Wanda L. Houston
Alfredo Narciso　Kristine Nielsen　Frank Pando
Scott Sowers　Will Toale　Teresa Yenque

Set Design by Robert Brill	*Costume Design by* William Ivey Long	*Lighting Design by* Donald Holder	*Original Music and Sound Design by* John Gromada
Hair and Wig Design by Paul Huntley	*Production Stage Manager* Jane Grey	*Dialect Coach* Deborah Hecht	*Fight Direction by* Rick Sordelet
Casting by Jim Carnahan, C.S.A.	*Associate Director* Barbara Rubin	*Technical Supervisor* Steve Beers	*General Manager* Sydney Beers
Founding Director Gene Feist	*Associate Artistic Director* Scott Ellis	*Press Representative* Boneau/Bryan-Brown	*Director of Marketing* David B. Steffen

Directed by

Edward Hall

**Major support for this production provided by JPMorgan Chase.
Additional support provided by the Eleanor Naylor Dana Charitable Trust and
the National Endowment for the Arts.**

Presented by arrangement with The University of the South, Sewanee, Tennessee
Roundabout Theatre Company is a member of the League of Resident Theatres. www.roundabouttheatre.org　　5/28/05

Kindness of Strangers: Natasha Richardson (as Blanche) and John C. Reilly (as Stanley).

A Streetcar Named Desire

Natasha Richardson
Blanche DuBois

John C. Reilly
Stanley Kowalski

Amy Ryan
Stella Kowalski

Chris Bauer
Harold Mitchell

Starla Benford
Street Person

John Carter
*Doctor,
Street Person*

Wanda L. Houston
Negro Woman

Alfredo Narciso
Street Person

Kristine Nielsen
Eunice Hubbell

Frank Pando
Pablo, Street Person

Barbara Sims
Nurse

Scott Sowers
Steve Hubble

Will Toale
*Young Collector,
Street Person*

Teresa Yenque
*Mexican Woman,
Street Person*

Charles Borland
*Standby Stanley,
Mitch*

Robert Emmet Lunney
*Standby Steve,
Doctor*

Angela Pierce
*Standby Blanche,
Stella*

Tennessee Williams
(1911-1983)
Playwright

Edward Hall
Director

Robert Brill
Set Design

William Ivey Long
Costume Design

Donald Holder
Lighting Design

Paul Huntley
*Hair and Wig
Design*

Rick Sordelet
Fight Direction

Jane Grey
*Production Stage
Manager*

Philip Cusack
Stage Manager

Barbara Rubin
Associate Director

Jim Carnahan
Casting Director

Gene Feist
*Founding Director,
Roundabout
Theatre*

2004-2005 AWARD

OUTER CRITICS CIRCLE AWARD
Featured Actress in a Play (Amy Ryan)

Todd Haimes
*Artistic Director
Roundabout Theatre*

A Streetcar Named Desire

Box Office
(L-R): Krystin MacRitchie, Steve Howe and Scott Falkowski.

Company Management
(L-R): Nancy Mulliner and Lauren Parker.

Stage Management
Philip Cusack and Jane Grey.

Photos by Ben Strohmann

Crew
(L-R): Dan Hoffman, John Wooding, Josh Weitzman, Erin Delaney, Greg Peeler, Lawrence Jenino.

Wardrobe
(L-R): Sandy Binion, Nadine Hettel, Kevin Mark Harris, Gerald Crawford and Jay Woods.

Front-of-House Staff
Front Row (L-R): Mary Ann Ehlshlager, Laconya Robinson, Jack Watanachaiyot.
Middle Row (L-R): Jonathan Martinez, Anthony Roman, Kate Longosky, Latiffa Marcus, Jay Watanachaiyot.
Back Row (L-R): Maman Garba, Ralph Mohan, Nick Wheatley, Jason Fernandez.

A Streetcar Named Desire

ROUNDABOUT THEATRE COMPANY STAFF

ARTISTIC DIRECTOR ....TODD HAIMES
MANAGING DIRECTOR ....ELLEN RICHARD
EXECUTIVE DIRECTOR,
EXTERNAL AFFAIRS ....JULIA C. LEVY
ASSOCIATE ARTISTIC DIRECTOR ....SCOTT ELLIS

ARTISTIC STAFF

DIRECTOR OF ARTISTIC DEVELOPMENT/
DIRECTOR OF CASTING ....Jim Carnahan
Artistic Consultant.........................Robyn Goodman
Resident Director ....Michael Mayer
Associate Artists ....Scott Elliott, Bill Irwin,
                                    Joe Mantello, Mark Brokaw
Consulting Dramaturg............................Jerry Patch
Artistic Associate ....Samantha Barrie
Casting Director ....Mele Nagler
Casting Associate ....Carrie Gardner
Casting Associate ............................J.V. Mercanti
Casting Assistant ....Kate Schwabe
Casting Assistant ....Stephen Kopel
Artistic Intern ....Corinne Hayoun

EDUCATION STAFF

EDUCATION DIRECTOR ....Megan Kirkpatrick
Director of Instruction and
Curriculum Development ....Renee Flemings
Education Program Associate ....Lindsay Erb
Education Program Associate ....Stacey L. Morris
Education Assistant ....Cassidy Jones
Education Interns ....Fumiko Eda, Tommy Marr,
                                         Catherine Taylor
Education Dramaturg ....Ted Sod
Teaching Artists ....Zakiyyah Alexander,
                    Phil Alexander, Cynthia Babak,
                    Victor Barbella, Brigitte Barnett-Loftis,
                    Caitlin Barton, Joe Basile, LaTonya Borsay,
                    Bonnie Brady, Mike Carnahan, Joe Clancy,
                    Melissa Denton, Stephen DiMenna, Joe Doran,
                    Tony Freeman, Shana Gold, Sheri Graubert,
                    Dennis Green, Susan Hamburger,
                    Karla Hendrick, Jim Jack, Alvin Keith,
                    Rebecca Lord, Erin McCready,
                    Andrew Ondrejcak, Laura Poe,
                    Nicole Press, Chris Rummel,
                    Drew Sachs, Anna Saggese, David Sinkus,
                    Vickie Tanner, Olivia Tsang,
                    Jennifer Varbalow, Leese Walker,
                    Eric Wallach, Diana Whitten,
                    Gail Winar, Kirche Zeile

ADMINISTRATIVE STAFF

GENERAL MANAGER ....Sydney Beers
General Counsel ....Laura O'Neill
Associate Managing Director ....Greg Backstrom
General Manager
of the Steinberg Center ....Don-Scott Cooper
Assistant to the General Manager ....Maggie Cantrick
Management Assistant ....Nicholas Caccavo
Office Operations Manager ....Bonnie Berens
Human Resources Manager ....Stephen Deutsch
Network Systems Manager ....Jeff Goodman
Manager of Corporate and Party Rentals ....Jetaun Dobbs
MIS Associate ....Lloyd Alvarez
MIS Assistant ....Anthony Foti
Receptionists...........Jennifer Decoteau, Andre Fortson,
                                Carolyn Miller, Elisa Papa
Messenger ....Robert Weisser
Management Intern ....Chris Aniello

FINANCE STAFF

CONTROLLER ....Susan Neiman
Assistant Controller ....John LaBarbera
Accounts Payable Administrator ....Frank Surdi
Customer Service Coordinator ....Trina Cox
Business Office Associate ....David Solomon
Business Assistant ....Yonit Kafka
Business Intern ....Chelsea Glickfield

DEVELOPMENT STAFF

DIRECTOR OF DEVELOPMENT ....Jeffory Lawson
Director, Institutional Giving ....Julie K. D'Andrea
Director, Individual Giving ....Julia Lazarus
Director, Special Events ....Steve Schaeffer
Manager, Donor Information Systems ....Tina Mae Bishko
Special Events Associate ....Elaina Grillo
Institutional Giving Associate ....Kristen Bolibruch
Annual Giving Associate ....Justin D. Steensma
Development Associate ....Adam Gwon
Development Assistant ....Stephenie L. Overton
Assistant, External Affairs ....Robert Weinstein
Patrons Services Assistant ....Dawn Kusinski
Development Intern ....Lauren Hoshibata

MARKETING STAFF

DIRECTOR OF MARKETING ....David B. Steffen
Marketing/Publications Manager ....Tim McCanna
Marketing Associate ....Sunil Ayyagari
Marketing Assistant ....Rebecca Ballon
Marketing Intern ....Alejandro Lojo
Website Consultant ....Keith Powell Beyland
DIRECTOR OF TELESALES
SPECIAL PROMOTIONS ....Tony Baksa
Telesales Manager ....Anton Borissov
Telesales Office Coordinator .................J.W. Griffin

TICKET SERVICES STAFF

DIRECTOR OF SALES OPERATIONS ....Jim Seggelink
Ticket Services Manager ....Ellen Holt
Subscription Manager ....Charlie Garbowski
Box Office Managers..................Edward P. Osborne,
                         Jaime Perlman, Jessica Bowser
Group Sales Manager ....Jeff Monteith
Assistant Box Office Managers ....Paul Caspary,
                         Steve Howe, Megan Young
Assistant Ticket Services Managers ....Robert Kane,
                         David Meglino, Robert Morgan
Ticket Services ....Solangel Bido,
            Andrew Clements, Johanna Comanzo,
            Sean Crews, Thomas Dahl, Nisha Dhruna,
            Adam Elsberry, Lindsay Ericson,
            Scott Falkowski, Catherine Fitzpatrick,
            Erin Frederick, Steven Gottlieb, Julie Hilimire,
            Bill Klemm, Talia Krispel, Alexander LaFrance,
            Krystin MacRitchie, Mead Margulies,
            Chris Migliaccio, Carlos Morris, Nicole Nicholson,
            Shannon Paige, Hillary Parker,
            Thomas Protulipac, Amy Robinson,
            Heather Siebert, Monté Smock,
            Melissa Snyder, Lillian Soto, Justin Sweeney,
            Greg Thorson, Pamela Unger
Ticket Services Intern ....Jesse Blum

SERVICES

Counsel ....Jeremy Nussbaum,
                         Cowan, Liebowitz & Latman, P.C.
Counsel ....Rosenberg & Estis
Counsel ....Rubin and Feldman, P.C.
Counsel ....Cleary, Gottlieb, Steen & Hamilton
Counsel ....Harry H. Weintraub,
                         Glick and Weintraub, P.C.
Immigration Counsel ....Mark D. Koestler and
                                    Theodore Ruthizer
House Physicians ....Dr. Theodore Tyberg,
                                    Dr. Lawrence Katz
House Dentist ....Neil Kanner, D.M.D.
Insurance ....Marsh USA Inc.
Accountant ....Brody, Weiss, Zucarelli &
                                    Urbanek CPAs, P.C.
Advertising...........Eliran Murphy Group/Denise Ganjou
Events Photography ....Anita and Steve Shevett
Production Photographer ....Joan Marcus
Theatre Displays ....King Displays, Wayne Sapper

GENERAL PRESS REPRESENTATIVES
BONEAU / BRYAN-BROWN

Adrian Bryan-Brown   Matt Polk
Jessica Johnson   Joe Perrotta

ROUNDABOUT THEATRE COMPANY
231 West 39th Street, New York, NY 10018
(212) 719-9393

CREDITS FOR A STREETCAR NAMED DESIRE

GENERAL MANAGER ....Sydney Beers
Associate General Manager/
Company Manager ....Nichole Larson
Associate Company Manager ....Nancy Mulliner
Production Stage Manager ....Philip Cusack
Stage Manager ....Philip Cusack
Assistant to the Technical Supervisor ....Elisa R. Kuhar
Assistant Set Designers ....Dustin O'Neill,
                                         Jenny Sawyers
Set Design Assistants ....Michael Byrnes,
                                         Erica Hemminger
Associate Costume Designer ....Rachel Attridge
Costume Shopper ....Matthew Pachtman
Associate Lighting Designer ....Hilary Manners
Assistant Sound Designer ....Christopher Cronin
Assistant Sound Designer ....Ryan Rumery
Additional Music Research ....Rian Murphy
Production Electrician ....Josh Weitzman
Assistant Production Electrician ....John Wooding
House Head Electrician ....Josh Weitzman
Deck Electrician ....John Wooding
Sound Engineers ....William Lewis, Greg Peeler
Wardrobe Supervisor ....Nadine Hettel
Dresser to Ms. Richardson ....Kevin Mark Harris
Dresser to Mr. Reilly ....Gerald Crawford
Dresser ....Jay Woods
Hair Supervisor ....Cynthia Demand
Makeup Artist ....Melissa Silver
Production Carpenter ....Dan Hoffman
House Head Carpenter ....Dan Hoffman
Production Properties ....Denise J. Grillo
Assistant Production Properties ....Keen Gat
House Head Properties ....Lawrence Jennino
Properties ....Erin Delaney
Assistant to the Stage Managers ....Ry Pepper
Production Assistant ....Sara Sahin
Intern to the Company Manager ....Lauren Parker
Ms. Richardson's Hair for
Production Designed by ....J. Roy Helland
Scenery Provided by ....Showman Fabricators
Additional Scenery Provided by ....Atlas Scenic Studios
Lighting Equipment
Provided by ....PRG, Production Resource Group
Sound Equipment Provided by ....Sound Associates
Natasha Richardson's Clothes by ....Euroco Costumes
Costumes and Alterations by ......Jennifer Love Costumes
Army Clothing by ....Kaufman's Army & Navy
Zippo Lighters Used
Rosebud matches by ....Diamond Brands, Inc.
Additional set
and hand props courtesy of ....George Fenmore, Inc.
Merchandising ....George Fenmore/
                         More Merchandising International

MUSIC CREDITS

"Doctor Jazz" (Walter Melorse, Joseph Oliver).
Administered by Edwin H. Morris & Co. Inc.,
Universal Music Publishing Group.
All rights reserved. Used by permission.

STUDIO 54 THEATRE STAFF

Theatre Manager ....Mary Ann Ehlshlager
House Manager ....LaConya Robinson
Assistant House Managers ....Jack Watanachaiyot,
                                    Jay Watanachaiyot
House Staff ....Onercida Concepcion, Elicia Edwards,
                    Linda Edwards, Jason Fernandez,
                    Jen Kneeland, Kate Longosky,
                    Latiffa Marcus, Nicole Marino,
                    Johnathan Martinez, Dana McCaw,
                    Kevin Owens, Nicole Ramirez,
                    Anthony Roman, Stella Varriale,
                    Nick Wheatley
Security ....Gotham Security
Maintenance ....Ralph Mohan, Maman Garba
Refreshments and Merchandising ... Studio 54 Promotions

Photos by Aubrey Reuben

Left: Amy Ryan and John C. Reilly at the opening night party at Gustavino. Right: Taking bows on opening night: Chris Bauer, Amy Ryan, John C. Reilly and Natasha Richardson.

Above left: Standbys Charles Borland, Angela Pierce. Center: Amy Ryan and Ian McKellen. Right: Richardson and Lynn Redgrave.

Best Opening Night Telegram Or Note: "Have a great opening! Please don't eat the grapes!"

Actor Who Has Done The Most Shows: John Carter

Favorite In-Theatre Gathering Place: The "Green Hall."

Favorite Off-Site Hangout: McCoy's on Ninth Avenue.

Special Backstage Ritual: Poker in the Green Hall.

Favorite Snack Foods: Swedish Fish and Nestle's Crunch.

Mascots: Buster (the dog) and Percy (the other dog).

Most Memorable Ad-Lib: "Who the hell's Shemp Humply?"

Record Number Of Cell Phone Rings During A Performance: 9-10. Someone in the mezzanine actually answered and had a conversation.

Memorable Stage Door Fan Encounter: "Can you give me voice lessons and your autograph?"

Latest Audience Arrival: Every performance at 8 PM. (Our show starts at 7:30.)

Fastest Costume Change: John C., from PJs to poker game

Who Wore The Heaviest/Hottest Costume: Frank Pando

Who Wore The Least: Natasha Richardson

Memorable Directorial Notes: "You need more sweat." "OK, now you're TOO drunk."

Company In-Jokes: "Shemp Humply."

Coolest Thing About Being In This Show: The people...we have the best cast and crew ever!

Correspondent: Nancy Mulliner, Company Manager

Left: Director Joe Mantello and Richardson. Center: Chris Bauer. Right: hair designer Paul Huntley and costume designer William Ivey Long.

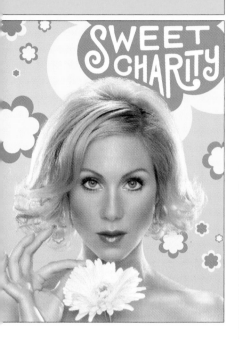

PLAYBILL®

CAST
(in order of appearance)

Charity Hope
Valentine ....CHRISTINA APPLEGATE
Charlie ....TYLER HANES
Policeman ....TIMOTHY EDWARD SMITH
Nickie ....JANINE LaMANNA
Helene ....KYRA Da COSTA
Herman ....ERNIE SABELLA
Ursula ....SHANNON LEWIS
Vittorio Vidal ....PAUL SCHOEFFLER
Frug Dancer ....CORINNE McFADDEN
Manfred ....TIMOTHY EDWARD SMITH
YMCA Receptionist ....TIMOTHY EDWARD
SMITH
Oscar Lindquist ....DENIS O'HARE
Daddy Johann Sebastian
Brubeck ....RHETT GEORGE
Daddy's All-Girl
Rhythm Choir ....JOYCE CHITTICK,
ANIKA ELLIS, MYLINDA HULL
Quartet.......................TODD ANDERSON,
BOB GAYNOR,
TYLER HANES,
TIMOTHY EDWARD SMITH
Rosie ....DYLIS CROMAN
The Company ....TODD ANDERSON,
JOYCE CHITTICK,
TIM CRASKEY,
DYLIS CROMAN,
ANIKA ELLIS,
BOB GAYNOR,

continued on the next page

continued on the next page

AL HIRSCHFELD THEATRE
A JUJAMCYN THEATRE
ROCCO LANDESMAN
PRESIDENT

PAUL LIBIN
PRODUCING DIRECTOR

JACK VIERTEL
CREATIVE DIRECTOR

Barry and Fran Weissler   Clear Channel Entertainment
IN ASSOCIATION WITH Edwin W. Schloss
PRESENT

Christina Applegate
AS

SWEET CHARITY

BOOK BY
Neil Simon

MUSIC BY
Cy Coleman

LYRICS BY
Dorothy Fields

Based on an original screenplay by Federico Fellini, Tullio Pinelli and Ennio Flaiano

STARRING

Denis O'Hare

Janine LaManna   Kyra Da Costa

WITH

Ernie Sabella

Shannon Lewis   Rhett George

AND

Paul Schoeffler

Timothy Edward Smith   Corinne McFadden
Todd Anderson   Alexis Carra   Joyce Chittick   Tim Craskey   Dylis Croman
Anika Ellis   Bob Gaynor   Tyler Hanes   Manuel I. Herrera   Kisha Howard   Mylinda Hull
Reginald Holden Jennings   Amy Nicole Krawcek   Marielys Molina   Seth Stewart

SCENIC DESIGN	COSTUME DESIGN	LIGHTING DESIGN
Scott Pask	William Ivey Long	Brian MacDevitt
SOUND DESIGN	HAIR DESIGN	MAKE-UP DESIGN
Peter Hylenski	Paul Huntley	Angelina Avallone
CASTING	ASSOCIATE DIRECTOR	ASSOCIATE CHOREOGRAPHERS
Jay Binder/Laura Stanczyk	Marc Bruni	Ted Banfalvi/Corinne McFadden

ORCHESTRATIONS	MUSIC DIRECTOR	ADDITIONAL MUSICAL & VOCAL ARRANGEMENTS	ADDITIONAL DANCE ARRANGEMENTS	MUSIC COORDINATOR
Don Sebesky	Don York	Michael Rafter	Jim Abbott	John Miller

GENERAL MANAGER	PRESS REPRESENTATIVE	PRODUCTION SUPERVISOR	PRODUCTION STAGE MANAGER
B.J. Holt	Barlow•Hartman	Arthur Siccardi	David O'Brien

EXECUTIVE PRODUCER	FOR CLEAR CHANNEL ENTERTAINMENT	ASSOCIATE PRODUCERS	IN ASSOCIATION WITH
Alecia Parker	Jennifer Costello	Daniel Posener Jay Binder	Hazel and Sam Feldman Allen Spivak Harvey Weinstein

CHOREOGRAPHY BY

Wayne Cilento

DIRECTED BY

Walter Bobbie

The producers wish to express their appreciation to Theatre Development Fund for its support of this production.
SWEET CHARITY IS LOVINGLY DEDICATED TO THE MEMORY OF CY COLEMAN.

5/4/05

I Could Touch the Sky: Christina Applegate and Denis O'Hare.

Photo by Paul Kolnik

2004-2005 AWARD

Drama Desk Award
Featured Actor in a Musical
(Denis O'Hare)

Sweet Charity

MUSICAL NUMBERS

Time: The 1960s
Place: New York City

ACT ONE

Overture
"You Should See Yourself" ....Charity
"Big Spender" ....Nickie, Helene and The Company
"Charity's Soliloquy" ....Charity
"Rich Man's Frug" ....The Company
"If My Friends Could See Me Now" ....Charity
"Too Many Tomorrows" ....Vittorio
"There's Gotta Be Something Better Than This" ....Charity, Nickie and Helene
"I'm the Bravest Individual" ....Charity and Oscar

ACT TWO

"The Rhythm of Life" ....Charity, Oscar, Daddy, Daddy's All-Girl Rhythm Choir
                                                                              and The Company
"A Good Impression" ....Oscar and The Quartet
"Baby Dream Your Dream" ....Nickie and Helene
"Sweet Charity" ....Oscar and The Company
"Big Spender" (Reprise) ....The Company
"Where Am I Going?" ....Charity
"I'm a Brass Band" ....Charity and The Company
"I Love to Cry at Weddings" ....Herman and The Company
"I'm the Bravest Individual" (Reprise) ....Charity

Christina Applegate
Charity

Denis O'Hare
Oscar

Paul Schoeffler
Vittorio

Janine LaManna
Nickie

Kyra Da Costa
Helene

Ernie Sabella
Herman

Shannon Lewis
Ensemble, Ursula

Rhett George
Ensemble, Daddy

Todd Anderson
Ensemble

Alexis Carra
Swing

Cast Continued

The Company ....RHETT GEORGE,
                                 TYLER HANES,
                                 MANUEL I. HERRERA,
KISHA HOWARD, MYLINDA HULL,
AMY NICOLE KRAWCEK, SHANNON LEWIS,
CORINNE McFADDEN, MARIELYS MOLINA,
      TIMOTHY EDWARD SMITH,
              SETH STEWART

UNDERSTUDIES

For Charity Hope Valentine: DYLIS CROMAN
for Oscar Lindquist: TIMOTHY EDWARD SMITH
for Nickie: JOYCE CHITTICK
for Helene: ANIKA ELLIS
for Vittorio Vidal: BOB GAYNOR
for Ursula: CORINNE McFADDEN

SWINGS:

ALEXIS CARRA
REGINALD HOLDEN JENNINGS

Dance Captain:
REGINALD HOLDEN JENNINGS

SWEET CHARITY ORCHESTRA

Orchestra conducted by Don York

Associate Conductor/Keyboards: John Samorian
Trumpets: Don Downs, Glenn Drewes
Trombones: Keith O'Quinn, Jeff Nelson
French Horn: Brad Gemeinhardt
Reeds: Chuck Wilson, Walt Weiskopf,
Tom Christensen, Roger Rosenberg
Guitar: Ed Hamilton
Bass: Bill Holcomb
Drums: David Ratajczak
Percussion: Charles Descarfino
Violins: Mineko Yajima, Cecelia Hobbs Gardner,
Jonathan Dinklage
Cello: Stephanie Cummins

Music Copyist: Kaye-Houston Music/
Anne Kaye and Doug Houston

Music Coordinator: John Miller

Joyce Chittick
Ensemble

Tim Craskey
Ensemble

Dylis Croman
Ensemble

Anika Ellis
Ensemble

Bob Gaynor
Ensemble

Tyler Hanes
Ensemble

Manuel I. Herrera
Ensemble

Kisha Howard
Ensemble

Mylinda Hull
Ensemble

Reginald Holden
Jennings
Swing, Dance Captain

Amy Nicole
Krawcek
Ensemble

Corinne McFadden
*Ensemble, Assoc.
Choreographer*

Marielys Molina
Ensemble

Timothy Edward
Smith
Ensemble

Seth Stewart
Ensemble

Neil Simon
Book

Cy Coleman
Music

Dorothy Fields
Lyrics

Walter Bobbie
Director

Wayne Cilento
Choreographer

Scott Pask
Scenic Design

William Ivey Long
Costume Design

Brian MacDevitt
Lighting Design

Peter Hylenski
Sound Design

Paul Huntley
Hair Design

Don Sebesky
Orchestrator

John Miller
Music Coordinator

Marc Bruni
Associate Director

Ted Banfalvi
*Associate
Choreographer*

Barry and Fran
Weissler
Producers

Edwin W. Schloss
Producer

Allen Spivak
Co-Producer

Harvey Weinstein
Co-Producer

SWEET
CHARITY
ALUMNI

Charlotte
D'Amboise
Charity

Photos by Ben Strohmann

Backstage Crew

Front Row (L-R): Tina Marie Clifton (Wardrobe), Amanda Duffy (Wardrobe), Bruce Morrow (Wardrobe).

Second Row (L-R): Veneda Trusdale (Dresser), Lisa Tucci (Wardrobe Supervisor), Beverly Jenkins (Stage Manager), Heather Richmond Wright (Hair Supervisor), Sunny Vridrine (Dresser), Jennifer Lerner (Asst. Production Electrician), Dana Calanan (Wardrobe), Billy Van De Bogart (Production Carpenter), Andy Trotto (Prop Man).

Third Row: (L-R): Francis Ehlers (Head Sound), David O'Brien (Production Stage Manager), Richie Fedeli (Asst. Carpenter), Eric Norris (Asst. Production Electrician), Mike Maher (Carpenter).

Fourth Row: (L-R): Bonnie Runk (Asst. Sound), John Blixt (Electrician), Tom O'Malley (Electrician), Dermot Lynch (House Electrician), Ron Fucarino (Carpenter), Sal Sclafani (House Propertyman), Gabe Harris (Automation Flyman).

Fifth Row: (L-R) Paul Reiner (Dresser), Stephen R. Gruse (Stage Manager), Dennis Sheehan (Carpenter), Dan Coey (Production Electrician), George Green Jr. (Production Prop Coordinator), Scott Dixon (Desk Automation), Joe Maher, Jr. (House Carpenter) and Losa Daniello (Wardrobe).

Stage Management
(L-R): David O'Brien (PSM),
Beverly Jenkins (SM),
Stephen R. Gruse (ASM)

Carpentry Department
Seated (L-R): Richie Fedeli (Asst. Carpenter), Billy Van De Bogart (Prod. Carpenter), Ron Fucarino.
Standing (L-R): Scott Dixon (Deck Automation, Mike Maher, Gabe Harris (Automation Flyman), Joe Maher Jr. (House Carpenter).

Photos by Ben Strothmann

Hair Department
(L-R): Heather Richmond Wright (Hair Supervisor), Amanda Duffy. Not pictured: Nathaniel Hathaway (Assistant Hair Supervisor).

Wardrobe Department
Seated (L-R): Veneda Truesdale, Tina Clifton, Lisa Tucci (Supervisor), Sunny Vidrine.
Standing (L-R): Dana Calanan, Bruce Harrow, Losa Daniello and Paul Riner.

Box Office
(L-R): Gloria Diabo and Linda Canavan.

Props Department
(L-R): Dennis Sheehan, George Green Jr. (Production Prop Coordinator), Sal Sclafani (House Propertyman) and Andy Trotto.

Front-of-House Staff
Front Row (L-R): Michele Fleury, Mary Marzan, Tristan Blacer.
Second Row (L-R): Alberta McNamee, Julie Burnham, Lorraine Feeks, Jose Nunez.
Third Row (L-R): Henry Menendez, Theresa Lopez, Janice Rodriguez, Amelis Tirado.
Back Row (L-R): Bart Ryan, Vladimir Belenky, Donald Royal.

Electrics and Sound Departments
Seated (L-R): Bonnie Runk (Asst. Sound), Tom O'Malley, Dermot Lynch (House Electrician), Eric Norris (Asst. Production Electrician).
Standing (L-R): Francis Elers (Head Sound), John Blixt, Dan Coey (Prod. Electrician), Jennifer Lerner (Asst. Production Electrician).

STAFF CREDITS FOR SWEET CHARITY

V.P. World Wide Marketing	Scott Moore
Marketing Manager	Ken Sperr
Company Manager	Hilary Hamilton
Stage Managers	Beverly Jenkins, Stephen R. Gruse
Associate General Manager	Michael Buchanan
Assistant Company Manager	Jeff Klein
Associate Scenic Designer	Orit Jacoby Carroll
Assistant Scenic Designers	Lauren Alvarez, Tal Goldin, Bryan Johnson
Associate Costume Designer	Martha Bromelmeier
Assistant Costume Designer	Rachel Attridge
Associate Lighting Designer	Charlie Pennebaker
Assistant Lighting Designers	Rachel Eichorn, Jennifer Schriever
Moving Lights Programmer	David Arch
Press Associates	Dennis Crowley, Ryan Ratelle
Casting Associates	Jack Bowdan CSA, Mark Brandon, Sarah Prosser, Megan Larche, Leah Alter
Associate Sound Designer	Tony Smolenski
Production Carpenter	William Van De Bogart
Automation Flyman	Gabe Harris
Deck Automation	Scott Dixon
Assistant Carpenter	Richard Fideli
Production Electrician	James Fedigan
Head Electrician	Daniel Coey
Followspot Operator	Jennifer Lerner
Assistant Electrician	Eric Norris
Sound Engineer	Francis Elers
Assistant Sound Engineer	Bonnie Runk
Production Prop Coordinator	George Green, Jr.
Production Prop Assistant	Angelo Torre
Production Prop Shopper	Kathy Fabian
Wardrobe Supervisor	Lisa Tucci
Assistant Wardrobe Supervisor	Fran Curry
Ms. Applegate's Dresser	Jane Rottenbach
Hair Supervisor	Heather Richmond Wright

Assistant Hair Supervisor	Nathaniel Hathaway
Notable Music, Inc./	Terrie Curran,
The Cy Coleman Office	Mark York, Jennifer Marik
Accounting	Rosenberg, Neuwirth & Kuchner/ Mark D'Ambrosi, Annemarie Aguanno,
Legal Counsel	Loeb & Loeb/ Seth Gelblum, Richard Garmise
Advertising	SPOTCo/Drew Hodges, Jim Edwards, Tom Greenwald, Amelia Heape, Jen McClelland, Vinny Sainato
Website/Internet Marketing	Situation Marketing/ Damian Bazadona, Ian Bennett
Artwork Photography	Jill Greenberg
Tour Marketing & Press	Anita Dloniak & Assoc.
Production Photography	Paul Kolnik
Merchandising	SFX Merchandising
Insurance	Stockbridge Risk Management, DeWitt Stern
Banking	JP Morgan Chase/Michelle Gibbons
Payroll Service	Castellana Services, Inc.
Booking	The Booking Group

NATIONAL ARTISTS MANAGEMENT COMPANY

Howie Cherpakov, Jack DePalma, Bob Williams, Marian Albarracin, Erin Barlow, Brett England, Suzanne Evans, Emily Dimond, Michelle Coleman, Victor Ruiz, Peter Ohsiek

CLEAR CHANNEL ENTERTAINMENT—THEATRICAL

Miles C. Wilkin, Scott Zeiger, David Anderson, Lauren Reid, Lynn Blandford, Bradley Broecker, Philip Brohn, Jennifer Costello, Jennifer DeLange, Joanna Hagan, Eric Joseph, Susan Krajsa, David Lazar, Hailey Lustig, Drew Murphy, Carl Pasbjerg, Debra Peltz, Denise Perry, Courtney Pierce, Dominic Roncace, Alison Spiriti, Dan Swartz

For Sweet Charity

Associate Producer	Tiffani Gavin

Marketing Directors	Jennifer DeLange, Carolyn Christensen

CREDITS

Scenery built and painted by Hudson Scenic Studios. Lighting equipment from PRG Lighting. Sound equipment from PRG Audio. Costumes executed by Carelli Costumes, Inc.; Euro Co Costumes.(com); Jennifer Love Costumes; JenKing; Brad Musgrove; Scafati, Inc.; Schneeman Studio, Limited; and Timberlake Studios. Millinery by Rodney Gordon, Inc. Shoes by T.O. Dey Shoes and J.C. Theatrical. Band uniforms by Fruhauf Uniforms. Rehearsed at the New 42nd Street Studios. Corporate sponsorship secured by Amy Willstatter's Bridge to Hollywood, LLC. Fitness equipment provided by Gym Source.

Thank you to Equinox at Greenwich Avenue.

Special thanks to
GRAN CENTENARIO TEQUILA
for their generous support.

JUJAMCYN THEATERS

Rocco Landesman
President

Paul Libin
Producing Director

Jack Viertel
Creative Director

Jerry Zaks

Daniel Adamian
General Manager

Jennifer Hershey
Director of Operations

STAFF FOR THE AL HIRSCHFELD THEATRE

Manager	Carmel Gunther
Treasurer	Carmine La Mendola
Carpenter	Joseph J. Maher, Jr.
Propertyman	Sal Sclafani
Electrician	Dermot J. Lynch

Best Opening Night Note: A framed Martha Graham quote. Somewhere in the middle it says, "No artist is satisfied ever. There is only a divine queer dissatisfaction."

Celebrity Visitor: Carol Burnett. I had worked with her last fall doing the TV remake of *Once Upon a Mattress*. She loved our show and said she wanted to have the elevator scene on a continuous loop so she could watch it at home.

Gypsy Robe: Dylis Croman, who understudies Charity and who went on for Christina when she broke her foot in Chicago.

Most Roles: Tim Smith, a marvelous actor. He plays many roles running throughout the show: the butler, the waiter, the man in Barney's Chili Hacienda, the man with the balloon. It's a wonderful device and Tim is winning and memorable in each part.

Backstage Ritual: Many of us meet before the show, during the overture. Since we have a curtain, we can actually be on stage during the overture. People meet and greet and occasionally Rhett George entertains us with his ice-skating routines.

Favorite Moment: Top of Act II. Christina and I get in the elevator (again, the curtain is down so we can hear the audience). I always get there first and I take a moment to just sit.

In-Theatre Gathering Place: Outside the stage door on the steps.

Snack Food: Zone Bars

Mascot: Christina's dog, Tallulah

Favorite Therapy: Ricola

Strangest Stage Door Fan Encounter: A woman who had me sign several old *Playbills* before the show. Then, after the show, she wanted me to sign three more *Playbills*. While I was signing, she said, "Make sure you spell your name out, make it legible, not just the way you did it on the others." I said, "but that's my signature, that's the way I do it." She argued with me, so I signed her *Playbill*, "Michelle Palooooooka" and walked away. Later she insisted that I come back and sign it again. Which I did.

Fastest Costume Change: The whole ensemble goes from "Brass Band" to the Fandango ballroom in about 30-45 seconds. It's absolute bedlam backstage. Seems like there are 14 dressers at that point.

Heaviest/Hottest Costume: All the guys wear suits at one point or another. Dancing in a suit is not the easiest thing in the world.

Who Wore The Least: The Fandango girls wear some pretty skimpy outfits.

Sweethearts: Manny Herrera and Corinne McFadden. They met on *Wicked* and now dance together in *Sweet Charity*.

Superstitions That Turned Out To Be True: Ummm…break a leg???

Phrase Which Sent Chills Through Everyone's Soul: "Today we're going to work on the Rosie scene."

Correspondent: Denis O'Hare, "Oscar"

Photo by Aubrey Reuben

Photo by Aubrey Reuben

Photo courtesy Denis O'Hare

Photo courtesy Denis O'Hare

Photo courtesy Denis O'Hare

Clockwise from top left: Christina Applegate and Denis O'Hare at a party to celebrate her first performance after her foot injury. Kyra Da Costa, Applegate and Janine LaManna at the opening night party at Gustavino. Applegate rehearsing "The Rhythm of Life." Applegate with choreographer Wayne Cilento. Applegate and O'Hare with producers Fran and Barry Weissler. O'Hare with Ernie Sabella. Walter Bobbie directs Applegate.

Photo by Aubrey Reuben

Photo by Aubrey Reuben

PLAYBILL®

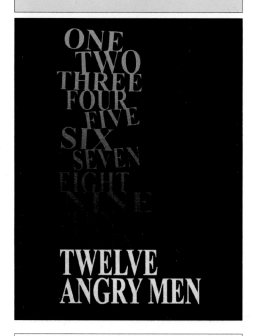

TWELVE ANGRY MEN

AMERICAN AIRLINES THEATRE

ROUNDABOUTTHEATRECOMPANY

TODD HAIMES, Artistic Director
ELLEN RICHARD, Managing Director
JULIA C. LEVY, Executive Director, External Affairs

Presents

TWELVE ANGRY MEN

by
Reginald Rose

with

Tom Aldredge   Mark Blum   Philip Bosco
Larry Bryggman   Robert Clohessy   Peter Friedman
Boyd Gaines   Kevin Geer   Michael Mastro
Matte Osian   John Pankow   James Rebhorn   Adam Trese

Set Design Allen Moyer	*Costume Design* Michael Krass	*Lighting Design* Paul Palazzo	*Sound Design* Brian Ronan
Original Compositions by John Gromada	*Production Stage Manager* Leslie C. Lyter	*Casting by* Jim Carnahan, C.S.A. *and* Mele Nagler	
Technical Supervisor Steve Beers	*General Manager* Sydney Beers	*Founding Director* Gene Feist	
Associate Artistic Director Scott Ellis	*Press Representative* Boneau/Bryan-Brown	*Director of Marketing* David B. Steffen	

Directed by
Scott Ellis

Major support for this production generously provided by The Blanche and Irving Laurie Foundation.
Roundabout Theatre Company is a member of the League of Resident Theatres.
www.roundabouttheatre.org

10/28/04

CAST

(in order of appearance)

Guard	MATTE OSIAN
Juror #1	MARK BLUM
Juror #2	KEVIN GEER
Juror #3	PHILIP BOSCO
Juror #4	JAMES REBHORN
Juror #5	MICHAEL MASTRO
Juror #6	ROBERT CLOHESSY
Juror #7	JOHN PANKOW
Juror #8	BOYD GAINES
Juror #9	TOM ALDREDGE
Juror #10	PETER FRIEDMAN
Juror #11	LARRY BRYGGMAN
Juror #12	ADAM TRESE
Voice of the Judge	ROBERT PROSKY

TIME AND PLACE

1954, Late Summer, a Jury Room of a
New York City Court of Law

UNDERSTUDIES/STANDBYS

for Juror #1, Juror #12, Juror #8:
KARL KENZLER
for Juror #2, Juror #3, Juror #9:
TERRY LAYMAN
for Guard, Juror #11, Juror #4, Juror #5:
GUY PAUL

Production Stage Manager: Leslie C. Tyler
Stage Manager: Jonathan Donahue

2004–2005 AWARDS

DRAMA DESK AWARDS:
Outstanding Revival of a Play

OUTER CRITICS CIRCLE AWARDS:
Outstanding Revival of a Play

DRAMA LEAGUE AWARDS:
Outstanding Revival of a Play

Kevin Geer, Philip Bosco and Michael Mastro.

Tom Aldredge
Juror #9

Mark Blum
Juror #1

Robert Clohessy
Juror #6

Larry Bryggman
Juror #11

Philip Bosco
Juror #3

Peter Friedman
Juror #10

Boyd Gaines
Juror #8

Kevin Geer
Juror #2

Michael Mastro
Juror #5

Matte Osian
*Guard/Standby for
Jurors #6, 7, 10*

John Pankow
Juror #7

James Rebhorn
Juror #4

Adam Trese
Juror #12

Karl Kenzler
*Understudy for
Jurors# 1, 8, 12*

Terry Layman
*Understudy for
Jurors #2, 3, 9*

Guy Paul
*Understudy Guard, &
Jurors #4, 5, 11*

Reginald Rose
Playwright

Scott Ellis
Director

Allen Moyer
Set Design

Paul Palazzo
Lighting Design

Brian Ronan
Sound Design

John Gromada
Original Music

Jim Carnahan
Casting

Gene Feist
*Founding Director
Roundabout Theatre
Company*

Todd Haimes
*Artistic Director,
Roundabout
Theatre Company*

Ellen Richard
*Managing Director,
Roundabout
Theatre Company*

Julia C. Levy
*Director, External
Affairs
Roundabout
Theatre Company*

ALTERNATE
JURORS
ALTERNATE
JURORS
ALTERNATE

Robert Foxworth
Juror #3

Byron Jennings
Juror #11

Box Office
(L-R): Mead Margulies, Solangel Bido and Ted Osborne.

Wardrobe
(L-R): Susan J. Fallon and Melissa Crawford.

Front of House
(L-R): Front Row: Eddie Camacho, Elsie Jamin-Maguire, Anne Ezell.
Back Row: Courtney Boddie, Jacklyn Rivera.

Crew
(L-R): Glen Merwede, Barbara Bartel, a cardboard cutout of Tom Aldredge, Amber Adams, Andrew Forste and Brian Maiuri.

Security: Adolf Torres.

Stage Managers
(L-R): Leslie Lyter (Production Stage Manager) and Jonathan Donahue (Stage Manager).

Twelve Angry Men

ROUNDABOUT THEATRE COMPANY STAFF

ARTISTIC DIRECTOR ....TODD HAIMES
MANAGING DIRECTOR ....ELLEN RICHARD
EXECUTIVE DIRECTOR,
EXTERNAL AFFAIRS ....JULIA C. LEVY
ASSOCIATE ARTISTIC DIRECTOR ...SCOTT ELLIS

ARTISTIC STAFF

Director of Artistic Development/
Director of Casting ....Jim Carnahan
Artistic Consultant ....Robyn Goodman
Resident Director ....Michael Mayer
Associate Artists ....Scott Elliott,
Bill Irwin,
Joe Mantello,
Mark Brokaw
Consulting Dramaturg ....Jerry Patch
Artistic Associate ....Samantha Barrie
Casting Director ....Mele Nagler
Casting Associate ....Carrie Gardner
Casting Associate ...........................J.V. Mercanti
Casting Assistant ....Kate Schwabe
Casting Assistant ....Stephen Kopel
Artistic Intern ....Corinne Hayoun

EDUCATION STAFF

Education Director ....Megan Kirkpatrick
Director of Instruction and
Curriculum Development ....Renee Flemings
Education Program Associate ....Lindsay Erb
Education Program Associate ....Stacey L. Morris
Education Assistant ....Cassidy Jones
Education Interns ....Fumiko Eda,
Tommy Marr, Catherine Taylor
Education Dramaturg ....Ted Sod
Teaching Artists ....Zakiyyah Alexander,
Phil Alexander, Cynthia Babak,
Victor Barbella, Brigitte Barnett-Loftis,
Caitlin Barton, Joe Basile, LaTonya Borsay,
Bonnie Brady, Mike Carnahan, Joe Clancy,
Melissa Denton, Stephen DiMenna, Joe Doran,
Tony Freeman, Shana Gold, Sheri Graubert,
Dennis Green, Susan Hamburger,
Karla Hendrick, Jim Jack, Alvin Keith,
Rebecca Lord, Erin McCready,
Andrew Ondrejcak, Laura Poe,
Nicole Press, Chris Rummel,
Drew Sachs, Anna Saggese, David Sinkus,
Vickie Tanner, Olivia Tsang,
Jennifer Varbalow, Leese Walker,
Eric Wallach, Diana Whitten,
Gail Winar, Kirche Zeile

ADMINISTRATIVE STAFF

General Manager ....Sydney Beers
General Counsel ....Laura O'Neill
Associate Managing Director ....Greg Backstrom
General Manager of
the Steinberg Center ....Don-Scott Cooper
Assistant to the General Manager ....Maggie Cantrick
Management Assistant ....Nicholas Caccavo
Office Operations Manager ....Bonnie Berens
Human Resources Manager ....Stephen Deutsch
Network Systems Manager ....Jeff Goodman
Manager of Corporate and Party Rentals ....Jetaun Dobbs
MIS Associate ....Lloyd Alvarez
MIS Assistant ....Anthony Foti
Receptionists ....Jennifer Decoteau,
Andre Fortson,
Carolyn Miller,
Elisa Papa
Messenger ....Robert Weisser
Management Intern ....Chris Aniello

FINANCE STAFF

Controller ....Susan Neiman
Assistant Controller ....John LaBarbera
Accounts Payable Administrator ....Frank Surdi
Customer Service Coordinator ....Trina Cox
Business Office Associate ....David Solomon
Business Assistant ....Yonit Kafka

Business Intern ....Chelsea Glickfield

DEVELOPMENT STAFF

DIRECTOR OF DEVELOPMENT ....Jeffory Lawson
Director, Institutional Giving ....Julie K. D'Andrea
Director, Individual Giving ....Julia Lazarus
Director, Special Events ....Steve Schaeffer
Manager, Donor Information Systems ....Tina Mae Bishko
Special Events Associate ....Elaina Grillo
Institutional Giving Associate ....Kristen Bolibruch
Annual Giving Associate ....Justin D. Steensma
Development Associate ....Adam Gwon
Development Assistant ....Stephenie L. Overton
Assistant, External Affairs ....Robert Weinstein
Patrons Services Assistant ....Dawn Kusinski
Development Intern ....Lauren Hoshibata

MARKETING STAFF

Director of Marketing ....David B. Steffen
Marketing/Publications Manager ....Tim McCanna
Marketing Associate ....Sunil Ayyagari
Marketing Assistant ....Rebecca Ballon
Marketing Intern ....Alejandro Lojo
Website Consultant ....Keith Powell Beyland
Director of Telesales Special Promotions ....Tony Baksa
Telesales Manager ....Anton Borissov
Telesales Office Coordinator ..................J.W. Griffin

TICKET SERVICES STAFF

DIRECTOR OF SALES OPERATIONS ...Jim Seggelink
Ticket Services Manager ....Ellen Holt
Subscription Manager ....Charlie Garbowski
Box Office Managers ....Edward P. Osborne,
Jaime Perlman,
Jessica Bowser
Group Sales Manager ....Jeff Monteith
Assistant Box Office Managers ....Paul Caspary,
Steve Howe,
Megan Young
Assistant Ticket Services Managers ....Robert Kane,
David Meglino,
Robert Morgan
Asst. to the Director of Sales Operations ...Nancy Mulliner
Ticket Services ....Solangel Bido,
Andrew Clements, Johanna Comanzo,
Sean Crews, Thomas Dahl,
Nisha Dhruna, Adam Elsberry,
Lindsay Ericson, Scott Falkowski,
Catherine Fitzpatrick, Erin Frederick,
Steven Gottlieb, Julie Hilimire,
Bill Klemm, Talia Krispel,
Alexander LaFrance, Krystin MacRitchie,
Mead Margulies, Chris Migliaccio,
Carlos Morris, Nicole Nicholson,
Shannon Paige, Hillary Parker,
Thomas Protulipac, Amy Robinson,
Heather Siebert, Monté Smock,
Melissa Snyder, Lillian Soto,
Justin Sweeney, Greg Thorson,
Pamela Unger
Ticket Services Intern ....Jesse Blum

SERVICES

Counsel ....Jeremy Nussbaum,
Cowan, Liebowitz & Latman, P.C.
Counsel ....Rosenberg & Estis
Counsel ....Rubin and Feldman, P.C.
Counsel ....Cleary, Gottlieb, Steen & Hamilton
Counsel ....Harry H. Weintraub,
Glick and Weintraub, P.C.
Immigration Counsel ....Mark D. Koestler and
Theodore Ruthizer
House Physicians ....Dr. Theodore Tyberg,
Dr. Lawrence Katz
House Dentist ....Neil Kanner, D.M.D.
Insurance ....Marsh USA Inc.
Accountant ....Brody, Weiss, Zucarelli &
Urbanek CPAs, P.C.

Advertising ....Eliran Murphy Group/
Denise Ganjou
Events Photography ....Anita and Steve Shevett
Production Photographer ....Joan Marcus
Theatre Displays ....King Displays/
Wayne Sapper

GENERAL PRESS REPRESENTATIVES
BONEAU / BRYAN-BROWN
Adrian Bryan-Brown, Matt Polk
Jessica Johnson, Joe Perrotta

ROUNDABOUT THEATRE COMPANY
231 West 39th Street, New York, NY 10018
(212) 719-9393

CREDITS FOR *TWELVE ANGRY MEN*

GENERAL MANAGER ....Sydney Beers
Company Manager ....Denys Baker
Associate General Manager ....Jean Haring
Production Stage Manager ....Leslie C. Lyter
Stage Manager ....Jonathan Donahue
Assistant Director ....Gwynn MacDonald
Assistant Set Designer ....Warren Karp
Assistant Costume Designer ....Tracy Christensen
Assistant Lighting Designer ....Dale Knoth
Assistant Sound Designer ....Mike Farfalla
Fight Director ....Rick Sordelet
Master Technicians ....Glenn Merwede,
Susan Goulet
Assistant Master Technicians ....Andrew Forste,
Brian Maiuri
Assistant to the Technical Supervisor ....Elisa R. Kuhar
Sound Operator ....Christopher Sloan
Wardrobe Supervisor ....Susan Fallon
Properties Supervisor ....Denise Grillo
Dresser ....Melissa Crawford
Props Associate ....Kevin Crawford
Production Assistant ....Angela DeGregoria
Costume Intern ....Ruby Randig
Set Built by ....Great Lakes Scenic Studio
Computer Motion Control and
Automation of Scenery and
Rigging by ....HYDE POWER SYSTEMS
Special Effects Equipment by ....Jauchem & Meeh, Inc
SHOWTRAK* Computer Motion Control
for Scenery and Rigging
Costume Rental ....ODDS Costumes
Some Suits Constructed by ....Scafati
Costume Alteration by ....Timberlake Studios
Period Eyewear by ....Fabulous Fanny's
Lighting Equipment by ....Fourth Phase
Sound Equipment by ....Sound Associates
Special Thanks to ....Jessica Barrios
Natural Herb Cough Drops .....Courtesy of Ricola U.S.A.

AMERICAN AIRLINES THEATRE STAFF

General Manager ....Sydney Beers
Master Technician ....Glenn Merwede
Master Technician ....Susan Goulet
Wardrobe Supervisor ....Susan J. Fallon
Box Office Manager ....Edward P. Osborne
House Manager ....Stephen Ryan
Associate House Manager ....Zipporah Aguasvivas
Head Usher ....Edwin Camacho
House Staff ....Courtney Boddie, Peter Breaden,
James Bruce, Oscar Castillo,
Ilia Diaz, Anne Ezell,
Danielle Fazio, Meghan Herbert,
Elsie Jamin-Maguire,
Sherra Johnston, Jacklyn Rivera
Security ....Julious Russell
Additional Security Provided by ....Gotham Security
Maintenance ....Kenrick Johnson,
Rafael Torres,
Maggie Western
Lobby Refreshments ....Sweet Concessions

Twelve Angry Men | Scrapbook

Opening Night Gifts: For publicity purposes there was a court appointed sketch artist in the back of the house one evening, and the sketch she produced was enlarged and framed by the cast and given to our director, Scott Ellis. It was rather amusing because he also had them reproduced and framed, and gave one to each person in the cast.

Celebrity Visitors: We have had quite a few: Jude Law, Sienna Miller, Chris Noth, Kevin Spacey, Pierce Brosnan, Henry Winkler, Colin Firth, Tracy Ullman, John Lithgow, Jeff Goldblum, Tony Shaloub, Michael J. Fox. They all said how glorious it was to watch such an extraordinary piece of ensemble work, and they all wanted desperately to be on the stage doing this show.

Who Has Done The Most Shows: By unanimous decision: Tom Aldredge.

"Easter Bonnet" Sketch: "Diss-Order in the Court" by Guy Paul.

Backstage Ritual: We have a Sunday brunch that is sort of becoming legendary. We cook all kinds of things: eggs Benedict, breakfast wraps, pancakes, waffles, pizza bagels.... You name it, we cook it. And we have guest chefs from the cast occasionally performing the cooking. It's quite special.

Favorite Moment During Each Performance: After the "jurors" file off the stage at the end of the play, they all line up and start a low mumbling about whether they are going to do two sets of bows or just one. After the first set, they run off and the mumbling becomes a full out tribal yell deciding if they are going to or not. It's quite glorious to hear all 13 of the men.

Favorite In-Theatre Gathering Place: The trap room in front of the TV.

Favorite Off Site Hangout: Angus McIndoe

Favorite Snack Food: To continue the brunch theme, because it's such a big part of our week, it's gotta be bacon. We have a LOT of carnivores over here.

Favorite Therapy: Ricolas (I can't keep the bowls filled!) and Throat-Coat tea.

Memorable Ad-lib: Phil Bosco has a line: "I think you're giving us a lot of mumbo-jumbo." One night it was "I think you're giving us a lot of hokey-pokey."

Cell Phone Rings: Unbelievably, during our Actors' Fund performance, we had at least four. We rarely get any at other times.

Strangest Press Encounter: At one of our private parties, two rather well known NY theatre critics were in attendance (invited, of course, which was also odd) and several company members endured pumping for information.

Strangest Fan Encounter: We had a student who insisted on studying the show in depth and "blackmailed" our cast into several kinds of interviews and comments.

Latest Audience Arrival: Our show is one hour and 45 minutes long. Several audience members arrived 9 PM for an 8 PM curtain.

Fastest Costume Change: Not necessarily a costume change, but at the five-minute call John Pankow takes a shower and then gets into his costume, and always makes it to places on time.

Busiest Day At The Box Office: New Year's weekend they turned away more than 350 patrons.

Infamous Directorial Note: When our director said to one the boys: "So, you're not planning on being in theatre again, right?"

Company In-Joke: It's a cast of 16 men (including understudies) and five men backstage, so what do you think? Fart jokes.

Sweethearts: All 16 of these beautiful men!

Correspondent: Susan Fallon, Dresser and Roundabout Wardrobe Supervisor

Left: Curtain calls on opening night. Right: James Rebhorn arriving at the cast party at the China Club.

Marquee of the American Airlines Theatre.

Boyd Gaines on opening night.

Director Scott Ellis at the China Club.

Tom Aldredge greets opening night guests J. Smith-Cameron and Frank Wood.

PLAYBILL®

CAST

(in alphabetical order)

Mitch Mahoney ....DERRICK BASKIN
Marcy Park ....DEBORAH S. CRAIG
Leaf Coneybear ....JESSE TYLER
FERGUSON
William Barfee ....DAN FOGLER
Rona Lisa Peretti ....LISA HOWARD
Olive Ostrovsky................................CELIA
KEENAN-BOLGER
Chip Tolentino ....JOSE LLANA
Douglas Panch ....JAY REISS
Logainne Schwartzandgrubenierre ....SARAH
SALTZBERG

UNDERSTUDIES

For William Barfee, Leaf Coneybear – TODD
BUONOPANE; for Mitch Mahoney – TODD
BUONOPANE, WILLIS WHITE; for Chip
Tolentino –WILLIS WHITE; for Douglas Panch –
TODD BUONOPANE, WILLIS WHITE; for
Olive Ostrovsky, Marcy Park – KATE WETHER-
HEAD, LISA YUEN; for Rona Lisa Peretti –LISA
YUEN; for Logainne Schwartzandgrubenierre –
KATE WETHERHEAD

The Barrington Stage Company workshop of
The 25th Annual Putnam County Spelling Bee
was originally co-directed by
Michael Barakiva and Rebecca Feldman.

CIRCLE IN THE SQUARE
UNDER THE DIRECTION OF THEODORE MANN and PAUL LIBIN

David Stone   James L. Nederlander   Barbara Whitman   Patrick Catullo
Barrington Stage Company   Second Stage Theatre

Present

The 25th Annual Putnam County
SPELLING BEE

Music & Lyrics by
WILLIAM FINN

Book By
RACHEL SHEINKIN

Conceived by
REBECCA FELDMAN

Additional Material by
JAY REISS

With

DERRICK BASKIN, DEBORAH S. CRAIG, JESSE TYLER FERGUSON, DAN FOGLER,
LISA HOWARD, CELIA KEENAN-BOLGER, JOSE LLANA, JAY REISS, SARAH SALTZBERG
TODD BUONOPANE, KATE WETHERHEAD, WILLIS WHITE, LISA YUEN

Set Design by
BEOWULF BORITT

Costume Design by
JENNIFER CAPRIO

Lighting Design by
NATASHA KATZ

Sound Design by
DAN MOSES SCHREIER

Orchestrations by
MICHAEL STAROBIN

Music Director
VADIM FEICHTNER

Vocal Arrangements by
CARMEL DEAN

Music Coordinator
MICHAEL KELLER

Press
THE PUBLICITY OFFICE

Casting
TARA RUBIN CASTING

Production Stage Manager
ANDREA "SPOOK" TESTANI

Production Manager
KAI BROTHERS

General Management
321 THEATRICAL MANAGEMENT

Choreographed by
DAN KNECHTGES

Directed by
JAMES LAPINE

Based on C-R-E-P-U-S-C-U-L-E, an original play by THE FARM.
Original Broadway Cast Recording on GHOSTLIGHT RECORDS.

LIVE BROADWAY

5/2/05

MUSICIANS

CONDUCTOR/Piano: VADIM
FEICHTNER
Associate Conductor/Synthesizer: Carmel
Dean
Reed: Rick Heckman
Cello: Amy Ralske
Drums/Percussion: Glenn Rhian

Music Coordinator: Michael Keller
Music Copying:
Emily Grishman Music Preparation
Emily Grishman/Katherine Edmonds

2004-2005 AWARDS

TONY AWARDS
Featured Actor in a Musical (Dan Fogler)
Book of a Musical (Rachel Sheinkin)

DRAMA DESK AWARDS
Ensemble Acting (The Entire Cast)
Book of a Musical (Rachel Sheinkin)
Director of a Musical (James Lapine)

OUTER CRITICS CIRCLE AWARD
Featured Actor in a Musical (Dan Fogler)

Derrick Baskin
Mitch Mahoney

Deborah S. Craig
Marcy Park

Jesse Tyler Ferguson
Leaf Coneybear

Dan Fogler
William Barfee

Lisa Howard
Rona Lisa Peretti

Celia Keenan-Bolger
Olive Ostrovsky

Jose Llana
Chip Tolentino

Jay Reiss
Douglas Panch

Sarah Saltzberg
*Logainne
Schwartzandgrubenierre*

Todd Buonopane
*Understudy for
Barfee, Coneybear,
Mitch, Mr. Panch*

Kate Wetherhead
*Understudy for Olive,
Marcy, Logainne*

Willis White
*Understudy for Mitch,
Chip, Mr. Panch*

Lisa Yuen
*Understudy for Olive,
Marcy, Ms. Peretti*

William Finn
Music/Lyrics

Rachel Sheinkin
Book

Rebecca Feldman
Conceiver

James Lapine
Director

Dan Knechtges
Choreographer

Darren Katz
Resident Director

Beowulf Boritt
Set Designer

Jennifer Caprio
Costume Designer

Natasha Katz
Lighting Designer

Dan Moses Schreier
Sound Designer

Michael Starobin
Orchestrations

Vadim Feichtner
*Musical Director/
Dance Arrangements*

Carmel Dean
*Vocal Arranger/
Associate
Conductor/Synthesizer*

Michael Keller
Music Coordinator

David Stone
Producer

**James L.
Nederlander**
Producer

Barbara Whitman
Producer

Front-of-House Staff
Back Row (L-R): Michael Trupia, Tammy Cummisky, Francine Kramer, Richard Berg (House Manager), Cody Perret (Asst. House Manager), Steve Chappell, Sharon Nelson and Zorro Joseph Guice.

Front Row (L-R): Laurel Bevoort, Raya Konyk, Margarita Caban, Sophie Koufakis, Patricia Kennedy, Orlando Powers-Rodriguez, Georgia Keghlian.

Photo by Ben Strohmann

Photo by Joan Marcus

The Cast: In Character and Ready to Spell
Back Row (L-R): Jose Llana, Deborah S. Craig, Jesse Tyler Ferguson.
Front Row (L-R): Celia Keenan-Bolger, Dan Fogler and Sarah Saltzberg.

The Orchestra
(L-R): Carmel Dean (Vocal Arranger/Associate Conductor/Synthesizer), Vadim Feichtner (Musical Director/Conductor/Piano), Amy Ralse (Cello), Rick Heckman (Reeds) and James Mack (Percussion sub).

Not pictured: Glenn Rhian (Percussion).

Photo by Ben Strohmann

Wardrobe Department
Susan Sigrist (Dresser), Cleon Byerly (Dresser) and Yvonna Balfour (Wardrobe Supervisor).

Stage Management
(L-R): Kelly Hance (Stage Manager), Andrea "Spook" Testani (Production Stage Manager), Darren Katz (Resident Director).

Stage Crew
Back Row (L-R): Stephanie Vetter (Monitor Engineer), Robert S. Lindsay (FOH Sound Engineer) and Stewart Wagner (Head Electrician).

Front Row (L-R): Billy Seelig (Sub Flyman), Robert Gordon (Head Carpenter), Owen Parmale (Propmaster).

Not pictured: Glenn Ingram (Flyman).

Volunteer Spelling Coordinators
(L-R): Keira Fromm and Chris Paseka.

STAFF FOR THE 25TH ANNUAL PUTNAM COUNTY SPELLING BEE

GENERAL MANAGEMENT
321 THEATRICAL MANAGEMENT
Nancy Nagel Gibbs
Nina Essman   Marcia Goldberg

GENERAL PRESS REPRESENTATIVE
THE PUBLICITY OFFICE
Bob Fennell   Marc Thibodeau
Michael S. Borowski

MARKETING
THE ARACA GROUP

CASTING
TARA RUBIN CASTING
Casting Associates:
Dunja Vitolic, Eric Woodall, Ron LaRosa

COMPANY MANAGER	**SETH MARQUETTE**
Resident Director	Darren Katz
Production Stage Manager	Andrea "Spook" Testani
Stage Manager	Kelly Hance
Assistant Stage Manager	Lisa Yuen
Assistant Choreographer	DJ Gray
Dance Captain	Derrick Baskin
Hair & Wig Design	Marty Kapulsky
Associate Lighting Designer	Philip Rosenberg
Assistant Set Designer	Jo Winiarski
Assistant Costume Designer	Brian Russman
Associate Sound Designer	David Bullard
Assistant Lighting Designer	John Viesta
Automated Lights Programmer	Laura Frank
Production Managers	Kai Brothers, Jason Block
Carpenter	Tony Hauser
Electrician	Randall Zaibek
Flyman	Glen Ingram
Monitor Engineer	Stephanie Vetter
Wardrobe Supervisor	Yvonna Balfour
Dressers	Cleon Byerly, Susan Sigrist
Costume Assistant	Jeffrey Hinchee
Set Design Assistants	John Conners, Camille Connolly, Mike Wade
Synthesizer Programming	Bruce Samuels
Music Preparation	Emily Grishman
Management Interns	Greg Pearl, Kimberly Jade Parker
Advertising	Serino Coyne, Inc./ Greg Corradetti, Ruth Rosenberg, Joaquin Esteva, Stephanie Santoso
Lobby Design	Beowulf Boritt
Web Design	Late August/ Jeff Prout, Jeff Bowen
Merchandising	The Araca Group/ Clint Bond, Karen Davidov, Julie Monahan, Edward Nelson, Daniel Pardes, James M. Pellechi, Jr.

Volunteer Spellers Coordinators	Chris Paseka, Keira Fromm
Lottery Coordinators	Bill Hubner, Michelle Schechter
Production Assistant	Benjamin J. Shuman
Legal Counsel	Schreck, Rose & Dapello/Nancy Rose
Accountant	FK Partners CPA's LLP/Robert Fried
Banking	JP Morgan Chase/ Richard Callian, Mic
Insurance	AON/Albert G. Ruben Insurance/ George Walden, Claudia Kaufman
Payroll Service	Castellana Services, Inc.
Production Photography	Joan Marcus
Opening Night Coordination	Tobak-Dantchik Events and Promotions, Inc./ Cathy Dantchik, Joanna B. Koondel

GROUP SALES – SHOWTIX
Patricia Daily
212.302.7000 or 800.677.1164

321 THEATRICAL MANAGEMENT
Lawrence Anderson, Bob Brinkerhoff, Emily Fisher,
Michele Helberg, Rachel Marcus, Erik Orton,
Chris Paseka, Susan Sampliner,
Greg Schaffert, Stephanie Wallis

SECOND STAGE THEATRE
Artistic Director: Carole Rothman
Executive Director: Timothy J. McClimon
Associate Artistic Director: Christopher Burney
General Manager: C. Barrack Evans
Production Manager: Jeff Wild

Board of Trustees
Anthony C.M. Kiser, Co-Chairman;
Stephen C. Sherrill, Co-Chairman;
Elizabeth H. Berger, Tavener Holmes Berry,
Maura Bulkeley, Suzanne Schwartz Davidson,
Bambi de la Gueronniere, Patricia D. Fili-Krushel,
Edward I. Herbst, Hamilton E. James,
Wendy Evans Joseph, Steven B. Klinsky,
George S. Loening, Patti LuPone,
Timothy J. McClimon, Mary P. Moran,
Anthony E. Napoli, Kirk A. Radke,
Lynne Randall, David Resnicow,
Donna Rosen, Mark Rosenthal,
Carole Rothman, Joshua Ruch,
John Schmidt, Denise V. Seegal,
Stacy Spikes, Ann Tenenbaum,
Michael Weinstein, Peter Weller,
Herbert S. Winokur, Jr.

BARRINGTON STAGE COMPANY
Board of Trustees
Mary Ann Quinson, President;
Richard Solar, Vice President;
James A. Papenn, Vice President;
Kusum Gaind, Secretary;
Jeananne Hauswald, Treasurer;

Julianne Boyd, Artistic Director;

Sydelle Blatt, Kathleen M. Chrisman,
Carl A. de Gersdorff, Chris Farrell,
Deann Simmons Halper, Nancy Humphreys,
Robert A. Marcus, Martha Piper,
Sheila Richman, Marion Simon,
Susan R. Simon, Ede Sorokoff,
Mark St. Germain, Tucker Welch,
Eileen Young

CREDITS
Scenery constructed by Showman Fabricators.
Lighting equipment by Production Resource Group.
Costumes by Tricorne, Martin Izquierdo Studios,
Matthew Hemesath and Carmen Gee. Sound Equipment
by Masque Sound. Props by Susan Barras, Kathy Fabian.
Ricola natural herb cough drops courtesy of Ricola USA,
Inc. Water courtesy of FIJI Water. Apple & Eve 100%
fruit juices used. Gummi Bears courtesy of Haribo
Gold-Bears. Wise pretzels and chips used. Additional
set and hand props courtesy of George Fenmore, Inc.
Piano by Steinway & Sons.

SPECIAL THANKS
Dana Harrel, Mimi Bilinski,
Daniel Heffernan, Jim Mack.
Steven, Mandy and Susan Fine.
Bayside Elementary in Stevensville, MD.
Robert Morris School, South Bound Brook, NJ.
Ridgefield Park Public Schools.

WWW.SPELLINGBEETHEMUSICAL.COM

ONSTAGE MERCHANDISING
George Fenmore/ More Merchandising International

CIRCLE IN THE SQUARE THEATRE
Thespian Theatre, Inc.
Under the direction of
Theodore Mann and Paul Libin

House Manager	Richard D. Berg
Head Carpenter	Robert Gordon
Head Electrician	Stewart Wagner
Prop Master	Owen E. Parmele
Sound Board Operator	Robert S. Lindsay
Box Office Treasurer	Ilene Towell
Controller	Susan Frankel
Assistant to Paul Libin	Patricia Michael
Assistant to Theodore Mann	Holly Ricciuti
Administrative Assistant	Cody Perret

Opening Night Memories: Vintage bottle of Dom in one hand, Elaine Stritch holding the other. She is clad head to toe in white with black dinner-plate size sunglasses. She is centimeters from my face, whispering something about "what a goddamned hard business this is." Jeff Goldblum is blowing odd little kisses at me from my dressing room door. Jay Reiss and I are pantless as we change for the opening night party. One of the most surreal moments of my life. (Fogler)

My Favorite Moment Of The Bee (Show): After I get eliminated from the Bee I give handshakes to each of the actors on stage as I exit. Dan Fogler always says something different to me. On the night of the first preview he said, "Welcome back to Broadway." On a night when the audience was really dead, he said, "You're always the lucky one." Celia always whispers, "I love you." (Ferguson)

Rituals: One of the strangest backstage rituals comes from Sarah Saltzberg. When we did the show in the Berkshires she had had to recite the lyrics of her song "Woe Is Me" while looking at an electrical box. When we moved to Second Stage there was no electrical box, so she used a fire hydrant. On Broadway, neither was backstage, so she now uses an "Exit" sign. She freaks out if she doesn't have time to do this ritual, so she has gotten really good at doing this very quickly. (Ferguson)

Musician Who Has Played The Most Performances Without A Sub: Vadim Feichtner has been at the piano every performance since Barrington Stage.

Backstage Songs: "These Are the Things That I Do to Get Ready for Coneybear" (comprised of a list of items Jesse puts on for his costume, sung to clapping).
"Everybody Grab Your Pecker"
"I Can't Hide Piranha Pride" (very Bon Jovi) Lyrics:
You can't hide...Piranha pride!
Come inside...
We're gonna bite your ankles!
We also like to sing the *Jurassic Park* theme song while looking right into each other's eyes.

Nicknames: Schwartzy, Salty, Fogiggley, Foglieries, C., Downtown, Tightsac, Hollywood, Short Stack, Hoser, Lee-Lee, Cocoa, Jester.

Catchphrases: "Okay Ladies!?" "Hoooh!"

Correspondents: Dan Fogler, "William Barfee" and Jesse Tyler Ferguson "Leaf Coneybear"

The cast takes a break from recording the original cast album at Avatar Studios. (L to R:) Dan Fogler, Lisa Howard, Jose Llana, Sarah Saltzberg, Jay Reiss, Celia Keenan-Bolger, Derrick Baskin, Jesse Tyler Ferguson, Deborah S. Craig.

Above Left: Craig and Llana at the opening night party at Cipriani. Right: Entrance to the Circle in the Square Theatre.

Above left: Producer David Stone and composer William Finn on opening night. Right: Saltzberg, Howard and Craig at the party.

Left: Fogler arrives at the cast party. Right: Donna Murphy greets Keenan-Bolger on opening night.

Photos by Aubrey Reuben

PLAYBILL®

⚙ LYCEUM THEATRE

A Shubert Organization Theatre
Gerald Schoenfeld, Chairman   Philip J. Smith, President
Robert E. Wankel, Executive Vice President

Mike Nichols

Hal Luftig   Leonard Soloway   Steven M. Levy   Tom Leonardis
Eric Falkenstein   Amy Nederlander

present

The 20TH Anniversary Show

Lighting Design	Sound Design	Production Stage Manager
Benjamin Pearcy	**Peter Fitzgerald**	**Barclay Stiff**

Production Supervisor	Press Representative	Marketing
Arthur Siccardi	**The Pete Sanders Group**	**HHC Marketing**

The producers would like to thank the Theatre Development Fund
for its support of this production.

LIVE BROADWAY

11/17/04

Whoopi Goldberg in character.

Whoopi performs her solo show.

Photos by Joan Marcus

341

Whoopi Goldberg

Benjamin Pearcy
Lighting Designer

Mike Nichols
Producer

Hal Luftig
Producer

Leonard Soloway
Producer

STAFF FOR WHOOPI

GENERAL MANAGEMENT
LEONARD SOLOWAY & STEVEN M. LEVY

PRESS REPRESENTATIVE
THE PETE SANDERS GROUP
Pete Sanders   Jeremy Shaffer
Glenna Freedman   Bill Coyle

Production Stage Manager ....Barclay Stiff
Assistant Lighting Designer ....Stephen Boulmetis
Assistant Sound Designer ....Wallace Florel
Technical Supervisor ....Arthur Siccardi
House Carpenter ....Adam Braunstein
House Electrician ....William K. Rowland
House Properties...........................Steve McDonald
Wardrobe Supervisor ....Veneda Truesdale
Advertising...............................Serino Coyne, Inc./
                                Roger Micone, Uma Sud
Marketing.................................HHC Marketing/
                                Hugh Hysell, Adam Jay
Assistant to Mr. Luftig ....Shannon R. Morrison
Press Assistant ....Heather Smith

Production Photographer ....Joan Marcus
Production Counsel ....Cowan DeBaets
                                Abrahams & Sheppard/
                                Frederick P. Bimbler
Comptroller ....Elliott Aronstam
Accounting ....Rosenberg Neuwirth & Kuchner/
                                Chris Cacace
Banking ....Commerce Bank/Barbara Von Borstel
Insurance ....Tannenbaum Harber Insurance Group/
                                Carol Bressi-Cilona
Payroll Service ...Castellana Services, Inc./Lance Castellana
Merchandising ....George Fenmore/
                                More Merchandising International
Opening Night Coordinator ....Tobak-Dantchik/
                                Joanna Koondel, Cathy Dantchik

CREDITS

Lighting equipment provided by
Production Resources Group.
Sound equipment by Sound Associates, Inc.
Natural herb cough drops courtesy of
Ricola USA Inc.
Water courtesy of FIJI Water.

 THE SHUBERT ORGANIZATION, INC.

Gerald Schoenfeld	**Philip J. Smith**
Chairman	President
John W. Kluge	**Lee J. Seidler**
Michael I. Sovern	**Stuart Subotnick**

Irving M. Wall

Robert E. Wankel
Executive Vice President

Peter Entin	**Elliot Greene**
Vice President	Vice President
Theatre Operations	Finance
David Andrews	**John Darby**
Vice President	Vice President
Shubert Ticketing Services	Facilities

House Manager ....Joann Swanson

Whoopi Goldberg and daughter Alex Martin at the opening night party at the China Club.

Outside the Lyceum Theatre, a poster charting Whoopi's "look" through the years.

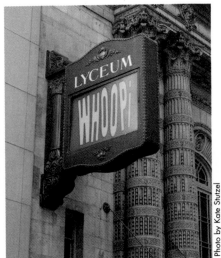

Cheering Goldberg at the opening night party were (L-R) Lea DeLaria, Christopher Sieber, Caroline Rhea, Ana Gasteyer and Katie Finneran.

Photos by Aubrey Reuben

Tony nominee S. Epatha Merkerson arrives on opening night.

Photo by Kate Stutzel

Left: Well-wishers on opening night include onetime Little Rascal Dickie Moore and his wife, film star Jane Powell. Center: The marquee of the Lyceum. Right: Raúl Esparza and Sally Ann Howes with producer Leonard Soloway at the opening night party.

PLAYBILL®

Edward Albee's
Who's Afraid
of Virginia Woolf?

CAST
(in order of appearance)

Martha	KATHLEEN TURNER
George	BILL IRWIN
Honey	MIREILLE ENOS
Nick	DAVID HARBOUR

THE SCENE

The living room of a house on the campus of a
small New England college, 1960

ACT I: "Fun and Games"
ACT II: "Walpurgisnacht"
ACT III: "The Exorcism"

STANDBYS

For Ms. Turner: JENNIFER REGAN
For Mr. Irwin: CHRISTOPHER BURNS
For Ms. Enos: STINA NIELSEN
For Mr. Harbour: DAVID FURR

The text used in this production
is based on the revised version of 2004.

2004-2005 AWARD

TONY AWARD:
Leading Actor in a Play (Bill Irwin)

⊛ LONGACRE THEATRE

220 West 48th Street
A Shubert Organization Theatre

Gerald Schoenfeld, *Chairman*   Philip J. Smith, *President*

Robert E. Wankel, *Executive Vice President*

Elizabeth Ireland McCann   Daryl Roth   Terry Allen Kramer
Scott Rudin   Roger Berlind   James L. Nederlander   Nick Simunek

Joey Parnes   Executive Producer

present

Kathleen   Bill
Turner   Irwin

in

Edward Albee's
Who's Afraid
of Virginia Woolf?

with

Mireille Enos   David Harbour

Scenic Design	Costume Design	Lighting Design	Sound Design
John Lee Beatty	Jane Greenwood	Peter Kaczorowski	Mark Bennett

Production Stage Manager	Casting	Fight Director
Susie Cordon	Jay Binder, CSA Jack Bowdan, CSA/ Laura Stanczyk, CSA	Rick Sordelet

Associate General Manager	Press Representative	Marketing
Elizabeth M. Blitzer	Shirley Herz Associates Sam Rudy	HHC Marketing

Directed By
Anthony Page

The producers wish to express their appreciation to
Theatre Development Fund for its support of this production.

LIVE BROADWAY   3/20/05

Get the Guests: Kathleen Turner (Martha) and Bill Irwin (George).

Who's Afraid of Virginia Woolf?

Kathleen Turner
Martha

Bill Irwin
George

Mireille Enos
Honey

David Harbour
Nick

Jennifer Regan
Standby for Martha

Christopher Burns
Standby for George

Stina Nielsen
Standby for Honey

David Furr
Standby for Nick

Edward Albee
Playwright

Anthony Page
Director

John Lee Beatty
Scenic Designer

Jane Greenwood
Costume Designer

Peter Kaczorowski
Lighting Designer

Mark Bennett
Sound Designer

Elizabeth Ireland McCann
Producer

Daryl Roth
Producer

Terry Allen Kramer
Producer

Scott Rudin
Producer

Roger Berlind
Producer

James L. Nederlander
Producer

Susie Cordon
Production Stage Manager

Allison Sommers
Stage Manager

Photos by Ben Strohmann

Understudies
(L-R): Christopher Burns, Stina Nielsen, David Furr and Jennifer Regan.

Photo by John Buryiak

The cast and crew of *Who's Afraid of Virginia Woolf?* on the stage of the Longacre Theatre.

STAFF FOR WHO'S AFRAID OF VIRGINIA WOOLF?

GENERAL MANAGEMENT
JOEY PARNES
John Johnson   Michelle Perna   S.D. Wagner

GENERAL PRESS REPRESENTATIVE
SHIRLEY HERZ ASSOCIATES
Shirley Herz   Sam Rudy   Kevin McAnarney
Dale Heller   Robert Lasko   Daniel Demello

CASTING
JAY BINDER CASTING
Jay Binder CSA, Jack Bowdan CSA, Mark Brandon,
Sarah Prosser, Leah Alter, Megan Larche

PRODUCTION PHOTOGRAPHER
Carol Rosegg

COMPANY MANAGER
ELIZABETH M. BLITZER

Production Stage Manager . . . . .Susie Cordon
Stage Manager . . . . .Allison Sommers
Assistant to the Director . . . . .Christina Huschle

Associate Set Designer . . . . .Eric Renschler
Associate Costume Designer . . . . .Maryann Smith
Associate Lighting Designer . . . . .Mick A. Smith
Associate Sound Designer . . . . .Michael Creason
Production Carpenter . . . . .Larry Morley
Production Electrician . . . . .Steve Cochrane
Production Props Supervisor . . . . .Mike Smanko
Production Sound . . . . .Wayne Smith
Fight Captain . . . . .David Furr
Hair Supervisor . . . . .John James
Wardrobe Supervisor . . . . .Dave Olin Rogers
Dressers . . . . .Dawn Marcoccia,
Francine Buryiak
Voice Consultant . . . . .Rebekah Maggor
Props Assistant . . . . .Charles Griffin
Production Assistant . . . . .Karyn Meek
Assistant to Mr. Albee . . . . .Jakob Holder
Assistant to Ms. Roth . . . . .Greg Raby
Assistant to Ms. Kramer . . . . .Sara Shannon
Assistant to Mr. Berlind . . . . .Jeffrey Hillock
Assistant to Mr. Rudin . . . . .Aaron Janus
Assistant to Mr. Nederlander . . . . .Ken Happel
Literary Manager . . . . .Gaydon Phillips
Management Interns . . . . .Rachel Levenson,
Alisa D. Sommer
Advertising . . . . .Spotco/Drew Hodges,
Jim Edwards, Tom McCann,
Kim Smarsh

Marketing . . . . .HHC Marketing/Hugh Hysell,
Adam Jay, Michael Redman,
Jillian Boeni, Matt Sicoli
Accounting . . . . .Rosenberg, Neuwirth &
Kuchner/Pat Pederson
Banking . . . . .JP Morgan Chase Bank/
Stephanie Dalton, Richard Callian,
Michele Gibbons
Insurance . . . . .AON/Albert G. Ruben/
George Walden, Claudia Kaufman,
nLegal . . . . .Robinson, Brog, Leinwand, Greene,
Genovese & Gluck P.C./
Richard Ticktin, Roy Jacobs
Travel . . . . .Road Rebel Entertainment Touring/
Chrissy Measley, Christine Paul,
Angie Schoenhard
Payroll . . . . .Castellana Services Inc./
Lance Castellana
Marketing Interns . . . . .Amanda Marcus,
Caitlin Strype, Jason Zammitt
Production Physician . . . . .Dr. Barry Kohn, MD

CREDITS

Scenery constructed by Showman Fabricators, Long Island City, NY. Costumes built by Eric Winterling, Inc. Lighting and sound equipment from PRG Lighting and PRG Audio. Books supplied by Ocean County (NJ) Library. County Antiques LP record by Shore Antiques. Special effects by Jauchem & Meeh.

SPECIAL THANKS

Almeida Theatre, Evan Williams, Kentucky Straight Bourbon Whiskey, San Faustino water, Ricola USA, Emer'gen-C super energy booster provided by Alacer Corp., Yamaha pianos, Tom Watson, Joan Jaffa, Richard Potter, Ben Pesner, Ben and Jerry's ice cream.

 THE SHUBERT ORGANIZATION, INC.

GERALD SCHOENFELD   PHILIP J. SMITH
Chairman   President

JOHN W. KLUGE   LEE J. SEIDLER

MICHAEL I. SOVERN   STUART SUBOTNICK

IRVING M. WALL

ROBERT E. WANKEL
Executive Vice President

PETER ENTIN   ELLIOT GREENE
Vice President   Vice President
Theatre Operations   Finance

DAVID ANDREWS   JOHN DARBY
Vice President   Vice President
Shubert Ticketing Services Facilities

House Manager . . . . .Michael Harris

Opening Night Gifts: Kathleen Turner gave us all beautiful hand-blown champagne stems. The guys got lapel pins of a howling wolf, all in silver. Bill Irwin gave everyone stationery with the Longacre Theatre logo. Our director, Anthony Page, sketched the cast during the rehearsal process, then painted them into a collage and made copies for everyone.

Backstage Rituals: Bill and Kathleen, just before they go on stage, clink their wedding rings. After every performance, we take a moment to hug each other so we know it was all just acting.

Favorite Moment: My favorite line in the play: "You get to the saddest of all points, the point where there is something to lose."

In-Theatre Gathering Place: We created a garden in the alley to the stage door. Everyone has brought in plants or patio furniture or lights or something to decorate it. The prop guy, Mike, brought huge banners from Japan. Chris Burns brought a punching bag. We have Sunday brunches there, weather-permitting, and invite our neighbors from *Doubt* and *Glass Menagerie*.

Off-Site Hangouts: Hurley's, Angus McIndoe's and sometimes Thalia.

Snack Food: Bread sticks! Atkins is dead.

Favorite Therapy: Ricolas are everywhere.

Memorable Stage Door Fan Encounter: Someone falsely claiming to be a member of Kathleen's family tried to get backstage. A personal favorite was a young girl from out of town who asked for my autograph and couldn't have been nicer about not feeling let down that she didn't get to see the whole regular cast.

Busiest Day At The Box Office: The day after the reviews came out.

Ad-Libs: Edward is a stickler for his lines. If you miss a line, you must go back and pick it up.

Cell Phone Rings: About eight. After four, people started yelling at the woman. Then, about a minute later, it started ringing again, and people booed her out of the theatre. As she left, they applauded.

Most Embarrassing Moment: Mireille accidentally did a spit take while drinking brandy.

Company In-Jokes: "Beware the touch of Dawn." "My idea of cleaning is to sweep the room with a glance."

Nicknames: "Bachelor" (David Harbour), "Mimi" (Mireille Enos), "Wilhelm" (Bill Irwin), "Kitten" (Chris Burns), "K.T." (Kathleen Turner).

Superstitions That Turned Out To Be True: We have a cabinet that's part of the set that can't be seen from audience. Everybody brought in a good luck charm or statue and we put them all in that cabinet, and it's given us good luck.

Coolest Thing About Being In This Show: Having Edward Albee backstage. You walk in and see him getting tea or coffee and say, "Hi, Edward," and meanwhile think, "You're *Edward Albee!*"

Also: The noisy rehearsal room. Bennigan's in Boston. The red nightclub in the basement of the Wilbur Theatre in Boston. The man who had a epileptic seizure in New York, but was enjoying the show so much that he refused to leave. The half-naked woman who was changing near the pass door because she said she was feeling hot.

Correspondent: Jennifer Regan, Standby for "Martha"

On stage opening night (L-R): Mireille Enos, Bill Irwin, Edward Albee, Kathleen Turner and David Harbour.

Marquee of the Longacre Theatre.

Director Anthony Page arrives at the opening night cast party at Bonds restaurant.

Bill Irwin and Kathleen Turner take curtain calls on opening night.

Set designer John Lee Beatty.

PLAYBILL®

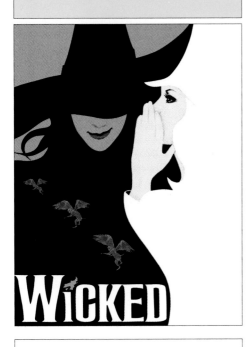

WICKED

CAST

(in order of appearance)

Glinda	JENNIFER LAURA THOMPSON
Witch's Father	SEAN McCOURT
Witch's Mother	CRISTY CANDLER
Midwife	JAN NEUBERGER
Elphaba	SHOSHANA BEAN
Nessarose	MICHELLE FEDERER
Boq	JEFFREY KUHN
Madame Morrible	CAROLE SHELLEY
Doctor Dillamond	WILLIAM YOUMANS
Fiyero	DAVID AYERS
Ozian Official	SEAN McCOURT
The Wonderful Wizard of Oz	GEORGE HEARN
Chistery	PHILLIP SPAETH

Monkeys, Students, Denizens of the Emerald City, Palace Guards and Other Citizens of Oz:
IOANA ALFONSO, JERAD BORTZ, JAMES BROWN III, BEN CAMERON, CRISTY CANDLER, KRISTY CATES, KRISTOFFER CUSICK, KATHY DEITCH, LORI ANN FERRERI, ASMERET GHEBREMICHAEL, LAUREN GIBBS, ZACH HENSLER, REED KELLY, KENWAY HON WAI K. KUA, STACIE MORGAIN LEWIS, SEAN McCOURT, JAN NEUBERGER, WALTER WINSTON ONEIL, ROBB SAPP, PHILLIP SPAETH, MARTY THOMAS, JENNIFER WALDMAN

continued on the next page

≫N≪ GERSHWIN THEATRE

UNDER THE DIRECTION OF
JAMES M. NEDERLANDER AND JAMES L. NEDERLANDER

Marc Platt
Universal Pictures
The Araca Group   and   Jon B. Platt
David Stone

present

Jennifer Laura Thompson   Shoshana Bean

WICKED

Music and Lyrics   Book
Stephen Schwartz   **Winnie Holzman**

Based on the novel by Gregory Maguire

Also Starring

Carole Shelley
David Ayers

Michelle Federer   Jeffrey Kuhn   William Youmans

Adinah Alexander Ioana Alfonso Clyde Alves Jerad Bortz James Brown III Ben Cameron
Cristy Candler Kristy Cates Kristoffer Cusick Kathy Deitch Lori Ann Ferreri Anthony Galde
Asmeret Ghebremichael Lauren Gibbs Kristen Leigh Gorski Zach Hensler Reed Kelly
Kenway Hon Wai K. Kua Stacie Morgain Lewis Sean McCourt Mark Myars Jan Neuberger
Walter Winston ONeil Robb Sapp Phillip Spaeth Marty Thomas Shanna VanDerwerker Jennifer Waldman

and

George Hearn
as the Wizard

Settings	Costumes	Lighting	Sound
Eugene Lee	**Susan Hilferty**	**Kenneth Posner**	**Tony Meola**

Projections	Wigs & Hair	Production Supervisor	Technical Supervisor
Elaine J. McCarthy	**Tom Watson**	**Steven Beckler**	**Jake Bell**

Music Arrangements	Music Director	Dance Arrangements	Music Coordinator
Alex Lacamoire & Stephen Oremus	**Alex Lacamoire**	**James Lynn Abbott**	**Michael Keller**

Associate Set Designer	Special Effects	Flying Sequences	Assistant Director
Edward Pierce	**Chic Silber**	**Paul Rubin/ZFX, Inc.**	**Lisa Leguillou**

Casting	Marketing	General Management	Press	Executive Producers
Bernard Telsey Casting	**TMG - The Marketing Group**	**321 Theatrical Management**	**The Publicity Office**	**Marcia Goldberg & Nina Essman**

Orchestrations
William David Brohn

Music Supervisor
Stephen Oremus

Musical Staging by
Wayne Cilento

Directed by
Joe Mantello

Grammy Award-winning Original Cast Recording on DECCA BROADWAY

LIVE ★
BROADWAY

4/11/05

New Witches Left: Shoshana Bean as Elphaba. Right: Jennifer Laura Thompson as Glinda.

MUSICAL NUMBERS

ACT I

"No One Mourns the Wicked" ....Glinda and Citizens of Oz
"Dear Old Shiz" ....Students
"The Wizard and I" ....Morrible, Elphaba
"What Is This Feeling?" ....Galinda, Elphaba and Students
"Something Bad" ....Dr. Dillamond and Elphaba
"Dancing Through Life" ....Fiyero, Galinda, Boq, Nessarose, Elphaba and Students
"Popular" ....Galinda
"I'm Not That Girl" ....Elphaba
"One Short Day" ....Elphaba, Glinda and Denizens of the Emerald City
"A Sentimental Man" ....The Wizard
"Defying Gravity" ....Elphaba, Glinda, Guards and Citizens of Oz

ACT II

"No One Mourns the Wicked" (reprise) ....Citizens of Oz
"Thank Goodness" ....Glinda, Morrible and Citizens of Oz
"The Wicked Witch of the East" ....Elphaba, Nessarose and Boq
"Wonderful" ....The Wizard and Elphaba
"I'm Not That Girl" (reprise) ....Glinda
"As Long As You're Mine" ....Elphaba and Fiyero
"No Good Deed" ....Elphaba
"March of the Witch Hunters" ....Boq and Citizens of Oz
"For Good" ....Glinda and Elphaba
"Finale" ....All

Cast Continued

UNDERSTUDIES AND STANDBYS

Standby for Glinda: MEGAN HILTY
Standby for Elphaba: SAYCON SENGBLOH
Understudy for Elphaba: KRISTY CATES; for Glinda: STACIE MORGAIN LEWIS; for Fiyero: JERAD BORTZ, KRISTOFFER CUSICK; for the Wizard and Dr. Dillamond: SEAN McCOURT, ANTHONY GALDE; for Madame Morrible: ADINAH ALEXANDER, JAN NEUBERGER; for Boq: WALTER WINSTON O'NEIL, ROBB SAPP; for Nessarose: CRISTY CANDLER, STACIE MORGAIN LEWIS; for Chistery: CLYDE ALVES, REED KELLY, MARK MYARS; for Witch's Father and Ozian Official: JERAD BORTZ, BEN CAMERON, ANTHONY GALDE.

SWINGS

ADINAH ALEXANDER,
ANTHONY GALDE,
SHANNA VANDERWERKER

DANCE CAPTAINS/SWINGS

CLYDE ALVES,
KRISTEN LEIGH GORSKI,
MARK MYARS

ORCHESTRA

CONDUCTOR: ALEX LACAMOIRE

Associate Conductor: David Evans
Assistant Conductor: T.O. Sterrett
Concertmaster: Christian Hebel
Violin: Victor Schultz
Viola: Kevin Roy
Cello: Dan Miller
Harp: Laura Sherman
Lead Trumpet: Jon Owens
Trumpet: Tom Hoyt
Trombones: Dale Kirkland, Douglas Purviance
Flute: Helen Campo
Oboe: Tuck Lee
Clarinet/Soprano Sax: John Moses
Bassoon/Baritone Sax/Clarinets: John Campo
French Horns: Theo Primis, Chad Yarbrough
Drums: Gary Seligson
Bass: Konrad Adderley
Piano/Synthesizer: T.O. Sterrett
Keyboards: Paul Loesel, David Evans
Guitars: Ric Molina, Greg Skaff
Percussion: Andy Jones

Music Coordinator: Michael Keller

Photo by Joan Marcus

George Hearn as the Wizard of Oz and Carole Shelley as Madame Morrible.

Jennifer Laura
Thompson
Glinda

Shoshana Bean
Elphaba

George Hearn
The Wizard

Carole Shelley
Madame Morrible

David Ayers
Fiyero

Michelle Federer
Nessarose

Jeffrey Kuhn
Boq

William Youmans
Doctor Dillamond

Megan Hilty
Standby for Glinda

Saycon Sengbloh
*Standby for
Elphaba*

Adinah Alexander
Swing

Ioana Alfonso
Ensemble

Clyde Alves
*Swing/Assistant
Dance Captain*

Jerad Bortz
Ensemble

James Brown III
Ensemble

Ben Cameron
Ensemble

Cristy Candler
Witch's Mother

Kristy Cates
Ensemble

Kristoffer Cusick
Ensemble

Kathy Deitch
Ensemble

Lori Ann Ferreri
Ensemble

Anthony Galde
Swing

Asmeret
Ghebremichael
Ensemble

Lauren Gibbs
Ensemble

Kristen Leigh Gorski
*Swing;/Dance
Captain*

Zach Hensler
Ensemble

Reed Kelly
Ensemble

Kenway Hon Wai
K. Kua
Ensemble

Stacie Morgain Lewis
Ensemble

Sean McCourt
*Witch's Father/
Ozian Official*

Mark Myars
*Swing/Dance
Captain*

Jan Neuberger
Midwife

Walter Winston
ONeil
Ensemble

Robb Sapp
Ensemble

Phillip Spaeth
Chistery

Wicked

Marty Thomas
Ensemble

Jennifer Waldman
Ensemble

Shanna
Vanderwerker
Swing

Stephen Schwartz
Music and Lyrics

Winnie Holzman
Book

Joe Mantello
Director

Wayne Cilento
Musical Staging

Eugene Lee
Scenic Designer

Susan Hilferty
Costume Designer

Kenneth Posner
Lighting Designer

Tony Meola
Sound Designer

Tom Watson
*Wig and Hair
Designer*

Stephen Oremus
*Music Supervisor/
Music Arrangements*

William David
Brohn
Orchestrations

Alex Lacamoire
*Music Director/
Music
Arrangements*

James Lynn Abbott
*Dance
Arrangements*

Michael Keller
Music Coordinator

Steven Beckler
*Production
Supervisor*

Lisa Leguillou
Assistant Director

Bernard Telsey
Casting
Casting

Paul Rubin
Flying Designer

Gregory Maguire
*Author of
Original Novel*

321 Management: Marcia Goldberg,
Nancy Nagel Gibbs and Nina Essman
General Management

Marc Platt
Producer

Jon B. Platt
Producer

David Stone
Producer

Wicked

ALUMNI

Kevin Aubin
Ensemble

Laura Bell Bundy
Standby for Glinda

Angela Brydon
Ensemble

Norbert Leo Butz
Fiyero

Alexis Ann Carra
Swing

Melissa Bell Chait
Ensemble

Kristin Chenoweth
Glinda

Marcus Choi
Ensemble

Eden Espinosa
Standby for Elphaba

Melissa Fahn
Ensemble

Christopher Fitzgerald
Boq

Rhett G. George
Ensemble

Joel Grey
The Wizard

Randy Harrison
Boq

Manuel Herrera
Chistery

Kisha Howard
Ensemble

L.J. Jellison
Ensemble

Corinne McFadden
Asst. Choreographer/ Ensemble

Joey McIntyre
Fiyero

Idina Menzel
Elphaba

Clifton Oliver
Ensemble

Andrew Palermo
Ensemble

Timothy Britten Parker
Standby for Dr. Dillamond

Andy Pellick
Ensemble

Eric Stretch
Swing

Lorna Ventura
Ensemble

Derrick Williams
Ensemble

Wicked

Front of House Staff
Back Row (L-R): Gaby Crawford, Maria Szymanski, Ivan Rodriguez, Rick Kaye, Martha Boniface, Joyce Pena, Lary Ann Williams, Fran Bennett, Michael King and Betty Friar.

Front Row (L-R): Mariana Casanova, Brenda Denaris, Peggy Boyles, James Gunn, Siobhan Dunne, Philippa Koopman, Joe Ortenzio, Gregory Woolard.

Orchestra
Back Row (L-R): Greg Skaff, Gary Seligson, Adam Ben-David, Andy Jones, Tuck Lee, Ric Molina, Paul Loesel, Melanie Bradford, Victor Schultz, Konrad Adderley.

Second Row (L-R): Jeff Adler, Laura Sherman, Dale Kirkland, Dale Turk, Alex Lacamoire (Music Director/Conductor), T.O. Sterrett, Matt Doebler.

Front Row (L-R): Chad Yarbrough, Tom Hoyt, John Campo, Jon Owens, David Evans, Sara Cyrus.

Photos by Ben Strohmann

The Crew
Back Row (L-R): Jim Carlson, Dennis Fox, Steve Shea, Dennis Peters, John Riggins, Don Savage, Paul Phillips.

Second Row (L-R): Kevin Anderson, Dan Viscardo, Bill Breidenbach, Colin Ahearn, Henry Brisen, Domenic Intagliato, James Connelly.

Kneeling (L-R): Mike Szymanski, Jordan Pankin, Mark Overton, Tommy Gloven, John Curvan, Val Gilmore, Pat Gilmore.

Wicked

STAFF FOR WICKED

General Management
321 THEATRICAL MANAGEMENT
Nina Essman   Nancy Nagel Gibbs
Marcia Goldberg

General Press Representative
THE PUBLICITY OFFICE
Bob Fennell   Marc Thibodeau
Michael S. Borowski

Casting
BERNARD TELSEY CASTING, C.S.A.:
Bernie Telsey, Will Cantler, David Vaccari,
Bethany Knox, Craig Burns,
Tiffany Little Canfield, Christine Dall,
Stephanie Yankwitt

Technical Supervision
JAKE BELL PRODUCTION SERVICES LTD.

COMPANY MANAGER .... SUSAN SAMPLINER

PRODUCTION .... KRISTEN HARRIS
STAGE MANAGER
Stage Manager .... Erica Schwartz
Assistant Stage Managers .... Chris Jamros,
Bess Marie Glorioso,
Jason Trubitt
Associate Company Manager .... Robert Brinkerhoff
Assistant Choreographer .... Corinne McFadden
Dance Captains .... Mark Myars,
Kristen Leigh Gorski
Assistant Dance Captain .... Clyde Alves
Assistant to Mr. Schwartz .... Michael Cole
Assistant Scenic Designer .... Nick Francone
Dressing/Properties .... Kristie Thompson
Scenic Assistant .... Christopher Domanski
Oz Map Design .... Francis Keeping
Draftsman .... Ted LeFevre
Set Model Construction .... Miranda Hardy
Associate Costume Designers .... Michael Sharpe,
Ken Mooney
Assistant Costume Designers .... Maiko Matsushima,
Amanda Whidden,
Amy Clark
Associate Lighting Designer .... Karen Spahn
Associate Lighting Designer/
Automated Lights .... Warren Flynn
Assistant Lighting Designer .... Ben Stanton
Lighting Assistant .... Jonathan Spencer
Associate Sound Designer .... Kai Harada
Sound Assistant .... Shannon Slaton
Projection Programmer .... Mark Gilmore
Assistant Projection Designers .... Jenny Lee,
Michael Patterson,
Jacob Daniel Pinholster
Projection Animators .... Gareth Smith,
Ari Sachter Zeltzer
Special Effects Associate .... Aaron Waitz
Associate Hair Designer .... Charles LaPointe
Fight Director .... Tom Schall
Production Carpenter .... Rick Howard
Head Carpenter .... C. Mark Overton
Deck Automation Carpenter .... William Breidenbach
Assistant Carpenter .... Dan Janssen
Production Electrician .... Robert Fehribach
Head Electrician .... Pat Gilmore
Deck Electrician/Moving Light Operator .... David Karlson

Follow Spot Operator .... Valerie Gilmore
Production Properties .... George Wagner
Property Master .... Joe Schwarz
Production Sound Engineer .... Douglas Graves
Sound Engineer .... Jordan Pankin
Assistant Sound Engineer .... Jack Babin
Production Wardrobe Supervisor .... Alyce Gilbert
Assistant Wardrobe Supervisor .... Kristine Bellerud
Dressers .... Bobbye Sue Albrecht, Artie Brown,
Kevin Hucke, Dianne Hylton,
Kim Kaldenberg, Michael Michalski,
Kathe Mull, Gayle Palmieri,
Laurel Parrish, Barbara Rosenthal,
Jason Viarengo, Randy Witherspoon
Hair Supervisor .... Alfonso Annotto
Assistant Hair Supervisor .... Monica Costea
Hairdressers .... Nora Martin,
Adenike Wright
Makeup Design .... Joseph Dulude II
Makeup Supervisor .... Jimmy Cortes
Music Preparation Supervisor .... Peter R. Miller,
Miller Music Service
Synthesizer Programming .... Andrew Barrett for
Lionella Productions, Ltd.
Rehearsal Pianists .... T.O. Sterrett,
Matthew Gallagher
Rehearsal Drummer .... Gary Seligson
Music Intern .... Joshua Salzman
Assistant to the General Managers .... Jesse Liebman
Production Assistants .... Timothy R. Semon,
David Zack, Jessica Allen,
Spencer Bell, Jack Little
Marketing .... TMG - The Marketing Group/
Tanya Grubich,
Laura Matalon,
Trish Santini,
Lesley Alpert,
Johanna Lindsay
Advertising .... Serino Coyne/
Greg Corradetti,
Joaquin Esteva,
Ruth Rosenberg
Website/Internet Marketing .... Late August Design/
Jeff Prout, Jeff Bowen
Merchandising .... The Araca Group/
Clint Bond, Jr., Karen Davidov,
Julie Monahan, Edward Nelson,
Daniel Pardes, James M. Pellechi, Jr.
Theatre Display .... King Displays
Opening Night Coordinator .... Tobak-Dantchik Events/
Cathy Dantchik,
Michael Lawrence
Group Sales .... Group Sales Box Office/
Ronald Lee (800-223-7565)
Banking .... JP Morgan Chase Bank/
Michele Gibbons
Payroll .... Castellana Services, Inc.
Accountant .... Robert Fried, C.P.A.
Comptroller .... Lawrence Anderson
Insurance .... AON/
Albert G. Ruben Insurance
Legal Counsel .... Loeb & Loeb/
Seth Gelblum
Legal Counsel for Universal Pictures .... Keith Blau
Physical Therapy .... P.T. Plus, P.C./
Marc Hunter-Hall
Onstage Merchandising .... George Fenmore, Inc.

Makeup provided by MAC Cosmetics

MARC PLATT PRODUCTIONS
President: Abby Wolf-Weiss
Adam Siegel, Nicole Brown, Josh Goldenberg,
Greg Lessans, Joey Levy, Jared Leboff

STONE PRODUCTIONS
Associate: Patrick Catullo

UNIVERSAL PICTURES

President & CEO,
(Vivendi Universal Entertainment) .... Ron Meyer
Chairman .... Stacey Snider
President of Production .... Scott Stuber
President of Marketing .... Adam Fogelson
Co-President of Marketing .... Eddie Egan

For additional WICKED merchandise, please visit
www.wickedthemusical.com

CREDITS

Scenery built by F&D Scene Changes, Calgary, Canada. Show control and scenic motion control featuring Stage Command Systems© and scenery fabrication by Scenic Technologies, a division of Production Resource Group, New Windsor, NY. Lighting and certain special effects equipment from Fourth Phase and sound equipment from ProMix, both divisions of Production Resource Group LLC. Other special effects equipment by Sunshine Scenic Studios and Aztec Stage Lighting. Video projection system provided by Scharff Weisberg Inc. Projections by Vermillion Border Productions. Costumes by Euroco Costumes, Barbara Matera Ltd., Parsons-Meares Ltd., Scafati, TRICORNE New York City and Eric Winterling. Millinery by Rodney Gordon and Lynne Mackey. Shoes by T.O. Dey, Frederick Longtin, Pluma and J.C. Theatrical. Flatheads and monkey wings built by Michael Curry Design Inc. Masks created and made by Matthew W. Mungle; lifecasts by Todd Kleitsch. Fur by Fur & Furgery. Undergarments and hosiery by Bra*Tenders, Inc. Antique jewelry by Ilene Chazanof. Specialty jewelry and tiaras by Larry Vrba. Custom Oz accessories by LouLou Button. Custom screening by Gene Mignola. Certain props by John Creech Designs and Den Design Studio. Additional hand props courtesy of George Fenmore. Confetti supplied by Artistry in Motion. Puppets by Bob Flanagan. Musical instruments from Manny's and Carroll Musical Instrument Rentals. Drums and other percussion equipment from Pearl, Sabian, Remo, Pro-Mark and Black Swamp. Cough drops supplied by Ricola, Inc. Emer'gen'C supplied by Alacer Corp. Rehearsed at the Lawrence A. Wien Center, 890 Broadway, and the Ford Center for the Performing Arts.

NEDERLANDER

CHAIRMAN .... JAMES M. NEDERLANDER
PRESIDENT .... JAMES L. NEDERLANDER

Executive Vice President
NICK SCANDALIOS

Vice President Corporate Development Charlene S. Nederlander	Senior Vice President Labor Relations Herschel Waxman
Vice President Jim Boese	Chief Financial Officer Freida Sawyer Belviso

www.nederlander.org

Yamaha is the official piano of the
Nederlander Organization.

STAFF FOR THE GERSHWIN THEATRE

Manager .... Richard D. Kaye
Assoc. Manager .... Steven A. Ouellette
Treasurer .... John Campise
Assistant Treasurer .... Anthony Rossano
Carpenter .... John Riggins
Electrician .... Henry L. Brisen
Assistant Electrician .... Tommy Gloven
Property Master .... Mark Illo
Flyman .... Dennis Fox
Fly Automation Carpenter .... Michael J. Szymanski
Head Usher .... Martha McGuire Boniface

Above: The Witch of the East gets clobbered again: Michelle Federer, as Nessarose, models the "Easter Bonnet" hat.

Left: Idina Menzel displays her 2004 Tony Award for Best Actress in a Musical on Tony night.

Right: Kristin Chenoweth and Idina Menzel rehearsing.

Photo by Aubrey Reuben

Photo by Aubrey Reuben

Photo by Joan Marcus

Tony Night Memory: It seems like only yesterday we were huddled together watching Nathan Lane open that fateful envelope. Ouch. The surprise on his face was nothing compared to ours. But the party went on and champagne was delivered to our dressing room tables the following Tuesday. Gregory Maguire, the author of the novel, "Wicked," wrote us a lovely note about "Charlotte's Web." "Charlotte's Web," he told us, received tepid reviews when it was published, and it didn't win any awards.

"Gypsy Of The Year": The Wicked company raised over $300,000 to handily win the competition. The sketch, "The WICKED Truth" by Anthony Galde, Stacie Morgain Lewis and Marty Thomas, imagined Britney Spears doing Wicked in Vegas. The real Britney declared on her Web site that Wicked changed her life. She worked so hard on the letter to her fans that she said she felt, "Like I had gone to Harvard."

"Easter Bonnet" Sketch: "Nessarose's Turn" by Bill Youmans, Kathy Deitch, Ben Cameron.

"Carols For A Cure" Carol: "Christmas Wrapping."

Memorable Ad-Libs: Although Kristin Chenoweth loved to veer from the script at every opportunity, it was Idina Menzel who came up with the classic ones. When Joey McIntyre made his entrance about 45 seconds late, Idina asked him how the game was. She was right. He had been watching the game. When Joey left the company, he gave everyone teabags with various backstage slogans. One of them said, "Joey McIntyre to the stage. Joey McIntyre to the stage."

One night, Kristin Chenoweth had to leave the show at intermission and her standby, Laura Bell Bundy, took over. Laura Bell is at least a head taller than Kristin. When the Witches met for the first time in Act II, Idina hugged her and said, "You've gotten so tall!"

Celebrity Visitors: Perhaps the best celebrity guest appearance happened the night Garth Brooks and Tricia Yearwood showed up backstage with their girls. No one mentioned to the cast that we would have guests just off stage after the curtain call. Shoshana Bean, the Elphaba with the trucker mouth, waltzed off the stage and trumpeted a curse that would make Joan Rivers blush. As soon as it came out of her mouth, she turned to see Garth in his big old cowboy hat and dear Ms. Yearwood with her girls. Elphaba turned a nice shade of green-red and said, gracefully, "Uh...I have to get out of makeup now."

Injuries: We had our share on the great raked stage, but none more frightening than the night Idina fell into the melting trap. We stopped the show for more than a half hour while EMS took her out on a stretcher. Thankfully, she only fractured a rib, but at the time, we thought it was much, much worse. When Idina got to the hospital, her green skin caused a few heads to turn. But this is New York. The nurses were merely annoyed at the attention she brought and the extra traffic that accompanied her at the ER. They were brusque with her dresser and rude to her parents. When someone announced that her husband had come to see her, the nurses were supremely annoyed. That is, until Taye Diggs walked into the room. Then, suddenly, they were more than accommodating.

Hangouts/Rituals/Snacks: Anthony Galde joined the cast this year and brought with him a decorator's eye and the organizational skills of Julie McCoy. He spearheaded most everything that needed to be spearheaded. He instigated a weekly Sunday Brunch in the Men's Ensemble room, which has become a tradition. We've had Italian Day, Soul Food Day, Irish Day and Jewish Day. On any given Sunday, you'll see George Hearn and Carole Shelley sharing doughnuts with the gypsies. Anthony even redid the green room to create a homey, chic, environment for birthday parties, company meetings and general napping.

Also: None of us will forget Idina's last performance. Although she was unable to do the show, she walked onstage in that now famous red sweatsuit and the audience cheered for minutes on end.

Also: Fictional newspaper correspondent Leo Donovan, who made a name for himself writing Wicked exposés for the call board, declared the Men's Ensemble dressing room to be the "Gayest Place on the Planet." We couldn't be more proud!

Correspondent: Sean McCourt, "Witch's Father/Ozian Official; understudy for Wizard/Dillamond."

Wonderful Town

| First Preview: November 5, 2003 | Opened: November 23, 2003 |
| Closed: January 30, 2005 | 16 Previews and 497 Performances |

PLAYBILL®

CAST

(in order of appearance)

Tour Guide	JAMES CLOW
Appopolous	TOM MARDIROSIAN
Officer Lonigan	TIMOTHY SHEW
Wreck	RAYMOND JARAMILLO McLEOD
Helen	KATE BALDWIN
Violet	LINDA MUGLESTON
Speedy Valenti	STANLEY WAYNE MATHIS
Eileen Sherwood	JENNIFER HOPE WILLS
Ruth Sherwood	BROOKE SHIELDS
Italian Chef, Italian Waiter	ALEX SANCHEZ, JORDAN CABLE
Drunks	MICHAEL O'DONNELL, DENNIS STOWE
Strange Man	DARRIN BAKER
Eskimo Pie Man	J.D. WEBSTER
Frank Lippencott	PETER BENSON
Robert Baker	GREGG EDELMAN
Associate Editors	DARRIN BAKER, JAMES CLOW
Mrs. Wade	MARTHA HAWLEY
Kid	JEFFREY SCHECTER
Chick Clark	RAY WILLS
Shore Patrolman, Man with the Sign	DARRIN BAKER
Cadets	JORDAN CABLE, MICHAEL O'DONNELL, ALEX SANCHEZ, JEFFREY SCHECTER, DENNIS STOWE, J.D. WEBSTER

continued on next page

AL HIRSCHFELD THEATRE

A JUJAMCYN THEATRE

JAMES H. BINGER CHAIRMAN	ROCCO LANDESMAN PRESIDENT
PAUL LIBIN PRODUCING DIRECTOR	JACK VIERTEL CREATIVE DIRECTOR

ROGER BERLIND   BARRY AND FRAN WEISSLER

IN ASSOCIATION WITH EDWIN W. SCHLOSS, ALLEN SPIVAK
CLEAR CHANNEL ENTERTAINMENT AND HARVEY WEINSTEIN
present

BROOKE SHIELDS
in
WONDERFUL TOWN

Book by
JOSEPH FIELDS AND JEROME CHODOROV

Music by	*Lyrics by*
LEONARD BERNSTEIN	**BETTY COMDEN & ADOLPH GREEN**

(Based upon the play "My Sister Eileen" by
JOSEPH FIELDS AND JEROME CHODOROV
and the stories by RUTH McKENNEY)

starring

JENNIFER HOPE WILLS

TOM MARDIROSIAN   RAY WILLS
RAYMOND JARAMILLO McLEOD   PETER BENSON

also starring

KATE BALDWIN   DARRIN BAKER   JAMES CLOW   MARTHA HAWLEY
STANLEY WAYNE MATHIS   LINDA MUGLESTON   TIMOTHY SHEW

CAROL BENTLEY   JORDAN CABLE   SUSAN DERRY   STEPHANIE FREDRICKS
ASHLEY HULL   J. ELAINE MARCOS   CAROLYN OCKERT   MICHAEL O'DONNELL
DENNIS STOWE   ALEX SANCHEZ   JEFFREY SCHECTER   MATTHEW SHEPARD
MELISSA SWENDER   J.D. WEBSTER   LEE A. WILKINS   LAURIE WILLIAMSON

and

GREGG EDELMAN

Scenic Design	*Costume Design*	*Lighting Design*
JOHN LEE BEATTY	MARTIN PAKLEDINAZ	PETER KACZOROWSKI

Sound Design	*Hair Design*	*Make-up Design*	*Script Adaptation*
LEW MEAD	PAUL HUNTLEY	ANGELINA AVALLONE	DAVID IVES

Casting by	*Original Orchestration*	*Music Coordinator*
JAY BINDER/LAURA STANCZYK	DON WALKER	SEYMOUR RED PRESS

Production Supervisor	*Production Stage Manager*
ARTHUR SICCARDI	PETER HANSON

Associate Director	*Associate Choreographer*
MARC BRUNI	VINCE PESCÉ

Executive Producer	*Associate Producers*
ALECIA PARKER	DANIEL M. POSENER JUDITH ANN ABRAMS

General Manager	*Musical Director*	*Press Representative*
B.J. HOLT	JOSHUA ROSENBLUM	THE PETE SANDERS GROUP

Supervising Music Director and Vocal Arranger

ROB FISHER

Directed and Choreographed by

KATHLEEN MARSHALL

The producers wish to thank City Center Encores! for the development production of *Wonderful Town*
and to express their appreciation to Theatre Development Fund for its support of this production.
New Broadway cast recording available on DRG Records.

1/17/05

One Hundred Easy Ways: Brooke Shields as Ruth Sherwood.

Wonderful Town

MUSICAL NUMBERS

Time: 1935
Place: New York City

ACT ONE

Overture ....The Orchestra

Christopher Street
"Christopher Street" ....Tour Guide, Tourists, Villagers

The Studio
"Ohio" ....Ruth, Eileen

All Around New York
"Conquering New York" ....Ruth, Eileen, Frank, New Yorkers

Christopher Street
"One Hundred Easy Ways" ....Ruth

Baker's Office
"What a Waste" ....Baker, Associate Editors
"Ruth's Story Vignettes" ....Baker, Ruth, Associate Editors

Christopher Street
"A Little Bit in Love" ....Eileen

The Studio
"Pass the Football" ....Wreck, Villagers
"Conversation Piece" ....Eileen, Frank, Ruth, Chick, Baker
"A Quiet Girl" ....Baker
"A Quiet Girl" (Reprise) ....Ruth

The Navy Yard
"Conga!" ....Ruth, Cadets

Christopher Street
"Conga!" (Reprise) ....The Company

ACT TWO

The Jail
"My Darlin' Eileen" ....Officer Lonigan, Eileen, Policemen

A Village Street
"Swing" ....Ruth, Villagers

The Studio
"Ohio" (Reprise) ....Ruth, Eileen

In front of the Vortex
"It's Love" ....Eileen, Baker, Villagers

The Village Vortex
Ballet at the Village Vortex ....Villagers
"Wrong Note Rag" ....Ruth, Eileen, Villagers
Finale ....The Company

Brooke Shields sings "Swing."

Wonderful Town

Brooke Shields
Ruth Sherwood

Jennifer Hope Wills
Eileen Sherwood

Gregg Edelman
Robert Baker

Tom Mardirosian
Appopolous

Ray Wills
Chick Clark

Raymond Jaramillo
McLeod
Wreck

Peter Benson
Frank Lippencott

Kate Baldwin
Helen

Darrin Baker
Strange Man/Editor

James Clow
Tour Guide/Editor

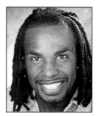
Martha Hawley
Mrs. Wade

Stanley Wayne
Mathis
Speedy Valenti

Linda Mugleston
Violet/
Understudy Ruth

Timothy Shew
Officer Lonigan

Carol Bentley
Ensemble

Jordan Cable
Ensemble

Susan Derry
Ensemble

Stephanie Fredricks
Swing

Ashley Hull
Ensemble

J. Elaine Marcos
Ensemble

Carolyn Ockert
Ensemble

Michael O'Donnell
Ensemble

Alex Sanchez
Ensemble

Jeffrey Schecter
Ensemble

Matthew Shepard
Swing

Dennis Stowe
Ensemble

Melissa Swender
Ensemble

J.D. Webster
Ensemble

Lee A. Wilkins
Swing

Laurie Williamson
Ensemble

Leonard Bernstein
Music

Betty Comden & Adolph Green
Lyrics

Kathleen Marshall
Director/
Choreographer

Rob Fisher
Supervising Musical
Director/Vocal Arrang

John Lee Beatty
Scenic Designer

Martin Pakledinaz
Costume Designer

Peter Kaczorowski
Lighting Designer

Paul Huntley
Hair Designer

Joshua Rosenblum
Musical Director

David Ives
Script Adaptation

Marc Bruni
Assistant Director

Wonderful Town

Roger Berlind
Producer

Barry and Fran Weissler
Producers

Edwin W. Schloss
Producer

Allen Spivak
Producer

Harvey Weinstein
Producer

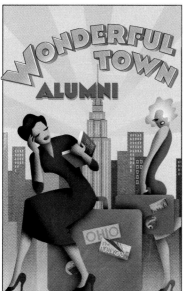

Nancy Anderson
Helen

Ken Barnett
Tour Guide/Editor

Joyce Chittick
Ensemble

Randy Danson
Mrs. Wade

Toni DiBuono
Mrs. Wade

Randy Donaldson
Swing

David Eggers
Ensemble

Sarah Jane Everman
Ensemble

Rick Faugno
Ensemble

Sarah Jayne Jensen
Ensemble

Lorin Latarro
Ensemble

Donald Margulies
Appopolous

Lisa Mayer
Swing

Michael McGrath
Chick Clark

Donna Murphy
Ruth Sherwood

Tina Ou
Ensemble

Vince Pesce
*Assoc. Choreographer/
Ensemble*

Devin Richards
Ensemble

Megan Sikora
Ensemble

Jennifer Westfeldt
Eileen Sherwood

Wonderful Town

Props
Back (L-R): Rich Anderson, Angel Torres, Sal Sclafani, Andy Trotto. Front: Laura McGarty.

Wardrobe
Back (L-R): Scott Shamaneck, Ryan Rosetto, Dana Calanan, Bruce Harrow. Front (L-R): Suzanne Delahunt, Sarah Hench, Penny Davis and Sarah Rocheforis.

Hair (L-R): Nathaniel Hathaway, Darlene Dannenfelser and Mary Mulligan.

Doorman: Neil Perez.

Photos by Ben Strothmann

Front of House
Back Row (L-R): Bart Ryan. 5th Row (L-R): Fidelis Kumbella (with Phillips), Aaron Kendall, Teresa Lopez. 4th Row (L-R): Cristin Whitlen. 3rd Row (L-R): Dorothy Walton, Lauren Hopkins, Janice Rodriguez, Amelia Tirado. 2nd Row (L-R): Tatiana Gomberg, Mary Francis Marzan. Front Row (L-R): Carmel Gunther (House Manager) and Alberta McNamee.

Wonderful Town

Stage Managers
(L-R): Valerie Lau-Kee Lai, Peter Hanson and Michael Wilhoite.

Sound and Electrics
Back Row (L-R): John Blixt, Dermot Lynch, Mike Barrow, Drayton Allison.
Front Row (L-R): Dan Robillard, Beth Berkeley and Bill Allison.

Carpentry Department
Back Row (L-R): Art Soyk, Bill Garvey, Karen Mooney.
Front Row (L-R): Kevin Lynch, Ronnie Fucarino, Joe Lynch.

Photos by Ben Strohmann

STAFF CREDITS FOR WONDERFUL TOWN

Press Associates ....Glenna Freedman, Jeremy Shaffer, Bill Coyle
Casting Associates ....Jack Bowdan, C.S.A./ Mark Brandon, Sarah Prosser, Megan Larche
Company Manager ....Bobby Driggers
Associate General Manager......................Michael Buchanan
Stage Managers ....Valerie Lau-Kee Lai, Michael Wilhoite
Assistant to the Choreographer ....Chase Brock
General Management Assistant ....Jeff Klein
Associate Scenic Designer ....Eric Renschler
Assistant Scenic Designer ....Chad Owens
Associate Costume Designer ....Tracy Christensen
Assistant Costume Designers ......Janine McCabe, Dennis Ballard
Associate Lighting Designer ....Mick Smith
Assistant Lighting Designers ....James Milkey, Ed McCarthy
Moving Light Programmer ....Josh Weitzman
Associate Sound Designers .....Anthony Smolenski, Sten Severson
Production Electrician ....James Fedigan
Production Prop Person ....Sal Sclafani
Head Carpenter ....William Van De Bogart
Flyman ....Ronald Fucarino
Automation Carpenter ....Richard Fideli
Head Electrician ....Drayton Allison
Assistant Electrician ....Greg Fedigan
Prop Persons ....George Green, Jr., Angelo Torre
Sound Engineer ....Daniel Robillard
Wardrobe Supervisor ....Penny Davis
Ms. Shields' Dresser ....Suzanne Delahunt
Hair Supervisor ....Darlene Dannenfelser
Assistant Hair Supervisor ....Shanah-Ann Kendall
Hairdresser ....Mary Elizabeth Micari
Makeup Consultant ....Deanna Nickel
Rehearsal Pianist ....Chris Fenwick
Production Assistants ....Matthew Murphy, Rachel Zack, Brendan Clifford
VP Worldwide Marketing ....Scott Moore
Marketing Manager ....Kenneth Sperr
Accounting ....Rosenberg, Neuwirth & Kuchner/ Mark D'Ambrosi, Annemarie Aguanno
Legal Counsel ....Loeb & Loeb/Seth Gelblum
Advertising ....SpotCo/ Drew Hodges, Jim Edwards, Amelia Heape
Website/Internet Marketing ....Late August Design/ Jeff Bowen, Jeff Prout
Production Photography ....Paul Kolnik
Insurance ....Stockbridge Risk Management/ DeWitt Stern Group, Inc.
Banking ....JP Morgan Chase/Stephanie Dalton
Payroll Service ....Castellana Services, Inc.
Displays ....King Displays
Press Intern ....Heather Smith

CREDIT AND ACKNOWLEDGEMENTS

Scenery and automation constructed by Hudson Scenic Studios, Inc. Lighting equipment from Fourth Phase. Sound equipment from ProMix. Costumes by Tricorne New York City; Barbara Matera, Ltd; Parsons-Meares, Ltd.; Studio Rouge; Timberlake Studios, Inc.; Scafati, Inc.; Paul Chang's Custom Tailor; Seams Unlimited, Ltd.; Virginia Johnson; Park Coats; Lynne Mackey; Rodney Gordon; JC Theatrical; LaDuca; Celebrity; C.C. Wei; Bessie Nelson; Gene Mignola; Early Halloween. Piano provided by Steinway & Sons. Musical materials by Boosey & Hawkes, Inc. Makeup provided by MAC.

🎭 JUJAMCYN THEATERS

James H. Binger
Chairman

Rocco Landesman
President

Paul Libin
Producing Director

Jack Viertel
Creative Director

Jerry Zaks

Daniel Adamian
General Manager

Jennifer Hershey
Director of Operations

STAFF FOR THE AL HIRSCHFELD THEATRE

Manager ....Carmel Gunther
Treasurer ....Carmine La Mendola
Carpenter ....Joseph J. Maher, Jr.
Propertyman ....Sal Sclafani
Electrician ....Dermot J. Lynch

Photos by Aubrey Reuben

The cast gathers for a final group photo at the closing night party at Tony's Di Napoli restaurant.

Above left: Nancy Anderson and Gregg Edelman at the June "Stars in the Alley" event. Above right: Brooke Shields and Anderson with the male ensemble at September's "Broadway on Broadway."

Above left: Producer Roger Berlind welcomes Shields to the cast. Above right: Cast members poke fun at Dame Edna in a "Gypsy of the Year" sketch.

Left: Jennifer Hope Wills and Shields kiss Edelman goodbye at the closing party. Right: Shields unveils the new poster as she joins the cast in October.

Celebrity Visitors: Whenever Betty Comden visited rehearsals, and she was at many, it was magical. She would sing along with every lyric of every song. At the sitzprobe she stood up, overcome with emotion, and said, "Adolph Green would be so happy!" It was an impromptu show of the love she had for her life and for Adolph.

Who Got The Gypsy Robe: Vincent Pesce

"Gypsy Of The Year" Sketch: "45th Street" by Lee Wilkins.

"Carols For A Cure" Carol: "We Three Kings"

Most Roles: Matt Shepard who is swing, covers Lonigan, Wreck, Bob Baker, both "Vignette" guys, and a "Conga" guy.

Most Shows: Vincent Pesce

Favorite Moment: I have an out-of-body experience during *Riverdance* sequence in "Darlin' Eileen." It's a dance joke, and people get it dead-on. Also, the moment Ruth climbs the chain-link fence in "Conga." Seeing Brooke on that fence every night is quite a sight. She really entertains all us middle-aged guys who grew up with her.

In-Theatre Gathering Place: The trap room under the stage is our clubhouse. We celebrate everybody's birthday down there. We also have Broadway's best baker, Stanley Wayne Mathis, in the cast. Every Saturday he bakes ten dozen cookies or peach cobbler or pineapple upside-down cake. On birthdays, he will bake special cakes and decorate them. We're all a couple of pounds heavier, thanks to him!

Off-Site Hangout: Some of the guys go to Charley O's, or go to a sports bar when there's a sports event.

Snack Food: Cookies

Mascot: Ray McLeod

Favorite Therapy: Richard Fideli, a stagehand, maintains a huge retro candy shop offstage right, completely stocked with every candy you can imagine: Red-Hots, Goobers, etc. Everything is free.

Memorable Ad Lib: On one put-in we had set difficulties. The main apartment drop failed to come in when Appopolous was talking about the apartment. It was supposed to appear as he was describing it, but all he had was a bare stage. So he ad-libbed, "You will soon have a sitting room…you are about to have a comfortable bathroom." Brooke went right with it and said, "I'm really, really so looking forward to it when these things arrive." It stopped the show. Audiences love it when those things happen.

Record Number Of Cell Phone Rings: Eight.

Superstitions: A lot of weird things keep happening backstage with no explanation. Props keep getting displaced—things nobody could have moved or touched. Speculation is that it's the ghost of Martin Beck, who is not happy that they had changed the name of the theatre from the Martin Beck to the Al Hirschfeld.

Correspondent: Tim Shew, "Officer Lonigan"

SPECIAL EVENTS

Stars in the Alley

June 2, 2004, Shubert Alley

"Stars in the Alley," Broadway's annual free live concert in Shubert Alley, featured performances from some of the latest shows and gave fans a chance to meet some of their favorites face-to-face. In addition to those pictured, performers included Elizabeth Berkley, Michael Cerveris, Mario Cantone, Frenchie Davis, Tovah Feldshuh, Swoosie Kurtz and Tonya Pinkins.

Above: Laura Michelle Kelly, Sally Murphy, Tricia Paoluccio, who play three of Tevye's daughers in *Fiddler on the Roof*. Below left, Phylicia Rashad of *A Raisin in the Sun* with Shirley Jones of *42nd Street*. Below right: Joey Fatone of *Little Shop of Horrors*.

Above left Laila Robins of *Frozen* and Alfred Molina of *Fiddler on the Roof*. Right: Christy Carlson Romano of *Beauty and the Beast*.

Left: James Barbour of *Assassins*. Right: Tom Wopat and Susan Egan.

Anisha Nagarajan and Manu Narayan of *Bombay Dreams*.

Broadway Bares XIV

June 20, 2004 at Roseland

Right: Two Broadway chorus girls get ready to make their entrances.

Below: Christopher Sieber (R) and a Broadway chorus boy backstage.

The 14th annual "Broadway Bares" fundraiser earned a record-setting $525,000 for Broadway Cares/Equity Fights AIDS. Executive produced by Jerry Mitchell, directed by Jodi Moccia, and hosted by Swoosie Kurtz, Shirley Jones and Patrick Cassidy, the event reimagined classic film scenes.

Two dancers prepare to go on.

John Tartaglia of *Avenue Q* with Rod.

A chorus girl sports the Janet Jackson look.

Seth Rudetsky flexes.

Photos by Aubrey Reuben

Broadway Show League

Championship Games: September 2, 2004
at Heckscher Fields in Central Park.

Producers pitcher (and real-life producer) Rocco Landesman leads his team in shaking hands with second-place *Beauty and the Beast*.

The softball team fielded by Broadway's *The Producers* won the 50th annual Broadway Show League championship—the show's third softball trophy in four years. The crew from the St. James beat the basemen from the previously undefeated *Beauty and the Beast* team in two successive games, first winning 9-8 and then, more decisively, 20-5. The championship was the culmination of a summer-long series of games played on the Heckscher Fields in Central Park by teams from Broadway's shows and organizations. Several Off-Broadway shows also competed.

Beauty and the Beast created a special logo for the team.

A *Producers* slugger.

Beast batter Frank Lopez (left) gets ready to swing. *Producers* hitter Tom McGinty Sr. (right) in the team Jersey.

Broadway on Broadway

September 12, 2004, Times Square

(Left) Co-host Christy Carlson Romano. (Right) The male chorus of *Wonderful Town* snuggles up to leading ladies Brooke Shields and Nancy Anderson.

More than 50,000 gathered September 12 in Times Square for the annual "Broadway on Broadway" free concert, at which hosts Wayne Brady (*Chicago*) and Christy Carlson Romano (*Beauty and the Beast*) sang and danced along with the representatives from the casts of nearly every production then on the boards, including special previews of the season's incoming musicals.

The cast of *Brooklyn* prepares for the show.

(Left) Kelli O'Hara and Tom Hewitt of *Dracula*. (Middle) Jennifer Laura Thompson and Idina Menzel of *Wicked*. (Right) Part of the chorus of *Hairspray*.

Photos by Aubrey Reuben

Broadway Flea Market and Grand Auction

September 19, 2004, Shubert Alley

(Left) An auctioneer hawks posters and Playbills. (Center) The official poster for the event. (Right) Some of the memorabilia up for auction.

Theatre lovers bid on cherished bits of Broadway memorabilia and earned $419,464 for Broadway Cares/Equity Fights AIDS at the 18th Annual Broadway Flea Market and Grand Auction. Favorite stars from Broadway, Off-Broadway and television serials took turns manning the celebrity table, signing autographs for the good cause and chatting with fans. Among goods and services up for bid: a walk-on appearance in *The Phantom of the Opera*; VIP tickets to the opening night of *La Cage aux Folles*, and a Hirschfeld drawing of Gwen Verdon. The table that earned the most for BC/EFA was run by the United Scenic Designers ($16,923), and the show that collected the highest amount was *Wicked* ($12,788). **Photos by Aubrey Reuben and Andrew Ku**

A fan (left) meets *Avenue Q* authors Robert Lopez and Jeff Marx.

(Left) Manu Narayan of *Bombay Dreams*. (Middle) Crew members man the *42nd Street* merchandise table. (Right) Laura Benanti.

Gypsy of the Year

December 6-7, 2004, Neil Simon Theatre

Don Richard as Officer Lockstock and Jennifer Cody as Little Sally, revisiting from *Urinetown*.

Photos by Aubrey Reuben

Nancy Lemenager in the opening number, "Ask a Gypsy."

Host Bruce Vilanch, of *Hairspray*.

Wicked snatched top fundraising honors in the 16th Annual "Gypsy of the Year" competition Dec. 6-7, raking in $365,918 toward a $2,754,631 total for the fundraising event to benefit Broadway Cares/Equity Fights AIDS. Gathered by 50 Broadway, Off-Broadway and touring shows over the past six weeks in nightly curtain-call appeals, the total was the second-highest ever, behind 2003's $3,359,000 but ahead of 2002's $2,265,000. The 2004 "Gypsy of the Year" competition was hosted by Bruce Vilanch, who was appearing at the theatre as Edna Turnblad in *Hairspray*. The event featured a mixture of satirical skits, inspirational songs, and virtuoso dance numbers, all performed by the "gypsies," the Broadway dancers who go from show to show and provide singing and dancing support to the leads. *The Lion King*'s "Driven," which featured Afro-jazz choreography by Gregory A. King, was named best skit of the year. Fundraising runners-up among musicals were *Avenue Q* ($154,208), *Mamma Mia!* ($154,032), *The Phantom of the Opera* ($151,124), *The Lion King* ($150,822) and *Rent* ($144,179). The top fundraising national tour was *Mamma Mia!* ($147,929), the top fundraising Off-Broadway show was *Menopause, The Musical* ($13,200), and the top fundraising Broadway play was *Twelve Angry Men* ($110,724).

Above: Gypsies from *Mamma Mia!* perform their sketch "Red State Ready."

Below: Michael Mastro (*Twelve Angry Men*), Kathleen Chalfant (*Five by Tenn*) and Kevin Cahoon (*The Foreigner*), recognize the non-musicals and Off-Broadway shows that raised money.

Theatre Hall of Fame

January 24, 2005
Gershwin Theatre/Sardi's Restaurant

Lyricist Tom Jones with Estelle Parsons.

Inductees (L-R): A.R. Gurney, Elizabeth I. McCann, Brian Murray, Len Cariou, Estelle Parsons and Santo Loquasto.

Brian Murray with Marian Seldes.

Edward Albee

The 34th annual induction ceremony for the Theatre Hall of Fame honored playwright A.R. Gurney, producer Elizabeth McCann, actor Brian Murray, actor Len Cariou, actress Estelle Parsons and designer Santo Loquasto. All of them were in attendance at the event, which began with speeches at the hall, housed at the Gershwin Theatre, and moved on to a reception at Sardi's restaurant.

Helen Stenborg and Barnard Hughes.

Michael Cumpsty, Tandy Cronyn and publisher Price Berkeley.

Easter Bonnet

April 18-19, 2005, New Amsterdam Theatre

Photos by Aubrey Reuben

Above: Tom Aldredge as a dredlocked judge in *Twelve Angry Men*'s skit, "Diss-Order in the Court." Right: Elizabeth Parkinson holds her baby and models *Movin' Out*'s bonnet in "Voices of Wings," which won Best Bonnet Presentation.

The 17-year-old Broadway production of *Phantom of the Opera* showed it could still hit the high notes, winning the grand prize at the Broadway Cares/Equity Fights AIDS' 19th annual Easter Bonnet Competition by raising $209,615. The prize for best bonnet presentation went to *Movin' Out*, which performed the dance number "Voices of Wings" ending with Elizabeth Parkinson in a cap flanked by a pair of white wings. All told, a new record $2,849,067 was raised by more than 50 participating shows in six weeks of post-show appeals from their respective stages, up sharply from last year's $2,149,744 and 2003's $1,826,392, and beating out the previous record, $2,275,659, raised in 2001. Special guests presented the awards at the New Amsterdam Theatre following two days of performances April 18 and 19. The Broadway play that raised the most money: *Twelve Angry Men*—$88,803. The national tour that raised the most: *Mamma Mia* tour #2—$154,441. Special award for Best Designed and Constructed Bonnet: *The Lion King*. The Off-Broadway show that raised the most: *Altar Boyz*—$22,888. Runners-up for fundraising: *Wicked* ($155,966), *Dirty Rotten Scoundrels* ($147,469), *The Lion King* ($144,829), *La Cage aux Folles* ($125,596).

Above: 101-year-old Ziegfeld Girl Doris Eaton Travis with Miss Mahogany in the opening number.

Below: Award presenters Jeff Goldblum, Jessica Lange and Harvey Fierstein.

Tony Honors

October 26, 2004, Tavern on the Green

Left: Members of the cast of *Big River*. Above: honorees Frances and Harry Edelstein, proprietors of the Edison Café.

Honoree Nancy Coyne.

The Tony Honors for Excellence in the Theatre, once part of the June Tony Awards ceremony, were bestowed October 26 in a ceremony at Tavern on the Green. Honorees for 2004 included Nancy Coyne (advertising executive), Frances and Harry Edelstein (of the Edison Café), Vincent Sardi, Jr. (of Sardi's restaurant), Martha Swope (production photographer) and the cast of Roundabout Theatre's 2003 *Big River*, which was performed by an ensemble consisting of hearing-impaired and hearing actors.

Honoree Martha Swope with guest Chita Rivera.

Left: Honoree Vincent Sardi Jr. Above: Doug Leeds, event host Brooke Shields, Sondra Gilman and the American Theatre Wing's Howard Sherman.

The 2005 Tony Awards

June 5, 2005   Radio City Music Hall

Here are the nominees and winners of the 2005 Tony Awards, which were presented June 5 at Radio City Musical Hall in New York City. Winners below are indicated by boldface type and an asterisk.

BEST MUSICAL
Dirty Rotten Scoundrels
The Light in the Piazza
Monty Python's Spamalot
The 25th Annual Putnam County Spelling Bee

BEST PLAY
Democracy
Doubt
Gem of the Ocean
The Pillowman

BEST PERFORMANCE BY A LEADING ACTOR IN A MUSICAL
Hank Azaria, *Monty Python's Spamalot*
Gary Beach, *La Cage aux Folles*
Norbert Leo Butz, *Dirty Rotten Scoundrels*
Tim Curry, *Monty Python's Spamalot*
John Lithgow, *Dirty Rotten Scoundrels*

BEST PERFORMANCE BY A LEADING ACTRESS IN A MUSICAL
Christina Applegate, *Sweet Charity*
Victoria Clark, *The Light in the Piazza*
Erin Dilly, *Chitty Chitty Bang Bang*
Sutton Foster, *Little Women*
Sherie Rene Scott, *Dirty Rotten Scoundrels*

BEST PERFORMANCE BY A LEADING ACTRESS IN A PLAY
Cherry Jones, *Doubt*
Laura Linney, *Sight Unseen*
Mary-Louise Parker, *Reckless*
Phylicia Rashad, *Gem of the Ocean*
Kathleen Turner, *Edward Albee's Who's Afraid of Virginia Woolf?*

The Winners' Circle: Norbert Leo Butz, Cherry Jones, Victoria Clark and Bill Irwin display their newly-won Tony Awards for the cameras.

BEST PERFORMANCE BY A LEADING ACTOR IN A PLAY
Philip Bosco, *Twelve Angry Men*
Billy Crudup, *The Pillowman*
Bill Irwin, *Edward Albee's Who's Afraid of Virginia Woolf?*
James Earl Jones, *On Golden Pond*
Brían F. O'Byrne, *Doubt*

BEST REVIVAL OF A PLAY
Edward Albee's Who's Afraid of Virginia Woolf?
Glengarry Glen Ross
On Golden Pond
Twelve Angry Men

BEST REVIVAL OF A MUSICAL
La Cage aux Folles
Pacific Overtures
Sweet Charity

BEST DIRECTION OF A MUSICAL
James Lapine, *The 25th Annual Putnam County Spelling Bee*
Mike Nichols, *Monty Python's Spamalot*
Jack O'Brien, *Dirty Rotten Scoundrels*
Bartlett Sher, *The Light in the Piazza*

BEST SPECIAL THEATRICAL EVENT
Dame Edna: Back with a Vengeance!
Laugh Whore
700 Sundays
Whoopi, the 20th Anniversary Show

(Continued on the next page.)

Above: Brian Stokes Mitchell announces the nominees May 10. Below: Nominees Gordon Clapp and Hank Azaria at the Tony Luncheon.

Nominee Erin Dilly blows a good-luck kiss as she arrives on Tony Night.

Photos by Aubrey Reuben

Events

Tony Awards continued.

BEST PERFORMANCE BY A FEATURED ACTOR IN A MUSICAL
*****Dan Fogler, *The 25th Annual Putnam County Spelling Bee**
Marc Kudisch, *Chitty Chitty Bang Bang*
Michael McGrath, *Monty Python's Spamalot*
Matthew Morrison, *The Light in the Piazza*
Christopher Sieber, *Monty Python's Spamalot*

BEST PERFORMANCE BY A FEATURED ACTRESS IN A MUSICAL
Joanna Gleason, *Dirty Rotten Scoundrels*
Celia Keenan-Bolger, *The 25th Annual Putnam County Spelling Bee*
Jan Maxwell, *Chitty Chitty Bang Bang*
Kelli O'Hara, *The Light in the Piazza*
*****Sara Ramirez, *Monty Python's Spamalot**

BEST DIRECTION OF A PLAY
John Crowley, *The Pillowman*
Scott Ellis, *Twelve Angry Men*
*****Doug Hughes, *Doubt**
Joe Mantello, *Glengarry Glen Ross*

BEST ORIGINAL SCORE (MUSIC AND/OR LYRICS) WRITTEN FOR THE THEATRE
Dirty Rotten Scoundrels
Music & Lyrics: David Yazbek
*****The Light in the Piazza**
Music & Lyrics: Adam Guettel
Monty Python's Spamalot
Music: John Du Prez and Eric Idle;
Lyrics: Eric Idle
The 25th Annual Putnam County Spelling Bee
Music & Lyrics: William Finn

BEST CHOREOGRAPHY
Wayne Cilento, *Sweet Charity*
Jerry Mitchell, *Dirty Rotten Scoundrels*
*****Jerry Mitchell, *La Cage aux Folles**
Casey Nicholaw, *Monty Python's Spamalot*

BEST BOOK OF A MUSICAL
Jeffrey Lane, *Dirty Rotten Scoundrels*
Craig Lucas, *The Light in the Piazza*
Eric Idle, *Monty Python's Spamalot*
*****Rachel Sheinkin, *The 25th Annual Putnam County Spelling Bee**

BEST PERFORMANCE BY A FEATURED ACTRESS IN A PLAY
Mireille Enos, *Edward Albee's Who's Afraid of Virginia Woolf?*
Heather Goldenhersh, *Doubt*
Dana Ivey, *The Rivals*
*****Adriane Lenox, *Doubt**
Amy Ryan, *A Streetcar Named Desire*

BEST PERFORMANCE BY A FEATURED ACTOR IN A PLAY
Alan Alda, *Glengarry Glen Ross*
Gordon Clapp, *Glengarry Glen Ross*
David Harbour, *Edward Albee's Who's Afraid of Virginia Woolf?*
*****Liev Schreiber, *Glengarry Glen Ross**
Michael Stuhlbarg, *The Pillowman*

(Continued on the next page.)

Left: Chita Rivera arrives at Radio City Music Hall. Right: Sara Ramirez with her Tony for Best Featured Actress in a Musical.

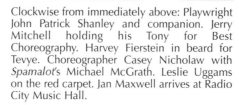

Clockwise from immediately above: Playwright John Patrick Shanley and companion. Jerry Mitchell holding his Tony for Best Choreography. Harvey Fierstein in beard for Tevye. Choreographer Casey Nicholaw with *Spamalot*'s Michael McGrath. Leslie Uggams on the red carpet. Jan Maxwell arrives at Radio City Music Hall.

Events

Class Photo: The nominees in the various performing categories gathered in Times Square.

Photos by Steve and Anita Shevett

Photos by Aubrey Reuben

Clockwise from above: Bill Irwin waves his Tony as Best Actor in a Play. Bernadette Peters and husband Michael Wittenberg on the red carpet. Robert Goulet and his wife Vera arrive at Radio City.

Tony Awards continued.

BEST SCENIC DESIGN OF A MUSICAL
Tim Hatley, *Monty Python's Spamalot*
Rumi Matsui, *Pacific Overtures*
Anthony Ward, *Chitty Chitty Bang Bang*
*Michael Yeargan, *The Light in the Piazza*

BEST SCENIC DESIGN OF A PLAY
John Lee Beatty, *Doubt*
David Gallo, *Gem of the Ocean*
Santo Loquasto, *Glengarry Glen Ross*
*Scott Pask, *The Pillowman*

BEST LIGHTING DESIGN OF A PLAY
Pat Collins, *Doubt*
Donald Holder, *Gem of the Ocean*
Donald Holder, *A Streetcar Named Desire*
*Brian MacDevitt, *The Pillowman*

BEST LIGHTING DESIGN OF A MUSICAL
*Christopher Akerlind, *The Light in the Piazza*
Mark Henderson, *Chitty Chitty Bang Bang*
Kenneth Posner, *Dirty Rotten Scoundrels*
Hugh Vanstone, *Monty Python's Spamalot*

BEST COSTUME DESIGN OF A PLAY
*Jess Goldstein, *The Rivals*
Jane Greenwood, *Edward Albee's Who's Afraid of Virginia Woolf?*
William Ivey Long, *A Streetcar Named Desire*
Constanza Romero, *Gem of the Ocean*

BEST COSTUME DESIGN OF A MUSICAL
Tim Hatley, *Monty Python's Spamalot*
Junko Koshino, *Pacific Overtures*
William Ivey Long, *La Cage aux Folles*
*Catherine Zuber, *The Light in the Piazza*

BEST ORCHESTRATIONS
Larry Hochman, *Monty Python's Spamalot*
*Ted Sperling, Adam Guettel and Bruce Coughlin, *The Light in the Piazza*
Jonathan Tunick, *Pacific Overtures*
Harold Wheeler, *Dirty Rotten Scoundrels*

SPECIAL TONY AWARD FOR LIFETIME ACHIEVEMENT IN THE THEATRE
Edward Albee

REGIONAL THEATRE TONY AWARD
Theatre de la Jeune Lune
Minneapolis, Minnesota

Total number of Tony awards won by each production:

The Light in the Piazza - 6
Doubt - 4
Monty Python's Spamalot - 3
Glengarry Glen Ross - 2
La Cage aux Folles - 2
The Pillowman - 2
The 25th Annual Putnam County Spelling Bee - 2
Dirty Rotten Scoundrels - 1
The Rivals - 1
700 Sundays - 1
Who's Afraid of Virginia Woolf? - 1

FACULTY

The Shubert Organization

Gerald Schoenfeld
Chairman

Philip J. Smith
President

Robert E. Wankel
Executive Vice President

Photos by Ben Strohmann

Jujamcyn Theaters

Rocco Landesman
President

Paul Libin
Producing Director

Jack Viertel
Creative Director

Photos courtesy Jujamcyn Theaters

Nederlander Organization

James M. Nederlander
Chairman

James L Nederlander
President

Photos by Ben Strohmann

Nederlander Staff
Seated (L-R): Maria Fajardo, Karen Fino, Angelica Misonet, Carol Eto, Lisa Lent, Nancy Salgado, Kim Angad-Jugmohan.
First Standing Row (L-R): Alice Gold, Thuy Dang, Alyce Cozzi, Dana Chie.
Second Standing Row (L-R): Brian Harasek, Blair Zwillman, Julia Barr, Rina Beacco, Aaron Kelley, Freddy Owens, Angelique Eto.
Back Row (L-R): Ken Happel, Josh Salez, David Perry.
Not Pictured: Janet Arvold, Phyllis Buono, Rachel Jukofsky, Jey Moore, Mitchell McCann.

Nick Scandalios

Herschel Waxman

Jim Boese

Freida Sawyer Belviso

Susan Lee

Jack Meyer

James M. Nederlander with daughter, Kristina Gustafson-Nederlander, and wife, Charlene Nederlander.

Kathleen Raitt

Disney Theatrical Productions

Photo by Ben Strothmann

Staff

Front Row (L-R): Jennifer Baker, Jay Kimbro, Dayle Gruet, Jeff Lee, Harry Gold, Sarah Norris.

Second Row (L-R): Seth Stuhl, Greg Gunter, Elliot Altman, Matt Cronin, Suzanne Jakel, Bill Hussey, Leslie Barrett.

Third Row (L-R): Kevin Snow, Ken Cerniglia, Janine McGuire, Suzanne Araneo, Shawn Baker, Amy Andrews, Antonia Barba.

Fourth Row (L-R): Alice Baeza, Karl Chmielewski, Todd Lacy, Jerome Kane, Eddie Pisapia, John Agati, Mark Nathman, Steven Downing.

Fifth Row (L-R): Clifford Schwartz, Anne Quart, Giovanna Primak, Tiffany Casanova, Jeff Parvin, Christian Trimmer, Gregory Bonsignore.

Sixth Row (L-R): Alan Levey, Joe McClafferty, Ron Kollen, Michele Holland, Rick Elice, Thomas Schumacher, Michele Steckler, David Schrader.

Seventh Row (L-R): Barbara Toben, Wilson Liu, Dana Amendola, Tara Engler, Kevin McGuire, Emily Powell, Jonathan Olson.

Eighth Row (L-R): Andrew Flatt, Juil Kim, Scott Hemerling, Gregory Hanoian, Suyin Chan, Ken Silverman, Alma La Marr, John Loiacono, Jonathan Hanson.

Clear Channel Entertainment

Photos by Ben Strohmann

(L-R): Carl Pasbjerg (Executive Producer, Theatrical Production), Jennifer Costello (Executive Producer, Theatrical Production) and Scott Zeiger (CEO North America, Theatrical Production). Not Pictured: Joanna Hagan (Executive Producer, Theatrical Production).

TKTS

(L-R): Steve Banovich, Kiki Hernandez, Bill Castellano, Mike Campanella, Liz Edell, Bill Roeder, Anthony Marin, Jim Divone and Lawrence Paone.

Roundabout Theatre Company

Todd Haimes
Artistic Director

Julia C. Levy
*Executive Director,
External Affairs*

Ellen Richard
Managing Director

Scott Ellis
*Associate Artistic
Director*

Ticket Services
Back Row (L-R): Charlie Garbowski, Ellen Holt, Erin Frederick, Steven Gottlieb, Pam Unger, Joseph Griffin
Middle Row (L-R): Ethan Ubell, Lindsay Erickson, Amanda Genovese, Julie Hilimire, Catherine Fitzpatrick, Robert Kane, Lily Soto
Front Row (L-R): Tom Protulipac, David Meglino, Tom Dahl, Adam Elsberry, Robert Morgan and Jeff Monteith.

Senior Staff
Standing (L-R): Susan Neiman (Controller), Tony Baksa (Director of Telesales Special Promotions), Jeffory Lawson (Director of Development), Don-Scott Cooper (General Manager of the Steinberg Center).
Seated (L-R): David B. Steffen (Director of Marketing), Sydney Beers (General Manager), Jim Carnahan (Director of Artistic Development/Director of Casting).

Development Office
Standing (L-R): Dominique Yacbozzi, Julie K. D'Andrea.
Middle Row (L-R): Dawn Kusinski, Kristen Bolibruch, Tina Mae Bishko, Lauren Hoshibata, Julia Lazarus
Seated (L-R): Justin D. Steensma, Steve Schaeffer and Corinne Hayoun,

Casting, Marketing and General Management
Standing (L-R): Kate Schwabe, Stephen Kopel, Mele Nagler, Nichole Larson
Seated (L-R): Greg Backstrom, Tim McCanna, Sunil Ayyagari and Becca Ballon.

Business Office
Top Row (L-R): Anthony Foti, Lloyd Alvarez. Middle Row (L-R): Jeff Goodman, Frank Surdi, Bonnie Berens, Elisa Papa, Trina Cox. Seated (L-R): Jennifer Decoteau, Yonit Kafka, John LaBarbera and David Solomon.

Photos by Ben Strohmann

Actors' Equity Association

Patrick Quinn
President

Alan Eisenberg
Executive Director

Right: National Council: Front Row (L-R): Conard Fowkes (Secretary/Treasurer), Patrick Quinn (President), Jean-Paul Richard (Second Vice President). Back Row (L-R): Ira Mont (Third Vice President), Arne Gundersen (Eastern Regional Vice President)

Photos by Ben Strohmann

Left: Executive Wing 16th Floor Group
First Row (L-R): Alan Eisenberg, Flora Stamatiades, Mary Lou Westerfield, Marie Gottschall, Amy Dolan, Karen Nothmann
Second Row (L-R): Ann Fortuno, Ellen Deutsch, Alex Barreto, Megann McManus, Jeff Stanley
Third Row (L-R): Tami Jean Lombardi, Stuart Levy, J.P. Bommel, John Fasulo
Fourth Row (L-R): Robert Fowler, Joe De Michele, Steve DiPaola, Chris Nee, Frank Horak and David Lotz.

Below: Auditions, Contracts and Membership
Front Row (L-R): Chris Landry, Barry Rosenberg, Diane Wright, Karlene Laemmie, Tom Hafner
Second Row (L-R): Diane Raimondi, Tatiana Kouloumbis, Adam Pitner, Jamie Blankenship
Back Row (L-R): J.P. Regit, Altravise Smith, Gisela Valenzuela, Lindsey Taub, and Robin Thomsen.

Above: 15th Floor Group
Front Row seated (L-R): Peter Mojica, Val LaVarco, Chris Lagalante, Zalina Hoosein, Rick Berg, Joe Erdey
Second Row seated (L-R): Dwane Upp, Kathy Mercado, Kathryn Herrera, Helene Ross, Deborah Johnson, Patrick Lee
Third Row standing (L-R): Sylvina Persaud, Catherine Jayne, Louise Foisy, Angelica Ybanez, Julie Posner, Nancy Lynch, Ken Greenwood
Back Row standing (L-R): Kevin Pinzon, Tom Kaub, Marc Kochanski, Kristin Wolf, Lawrence Lorczak, Gary Dimon, William Adriance, Beverly Sloan, Trevor Burrowes and Walt Kiskaddon.

Dramatists Guild

John Weidman
President

Marsha Norman
Vice President

Photos by Ben Strohmann

The Dramatists Guild Council
Seated (L-R): Christopher C. Wilson, Sheldon Harnick, Arthur Kopit, Susan Birkenhead, Stephen Schwartz
Standing (L-R): Carol Hall, Marsha Norman, John Weidman and Ralph Sevush.

Jonathan Reynolds
Treasurer

Arthur Kopit
Secretary

The Dramatists Guild Staff
Front Row (L-R): Ralph Sevush (Executive Director), Doug Green (Director of MIS, Webmaster),
Tari Stratton (Director of Outreach), Gregory Bossler (Director of Publications)
Back Row (L-R): Tom Epstein (Director of Membership), Joel Szulc (Managing Director)

Association of Theatrical Press Agents and Managers

Photos by Ben Strohmann

Seated (L-R): President Maria A. Somma, Secretary/Treasurer Gordon G. Forbes, Vice President David R. Calhoun
Second Row (L-R): Press Agent Chapter Chair Shirley R. Herz, Board Member Emeritus Richard Seader, Chicago
Steward Maury Collins, Barbara Carroll, Manager Chapter Chair Robert Nolan, Susan Elrod
Third Row (L-R): Board Member and Philadelphia Steward Mark Schweppe, Manager Alternate Howard Rogut,
President Emeritus Merle Debuskey, Jim Baldassare, Kevin McAnarney, David Gersten, Press Agent Alternate Bruce
Cohen, Mary K. Witte

American Federation of Musicians, Local 802

Front Row (L-R): Jay Blumenthal (VP), David Lennon (President), Bill Dennison (VP)
Middle Row (L-R): Bobby Shankin, John Babich, Mary Whitaker, Mary Landolfi
Back Row (L-R): John Bogert, Tino Gagliardi, Art Weiss, Jack Gale
(Not Pictured: Maura Giannini, Jay Schaffner, Jimmy Owens)

Society of Stage Directors and Choreographers

Photos by Ben Strohmann

Seated (L-R): Doug Hughes (Treasurer), Ron Shechtman (Counsel), Pamela Berlin (President), Barbara Hauptman (Executive Director), Sue Lawless (Secretary), Hope Clarke, John Dillon
Standing (L-R): Tisa Chang, Austin Pendleton (Vice President), Richard Hamburger, Will Parker, Lisa Peterson, Karen Azenberg (Executive Vice President), Mark Brokaw, Renee Lasher, Mauro Melleno, Edie Cowan, Tracy Dickson, Sam Bellinger, Barbara Wolkoff, Kathryn Haapala (Deputy Executive Director), James Graves, Lena Abrams, Lonny Price

Theatrical Stage Employees, IATSE Local 1

Executive Board
Seated (L-R): Legitimate Theatre Business Manager Michael Wekselblatt, Secretary Robert Score, President James J. Claffey, Jr., Vice President William Walters, Treasurer Donald B. Kleinschmidt
Standing (L-R): Television Business Managers Edward McMahon III and Robert Nimmo, Legitimate Theatre Business Manager Kevin McGarty, Chairman of Trustees John Diaz, Sr., Trustees William Ngai, Daniel Thorn

Treasurers & Ticket Sellers Union, IATSE Local 751

(L-R): Jim Sita, Kathy McBrearty, Patricia Quiles

Seated (L-R): Greer Bond, Matthew Fearon, Joseph Scanapicco, Jr., Gene McElwain, Noreen Morgan
Second Row (L-R): David Heveran, Paul Posillico, Karen Winer, Diane Heatherington
Third Row (L-R): John Nesbitt, William Castellano, Michael Loiacono, Harry Jaffie, Stanley Shaffer, Peter Attanasio, Jr. Fred Santore, Jr.
Left of Flag: Robert Begin
Right of Flag: Lawrence Paone

Theatrical Wardrobe Union, IATSE Local 764

Photos by Ben Strothmann

Back Row (L-R): Business Representative James Hurley, Alyssa Kabel, Dennis Birchall, Marilyn Knotts, Fund Manager Mary Ferry, James Kabel, Staff member Joan Boyce, Staff member Rosemary McGroarty, Trustee Charles Catanese, Staff member Jon Kelib, Assistant Fund Manager Carletta Pizzorno, Staff member Michael Gemignani, President Patricia A. White.
Third Row (L-R): Trustee Veneda Truesdale, Trustee Margaret Kurz, Tree Sarvay, Anthony Hoffman, Michael Sancineto, Frank Sancineto, Vice President Kristin Gardner, Secretary-Treasurer Jenna Krempel.
Second Row (L-R): Trustee Rochelle Friedman, Michael Fisher, Jay Woods, Linda McAllister, Anita-Ali Davis, Eileen Casey, David Gevengoed, Rene Irwin, Soomi Marano, Laura Ellington.
Front Row (L-R): Ginnie Wiedmann, Brenda Green, Dolores Jones, Cindy Chock, Barbara Hladsky, Trustee Patricia Sullivan and Sergeant at Arms Terry La Vada.

United Scenic Artists, IATSE Local 829

Front Row (L-R): Cecilia Friederichs, Beverly Miller.
Back Row (L-R): Michael McBride, F. Mitchell Dana, Tony Quintavalla, Joe Saint.

Local 306 Motion Picture Projectionists, Video Technicians and Allied Crafts (Ushers)

Seated (L-R): Maureen Huff, Rosaire Lulu Caso, Mim Pollock, Susan Lehman.
Standing (L-R): Mike Terr, Dotty Rogan, John Livanos, Michael Goucher, Rita Russell, Hugo Capra, Ken Costigan.

Theatrical Teamsters, Local 817

Executive Board of Theatrical Teamsters Local 817
Standing (L-R):
Kevin Keefe,
Mike Hyde,
Ed Iacobelli,
T.J. O'Donnell,
Jim Leavey,
Frank Connolly, Jr.
Seated:
Thomas R. O'Donnell

Theatrical Teamsters Staff
(L-R):
Tina Gusmano,
Christine Harkerss,
Marge Marklin

SEIU Local 32BJ

Mike Fishman,
President of Local 32BJ
Service Employees
International Union

Local 30 IUOE

Jack Ahern,
Business Manager of
Local 30,
International Union
of Operating
Engineers

Coalition of Broadway Unions and Guilds

Photos by Ben Strohmann

Board Members

First Row (L-R): Ray Polgar (Broadway Business Representative, Local 798 IATSE), Frank Connolly, Jr. (Business Representative, Theatrical Teamsters Local 817), Anthony M. DePaolo (International Vice President, IATSE), Carol Waaser (Eastern Regional Director, Actors' Equity Association), Michael Manley (Director, Touring Division, American Federation of Musicians)

Second Row (L-R): Deborah J. Allton (New York Area Counsel, American Guild of Musical Artists), Alex Barreto (Assistant to Executive Director, Actors' Equity Association), Lynne Bond (Theatre Representative, AFM Local 802), Frank Gallagher (Business Representative, Local 764 IATSE), Joe Delia (Assistant to the President, AFM Local 802), Ralph Sevush (Executive Director, Dramatists Guild)

Third Row (L-R): Miriam "Mim" Pollock (Theatrical Business Representative, Local 306 IATSE), John M. Diaz (Chairman of Trustees, Local One IATSE), Michael Wexelblatt (Business Manager, Local One IATSE), Barbara B. Hauptman (Executive Director, Society of Stage Directors and Choreographers), Kathryn Haapal (Deputy Executive Director, Society of Stage Directors and Choreographers) and James P. Hurley (Business Representative, Local 764 IATSE).

Fourth Row: Maria A. Somma (President, ATPAM Local 18032 IATSE), Gordon G. Forbes (Secretary Treasurer, ATPAM, Local 18032 IATSE)

Not pictured: (Business Representative, Local 30 Engineers), Mary Donovan (Theatre Representative, AFM Local 802), Alan Eisenberg (Executive Director, Actors' Equity Association), Cecilia Friederichs (Financial Secretary, USA Local 829 IATSE), Alan Gordon (Executive Director, American Guild of Musical Artists), Ken Greenwood (Senior Business Representative, Actors' Equity Association), David Lennon (President, AFM Local 802), Michael McBride (National Business Agent, USA Local 829 IATSE), Gene McElwain (Secretary Treasurer/Business Representative, Local 751 IATSE), Tom J. O'Donnell (Secretary Treasurer, Local 817 Teamsters), Patrick Quinn (President, Actors' Equity Association), Mike Spillane (Legal Counsel Local 30 Engineers), Tom Walsh (Senior Business Representative, ATPAM Local 18032 IATSE), Patricia White (President, Local 764 IATSE)

Makeup Artists and Hair Stylists, IATSE Local 798

Ray Polgar, Broadway Business Representative.

Boneau/Bryan-Brown

Jim Byk

Brandi Cornwell

Erika Creagh

Jackie Green

Juliana Hannett

Rick Hayashi

Chris Boneau

Adrian Bryan-Brown

Photos by Ben Strothmann

Hector Hernandez

Amy Jacobs

Jessica Johnson

Don Marazzo

Aaron Meier

Linnae Petruzzelli

Joe Perrotta

Matt Polk

Susanne Tighe

Barlow•Hartman Public Relations

John Barlow

Michael Hartman

Leslie Baden

Carol Fineman

Guido Goetz

Bethany Larsen

Mark Pino

Barlow•Hartman Staff (L-R): Bethany Larsen, Andy Snyder, Carol Fineman, Leslie Baden, Michael Hartman, Guido Goetz, Wayne Wolfe, Mark Pino and John Barlow.

Rick Miramontez

Ryan Ratelle

Miguel Raya

Andy Snyder

Gerilyn Shur

Wayne Wolfe

Photos by Ben Strohmann

Richard Kornberg & Associates

Richard Kornberg

Don Summa

Carrie Friedman

Tom D'Ambrosio

Photos by Ben Strothmann

The Pete Sanders Group

Pete Sanders

Glenna Freedman

Heather Smith

Jeremy Shaffer

Jeffrey Richards Assoc.

Irene Gandy

The Publicity Office

Michael Borowski

SERINO COYNE, INC.
Class of 2004-05

Twenty-seven years on Broadway sure have aged this gang! These kids lead a team of 100 in three cities to create the logos, posters, billboards, and TV and radio commercials that help encourage the world to come on along and listen to the lullaby of Broadway.

NANCY COYNE
Class co-President

MATTHEW SERINO
Class co-President

ANDY APOSTOLIDES

SANDY BLOCK

TOM CALLAHAN

GREG CORRADETTI

ANGELO DESIMINI

SCOTT JOHNSON

DAVID KANE

BURT KLEEGER

ROGER MICONE

JIM MILLER

THOMAS MYGATT

RUTH ROSENBERG

JIM RUSSEK

SUE TAYLOR

GINGER WITT

Text and page design by Serino Coyne

G. Anderson   B. Aquart   J. Aquino   D. Cox   T. Coppola   A. Cruz   A. Davis   J. Disbrow

S. Eckersley   T. Francis   A. Heape   L. Hunter   W. Hutton   L. Johnson   L. Kaiser   R. Kolb

SpotCo Class of 2005

B. Berk   J. Edwards   T. Greenwald   D. Hodges

J. Lanasa   R. Lederman   T. Licorish   M. Littell   M. Masyga   D. Melchiorre   T. McCann

J. McClelland   J. McNicholas   P. Milano   W. Mitchell   G. Montalvo   D. Preston   M. Rheault

I. Rosen   V. Sainato   K. Smarsh   L-A Stone   D. Tandet   E. Vicioso   G. Wingfield

Text and page design by SpotCo

The Actors' Fund of America

Photos by Ben Strohmann

Seated (L-R): Icem Benamu, Stephanie Linwood Coleman, Patch Schwadron, Lucy Seligson, Liz Lawlor, Erica Chung, Josh Levine, Ryan Dietz
Second Row (L-R): Victor Mendoza, Debbie Schaum, Judy Fish, Belinda Sosa, Joe Benincasa, Sue Composto, Tamar Shapiro, Sara Meehan
Third Row (L-R): Jose Delgado, Gloria Jones, Dave Gusty, Billie Levinson, Wally Munro, Catherine Cooke, Ruth Shin
Fourth Row (L-R): Melissa Haslam, Sylvian Underwood, Lorraine Chisholm, Lisa Naudus, Helene Kendler, Thomas Pileggi
Fifth Row (L-R): Barbara Davis, Sam Smith, Charlene Morgan, Vicki Avila, Carol Wilson, Rick Martinez, Tim Pinckney, Israel Duran, Janet Pearl
Back Row (L-R): Dr. Jim Spears, David Engelman, Jonathan Margolies, Keith McNutt, Bob Rosenthal

Lincoln Center Theater

(L-R): André Bishop (Artistic Director), Bernard Gersten (Executive Producer).

League of American Theatres and Producers

Jed Bernstein
President

Gerald Schoenfeld
Chairman

Staff

Front Row (L-R): Jazmine Estacio (Manager of Labor Relations), Harriet Slaughter (Co-Director of Pension & Health), Laura Fayans (Comptroller), Irving Cheskin (Co-Director of Pension & Health), Ben Pesner (Manager, Creative Services).

Second Row: Zenovia Varelis (Secretary to Labor), Jessica Storm (Research Assistant), Christina Warner (Administrative Assistant), Ed Sandler (Director of Membership), Tahra Millan (Manager of Marketing and Promotions), Jan Svendsen (Director of Marketing, Events and Development), Melanie Seinfeld (Assistant Comptroller), Colin Gibson (Director of Finance and Administration), Rachel Reiner (Manager of Membership Services), Jennifer Stewart (Membership Services Associate), Roger Calderon (Supervisor of Broadway Ticket Center).

Back Row: Jed Bernstein (League President), Jim Echikson (Director of Corporate Sponsorship), Karen Hauser (Director of Research), Neil Freeman (Manager of Research), David Carpenter, (Manager Ticket Center Operations), Seth Popper (Director of Labor Relations), Robert Davis (Manager of Information Technology), Edward Forman (Marketing Manager, Sponsorship), Michel Kinter (Manager of Labor Relations), Britt Marden (Marketing Manager, Events), Alan Cohen (Director of Communications).

Not Pictured: Gerald Schoenfeld (Chairman), Patricia Casterlin (Assistant to the President), Jean Kroeper (Manager of Tony Awards Administration & Office Management), Robin Fox (Receptionist), Barbara Janowitz, (Director of Government Relations), Erica Ryan (Manager of Government Relations), Jim Lochner (Marketing Coordinator).

American Theatre Wing

Photo by Ben Strohmann

Front Row (L-R): Liz Jurist, Rose Wohlstetter
Middle Row (L-R): Robb Perry, Randy Ellen Lutterman, Lesley-Anne Stone, Peter Schneider, Dasha Epstein, Doug Leeds, Sondra Gilman and Ron Konecky.
Back Row (L-R): David Brown, Mallory Factor, Ted Chapin (pointing at a Sardi's sketch of longtime Wing leader Isabelle Stevenson), Matt Jarrett, Stephen Abrams and Jay Harris.

Not pictured:
Board Members: Lucie Arnaz, Donald Brooks, Bill Craver, Marlene Hess, Henry Hewes, Anita Jaffe, Jeffrey Eric Jenkins, Jo Sullivan Loesser, Michael Price, Lloyd Richards, Jane Safer, Alan Siegel and Howard Stringer.
Staff Members: Howard Sherman and Raisa Ushomirski.

Photo by Elaine Ubina

(L-R): Executive Director Howard Sherman, Board Chairman Sondra Gilman and Board President Doug Leeds at the American Theatre Wing Spring Dinner.

Broadway Cares/Equity Fights AIDS

Tom Viola
Executive Director

Michael Graziano
Producing Director

Larry Cook
*Director of Finance
and Administration*

First Row (L-R): Jamie Bishton, Keith Bullock, Dennis Henriquez, Michael Kumor
Second Row (L-R): Wendy Merritt-Kaufmann, Peter Neufeld, Brian Schaaf, Yvonne Ghareeb, Kevin Burke, Denise Roberts Hurlin, Carol Ingram, Jane Smulyan
Third Row (L-R): Trish Doss, Michelle Abesamis, Ngoc Bui, Chris Economakos, Mary-Shannon Ryan, Frank Conway, Andy Halliday, Tom Viola
Fourth Row (L-R): Frank Sonntag, Chris Kenney, Andy Smith, Rose James, Raymond Shelton, David Finch, Joe Norton, Larry Cook
Fifth Row (L-R): Peter Borzotta, Ariadne Villarreal, Nathan Hurlin, Brian O'Donnell, Roy Palijaro, Michael Graziano, Charles Hamlen, Ed Garrison, Anthony LaTorella. Not pictured: John Lytton.

Playbill / Manhattan

Philip S. Birsh
President and Publisher

Clifford S. Tinder
Senior Vice President/ Publisher, Classic Arts Division

Photos by Ben Strohmann

The Manhattan Staff

Back Row (L-R): Anderson Peguero, Philip S. Birsh, Andy Buck, Bruce Stapleton, Timothy Leinhart, Glenn Asciutto, Ari Ackerman, Susan Ludlow, Irv Winick, Robert Viagas.
Middle Row (L-R): Clara Barragan-Tiburcio, Gary Pearce, Terry Wilson, Joel Wyman, Mariah Woodruff, Amy Asch, Valerie Allen, Louis Botto, Oldyna Dynowska, Orlando Pabon, Arturo Gonzalez, Julie Nemitz.
Front Row (L-R): Maude Popkin, Ira Pekelnaya (Holding Banner), Jolie Schaffzin, Cliff Tinder, Ruthe Schnell, Jane Katz, Judy Samelson, Theresa Holder (Holding Banner), Lilian Richman, Esvard D'Haiti, Lavdi Sofia.

Editorial Staff

(L-R): Ira Pekelnaya, Maude Popkin, Louis Botto, Andy Buck, Gary Pearce, Silvija Ozols and Editor-in-Chief Judy Samelson.

Not pictured: Kesler Thibert, David Gewirtzman and Melissa Merlo.

Advertising Staff

(L-R): Glenn Shaevitz, Irv Winick, Jolie Schaffzin, Susan Ludlow, Julie Nemitz, Glenn Asciutto, Jane Katz, Ari Ackerman and Valerie Allen.

Not pictured: Michael Griffin.

Playbill / Woodside

Printing and Binding: Back Row (L to R): Philip S. Birsh, Elias Garcia, Thomas McClenin, John Matthews. Third Row (L-R): James Allen, Kenneth Gomez, Sadu Greene, Patrick Cusanelli, Robert Cusanelli, Louis Cusanelli, Ramdat Ramlall, Manuel Guzman, Michael Rotundo, Scott Cipriano. Second Row (L-R): Cliff Tinder, Raymundo Sierra, Wilfredo Lebron, James Ayala, Gary Pope, Frank Dunn, Larry Przetakiewicz, Carlos Moyano, David Rodriguez, Gilberto Gonzalez, Lennox Worrell. Front Row (L-R): Nancy Galarraga, Mary Roaid, Maheshwari Moti and Domingo Pagan.

Playbill.com Staff (L-R): Morgan Allen, Ken Jones, Robert Simonson, Kate Stutzel (intern), Andrew Gans and Andrew Ku.

Accounting (L-R): Beatriz Chitnis, James Eastman, Lewis Cole (Treasurer), Theresa Bernstein and John LoCascio. Not pictured: Joann D'Amato.

Classic Arts Division Program Editors (L-R): Jonny Segura, Scott Sepich, Cliff Tinder (Publisher), Evan Dashevsky, Kristy Bredin and Claire Mangan.

PlaybillArts.com Staff (L-R): Editor Ben Mattison, Online Director Andrew Ku and Assistant Editor Emily Hall.

Photos by Ben Strothmann

Playbill / Miami

Arthur T. Birsh
Chairman

Joan Alleman
Corporate Vice President

Les Feldman
*Publisher/
Southern Division*

Publishing and Advertising Staff
Front Row (L-R): Sara Smith, Arthur T. Birsh,
Leslie J. Feldman, Donald Roberts
Back Row (L-R): Tom Green, Jeff Ross, Ed Gurien

Southern Playbill Staff: First Row (L-R): Sara Smith, Mark Hamilton, Ruth Ingram, Laura Goldman, Maria Moreno, Maritza Lopez, Sally Coscia
Second Row (L-R): Raquel Romero, Jeff Ross, Michelle Campos, Leslie J. Feldman, Arthur T. Birsh, Joan Alleman, Donald Roberts, Kevin Keegan
Third Row (L-R): Tom Green, Silvia Cañadas, Christopher Diaz, Carolina Diaz, Milton McPherson, Eric Schrader, Lance Lenhardt, Ed Gurien,
Baldemar Albornoz. (Photos taken at the Jackie Gleason Theatre in Miami Beach.)

Art Staff
Front Row (L-R): Maria Moreno, Carolina Diaz,
Joan Alleman (Vice President), Maritza Lopez, Silvia Cañadas.
Back Row (L-R): Lance Lenhardt, Christopher Diaz, Milton McPherson,
Sally Coscia, Baldemar Albornoz

Production Staff
Front Row (L-R): Raquel Romero, Laura Goldman, Linda Clark,
Ruth Ingram
Back Row (L-R): Mark C. Hamilton, Eric Schrader, Michelle Campos,
Kevin Keegan

401

Playbill

Steven Suskin
Playbill.com Columnist

Production Chiefs
(L-R): Louis Cusanelli, Robert Cusanelli, Patrick Cusanelli.

Harry Haun
Staff Writer

Photos by Ben Strohmann

Marilyn A. Miller
*Sales Manager/
Minneapolis, Minnesota*

Playbill Programs
(L-R): Scott Hale (Off-Broadway program editor), Pam Karr (Broadway program editor), Marie Amsterdam (subscription manager).

Wayman Wong
Playbill.com Columnist

Ron Friedman
*Sales Manager/
Columbus, Ohio*

Not pictured: Tom Green, Karen Kanter, Judy Pletcher, Kenneth R. Back, Nancy Hardin, Margo Cooper, Elaine Bodker, Michael Manzo and Dave Levin.

Playbill Production
(L-R): Benjamin Hyacinthe, Sean Kenny, Patrick Cusanelli, David Porrello

Your Yearbook Committee (June 2005):
(L-R): Assistant Editor Amy Asch, Photographer Ben Strothmann, Editor Robert Viagas, Production Assistant David Gewirtzman, Art Director James Babbin and Editorial Assistant Melissa Merlo.

Bob Caulfield
*Sales Representative/
San Francisco*

Not pictured: Betsy Gugick, Kenneth A. Singer, Abigail Bocchetto, Megan Boles, John Rosenow, Linda Clark, Lacy Carter, Carol Brumm and Maureen Umlauf.

In Memoriam

May 2004 to May 2005

Charles Antalosky
Victor Argo
Louis Armstrong
Hartney J. Arthur
Phil Arthur
Mark Arvin
Norm Berman
Elmer Bernstein
James H. Binger
Don Blakely
Frank Borgman
Robert Brand
Phoebe Brand
Marlon Brando
Victoria Lynn Burton
Virginia Capers
Natalie Chilvers
Tim Choate
Jerome Chodorov
David Clarke
Caitlin Clarke
Richard Clarke
Patience Cleveland
Carolyn Coates
Cy Coleman
Jack Collins
William Conn, Jr.
Georgine Darcy
Ossie Davis
Hannah Dean
Peter Deign
Sally Demay
Steve Denaut
Tom Dillon
Mary Diveny
Maree Dow
Doris Dowling
Olga Druce
Fred Ebb
Gordon Ewing

Darryl Ferrer
Howard Feuer
Posy Feuer
Mary Helen Fisher
Peter Foy
Gene Frankel
Dick Gallagher
Kurt Garfield
Haskell Gordon
Pamela Gordon
Clarke Gordon
Frank Gorshin
Bernard Granville
Mel Gussow
Richard Hamilton
Blair Hammond
John Hammond
Paul Harding
Dee Harless
Wally Harper
Julius W. Harris
Stephen Hart
Rufus Hill
Jane Hoffman
Mildred Hughes
Ruth Hussey
Eric Hutson
Frances Hyland
Art James
Todd Jamieson
Timothy Jecko
Joyce Jillson
Richard Karlan
Howard Keel
R.D. Kennedy
Lincoln Kilpatrick

Alan King
Tom Kneebone
Julie Kurnitz
Heath Lamberts
William Leach
Anna Lee
Janet Leigh
Lu Leonard
Jacques Levy
Richard Lupino
Ruth Manning
Irene Manning
Lilene Mansell
Janice Mars
Barney Martin
Frank Maxwell
Virginia Mayo
William J. McCarthy
Arthur Miller
Betty Miller
John Mills
Gregory Mitchell
Robert Molnar
John Monks, Jr.
Benjamin Mordecai
David Neuman
Helen Noyes
Jerry Orbach
Elizabeth Owens
Hildy Parks
Donna Pearson
Susan Peretz
Barbara-Mae Phillips
William Pierson
Dan Priest
Phillip Pruneau

John Raitt
Christopher Reeve
Dorothy Richards
Trude Rittman
Eugene Roche
Chev Rodgers
Eddie Roll
Norman Rose
David Russell
Isabel Sanford
Jonathan M. Scharer
Bobby Short
Nancy Simons
Margot Skinner
Ben Slack
Charles Rome Smith
Archie Smith
Roger Spivy
Geraldine Teagarden
Manu Tupou
Jerry Turner
Jim Tyler
Tony Van Bridge
Richard Vath
John Vernon
Ruth Warrick
Stan Watt
Charles C. Welch
Louise Westergaard
Thelma White
Onna White
Keith Williams
Simon Wincelberg
Helene Winston
Iggie Wolfington
Peter Woodthorpe
Joyce Worsley
Teresa Wright
John Wylie
Peter Zeisler

INDEX

Gannon, Ben 49, 50
Gannon, Kim 287
Gans, Andrew 400
Garba, Maman 20, 257, 320, 321
Garber, Victor 21
Garbowski, Charlie 3, 20, 257, 321, 381
Garcia, Ana M. 79
Garcia, Aymee 22, 23, 25, 26, 27
Garcia, Elias 400
Garcia, Gabriela 66, 68, 71
Garcia, Gonzalo 78
Garcia, Jordan 161
Garcia, Jordon 128
Garcia, Laurie 98, 99
Garcia, Liza 225, 226
Garcia-Suli, Hilda 115, 117
Gardella, Verónica 119, 120
Gardner, Alyssa 107, 179
Gardner, Carrie 3, 20, 79, 85, 189, 257, 272, 321
Gardner, Cecelia Hobbs 47, 324
Gardner, Dean 63, 161
Gardner, Earl 47, 186
Gardner, James 98, 99, 100
Gardner, Kristin 386
Gardner, Michael 310, 311
Gardner, Philip 235, 236, 237
Garfield, Kurt 403
Garib, Krystal Kiran 38, 39
Garland, Jill 173
Garment, Paul 62
Garmise Esq., Richard 60, 193, 328
Garner, Bob 34
Garner, Sandra 151
Garner, Steve 179
Garner, Travis 54
Garnett, Kim 82
Garrett, Tre 179
Garrison, Ed 398
Garrison, Mary Catherine 17, 18, 19, 21
Garrity, Matt 128
Garro, Michael 78
Garside, Brad 117, 226
Garson, Judith 136
Gartman, Lev 169, 278
Garvey, Bill 361
Garvey, Jennifer 25
Garvey, Joseph P. 206, 207
Garvey, Justin 25
Gary, Tanesha 62, 64
Gaschen, David 259, 260, 261
Gaspar, Dorothy 15
Gasteyer, Ana 343
Gaston, Jose 107, 128
Gat, Keen 321
Gates, Thomas J. 58, 60
Gatling, Zipporah G. 201, 203
Gaughan, John 35
Gavin, Tiffani 128, 328
Gayheart, Rebecca 313, 314, 317
Gayle, Jack 69
Gaylor, Angela 185, 187, 190, 191
Gaynair, Brian 120, 232
Gaynor, Bob 323, 324, 325
Gayol, Roxanne 244
Geanolaes, Helen 14
Gee, Carmen 179, 339
Gee, Justin 8, 207
Geer, Kevin 330, 331
Gehan, Nathan 128, 232
Geiger, Denise 50, 266
Gelbart, Larry 310, 312
Gelber, Jordan 22, 23, 27
Gelblum Esq., Seth D. 60, 71, 94, 193, 328, 354
Gelblum, Seth D. 60
Gelfand, Steve 210
Gemeinhardt, Brad 324
Gemignani, Alexander 17, 18, 19, 21, 24
Gemignani, Michael 386
Gemignani, Paul 19, 131, 132, 252, 253

Genece, Naomi 206
Genelle, Joanne 79
Generalovich, Tracy 28, 29, 30
Genovese, Amanda 381
Gensler, Louis 303
Gentile, John 127, 128
Gentry, Ken 216
George, Daniel 20
George, Rhett 323, 324, 329, 352
George, Scott 183
Geralis, Antony 229, 232
Gerber, Tony 290
Gerschefski, Ann 38
Germain, Mark St. 339
Gerrard, Lisa 241
Gershwin, George 303
Gershwin, Ira 303
Gerson, David R. 295
Gersten, Bernard 133, 199, 299, 300, 395
Gersten, David 384
Gesele, Michael 50, 148
Gettelfinger, Sara 89, 91, 93, 95
Gettinger, Ben 221, 223
Gevengoed, David 386
Gewirtzman, David ii, 194, 399, 402
Ghareeb, Yvonne 398
Ghebremichael, Asmeret 348, 350
Ghebresillassie, Susie 278, 280
Ghelfi, Chris 111, 112
Ghoukassian, Adrineh 8, 35, 207
Giannini, Maura 229, 384
Gianono, Eva 295
Giant, Bill 15
Giattino, Melissa 122, 123
Gibbons, Adrienne 277
Gibbons, Frank 207
Gibbons, Maggie 307
Gibbons, Michele 15, 60, 63, 100, 117, 179, 189, 193, 212, 219, 249, 283, 346, 354
Gibbons, Michelle 139, 143, 154, 278, 328
Gibbs, James W. 82
Gibbs, Lauren 348, 350
Gibbs, Nancy Nagel 13, 339, 354
Gibson, Colin 396
Gibson, John R. 43, 79, 126, 128
Gibson, Julia 242, 243
Gibson, Michael 12, 49
Gibson, William 151
Giebler, Sue 226
Gifford, Gene 143
Gifford, Vanessa 25
Gigerich, A.J. 25
Gigliobianco, Jodie 198
Gilbar, Lisa 232
Gilbert, Alyce 354
Gilbert, Amy 219
Gilbert, Julian 8
Gilbert, Michael 206
Gilbert, Ryan 128
Gilkison, Jason 82
Gill, Jaymes 43, 78, 79
Gill, Len 43
Gillentine, Meg 130, 131, 132, 134
Gillerman, Ambassador Dan 151
Gillespie, Kevin 151
Gillespie, Sarah 212
Gillett, Eric Michael 131, 132
Gilliam, Michael 58
Gilliam, Terry 233
Gillies, Thea Bradshaw 173, 271, 272
Gillispie, Betty 240
Gillman, Jason 89, 91, 93
Gilloon, Dan 265
Gilman, Sondra 372, 397
Gilmore, Mark 354
Gilmore, Pat 353, 354
Gilmore, Rachael 249

Gilmore, Valerie 353, 354
Gilpin, Nicholas 222
Gilroy, Katrina 272
Ginsberg, Ned 35
Giordano, Vince 143
Giorgianni, Joe 11, 14
Giovanni, Kearran 73, 75
Girman, Michael 265, 266
Giurecio, Gina 183
Gladstone, Valerie 34, 35, 249
Glassberg, Deborah 25
Glassburn, Leslie A. 272
Glatzer C.P.A., Kenneth D. 148
Gleason, Jackie 401
Gleason, Joanna 89, 91, 93, 95, 374
Gleason, Kate 269, 270
Glendening, Sarah 156, 157, 158, 162
Glendinning, Hugo 181, 183
Glenn, Pia C. 130, 131, 132
Glennie-Smith, Nick 207
Glickfield, Chelsea 257, 321
Glorioso, Bess Marie 354
Gloven, Tommy 353, 354
Glover, Marjorie 271
Glover, Tim 241
Glynn, Patrick 74, 77
Goble, Patty 186, 187
Goddard, Leslie 164, 165
Godsey, Jimmy 63
Godwin, Joe 232
Goertz, Lonnie 278
Goetschius, Elissa 307
Goetz, Guido 43, 391
Goings, Wendall 115, 117
Gold, Alice 378
Gold, Harry S. 8, 35, 207, 379
Gold, Michele 8, 35, 207
Gold, Shana 321
Gold, Victoria 117
Gold, Wally 15
Goldberg Esq., Jay 71
Goldberg, Alexis 257
Goldberg, Andy 54, 287, 307
Goldberg, Hal 160, 161, 243, 282
Goldberg, Jon-Erik 224
Goldberg, Marc 111
Goldberg, Marcia 13, 339, 354
Goldberg, Whoopi 341, 342, 343
Goldblum, Jeff 95, 269, 270, 273, 334, 340, 371
Golden, Annie 21
Goldin, Tal 20
Goldenberg, Josh 354
Goldenhersh, Heather ii, 97, 98, 101, 374
Goldensohn, Suzanne 128
Goldfeder, Laurie 183
Goldin, Tal 189, 328
Golding, Cherito 78
Goldman, Laura 401
Goldman, Nina 89, 91, 93
Goldrich, Zina 24
Goldsmith, Noah 193, 245
Goldsmith, Russell 183
Goldstein, Allison 54, 287, 307
Goldstein, Daniel 15
Goldstein, Jeff 198
Goldstein, Jess 53, 151, 158, 178, 298, 306
Goldstein, Jonathan 3, 20, 257
Goldstein, Neil 43, 63
Goldstein, Seth 25
Goldstein-Breyer, Kate 63
Golia, Nanette 8, 159, 161
Gomberg, Tatiana 360
Gomez, Kenneth 400
Gomez, Lino 357
Gomez, Susan 189, 311
Gonda, Eli 117, 143, 144
Gonzales, Marie 302
Gonzalez, Aldrin 28, 30, 36

Gonzalez, Andrea 255, 256
Gonzalez, Arturo 399
González, Claudio 119, 120
Gonzalez, Gilberto 400
Gonzalez, Jessica 32
Gonzalez, Richard 207
Gonzalez, Thom 33, 35
Good, Brian 244
Good, Tara 151, 152
Goode, Olivia 175
Goodfriend, Dana 50
Goodman, Hazelle 155
Goodman, Jeff 3, 8, 20, 257, 321, 381
Goodman, Matthew 261, 265
Goodman, Robyn 3, 20, 24, 25, 257, 314, 321
Goodman, Sue 62, 64
Goodrum, Liz 169
Goodwin, Will 82
Googe Esq., Charles H. 133, 199, 299
Gopal, Tanvir 37, 38, 39
Gordon, Alan 389
Gordon, Allan S. 166, 231, 291, 295
Gordon, Bob 42
Gordon, Charles 74, 77
Gordon, Clarke 403
Gordon, Haskell 403
Gordon, Mark R. 106, 107
Gordon, Matthew 183
Gordon, Mindy 107, 128, 161
Gordon, Pamela 403
Gordon, Robert 136, 338, 339
Gordon, Rodney 8, 15, 50, 79, 107, 128, 266, 278, 328, 354, 361
Gore, Michelle 207
Gorin, Stephanie 43, 226
Gorman, Greg 82
Gornik, Gina 98, 99, 100
Gorruso, Anthony 122, 127, 229
Gorshin, Frank 403
Gorski, Kristen Leigh 349, 350, 354
Gorzell, Andrea 54
Gottesman, Joseph 5
Gottlieb, Steven 257, 321, 381
Gottschall, Marie 382
Gotwald, David 278
Goucher, Michael 387
Gough, Michael 125
Gough, Shawn 133
Goulet, Robert 187
Goulet, Susan 178, 219
Gountas, George 311
Govich, Milena 156, 158, 162
Gowenlock, Kay 168, 169
Goya, Ruth 240
Grace, Kathleen 287
Graf, Douglas 206, 207
Graff, Randy 114
Graham, Greg 89, 90, 91, 93, 94, 95, 167
Graham, Martha 329
Graham, Somer Lee 224
Graham, William 169
Graney, Pat 199
Granger, Milton 74, 77
Granger, Phil 131
Grant, Christina 33
Grant, Emily 107, 128, 161
Grant, Sharon 32
Granville, Bernard 403
Grasso, Angelo 240
Grasso, Thomas B. 249
Graubert, Sheri 321
Grausam, James 307
Graves, Douglas 354
Graves, James 385
Gravitte, Beau 195, 197, 200
Gravitte, Debbie 193, 200
Gray, DJ 339
Gray, Glen 143
Gray, James 277
Gray, Jeffry 50, 212, 240

Gray, Tamyra 37, 39
Graynor, Ari 52, 53, 55
Grayson, Bobby 50
Grayson, Bobby H. 315, 316
Graziano, Michael 398
Greaves, Danielle Lee 289, 291
Grecki, Victoria 117
Green Jr., George 326, 327, 328, 361
Green, Adolph 183, 358, 362
Green, Amanda 25
Green, Brenda 386
Green, Bud 183
Green, Dennis 321
Green, Doug 383
Green, Jackie 35
Green, Jackie 8, 50, 85, 183, 207, 232, 245, 316, 390
Green, Jennifer 232
Green, Julius 143
Green, Laura 169, 212, 278
Green, Stacey 43
Green, Thomas 169
Green, Tom 168, 401
Greenberg, Edward M. 206, 207
Greenberg, Jill 328
Greenberg, Kimberly 207
Greenberg, Steven 25
Greenblatt, Kenneth D. 188
Greene, Ana-Rose 5, 211, 277
Greene, Ellen 213
Greene, Elliot 25, 50, 43, 60, 71, 94, 107, 120, 143, 148, 154, 173, 179, 193, 226, 232, 245, 249, 266, 272, 283, 311, 316, 342, 346
Greene, Frank 275
Greene, Lara 240
Greene, Michelle 249
Greene, Sadu 400
Greenfield, Mandy 54, 100, 287, 307
Greenfield, Steven J. 275
Greenhouse, Burton 173
Greenhouse, Ed 173
Greenwald, Tom 15, 60, 94, 328, 394
Greenwood, Jane 248, 345
Greenwood, Ken 382, 389
Greer, Dean R. 225, 226
Greer, Justin 275, 276
Greer, Ryan 226
Greer, Steve 266
Greer, Timothy 115, 117
Grego, David 69
Gregor, Helen 79
Gregory II, Chester 163, 165
Gregory, Michael 183
Gregory, Wanda 15, 34, 107
Greif, Michael 199, 291, 296
Grekin, Douglas 82
Grennes, Dan 192
Gretchen Metzloff 25
Grevengoed, David 13
Grey, Jane 318, 319, 320, 321
Grey, Joel 352
Grieco, Charles 71, 143
Grieco, Jeri 126, 128
Grier, Jean Michelle 201, 203
Griff, Eddie 265
Griffenkranz, Joan 50
Griffin, Charles 346
Griffin, Dennis 43
Griffin, Gerard 94
Griffin, J.W. 3, 257, 321
Griffin, Joseph 381
Griffin, Jung 173
Griffin, Michael 399
Griffin, Wylie 311
Griffing, Lois L. 8, 13, 15
Griffith, Laura 195, 196, 197, 199, 200
Griffith, Marey 207

Griffith, Melanie 72
Griffiths, Heidi 63, 64
Griggs, Jennifer 240
Grigsby, Kimberly 62, 64
Grilikhes-Lasky, Antonia 63
Grillman, Denise 25
Grillo, Denise 8, 85, 87, 212, 245, 257, 271, 321
Grillo, Elaina 3, 20, 257, 321
Grillos, Nicole 311
Grimes, Peter 54, 287, 307
Grimminck, Marti Wigder 15
Grindrod, David 224, 226
Grisdale, Ashley 226
Grishman, Emily 20, 25, 60, 74, 90, 94, 117, 133, 165, 199, 229, 257, 335, 339
Gromada, John 306, 331
Groomes, Ron 25, 161
Grossman, Harry 8, 207
Grossman, Kory 122, 127
Grossman, Randi 25, 183
Grother, William C. 82
Grove, Barry 53, 54, 98, 100, 286, 287, 306, 307
Growler, Michael 53, 54, 286, 287, 307
Gruber, Larry 94, 107, 117, 143, 161
Grubich, Tanya 15, 25, 54, 63, 100, 169, 212, 219, 226, 240, 249, 287, 295, 307, 354
Gruet, Dayle 35, 207, 212, 379
Grunder, Kay 244, 245, 315, 316
Gruse, Stephen R. 326, 328
Guare, John 199
Guay, Anne 316
Gubin, Ron 107, 128, 161
Guercio, Tanya 169
Guercy, Tanya 168
Guerin, Denis 133, 199, 299
Guerra, Cathy 35
Guerzon, Albert 221, 223
Guettel, Adam 195, 197, 200, 374, 375
Guggino, Michael 71
Gugino, Carla 1, 2, 3, 4
Gugliero, Michele 174
Guida, Kathryn B. 41, 43, 249, 311
Guiher, Catharine 20
Guip, Amy 295
Gulan, Timothy 131, 132
Gulorry, Eric 93
Gulsvig, Becky 164, 165
Gulzar 43
Gumley, Matthew 28, 30
Gundersen, Arne 382
Gunhus, Eric 274, 275, 276
Gunn, Chris 214, 216
Gunn, James 353
Gunter, Greg 8, 35, 207, 379
Gunther, Carmel 328, 360, 361
Guralchuk, Keith 35, 206, 207
Gurien, Ed 401
Gurney, A.R. 370
Gurry, Matt 98, 99
Gurwin, Danny 214, 215, 220
Gushin, Alex 115
Gusmano, Tina 388
Gussow, Mel 403
Gustafson, Bob 5
Gustafson-Nederlander, Kristina 378
Gusty, Dave 395
Guthertz, Elisa 154
Gutierrez, Alex 53, 54
Gutierrez, Gerald 133, 199, 299
Gutierrez, Michelle 160
Gutman, Hally 60
Gutterman, Jay and Cindy